Essentials

AutoCAD®
Mechanical 2017 (R1)

September 2016

AUTODESK.
Authorized Publisher

Contents

Introduction

Welcome to the *AutoCAD® Mechanical 2017 (R1) Essentials* student guide for use in Authorized Training Center (ATC®) locations, corporate training settings, and other classroom settings.

Although this student guide is designed for instructor-led courses, you can also use it for self-paced learning. The student guide encourages self-learning through the use of the AutoCAD® Mechanical Help system.

This introduction covers the following topics:

- Course objectives
- Prerequisites
- Using this guide
- Downloading and installing the Practice Files
- Notes, tips, and warnings
- Feedback
- Free Autodesk software for students and educators

This student guide is complementary to the software documentation. For detailed explanations of features and functionality, refer to the Help in the software.

Course Objectives

After completing this student guide, you will be able to:

- Identify the main interface elements, their setup and what Help information is available, and to create and use drawing template files.
- Describe the object property management system in which layers are configured and the tools for manipulating layers.
- Describe the workflows for organizing drawing geometry and create a Mechanical structure in a drawing by creating components, component views, and folders.
- Describe the core mechanical design tools of rectangle, hatch, fillet, chamfer, holes, slots, and threads and how to use them to create and modify geometry in your drawings.
- Modify and edit drawing objects by creating multiple offset copies, scaling them with separate values for the X and Y direction, or using a power command.
- Insert industry standard parts into your assembly designs.
- Create production-ready drawings in model space and layouts of structured and non-structured geometry and insert title blocks and borders.
- Notate a drawing through the creation and editing of dimensions, hole charts, fits lists, and mechanical symbols.

- Explain how to create and edit a bill of materials, parts list, and balloons.
- Describe the tools that you can use to verify whether or not the standard parts or custom parts within your design meet or exceed the requirements for operational use.
- Exchange data between CAD systems in the form of Mechanical DWG™ and IGES files and create Mechanical drawings using Inventor Link.
- Create a custom drafting standard and drawing template that includes the configuration settings for layers, object properties, symbols, text, BOMs, parts list, balloons, and other annotation tools.

Prerequisites

This guide is designed for users who are new to the AutoCAD® Mechanical 2017 (R1) software.

- A basic understanding of mechanical drafting or design.
- A working knowledge of the AutoCAD® software.
- A working knowledge of the Microsoft® Windows® 7 operating system.

Using This Guide

The lessons are independent of each other. However, it is recommended that you complete these lessons in the order in which they are presented unless you are familiar with the concepts and functionality described in those lessons.

Each chapter contains:

- **Lessons** - Usually two or more lessons in each chapter.
- **Exercises** - Practical, real-world examples for you to practice using the functionality that you have just learned. Each exercise contains step-by-step procedures and graphics to help you complete the exercise successfully.

Downloading and Installing the Practice Files

The Practice Files page in this Student Guide contains a link to all of the data and drawings required to complete the exercises. To install the data files for the exercises:

1. Type or click the link, provided in the Practice Files page of the student guide, into a web browser and download the .EXE file containing the Practice Files.

2. Extract the .EXE file to *C:*. This should be a directory for which you have read\write privileges for your user account. A folder called *C:\AutoCAD Mechanical 2017 Essentials Practice Files* is created, containing the files that are required for each exercise in this student guide.

Notes, Tips, and Warnings

Throughout this student guide, notes, tips, and warnings are called out for special attention.

Notes contain guidelines, constraints, and other explanatory information.

Tips provide information to enhance your productivity.

Warnings provide information about actions that might result in the loss of data, system failures, or other serious consequences.

Feedback

We always welcome feedback on Autodesk Official Training Courseware. After completing this course, if you have suggestions for improvements or want to report an error in the student guide or with the Practice Files, please send your comments to *feedback@ascented.com*.

Free Autodesk Software for Students and Educators

The Autodesk Education Community is an online resource with more than five million members that enables educators and students to download for free the same software used by professionals worldwide (see website for terms and conditions). You can also access additional tools and materials to help you design, visualize, and simulate ideas. Connect with other learners to stay current with the latest industry trends and get the most out of your designs.

Get started today. Register at the Autodesk Education Community (*www.autodesk.com/joinedu*) and download one of the many available Autodesk software applications.

Note: Free products are subject to the terms and conditions of the end-user license and services agreement that accompanies the software. The software is for personal use for education purposes only and is not intended for classroom or lab use.

Exercise Files

To download the practice files for this student guide, use the following steps:

1. Type the URL shown below into the address bar of your Internet browser. The URL must be typed **exactly as shown**. If you are using an ASCENT ebook, you can click on the link to download the file.

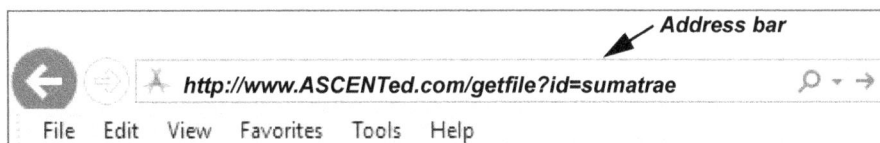

Address bar

http://www.ASCENTed.com/getfile?id=sumatrae

File   Edit   View   Favorites   Tools   Help

2. Press <Enter> to download the .ZIP file that contains the Practice Files.

3. Once the download is complete, unzip the file to a local folder. The unzipped file contains an .EXE file.

4. Double-click on the .EXE file and follow the instructions to automatically install the Practice Files on the C:\ drive of your computer.

   Do not change the location in which the Practice Files folder is installed. Doing so can cause errors when completing the practices in this student guide.

http://www.ASCENTed.com/getfile?id=sumatrae

Autodesk

Getting Started

In this chapter, you learn how the AutoCAD® Mechanical interface is set up. You become familiar with where to find various commands, and learn how to create drawing template files and to use them when creating new drawings.

Objectives

After completing this chapter, you will be able to:

- Identify the main interface elements, their setup, and the available Help information.
- Create and use drawing template files.

Lesson: Interacting with the User Interface

Overview

This lesson describes the AutoCAD Mechanical interface, how to change different parts of it, and how to access helpful information when required.

To work comfortably, confidently, and quickly in any software application, you need to learn the different parts of its user interface. When you know how to adjust the user interface to match your workflow requirements, you can work comfortably and efficiently. Learning where to access information when you need it helps you to continue to improve your abilities and skills.

The following illustration shows the upper-left area of the user interface in its default configuration.

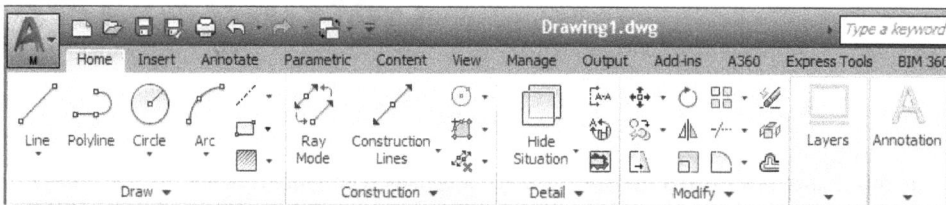

Objectives

After completing this lesson, you will be able to:

- Describe the parts of the user interface.
- Explore and explain the purpose of the Ribbon and control its display.
- Access Help and other useful information using the InfoCenter.

The User Interface

The AutoCAD Mechanical software has a similar look and feel to the standard AutoCAD® software because it uses the AutoCAD software at its core. You interact with the AutoCAD Mechanical user interface to create and modify geometry as you do in the standard AutoCAD software. The Ribbon, drop-down lists, toolbars, drawing window, shortcut menus, Command Line, and Status Bar all function as they do in the standard AutoCAD software, depending on which workspace is selected. However, although the interface might feel the same and you can use the commands that you are accustomed to, you need to learn how to interact with the AutoCAD Mechanical software. It contains a number of commands, tools, and workflows that were specifically established to help you create mechanical designs and drawings more quickly while meeting the requirements of industry and company standards.

Start Screen

The initial Start window, shown in the illustration below, displays when you launch the software or when you click on the Start tab while working in an active drawing. It contains two frames: Learn and Create.

- The Learn frame: Contains videos, tips, and online resources to help you learn about new items in the software and how to start using the software.
- The Create frame: Contains tools to enable you to create new drawings, open existing drawings or samples, and view recently used files. You can also access product updates and connect to Autodesk® A360 to access online services.

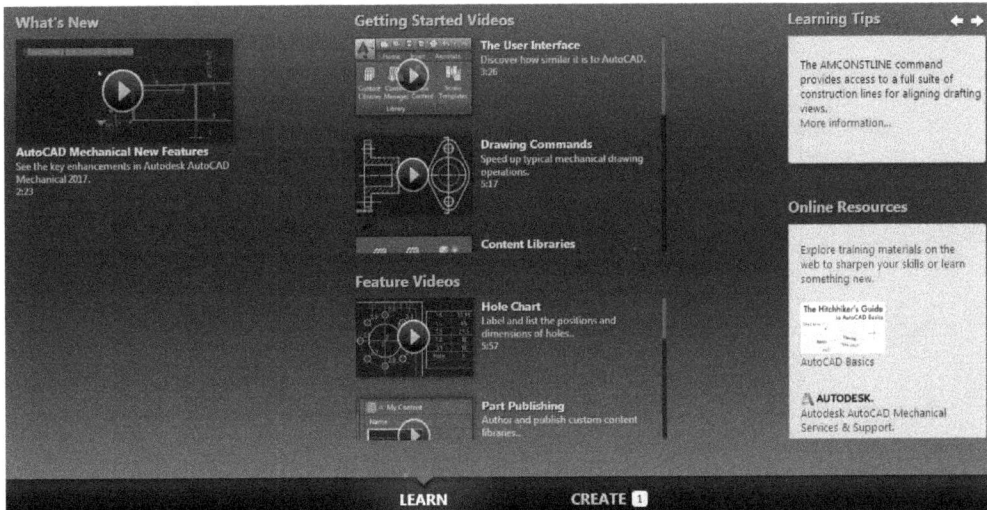

Parts of the User Interface

The initial display and position of the Ribbon, menus, toolbars, and palettes in the user interface depends on the active workspace. The AutoCAD Mechanical Ribbon is organized to align with the AutoCAD Ribbon where possible and includes additional tabs and panels for unique AutoCAD Mechanical commands. The Ribbon panels are organized to align with the tasks for completing a mechanical design and include the unique tools and commands of the AutoCAD Mechanical software.

As you create and edit geometry in the AutoCAD Mechanical software, using the various palettes can be beneficial. Different palettes help you access commands more efficiently and others make it easier and faster to change the properties of objects. Each palette can be independently set to dock, anchor, float, or auto hide at a specific location within the user interface.

The Ribbon, Quick Properties, and Properties palettes are all palettes that are available in the standard AutoCAD software and in the AutoCAD Mechanical software. You can use the Ribbon to access a number of AutoCAD and AutoCAD Mechanical commands from a single location. The Properties and Quick Properties palettes enable you to make various edits to all types of existing drawing objects.

When you are creating and editing drawings that use the Mechanical structure, you interact with two additional palettes that are unique to the AutoCAD Mechanical: Browser and Structure Catalog. The Browser palette is used to display, hide, move, and edit 2D mechanically structured content. You also use it to create and modify viewports in a layout. The Structure Catalog palette enables you to access and reuse structured geometry.

In the following illustration, the default workspace Mechanical is active and the different primary areas of the user interface are identified.

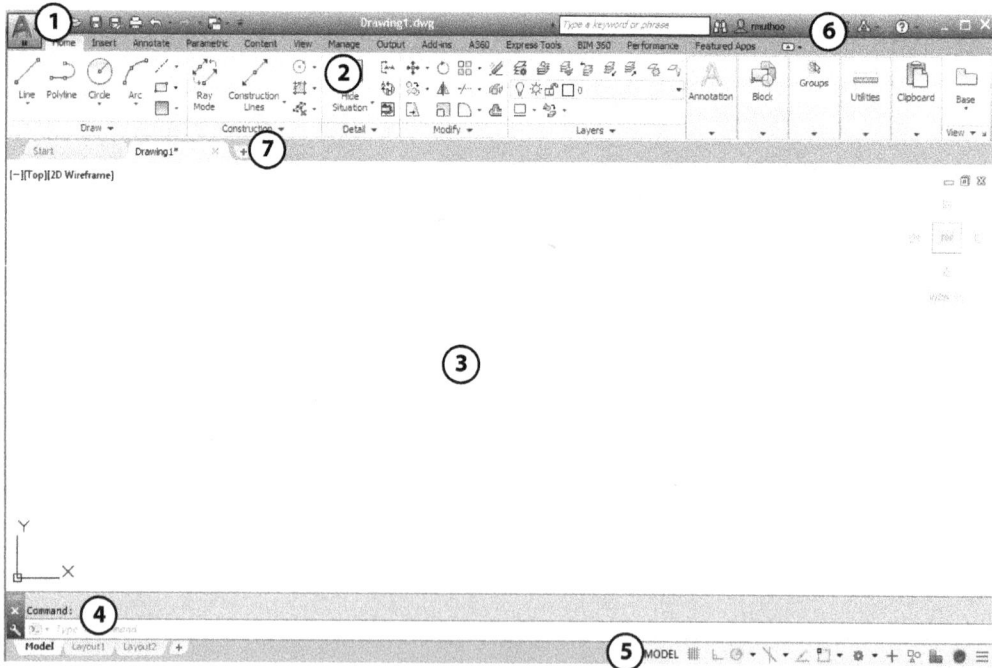

1. Application Menu and Quick Access Toolbar

2. Ribbon

3. Drawing Area

4. Command Window

5. Status Bar and workspace

6. InfoCenter and Communication Center

7. File Tabs

Application Menu

You can use the Application Menu to access several key commands as shown in the following illustration. Most of these commands contain submenus with more detailed options.

Tasks that you can accomplish include:

- Saving or exporting files.
- Opening recently opened documents.
- Accessing the options.
- Searching for a command.
- Printing documents.

Using the Search function, you can locate one or more commands that are related to the keyword that you in the Search field. For example, if you want to know which commands are available to draw centerlines, entering **centerline** returns all commands that contain the word centerline, as shown in the following illustration. The search results list the commands and the menu in which they are located. Clicking a listed search result starts that command.

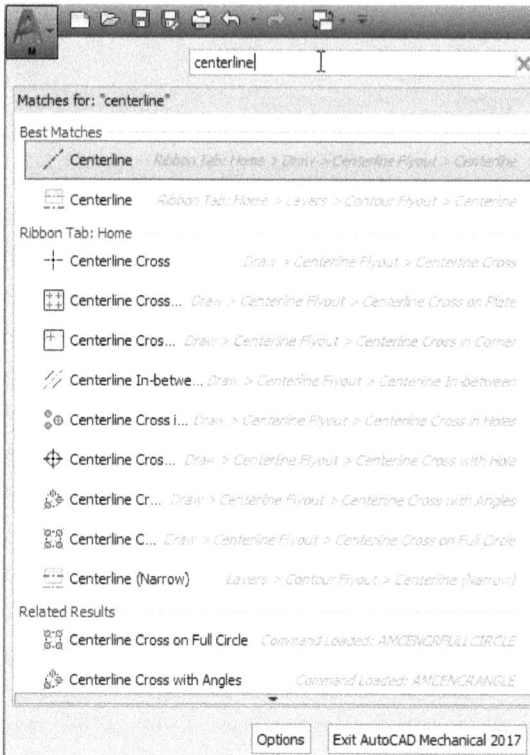

Workspaces

To help you access the commands that you want to use, the AutoCAD Mechanical software has several preset workspaces you can use. Each workspace controls the display settings and location of the Ribbon, toolbars, and Browser. The tabs that are available on the Ribbon also change, depending on the selected workspace. These different workspaces can help you work more efficiently, and enable you to create a design environment that suits your needs. You can create a custom workspace from one of the preset workspaces to further refine the interface with the tools that you want to use. If you change the display settings or position of items in the interface, you can quickly reset the interface by reselecting the workspace.

By default, the software includes the following workspace configurations:

- Mechanical
- Structure
- 3D Basics
- 3D Modeling

You can switch between defined workspaces by selecting the required workspace from the Workspace Switching icon in the Status Bar, as shown in the following illustration.

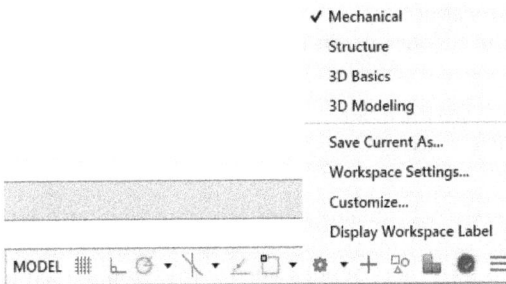

Exploring the Ribbon

The Ribbon is an important part of the user interface and it enables you to efficiently access multiple commands. As you become increasingly familiar with the Ribbon, you can use it to improve your design creation and editing time.

The Ribbon supports the heads-up design process because it is space efficient and eliminates the clutter of tool palettes and toolbars. Using the Ribbon alone provides you with more space on your screen in the drawing area and enables you to maintain access to the tools and controls you need.

About the Ribbon

The Ribbon is a special tool palette that contains the tools and controls that are relevant to the active workspace. It is divided into areas that contain groups of tools called panels. Each separate panel contains related tools, such as those used for adding dimensional constraints, adding symbols, or adding hole features. Some panels can be expanded to display more tools. You can also customize and save your Ribbon configuration.

Examples of the Mechanical and Structure Ribbons

The following illustration shows the contents of the Ribbon when the Mechanical workspace is active.

The following illustration shows the contents of the Ribbon when the Structure workspace is active. Note the extra tab on the Ribbon for managing Structure.

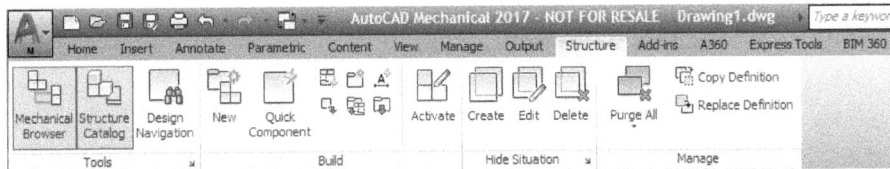

Ribbon Controls

The Ribbon is toggled on by default when you start the software in either the Mechanical or Structure workspace. The Ribbon is organized into a series of tabs. Each tab includes a different set of panels with related commands and controls that can be found on the Mechanical Classic toolbars and dialog boxes.

You can toggle the tabs and associated panels in the Ribbon on or off by right-clicking in the Ribbon area and selecting Show Tabs or Show Panels. You can also toggle panel titles on or off by right-clicking on the panel tabs. Additionally, you can save your Ribbon configuration.

Each tab in the Ribbon has its own set of panels that contain groups of related tools, such as those for using content, adding text, or adding dimensions. Some panels can be expanded to display more tools. Some tools can also be expanded to display more options (such as the Power Dimension tool), as indicated by an arrow in the corner of the icon.

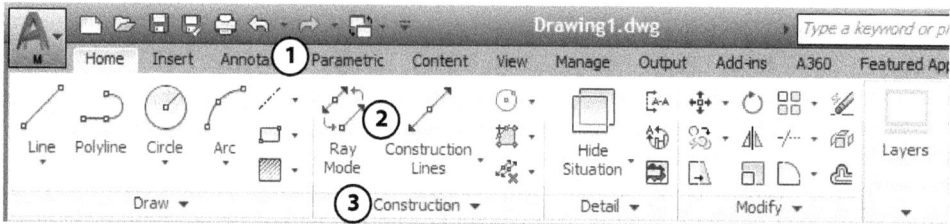

1. Identifies the name of the tabs.

2. Contains groups of related tools that are associated with the selected tool.

3. Identifies the name of the panels. Click and hold the down arrow to display more tools and options in the selected panel.

Add or Remove Tabs

To toggle specific tabs on or off, right-click on the Ribbon and select Show Tabs. You can then select a tab name to display or remove tabs from the Ribbon. Tabs that are currently displayed are indicated by a checkmark as shown in the illustration below.

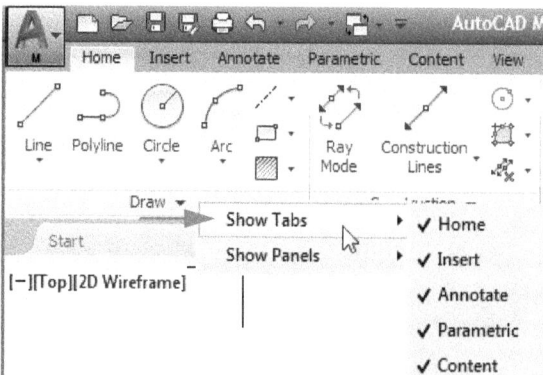

Panels

The AutoCAD Mechanical software uses Ribbon panels as one method of accessing commands and settings. Each panel consists of a collection of tools that perform related or similar tasks.

When using the Mechanical workspace, a standard set of panels is displayed on each of the tabs in the Ribbon at the top of the drawing area. Note that when you select a different tab, a different set of panels is displayed.

By default, each panel is docked at the top of the drawing area in the Ribbon.

Panel Visibility

To toggle specific panels on or off, right-click in the Ribbon and select Show Panels. Select to display or remove panels from the Ribbon tab. Panels that are currently displayed are indicated by a checkmark, as shown in the illustration below. Panels containing toolbars display in the last position (docked or floating) that they were in before they were removed from the display.

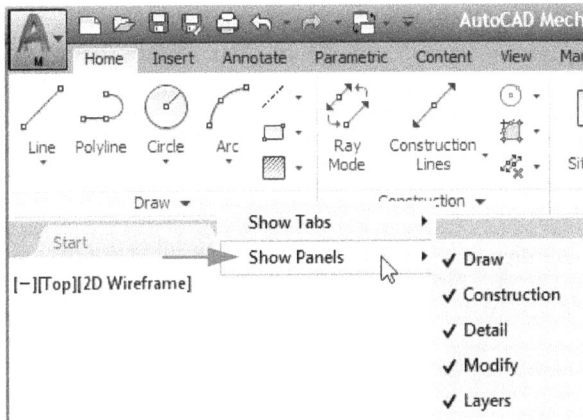

Panel Tools Visibility

Some panels cascade to reveal additional tools when you select the black arrow in the lower right corner of the panel. You can keep these panels open to display all of the tools by selecting the thumbtack located in the lower left corner of the expanded panel.

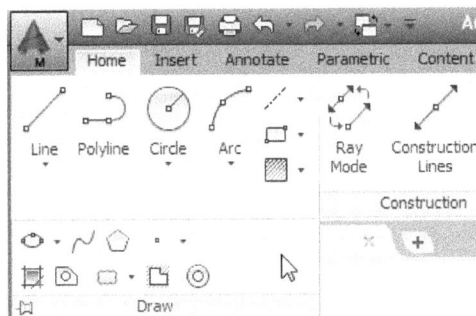

File Tabs

The drawing File Tabs enable you to quickly open and close drawings, or create new ones. If you close all of the drawings that are currently open or click the Start tab, the initial Start window displays containing two content frames: Learn and Create. By default, the Start tab is always the first tab in the File Tabs. Clicking 🔲 (New Drawing) in the File Tabs starts a new blank drawing, which also becomes the active drawing. You can close a drawing by clicking ⊗ (Close) in the File tabs. You can also close a single drawing or close all the open drawings together by right-clicking on a drawing filename in the File Tabs and selecting either Close, Close All, or Close All Other Drawings.

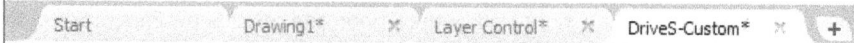

| Start | Drawing1* | × | Layer Control* | × | DriveS-Custom* | × | + |

Accessing Help Information

A key part of your continual learning is knowing how and where to get more information when you need it. In the AutoCAD Mechanical software, you can access different areas and types of information that you can use to help you relearn a topic, expand your understanding of a topic, or learn a new topic.

Accessing Help Information

Your point of access for additional information is through the InfoCenter toolbar, which is located on the title bar of the main AutoCAD Mechanical interface. From the InfoCenter, you can search the Help System, sign in to A360, launch the Autodesk Exchange Apps website, and download offline help.

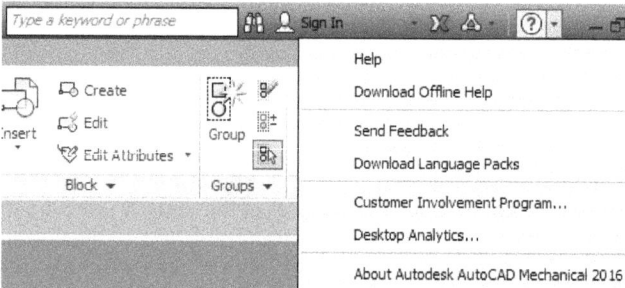

Type a keyword or phrase		Sign In				?	
			Help				
Insert	Create	Group	Download Offline Help				
	Edit		Send Feedback				
	Edit Attributes		Download Language Packs				
Block ▾		Groups ▾					
			Customer Involvement Program...				
			Desktop Analytics...				
			About Autodesk AutoCAD Mechanical 2016				

The AutoCAD Mechanical Help system window gives you access to a variety of topics on the Home page. You can directly access product information on specific topics, learn what's new in the latest version of the AutoCAD Mechanical software, and access the online community. If you need to access the Help system when you are not connected to the internet, you can download the Offline Help system for use during that time.

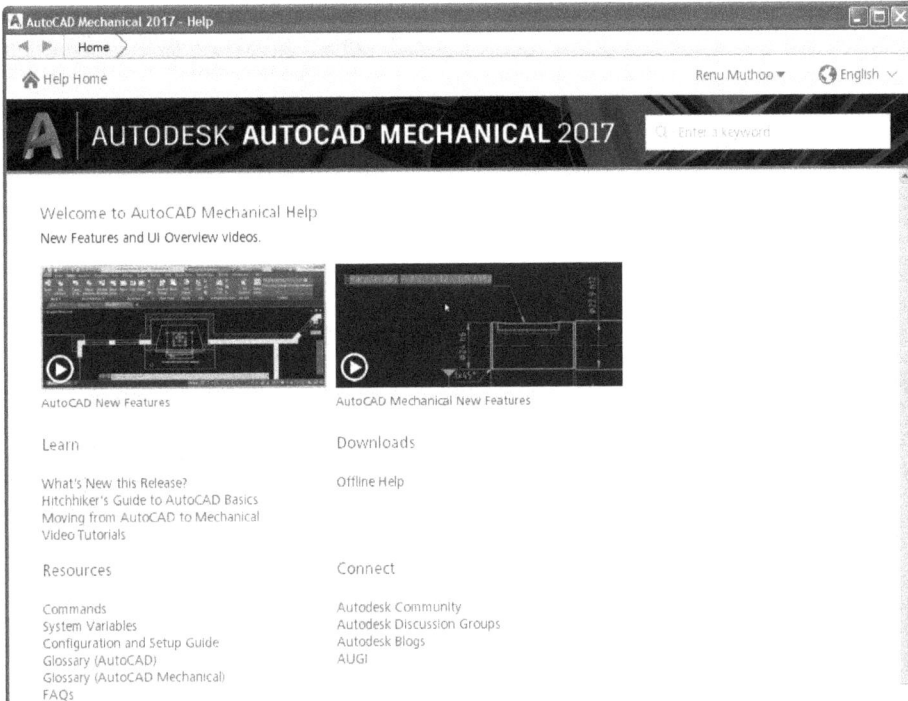

Procedure: Accessing Help Information

To access help information in the AutoCAD Mechanical software, complete the following steps:

1. On the InfoCenter toolbar, type a keyword or phrase and press ENTER. Alternatively, to the right of Help, click the drop-down arrow and select Help.

2. Determine the topic or type of information you need assistance with or are trying to learn more about.

Exercise: Interact with the User Interface

In this exercise, you will interact with the AutoCAD Mechanical user interface by accessing commands using different workflows and changing the display of different parts of the user interface

1. Open *Interact with the User Interface.dwg*.

2. To begin drawing a rectangle, click Home tab > Draw panel > expand the Rectangle drop-down list.

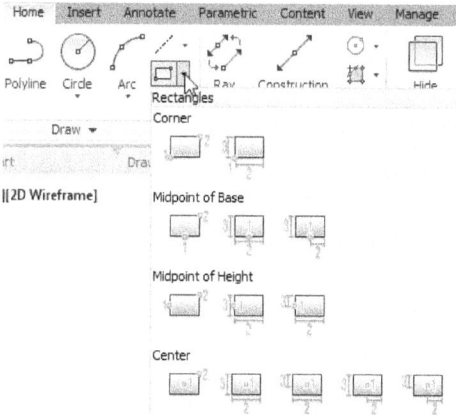

3. All of the rectangles are displayed with their icons. To create a rectangle with its middle aligned with the center of the existing circle, select the second rectangle in the *Center* area.. Click OK.

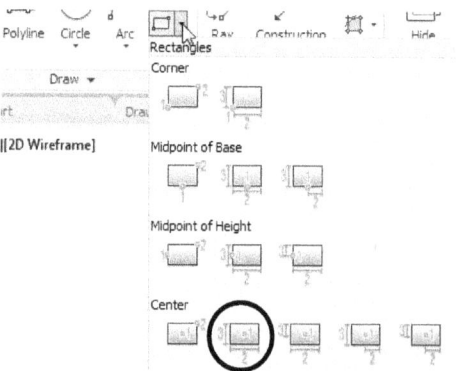

4. To set the rectangle location and size:
   - In the drawing area, object snap to the center of the circle.
   - Move the cursor horizontally, enter **400** in the edit box, and then press ENTER.
   - Move the cursor vertically, enter **100** in the edit box (as shown in the illustration below) and then press ENTER.

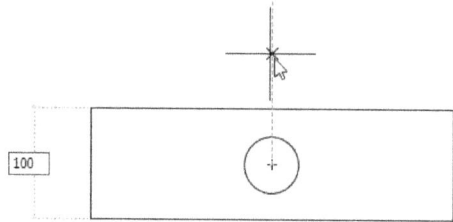

5. In the Status Bar, click the workspace switching icon. In the list of workspaces, select **Structure**. The Ribbon and Mechanical Browser should display as shown in the following illustration.

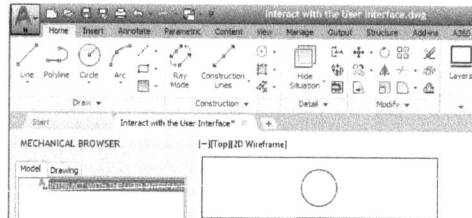

6. To minimize the Ribbon so that only the panel titles are displayed, click on the Ribbon title bar twice to cycle through different minimizing options. You can also select the Minimize to Panel Titles from the arrow drop-down list.

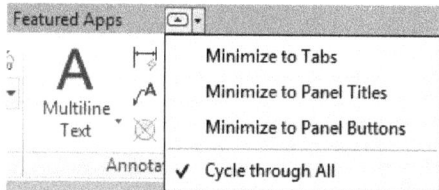

7. To remove the Parametric tab from the Ribbon, right-click on one of the tab titles in the Ribbon, select **Show Tabs**, and then select **Parametric** to uncheck the box. Review the Ribbon to see that the Parametric tab has been removed.

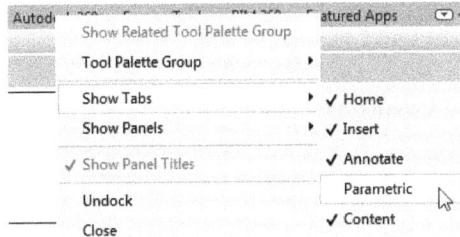

8. To restore the Ribbon, double-click on the Ribbon title bar until the required display method is restored.

9. To search for the commands that enable you to draw centerlines, do the following:

   - Click Application Menu.
   - In the Search field, enter **centerline**.
   - In the Matches list, click **Centerline Cross** to start the command.

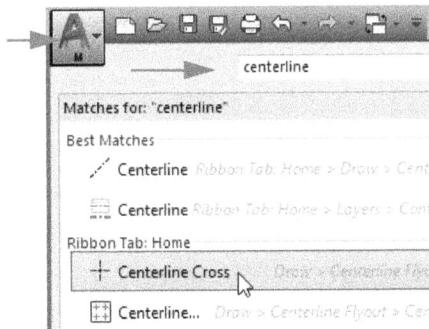

10. In the drawing area, object snap to the center of the circle and then to a quadrant on the circle to create the centerline as shown in the following illustration.

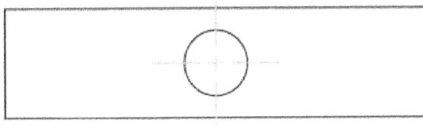

11. Save and close the file.

Lesson: Common Drawing Setup

Overview

This lesson describes the creation of drawing template files and the use of drawing templates for the creation of a new drawing.

Using drawing template files, you can maintain a consistent look and style across your drawings. Template files can also improve your productivity by decreasing the repetitive task of configuring the settings in a new drawing.

Objectives

After completing this lesson, you will be able to:

- Describe the purpose and benefit of drawing template files.
- Explain how mechanical standards impact the creation of drawing geometry.
- Create a new drawing based on an existing template file.
- Create a new drawing template file.
- Change the default location from which template files are accessed and saved.

About Drawing Templates

Learning to create and use template files is easier and more understandable if you know the purpose and benefits of using drawing templates.

Definition of Drawing Templates

You use drawing templates to provide a starting point for all of the new drawings that you create. In most design environments, the drawings that you create share some common properties and settings. Your company might have specific standards that each drawing must match, or your client might have specific requirements to which your drawing must adhere.

Several drawing templates are included with the software. Most of them are suitable for getting started and you can build on them to create a custom set of templates that are specific to your drawing requirements. When you save a drawing template, you save all of the drawing commonalities, eliminating the need to create or adjust properties and settings each time you create a new drawing.

Commonalities between drawings include:

- Configuration settings in the drawing, such as text styles and unit precision.
- Common blocks that you use to annotate drawings.
- Layout configurations and the insertion of borders and title blocks.
- Various settings in the Options dialog box. If the AutoCAD drawing symbol precedes a setting in the Options dialog box, any changes you make to that setting are specific to that drawing or template file. Therefore, ensure that the settings you change from the defaults are saved as part of your template. The AutoCAD Mechanical software adds seven tabs to the Options dialog box with additional configuration options and settings. Each of these tabs has *AM:* as a prefix to its name.
- The standard on the *AM:Standards* tab that you want active in the drawing. Within that standard, the different categories, such as layers, dimensions, borders, title blocks, parts lists, etc., would have their settings configured to match your requirements for the use of this template.

Drawing template files are differentiated from drawing files by their DWT file extension.

Example of Drawing Templates

You can set and save many options in a template file so that they are already configured in any drawing created from that template file. For AutoCAD Mechanical software drawing files, one of the most important items to configure and set to be current is the mechanical standard.

In the following illustration, the template file being created has the custom mechanical Standard of COMPANY XYZ set to active. This standard is based on the ISO standard and is configured to have all layers, dimensions, hole charts, drawing sheets, etc., match the final requirements for the drawings that use this template as a starting point.

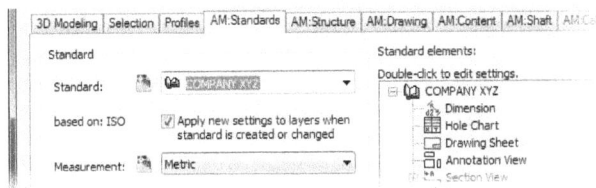

About Standards Based Design

To assist in the communication of design data, different industry organizations have established different standards. By learning how to configure and use the AutoCAD Mechanical software, your drawings conform to these standards and to any variations specified by your company.

In the following illustration, the custom standard called COMPANY XYZ is being selected to make it the active standard. This custom standard is initially based on one of the industry standards.

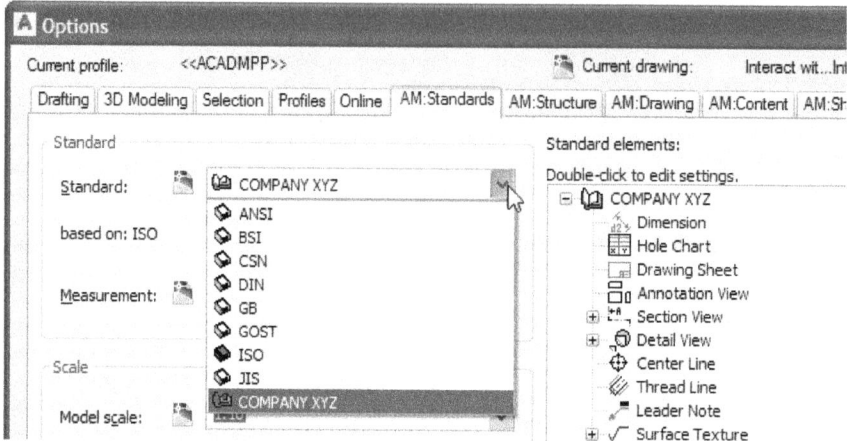

Definition of Standards Based Design

Standards-based design means that you create geometry and annotation that meets industry-accepted standards, such as ANSI, ISO, and DIN. It also means that you meet any company-specific variation to those industry standards. A standard contains multiple elements that you can edit to achieve the settings specific to your requirements. Customizing an existing standard can include, but is not limited to, changing the assigned layer geometry, changing how dimensions are to display, selecting which welding symbols can be added to the drawing, and defining the information to be stored in the BOM. You can activate or modify a standard on the *AM:Standards* tab in the Options dialog box.

To create design data that meets these standards, you can use the AutoCAD Mechanical software tools in place of the AutoCAD software drawing and modifying tools. You can apply your drawing standards to all new drawings that you create in the AutoCAD Mechanical software and to previously existing AutoCAD software drawing (DWG™) files that are opened in the AutoCAD Mechanical software.

In the following illustration, the Object Property Settings dialog box displays a list of some of the layer and object property configuration settings for the active standard. The settings in the active standard help you to ensure that all of the geometry that you create in the drawing is created on the correct layer with the correct properties. Because the objects are mapped to a layer that you configure to meet your company standards, you can focus on creating the design geometry and not on the layer on which you are creating the geometry.

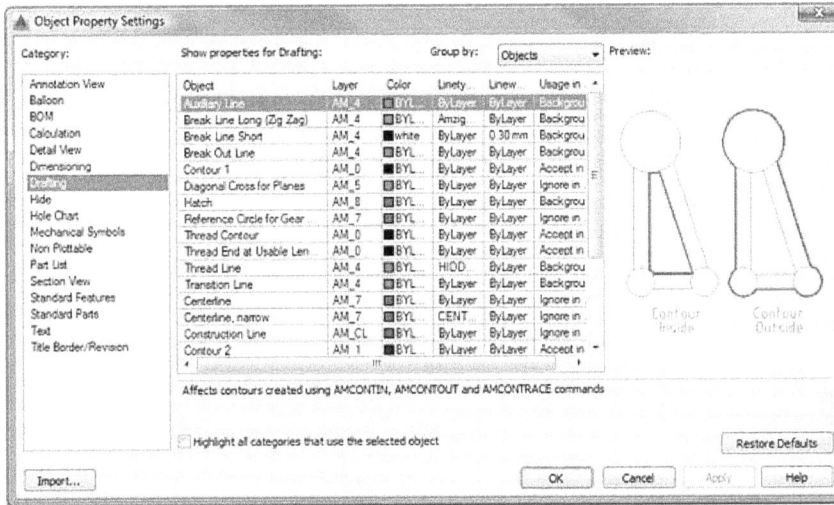

Example of Standards Based Design

Using the standards-based drafting and design tools in the AutoCAD Mechanical software, the two views of a spacer plate for planting corn seed were created following both the industry standards for notation and the company standards for layer settings and use.

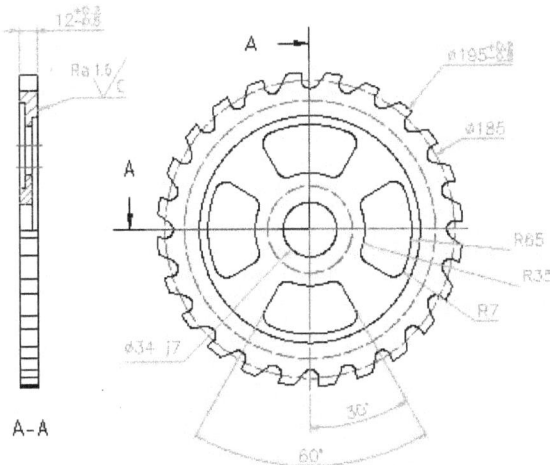

Creating a New Drawing Based on a Template

To realize how much time you save when using a template file, you must know how to create a new drawing that is based on an existing template.

In the following illustration, the AutoCAD Mechanical software default templates are shown in the Select template dialog box.

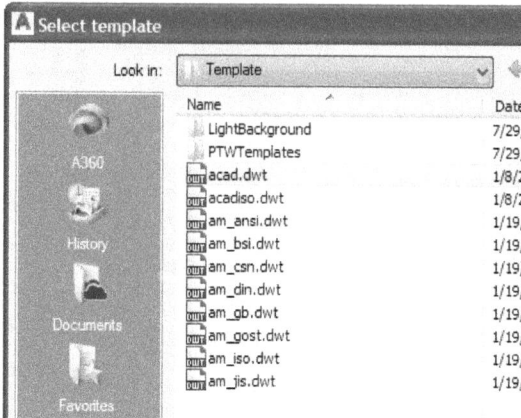

Access

Command Line: NEW

Menu Bar: File > New

Toolbar: Quick Access Toolbar

Application Menu: New

If you use the QNEW command, and the Default Template File Name for QNEW option is set to a value other than the default None, you are not prompted to select which template to use for the new

drawing. Also, starting a new drawing from the Start window or clicking ⊞ (New Drawing) in the File Tabs uses the most recently used drawing template and does not open the Select template dialog box.

Procedure: Creating a New Drawing Based on a Template

To create a new drawing based on an existing template file, complete the following steps:

1. In the Quick Access toolbar, click New.

2. In the Select Template dialog box, select the DWT template file that best matches your starting configuration requirements in the default folder or a folder to which you navigate.

Creating a New Template

You can create multiple templates when your setting requirements for new drawings vary. Each of the multiple templates contains the settings that match the requirements for those new drawings. To create a single template or multiple templates with varying settings, you need to learn how to create a new drawing template.

In the following illustration, a new drawing template file is being saved with the name COMPANY XYZ.

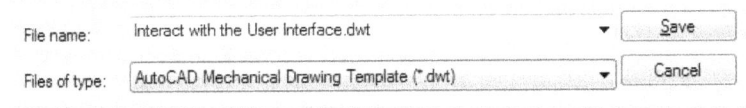

File name:	Interact with the User Interface.dwt	▼	Save
Files of type:	AutoCAD Mechanical Drawing Template (*.dwt)	▼	Cancel

Access

Command Line: SAVEAS

Menu Bar: File > Save As

Toolbar: Quick Access Toolbar

Application Menu: Save As

To save the file as a template after executing the Save As command, you must select AutoCAD Mechanical Drawing Template (*.DWT) from the Files of type drop-down list in the Save Drawing As dialog box. When you select this file format, the active folder for saving this file is changed to the folder specified in the Options dialog box.

> To edit a template file, you can open the file as you would any other standard drawing file. The exception is in the Select File dialog box in which you can select Drawing Template (*.DWT) from the Files of type drop-down list. Selecting this file format can change the active folder from which you are opening files.

Procedure: Creating a New Template

An overview of creating a new drawing template file is shown in the following steps:

1. Open a drawing or template on which you want to base a new template.

2. Change the mechanical standard and other settings in the opened file to match your requirements for the new template file.

3. Click Application Menu > Save As.

4. In the Save Drawing As dialog box, in the Files of type drop-down list, select AutoCAD Mechanical Drawing Template (*.DWT).

5. Navigate to the folder in which you want to save the template.

6. Enter a filename for the new template.

7. In the Template Options dialog box, click OK.

Changing the Location of Templates

For file security and productivity, you should learn why and how to change the default location from which template files are accessed and saved.

In the following illustration, the default folder location from which the template files are accessed and saved has been changed. Now when the Select Template dialog box opens, it automatically accesses this new location. This new location only contains the template files that are used by you and members of your design team.

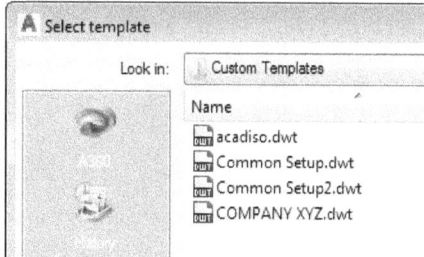

CAD Management of Templates

For file management purposes, you should save your template files in a central location within your file backup system. You can then change the path in your installation of the AutoCAD Mechanical software so that each time you create a new drawing, you can select the templates from that central location. If you are working in an environment in which multiple people need to create new drawings using the same template or set of templates, you can locate that central storage for the templates on a network drive and then change the template file location path to point to that network location.

It is easy to update templates when they are stored in a single location because you only need to edit a single file in a single location. Because everyone who uses the template accesses it from a single location, when you save the template with the changes, people automatically use that template's current settings when they create a new drawing.

Drawing Template File Location

To change the location from which the template files are accessed and saved, you can specify a new path in the Options dialog box. To access this path setting on the Files tab, click the plus sign (+) to expand the tree view for Template Settings and then select Drawing Template File Location, as shown in the following illustration. To specify a new path, click on the current path and a new one, or click Browse to navigate to and select the folder.

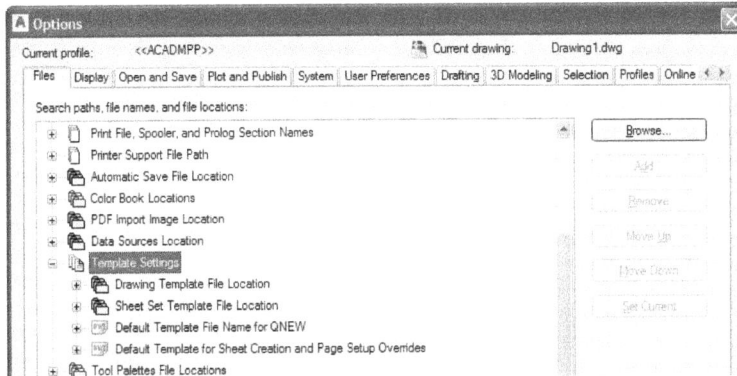

By changing the path under the Default Template File Name for QNEW category, you can specify which template file should be used automatically when the QNEW command is executed.

Procedure: Changing the Location of Templates

To change the folder location for accessing and saving template files, complete the following steps:

1. In the Options dialog box, click the Files tab.

2. In the Search paths, filenames, and file locations drop-down list, expand the tree view for Template Settings and then select Drawing Template File Location.

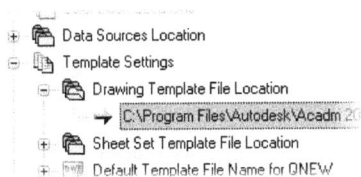

3. Enter a new local or network folder location or click Browse to select one.

Exercise: Create and Use Template Drawings

In this exercise, you will create template drawings and new drawings using one of the template files. You will also set a new folder location for saving and accessing template files.

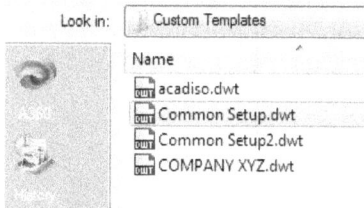

The completed exercise

1. Open *Common Drawing Setup.dwg*.

2. To change the active mechanical standard, do the following:

   - On the Application Menu, click Options.
   - In the Options dialog box, AM:Standards tab, on the Standard list, click PROJECT ABC.
   - Click OK.

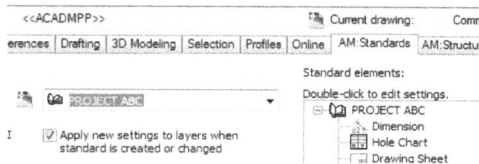

3. To change the display precision for the units, on the Application Menu, click Drawing Utilities > Units. In the Drawing Units dialog box, change the precision to three decimal places and click OK.

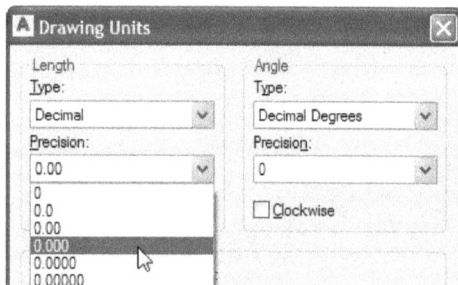

4. To create a template from this open drawing, do the following:

   - On the Application Menu, click Save As.
   - In the Save Drawing As dialog box, from the Files of type list, select AutoCAD Mechanical Drawing Template (*.DWT). Note the template files listed in the current folder.
   - Enter **Common Setup** in the File name box.
   - Click Save.

5. In the Template Options dialog box, click OK.

6. Close all open files.

7. To create a new drawing based on the template you just created, do the following:

   - On the Quick Access Toolbar, click New.
   - In the Select template dialog box, review the list of available templates from which you can select.
   - Select *Common Setup.dwt*.
   - Click Open.

8. On the Application Menu, click Options to ensure that PROJECT ABC is the active standard.

9. To change the folder in which template drawings are saved and accessed, do the following:

   - In the Options dialog box, click the left scroll arrow to the right of the tabs to scroll and view the Files tab.
   - Click the Files tab.

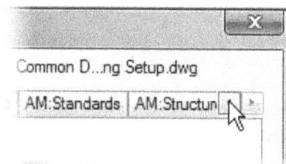

10. On the Files tab, in the Search paths, filenames, and file locations list, expand the tree view for Template Settings and expand Drawing Template File Location. Click the listed path.

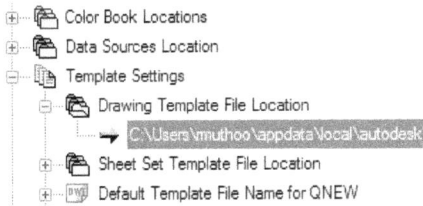

11. Note the current folder location and path so that you can specify it again after completing this exercise. The default path is *C:\Users\<User Name>\appdata\local\autodesk\autocad mechanical<version>\<revision>\<language>\acadm\template*.

12. To specify a new folder location, do the following:
    - Click Browse.
    - In the Browse for Folder dialog box, expand the folders to the location in which you installed the dataset for this training guide (*C:\AutoCAD Mechanical 2017 Essentials Practice Files*) and select the Custom Templates folder.
    - Click OK.

    Note that the Drawing Template File Location changes to the selected path.

13. In the Options dialog box, click OK.

14. On the Application Menu, click Save As.

15. To save the file as a template, do the following:
    - In the Save Drawing As dialog box, in the Files of type list, select AutoCAD Mechanical Drawing Template (*.DWT).
    - Note the folder location (Custom Templates) in which this template will be saved.
    - Enter **Common Setup2**.
    - Click Save.

16. In the Template Options dialog box, click OK.

17. Close all open files.

18. Using Windows Explorer, copy the *Common Setup.dwt* file from the default template file location (*C:\Users\<user name>\AppData \Local\Autodesk\AutoCAD Mechanical <version>\<revision>\<language>\Acadm\Template*) to the new template path (*C:\AutoCAD Mechanical 2017 Essentials Practice Files\Custom Templates*).

    Note: You might need to enter all or part of the path if the Appdata subfolder is not visible.

19. In the software, on the Quick Access Toolbar, click New. Do the following:
    - Review the available templates.
    - Select *Common Setup.dwt*.
    - Click Open.

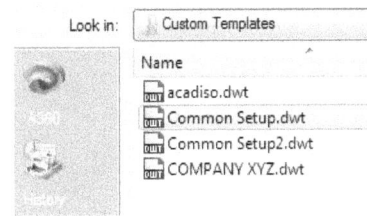

20. Close all open files.

Chapter Summary

In this chapter, you learned how to use the AutoCAD Mechanical interface. You also became familiar with finding various tools and menus, learned how to create drawing template files, and how to use drawing templates for the creation of a new drawings.

Having completed this chapter, you can:

- Identify the main interface elements, their setup, and the available Help information.
- Create and use drawing template files.

Object Property and Layer Management

In this chapter, you learn about the AutoCAD® Mechanical layer management system and how to control the display of geometry based on its layer type, change geometry to different layers, and set a layer to be current.

Objectives

After completing this chapter, you will be able to:

- Use coordinate geometry to draw a parcel and to list line and arc information.
- Use drawing cleanup to fix errors in a drawing.

Lesson: Property Management

Overview

This lesson describes the AutoCAD Mechanical object property and layer management system, where layers are initially configured, where the initial properties of objects are configured, and the interface you use to view and interact with the configurations.

You use intelligent, automated layers and object properties in the AutoCAD Mechanical software. When you use a Mechanical command, the current layer might change, or the layers might automatically be set to on or off, become locked or unlocked, or be filtered out of a selection set. The geometry you create is placed on the correct layer with the correct properties. When you understand where layers and object properties are configured, how the layer management system works, and how the interface you use in the drawing interacts with the configured layers, you can use the AutoCAD Mechanical software to create and manage layers and objects without having to manage them manually.

Objectives

After completing this lesson, you will be able to:

- Describe the automatic management of layers and object properties in the AutoCAD Mechanical software.
- Explain the process for managing layers using the Mechanical Layer Manager.
- Describe the process for preconfiguring the properties of objects in a standard.

About Automatic Management of Layers

To meet the drafting standards in most companies, it is critical that drawing geometry be created on the correct layer and with the correct properties, such as color and linetype. In the AutoCAD Mechanical software, a layer and the properties of a layer are the same as they are in the standard AutoCAD® software. The primary difference is in the way the layers are configured, created, and managed and that geometry is automatically created with the correct properties. To work efficiently with the AutoCAD Mechanical software, you need to understand its system of automatic management of layers and object properties.

In the following illustration, a drawing view of a design is shown with the geometry required to communicate its shape and characteristics, and with dimensions that identify its size. Using the AutoCAD Mechanical software commands, the geometry was created and automatically adhered to the standard. It was placed on the correct layer other properties were modified as well.

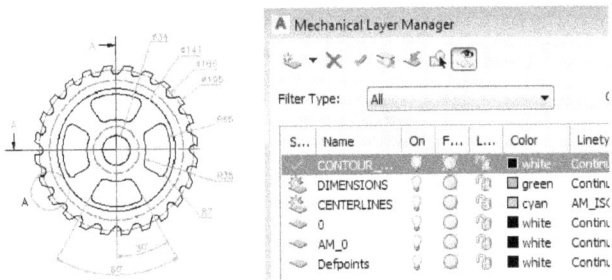

Definition of Automatic Management of Layers and Object Properties

Automatic management of layers and object properties is done as part of automatic property management. Automatic property management refers to the process where every AutoCAD Mechanical command checks a group of settings known as the object property settings and honors them during execution. This enables each command to be "aware" of the other commands and intelligently react to objects in the drawing area.

Automatic property management and the object property settings are central to the intelligence behind AutoCAD Mechanical commands. Each command has its own unique logic for dealing with object property settings. If you toggle off automatic property management, these commands stop checking object property settings and the intelligence built around object property settings is disabled. Instead of toggling off automatic property management, it is recommended that you modify the object property settings to suit your particular requirements. Your configuration settings associated with automatic property management are saved as part of the active standard.

You predefine the properties of objects that AutoCAD Mechanical commands create in the Object Property Settings dialog box. Within this dialog box, you can specify which layer the object should be created on. When automatic property management is enabled, AutoCAD Mechanical commands honor this setting and always create objects on the preassigned layer. If the layer does not exist, it is created automatically. Layers that are created by AutoCAD Mechanical commands in this manner are referred to as Mechanical layers.

You create and manage the layers that the objects are assigned to in the Mechanical Layer Manager dialog box. Within this dialog box, you can add layers and change properties such as their name, visibility settings, color, linetype, and lineweight.

Example of Automatic Management of Layers and Object Properties

A final drafted drawing is composed of geometry drawn with different types of lines, widths, and colors to help visually communicate the information in that design. In some cases, all aspects of the display of geometry are based on the layer it is created on and the properties of that layer. In other cases, the geometry might require a unique property such as a different color or lineweight. Because you configured the settings to the standard, AutoCAD Mechanical commands create the geometry with those settings.

The command for creating centerlines is an ideal example of AutoCAD Mechanical automatic property management in action. The command automatically creates the centerline on the correct layer regardless of what layer is current. Other geometry such as dimensions, weld symbols, surface texture symbols, and hatching can be assigned so that the software automatically creates the geometry according to the current settings in the standard.

In the following illustration, drawing views of a simple part are shown with the geometry required to communicate the shape and size of the part. The layers that were created in the drawing and the properties of the objects were automatically set as the geometry was being added to the drawing.

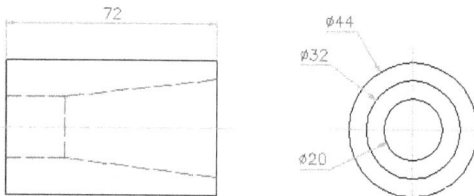

Managing Layers Using the Mechanical Layer Manager

When you are working on a drawing that was correctly configured when started, it should contain the correct layers and their properties should already be configured. With these items configured, your drawing tasks should only require you to access and use the configured layers. To focus your tasks and have access to the configured layers, use the Mechanical Layer Manager dialog box instead of the traditional AutoCAD software's Layer Properties Manager. To efficiently use the Mechanical Layer Manager, you need to understand the information it is showing and its available options.

Mechanical Layer Manager

When you start a drawing in the AutoCAD Mechanical software, it might only contain one or two layers. As you access an AutoCAD Mechanical software drawing and annotation tools, predefined Mechanical layers are automatically added to the list. You can use the Mechanical Layer Manager dialog box to control the layer states, set layers to be current, add predefined layers to the drawing, and create new layers.

From within the Mechanical Layer Manager, you can do the following:

- Create and edit AutoCAD and AutoCAD Mechanical software layers and properties.
- Convert AutoCAD software layers to AutoCAD Mechanical software layers.
- Import layer information and settings.
- Set a layer definition as the current layer and have the predefined layer added to the drawing file.

You can determine whether a layer is an AutoCAD software layer or an AutoCAD Mechanical software layer based on the differences between the icons displayed in the Status column for each layer.

Layers either already exist in the drawing or are only defined in the drawing and not yet created. You can identify layers that exist or layers that are only defined based on the way they display in the Mechanical Layer Manager. Mechanical layers that are only defined in the drawing file have their layer names displayed in the layer list in a light gray text and no icons are displayed in the Freeze, Lock, or Plot property columns. You can add a predefined layer to the drawing by double-clicking on its name in the layer list.

By default, only the layers used in the drawing are displayed in the layer list to make it more concise and easier to work with when editing a drawing. You can toggle on the display of all AutoCAD Mechanical software layer definitions to preconfigure a layer's properties or to make it current and add it to the drawing.

In the following illustration, a section of the Mechanical Layer Manager is shown with and without listing the Mechanical layers that were predefined in the drawing. The inclusion or exclusion of all of the defined layers in the layer list is based on the Show/Hide Layer Definitions option. You can toggle the setting for this option by clicking the identified button.

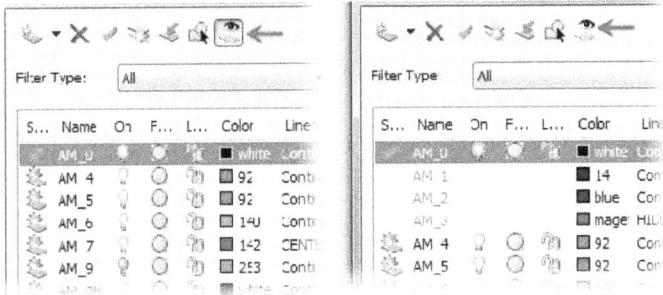

Predefined Mechanical Layers

Because Mechanical layers are created on the fly as they are required by the geometry creation commands that you execute, the layers to be created must be predefined in the drawing.

The AutoCAD Mechanical software includes several predefined Mechanical layers. By default, the naming format of layers follows a convention of AM_*. The actual layer name in a drawing depends on its configuration in the active standard. The layer names and settings can be different between drafting standards and between drawing files.

Each layer in the standard has its own designated use. Some layers are shared among several objects while other layers are exclusive to specific objects. The default layer assignments have been tried and tested for optimum use over several releases of the AutoCAD Mechanical software. If required, you can change the configuration settings for object properties so that you automatically adhere to your company standards or customer requirements.

There are two ways to customize layer assignments: rename existing layers to reflect the company standards or create a custom set of Mechanical layers and assign them to objects.

In the following illustration, the default layer names are shown on the left and the same layers are shown on the right after they have been renamed to match company standards. In this example, only the first layer (AM_0/CONTOUR_LINES) is actually created in the drawing. The other layers are only defined in the standard and are ready to be added.

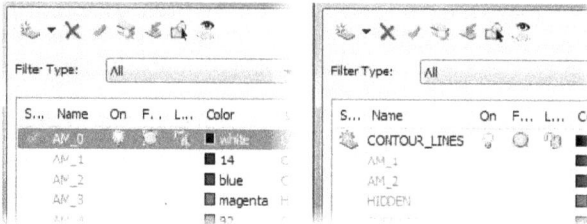

Access

Command Line: AMLAYER

Ribbon: Home tab > Layers panel > Mechanical Layer Manager

Menu Bar: Format > Mechanical Layer Manager

Mechanical Layer Manager Options

There are two key tasks to be done in the Mechanical Layer Manager. You can either configure the layer definitions and their properties and save them as part of your template drawing, or make changes to the properties of layers in a drawing in which you are actively working.

If the drawing you are working on was initially created in the traditional AutoCAD software, the layers that were created can be converted to Mechanical layers, enabling you to map objects to that layer. You can convert a layer to a Mechanical layer by right-clicking the AutoCAD software layer in the list and clicking Convert To Mechanical Layer. If the layers do not adhere to your standards because they were created without using your drawing template, you can import the layer and object property settings.

You set a layer to be the current layer by double-clicking on it, selecting the layer, and then clicking the Set Current option, or by right-clicking on the layer and clicking Set Current. Setting a Mechanical layer definition to be current when it has not yet been created in the drawing causes that layer to be created in the drawing and set to be current.

The properties that you can set for a layer are On/Off, Freeze/Thaw, Lock/Unlock, Color, Lineweight, Plot/No Plot, Replicate in Layer Groups, or enable overriding of color by a layer group.

To make it easier to view the list of layers and make changes, you can toggle on and off the display of Mechanical layer definitions and limit the layers that are listed to those that pertain to a specific mechanical category.

In addition to configuring layers, more options are available in the shortcut menu and in the top row of buttons. These can be used to visually identify the geometry that is on a layer by highlighting it in the drawing window. You can also move geometry to a specific layer and select all of the objects that are on a layer.

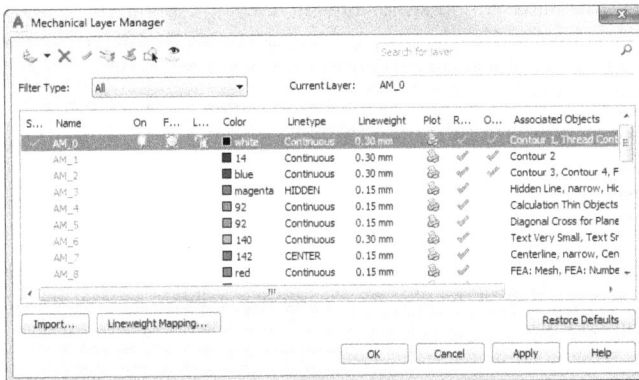

Full View/Simple View

You can display the layer list information in two different ways: Full or Simple. You can toggle between these views by clicking the corresponding option in the shortcut menu.

Full is the default and is similar to the AutoCAD software option in that it lists all of the layer's properties. Simple removes columns of information so that only the properties of On/Off, Freeze/Thaw, Lock/Unlock, and Description are displayed. You might want to switch to Simple if the layers are configured correctly and you no longer require the additional information.

In the following illustration, a portion of the left side of the Mechanical Layer Manager is shown in Full and Simple views.

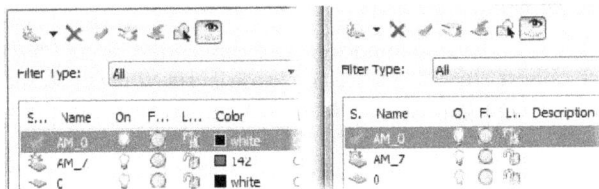

Process: Managing Layers Using the Mechanical Layer Manager

An overview of managing Mechanical layers with the Mechanical Layer Manager for use with automatic property management for mechanically created objects is shown in the following steps:

1. Open the Mechanical Layer Manager.

2. Convert existing AutoCAD software layers to Mechanical layers, change the property settings for layers that are created in the drawing or defined in the standard, or create a layer in the drawing from a Mechanical layer definition by setting that layer definition to be the current layer.

How to Configure Object Property Settings in a Standard

When you create and edit a drawing in the AutoCAD Mechanical software, properties for mechanically created geometry are set automatically based on the options that were configured for automatic property management. Because the initial configuration of your drawings should be based on a template file in which the drafting standard has been completely set to meet your requirements, you typically do not need to access and edit object property settings as you are working on a drawing.

Although you typically do not need to make changes to the configuration of object property settings, you should know and understand what it means to have object properties set in the standard, where object properties are configured, and the process of configuring them. This knowledge is helpful in understanding why the different mechanical objects you create automatically include specific properties.

The following illustration shows the centerlines are being created for the end view of an object and the results of their creation. The properties of the objects are automatically set as they are created using different Mechanical commands.

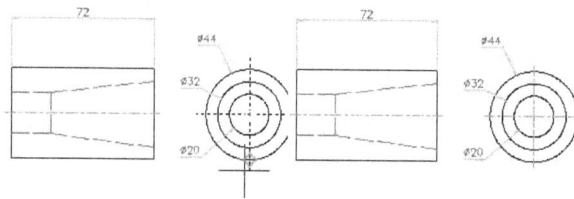

Object Property Settings

When the AutoCAD Mechanical software manages object properties, those properties are automatically applied to the mechanical objects and content that you create in the drawing, including placement on the correct layer. You can configure the settings separately for automatic object property management and for layer configuration.

When you are configuring your drawing or drawing template, you typically start by configuring the layers so you can then specify what objects are to be created on those layers. While the settings for layers are done in the Mechanical Layer Manager, you use the Object Properties dialog box to assign what layer an object is created on and if the object should have a different color, linetype, or lineweight from that specified layer. You also set whether that object should be ignored when calculating hidden geometry.

The configuration of the object property settings is part of the configuration of a drafting standard. Because it is part of a drafting standard, you should save your custom object property settings as part of the drawing template file that you use to create new drawings. You can open the Object Properties dialog box from the Standards Settings dialog box when editing the active standard.

Active Standard

In the Options dialog box, in the AM:Standards tab, you can select the standard that you want to activate for a drawing. The name that is displayed in the Standard list is the active standard in the drawing. When you select the standard from the list of available standards, the list under Standard elements displays all of the elements for that standard. The name of the selected standard is listed as the top element. After you double-click on the standard's name at the top of the list, the Standards Settings dialog box opens.

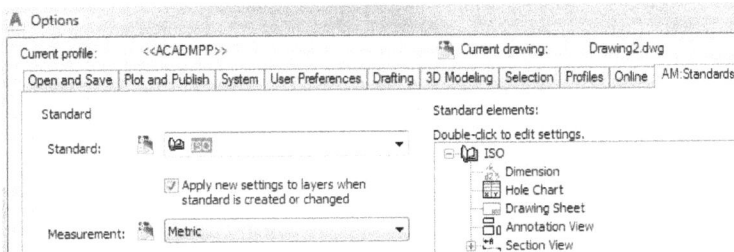

In the Standards Settings dialog box, click Settings under Object Properties to display the Object Property Settings dialog box. You can change the settings for objects created by mechanical tools in this dialog box.

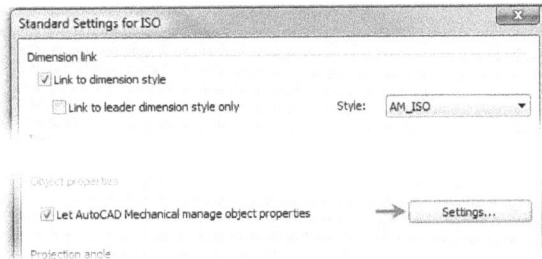

Object Property Settings Dialog Box

The Object Property Settings dialog box is set up to help you understand and identify the relationships and properties associated with the different objects.

The Object Property Settings dialog box has three distinct areas. The area on the left contains a list of object categories (1). When you select a category, the associated objects for that category are listed in the table in the middle of the dialog box (2). This table also displays the objects in a tree structure to help identify the relationship between objects. You can group this list by object or layer.

After you select an object in the middle table, the associated object is highlighted in the preview on the right (3). If the Highlight All Categories That Use the Selected Object checkbox is selected and the selected object participates in other categories, these categories are highlighted in the categories list on the left. An explanation displays below the properties table describing the purpose of a selected object in the properties list.

You can also use the middle table to change the properties of the selected object. When you change an object's properties, the preview on the right updates. If a property changes for an object that is shared between multiple categories, a dialog box opens prompting you about the other categories that are affected by the change.

If you have made property changes and want to have all properties revert to the default settings, click Restore Defaults. However, clicking Restore Defaults also resets the layer settings in the Mechanical Layer Manager. Any custom layer name is converted to an AutoCAD layer.

Process: Configuring Object Property Settings in a Standard

An overview of configuring the default object property settings in a standard for automatic property management of mechanically created objects is shown in the following steps:

1.   Select the drafting standard that you want to configure and open the Object Property Settings dialog box.

2.   In the Object Property Settings dialog box, in the Category list, select the object category that you want to configure.

3.   In the properties list for the selected category, in the Layer, Color, Linetype, Lineweight, and Usage In Hide columns, set the properties for the objects as required.

Exercise: Automatic Property Management

In this exercise, you will review the layer and object settings for automatic property management in two different drafting standards. You will then create additional geometry in the drawing file and review the layers and properties for that geometry.

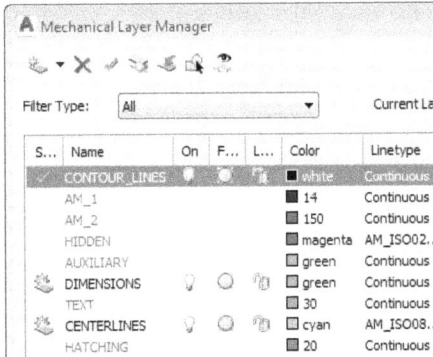

The completed exercise

1. Open *Property Management.dwg*.

2. To begin reviewing the layer configuration in the active standard:

    - Click Home tab > Layers panel > Mechanical Layer Manager.
    - In the Mechanical Layer Manager, review the list of layers that are currently in the drawing.

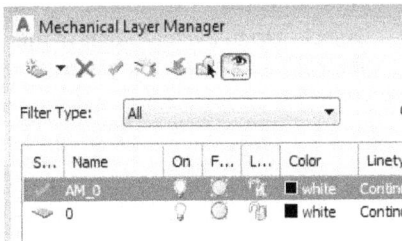

3. To review the list of all defined Mechanical layers:

    - In the Mechanical Layer Manager, click Show/Hide Layer Definitions.

    Review the list of layer names and colors. Note layers AM_0, AM_5, and AM_7.

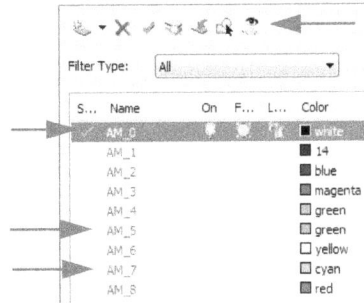

4. Click OK to close the dialog box.

5. To change the active standard:

    - Right-click anywhere in the drawing window and click Options.
    - In the AM:Standards tab, in the Standard list, select COMPANY XYZ.
    - Click OK.

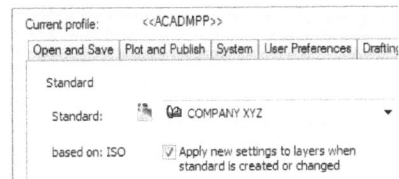

6. Review the new configured layer settings by doing the following:

    - Open the Mechanical Layer Manager.
    - In the Mechanical Layer Manager, scroll up the list of layer definitions to review their names and colors. Note the names that replaced layers AM_0, AM_5, and AM_7.

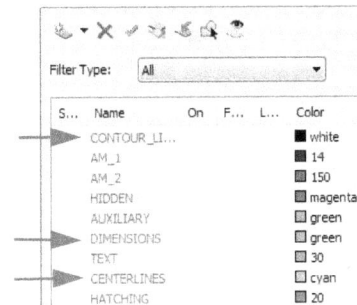

7. To review the list of layers that are currently in the drawing:

   - In the Mechanical Layer Manager, click Show/Hide Layer Definitions.
   - Review the list of displayed layers.
   - Click OK.

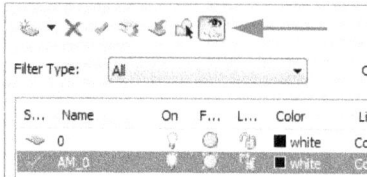

8. To begin reviewing the current object property settings:

   - Right-click anywhere in the drawing window and click Options.
   - In the AM:Standards tab, in the list of Standard elements (on the right side of the dialog box), double-click on COMPANY XYZ.

9. In the Standard Settings for COMPANY XYZ dialog box, under Object properties, click Settings.

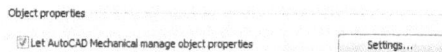

10. In the Object Property Settings dialog box, under Category, click Drafting.

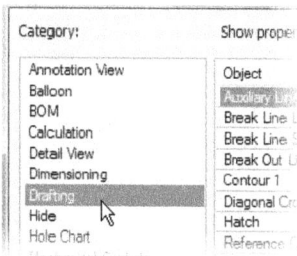

11. In the table of objects for the Drafting category, review the layer and color property settings for the Contour 1 and Centerline objects.

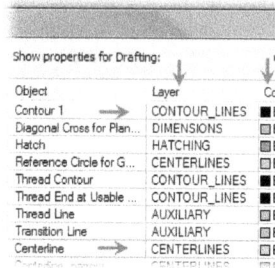

12. Click OK in each of the open dialog boxes to close them.

13. Click Home tab > Layers panel and expand the Mechanical Layers drop-down list. Select Contour to set the CONTOUR_LINES layer to be current. Note that it changes to CONTOUR_LINES in the Layer list.

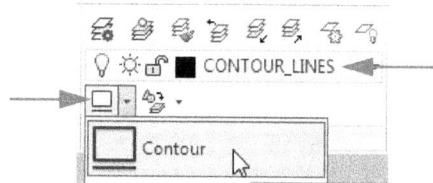

14. To add a centerline to the existing rectangle:

   - Click Home tab > Draw panel> Centerline.
   - Object snap to the midpoints of the vertical lines of the rectangle to create the centerline.

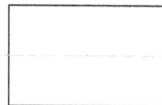

15. Begin to add a dimension:

- Click Annotate tab > Dimension panel > Power Dimension.
- For the first and second extension line origin points, object snap to the top two corners of the rectangle.

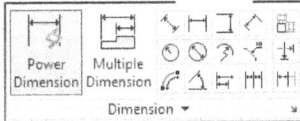

16. To position the dimension:

- Move the cursor up and click when the dimension display snaps into position and displays in red.
- On the Power Dimensioning contextual Ribbon tab, click Close Editor.
- Press ESC.

17. Review the current list of layers defined in the drawing:

- Click Home tab > Layers panel > Layer drop-down list.
- Note the listed layers.
- Press ESC.

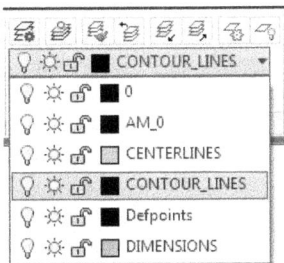

18. Review the list of layers created in the drawing with the list of layer definitions by doing the following:

- Open the Mechanical Layer Manager.
- Click Show/Hide Layer Definitions.
- Review the list of displayed layers.
- Click OK.

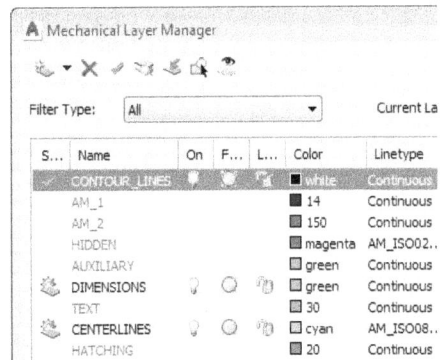

19. Save and close all files.

Lesson: Layer Control

Overview

You can control the display of geometry based on its layer type. You can also change geometry to different layers and set a layer to be current.

You can create geometry on different layers so that your drawings meet your company's drawing requirements. These standards are set to ensure consistency between the drawings regardless of who created or last modified them. The drawings have the same general style of appearance when plotted to paper, and anyone who opens the drawing can select the information that they want to display based on the layers that are currently visible. By learning how to change layer visibility, the layer on which the geometry is located, and the current layer, you can complete your work more quickly and easily.

In the following illustration, the assembly view is shown with and without geometry based on toggling off the construction and standard parts layers.

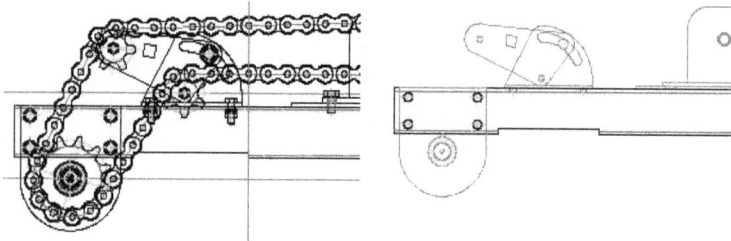

Objectives

After completing this lesson, you will be able to:

- Set the current layer based on the type of geometry that you want to create.
- Reset the layer settings to match the standard and move the geometry to another layer.
- Identify the commands that you use to toggle on and off the display of specific layer types.

Changing the Current Layer

Setting a layer to be current is not difficult but can be time-consuming when you are creating geometry that needs to be on different layers, or if you are not familiar with the layer-naming convention used in the drawing. By knowing how to change the current layer based on the type of geometry you want to create, you can quickly set the appropriate layer to be current while ensuring that the setting adheres to the active standard.

In the following illustration, the layer for hidden lines is in the process of being selected to become the current layer. The layer name that actually becomes current is based on the layer name in the active standard.

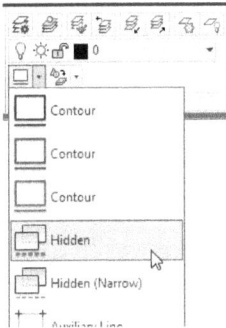

About Changing the Current Layer

You can change the current layer with the Mechanical Layer Manager or the Mechanical Layers drop-down list on the Home tab>Layers panel.

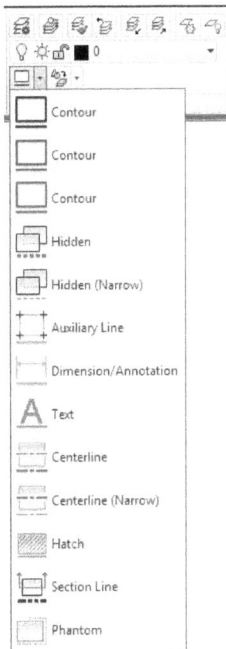

Selecting a layer in the Layers drop-down list is the quickest method of setting a layer to be current. Layers that you set to be current that do not yet exist in the drawing are automatically created and then set to be current. The types of objects that the layer is used for are indicated in the tooltips on the buttons.

Change Layer Buttons

All layers have specific purposes. For example, you can use contour layers for drawing solid object lines. The following table shows the layer buttons, what object type they are used for, the layer name, and the linetype used. If you change the layer name in the standard from the defaults listed here, these buttons set that new layer name to be current.

Icon	Option	Description
	Contour	Sets the current layer to AM_0. This is the first default contour layer. The linetype is set to Bylayer.
	Contour	Sets the current layer to AM_1. This is the second default contour layer. The linetype is set to Bylayer.
	Contour	Sets the current layer to AM_2. This is the third default contour layer. The linetype is set to Bylayer.
	Hidden	Sets the current layer to AM_3. The linetype is set to Bylayer.
	Hidden (Narrow)	Sets the current layer to AM_3. The linetype is set to an override. The linetype style uses a shorter length dash and space. The name of the linetype used for the override varies depending on which standard is current.
	Auxiliary Line	Sets the current layer to AM_4. The linetype is set to Bylayer.
	Dimension/ Annotation	Sets the current layer to AM_5. The linetype is set to Bylayer.
	Text	Sets the current layer to AM_6. The linetype is set to Bylayer.
	Centerline	Sets the current layer to AM_7. The linetype is set to Bylayer.
	Centerline (Narrow)	Sets the current layer to AM_7. The linetype style uses shorter dashes and spaces. The name of the linetype used for the override varies depending on which standard is current.
	Hatch	Sets the current layer to AM_8. The linetype is set to Bylayer.
	Section Line	Sets the current layer to AM_10. The linetype is set to Bylayer.
	Phantom	Sets the current layer to AM_11. The linetype is set to Bylayer.

Procedure: Setting a Layer to be Current from the Layers Panel

An overview of setting a layer to be current in the drawing by selecting its layer type from the Layer drop-down list is shown in the following steps:

1. Click Home tab > Layers panel > Mechanical Layers drop-down list.

2. On the drop-down list, click the button for the layer that you want to set to be current.

Procedure: Setting a Layer to be Current in the Mechanical Layer Manager Dialog Box

An overview of setting a layer to be current in the drawing by selecting its layer in the Mechanical Layer Manager is shown in the following steps:

1. Click Home tab > Layers panel > Mechanical Layer Manager.

2. In the Mechanical Layer Manager, double-click on the layer that you want to set to be current. To set a layer to be active, that is currently only defined in the standard and has not yet been created in the drawing file, toggle on the Show/Hide Layer Definitions option.

Layer Functions

As you are working on a drawing, you might note that some of the geometry does not reside on the correct layer, or that the layer properties have been changed from the settings in the active standard. To move the geometry to the correct layer or set the layer properties so that they match the settings in the active standard with minimal effort, you need to learn how to use the commands that are available for such tasks.

Reset Layers to the Current Layer Configuration

You can use the Reset All Layers command to reset the layer properties in the drawing. When you do so, the layers update to match the configuration in the current standard.

If any of the layer properties have been modified using the AutoCAD software layer tools, the layer properties are reset to follow the current standards in the AutoCAD Mechanical software. If you have overridden the properties for individual objects using the Properties Override dialog box, the properties are not changed back to the current configuration.

Access

Reset All Layers	Command Line: AMLAYRESET
	Ribbon: N/A
	Menu Bar: Format > Layer Tools > Reset All Layers

Move Objects to Another Layer

You can use the Move to Another Layer command to move drawing objects to another layer, which enables you to select the objects that you want to move and then select the layer to which you want them to be moved. If the layer does not yet exist, it is created.

Access

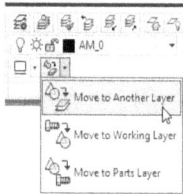

Command Line: AMLAYMOVE

Ribbon: Home tab > Layers panel > Move to Another Layer drop-down list > Move to Another Layer

Menu Bar: Modify > Properties > Move to another Layer

Move Objects to the Parts Layer

The Move to Parts Layer command enables you to move objects that are on working layers onto the corresponding standard parts layer of the same layer group. Use this command if you have created a part that you want to locate on the layers with standard parts. This command enables you to change to the appropriate layer in the active standard without having to know the layer names.

Access

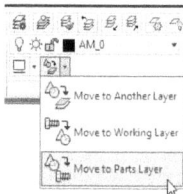

Command Line: AMLAYMOVEPL

Ribbon: Home tab > Layers panel > Move to Another Layer drop-down list > Move to Parts Layer

Menu Bar: Modify > Properties > Move to Parts Layer

Move Objects to the Working Layer

You can use the Move to Working Layer command to move objects that are on standard parts layers onto the corresponding working layer of the same layer group. Use this command when a part resides on the layers for standard parts and you do not want it to be on those layers. This command enables you to change to the correct layer in the active standard without having to know the layer names.

Access

Command Line: AMLAYMOVEWL

Ribbon: Home tab > Layers panel > Move to Another Layer drop-down list > Move to Working Layer

Menu Bar: Modify > Properties > Move to Working Layer

Layer Display

A primary benefit of creating geometry on different layers is to control what you see in the drawing. You can access specific commands that speed up the task of toggling off and on the geometry's visibility on specific types of layers. To accomplish these quick changes in layer visibility, you must learn what types of layers you can toggle on and off and how to access the commands.

Toggling the Visibility of Standard Parts On and Off

You can use the Standard Parts On/Off command to control the visibility of standard parts. When you use the command, all of the layers for the standard parts (AM_*N) are toggled on or off. However, only standard parts placed from the standard parts library or any object drawn on the AM_*N layers are toggled on or off. If you move standard parts to a different layer, the Standard Parts On/Off command does not change the visibility of the parts. When you use the command, you do not have to know all of the layer names.

Access

Command Line: AMLAYPARTO

Ribbon: Home tab > expanded Layers panel > Standard Parts On/Off

Menu Bar: Format > Layer Tools > Standard Parts On/Off

Toggling the Visibility of Construction Lines On and Off

You can use the Construction Line On/Off command to toggle construction line layers (AM_CL) on or off. Use this shortcut to avoid sorting through all of the layers to find the layer to toggle on or off. You can set up construction lines early in the drawing process, and then toggle them on and off as you create the drawing.

Access

Command Line: AMCLINEO

Ribbon: Home tab > expanded Layers panel > Construction Lines On/Off

Menu Bar: Format > Layer Tools > Construction Line On/Off

Locking and Unlocking Construction Lines

You use the Construction Lines Lock/Unlock command to lock or unlock construction line layers.

When you are modifying other geometry that is around construction lines, you might want to lock the construction lines to prevent the lines from being moved accidentally. You can use the Construction Line Lock/Unlock command as a shortcut for finding the AM_CL layer and manually locking or unlocking it. When you use the command, you do not have to know all of the layer names.

Access

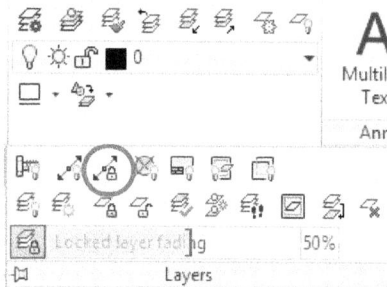

Command Line: AMCLINEL

Ribbon: Home tab > expanded Layers panel > Construction Lines Lock/Unlock

Menu Bar: Format > Layer Tools > Construction Line Lock/Unlock

Toggling the Visibility of the Title Block On and Off

You can use the Title Block Layer On/Off command to control the title block visibility. This command toggles the title block and border layer on or off. For this command to work, the title block must be on the layer defined for borders and title blocks as set in the current standard.

Access

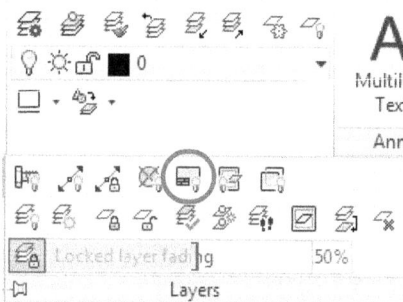

Command Line: AMLAYTIBLO

Ribbon: Home tab > expanded Layers panel > Title Block Layer On/Off

Menu Bar: Format > Layer Tools > Title Block Layer On/Off

Toggling the Visibility of Viewports On and Off

You can use the Viewport Layer On/Off command to control the visibility of the viewport layer (AM_VIEWS). For this command to work, the viewport must be created on the AM_VIEWS layer. Using this command lessens the need for knowing all of the layer names.

Access

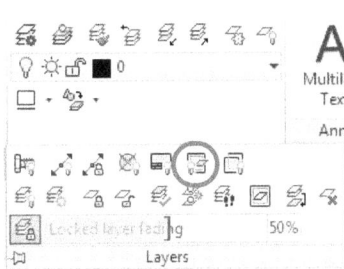

Command Line: AMLAYVPO

Ribbon: Home tab > Layers panel > Viewport Layer On/Off

Menu Bar: Format > Layer Tools > Viewport Layer On/Off

Exercise: Control Layer Display and Geometry on Layers

In this exercise, you will change the display of layers and set different layers to be current during the process of adding and modifying geometry to a part in an assembly.

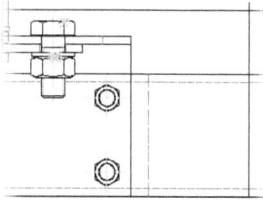

The completed exercise

1. Open *Layer Control.dwg*.

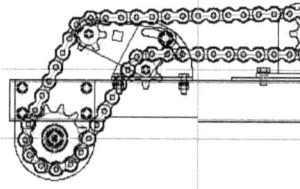

2. On the Home tab > expanded Layers panel, click the push pin icon in the lower left corner to pin the panel open to easily access all of the commands that are used in the exercise.

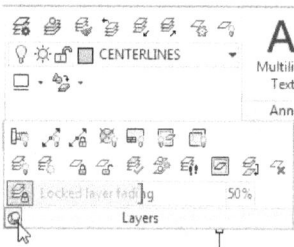

3. In the expanded Layers panel, click Construction Lines On/Off. Note that the red construction lines are removed. Zoom in near the bottom and note the missing vertical line between the two horizontal lines.

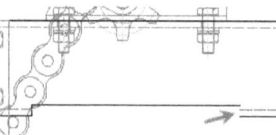

4. In the open Layer panel > Mechanical Layers drop-down list, select the first contour button. The layer CONTOUR_LINES should now be set to be current.

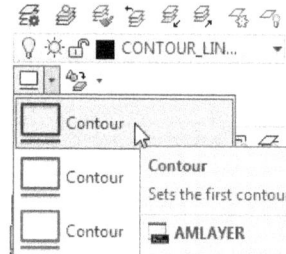

5. Draw a line from end point to end point to join the two horizontal lines.

6. In the expanded Layers panel, click Standards Parts On/Off. Note which geometry is no longer displayed and that the left end line for the square tube part is now missing.

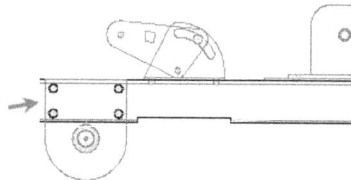

7. In the expanded Layers panel, click Standards Parts On/Off again to toggle the standard parts back on to edit that line.

8. To change the layer on which the end line resides, do the following:

    - In the expanded Layers panel > Move to Another Layer drop-down, click Move to Working Layer.
    - Select the left end vertical line that was not previously displayed.
    - Press ENTER.

9. In the expanded Layers panel, click Standards Parts On/Off. Note that some of the geometry is no longer displayed but the end line remains displayed when this layer is off.

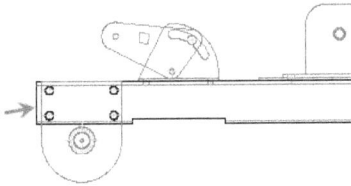

10. Click Standards Parts On/Off again.

11. Pan upwards until the upper parts are visible in the view.

12. Click Construction Lines On/Off. Zoom into the rectangular part.

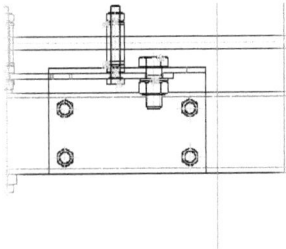

13. In the Layers panel, click Mechanical Layers drop-down list > Hidden. The layer HIDDEN is now set to be current.

14. On the right side of the rectangular part, draw a line on the square tube part using the construction line intersection locations as your start and end points.

15. Click Construction Lines On/Off and note the new line (dashed magenta line).

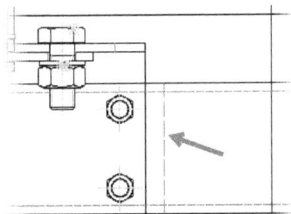

16. Unpin the Layers panel. Save and close all files.

Chapter Summary

In this chapter, you learned about the AutoCAD Mechanical layer management system and how to control the display of geometry based on its layer type, change geometry to different layers, and to set a layer to be current.

Having completed this chapter, you can:

- Describe the object property and layer management system, where layers are configured, and the interface.
- Change layer visibility, which layer the geometry is on, and which layer is current.

Organizing Drawing Geometry

In this chapter, you learn about the workflows available in the AutoCAD® Mechanical software for organizing drawing geometry. You then learn how to use Mechanical structure for the creation of components, component views, and folders within Mechanical structure. You also learn how to insert instances of structure definitions into a drawing and how to edit structure definitions.

Objectives

After completing this chapter, you will be able to:

- Identify and describe the different ways of creating and organizing drawing geometry in the AutoCAD Mechanical software.
- Create Mechanical structure in a drawing by creating components, component views, and folders.
- Insert instances of structure definitions into the drawing and edit structure definitions.

Lesson: Drawing Creation Workflows and Organization

Overview

This lesson describes the different workflows that you can use to organize your drawing geometry as you create and reuse it in the AutoCAD Mechanical software.

When you have more than one way of accomplishing something, you should understand all of the methods so that you can select the most appropriate one for your needs. For example, when you create a drawing, you can create it so that you plot the geometry directly from model space or from individual layouts. The method you use depends on your requirements. To work efficiently with the geometry in a drawing while meeting your requirements, you need to understand the different ways of creating and organizing drawing geometry in the AutoCAD Mechanical software.

Objectives

After completing this lesson, you will be able to:

- Explain the differences between the workflows for organizing drawing geometry in the AutoCAD Mechanical software.
- Describe the purpose and benefit of Mechanical structure.

About the Organization Methods

The AutoCAD Mechanical software has different methods and workflows that you can use to organize your drawing geometry, and various tool sets to accomplish these tasks. By understanding the differences between the workflows, you can select the workflow that you want to follow when creating your designs. By understanding the workflows before learning the AutoCAD Mechanical tools and techniques, you can learn whether they apply to all workflows or only to a specific workflow. This makes it easier to understand the importance and use of the tool or technique you are learning at the time.

Organization Methods Defined

When you use the AutoCAD Mechanical software, there are three primary ways in which you can create and organize the drawing geometry. The three methods are:

- Follow the traditional AutoCAD® software workflow.
- Use layer groups to organize the geometry.
- Use Mechanical structure to organize and reuse the drawing geometry.

When you follow the traditional AutoCAD software method of geometry organization, a completed drawing of different parts consists of separate individual objects intermixed with some blocks. To move any part, you have to ensure that you select each individual object segment that makes up that part. If you want to change the visibility of one part, you have to manually create unique sets of layers for each part.

When you use layer groups, the creation and organization of geometry in a drawing is almost exactly is it is done in the AutoCAD software. The difference is that layer groups have tools and options that enable you to automate the creation of unique layers for different parts.

When you use Mechanical structure, the completed drawing consists of definitions of parts and assemblies. You can create the visible, hidden, and centerline geometry that defines a part within the part definition. The assembly design then consists of bringing the parts together. You can add, modify, or remove geometry or parts from a part or assembly definition at any time. To change the position or orientation of a part or assembly definition, you need to select one piece of geometry in that definition to select all of it, instead of having to select every individual object that shows the part or assembly. If you want to change the visibility of a part or subassembly, you can toggle on and off the visibility of just that part or assembly definition without having to manage or manipulate layers.

Example Comparing Creation Workflows

The following example compares the traditional AutoCAD software workflow of creating and organizing drawing geometry with the Mechanical structure workflow. For this comparison, a simple hanger assembly that clamps to a pipe is used. This hanger design consists of three parts that are bolted together.

In the following illustration, the traditional AutoCAD workflow was followed to complete the design, with the final design shown on the left. The objects are drawn as individual objects and remain as such. Selecting an object activates the grips for that object. Moving the geometry apart shows how the geometry is created to represent the assembly design.

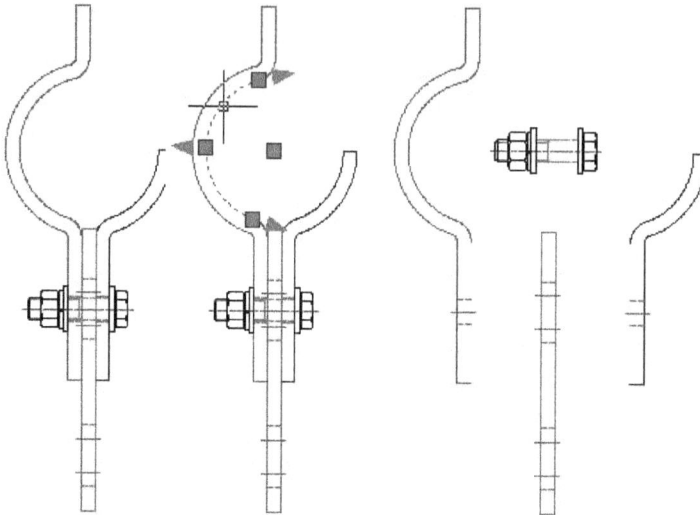

In the following illustration, Mechanical structure was used to complete the design with the final design shown on the left. The objects are drawn as individual objects within different part definitions. When you select an object, the grip for that entire part definition becomes active. The illustration on the right shows the individual part definitions moved apart with the contents of the Browser included to show how each part is a separate definition.

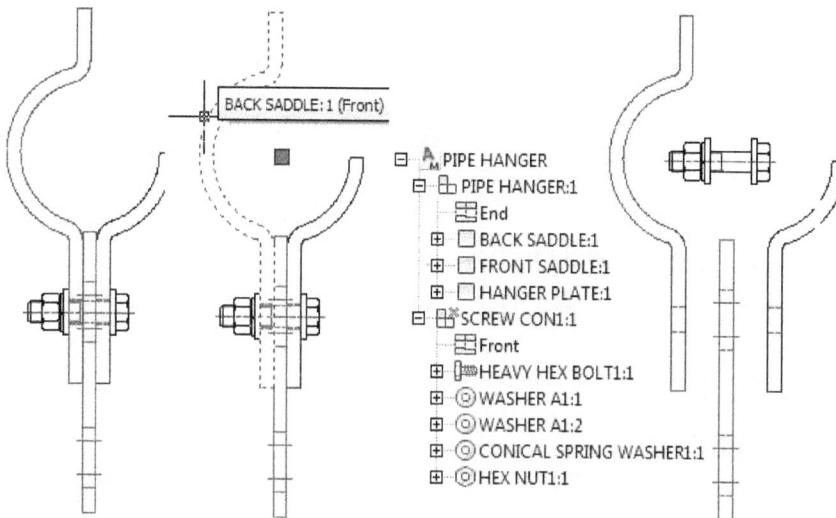

About Mechanical Structure

Once you understand Mechanical structure and how it can benefit you during the creation and modification of a 2D design, you can decide whether you want to learn more about the commands and options for creating and leveraging Mechanical structure in your designs.

Using Mechanical structure, the different parts of the chain drive system shown in the following illustration were created, manipulated, and modified as a part and not as a line, arc, and circle that represent a view of the overall assembly. Using Mechanical structure, the completed view becomes the byproduct of creating and positioning its parts. Additional views of the parts in the assembly were inserted into the drawing to show how the same part can be displayed multiple times and in different ways.

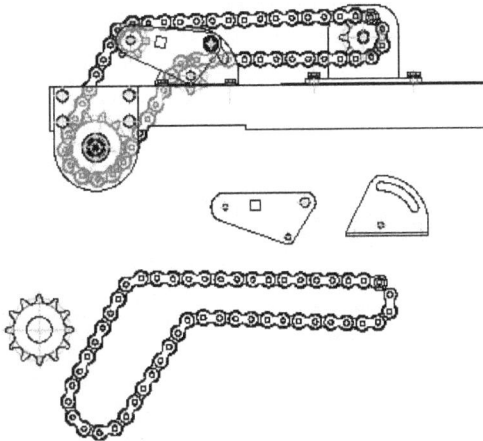

Definition of Mechanical Structure

Mechanical structure is a combination of commands, capabilities, and workflow that assists you when creating, modifying, and documenting your design. Mechanical structure enables you to logically create and organize your 2D geometry into parts and assemblies. It uses components and folders to logically define how independent geometry relates to each other. It helps you to concentrate on the parts and assemblies within your design instead of on the individual lines, arcs, and circles that make up the different views of the design. Using Mechanical structure, you can create the same hierarchical part to assembly structure relationship during the design process that you intend to use during the manufacture and assembly of the product.

After the part and assembly data has been defined as having a Mechanical structure, you can quickly reuse different views in other designs and populate the data in parts lists and bill of materials (BOM). By adding or deleting instances of the same part or assembly to the design, the quantity in the BOM updates to reflect the correct current count.

When it comes time to modify a part or assembly, editing one instance updates all instances of that view. This means you do not need to edit the part or assembly geometry in each location in which it is used in your design.

Organization of Geometry Using Mechanical Structure

When you create Mechanical structure to represent a part, you can define the part as a component in the drawing. In that part component, you can create special folders called component views. These component views contain the geometry that represents a specific view of the part. Examples of specific views include top, front, right, and left. An assembly is also a component and is composed of part and subassembly components. The drawing views of the assembly are then defined based on the collection of part and subassembly component views.

To help you access and reuse this logical organization of information, the AutoCAD Mechanical software displays the organizational structure in a hierarchical fashion in a palette called the Mechanical Browser. The drawing geometry associated with a part is organized into different views of that part and are nested below the part in the Browser. To further refine the structure and organize the geometry within a part or assembly component view, you can create folders and define geometry within them. Individual parts are nested below the overall assembly or under subassemblies.

In the following illustration, the same Mechanical structure that is displayed in the Browser is shown with and without balloon callouts.

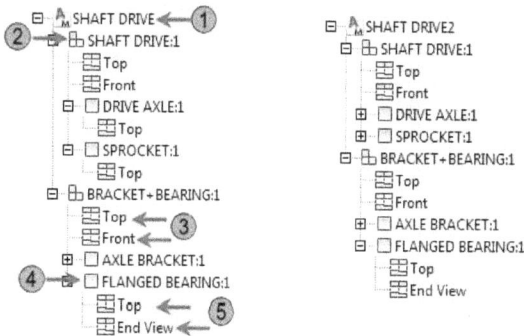

1. The top drawing node for the Mechanical structure. Right-click to access commands to create and insert structure content at the upper level of the structure. You can also right-click and click Browser Options to adjust the display options applied to the Browser content.

2. Assembly component icon indicating an assembly component.

3. Component views for the subassembly component.

4. Part component icon indicating a part component.

5. Component views for the part component.

Structure is Like Packaging Wrappers

Mechanical structure can be thought of as a special wrapper around your data and geometry. The component is the overall organizing wrapper for a part or assembly. An assembly component is a single wrapper containing part components, subassembly components, and the views of those parts or subassemblies. A part component is a wrapper that contains the different component views showing the part in different ways and directions. The component view within a part component wraps up the individual pieces of geometry that represent that part in a specific viewing direction.

Example of Mechanical Structure

When creating a design of an assembly, Mechanical structure makes the task of organizing and manipulating the geometry that represents different parts in different views easier and more logical. In the following illustration, two views of a mechanical gripper are shown with the Mechanical Browser. In the Browser, the part titled LEVER is selected. The geometry defined within its two views is shown is highlighted with bold lines in the drawing area in the two views. This structure enables you to move and rotate each view as if all line, circle, and arc objects in that view were a single part object. You can manipulate them all as a single part while still being able to edit the individual objects in the view.

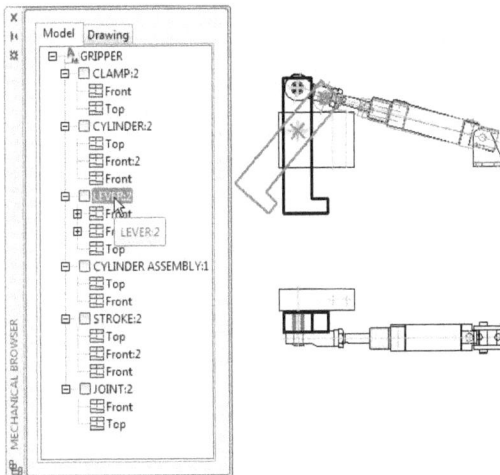

Lesson: Structuring Data in Drawings

Overview

This lesson describes Mechanical structure and the creation of components, component views, and folders within Mechanical structure.

You can create different drawing views of a design to communicate its shape, size, position, orientation, and purpose. Mechanical structure helps you to create, manage, and reuse your design data by bringing logical organization to the independent lines, arcs, and circles that you create to represent your design in those different views.

In the following illustration, a section of the Browser shows the parts and subassemblies that collectively create the machine drawing shown to the right.

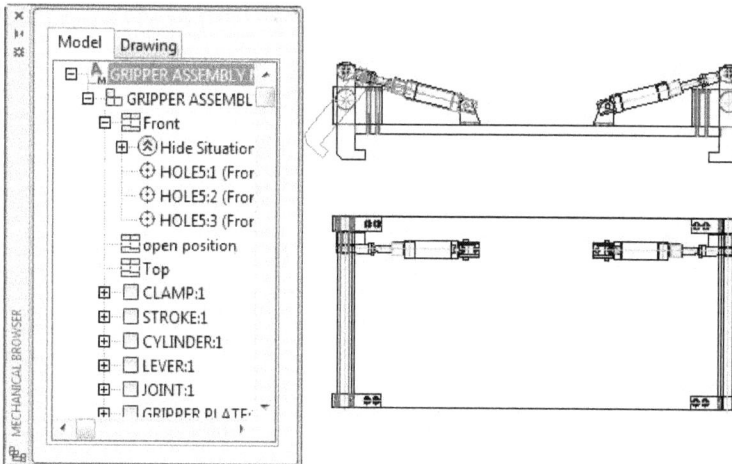

Objectives

After completing this lesson, you will be able to:

- Describe the process for creating a Mechanically structured design.
- Create a new component and new component view.
- Create Mechanical structure folders within a component view.
- Restructure components in the Browser.
- Identify the settings that control structure creation.

How to Create a Structured Design

When you use Mechanical structure to create, modify, and document your design, you benefit in a number of ways from having your 2D geometry organized into logical parts and assemblies. These include the ease of reuse in one or more designs, the ease of modifying a part and having all instances reflect those changes, the automatic population of the bill of materials, and the ability to show the same design in multiple ways. To effectively use Mechanical structure and reap these benefits, you must first learn the order in which you can define structure, data, and geometry within the structure.

How to Create a Structured Design

There are three primary workflows for the creation of a Mechanical structure. Regardless of which workflow you use, the order in which you create Mechanical structure is very flexible.

Following one workflow, you can define the assembly component and part components within the assembly. When you have defined the structure relationship from the assembly down to the part, you begin to create the geometry within the part component.

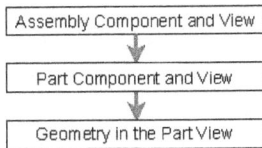

Following another workflow, you begin by creating the geometry for a part. With the geometry created, you then create a part component and define the geometry as a component view of that part. You then combine part components to create an assembly component.

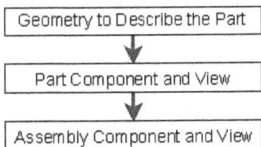

The third workflow is a combination of the first two workflows. Here you create some of the assemblies and parts by first defining their structure, but for other parts you begin by creating their geometry.

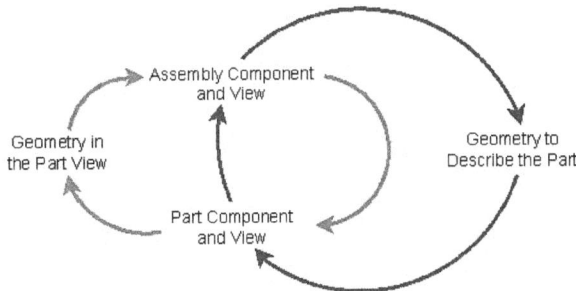

Workflow Example

In the following illustration, the two primary workflows are indicated by the information being populated in the Browser to create the drawing shown on the right. The top workflow shows the assembly components being created, followed by the part components within the assembly. After the part is created at the correct structure level, the view geometry would be created for that part. The bottom workflow shows the part components and their views with the geometry being created first. Once the parts and their views have been created, the assemblies in which they belong are created. Regardless of which workflow method you use, the end result is the same.

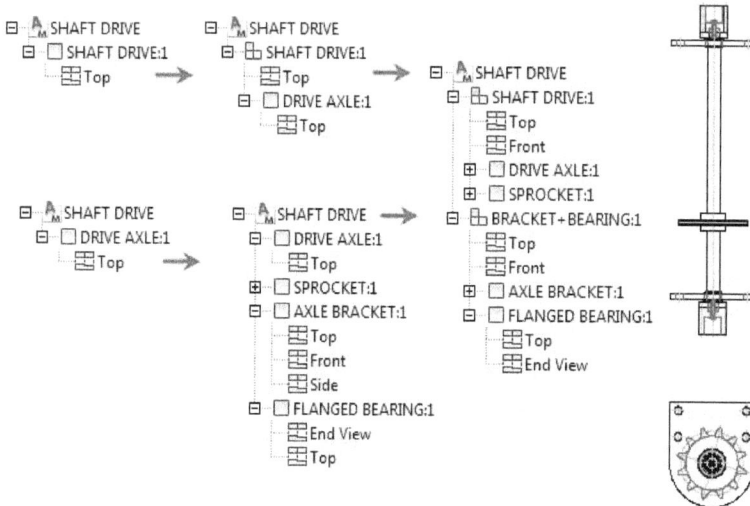

Creating Components and Component Views

The products you design and create include parts and assemblies. To create the same part and assembly structure relationship in your drawings, you must learn how to create new components and component views.

In the following illustration, the drawing is structurally defined as an assembly consisting of parts, a subassembly, and associated drawing views.

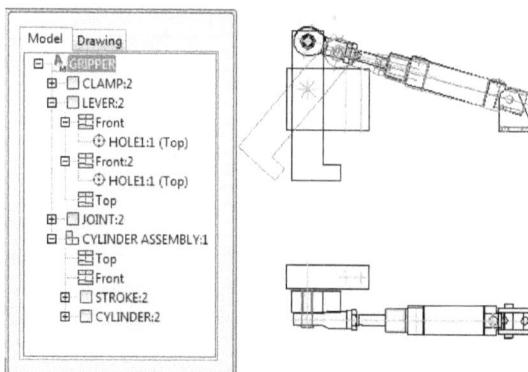

About Creating Components and Component Views

When you create a new component, you also create its component view. Components are displayed in the Browser with an icon and always have at least one component view listed under them. A part component icon displays as a single square, while an assembly component icon displays as three squares stacked together.

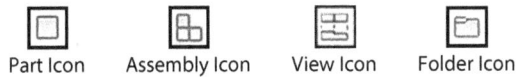

Part Icon   Assembly Icon   View Icon   Folder Icon

As with almost all commands in the AutoCAD software, there are many different ways in which you can execute the commands to create new components or new component views. There are some key benefits to using the Browser shortcut menu for the component and component view creation commands. First, this workflow follows the logical progression of focusing on which part you need to create or which view in a part you need to create. Second, you define where in the structure this new item should be created based on the node in the Browser on which you right-click.

For example, right-clicking in the Browser on a component or component view and clicking New > Component in the shortcut menu, creates a new part component nested below the component on which you right-clicked. For example, if you right-clicked on a part component, it would change to an assembly component because the new part component is now defined within it.

To create a new component at the highest level in the structure, right-click on the node for the drawing filename as shown in the following illustration.

To create a new component view from the Browser shortcut menu, you can right-click on the part or assembly component within which you want the new component view to be defined.

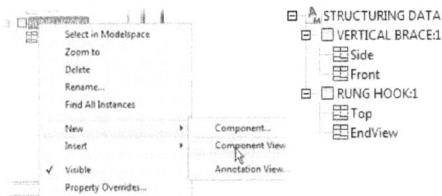

By default, after you execute the command from the Browser, you complete the command by responding to the prompts at the Command Line. Alternatively, in the Options dialog box, on the AM:Structure tab, in the Browser Right-Click For Creation list, select the Use Dialog Box (AMSNEW) option to open with the New dialog box instead.

When you are creating a component or component view, default names are automatically displayed for the new items. When prompted for a name, one that better matches the part, assembly, view orientation, or purpose of the view. You can change these default names on the AM:Structure tab in the Options dialog box.

Toggling the Structure Workspace

By default, Mechanical structure is toggled off for all new drawings, unless you are using a template drawing in which structure has been enabled. You can enable Mechanical structure for all new drawings in the Options dialog box in the AM:Structure tab.

For drawings in which Mechanical structure is toggled off, you can enable it by toggling the option on manually, by executing one of the commands that creates structure, or by inserting mechanically structured content into the drawing. Once on, you can toggle off Mechanical structure in a drawing file at any time, but only if all mechanically structured content or definitions have been deleted and removed from the drawing file.

You can toggle Mechanical structure on and off in the Status Bar by opening the Workspace Switching drop-down list and selecting Structure.

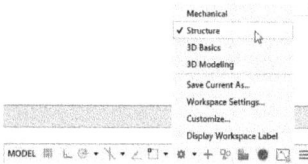

Command Access and Workspace

Although you can toggle on and off the visibility of toolbars and organize their positions to suit your preferences, the commands associated with Mechanical structure have also been prearranged for you in the workspace titled Structure. In this workspace the Mechanical Browser is visible. The Ribbon includes the Structure tab, which then becomes the primary location for accessing the commands you need to use when creating and modifying structured data. It is also the location for accessing many of the mechanical commands for creating and annotating your designs.

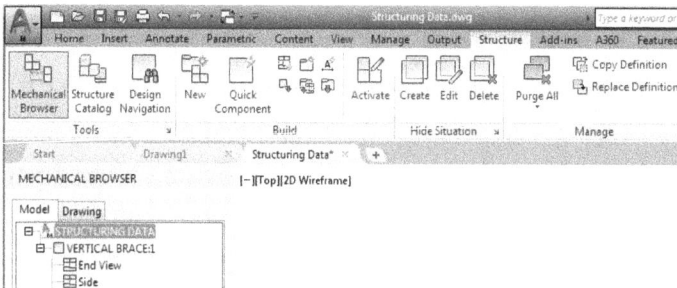

Access

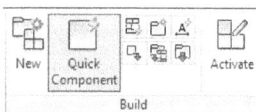

Command Line: **AMSCREATE**

Ribbon: Structure tab > Build panel > Quick Component

Menu Bar: Structure > Create > Component

Access

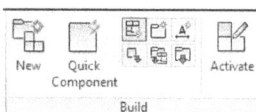

Command Line: **AMSCREATE**

Ribbon: Structure tab > Build panel > Quick View

Menu Bar: Structure > Create > Component View

Access

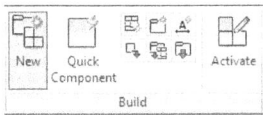

Command Line: **AMSNEW**

Ribbon: Structure tab > Build panel > New

Menu Bar: Structure > Structure

Note that the Quick Component and Quick View commands in the Ribbon, are a variation of the Menu Bar commands for creating a new component and new component view. When you use the quick commands, a new part or view is created using the names configured in the AM:Standards tab in the Options dialog box. The new views default to having an insertion point of 0,0.

New Dialog Box

The New dialog box opens when you start the AMSNEW command. You can use it to specify whether you want to create a new component or new component view and at the level in the structure at which this new item should be created. You can also select the existing objects that should be defined in the component view and where the view's insertion base point is located.

After components and component views have been created, you can use this dialog box again to reuse the component views in the drawing.

You can follow a linear and descending workflow when working with the options within this dialog box to create or insert structured data. You can work from the top area to the bottom area.

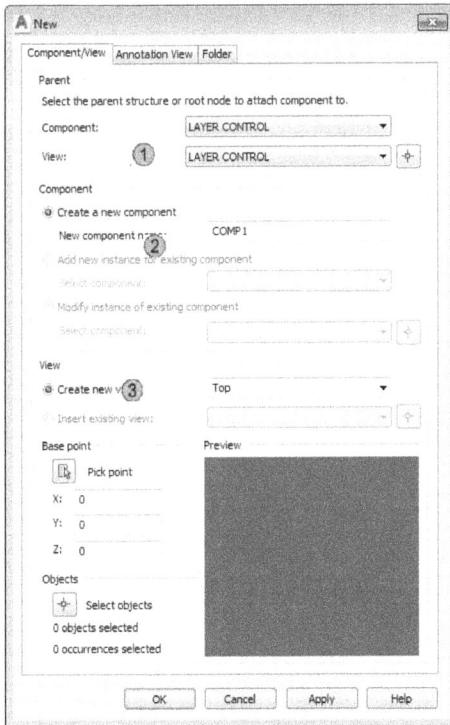

1. Select the component and view under which the new component or component view is going to be nested. Click Select Objects to select the component and view from the drawing window instead of using the lists.

2. Select to create a new component, add a new instance of a component, or modify an existing instance. When creating a new component, enter the name of the component.

3. Specify the name of the view for the new component and the view's base point. You can also select any existing geometry that belongs in the new view.

Procedure: Creating a New Component

1. In the Browser, right-click on the drawing filename or component below which you want to nest the new component. Click New > Component.

2. Enter a name for the new component.

3. Enter a name for the view that you are initially creating for this component. Press ENTER to accept the default view name.

4. Select any existing drawing objects that should be part of this component view. Press ENTER to skip adding any geometry to the component view.

5. Specify the base point for the component view.

Procedure: Creating a New Component Under an Assembly with Multiple Component Views

1. In the Browser, right-click on the assembly component below which you want to nest the new part component and click New > Component.

2. Enter a name for the new component.

3. Enter a name for the view that you are initially creating for this component.

4. Enter the name of the assembly's component view in which this part's component view should be included.

5. Select any existing drawing objects that should be wrapped into this component view. Press ENTER to skip adding any geometry to the component view.

6. Specify the base point for the component view.

Procedure: Creating a New Component View

1. In the Browser, right-click on the part or assembly component for which you want to create a new part component view. Click New > Component View.

2. Enter a name for the new component view.

3. Select any existing drawing objects that should be part of this component view. Press ENTER to skip adding any geometry to the component view.

4. Specify the base point for the component view.

Creating Folders Within a Component View

As you structure your designs into components and component views, you might need to further define and organize your design geometry. By learning about folders in Mechanical structure and how to create them, you can add an extra level of definition and organization to your designs.

In the following illustration, the slot punches in the top view were created by drawing the geometry of one slot punch in a folder and then inserting the folder once more. By using folders and structure in this manner, both slot punches can be modified and updated by editing the contents of one of the folders. In addition, when using folders an entire slot can be quickly selected to change its position or orientation.

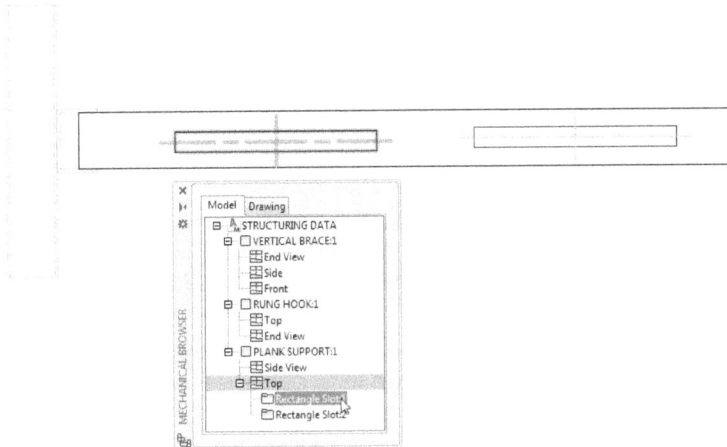

About Folders

You can create folders at the upper level of the drawing, in other folders, and in component views. To create a folder nested under the drawing filename, a folder, or a component view, right-click on that node in the Browser and select the appropriate command.

Folders within a component view are usually used to organize and combine related geometry. This might be a feature on the part, such as pocket cuts, punches, and stamped shapes. It might also be the geometry of the section of an edge of the part, such as one half of a symmetrical part. It might also be the geometry that was added to an assembly component view to represent features created during pre- or post-assembly of the parts.

Although you can use folders to structure parts and assemblies and not use components and component views, you would lose some of the benefits and capabilities for geometry and data reuse. Therefore, you should implement the use of folders where it provides more organization and data reuse to your components and component views.

Access

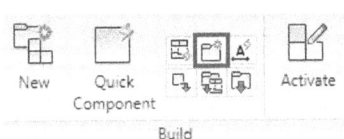

Command Line: AMSCREATE

Ribbon: Structure tab > Build panel > Create Folder

Menu Bar: Structure > Create > Folder

Procedure: Creating Folders

An overview of using the Browser and command-line prompts to create a new folder is shown in the following steps:

1. In the Browser, right-click on the drawing filename, folder, or component view below which you want the folder to be created. If you right-click on a drawing filename or component view, click New > Folder. If you right-click on an existing folder, click New Folder.

2. Enter a name for the new folder.

3. Select any existing drawing objects that should be part of this folder. Press ENTER to skip adding any geometry to the folder.

4. Specify the insertion base point for the geometry in this folder.

Restructuring Components

As you create a design, you might decide to change the existing subassemblies and how the parts are structured relative to the assembly and subassemblies. To restructure components to match your requirements, you must learn how to restructure them from one level of the structure to another. You must also have the component views of the component that is being restructured assigned to the correct view of the assembly component to which it is being restructured.

In the following illustration, the tree view on the left shows a one-level component structure. The tree view on the right shows the structure following restructuring. During restructuring, existing views for part components that are being restructured are assigned to the assembly component view into which the part component is being restructured. The partial dialog box at the bottom of the image shows this being done for one of the components.

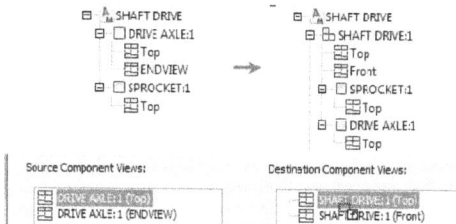

Rearranging and Restructuring Components

You can rearrange or restructure components, component views, and folders in the Browser tree by dragging and dropping them to another location in the hierarchy. You can select and manipulate one object at a time or multiple objects by holding SHIFT or CTRL while you click in the Browser.

You can rearrange the order structure of objects in the Browser by holding SHIFT when dragging the object. When you are rearranging structure content, a horizontal line displays at the target location.

You can create subassemblies by dragging a component over another component, or by dragging a component view over another component view. You can remove a nested object from an assembly or folder by dragging it over another component or over the drawing filename at the top of the Browser.

The Component Restructure dialog box opens when you restructure a component under another component by dragging and dropping it in the Browser. You can use this dialog box to map the views from the source (dragged) component to views of the destination component. If both the source and destination only have one view, the dialog box does not open. You can right-click under Source Component and click Auto Map Views to automatically map all of the views if they have the same view names and number of views.

> To maintain the integrity of the design you cannot perform some operations when reordering structure. For example, you cannot drag component views to components. Nor can you drag components or component views to folders, because folders can never be parents of components. You also cannot drag components or component views to an externally referenced component.

Ghost Components

You might find ghost components in the Browser when you restructure components with more than one view and do not map all of the views. When you map a component's views to a subassembly, and keep one or more views unmapped, the component becomes a ghost component. These are only intermediate holders of component views while you restructure your design. The ghost component is displayed with an icon that is empty of color.

Ghost components hold the unmapped views until you map them to the parent. To remove the ghost component and complete the component restructure, drag the ghost component view to a view in the parent subassembly.

Because ghost components are temporary holders of information and not required for your design, you should ensure that all views are mapped to the correct assembly.

In the following illustration, the part component DRIVE AXLE:1 was restructured to be a part in the assembly component SHAFT DRIVE:1. At the time of the restructure, the assembly component only contained one component view. Therefore, only one of the part's component views was mapped. The part's other component view is shown below the ghost entry for the DRIVE AXLE:1 component.

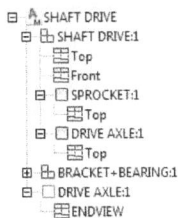

Procedure: Restructuring Components

An overview of restructuring part components in the Browser is shown in the following steps:

1. In the Browser, drag the component to the component within which you want it to be nested.

2. In the Component Restructure dialog box, map the views from the Source Component Views list to the Destination Component Views. Click and drag the component view that is being restructured and drop it on the component view of the component that is being restructured below.

Settings that Control Structure Creation

To further improve your productivity with Mechanical structure, you can change the structure creation settings to suit your requirements and workflow. To make these changes, you must understand where to access these settings and which settings to change.

Options Dialog Box - AM:Structure Tab

You can change the settings for the creation of components, component views, and folders on the *AM:Structure* tab in the Options dialog box.

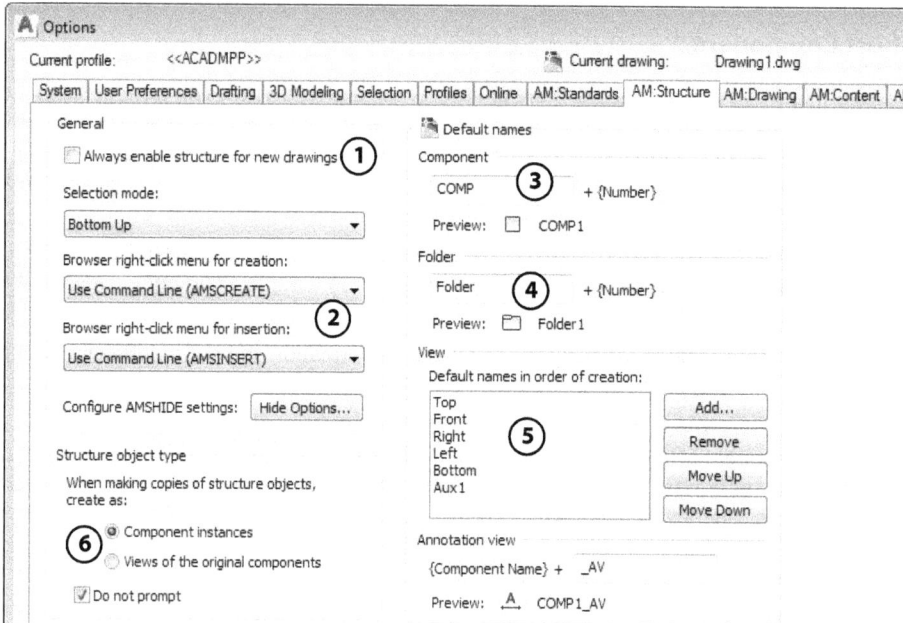

1. Select this option so that Mechanical structure is automatically enabled in all new drawings.

2. Use these lists to control the user interaction for the creation of new components, component views, and folders when the creation is initiated from the Browser. The default is to information in the Command Line.

3. Set this box to be the default prefix for component names. Unless you change the name during component creation, the next incremental number is automatically added to the name that is used here.

4. Set this box to be the default prefix for folder names. Unless you change the name of the folder during its creation, the next incremental number is automatically added to the name that is used here.

5. Sets the order in which the default component view names are prompted for creation within a component. You can add, remove, and reorder names in this list.

6. Set the creation results when copying, arraying, mirroring, or pasting Mechanical structure component views to create a new instance or add additional views of the same part instance.

In the following illustration, a simple structure was created to show the default automatic naming of objects as they are created. The component views under COMP2:1 also show the default creation order for the component views.

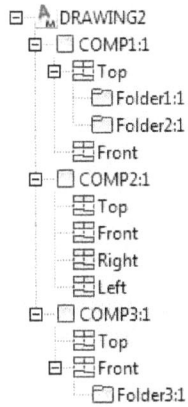

- DRAWING2
  - COMP1:1
    - Top
      - Folder1:1
      - Folder2:1
    - Front
  - COMP2:1
    - Top
    - Front
    - Right
    - Left
  - COMP3:1
    - Top
    - Front
      - Folder3:1

Exercise: Create a Drawing Using Structure

In this exercise, you will create components, component views, and a folder while creating and defining parts and an assembly. The drawing geometry already exists for one part and you create the geometry as you define the other part. You will also restructure two parts into an assembly.

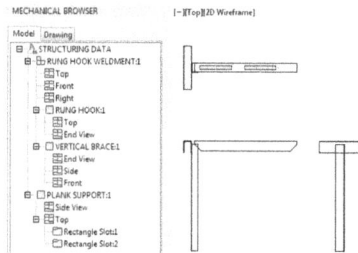

The completed exercise

Create Components and Component Views

In this section of the exercise, you will create new components and component views from existing drawing geometry and from all new geometry. You will also define geometry within a folder in a component view and copy that folder.

Note: This exercise assumes that the Structure workspace is active. You can activate it in the Status Bar by opening the Workspace Switching drop-down list and selecting Structure.

1. Open *Structuring Data.dwg*.

2. In the Mechanical Browser, expand the tree view and click the listing of the component and component views to review the currently defined data. Click on a view and note that the associated geometry is highlighted in the drawing window.

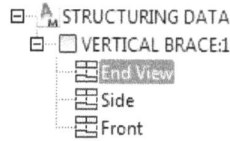

3. In the Browser, right-click on VERTICAL BRACE:1 and click Visible to clear the checkmark and note the components that are hidden in the drawing window.

4. To begin creating a component for the three views of the cross-channel part, do the following:

   - In the Browser, right-click on the drawing name (STRUCTURING DATA) and click New > Component.
   - When prompted for the component name, enter **RUNG HOOK** and press ENTER.

5. To specify the component view and its base point, do the following:

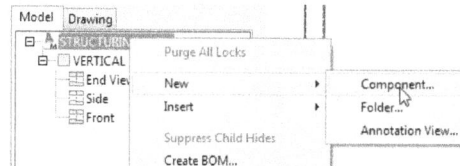

   - When prompted to the view name, press ENTER to accept the default of Top.
   - Select the geometry shown in the following illustration and press ENTER.
   - For the base point, object snap to the midpoint of the vertical line on the right.

6. To begin creating another component view for this new part, in the Browser, right-click on RUNG HOOK:1 and click New > Component View.

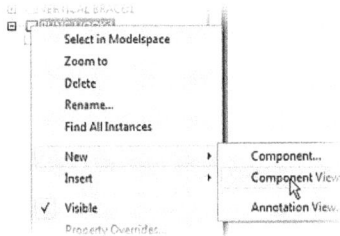

7. To specify the component view and its base point, do the following:

- For the view name, enter **End View** and then press ENTER.
- Select the objects directly below the top view, and then press ENTER.
- For the base point, object snap to the lower-right corner.

8. To toggle the display of the vertical brace part back on, in the Browser, right-click on VERTICAL BRACE:1 and click Visible.

9. To create a new component for all new geometry, do the following:

- In the Browser, right-click on the drawing name (STRUCTURING DATA) and click New > Component.
- For the component name, enter **PLANK SUPPORT**.
- For the view name, enter **Side View**.
- When prompted to select the objects for the view, press ENTER.
- For the base point, enter **0,0**.

10. In the Browser, under PLANK SUPPORT:1, double-click on Side View.

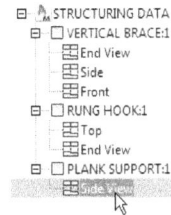

11. Draw the part as shown in the following illustration. For this exercise, do not add the dimensions.

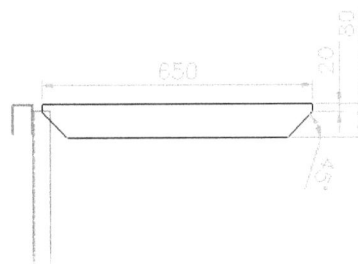

12. In the Browser, double-click on the drawing name node at the top so that the Side View component view is no longer active.

13. In the top view, draw a rectangle that fits between the C channel and aligns to the edges of the part view that you just created, as shown in the following illustration.

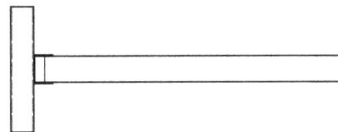

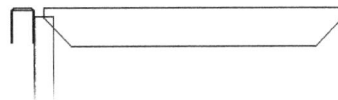

14. To create a top component view for the PLANK SUPPORT part, do the following:

- In the Browser, right-click on PLANK SUPPORT:1 and click New > Component View.
- For the view name, press ENTER to accept Top .
- Select the rectangle that you created and press ENTER.
- For the base point, object snap to the midpoint of the vertical line on the left.

15. In the Browser, under PLANK SUPPORT:1, double-click on the Top component view to make it active.

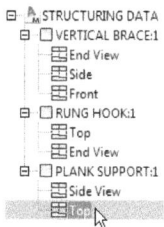

16. Draw a rectangle closer to the left vertical line of the rectangle, as shown in the following illustration. For this exercise, do not add the dimensions.

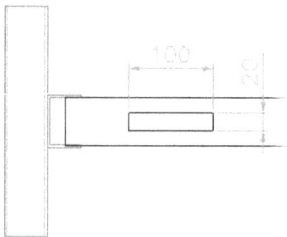

17. To draw centerlines for the rectangular slot, do the following:

- Click Home tab > Draw panel > Centerline.
- Object snap to the midpoints of the vertical lines.
- Repeat the command to draw a vertical centerline through the slot.

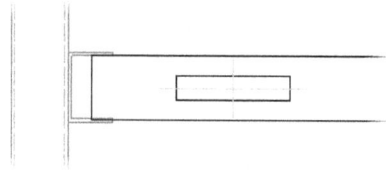

18. To begin putting the rectangle and two centerlines in a single folder, do the following:

- In the Browser, under PLANK SUPPORT:1, right-click on Top. Click New > Folder.
- For the folder name, enter **Rectangle Slot**.

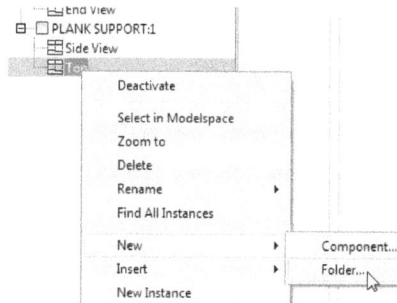

19. To define the geometry and base point for the folder, do the following:

- Select the rectangle and two centerlines.
- For the base point, object snap to the intersection of the two centerlines.

20. To copy the rectangular slot and place it to the right of the initial slot, do the following:

- In the Browser, under PLANK SUPPORT:1, expand the Top tree view. Right-click on Rectangle Slot:1 and select New Instance.
- For the parent, select the rectangle slot in the drawing and place it to the right.

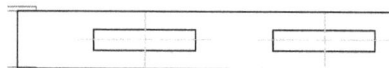

21. Review the contents of the Browser. Note the addition of a second folder for the copied rectangular slot.

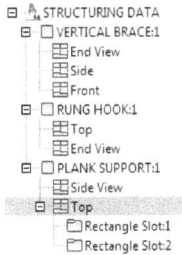

22. In the Browser, double-click on the drawing name node at the top so that the Top component view is no longer active.

Restructure Components

In this section of the exercise, you will create a new component with component views and then restructure existing components to be defined within that new component, thereby converting the new component into a subassembly component.

1. To create a new component that becomes an assembly component for the welded parts, do the following:

- In the Browser, right-click on the drawing name and click New > Component.
- For the component name, **RUNG HOOK WELDMENT**.
- For the view name, press ENTER to accept Top.
- For the objects for the view, press ENTER.
- For the base point, enter **0,0**.

2. To create another component view for the new component, do the following:

- In the Browser, right-click on the component RUNG HOOK WELDMENT:1 and click New > Component View.
- For the view name, press ENTER to accept Front.
- For the objects for the view, press ENTER.
- For the base point, enter **0,0**.

3. To begin restructuring the components, in the Browser, drag RUNG HOOK onto RUNG HOOK WELDMENT.

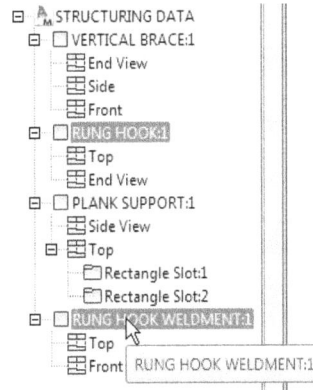

4. In the Component Restructure dialog box, drag the component views from the left list onto the right list as shown in the illustration. Click OK.

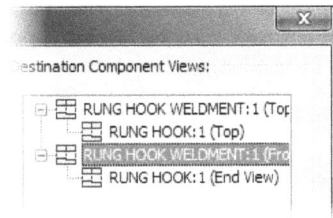

5. In the Browser, drag VERTICAL BRACE onto RUNG HOOK WELDMENT to restructure it.

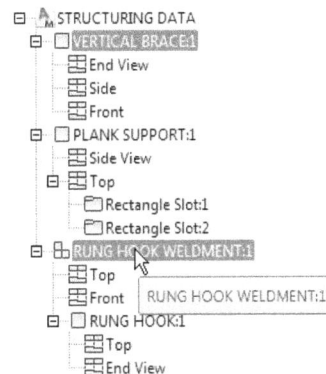

6. In the Component Restructure dialog box, drag the component views from the left list onto the right list as shown in the following illustration. This leaves one VERTICAL BRACE:1 (Front) unmapped. Click OK.

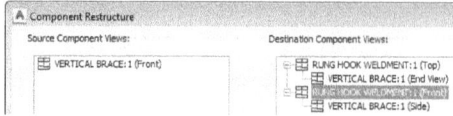

7. To create another component view for the assembly component, do the following:

- In the Browser, right-click on RUNG HOOK WELDMENT and click New > Component View.

- For the view name, press ENTER to accept Right.

- For the objects for the view, press ENTER.

- For the base point, enter **0,0**.

8. In the Browser, under the ghost entry for the component VERTICAL BRACE, drag the Front component view onto the Right component view of RUNG HOOK WELDMENT.

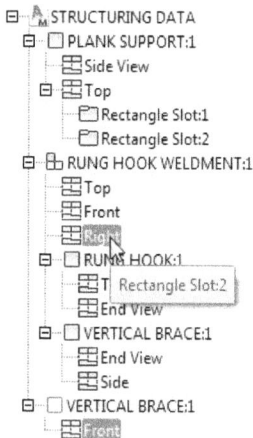

9. To reorder the components in the Browser, select the assembly component (RUNG HOOK WELDMENT), press and hold SHIFT, and drag the assembly component above the top part component (PLANK SUPPORT). Collapse both trees as shown in the illustration

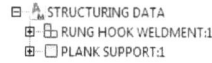

10. Save and close all of the files.

Lesson: Reusing and Editing Structured Data

Overview

This lesson describes how to insert instances of structure definitions into a drawing and how to edit structure definitions.

Using Mechanical structure is useful when you need to use the same part or assembly multiple times in a design or in other designs. It saves time and provides design consistency. You need to learn how to reuse and edit the available structured data.

In the following illustration, the initial state of a bleacher frame design is shown on the left. Additional parts were added to the drawing view of the assembly by reusing the existing defined structure. Because the cross bracket to which the bench seat bolts is defined as a structured component, the geometry in one instance was modified and all other instances automatically reflected that change, which saved editing time.

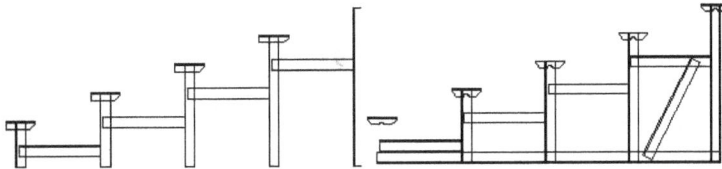

Objectives

After completing this lesson, you will be able to:

- Describe the difference between a definition, instance, and occurrence in Mechanical structure.
- Add instances of components, component views, and folders form the Browser.
- Instance component views and folders into the drawing using the Structure Catalog.
- State the available methods and options for editing a structure definition.
- State how the display of an instance of a definition can be changed.

About Structure Definitions, Instances, and Occurrences

As you reuse your structured data, you must know the difference between its definition, its instances, and its occurrences. By understanding their differences and purposes, you can identify the display differences in the Browser and Structure Catalog, learn the ramifications of an edit on structured data, and learn what occurs when you delete the structure's definition from a drawing.

In the following illustration, part of the Browser shows some of the instances and occurrences of components and folders that are within this subassembly's definition and instance.

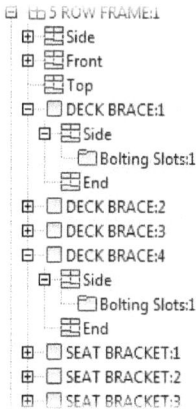

Definition of Structure Definitions, Instances, and Occurrences

When you create a component, component view, or folder within Mechanical structure, you are creating a definition of that item. The definition stores the name, insertion point, and all of the geometry. BOM Attribute values are also stored in a component's definition. These definitions can be stored in the drawing file regardless of whether they are used graphically in the drawing or not.

When you graphically place a definition in the drawing, an instance of that definition has been created. By copying the instance or inserting the definition multiple times, multiple instances of the same definition are placed in the drawing. Because each instance refers back to the same definition, if you change the geometry in one instance, all instances update to reflect these changes. The only exception to the automatic update for instances is if you apply property overrides. For each instance of a definition, you can override the visible geometry and the color it should display.

An instance of a definition adds a colon (:) and a number to the end of the component, component view, or folder name. The number is automatically incremented and added as each instance is added. While the first instance of a part or assembly component displays in the Browser with a suffix of :1, the first instance of a component view does not display the colon and number as a suffix to its name. For all other instances of the component view, the next incremental number has been added to the name. In the Browser the first instance of the component view called Top is displayed as Top and the next instance of that component view definition is displayed as Top:2. Each time you add an instance of a component to the drawing, the BOM quantity value for that component increases automatically. If a component definition is not instanced into the drawing, it is not included in the BOM.

When is the graphical display of a definition not an instance? When it is an occurrence. An occurrence of a definition happens when an instance of that definition is nested within another definition and you add multiple instances of that overall definition. Instead of more instances of the nested definition being created, occurrences of the same instances are created. Regardless of whether it is an instance or an occurrence, they all refer back to the same definition stored in the drawing file. If you change the geometry in an instance or occurrence, that definition changes and the geometry changes for all of them. The primary difference with an occurrence is its property display and Browser display. Unlike instances, the property display cannot be different between occurrences. Additionally, the names in the Browser for an occurrence are identical to its original instance. The numbers do not increment to a new higher number.

Similar to Blocks

Mechanical structure definitions, instances, and occurrences are somewhat similar to block definitions and instances of blocks. Block definitions can be defined in a drawing file but not used graphically in the drawing, and the geometry displayed for each placement of the block is the same. If you change the geometry in the block definition, all of the blocks inserted in the drawing change to reflect the new definition.

Example of Definitions, Instances, and Occurrences

In the following illustration, a small bleacher substructure has been designed using Mechanical structure and two different views have been created. The substructure uses four welded frames bolted together by cross braces. In the Browser tree on the left, the welded 5 ROW FRAME is a subassembly to the design and has been instanced into the drawing four times as indicated by the number after the component name.

Expanding the Browser for the first and second instances of 5 ROW FRAME displays the part components in the subassembly. Reviewing the component names and instance numbers for the components in the two subassemblies reveals that the names and instance numbers are identical. Because of this, the components listed under the second instance of the subassembly are occurrences of the original instances and not new instances.

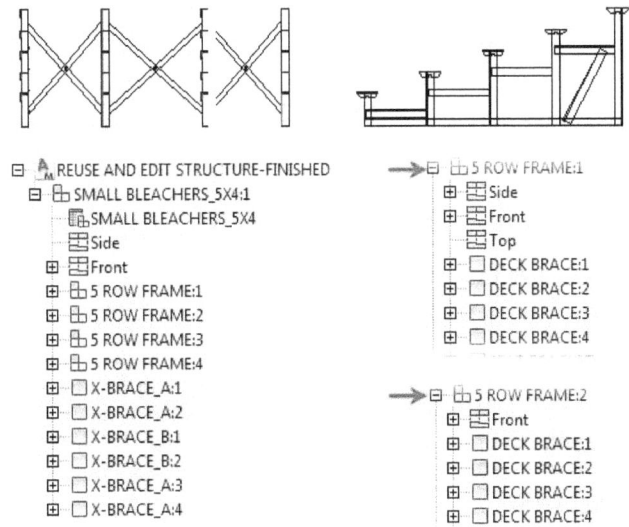

Key Points

- **Definition** - Describes all of the information stored in the drawing file about a component, component view, and folder. The definition can reside in the drawing file without being graphically represented in the drawing window or Browser.

- **Instance** - Each component, component view, or folder definition that you place graphically in the drawing is represented in the Browser. When more than one instance of a definition is placed in the drawing, the definition names include a suffix of a colon (:) and a number. They can have unique property display settings between the instances. BOM quantity is based on the number of instances of a component.

- **Occurrence** - The structured item that is automatically added to the drawing because it is nested in a component view or folder that also has another instance added to the drawing. The Browser entry name is identical to the original name and instance number. The instance number after the name does not change. The display properties between multiple occurrences are always identical.

Reusing Structured Data from the Browser

You can use the Browser to view the Mechanical structure of your design and to add additional instances to your drawing. By learning how to add instances of components, component views, and folders to the drawing from the Browser, you can quickly reuse the existing structured geometry and complete your designs and drawings.

In the following illustration, the fifth instance of the SEAT BRACKET component is being selected to have another component view added. Currently, this component instance indicates that only one of its three possible component views has been inserted into the drawing.

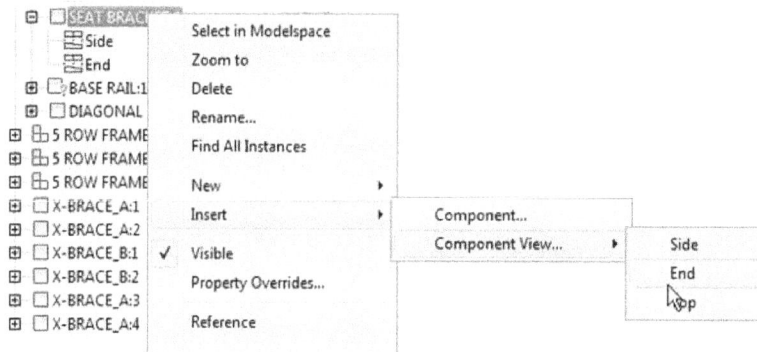

Reusing Structured Data from the Browser

You can reuse structured data from the Browser by inserting instances of a component, component view, or folder. To use the option to insert any of these items, right-click on a node for the drawing, component, component view, or folder in the Browser. The commands available for inserting instances then depend on the object on which you right-clicked. On the shortcut menu, expand the Insert menu. You might have the option to click Component, Component View, or Folder. The component, component view, or folder that you selected to insert is then inserted and nested below the node on which you initially right-clicked.

If you want to insert a component, right-click on the component below which you want to insert the new component, rather than the component that you want to insert. When you select to insert a component, the component under which it is being inserted becomes an assembly component if it is not already one. In the following illustration, another instance of SEAT BRACKET was added to the design after the insert was initiated by right-clicking on the assembly component BLEACHER FRAME.

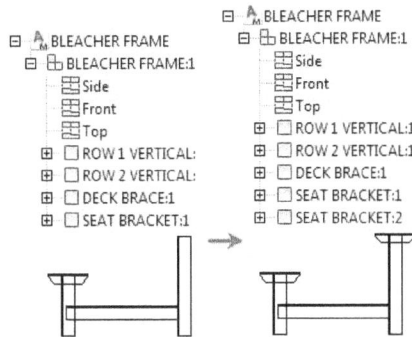

The option to insert a component view is only available on the Browser shortcut menu when you right-click on a part or assembly component. If the component on which you right-clicked is nested in another assembly and has more than one component view, you are prompted to the name of a component view from that parent assembly. You are prompted for the parent component view so that the instance of the component view you are inserting is automatically mapped to that parent component view. That mapping adds more intelligence and relationship to the structured data that you are creating.

When inserting an instance from the Browser, note the object that you want to insert and the structure item below which you want the instance to be nested. You can then right-click on the Browser entry for the structure item below which you want the instance to be inserted and click the shortcut menu option for the object that you want to insert.

Procedure: Inserting an Instance of a Component from the Browser

An overview of using the Browser and Command Line to insert an instance of a component is shown in the following steps:

1. In the Browser, double-click on the component view into which you want to insert the component so that view is active.

2. In the Browser, right-click on the active component view and click Insert > Component.

3. Enter the name of the component that you want to insert.

4. If more than one component view exists for the specified component, enter the name of the component view to insert.

5. Specify the insertion point for the component view.

6. Specify the rotation angle for the component view.

Procedure: Inserting an Instance of a Component View from the Browser

An overview of using the Browser and Command Line to insert an instance of a component view is shown in the following steps:

1. In the Browser, right-click on the component containing the component view of which you want to insert another instance. Click Insert > Component View > and the name of the view that you want to insert.

2. If the component that you right-clicked is nested in another assembly and has more than one component view defined, enter the name of the component view for which you want to associate the instance of this component view.

3. Specify the insertion point for the component view.

4. Specify the rotation angle for the component view.

Procedure: Inserting an Instance of a Folder from the Browser

An overview of using the Browser and Command Line to insert an instance of a folder is shown in the following steps:

1. In the Browser, right-click on the node for the drawing filename or component view for which you want to insert an instance nested below. Click Insert > Folder.

2. Enter the name of the folder that you want to insert.

3. Specify the insertion point for the folder.

4. Specify the rotation angle for the folder.

Strategy for Instancing Component Views

Although you can add multiple instances of a component view from any of the instances of the component, you should try to maintain a consistent method for inserting component views into the different views of an assembly. By using a consistent method, you and other users of the drawing can more easily understand the implemented structure.

In the following illustration, the tall narrow view of the 5 ROW FRAME assembly has been labeled as the Front view. This view shows five End views of the SEAT BRACKET part. In this case all five component views were added to the assembly's view from the first instance of the SEAT BRACKET component. While this is an efficient way of initially creating the view, trying to correlate where a part is located in different views is more difficult.

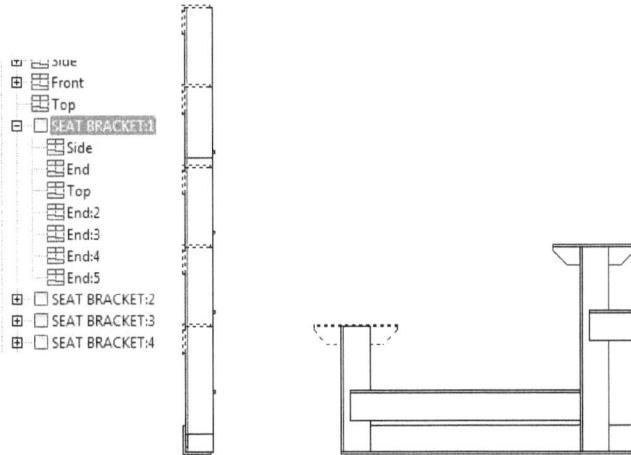

In the following illustration, the Browser shows that for each instance of the SEAT BRACKET an End view has been placed. By inserting instances of the views in this way, you can click the instance in the Browser and have the component views highlight in each of the views in which they are placed. In this case, selecting the first instance of the SEAT BRACKET only highlights the geometry for its Side and End views. The other End views are only highlighted if you select their corresponding component instance. By adding the component views to the other view of the assembly design in this way, it is easy to identify and understand what is used where. This also helps you to edit the design more quickly while maintaining the integrity of the Mechanical structure.

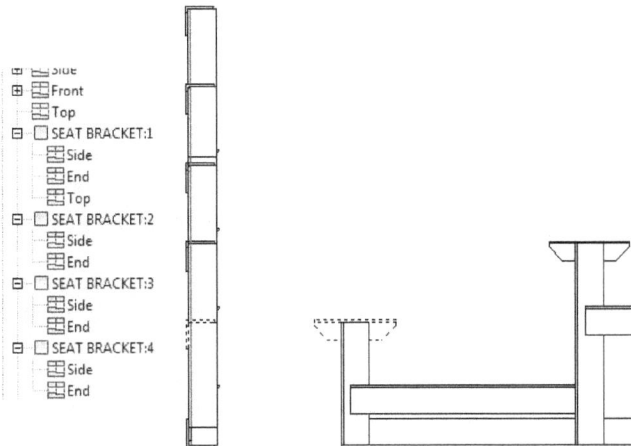

Reusing Structured Data From the Structure Catalog

The Structure Catalog is an important tool that you can use to create structured drawings through reusing existing structured data. By learning about the Structure Catalog and how to use it to reuse Mechanical structure data from the current drawing and other drawings, you can quickly complete your designs and drawings by not having to recreate the geometry and associated data.

About Reusing Structured Data From the Structure Catalog

You can use the Structure Catalog to view and retrieve structured data from other drawings and the currently open drawing. The Structure Catalog has three different tabs for viewing and accessing structured data. You can use two of the tabs to access other drawings and one to access data in the current drawing. Not only can you access and reuse structured data in drawing files that are stored locally on your computer or out on the network, but you can also directly access and reuse structured data in drawing files that are stored in the Autodesk® Vault software.

When you reuse a component view or folder from another drawing file, you can either establish an external reference to the other drawing or insert the content into the active drawing. The default behavior of a drag creates an external reference to the originating drawing file. By pressing CTRL when you drag, you insert the content into the active drawing.

You cannot directly drag a component. You can only drag the component views. However, when you insert or reference an assembly component view, the components associated with the view are automatically inserted into the drawing and represented in the Browser.

The external references that you establish through the Structure Catalog are more versatile and efficient than traditional external references. This is because when you reference structured content from an external file, only that information is loaded into the drawing and into memory. Any externally referenced component or folder displays a paper clip in the corner of its Browser icon.

In the following illustration, the tree view in the Structure Catalog shows a drawing that contains both internally and externally defined components. The first arrow shows a locally defined component while the bottom arrow shows the external component.

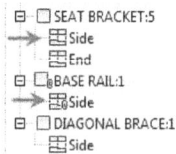

Structure definitions that exist in the drawing file but have not been instanced into the drawing display as a light green icon on the *Current Drawing* tab in the Structure Catalog.

Access

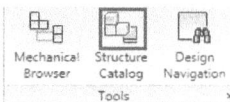

Command Line: AMSCATALOG

Ribbon: Structure tab > Tools panel > Structure Catalog

Menu Bar: Tools > Palettes > Structure Catalog

Structure Catalog - External Drawings Tab

You can use the *External Drawings* tab to open a selected drawing, search for a drawing file, insert selected structured definitions as an external reference component or annotation view, or import the definition into the drawing. You can also use the *External Drawings* tab to define the folders that are listed on the Library tab and to access drawings directly from the Autodesk Vault software.

The pane areas can be resized by clicking and dragging the dividing bars. You can also collapse and expand the two panes on the right to quickly adjust the available area to match your immediate requirements.

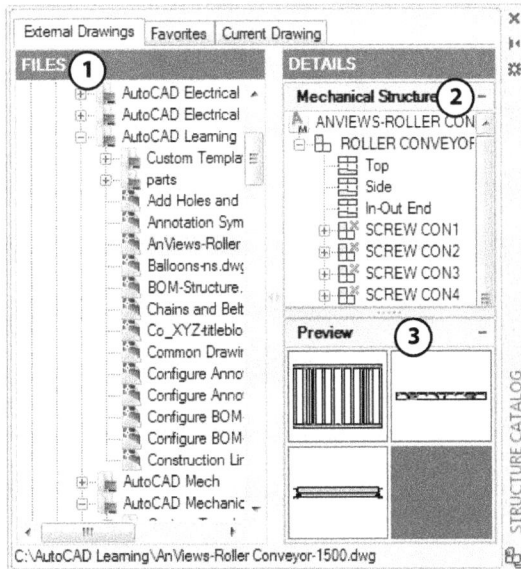

1. A listing of local and network folders and drawings that you navigate through to select the drawing that contains the structure that you want to reuse. Open a drawing file directly from this list by double-clicking on it or by clicking Open in the shortcut menu. Use the Get From Vault option in the shortcut menu to display the drawings in the vault that you are currently logged in to and to select a vaulted drawing to reuse. Right-click on a folder and click Add to Favorites to display the folder and its contents in the Favorites tab.

2. Displays the structured data for the drawing that you selected in the Files pane. Expand the structure so that you can select the item that you want to reuse in the current drawing. Drag and drop the component view or folder to the drawing window to create an instance that is an external reference to this drawing file. Press CTRL while dragging and dropping the component view or folder to import it rather than creating an externally reference. To import an entire component definition, right-click on the component and click Import Definition. This import does not immediately place an instance of the component in the drawing. Instead, the definition exists in the drawing and you must insert an instance from the Structure Catalog *Current Drawing* tab or from the Browser.

3. A preview of the drawing file, component views, or folders.

> Any drawing that you access from the Autodesk Vault software is copied to the working folder in the Vault and referenced into your assembly from that location.

Structure Catalog - Favorites Tab

You can use the *Favorites* tab to access drawing files in the folders that you have added to the *Favorites* tab using the Add to Favorites shortcut menu option in the *External Drawings* tab. You can access and reuse structured data from the drawings listed on this tab as you would do in the *External Drawings* tab.

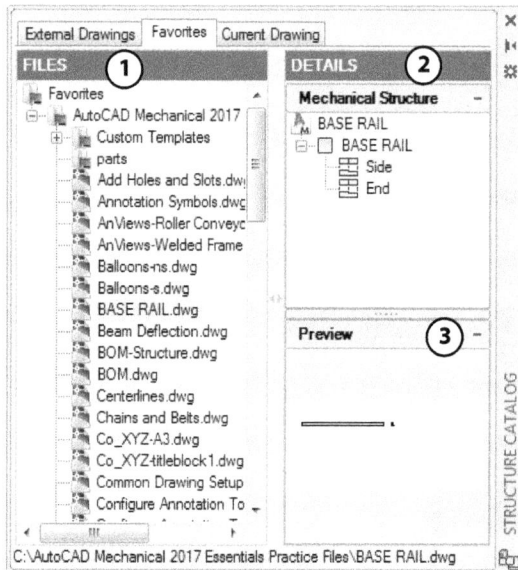

1. Use to navigate through the folders that you added to the library and select a drawing containing the structured data that you want to reuse. Double-click on the drawing file to open it directly.

2. Displays the structured data for the drawing that you selected in the Files pane. Expand the structure so that you can select the item that you want to reuse in the current drawing. Drag the component view or folder to the drawing window to create an instance that is an external reference to this drawing file. Press CTRL while dragging the component view or folder to import it rather than creating an external reference. To import an entire component definition, right-click on the component and click Import Definition. This import does not immediately place an instance of the component in the drawing. Instead, the definition exists in the drawing and you must insert an instance from the Structure Catalog Current tab or from the Browser.

3. A preview of the drawing file, component views, or folders.

Structure Catalog - Current Drawing Tab

You can use the *Current Drawing* tab to view, manage, and instance the structure definitions and external references in the drawing file that you are currently editing.

The options for managing externally referenced files are accessed from the shortcut menu. Types of management activities include unloading, reloading, and repathing external references along with checking in and out referenced files from the vault when you are logged in. When you hover the cursor over the vault status icon, a tooltip displays the status information of that file. This enables you to review the status information without having to scroll to the right or expand the File References area to see the information.

The Mechanical Structure pane lists all of the component definitions in the drawing file. This structure display lists all of the component views of a component, even ones that might not currently be instanced into the drawing file.

For local assembly components, you can set their BOM representation to Normal, Phantom, or Phantom in Current Drawing. Setting an assembly component to phantom enables you to organize data and geometry together into a single component definition while still having the components in the phantom assembly component display as their own line item entries in the BOM. This is often done to make it easier to reuse and manipulate the geometry as a single item while maintaining the separation of its BOM data.

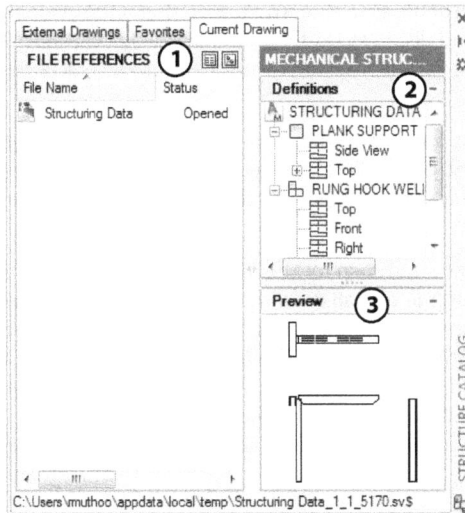

1. Lists the external references into the current drawing and their current status. Use the shortcut menu options to reload, unload, open, change the path, or check in or out externally referenced files.

2. Insert additional instances of a component view or folder by dragging it from this structure tree to the drawing window. Using the options in the shortcut menu, you can rename, delete, externalize, localize, open, set the BOM representation, or insert the structured data. Deleting the structure definition here completely removes the definition and all of its instances from the drawing.

3. A preview of the drawing file, component views, or folders.

By changing the File References display pane to a tree view, you can view the relationship of the referenced files rather than the properties.

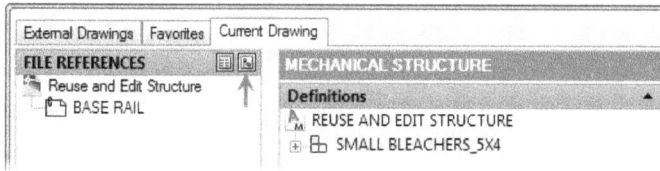

Targeting the Instance Location Within the Structure

When you insert an instance of a component view or folder into the drawing from the Structure Catalog, the instance is placed in the active level of the structure. This means that if the overall drawing is active, any component or folder is inserted and displayed at the uppermost level of the structure. If you have a component view active, the instance for the inserted component or folder is added under that component view.

Because of this insertion behavior, set the component view into which you want the instance to be placed to be active before inserting it from the Structure Catalog. Having the correct component view set to be active before adding the instance saves time because you do not need to restructure the instance after it has been inserted.

In the following illustration, two different results are shown for the insertion of the same component view. In the Browser tree view shown on the left, the overall drawing file was active when the SEAT BRACKET component was being instanced. This caused the instance to be inserted at the uppermost level of the structure. The Browser tree view on the right shows the same component when it was inserted with the Side component view active during the insertion. In this case the component instance is now part of the 5 ROW FRAME assembly component definition.

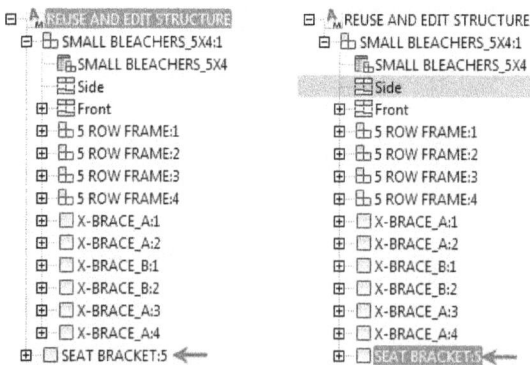

Procedure: Adding Folders to the Structure Catalog Favorites

An overview of adding local or network folders to the Structure Catalog Favorites tab for faster and easier access of structure reuse is shown in the following steps:

1. Open the Structure Catalog and click the *External Drawings* tab.

2. In the Files pane, in the *Favorites* tab, navigate to the local or network folder that contains the drawings to which you want access.

3. Right-click on the folder you want listed on the *Favorites* tab. Click Add to Favorites.

Procedure: Reusing the Structured Data in Other Drawings

An overview of using the Structure Catalog to reuse the structured data in another drawing by externally referencing it into the current drawing is shown in the following steps:

1. In the Browser, click the structure level on which you want to insert the instance.

2. Open the Structure Catalog and click the *External Drawings* or *Favorites* tab.

3. In the Files pane, select the drawing that contains the structured data that you want to reuse so that it is highlighted.

4. In the Mechanical Structure pane, click the plus sign (+) to expand the tree view of the previously selected drawing. Select the component view or folder that you want to insert.

5. In the Mechanical Structure pane, click and drag the component view or folder to the drawing window.

6. Specify the insertion point for the instance.

7. Specify the rotation angle for the instance.

> You cannot use the External Drawings or Favorites tabs in the Structure Catalog to directly insert instances of mechanical content, such as bolts, bearings, gears, and structural steel, from another drawing file into the current drawing.

Procedure: Reusing the Structured Data in a Vaulted Drawing

An overview of using the Structure Catalog to reuse structured data in a drawing file that exists in Autodesk Vault by externally referencing it into the current drawing is shown in the following steps:

1. In the Browser, click the structure level on which you want to insert the instance.

2. Open the Structure Catalog and click the *External Drawings* or *Favorites* tab.

3. Right-click in the left pane and click Get from Vault.

4. If you are not logged in to the Autodesk Vault software, log in to the server and database that contains the structured data that you want to reuse.

5. In the Select File dialog box, navigate through the vault folders and select the vaulted drawing that contains the structured data.

6. With the file highlighted in the Files pane on the *External Drawings* or *Favorites* tab, in the Mechanical Structure pane, expand the tree view to display the component view or folder that you want to insert.

7. In the Mechanical Structure pane, click and drag the component view or folder to the drawing window.

8. Specify the insertion point for the instance.

9. Specify the rotation angle for the instance.

Procedure: Reusing the Structured Data in the Current Drawing

An overview of using the Structure Catalog to reuse the structured data that exists in the current drawing is shown in the following steps:

1. In the Browser, click the structure level on which you want to insert the instance.

2. Open the Structure Catalog and click the *Current Drawing* tab.

3. In the Mechanical Structure pane, expand the tree view to display the component view or folder that you want to instance into the drawing.

4. In the Mechanical Structure pane, click and drag the component view or folder to the drawing window.

5. Specify the insertion point for the instance.

6. Specify the rotation angle for the instance.

Edit a Structure Definition

As your designs change, you need to be able to edit the geometry in a definition and change what should and should not be part of a definition. After creating a definition, you might decide that you want to change a definition's base point to make it easier to position the definition as it is reused. Changing the name of a component definition helps you and others identify what the component is, thereby making the task of selecting it for reuse or editing that much easier.

To make edits and changes to a structure definition, you must learn what methods and options are available for you to use.

Typical Editing Tasks and Methods

You must do the following to edit the structured data of a component view or folder:

- Redefine its insertion point.
- Change the size or position of the geometry.
- Delete or add geometry.
- Rename the definition.
- The following two methods or workflows can be used when you need to modify geometry in a definition to change its size or position or to delete it completely.

- You can activate the component view or folder. Once it is active, you can modify the geometry in the definition using the standard editing commands. Any geometry that you create while the definition is active is automatically added to this active definition.
- You can select the geometry object that you want to modify by directly selecting it. To select the geometry, you need to cycle from its uppermost structure level down to the geometry object that you want to edit. Alternatively, before trying to select the geometry, you can change the selection order to start selecting at the bottom of the structure.

Redefine the Base Point

When you drag a new instance of a component view or folder into the drawing from the Structure Catalog, you can position the instance based on that definition's defined base point. A component view or folder that is selected in the drawing window displays a single grip point at that insertion base point.

Sometimes, you might decide that having the base point defined to a different location is more useful than the one that is currently defined. To change the base point, right-click on the component view or folder in the Browser, and click Change Basepoint. You can then specify a new base point by entering the coordinate value or object snapping to the geometry. You can also access the Change Basepoint command in the Ribbon. On the Structure tab > Edit Structure panel, click Change Basepoint. **Note:** The Edit Structure panel is only available when a component view has been activated.

In the following illustration, one instance of the side view of the seat bracket component has been selected. Initially, the base point was defined at an arbitrary point as shown on the left. After redefining the base point, the insertion location and single grip are now positioned in a more appropriate location for positioning the component in the assembly.

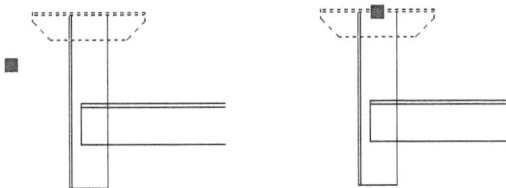

Activating Structure

You can activate a component view or folder to focus your tasks to that definition. To activate a component view or folder, double-click on the component view or folder in the Browser that requires modification. You can also select the component view or folder in the Browser or drawing window, right-click on it, and click Activate. Selecting the component view in the drawing window and then activating it can be an efficient method of activating a component view or folder when you have a design in which there are a large number of components from which to select.

To return the focus back to the overall drawing file from a component view or folder, double-click on a blank area or drawing name in the Browser.

When you create, modify, or erase geometry in the active component view or folder, the definition immediately changes and all instances of the definition update, thereby reflecting the changes you have made. Creating a new component or folder when a component view is active automatically establishes the active definition as the parent level to the newly created component or folder.

After you have activated a definition, geometry not included in the active definition remains visible but the display is dimmed. The Status Bar setting S-LOCK controls your ability to select geometry that is not part of the active definition. When S-LOCK is on (highlighted on the Status Bar), you cannot select geometry that is not at or below the level of the active definition. If it is off, you can select and manipulate all of the geometry.

In the following illustration, the Front component view in the component STROKE:2 is active. The active component view or folder is highlighted in the Browser by a blue bar. In the drawing window, the geometry not in the active component view displays in light gray.

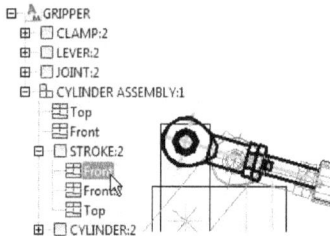

Top-Down Versus Bottom-Up Selection Order

The structure that you create can be as simple as a single level of geometry wrapped into a component view or as complex as an entire assembly containing multiple levels of subassemblies and parts. When you want to select individual pieces of geometry or a component view nested within the structure, you might need to cycle through the levels of structure to select the correct one. The selection order setting on the Status Bar of TOP-DN and BTM-UP enables you to specify the direction in which you want to begin cycling through the levels of structure associated with a piece of geometry.

To change the order in which you cycle through the levels of structure, on the Status Bar, click TOP-DN or BTM-UP. The label on this button changes to display the current selection order setting. To cycle through the structure, when a command prompts you to select objects, click the object. To cycle up or down the structure for this object, click again until the correct level is highlighted.

In the following illustration, the tree view is shown in the middle of the image and indicates the levels of structure that are being cycled through in the upper and lower examples. In the selection order shown at the top, selection order is set to TOP-DN. Clicking the geometry starts the selection from the uppermost structure level associated with the geometry down to the geometry defined within the component view. In the illustration shown at the bottom, the selection order is set to BTM-UP. Clicking the geometry starts the selection of the geometry in the component view and works up to the uppermost structure level.

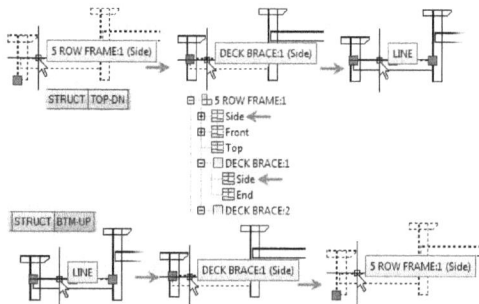

Design Navigation Mode

To assist you in identifying the folders and component views that exist in your design, you can toggle on Design Navigation mode to enable the dynamic highlighting of component view geometry and the display of tooltips listing the component view name. The order of highlighting is controlled by the Top-down or the Bottom-up Status Bar settings.

When you hover the cursor over geometry that is within multiple definitions, you can cycle through those levels of structure by clicking or hovering over the plus or minus symbol on the left end of the tooltip. Clicking the name in the tooltip causes that component view to be selected.

In the following illustration, the design navigation mode is on and the selection order on the Status Bar is set to Top-down. Hovering the cursor over the seat bracket caused the overall assembly to highlight. By hovering over or clicking the plus symbol on the tooltip, the tooltip expanded to the next level of structure. The current focus in this illustration is the End view of the fourth instance of SEAT BRACKET. The associated view is also highlighted in the Browser by a red rectangle around its name.

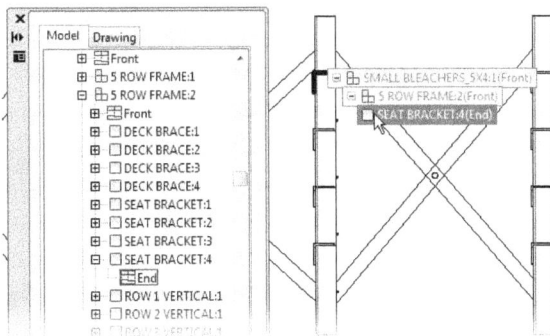

In the following illustration, the selection order status setting is set to Bottom-up. In this case the first identified component is the individual part and then it expands up to the next assembly level.

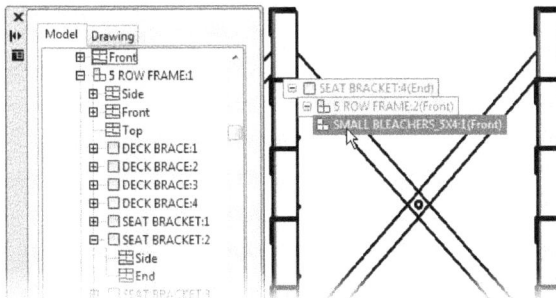

Access

Command Line: AMSNAVMODE, CTRL+D

Ribbon: Structure tab > Tools panel > Design Navigation Mode

Menu Bar: Structure > Design Navigation Mode

> In addition to the Design Navigation Mode setting, the highlighting of geometry is controlled by the PREVIEWEFFECT and SELECTIONPREVIEW system variables.

Edit the Contents of Structured Data

During the process of creating geometry and defining the structure of your data, you might have geometry in a structure definition you want to remove or you might want to add a copy to another structure definition. You might also have existing geometry that is not part of the definition and that you want to be part of the definition. You can use the AMSEDIT command to make these changes to structure definitions.

You can launch this command in the Browser by right-clicking on the component view or folder and clicking Edit Objects or you can launch it from the Edit Structure panel in the Ribbon. When you launch the command from the Browser, you can select the Add, Remove, or Copy option as well depending on what you want to modify. When you launch the command from the Edit Structure panel in the Ribbon, you can select Add or Remove. To use the Ribbon commands, you must first set the component view or folder that you want to edit to be active.

Option	Description
Add	Enables you to select and add geometry or components to the current definition. You can only add geometry to folders, but you can add geometry or components to component views. Any association to other structure definitions that a piece of geometry might have had is replaced with the new definition information. Selecting a component to add forces a restructure and the opening of the Component Restructure dialog box.
Remove	Removes all structure definition information from the geometry causing it to be standard model space geometry.
Copy	Enables you to copy geometry that is not currently associated to any definition to the component view or folder in which the command was executed. Unlike the Add option, Copy leaves the original copy of the geometry and cannot add geometry from other definitions.

Access

Command Line: AMSEDIT

Ribbon: Structure tab > contextual Edit Structure panel > Add

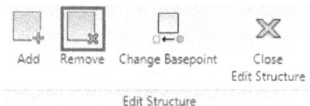

Command Line: AMSEDIT

Ribbon: Structure tab > contextual Edit Structure panel > Remove

Rename the Definition

When you create a component, component view, or folder definition, you might a general name as a temporary name for the definition or you might accept the default name. You can specify a more accurate or describing name later.

For example, your standard is to use manufacturing part numbers for the part and assembly component names but you might not have part numbers for the new part and assemblies for a new design that has not yet been accepted. This means you need a method of renaming the definitions after the design has been approved.

You can rename a definition in the Browser or Structure Catalog by right-clicking on it and selecting the Rename option. If you right-click on a component view in the Browser, the Rename option expands, enabling you to select between renaming the component or component view.

Break Link to Create a New Definition

When you use the Copy command to duplicate a part or assembly component, you create another instance of the component or component view definition. Any changes that you make in the copy also change the definition. Therefore, both instances change. To use an existing definition to create a unique and separate definition, right-click on the instance in the Browser and click Break Link. You can then enter a new and unique name for the definition.

You can use the Break Link option to create new component, component view, or folder definitions from an existing instance of the definition. The data within that structure definition is based on what was in the instance when the link was broken. The new definition created from a part component is now completely separate and unique from its original definition. If you break the link to an assembly component, the assembly definition is unique but the part and assembly components nested below it are still linked to their original definitions.

Changing the Display of Instances

As you use Mechanical structure, you focus more on what the geometry you are creating pertains to. When you follow the workflow of focusing on an object's purpose in a design, different options are available that help you to locate and change the display of an instanced definition. Understanding how the display of an instance of a definition can be changed helps you to become more productive in creating and modifying your design using Mechanical structure.

Locating an Instance in the Drawing Window or Browser

Although locating an instance of a definition in the drawing window or Browser does not change the display of the instance, it helps to ensure that you are working on the correct one. If you have selected an instance in the drawing window and want to highlight it in the Browser, right-click in an open area and click Find in Browser. To locate and display an instance of a definition in the drawing window based on its entry in the Browser, right-click on the instance in the Browser and click Zoom To.

You can select the Find All Instances option when you want to locate and identify all of the instances of a component view or folder, or all of the component views of a component. You can access this option from the shortcut menu after selecting the component, component view, or folder in the Browser or drawing window. After selecting the Find All Instances option, all of the instances are selected in the drawing window and in the Browser. The view in the drawing window also changes to display the extents of the selected instances.

In the following illustration, all of the component views for the DECK BRACE component have been found and selected, as indicated by their displayed grip.

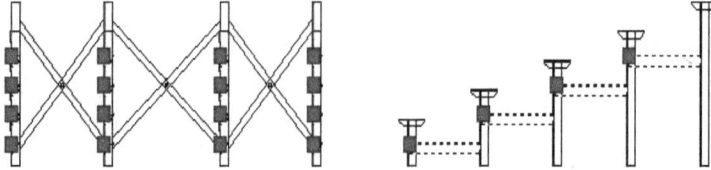

Visibility of Instances

If you want to focus on a specific area of your design, you might want to toggle off the display of some parts or assemblies as you create or modify others. With your designs defined with structure, you can toggle on and off the display of individual instances of a definition so that you are only displaying a specific set of objects.

When you want the instance of a definition to be visible or hidden in the drawing, you can toggle that instance's Visible setting. To change the setting, right-click on the instance in the Browser that you want to hide or make visible and click Visible. The visibility for the selected structure and any nested structure automatically changes.

Instances with their visibility toggled off are identified by a gray icon in the Browser.

Property Overrides for an Instance

The geometry that is displayed for an instance of a definition is the exact size and location that is specified in the definition and is the same color by default. Although the geometry size and location is always the same as the definition, you can override the display properties of visibility and color for each instance of a definition.

To override the properties of an instance, right-click on the instance in the Browser and click Property Overrides. In the Property Overrides dialog box, select the Override Properties checkbox to be able to select or clear the checkboxes for the settings that you want to be visible or overridden.

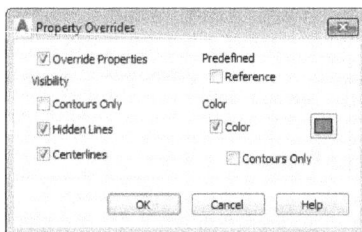

Scale Factor of an Instance

Each instance of a component view or folder that you insert into the drawing is displayed at its true full scale size. You can display an instance of a component view or folder at a larger or smaller scale if required. Changing the scale factor changes the display of the instance by the same amount in both the X and Y directions.

To change the scale factor at which a component view or folder instance is being displayed, right-click on the instance in the Browser and click Edit Scale. In the Scale dialog box, the numeric factor by which the instance should get larger or smaller.

Exercise: Reuse and Edit Structured Data

In this exercise, you will work on two drawing views of the structure of a bleacher. You will insert instances of components and component views and modify a component definition.

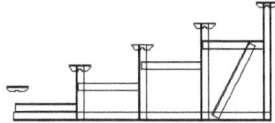

The completed exercise

Note: This exercise assumes that the **Structure** workspace is active.

Copy and Insert Views

In this section of the exercise, you will add an instance by copying an existing part and then add a component view for that copied component.

1. Open *Reuse and Edit Structure.dwg*.

2. On the Status Bar, ensure that the Structure selection order is **Top-down**. If it is Bottom-up, click to toggle it to Top-down.

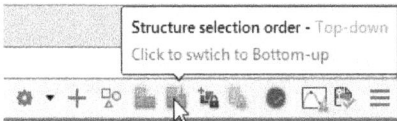

3. You will now prepare to add another instance of the component SEAT BRACKET to the Side component view in the assembly 5 ROW FRAME. In the Browser, expand the tree view and under 5 ROW FRAME:1, double-click on the Side component view to activate it.

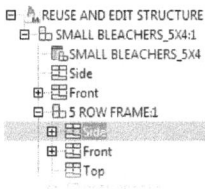

4. Zoom in to the upper right corner of the right side view.

5. To add another instance of the component SEAT BRACKET, do the following:

   - Run the standard COPY command by entering **copy** and pressing ENTER.
   - In the drawing window, select the instance of the SEAT BRACKET.
   - For the base point, object snap to the midpoint along the top.
   - For the second point, object snap to the midpoint of the horizontal line on the component to the right, as shown in the following illustration.
   - Press ENTER.

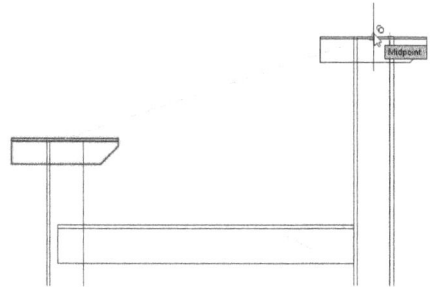

6. In the Browser, under the assembly component 5 ROW FRAME:1, expand SEAT BRACKET:5. Note that it currently only has one component view instanced.

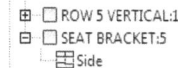

7. To begin adding one of the other component views that are defined for SEAT BRACKET, do the following:

   - In the Browser, right-click on SEAT BRACKET:5 and click Insert > Component View > End.
   - For the parent view, enter **Front**.

8. To specify the insertion point for the view, do the following:

- Pan to the left until the other drawing view of the overall assembly is displayed.
- Object snap to the upper left corner of the tallest component.
- For the rotation angle, press ENTER.

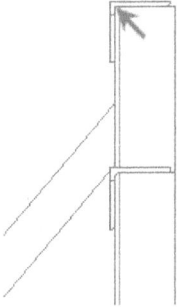

9. Pan and zoom so that the side view is displayed again.

Reuse Data Using the Structure Catalog

In this section of the exercise, you will reuse structured data by using the Structure Catalog. Specific tasks include adding a folder to the Favorites, adding a component from an external drawing, and adding a view of a non-instanced definition.

1. To display the Structure Catalog (if not displayed), in the Structure tab > Tools panel, click Structure Catalog.

2. To add a favorites folder to the Structure Catalog, do the following:

- In the Structure Catalog, on the *External Drawings* tab, Files pane, navigate to the location in which you downloaded and stored this dataset. For example, *C:\AutoCAD Mechanical 2017 Essentials Practice Files*.
- Right-click on the *AutoCAD Mechanical 2017 Essentials Practice Files* folder.
- Click Add to Favorites.

3. To begin inserting a component view from a drawing in the newly created Favorites path, do the following:

- In the Files pane, on the *Favorites* tab, in the *AutoCAD Mechanical 2017 Essentials Practice Files* folder, click *BASE RAIL.dwg*.
- In the DETAILS>Mechanical Structure pane, expand the component BASE RAIL. Click, drag, and drop the Side component view into the drawing window, as shown in the illustration below. The horizontal plank is attached to the cursor

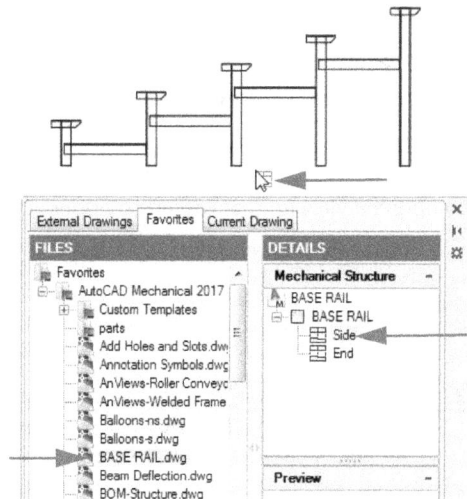

4. To place the instance of this externally referenced component view, do the following:

- For the insertion point, in the side view, object snap to the lower left corner of the left most vertical part.
- For the rotation angle, press ENTER.

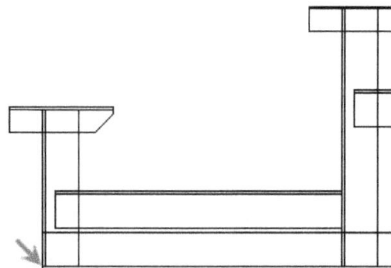

5. You will now begin adding an instance of the DIAGONAL BRACE component that is defined in this drawing but not yet instanced. Zoom into the right most upper horizontal part and note a diagonal green line as shown in the illustration.

- In the Structure Catalog, on the *Current Drawing* tab, in the Definitions pane, under DIAGONAL BRACE, drag the Side component view to the drawing window.

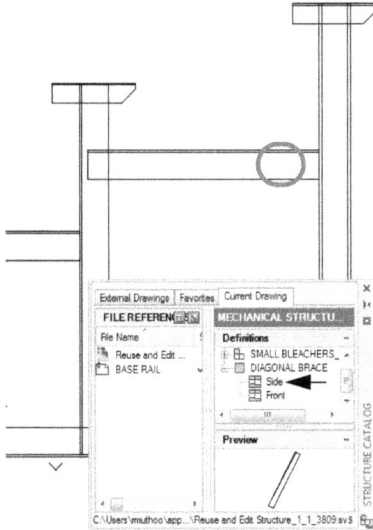

6. To place the instance, do the following:

- For the insertion point, object snap to the left endpoint of the green line.
- For the rotation angle, press ENTER.

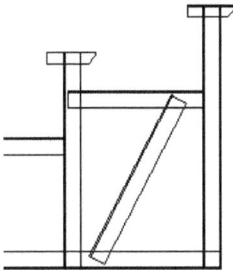

7. In the Browser, double-click on the drawing filename to set the overall drawing file to be active.

View the Data and Edit a Definition

In this section of the exercise, you will use different tools to view the data and change its display. You will also edit the definition of a component view.

1. In the Browser for 5 ROW FRAME:1, under SEAT BRACKET:1, right-click on the component view Side and click Zoom to.

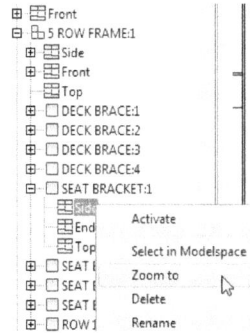

2. Zoom out to view the entire length of this seat's vertical member as shown in the following illustration.

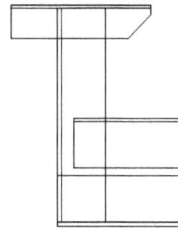

3. Click the vertical component and keep clicking to cycle through the levels of structure until only the vertical component (ROW 1 VERTIVCAL:1 (Side)) is highlighted as shown in the following illustration. Right-click anywhere and click Find in Browser.

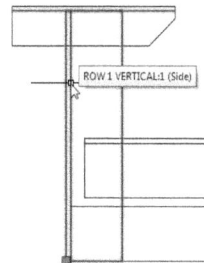

4. To hide the display of this component view, do the following:

- In the Browser, right-click on the highlighted Side view under ROW 1 VERTICAL:1 and click Visible to clear it.
- Press ESC to cancel the grip selection.

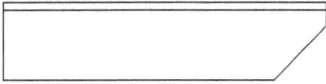

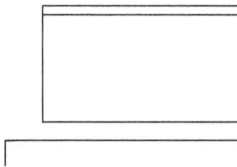

5. To edit the corner of the SEAT BRACKET component by adding a chamfer, do the following:

- Enter **CHAMFER** to start the command.
- Set the chamfer distance to 35.
- Select the left line and hover the cursor over the bottom line to display the preselection display as shown on the left in the illustration.
- Select the bottom line to have the chamfer displays as shown on the right in the illustration.

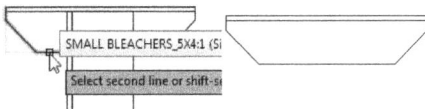

6. Review the other instances of this definition and note how they have all updated to reflect these changes.

7. On the SEAT BRACKET component, draw a circle with its center at the midpoint of the bottom line and a diameter of 35.

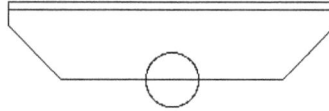

8. Run the **Trim** command, select the line and circle as the cutting objects, and trim the line and then the circle. Note that the resulting arc and a line segment are not displayed in the other instances of the SEAT BRACKET, and that the right half portion of the horizontal line is missing.

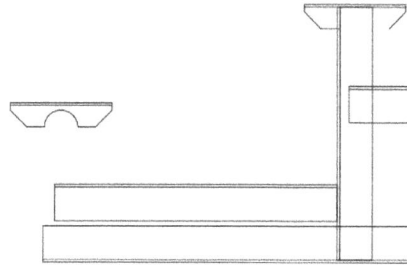

9. To begin adding the arc to the component view definition, in the Browser, under SEAT BRACKET:1, double-click on the Side component view to make it active. Note that in the seat bracket, the missing arc and line display as light gray.

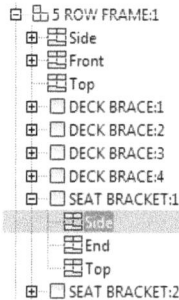

10. To add the arc to the active view definition, do the following:

   - In the Ribbon, on the Structure tab > Edit Structure panel, click Add.
   - Select the missing arc and line segment.
   - Press ENTER.

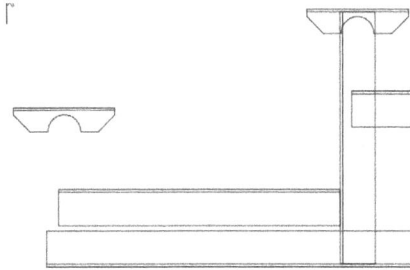

11. In the Browser, double-click on the drawing filename to set the overall drawing file to be active.

12. Save and close all of the files.

Chapter Summary

In this chapter, you learned about the workflows that are available in the AutoCAD Mechanical software for organizing drawing geometry. You then learned how to use Mechanical structure for the creation of components, component views, and folders within Mechanical structure. You also learned how to insert instances of structure definitions into a drawing and edit structure definitions.

Having completed this chapter, you can:

- Identify and describe the different ways of creating and organizing drawing geometry in the AutoCAD Mechanical software.
- Create Mechanical structure in a drawing by creating components, component views, and folders.
- Insert instances of structure definitions into the drawing and edit the structure definitions.

Tools for Creating Key Geometry

This chapter describes the core mechanical design productivity tools for creating rectangles, hatching, fillets, chamfers, holes, slots, and threads. This chapter also covers the AutoCAD® Mechanical power snap configuration and its use with the geometry creation and editing tools.

Objectives

After completing this chapter, you will be able to:

- Create and modify geometry using rectangle, hatch, fillet, chamfer, and contour finder.
- Configure and activate power snaps.
- Add centerlines, holes with centerlines, and circles with centerlines to a drawing.
- Create, erase, and change the visibility of construction lines.
- Create polylines based on existing contour geometry.
- Add holes, slots, and threads to a drawing.

About the Design Productivity Tools

You can use design productivity tools to focus on creating your design while spending less time on routine drafting tasks, such as creating hole patterns, adding centerlines, and adding section lines.

In the following illustration, the holes, centerlines, and section line were added to the part using different design productivity tools. Each of these objects was automatically placed on the correct layer.

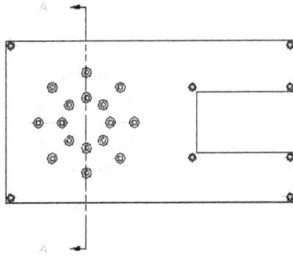

Definition of Design Productivity Tools

Design productivity tools are commands and options that help you to create geometry that represents mechanical designs. By using these tools, the geometry is created on the appropriate layers based on your standard, and your ability to edit the geometry is enhanced.

The design automation tools include those used to create rectangles, hatches, fillets, chamfers, construction lines, symmetric lines, breakout lines, section lines, and centerlines. Power commands are also available for dimensioning, creating views, snapping to geometry, and copying, editing, and erasing geometry.

In the following illustration, construction lines are projecting from the front view and top view to assist in locating and sizing the geometry for the right side view.

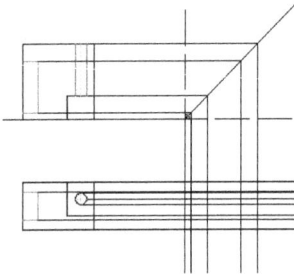

Example of Design Productivity Tools

Part of the centerline productivity tool enables you to define and create a pattern of holes. A circular centerline can be created based on a specified diameter and the number of holes determines the position and angle of the linear centerlines. Countersink holes based on industry sizes can now be defined to be positioned at the intersection of these centerlines.

Lesson: Core Design Tools

Overview

This lesson describes the core mechanical design tools of Rectangle, Hatch, Fillet, Chamfer, and Contour Finder, and how to use them to create and modify geometry in your design.

As you create your mechanical designs, note that they are composed of common mechanical shapes and features. The mechanical tools of Rectangle, Hatch, Fillet, Chamfer, and Contour Finder make it easier and faster to create and modify those types of shapes and features. The tools add versatility to your designs.

In the following illustration, the geometry in the different drawing views of the part was created using the primary tools of Line and Circle and some additional core tools of Rectangle, Fillet, Chamfer, Hatch, and Contour Finder.

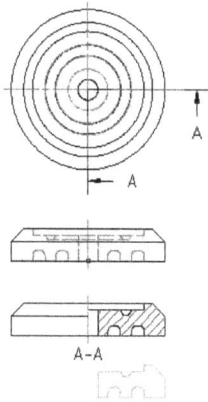

Objectives

After completing this lesson, you will be able to:

- Create rectangles using different defining methods.
- Place different hatch styles in a drawing.
- Add and modify fillets.
- Add and modify chamfers.
- Create polylines based on existing contour geometry.

Creating Rectangles

Along with the line and circle, the rectangle is the most common shape that is used when you create a drawing. Because the location and size of the rectangles varies, you need to be able to create them in many different ways. By learning about the types of rectangles that you can create and how to access their commands, you can create the rectangles in the drawing by entering specific information about them.

About Creating Rectangles

With the Rectangle command, you can create rectangles and squares quickly and easily from different insertion points. The easiest way to draw a rectangle is to select two diagonal corner points. You can define the size of the rectangle by selecting the opposite corner locations or entering coordinates. You can define the start point of the rectangle in different ways. For example, from the baseline, from the height, or from the center. You can use the Rectangle drop-down list in the Draw panel or the Rectangles dialog box to select the rectangle options.

Editing Rectangles

To edit the size or location of a rectangle, double-click on it so that you can reselect the rectangle insertion point and dimensions according to how the rectangle was originally placed.

Rectangles

When you expand the Rectangle drop-down list in the Draw panel, you can access a number of methods for creating a rectangle and a square. The tools are categorized under subheadings, such as Center and Corner. The icon on the button indicates the insertion location and additional defining information that is required to create that rectangle.

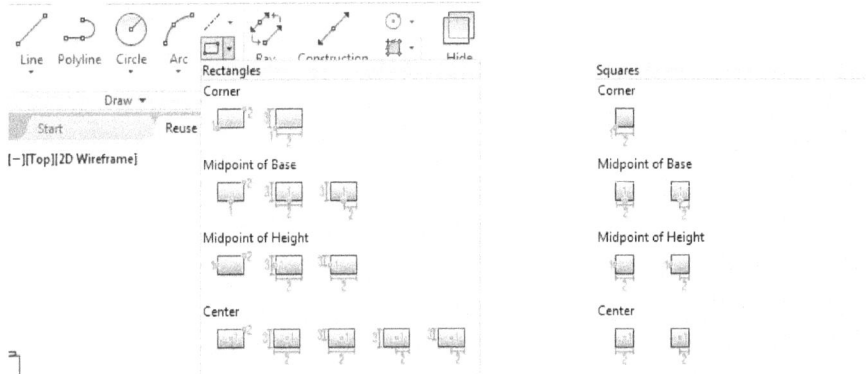

The creation methods are listed on two tabs: one for creating rectangles and the other for creating squares. Each creation method shows an icon indicating the criteria required to create that rectangle or square. The blue dots and numbers correspond to the location and order in which you pick the points required to define the rectangle in your drawing. The green dimensions identify the values that you enter at the Command Line to define the size.

Procedure: Creating Rectangles and Squares

1. In the Ribbon, expand Rectangle.

2. Select the required creation method of the rectangle/square.

3. Specify the insertion base point.

4. Specify the values or locations as required by the creation method being used.

Placing Hatch

When you create a section or breakout view, you need to hatch the areas of the part that are to appear as though they were cut through. Based on the shape and size of the part being hatched and whether multiple parts in an assembly are being hatched, your requirements might vary. By understanding how to add mechanical hatches, you can complete your drawings and create various hatch styles.

In the following illustration, the hatch lines showing the location of a half section were easily added by selecting a preconfigured pattern and size.

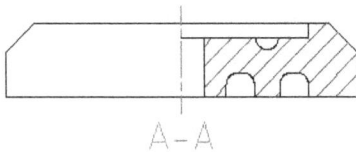

About Placing Hatch

When you place a mechanical hatch in your drawing, you can use one of three hatching tools. The tools allow you to do the following:

- Place a predefined nonassociative hatch.
- Place a custom nonassociative hatch.
- Place a custom associative hatch.

Editing Hatch

After you have placed a hatch in the drawing, you can edit it and change its style and properties. You can edit a hatch by double-clicking on it in the drawing area.

When the boundary defining an associative hatch changes, the hatch automatically adjusts to the boundary's new position, as long as the boundary continues to define a closed area. If the boundary defining a nonassociative hatch changes, you can update only it after you double-click on the hatch, click OK in the Hatch dialog box, and press ENTER.

Placing Predefined Hatch Patterns

The AutoCAD Mechanical software contains a set of six predefined hatch patterns with left and right directions and one double-hatch pattern. There are three predefined hatch widths at an angle of 45 degrees and three at an angle of 135 degrees. Each pattern is applied to objects in the same manner. You can select a hatch pattern and then select an object or click on a point. The hatch pattern is drawn but is not associative.

Access

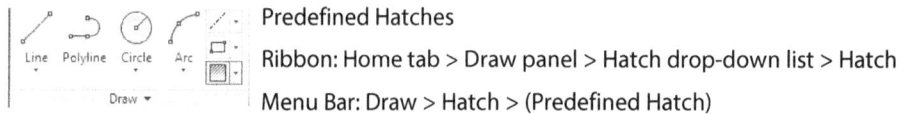

Predefined Hatches

Ribbon: Home tab > Draw panel > Hatch drop-down list > Hatch

Menu Bar: Draw > Hatch > (Predefined Hatch)

Predefined Hatches on the Draw Tools Panel

When you click Home tab > Draw panel > Hatch drop-down list, you can access some predefined hatches and the user-defined hatch. The icon and tooltip for predefined hatches indicate the direction and spacing between the hatch lines as shown in the following illustration.

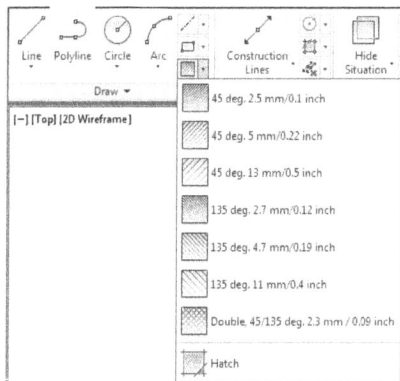

Process: Adding Predefined Hatch Geometry

The following steps describe how to create a hatch in a drawing based on a predefined pattern.

1. Click *Home* tab > Draw panel > Hatch drop-down list and select the predefined pattern that you want to use.

2. In the drawing window, click a point inside a closed area as defined by contours.

Placing User-Defined Hatch

With the User-Defined Hatch command, you can create custom hatch patterns. You can use the User-Defined Hatch command to select from additional hatch patterns and still have the hatch follow the layer defined in the standard and the drawing scale. If you change the drawing scale, the scale of the user-defined hatch is updated.

Access

Command Line: AMUSERHATCH

Ribbon: Home tab > Draw panel > Hatch drop-down list > Hatch

Menu Bar: Draw > Hatch > User-Defined Hatch

User-Defined Hatch Dialog Box

If you launch the **AMUSERHATCH** command from the Command Line or the Menu Bar, the Hatch dialog box opens when you click to place a user-defined hatch, enabling you to select a hatch pattern and to set its properties. When the Adapt hatch distance at less than option is selected, if you place a hatch that has less than the specified number of lines, its scale value changes so that it has the specified number of hatch lines.

Hatch Creation Contextual Tab

When you launch the **Hatch** command from the Ribbon, the Hatch Creation contextual tab displays, enabling you to select the pattern that you want to use in the drawing and to set its properties. In the Hatch Creation contextual tab, you can set the hatch to be associative. This enables it to adjust to the selected boundary geometry if the boundary changes and maintains a closed loop around the hatch.

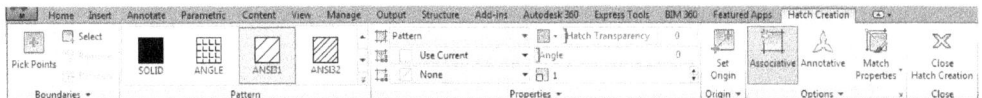

The hatch that is placed in the drawing is automatically placed on the layer specified in the active standard.

Adding Fillets

In a drawing view, you can quickly create an arc that is tangent to two existing objects using the **Fillet** command. The AutoCAD Mechanical **Fillet** command is designed for use in mechanical part drawings. By knowing how to create a mechanical fillet, you can correctly represent the parts and gain the greatest flexibility for editing the arc in the future. You can use the cursor to display a preview of the fillet and when satisfied with how the fillet looks, click to accept your selection.

In the following illustration, the radius dimension for the fillet was automatically added to the drawing after the fillet was created.

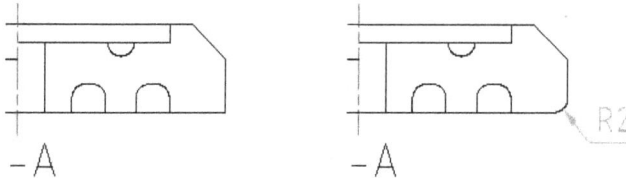

About Adding Fillets

You can add a fillet arc at the intersection of lines, arcs, or circles or at all of the corners of a selected polyline. By selecting the Polyline option, you can create fillets in all of the corners of the selected polyline.

When adding a mechanical fillet, you can set its size by selecting it from a list of common sizes in the Fillet contextual tab in the Ribbon. You can also set the arc to be automatically dimensioned after it is created. To save time using mechanical fillets, you can double-click on a fillet, change its size, and have the arc and its tangent geometry update automatically.

Access

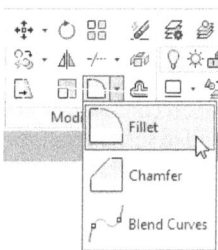

Command Line: AMFILLET2D

Ribbon: Home tab > Modify panel > Fillet drop-down list > Fillet

Menu Bar: Modify > Fillet

Fillet Options

To set the fillet radius size and other filleting options, use the Fillet Options contextual tab in the Ribbon. You can also use the Setup command option after launching the Fillet command, which only becomes available when the AMFILLET2DTAB system variable is set to 0. The Setup option opens the Fillet dialog box.

You can set the size for the radius by selecting a value in the Fillet Size list, by entering a value in the Fillet Size list, or by selecting an existing arc. To select an existing arc, click the select button to the right of the size list.

To configure the sizes that are displayed in the Fillet Size list and the order in which they are listed, click Configure to open the Fillet List Configuration dialog box. The changes you make here apply directly to the active standard.

In the Fillet Options contextual tab, you can select whether or not to trim or extend the selected geometry to the endpoint of the fillet arc. You can also select to add dimensions to the fillet after it has been created. The format for the radius dimensions is based on the configuration in the active standard for radius representation and the active dimension style.

When the Trim Geometry checkbox is selected, the selected geometry automatically trims or extends to the arc, and you can select either of the trimmed or extended objects to have them return to their original lengths.

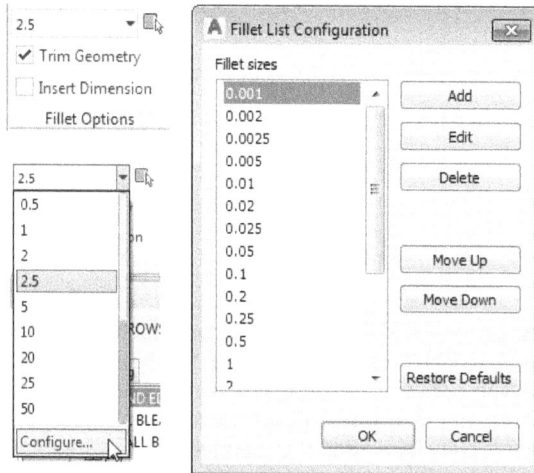

Editing Fillets

The method used to edit a fillet depends on whether the fillet is part of a polyline.

To begin editing an arc that was previously created by the Fillet command, select the non-polyline objects and double-click on the arc. In the Fillet dialog box, select a value or a new one and click OK. The fillet arc changes to the new value. You can then select additional fillets of the same initial size to change them to the new value.

If the fillet was added to a polyline, you change the fillet radius by creating a new one in its place. For a polyline with multiple vertices or fillets, you can change the size of one fillet by starting the Fillet command again, setting the required radius, and then selecting the polyline segments on either side of the fillet that you want to change. The arc radius then increases or decreases accordingly. If you want to change all vertices or fillets for a polyline to have the same radius, after starting the Fillet command and setting the radius, select the Polyline command suboption and then select the polyline that you want to change.

Procedure: Adding Fillets

To set the fillet size and fillet objects, complete the following steps:

1. Start the **Fillet** command.

2. In the Fillet Options contextual tab, set the required fillet size.

3. Select or clear the options for trimming geometry and inserting dimensions.

4. In the drawing area, select the first object.

5. Hover the cursor over the second object to preview how the fillet will display. If it displays correctly, select the second object. (You can change the fillet radius before selecting the second object.)

6. If you have the option to insert the selected dimensions, position the dimension.

7. Continue selecting additional objects to fillet.

8. Press ESC to end the command.

Adding Chamfers

There are two options for removing the sharpness of a part's edge: Fillet or Chamfer. A part that has a chamfered edge has a small flat transition between two of its surfaces. In the drawing view, the chamfer is indicated by a straight line angling between two other line segments and connecting the two. By knowing how to create a mechanical chamfer, you can correctly represent the parts in the drawing view while gaining the greatest flexibility for editing the chamfer in the future.

In the following illustration, chamfers were added to the top two corners of the part. For one of the chamfers, the Dimension setup option was selected so that the dimension would automatically be added after the creation of the chamfer.

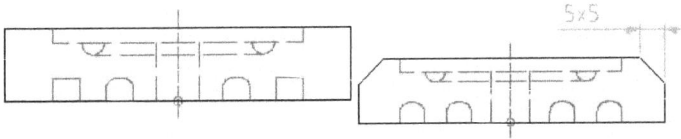

About Adding Chamfers

You can add a chamfer between two intersecting lines, at one corner of a polyline, or at all of the corners of a selected polyline. To chamfer all of the corners of a polyline, select the Chamfer command's Polyline suboption and then select the polyline that you want to chamfer.

When adding a mechanical chamfer, you can select its size from a list of common sizes in the Chamfer contextual tab in the Ribbon and have it automatically dimensioned after it has been created. You can also define the size by two distances or a distance and an angle. You can also double-click on an existing chamfer, change its size, and have the segment and its adjoining geometry update automatically.

You can use the cursor to display a preview of the chamfer and when satisfied with how the chamfer displays, click to accept your selection.

Access

Command Line: AMCHAM2D

Ribbon: Home tab > Modify panel > Fillet drop-down list > Chamfer

Menu Bar: Modify > Chamfer

Chamfer Options

To set the chamfer size and other options, use the Chamfer Options contextual tab in the Ribbon. You can also use the Setup command option after launching the Fillet command, which only becomes available when the AMCHAMFER2DTAB system variable is set to 0. The Setup option opens the Chamfer dialog box.

In the Chamfer Options contextual tab, you can set the chamfer size by specifying the first chamfer length and then the second length or angle. You can set the chamfer method by selecting the Distance or the Angle options. To specify the length or angle values, you can select from the lists or the required values. You can also specify the length or angle value by clicking Select to the right of that length or angle list.

When you create a chamfer based on two lengths, the chamfer lengths are measured from the point of intersection. A chamfer created using an angle has its size based on one distance from the point of intersection and an angle from the first selected object.

To configure the sizes that are displayed in the chamfer length lists and their order in which they are listed, click Configure to open the Chamfer List Configuration dialog box. The changes you make here apply directly to the active standard.

In the Chamfer Options contextual tab, you can also select whether or not to trim or extend the selected geometry to the endpoints of the chamfer line and select to add dimensions to the chamfer after it has been created. When the Trim Geometry checkbox is selected, not only does the selected geometry automatically trim or extend to the chamfer line, but you can also select either of the trimmed or extended objects to have them return to their original lengths.

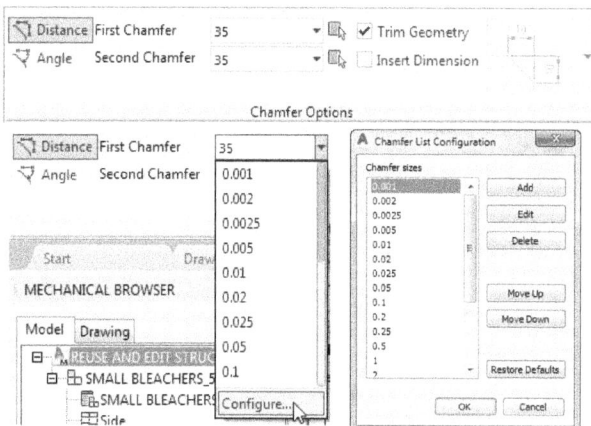

Chamfer Dimension Methods

The default format for the chamfer dimension is based on the configuration in the active standard for chamfer representation and the active dimension style. You can select a different chamfer dimension style by selecting that style in the Chamfer Dimension Style list.

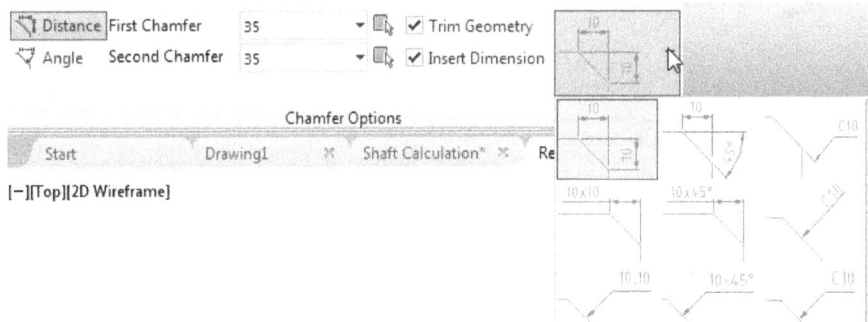

Editing Chamfers

To change the size of a chamfer, it must have been created by selecting individual line segments and not a polyline. For all chamfers created between line segments, double-click on the chamfer line segment that was previously created by the Chamfer command. In the Chamfer dialog box, select or a new value and click OK. The chamfer changes to the new value and you can select additional chamfers of the same initial size to also have them change to the new value.

Procedure: Adding Chamfers

To set the chamfer size and chamfer objects, complete the following steps:

1. Start the **Chamfer** command.

2. In the Chamfer Options contextual tab, set the required chamfer method and size.

3. Select or clear the options for trimming geometry and inserting dimensions. If the option to add dimensions is selected and you want to dimension with a style other than the default style, set the dimension display style.

4. In the drawing window, select the first object.

5. Hover the cursor over the second object to preview how the chamfer will display. If it displays correctly, select the second object. (You can change the chamfer options before selecting the second object.)

6. If you have selected the Trim Geometry option and do not want a segment to be trimmed, click the trimmed object to return it to its original length or press ENTER.

7. Continue selecting additional objects to chamfer.

8. Press ESC to end the command.

Creating Contours

As you design parts in relation to their position in an assembly, the outer size and shape or internal features are often based on the size, position, and shape of other part geometry. If you create a single polyline outline of the part or feature from the existing geometry, the new part matches its use and is easy to select and manipulate. By knowing how to create contours from existing geometry, you can efficiently create outlining polylines.

In the following illustration, the closed loop shown below the section view represents the closed boundary edges around a point specified in the section view. Clicking a point inside the closed loop area was much easier than trying to draw over or modify the existing geometry. This closed polyline loop can now be used as the basis of other parts or for future cross-sectional analysis.

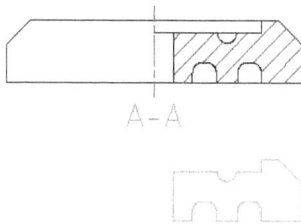

About Creating Contours

You use one of the contour tools to create a polyline boundary around a defined area. Four contour tracing commands are available: Contour Outside, Contour Inside, Contour Trace, and Trace Contour.

The first three commands are used to automatically analyze the boundary and create a polyline, while the Trace Contour command is used to manually create a polyline by tracing existing geometry. Using the Contour Outside, Contour Inside, and Contour Trace commands all of the construction geometry is ignored when the boundary is calculated as these commands automatically analyze the geometry in the drawing. Use the contour commands to create new parts from the boundaries of existing parts.

You can then use the polylines where they are created or move them to another area of the drawing and edit them as required.

Contour Outside

You can use the Contour Outside command to create a polyline based on the closed outer boundary defined by selected objects. The Contour Outside command only recognizes objects created on the contour layers AM_0, AM_1, or AM_2, or on other custom contour layers. The created polyline is placed on layer AM_4.

Access

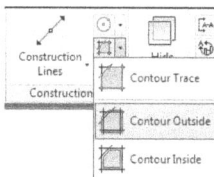

Command Line: AMCONTOUT

Ribbon: Home tab > Construction panel > Contour Trace drop-down list > Contour Outside

Menu: Draw > Boundary > Contour Outside

Procedure: Creating Outside Contours

To create a polyline based on the outside contour of selected geometry that defines a closed loop, complete the following steps:

1. Start the **Contour Outside** command.

2. Select the objects for which you want to calculate an outer boundary and press ENTER.

3. Press ENTER to create the polyline.

Contour Inside

You can use the Contour Inside command to calculate and create a polyline based on a closed boundary that was created using existing drawing geometry. To specify the location required to calculate the boundary, click a point inside the boundary that you want to create. The Contour Inside command only recognizes objects created on the contour layers AM_0, AM_1, or AM_2, or on other custom contour layers. The created polyline is placed on layer AM_4.

Access

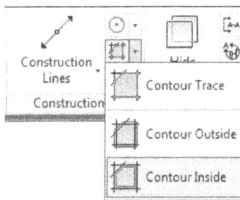 Command Line: AMCONTIN

Ribbon: Home tab > Construction panel > Contour Trace drop-down list > Contour Inside

Menu: Draw > Boundary > Contour Inside

Procedure: Creating Inside Contours

To create a polyline based on the inside contour of a selected point within a closed boundary, complete the following steps:.

1. Start the **Contour Inside** command.

2. In the drawing area, click a point inside the contour.

Contour Trace

You can use the Contour Trace command to identify endpoints on analyzed geometry and to create a polyline when a closed boundary is calculated from existing geometry.

The Contour Trace tool analyzes the perimeter of your boundary. If the tool finds an opening in the contour, you are prompted to have the open points displayed on screen. You can select a point inside a boundary for inside contours or select the objects to create outside contours.

The Contour Trace command only recognizes objects created on the contour layers AM_0, AM_1, or AM_2, or on other custom contour layers. The polylines created by the Contour Trace command are placed on layer AM_4.

Access

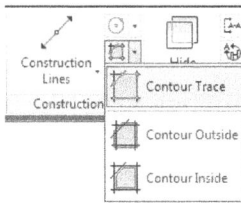

Command Line: AMCONTRACE

Ribbon: Home tab > Construction panel > Contour Trace drop-down list > Contour Trace

Menu: Draw > Boundary > Contour Trace

Procedure: Creating Contour Traces

To identify the endpoints of all of the geometry that is analyzed to calculate a closed loop based on the geometry surrounding a selected point, complete the following steps:

1. Start the **Contour Trace** command.

2. Press ENTER to accept the default contour type inside.

3. In the drawing area, click inside the contour.

4. - In the AutoCAD Question dialog box, click Yes.

5. Review the rectangles identifying the open ends of the contour.

Trace Contour

You can use the Trace Contour command to manually draw a polyline boundary around a specific region of your design. You can create the polyline by object snapping to existing geometry in the drawing. A key function of the Trace Contour command is the ability to create a polyline that overlaps part of a circle or arc. By using the Draw Arc command option, the radius and orientation of the arc segment that you create when tracing, matches the radius and direction of the circle or arc you selected after launching the command option.

Although this command is part of the construction editing tools, when you use Trace Contour the polylines are placed on the current layer.

Access

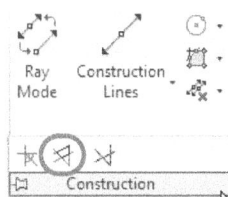

Command Line: AMTRCONT

Ribbon: Home tab > expanded Construction panel > Trace Contour

Menu: Draw > Construction Lines > Trace Contour

Procedure: Tracing a Contour

To create a polyline by object snapping to existing geometry and selecting arcs and circles to trace over, complete the following steps:

1. Start the **Trace Contour** command.

2. Object snap to the points that you want to trace over. Press ENTER to select an arc or circle and have the next segment be an arc with that radius and direction.

3. Continue to select additional points or segments.

4. Press ENTER twice to end the Trace Contour command.

Exercise: Create Geometry Using the Core Design Tools

In this exercise, you will work toward completing the drawing views of a cylindrical part. You will add a rectangle, chamfers, fillets, a new component view, hatch, and closed polyline based on a closed inner contour.

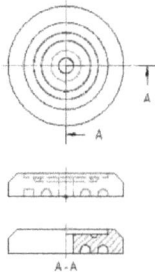

The completed exercise

1. Open *Core Design Tools.dwg*.

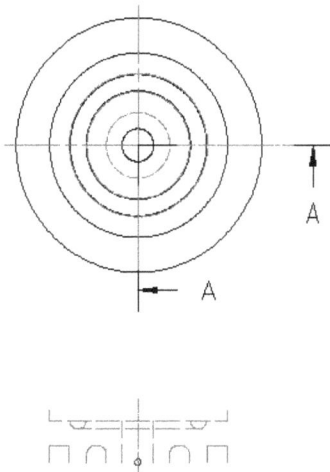

2. To begin drawing the outer rectangle shape for the front view based on the midpoint location of the rectangle's base and its width and height dimensions, do the following:

   ▪ Click *Home* tab > Draw panel > Rectangle drop-down list.
   ▪ In the *Midpoint of Base* category, click the middle option, as shown in the following illustration.

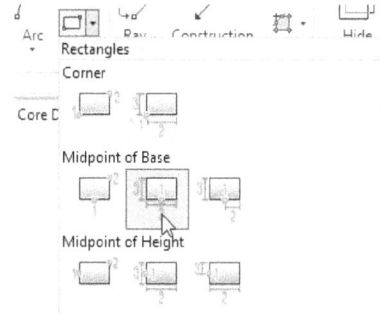

3. To draw the rectangle, do the following:

   ▪ In the front view, for the base point, object snap to the center of the small blue circle.
   ▪ For the full base value, enter **62**.
   ▪ For the full height value, enter **12.50**.

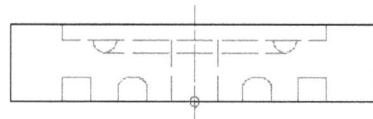

4. To begin chamfering the edges of the rectangle, click *Home* tab > Modify panel > Chamfer.

5. To set the chamfer size, do the following:

   ▪ In the Chamfer contextual tab, in the Chamfer Options, in the First Chamfer drop-down list, select **5**.
   ▪ In the Second Chamfer drop-down list, select **5**.
   ▪ Verify only Trim Geometry is selected and Insert Dimension is cleared.

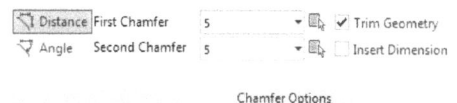

6. To chamfer the top corners in the front view, do the following:

   - Click the left vertical line.
   - Hover the cursor at the top horizontal line to preview and then click to accept the chamfer.
   - Similarly, click the right vertical line and the top horizontal line.
   - Press ESC.

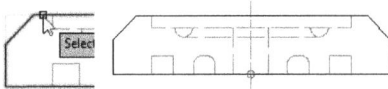

7. To begin filleting the bottom groove slots in the front view, click *Home* tab > Modify panel > Fillet.

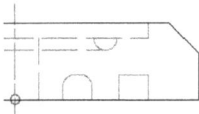

8. To set the fillet size, do the following:

   - In the Fillet contextual tab, in the Fillet Options, in the Fillet size drop-down list, select 2.
   - Verify only Trim Geometry is selected and Insert Dimension is cleared.

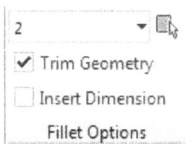

9. To fillet the top-right corner of the slot, do the following:

   - Click the right vertical line (hidden-magenta) of the right-most slot.
   - Hover the cursor at the adjoining horizontal hidden line to preview and then click to accept the fillet.
   - Press ENTER.

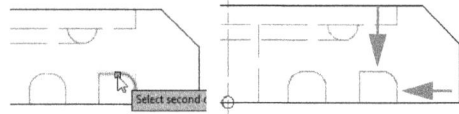

10. Still in the Fillet command, click on the left horizontal hidden line of the right-most slot and then the adjoining left vertical hidden line. Press ESC.

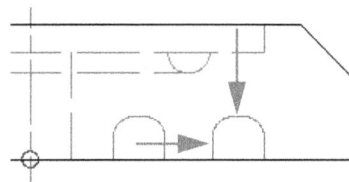

11. Using the standard **Copy** command, copy all of the objects except the small blue circle in the front view to just above the A-A label as shown in the following illustration.

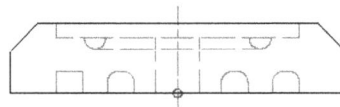

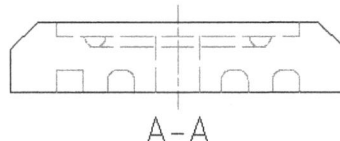

A – A

12. Erase and trim the lines in this view to have it display as shown in the following illustration.

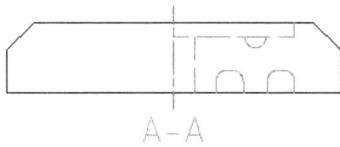

A – A

13. In the drawing window, select all of the hidden lines (magenta) and hidden shapes. Click Home tab > Layers panel > Layers drop-down list, and select AM_0. The lines should now be visible contour lines.

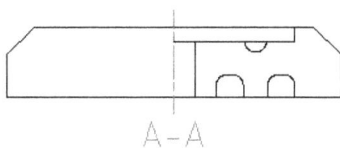

A – A

14. To hatch this section view, do the following:

- Click *Home* tab > Draw panel > Hatch.
- Click inside the closed bounded area.

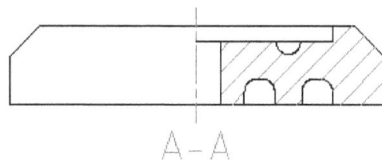

A – A

15. To create a closed polyline loop of the previously hatched area, do the following:

- Click *Home* tab > Construction panel > Contour Inside.
- Click in the hatched area. A green boundary is created.

16. To move the new polyline below the section view, do the following:

- On the Modify panel, click Move.
- For Select objects, enter **L.**
- Press ENTER.
- For the base point and second point, click in the drawing window to position the preview below the section view as shown in the following illustration.

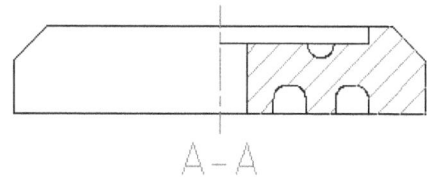

A – A

17. Save and close all of the files.

Lesson: Power Snaps

Overview

This lesson describes how to configure and use power snaps.

As you are creating or manipulating geometry, you might find that your requirements for snapping to geometry change throughout the task or between tasks. By knowing how to configure power snaps to meet your design needs, you can use them to assist in locating precise positions in your designs.

In the following illustration, a different power snap configuration was activated so that the object snap settings most often used with circle and arc geometry became active. The size of the cursor for this configuration was set differently than the other power snap configurations so that it would indicate the active power snap configuration.

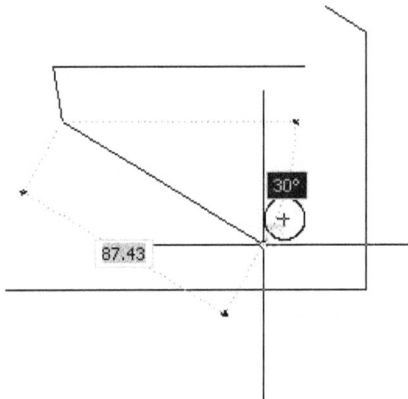

Objectives

After completing this lesson, you will be able to:

- Describe the purpose and benefits of power snaps.
- Establish different settings for the power snap configurations.
- Activate different power snap configurations.

About Power Snaps

To create accurate drawings, you need to precisely position geometry during its creation and manipulation. In many cases, the precise position is based on existing geometry. Object snaps locate points relative to objects in the drawing. Toggling on multiple object snaps for use while a creation or modification command is active makes it easier for you to snap to the geometry because you do not have to specify the object snap mode for each click. By learning about power snaps, you can extend your capabilities and use of object snaps, object tracking, and polar tracking.

In the following illustration, the Arc Radial object snap is being used to locate a point that is along the arc's radius line in alignment with the endpoint of the arc.

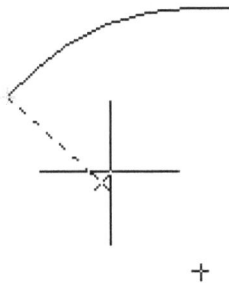

Definition of Power Snaps

Power snaps include additional object snap modes that are not available in standard AutoCAD® software. By using these additional modes when required, you can locate the required point without having to create more geometry to identify the location. Using power snaps, you can do the following:

- Set and save up to four different configurations that you can activate at any time while you are creating or modifying geometry. You can preconfigure object snap combinations once and use them often throughout the creation of your design.

- Filter out object snapping to specific types of geometry or ignore any Z values. Filtering out specific types of geometry ensures that you do not accidentally snap to it when you want to snap to a piece of geometry nearby.

The primary items stored in a power snap configuration include the snap modes that you want set as running object snaps, what the polar tracking and object snap tracking settings should be, and whether or not entity or Z value filtering should be active. The additional power snap modes that can be saved in a configuration are Symmetry, Arc Radial Lines, and Arc Tangent Lines. On demand, you can also access the Rectangle Center and Mid of 2 Points snap modes.

Example of Power Snaps

When multiple objects reside in an area to which you are snapping, you must ensure you snap to the appropriate object and location. In the following illustration, a dimension is being created from the far right endpoint to the far left endpoint. Without the power snap entity filters, you might snap to the endpoint of the extension line as shown in the bottom left of the illustration. With entity filters on and set, the correct results are achieved, as shown in the bottom right. In this power snap configuration, the entity filter is toggled on and is filtering out specific object types to which it is not going to snap. This makes selection of the points faster and easier.

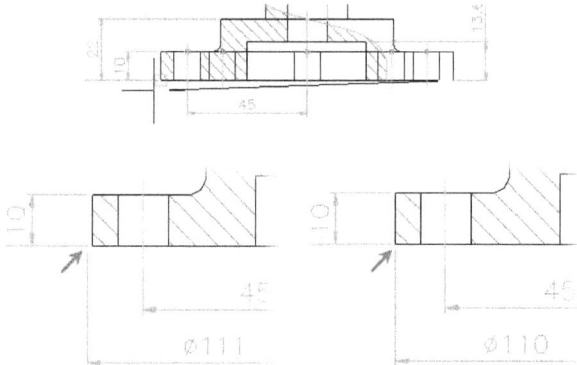

Configuring Power Snaps

Power snaps are set specifically for your installation of the AutoCAD Mechanical software. To use power snaps, you need to learn about the different items that can be configured and how to configure them.

Access

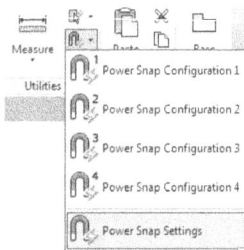

Command Line: AMPOWERSNAP

Ribbon: Home tab > Utilities panel > Power Snap drop-down list > Power Snap Settings

Menu: Tools > Drafting Settings > Osnap Settings

Power Snap Settings Dialog Box

You can preconfigure the power snap configurations and change the current power snap configuration in the Power Snap Settings dialog box. The typical workflow for configuring the power snap settings is to select the options and settings in the dialog box. First, select the setting that you want to configure in the Power Snap Configuration list. Next, select the required settings on the Power Snap tab and Polar Snap tab. The selected settings are then applied to the previously selected power snap configuration.

The following illustration shows the list of power snap configurations that you can select to configure in the Power Snap Settings dialog box. You can select the current configuration or one of four specifically defined setting configurations.

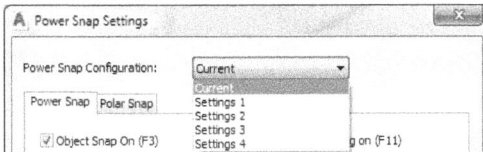

When you select a power snap mode on the Power Snap tab, you are setting that object snap to be used as a running object snap as you would set running object snaps in the AutoCAD software. However, with power snaps you can create four different preconfigurations of snap modes. This enables you to select a power snap configuration to change the settings instead of selecting and clearing the modes to achieve the required configuration. In addition to selecting the object snap modes, power snap configurations enable you to use polar snap settings to configure the size of the crosshair, and to control whether the snap settings should be listed on the status line, whether the Z value should be ignored for the location that is being snapped to, and whether various objects should be filtered out so that they are not snapped to.

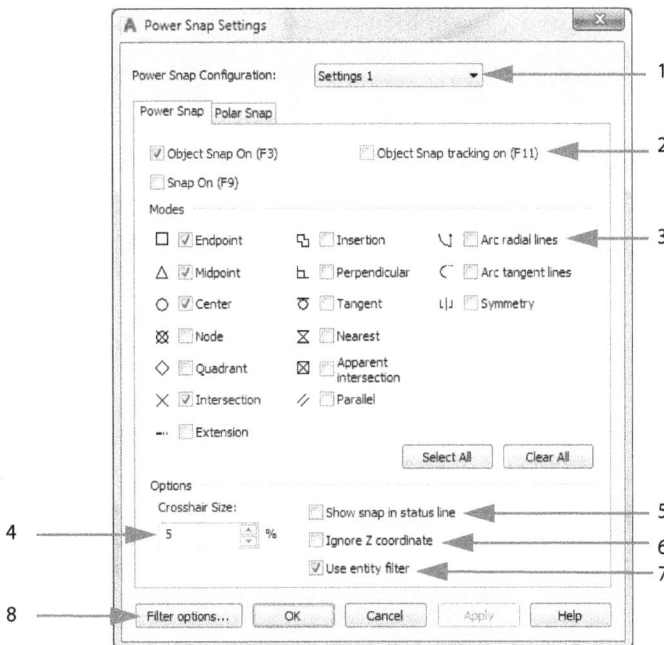

1. Use to select the setting number that you want to configure. Change this setting when you need to have specific settings for the current design operations. Activate one of the numbered settings to configure different typical object snap conditions. For example, Settings 1 and Settings 2 have object snaps that are typically used for line geometry, while Settings 3 and Settings 4 have settings that are typically used to interact with circles and arcs.

2. Toggle on or off the settings for running object snaps, grid snap, or object snap tracking to match your requirements for the currently selected power snap configuration.

3. Use to select which object snap modes are to be considered when clicking a location in the drawing window. This list includes three snap modes specific to power snaps.

4. Use to set the size of the crosshair. Each power snap configuration can have a different crosshair size setting. By setting different sizes per configuration, you can have a visual indicator as to which power snap configuration is active.

5. Select to have the three letter abbreviations for the selected snap modes list on the far left side of the status line.

6. Use to ignore the Z value returned from an object snap location.

7. Use to have the object snap modes ignore any object that is determined to be in the Filters list.

8. Click to open the Entity Filter dialog box to select or clear defined filters, create new filters, and edit or delete existing filters.

If you change the object snap, object snap tracking, or polar tracking settings in the Drafting Settings dialog box, the changes are indicated on the Current Settings tab in the Power Snap Settings dialog box. Any changes to the settings on this tab are also indicated in the Drafting Settings dialog box.

> If you want to define a power snap configuration that does not use object snaps but sets specific polar snap settings, clear the Enable Object Snap checkbox when that numbered settings tab is active. The object snap configuration then uses the settings from the Polar Snap tab.

Entity Filters

Click Filter options in the Power Snap Settings dialog box to open the Entity Filter dialog box in which you can select or clear any existing defined filter. When you click New, you can enter a new filter name and the conditions in which geometry should be identified for filtering from object snap consideration. By selecting an existing filter and clicking Edit, you can change the name of the filter and its filtering conditions.

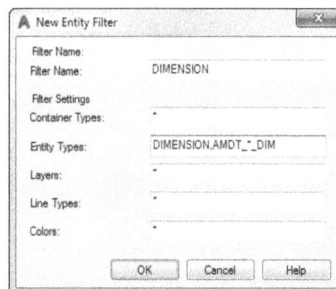

Snap Settings

The Power Snap Settings dialog box can also be opened from within the Options dialog box, on the AM:Preferences tab. When you click Snap Defaults, you can also preset the four power snap configurations.

The AutoCAD Mechanical software also enables you to assign object snap modes to specific commands. When you launch those commands, the assigned snap modes are automatically activated as running object snap modes along with any other settings that you might have set. Under Snap Settings, on the AM:Preferences tab, you can set whether the assigned snap modes to AutoCAD software commands are included with your current object snap settings. The default setting is System Settings, which includes the assigned snap modes. By selecting User Settings, only the object snap settings that you have configured are active after the command is executed.

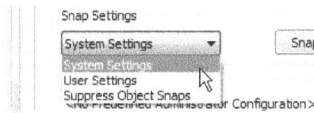

Procedure: Configuring Power Snaps

To preset power snap configurations for future use, complete the following steps:

1. Open the Power Snap Settings dialog box.

2. In the Polar Snap Configuration list, select the polar snap numbered setting for which you want to set the values.

3. Configure the snap modes, polar snap settings, and crosshair size to match your requirements.

4. Select or clear the options for using entity filters, ignoring Z coordinate values, and displaying the active snap modes in the status line.

Activating Power Snap Configurations

After you have configured the power snap settings, you can select them to use while creating your designs. Because the settings are saved with your installation of the AutoCAD Mechanical software, they are consistent from one drawing to another. You can change them at any time as your requirements change.

To benefit from the power snap configurations you have established, you need to be able to activate them. In the following illustration, Power Snap Configuration 3 is being activated. The settings saved within this configuration are can be used during the creation or modification of geometry until you change to a different configuration.

Access

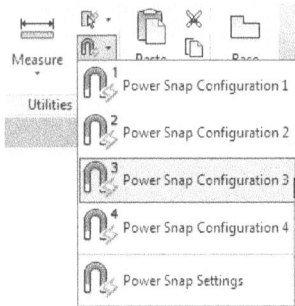

Command Line: AMPOWERSNAP (to select in Power Snaps Settings dialog box)

Ribbon: Home tab > Utilities panel > Power Snap drop-down list > Power Snap Configuration 1-4

Menu: Tools > Drafting Settings > Power Snap Configuration 1-4

Procedure: Activating Power Snap Configurations

To activate a saved power snap configuration to restore the saved settings associated with the configuration, complete the following steps:

- On the Home tab > Utilities panel > Power Snap drop-down list, or on the Tools menu > Drafting Settings flyout, or in the Power Snap Settings dialog box, select the numbered power snap configuration that you want to restore.

Key Points When Using Power Snaps

As you activate and use power snap configurations, remember the following key points:

- When the AM:Preferences Snap Settings is set to System Settings, the object snaps that are active when you execute a command might include ones that you have not configured in the activated power snap configuration. System setting object snaps are END, MID, CEN, and INT.
- If you change the object snap settings in the Drafting Settings dialog box, it only changes the power snap settings that are currently being used and not the saved configuration.
- When you activate a numbered power snap configuration, the current settings are replaced by the saved configuration settings. This includes all object snap, object snap tracking, and polar tracking settings.

Exercise: Configure and Activate Power Snaps

In this exercise, you will configure two of the four power snap configurations and activate them during the creation of basic line geometry.

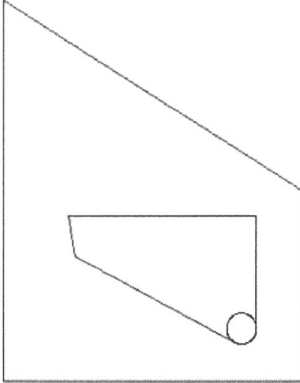

The completed exercise

1. Open *Power Snaps Configurations.dwg*.

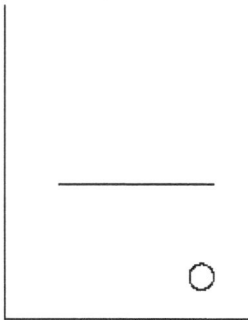

2. To edit the AutoTrack Settings, do the following:

   - Right-click in the drawing area gz80
   - and click Options.
   - In the Options dialog box, click the *Drafting* tab.
   - In AutoTrack Settings, clear the Display AutoTrack tooltip checkbox and click OK.

3. By default, Dynamic Input is toggled off and not displayed in the Status Bar. To toggle it on and display Dynamic Input on the Status Bar, click on Customization and select Dynamic Input in the list.

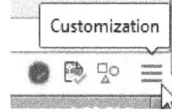

4. To begin editing the Dynamic Input settings, on the Status Bar, right-click on Dynamic Input and click Dynamic Input Settings.

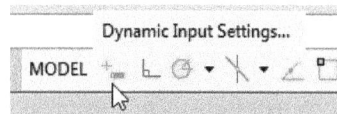

5. To set the Dynamic Input settings, do the following:

   - In the Drafting Settings dialog box > Dynamic Input tab, under Dimension Input, click Settings.
   - In the Dimension Input Settings dialog box, adjust the setting to match the values shown in the following illustration.
   - Click OK to close both dialog boxes.

6. To open the Power Snap Settings dialog box:

- Right-click in the drawing area and click Options.
- In the Options dialog box, select the *AM:Preferences* tab.
- In the *AM:preferences* tab, select Snap Defaults.

7. To begin configuring the settings for one power snap configuration, in the Power Snap Configuration list, verify that Settings 1 is selected.

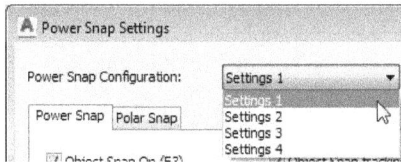

8. Set additional options for Settings 1 by doing the following:

- On the *Power Snap* tab, select the Object Snap tracking on checkbox.
- On the *Polar Snap* tab, select the Polar tracking on checkbox.
- Click Apply.

9. To begin configuring the settings for another power snap configuration, in the Power Snap Configuration list, select Settings 3.

10. On the *Polar Snap* tab:

- Ensure that the Polar tracking on checkbox is selected.
- In the Increment angle list, select 10.

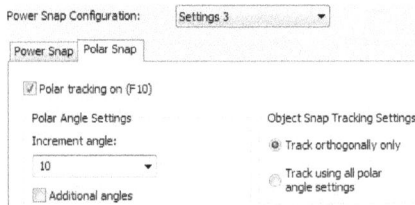

11. On the *Power Snap* tab, in the Crosshair Size field, enter **15**. Click OK. Click OK in the Options dialog box as well.

12. To activate the settings for the power snap configuration 1, on the *Home* tab > Utilities panel > Power Snap drop-down list, click Power Snap Configuration 1.

13. Begin to draw line segments using the current power snap configuration:

- Click Home tab > Draw panel > Line.
- For the first point, object snap to the right endpoint of the lower horizontal line.

14. To the next point 90 degrees above the start point and horizontally aligned to the midpoint of the left vertical line, do the following:

- Hover the cursor over the midpoint area of the left vertical line to acquire its midpoint as an object snap tracking location.
- Move the cursor above the first entered point and note that polar snap only occurs when it is within the 90 degree range.
- Click to accept this point when the tracking projection lines are displayed.

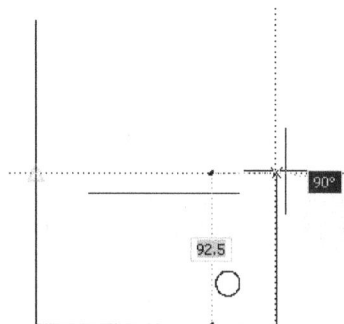

15. Object snap to the top end point of the left vertical line and press ENTER.

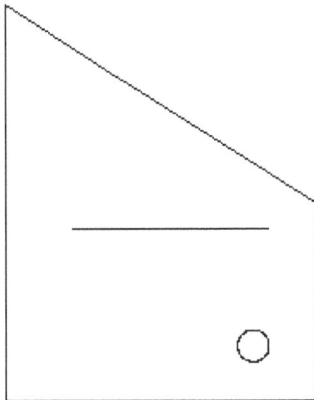

16. Begin to draw the inner contour lines, as follows:

- Press ENTER to start drawing another line.
- Object snap to the left endpoint of the middle horizontal line.
- Move the cursor down and to the right, and note that polar tracking does not occur at any angle except at the 90 degree increment.

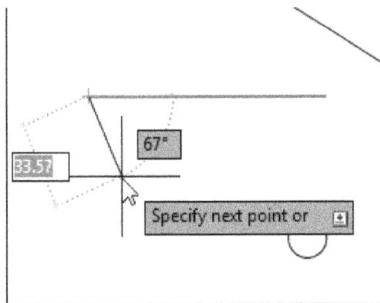

17. To activate the other power snap configuration settings that you have created, on the *Home* tab > Utilities panel > Power Snap drop-down list, click Power Snap Configuration 3.

18. To continue drawing the line segments, do the following:

- Move the cursor down and to the right so that polar tracking locks in at 80 degrees. Note that polar tracking occurs at every 10 degree increment.
- Enter **20**.

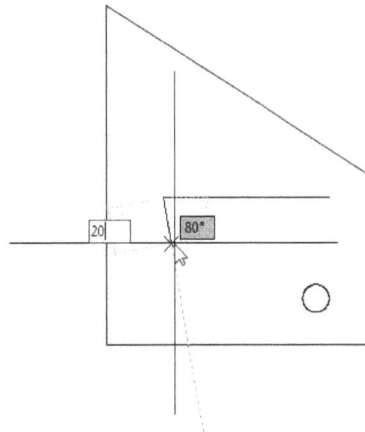

19. Object snap to the tangency of the circle to create another line segment. Press ENTER.

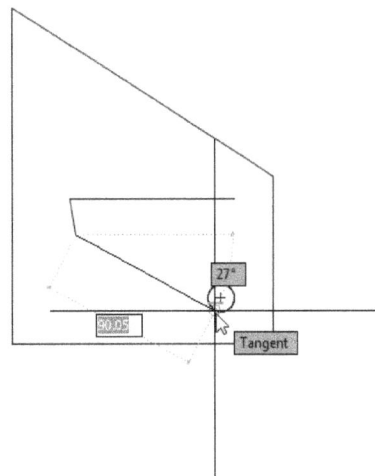

20. Complete the drawing view by drawing one more line segment from the right quadrant of the circle to the right endpoint of the line above.

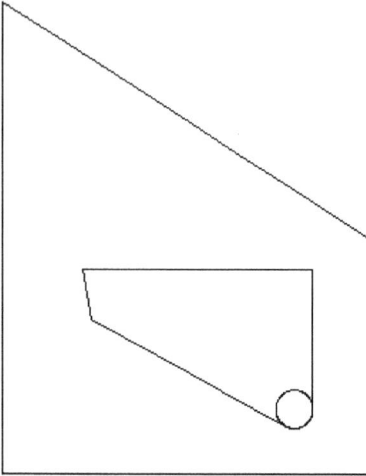

21. To restore your system to the default settings, reverse the settings made in Steps 2 - 10.

22. Save and close all of the files.

Lesson: Centerlines

Overview

You can create individual and patterned centerlines, centerlines and holes, and centerlines and circles.

You can place centerlines in a drawing to indicate symmetry, hole centers, and alignment. To add centerlines, holes with centerlines, and circles with centerlines to the drawing as efficiently as possible, you need to learn the available centerline creation methods.

As shown in the following illustration, you can use the Mechanical centerline tools to add centerlines to indicate the center of holes, create the circles and centerlines for the pin post, add circular and radial centerlines, add holes that follow industry standards for sizing, and add a centerline to indicate the center axis of the part.

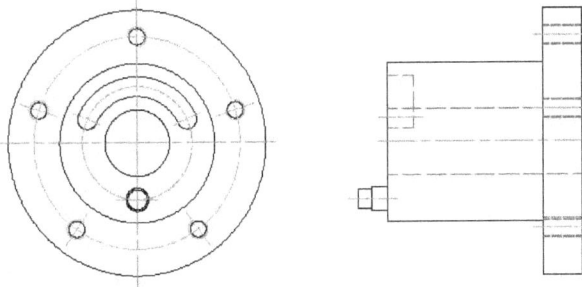

Objectives

After completing this lesson, you will be able to:

- Describe the types of centerlines that you can add to a drawing.
- Create centerlines and holes with centerlines.
- Set the centerline overshoot method and value in the standard.

About Mechanical Centerlines

Centerlines are one of many important items that you add to a drawing to help communicate the design of a part or assembly to others. With an understanding of the types of centerlines that you can create in a drawing and the available centerline tools, you can complete your drawings more quickly while ensuring conformance to your company standards.

In the following illustration, the centerlines identify the center points of the circles and arcs.

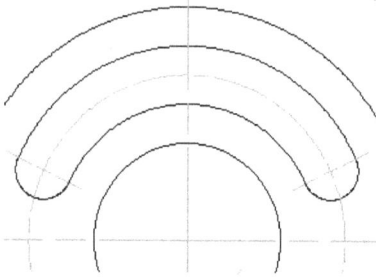

Definition of Centerlines

Two types of centerlines can be added to your drawings. One is the crossing of centerlines at 90 degrees to each other to indicate the center point of a circle or arc at the intersection of the centerlines. The other is a single linear centerline to indicate the center axis of a cylinder or hole when viewing it from the side, or to show symmetry of the part about that centerline.

To conform to drafting practices and standards, when you create centerlines they automatically extend past the selected geometry or points. They also automatically reside on the layer that has been specified for centerlines. Both the extension and layer are part of the configuration of the active standard.

In most cases you can create a linear centerline as you would draw a regular line, by specifying a start point and endpoint. You can select two lines to create a single linear centerline that is positioned halfway between two parallel lines or bisecting the angle of converging lines.

The majority of centerline commands are used to create crossing centerlines. You can do the following:

- Add a centerline cross to an existing arc or circle.
- Insert a centerline cross and multiple circles at the centerline cross.
- Create the centerlines in a pattern or offset position.
- Insert multiple circles at the centerline cross position of a centerline pattern or offset.
- Insert holes or external threads based on industry standards at the centerline cross position of a centerline pattern or offset.

Example of Centerlines

In the following illustration, the centerlines in the drawing views of the part help to identify the shape of the part and the location and relationship of the features on the part. The centerlines indicate that the slot follows a true arcing path with the arc's center coincident to the center of the part. The center of the circular post is located 17 mm directly below the center of the part, and is in exact alignment with the threaded hole on the upper area of the part.

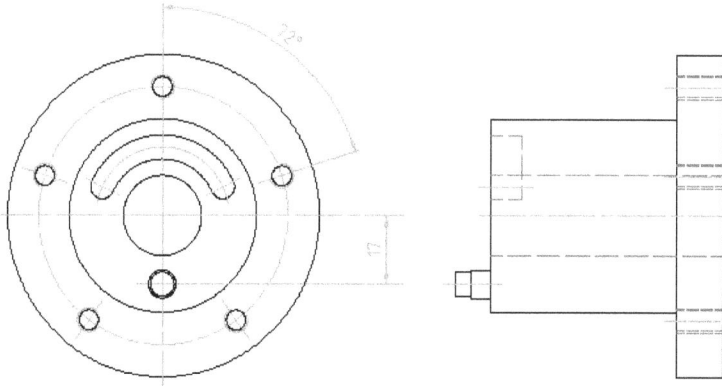

Creating Centerlines

When you create a drawing of a part and are following standard drafting practices, you need to include centerlines when representing circular edges. These circular edges might be a cylindrical flange and the holes for bolting it to another part, or the center location of a slot. To add these centerlines to the drawing using the most efficient method possible, you need to learn about the different centerline creation tools and how to use them to create centerlines and holes with centerlines.

In the following illustration, the drawing view of the part shows the results of adding centerlines to a drawing using Centerline Cross, Centerline Cross with Hole, and Centerline Cross on Full Circle. When the circular bolting pattern was created with Centerline Cross on Full Circle, standard-sized threaded holes were selected and then placed automatically.

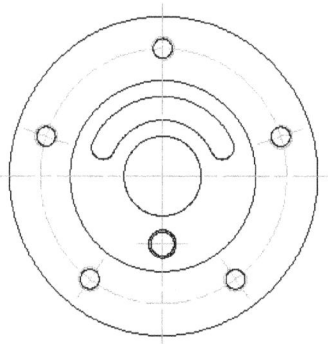

Access of Centerline Commands

You can access the commands for creating centerlines in the Home tab > Draw panel > Center Line drop-down list.

In the Center Line drop-down list, the icons for the centerline creation methods display with light blue and gray geometry. The gray geometry indicates the geometry that needs to be referenced. The light blue geometry indicates what is created with that option. In addition, when you hover the cursor over an option, a tooltip displays explaining the option.

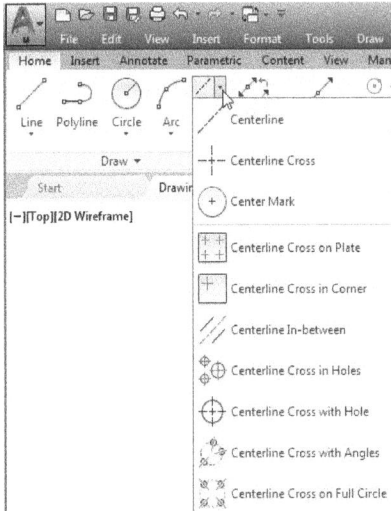

After you have added a centerline or pattern of centerlines with holes to a drawing view, you can edit them following the prompts that you followed when you initially created them. To edit a centerline, double-click on one of the centerline segments in the drawing window. The options and procedures that display depend on which command was initially used to create the centerline.

Centerline Line

You can use the **Centerline** command to create a single linear centerline from one specified point to another. You can specify those points using object snapping or by entering the coordinates. The centerline that is created extends past the specified points by a distance that is set in the active standard.

Access

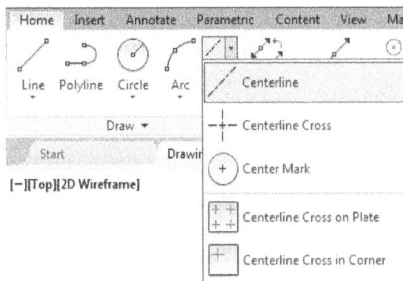

Command Line: AMCENTLINE

Ribbon: Home tab > Draw panel > Centerline drop-down list > Centerline

Menu: Draw > Centerlines > Centerline

Procedure: Creating a Centerline

To create a single centerline line segment, complete the following steps:

1. Start the **Centerline** command.

2. Specify the centerline start point.

3. Specify the centerline endpoint.

Centerline Cross

You can use the **Centerline Cross** command to draw a crossing centerline through a specified point with a specified diameter or radius. If you specify the size by clicking in the drawing window, you can set the crossing centerline size by entering the radius from the center to the second point that you clicked. This centerline creation command is useful for adding a centerline on an existing circle or arc that does not already have a centerline.

The centerline cross is drawn from the center point and extends outward through the creation of four separate lines. These run parallel to the axis of the current user coordinate system (UCS). Therefore, if you want an angled cross, change the UCS alignment before using this command.

Because the crossing centerlines are separate segments, when you add a centerline cross to an arc, you can delete the line segments that are not required for identifying the arc.

Access

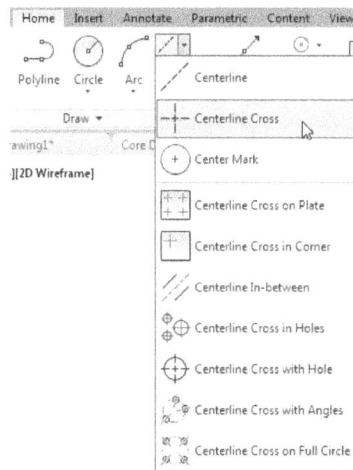

Command Line: AMCENCROSS

Ribbon: Home tab > Draw panel > Centerline drop-down list > Centerline Cross

Menu: Draw > Centerlines > Centerline Cross

Procedure: Inserting a Centerline Cross

To create a crossing centerline, complete the following steps:

1. Start the **Centerline Cross** command.

2. Specify the center point.

3. Enter the diameter or object snap to a point on the arc or circle.

Centerline Cross with Hole

You can use a centerline cross with a hole to create a centerline and the hole geometry at the same time. You can enter a value for the diameter of the hole. The size of the cross is automatically modified to match the size of the hole. A centerline cross with a hole is drawn from a center point and extends outward.

To create multiple concentric circles at the hole position, separate each value you with the pipe symbol (|).

After you specify a diameter, you can continue to insert centerline crosses with the same-sized hole definitions. The diameter values that you enter become the default diameter values the next time you use the command.

Access

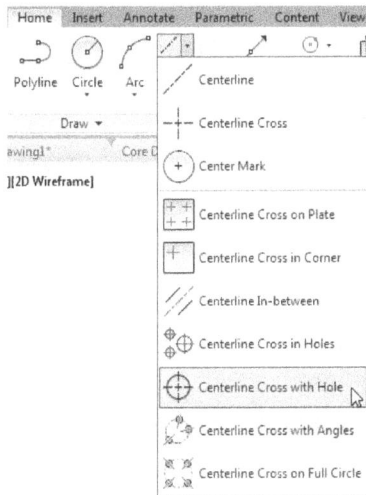

Command Line: AMCENCRHOLE

Ribbon: Home tab > Draw panel > Centerline drop-down list > Centerline Cross with Hole

Menu: Draw > Centerlines > Centerline Cross with Hole

Procedure: Inserting a Centerline Cross with Hole

To create a crossing centerline with circles, complete the following steps:

1. Start the **Centerline Cross with Hole** command.

2. In the drawing area, click the center point for the circles and centerline.

3. Enter the diameter of the hole to insert the centerline cross with a hole.

4. In the drawing area, click to insert additional circles and centerlines of the same definition. Press ESC to end the command.

Centerline Cross with Angles

You can use the **Centerline Cross with Angles** command to create one or more centerline circles with a pattern of holes at specified angles. At each specified angle, a linear centerline is created radial to the centerline circle. The holes are then positioned at the intersection of the centerline circle and the radial centerline. The holes can be one or more concentric circles or an industry standard hole or external thread.

To create multiple concentric centerline circles or multiple circles at the hole positions, separate each value you with the pipe symbol (|).

Access

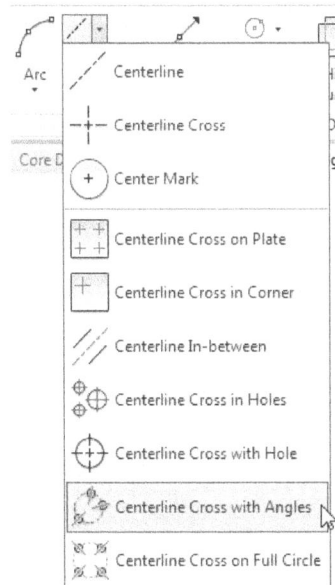

Command Line: AMCENCRANGLE

Ribbon: Home tab > Draw panel > Centerline drop-down list > Centerline Cross with Angles

Menu: Draw > Centerlines > Centerline Cross with Angles

Procedure: Inserting a Centerline Cross with Angles

To create a circular pattern of holes and corresponding centerlines with a specified angle, complete the following steps:

1. Start the **Centerline Cross with Angles** command.

2. Specify the center point of the circular centerlines.

3. Enter the diameters of the circular centerlines. If there is more than one, separate the diameter values with the pipe (|) symbol.

4. Enter the diameter of the holes. If there is more than one, separate the diameter values with the pipe (|) symbol. Alternatively, select the Standard Parts option to select a standard hole type and size.

5. Enter the angles separated by a pipe (|) symbol. Press ENTER to accept the default angles for the holes (45|90|135).

Centerline Cross on Full Circle

With the **Centerline Cross on Full Circle** command, you can create one or more centerline circles with evenly spaced holes along those circles. At each evenly spaced angular position along the circle, a linear centerline is created radial to the centerline circle. The holes are then positioned at the intersection of the centerline circle and the evenly spaced radial centerline.

To create multiple concentric centerline circles or multiple circles at the hole positions, separate each value you with the pipe symbol (|).

Access

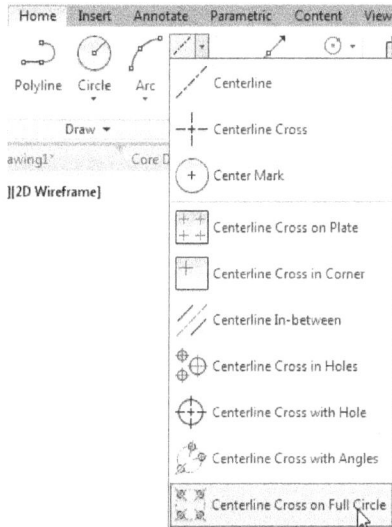

Command Line: AMCENCRFULLCIRCLE

Ribbon: Home tab > Draw panel > Centerline drop-down list > Centerline Cross on Full Circle

Menu: Draw > Centerlines > Centerline Cross on Full Circle

Procedure: Inserting a Centerline Cross on Full Circle

To create a circular pattern of holes and corresponding centerlines spaced evenly through a full 360 degrees, complete the following steps:

1. Start the **Centerline Cross on Full Circle** command.

2. Specify the center point of the circular centerlines.

3. Enter the diameters of the circular centerlines. If there is more than one, separate the diameter values with the pipe (|) symbol.

4. Enter the diameter of the holes. If there is more than one, separate the diameter values with the pipe (|) symbol. Alternatively, select the Standard Parts option to select a standard hole type and size.

5. Enter the number of holes to be inserted through 360 degrees.

6. Enter the angle at which the first set of holes should be positioned. Alternatively, press ENTER to accept the default rotation angle from which to start the pattern.

Centerline Cross on Plate

With the **Centerline Cross on Plate** command, you can create holes that are positioned an offset distance from the corners of a closed boundary of geometry. You can specify the offset to be inside or outside the closed boundary area.

For the hole, you can multiple diameters to create multiple concentric circles at each centerline location. You can specify an industry standard hole or external thread, or set it to only create the centerlines and no holes.

Access

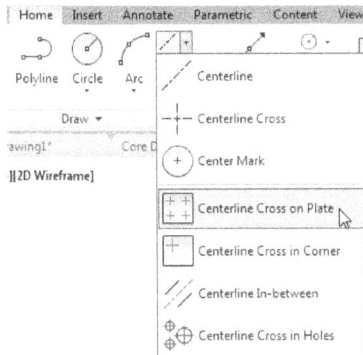

Command Line: AMCENCRPLATE

Ribbon: Home tab > Draw panel > Centerline drop-down list > Centerline Cross on Plate

Menu: Draw > Centerlines > Centerline Cross on Plate

Procedure: Inserting a Centerline Cross on Plate

To create crossing centerlines with circles or holes at an offset distance from existing contour geometry, complete the following steps:

1. Start the **Centerline Cross on Plate** command.

2. Specify the offset distance from the contour geometry where the center of the centerline cross is located.

3. Select the existing contour geometry and press ENTER.

4. Specify a point inside or outside the contour.

5. Enter the diameter of the circles that you want to insert at each centerline cross. If there is more than one, separate the diameter values with the pipe (|) symbol. Alternatively, select the Standard Parts option to select a standard hole type and size.

Centerline Cross in Corner

With the **Centerline Cross in Corner** command, you can create one or more concentric circles or insert a hole at an offset distance from two intersecting lines.

After starting the command and selecting two lines that intersect, you can specify an offset distance from each line, distance, or click it in the drawing window. With the centerline position set, you can specify the diameters of circles, an industry standard hole or external threads, or no hole at all to be placed at that centerline position.

To specify the diameters of multiple concentric circles, separate each value with the pipe symbol (|). If you select no hole, only the centerline cross is created.

Access

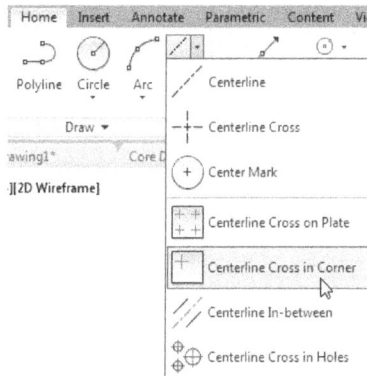

Command Line: AMCENCRCORNER

Ribbon: Home tab > Draw panel > Centerline drop-down list > Centerline Cross in Corner

Menu: Draw > Centerlines > Centerline Cross in Corner

Procedure: Inserting a Centerline Cross in a Corner

To create crossing centerlines with circles or holes at an offset distance from two selected contour lines, complete the following steps:

1.   Start the **Center line Cross in Corner** command.

2.   Select the first contour line.

3.   Select the second contour line.

4.   Specify the offset distance from the first contour line to the center of the centerline cross.

5.   Specify the offset distance from the second contour line to the center of the centerline cross.

6.   Enter the diameter of the holes. If there is more than one, separate the diameter values with the pipe (|) symbol. Alternatively, select the Standard Parts option to select a standard hole type and size.

Centerline Cross in Holes

Use the **Centerline Cross in Holes** command to quickly add a corresponding centerline cross to existing holes (circles). After you access the command, you can specify the hole or holes that require centerlines. The centerline is created automatically and displayed in the hole at the correct size and with the correct oversize extensions.

Access

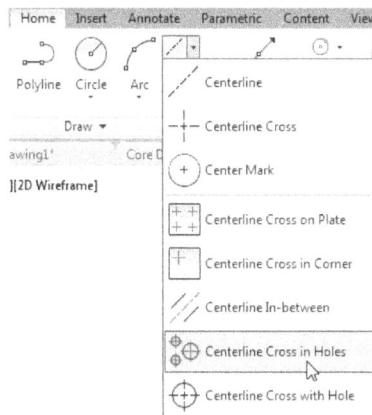

Command Line: AMCENCRINHOLE

Ribbon: Home tab > Draw panel > Centerline drop-down list > Centerline Cross in Holes

Menu: Draw > Centerlines > Centerline Cross in Holes

Procedure: Inserting a Centerline Cross in Holes

To add crossing centerlines to existing circles and size the centerline automatically according to the size of the selected circle, complete the following steps:

1. Start the **Center Line Cross in Holes** command.

2. Select the circles.

3. Press ENTER to insert the centerlines.

Centerlines Between Two Lines

Use the **Centerline In-between** command to place a bisecting centerline between two parallel or nonparallel lines. If you already have two lines in your drawing that you want to mark as symmetric, you can create a centerline between them automatically. In this case, the length of the centerline depends on the length of the first line that you select.

Access

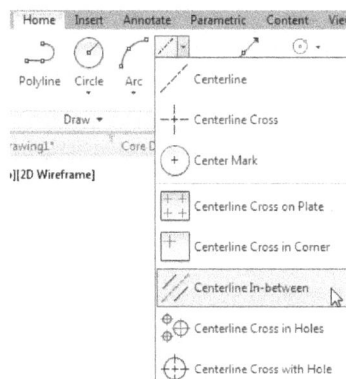

Command Line: AMCENINBET

Ribbon: Home tab > Draw panel > Centerline drop-down list > Centerline In-between

Menu: Draw > Centerlines > Centerline In-between

Procedure: Inserting a Centerline Between Two Lines

To add a straight centerline segment that bisects the angle created by two intersecting lines, complete the following steps:

1. Start the **Centerline In-between** command.

2. Select the first contour line.

3. Select the second contour line to insert the centerline.

Centerline Settings

To control how far the centerlines extend past the arcs and circles, you need to know where and how to configure the properties of centerlines.

The following illustration shows two different results of the same drawing view. The centerline overshoot was set to different values.

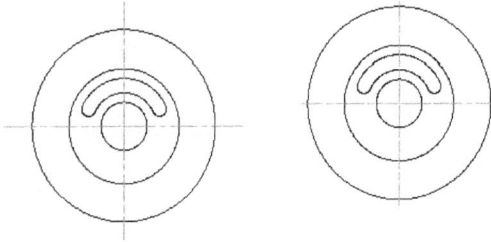

Center Line Settings Dialog Box

You can change the overshoot extension distance of the centerlines in the Center Line Settings dialog box for the active standard. In the Options dialog box, select the *AM:Standards* tab. In the tree view on the right, double-click on Center Line to open the Center Line Settings dialog box.

1. Select the **Type** that you want to use from: Fixed, Proportional, and Automatic. Depending on the selected Type, different options become available.

2. Fixed is used to a set distance by which the centerline extends past a specified point or past the selected circle.

3. Proportional is used to have the distance the centerline extend past the object based on the size of the geometry. Entering a value of **0.1** adds 10 percent to the overall length of the centerline. Half of that percentage distance is added to each end of the line to create the amount of extension. This causes a varying overshoot distance for each centerline added because the size of the geometry varies.

4. **Automatic** is used to define both a fixed value (1) and a proportional value (2). The extension distance is the larger of the two values.

5. Select the **Ignore drawing scaling** checkbox to maintain the overshoot value established by the fixed or proportional size regardless of the scale factor.

6. **Restore Defaults** sets the values in this dialog box back to the default values.

Exercise: Add Centerlines and Holes

In this exercise, you will add centerlines, circles with centerlines, and holes with centerlines to existing views of a part.

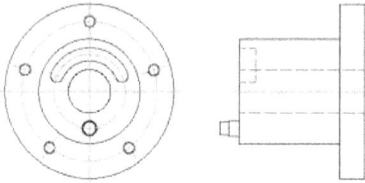

The completed exercise

1. Open *Centerlines.dwg*.

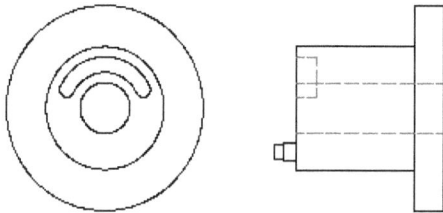

2. To add a crossing centerline to the front view, do the following:

- Click Home tab > Draw panel > Centerline drop-down list > Centerline Cross.
- Object snap to the center of any circle in the front view.
- Object snap to the quadrant of the largest circle.

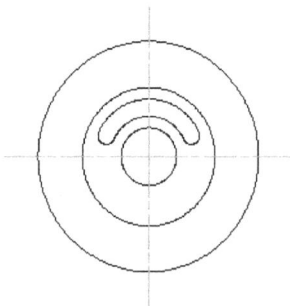

3. Begin to change the overshoot setting in the standard, as follows:

- Right-click anywhere in the drawing window and click Options.
- In the Options dialog box, in the AM:Standards tab, in the Standard elements list, double-click on Center Line.

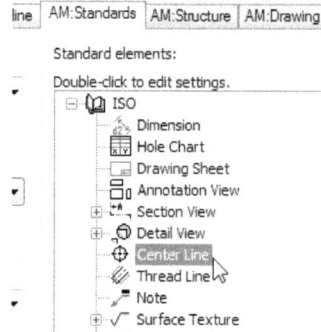

4. To set the overshoot size, do the following:

- In the Center Line Settings dialog box, in the Fixed field, enter **3**.
- In the Center Line Settings dialog box, click OK.
- In the Options dialog box, click OK.

5. Edit the centerline. In the front view, double-click on the centerline that you placed previously to highlight it and then object snap to the quadrant on the outer circle. Note the decrease in the distance by which the centerline extends past the circle.

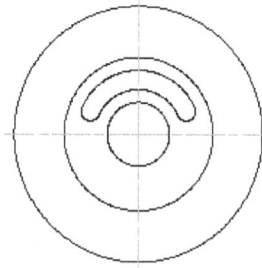

6. To draw a straight centerline in the side view to indicate the center axis position, do the following:

   - Click Home tab > Draw panel > Centerline drop-down list > Centerline.
   - In the right view, object snap to the midpoints of the right most and left vertical lines to create a centerline as shown in the following illustration.

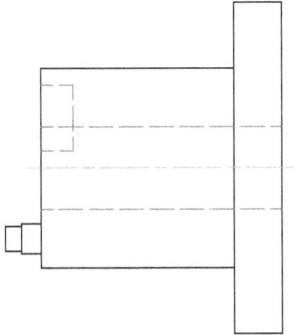

7. On the Home tab, expand the Layers panel to view all of the tools. Click Construction Line On/Off to toggle on the visibility of construction lines (red line).

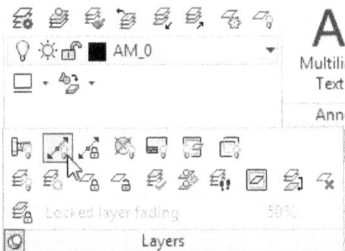

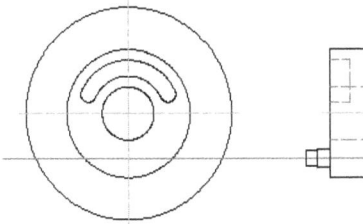

8. To begin drawing the two circles and the centerlines for the extruding posts shown in the side view, do the following:

   - Click Home tab > Draw panel > Centerline drop-down list > Centerline Cross with Hole.

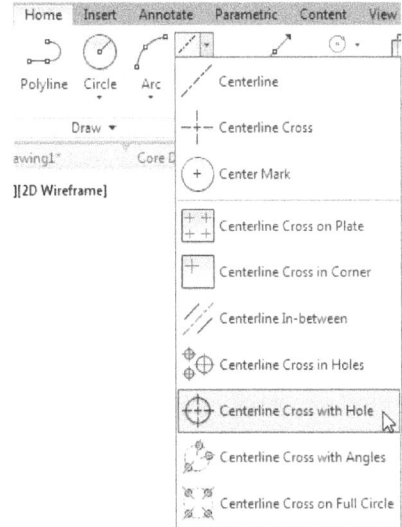

9. To position the holes and centerlines in the front view, do the following:

   - Object snap to the intersection of the construction line and centerline.
   - For the hole diameter, enter **6**.
   - Press ENTER.
   - Press ESC.

10. Repeat Steps 8 and 9 and enter **7** for the second hole diameter.

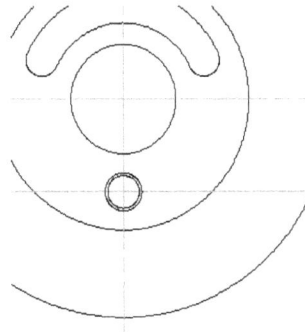

11. Click Home tab > expanded Layers panel > Construction Line On/Off to toggle off the visibility of construction lines.

12. To begin creating a circular tapped hole pattern that includes circular and radial centerlines, click Home tab > Draw panel > Centerline drop-down list > Centerline Cross on Full Circle.

13. To set the position of the centerlines, their diameter, and number of holes, do the following:

   - Object snap to the center of the front view.
   - For the diameter of the circle, enter **64**.
   - For the diameter of the hole, enter **S** for Standard part.
   - For the centerline cross diameter, enter **6**.
   - For the number of centerlines, enter **5**.
   - For the rotation angle, enter **90**.

14. To select a standard tapped hole to insert at the locations that you just specified, do the following:

   - In the Select a Hole/Thread dialog box, in the Details area, click Tapped Holes.
   - In the Details area, click Through.
   - In the Details area, click ISO 262 (Regular Thread).
   - In the Select a Size list, click M6.
   - Click Finish.

15. Review the centerlines and holes that were just added to the drawing view.

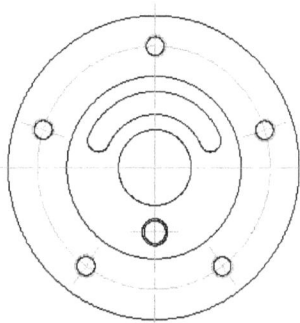

16. Begin to create centerlines through the arcing slot, as follows:

   - Click Home tab > Draw panel > Centerline drop-down list > Centerline Cross with Angles.
   - Object snap to the center of the front view.
   - For the diameter of the circle, object snap to the center of the arc as shown in the following illustration.

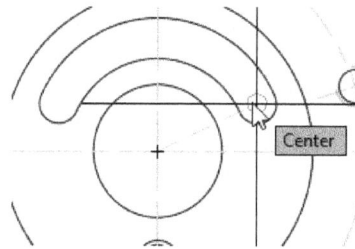

17. To define the rest of the centerline, do the following:

   - For the diameter of the hole, enter **N** for No hole.
   - For the centerline cross diameter, enter **3**.
   - For the angle of the radial centerlines, enter **25|155**.

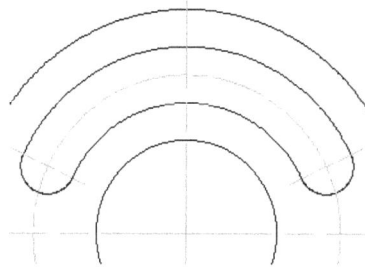

18. Save and close the file.

Lesson: Construction Lines

Overview

This lesson describes the use and creation of construction lines.

To communicate the design of a part or assembly, you need to create drawings that view the design from different directions. Following drafting practices, the views you create are orthographic projections, meaning that the viewing direction is 90 degrees around the part or assembly. For drawing views that are directly above and below or left and right to each other, features on the parts align horizontally or vertically between the views. By using construction lines, you can project the location of something in one view to another view. Therefore, its location is already identified in the other view.

In the following illustration, different aspects of the right-side view are being located and created by projecting construction lines horizontally from the front and top views. Using a projection crosshair, vertical construction lines are automatically created that correspond to the horizontal construction lines in the top view.

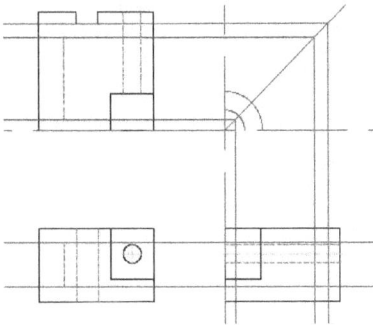

Objectives

After completing this lesson, you will be able to:

- Describe the purpose of construction lines and their display.
- Add construction lines to your drawing.
- Automatically place construction lines based on selected geometry.
- Insert a construction line projection crosshair for orthographic view creation.
- Erase construction lines without erasing other geometry.

About Construction Lines

Construction lines are intended to help you complete your drawings. Once you understand construction lines, you can learn how to use them in your drawings.

Definition of Construction Lines

Construction lines refer to the construction geometry that you add to your drawings to help locate and align points between views and within a view. The construction geometry that you create can include xlines, rays, circles, and rectangles. When you use commands to define the construction geometry while meeting specific geometric conditions, such as being parallel, perpendicular, or tangent to something, the geometry is automatically placed on the layer AM_CL, which is also referred to as the cline layer.

Construction lines automatically follow the layer management system. You can toggle on and off the visibility of the construction geometry to match your requirements. If you want to remove the construction geometry, you can select and erase it without removing other geometry in the selection window. You can also erase all of the construction geometry without having to select it. Construction geometry that is visible in the drawing area that is being plotted is also visible in the plot. Therefore, if you do not want to include it in the plot, you need to toggle its visibility off or erase it before plotting.

If a structured component view or folder is active when you create construction geometry, a message prompts you that the construction geometry is unsupported in structure. The construction geometry is then created at the uppermost level of the drawing outside the component views or folders. Because construction lines are mostly used to project locations between views, so the construction lines should not be a part of a component view that can be reused separately from the other views.

> Construction lines are ignored by commands that affect the viewing extents of the drawing.

Example of Construction Lines

The following example shows how construction lines can be used to project the location of a part's feature from one view to another. In this case, the square notch shown in the front and top views was quickly located and drawn in the right-side view based on the intersection of the construction lines.

The construction lines were created as lines and rays that were automatically added after the geometry in the front and top views was selected. The vertical lines were created automatically because the projection crosshair had been inserted and was set to on.

Note: The lineweight for the right-side view was changed to help with visualization of the view's geometry over the construction lines.

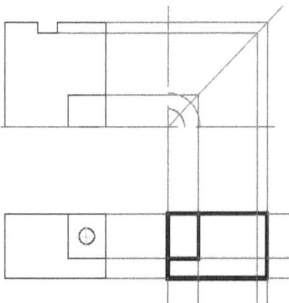

Drawing Construction Lines

To create construction geometry, you need to know where to access the commands for adding xlines, rays, circles, or rectangles to your drawing.

Accessing Construction Line Commands from the Ribbon

To access the commands for creating construction geometry from multiple locations, click Home tab > Construction panel > Construction Lines drop-down list.

The icons in the drop-down list identify the construction geometry that you can create with the command. Refer to the AutoCAD Mechanical software's Help for specific information on each of the construction geometry creation commands.

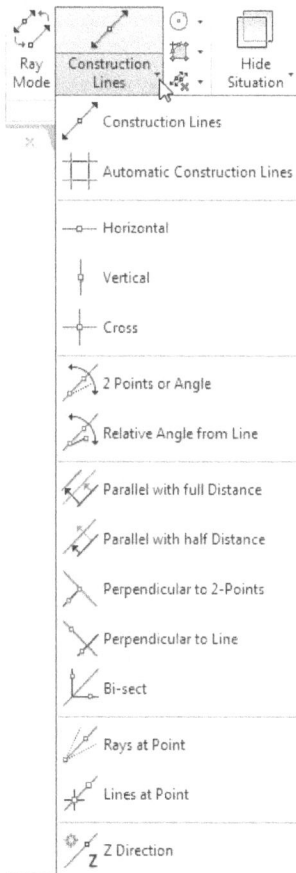

Access

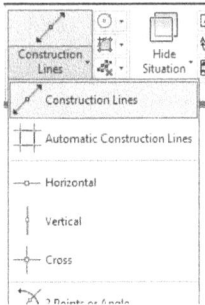

Command Line: AMCONSTLINES

Ribbon: Home tab > Construction panel > Construction Lines drop-down list > Construction Lines

Menu: Draw > Construction Lines > Draw Construction Lines

Procedure: Drawing Construction Lines

To add construction geometry to your drawings, complete the following steps:

1.   Start the **Construction Lines** command for the construction geometry that you want to create in your drawing.

2.   Specify the inputs required to create the construction geometry for the selected tool.

Placing Construction Lines Automatically

Instead of adding horizontal or vertical construction lines to the drawing one at a time, you can use automatic construction line tools to generate construction lines from all relevant points of selected objects. You can automatically create horizontal and vertical construction lines, projecting logical snap points (intersections, quadrants, endpoints, etc.) with construction lines and rays. You can project construction lines in any combination of directions.

Access

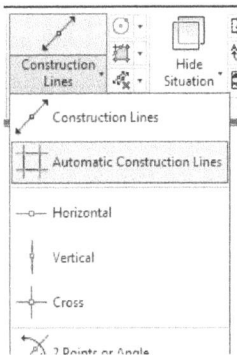

Command Line: AMAUTOCLINES

Ribbon: Home tab > Construction panel > Construction Lines drop-down list > Automatic Construction Lines

Menu: Draw > Construction Lines > Automatic Construction Lines

Automatic C-Line Creation Dialog Box

When you start the **Automatic Construction Lines** command, the Automatic C-Line Creation dialog box opens, enabling you to select the direction in which the construction lines should be projected from the selected geometry.

The geometry that you select to which to automatically add construction lines must be on the AM_0, AM_1, AM_2, AM_3, or AM_7 layers, or any AutoCAD layer. Objects placed on AutoCAD Mechanical layers that are reserved for construction lines, standard parts, and general annotation are filtered out.

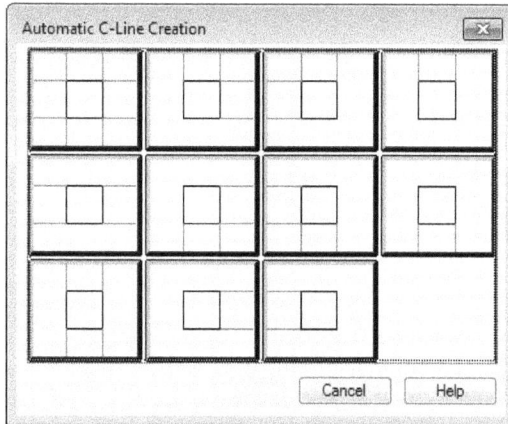

Procedure: Placing Construction Lines Automatically

To automatically place horizontal and vertical construction lines in the drawing based on the selected geometry, complete the following steps:

1. Start the **Automatic Construction Lines** command.

2. In the Automatic C-Line Creation dialog box, select the creation and direction method that you want to use.

3. In the drawing window, select the objects from which you want construction lines to be automatically projected.

Inserting and Using Projection Crosshairs

When you create orthographic views, you can use first- or third-angle projection drafting practices to lay out the different viewing directions of the part or assembly. When using these view project alignments, some of the views might not be directly in line or might not have the same rotation to each other, interfering with directly projecting construction lines horizontally or vertically. For example, using third-angle projection, the top and right-side views are rotated 90 degrees out of alignment for direct projection. However, the alignments enable you to project vertically or horizontally to a line drawn at 45 degrees. You can then project horizontally or vertically through that intersection point to the other view.

To make it easier and faster to project between views that rotate 90 degrees from their true projection alignment, you need to learn how to insert and use the projection crosshair.

In the following illustration, the projection crosshair was added to the drawing first and then the horizontal construction lines were added. When the construction lines in the top view were added, the projection crosshair automatically created the construction lines downward from the miter line. The intersection of these vertical construction lines and the front view construction lines defines the points in a third-angle right-side orthographic view.

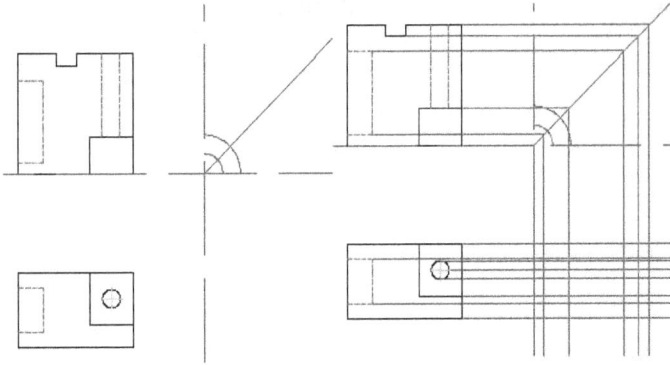

About Projection Crosshairs

You can insert construction line projection crosshairs to help with projecting locations in one orthographic view to another. You can insert the crosshair and define the quadrant to place the 45-degree bisecting projection angle. As you insert construction lines that are parallel to the crosshair axes and intersect the 45-degree bisecting construction line, the projection tool automatically creates construction rays in the other direction.

For example, following third-angle projection practices, you can draw a front view and top view of a component. To start creating the side view, place the projection tool in the upper right part of the drawing. As you add a horizontal construction line from the top view, it is automatically projected down to the side view that you are trying to generate.

■ To insert the projection crosshair, use the Projection On/Off command.

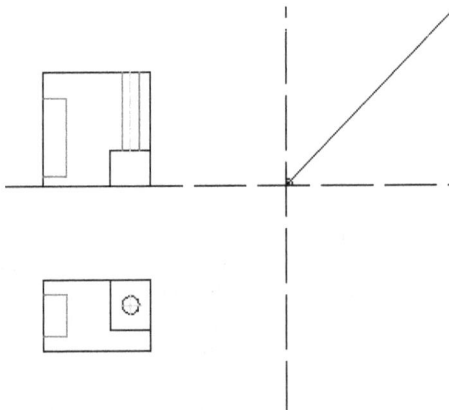

Access

Command Line: AMPROJO

Ribbon: Home tab > expanded Construction panel > Projection

Menu: Draw > Construction Lines > Projection On/Off

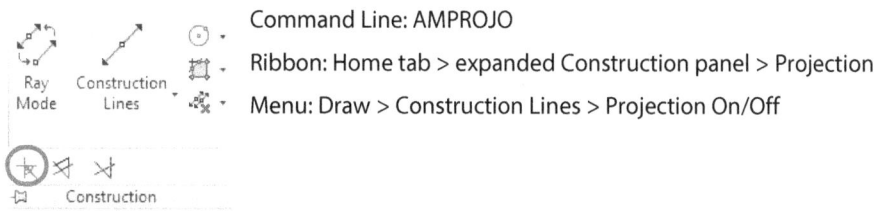

Procedure: Inserting Projection Crosshairs

To insert a projection crosshair, complete the following steps:

1. Start the **Projection On/Off** command.

2. Click **ON** in the Projection ON/OFF display.

3. Specify the insertion point for the crosshair.

4. Specify the rotation angle for the bisecting projection line.

> To place the projection crosshair so that it projects correctly from one view to another, use object snap tracking when prompted to specify the insertion point.

Erasing Construction Lines

When you no longer require some or all of the construction geometry that you have created, you need a quick and easy way to erase it from your drawing. You can do this using the Erase Construction Lines and Erase All Construction Lines tools.

In the following illustration, a set of drawing views is shown before and after the selection and deletion of some of the construction lines in the drawing. The arrows on the left show the defining corners of the selection window that was defined to erase the construction lines. Note how the right-side view still has the part geometry and that the construction lines have been erased.

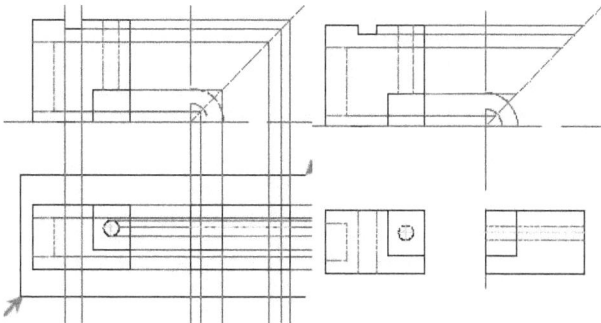

About Erasing Construction Lines

You can only use the Erase Construction Lines and Erase All Construction Lines tools to erase construction geometry from the drawing. They only select geometry on the AM_CL layer. Therefore, all non-construction geometry is not erased.

The Erase Construction Lines tool enables you to use a selection window to specify the construction geometry that is erased. Because only geometry on the AM_CL layer is selected, non-construction geometry within the selection window does not get erased. The Erase All Construction Lines tool erases all geometry on the AM_CL layer.

Access

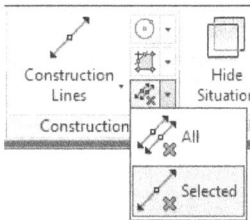

Command Line: AMERASECL

Ribbon: Home tab > Construction panel > Erase Construction Lines drop-down list > Selected

Menu: Modify > Erase > Erase Construction Lines

Procedure: Erasing Selected Construction Lines

To erase only the construction lines within a selection window, complete the following steps:

1. Start the **Erase Construction Lines** command.

2. Specify two opposite corners of the selection window so that the construction geometry is in or passes through the window area.

Access

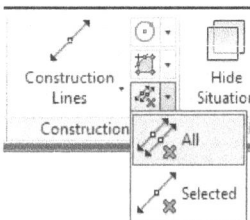

Command Line: AMERASEALLCL

Ribbon: Home tab > Construction panel > Erase Construction Lines drop-down list > All

Menu: Modify > Erase > Erase all Construction Lines

Exercise: Create and Use Construction Lines

In this exercise, you will work with construction-line tools to create an orthographic view of a part.

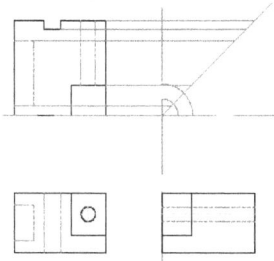

The completed exercise

1. Open *Construction Lines.dwg*.

2. To place the projection crosshair, in the Home tab > expanded Construction panel, click Projection and do the following:

   - Click **ON** in the Projection ON/OFF display.
   - Track from the lower-right corner of the top view, 20 units to the right.
   - Enter **90** for the rotation angle.

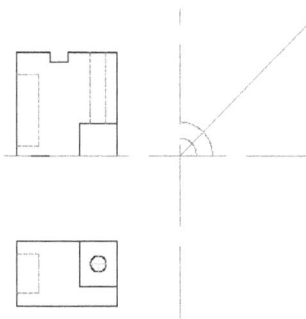

3. Begin to create horizontal construction lines from the existing views, as follows:

   - Click Home tab > Construction panel > Construction Lines drop-down list > Automatic Construction Lines.
   - Click the button shown in the illustration to create horizontal construction lines.

4. In the drawing window, use a selection or crossing window to select all of the geometry in both views. Right-click to create the construction lines as shown in the following illustration.

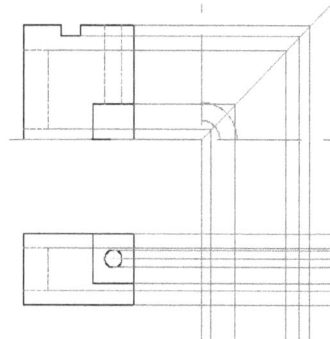

5. In the area for the right-side view, draw a rectangle from the lower-left intersection corner to the upper-right intersecting corner of the construction lines.

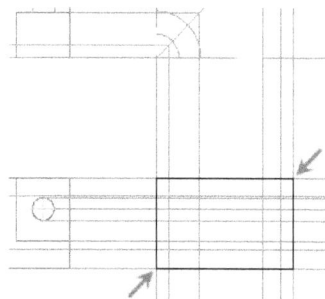

6. To draw the centerline for the hole, do the following:

- Click Home tab > Draw panel > Centerline drop-down list > Centerline.
- Object snap to the intersection points identified.

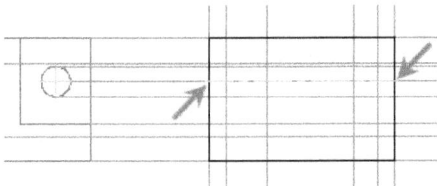

7. To view the geometry that you just created without visible construction lines, click Home tab > expanded Layers panel > Construction Lines On/Off.

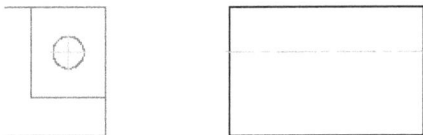

8. To toggle the visibility of the construction lines back on, click Home tab > expanded Layers panel > Construction Lines On/Off.

9. To draw the hidden lines to show the sides of the holes, do the following:

- Click Home tab > Layers panel > Mechanical Layers (Contour) drop-down list > Hidden. (AM_3 should display in the Layer Control).
- Draw two horizontal lines from the intersection points shown in the following illustration (on the construction lines that extend for top and bottom of the circle).

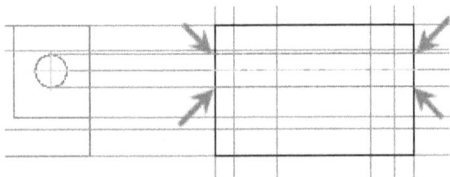

10. To draw the square notch shown in the front and top views, do the following:

- Click Home tab > Layers panel > Mechanical Layers (Contour) drop-down list > Contour. (AM_0 should display in the Layer Control).
- Draw two lines (lower horizontal and right vertical) through the three intersection points shown in the following illustration.

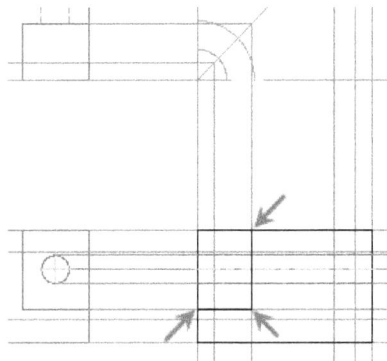

11. To draw two vertical construction lines through two points in the top view, do the following:

- Click Home tab > Construction panel > Construction Lines drop-down list > Vertical.
- Object snap to the points shown in the following illustration to draw the two vertical lines.

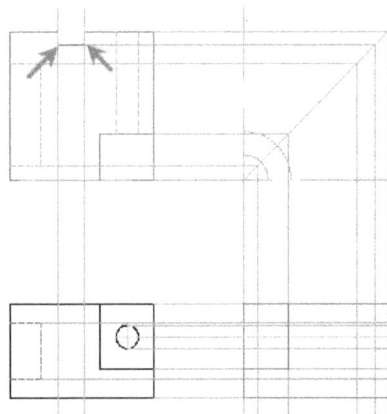

12. To draw the hidden lines in the front view to show the location of the back notch, do the following:

- Click Home tab > Layers Panel > Mechanical Layers (Contour) drop-down list > Hidden. (AM_3 should display in the Layer Control)
- Draw two vertical lines from the intersection points shown in the following illustration.

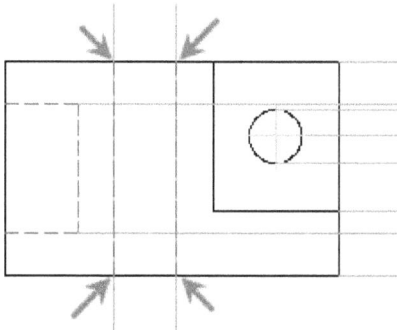

13. To erase some of the construction lines in the drawing, do the following:

- Click Home tab > Construction panel > Erase Construction Lines drop-down list > Selected.
- Define a selection window around the front and side views, as shown in the following illustration.

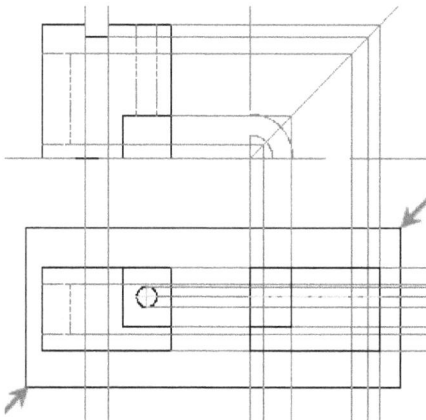

14. Review the geometry that you just created and the results of the erased construction lines.

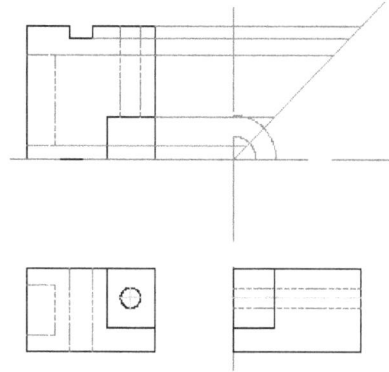

15. Save and close all of the drawings.

Lesson: Designing with Lines

Overview

This lesson describes the creation of section, zigzag, breakout, and symmetrical lines.

When you create a production drawing of a part or assembly, many lines with different appearances and purposes are drawn. The AutoCAD Mechanical software has specific line creation tools that help create lines for identifying section view cutting lines, breaks in long parts, breakout areas, and lines that are symmetrical about an axis. By using these tools, you can greatly increase your drawing productivity.

In the following illustration, the section, breakout, and symmetrical line creation tools were used to create the two views of the part. The section line A identifies where the part is being cut through for the section view A-A. The section view is symmetrical about the center axis. The irregular path of the breakout lines defines an area in which the view can be edited to show the internal aspects of the part as visible lines rather than hidden lines.

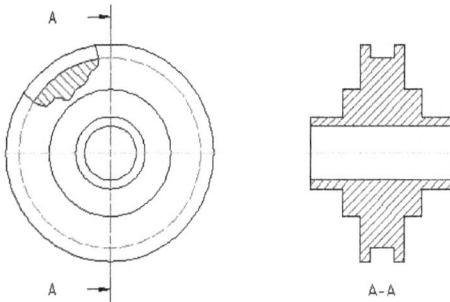

Objectives

After completing this lesson, you will be able to:

- Create section lines.
- Create zigzag lines.
- Create breakout lines.
- Create symmetrical lines.

Creating Section Lines

Use the AMSECTIONLINE command to create a cutting plane line. The section line is an imaginary cutting line through a work piece. The arrows and reference letter determine the cutting direction. The section line and reference letter are inserted on layer AM_10. The Section Line command only create the line and the section-view description. It does not create a section view.

When creating a section line, you do not draw end lines with attached arrowheads. They are created automatically.

Access

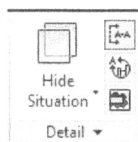

Command Line: AMSECTIONLINE

Ribbon: Home tab > Detail panel > Section Line

Menu Bar: Draw > Section Line

Section Line Command Options

Multiple command-line options are available when adding section lines. Before placing the first point, you can use the Visibility option to change the visibility of arrowheads and lines. After selecting the first point of the section line, you can select the Center option. After selecting the second point of the section line, you can select the Half, Name, or Arc options.

You can use the following options with the command:

Option	Description
Visibility	Select to change the visibility settings for the section line's arrows, line, name, and plane names from the default settings in the standard.
Center	Use to create a section line for a cylindrical shape. This creates a center point that enables you to specify an angle for the next segment.
Half	Creates a perpendicular line to the last segment and prompts you for a section symbol.
Name	Prompts you for a section name.
Arc	Creates an arc segment by prompting you for the center point and endpoint of the arc.

Section Line Properties Dialog Box

In the Section Line Properties dialog box, you can configure the text and line properties associated with the annotation of section views. You can open the dialog box from the Options dialog box on the *AM:Standards* tab by double-clicking on the element Section View.

The settings that you establish in the current standard for the Section View element control the appearance of the section line and annotation label when you draw a section line using the AMSECTIONLINE command.

The initial text height and style is based on the text property settings for the overall standard. You can only change the text style or a custom height value if you are editing a custom standard.

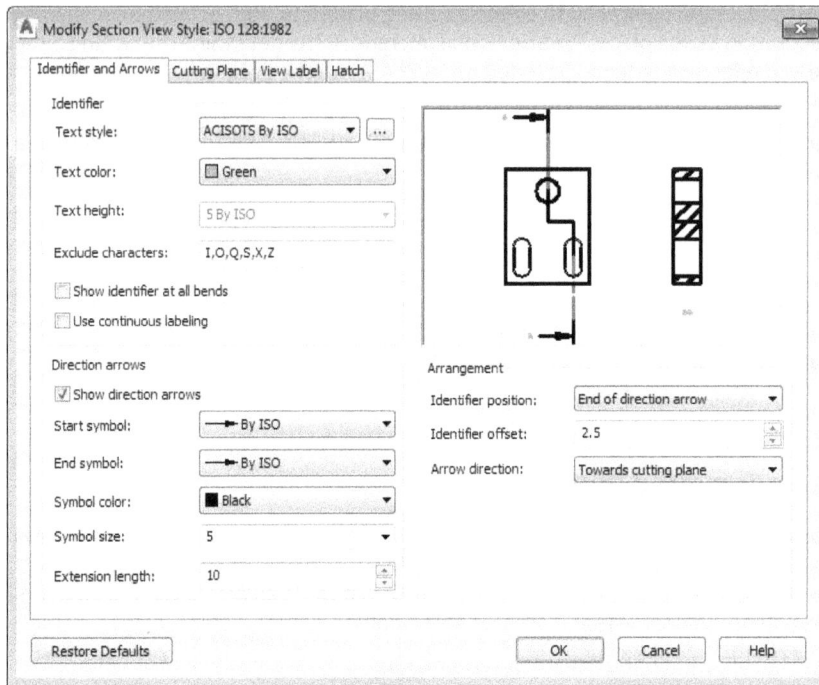

Procedure: Creating Section Lines

To create a section line in a drawing view, complete the following steps:

1. Start the **Section Line** command.

2. In the drawing area, click the start point.

3. Click the next section line point.

4. Click additional points or press ENTER to finish the section line determination.

5. Press ENTER to accept the default reference letter at the start point.

6. Click the right or left side of the first line to specify the section view direction.

7. Specify the origin (insertion point) of the letter view label to be placed with the section view.

Creating Zigzag Lines

Use the AMZIGZAGLINE command to create a unique zigzag line on layer AM_4. A zigzag line is often used instead of a breakout line. You can use the Zig-Zag Line command as you would use the regular line command. Specify the start point and endpoint and the zigzag line displays between those points. The scale of the zigzag line is determined by the model scale in the mechanical standard.

In the following illustration, the redundant information in the middle of the drawing view of the welded assembly was removed so that the ends could be shown. The start and end locations of where the material was removed are indicated by the zigzag line.

Access

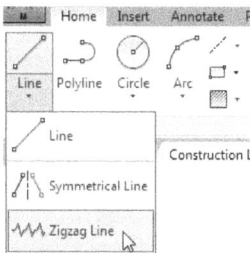

Command Line: AMZIGZAGLINE

Ribbon: Home tab > Draw panel > Line drop-down list > Zigzag Line

Menu Bar: Draw > Zig-Zag Line

Procedure: Creating Zigzag Lines

To create a zigzag line in a drawing view, complete the following steps:

1. If you are using structure, activate the structured view to which the zigzag line is associated.

2. Start the **Zigzag Line** command.

3. Specify the first point of the zigzag line.

4. Specify the next point of the zigzag line.

5. Press ENTER to create the zigzag line and end the command.

Creating Breakout Lines

With the Break Out Line command, you can create a sectional view of a drawing area using data points. Use AMBROUTLINE to create a breakout line. This only requires a few reference points to create a smoothed curve line on layer AM_4.

To use the breakout line as a boundary edge when using a predefined hatch command, you must move the breakout line to a contour layer, such as AM_0.

In the following illustration, a breakout line was added to a drawing view of a part. The view of the part was then edited so that the material within the breakout area displays with the correct linetype and hatch to signify solid material in that area.

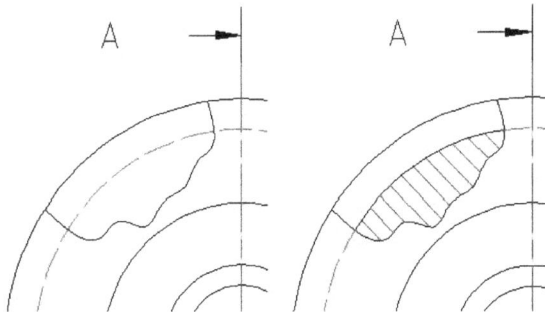

Access

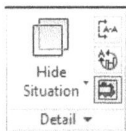

Command Line: AMBROUTLINE

Ribbon: Home tab > Detail panel > Break-out Line

Menu: Draw > Break-out Line

Procedure: Creating Breakout Lines

To create a breakout line, complete the following steps:

1. If you are using structure, activate the structured view to which the breakout line is associated.

2. Start the **Break-out Line** command.

3. Specify the start point.

4. Specify the next point.

5. Continue specifying points for the breakout area as required.

6. Press ENTER to create a smoothed breakout line.

If you use ESC instead of ENTER to end the command, the breakout line is not smoothed.

Creating Symmetrical Lines

Use the **Symmetrical Line** command to generate line segments that are mirrored about a centerline. First, define the axis of symmetry. If there is an existing AutoCAD Mechanical centerline on layer AM_7, you can reuse it by selecting the centerline. If you do not have a centerline, you can create one by clicking two points that define its orientation. You then specify the start point and endpoint or other points of the line to be mirrored. Line segments for the Symmetrical Line command are placed on the current layer. The centerline is placed on layer AM_7.

You can edit any of the lines created with the Symmetrical Line command independent of the others. When one side of the centerline is modified, the other side is not automatically modified to match.

In the following illustration, a set of symmetrical lines are being created. The line being directly defined started at the intersection of the centerline and the construction line on the far left. It is being defined in a clockwise direction. The illustration shows the before and after of the creation of one of the symmetrical line segments. The symmetrical lines are automatically being created below the horizontal centerline and display as a mirror image of the top line.

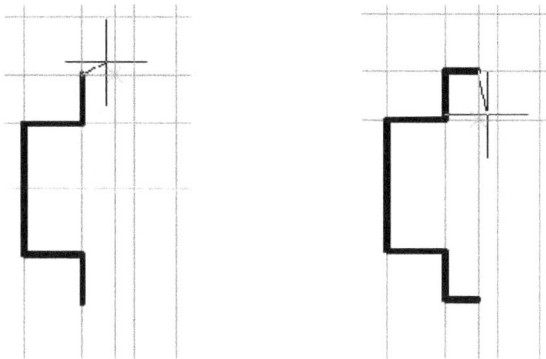

Access

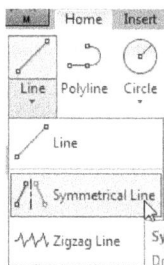

Command Line: AMSYMLINE

Ribbon: Home tab > Draw panel > Line drop-down list > Symmetrical Line

Menu: Draw > Symmetrical Line

Procedure: Creating Symmetrical Lines

To create two sets of lines that are symmetrical about a centerline by drawing one set of the lines, complete the following steps:

1. If you are using structure, activate the structured view to which the lines are associated.

2. Start the **Symmetrical Line** command.

3. Select a centerline. If one does not already exist, click two points to define the centerline orientation.

4. Specify the first point.

5. Specify the second point. The line is displayed with a mirrored line on the other side of the centerline.

6. Continue specifying additional points as required.

7. Press ENTER to complete the line.

Exercise: Draw with Different Line Tools

In this exercise, you will create part of a right-side view of a part, add a section plane line to an existing view, and add a breakout line.

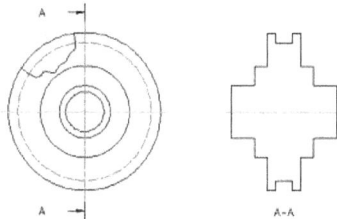

The completed exercise

1. Open *Designing with Lines.dwg*.

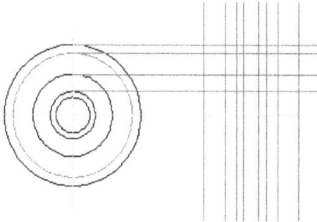

2. Begin to draw a right-side full-section view of the part, as follows:

    ▪ Click Home tab > Draw panel > Line drop-down list > Symmetrical Line.

    ▪ Click anywhere along the horizontal centerline on the right to select it.

3. Draw line segments for the top half of the part by object snapping to the intersection points. Start at point 1 and work around the top half of the centerline to point 2. After clicking at point 2, press ENTER. The lower half is automatically created below the horizontal centerline.

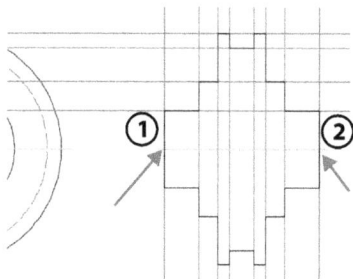

4. Click Home tab > Construction panel > Erase Construction Lines drop-down list > All to remove the construction lines.

5. Begin to define the section plane line and view label. Click Home tab > Detail panel > Section Line.

6. To specify the section line location, do the following:

    ▪ Object snap to the top and bottom endpoints of the vertical centerline in the front view.

    ▪ Press ENTER.

    ▪ Press ENTER again to accept the default section symbol.

    ▪ To specify the arrow and label side, click the left side of the vertical centerline.

7. At the prompt to specify the origin of the section view, click under the right-side view to locate the view label. The section line and view label should now display as shown in the following illustration.

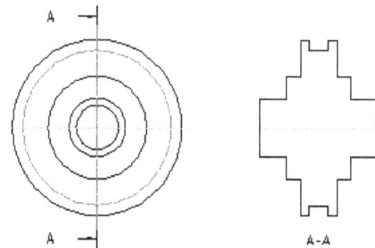

8. To create a breakout line in the front view, do the following:

- Click Home tab > Detail panel > Break-out Line.
- Click the points to define a breakout similar to the one shown in the following illustration.

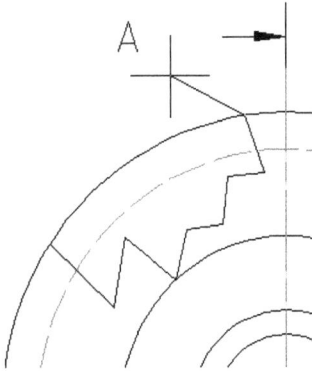

9. Right-click to end the Break Out Line command and the lines are changed to smoothed breakout lines.

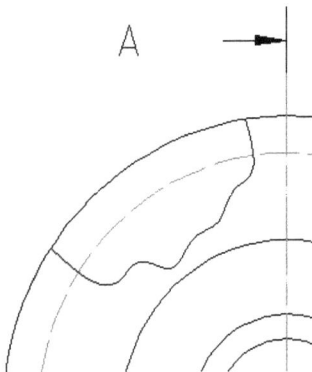

10. Save and close all of the files.

Lesson: Adding Standard Feature Data for Holes and Slots

Overview

You can add industry-standard holes, slots, and threads to your drawings.

Including holes, slots, and threads in a part's design helps to ensure that the part can be positioned, assembled, and function as it is intended. By adding these features using AutoCAD Mechanical commands, you can use common industry sizes by selecting them from a predefined list based on the selected standard. Selecting from a predefined list helps save time by reusing previously-defined geometry and having the threads and centerlines automatically placed on the correct layer.

In the following illustration, the top view shows a different view of the counterbore hole from the uppermost part of the three different parts. The front view of the assembled three parts also shows a slot and a tapped hole in the parts below the uppermost part.

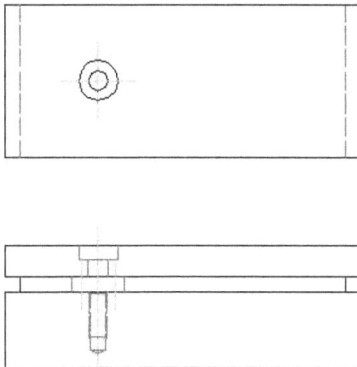

Objectives

After completing this lesson, you will be able to:

- Define standard content and describe the benefits of using it in your designs.
- Explain what standard features are, how you select them, how they interact with structure, what
- their layering properties are, and how to edit the features that are already present in the drawing.
- Insert basic through and blind holes, tapped holes, counterbore holes, and countersink holes.
- Insert externally threaded features and internal or external pipe threads.
- Insert through and blind slots.

About Standard Content

When you create a design that includes holes, slots, bolts, or screws, it is a lot more efficient to select them from a list and place them in your drawing than to draw them. The standard content in the AutoCAD Mechanical software enables you to do so.

In the following illustration, the Standard Parts Library palette lists some of the standards and categories of geometry that you can include in your design. This geometry includes features for parts you are designing and an entire part that you can add to an assembly.

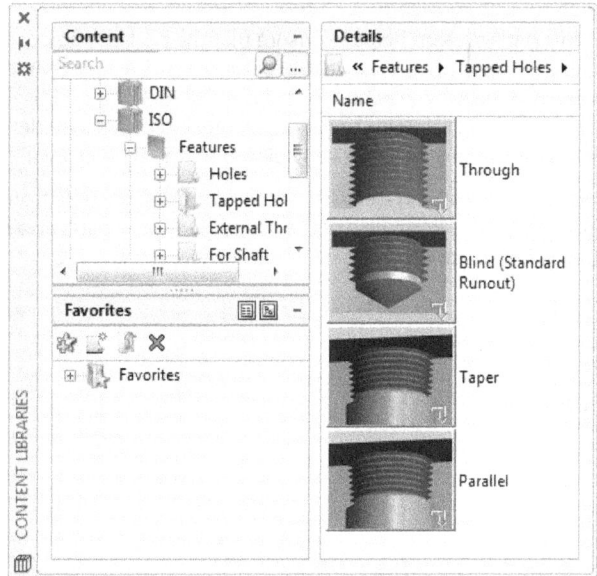

Definition of Standard Content

Standard content refers to the more than 700,000 parametric standard parts and predrawn features that you can use in your assembly and part designs. When using this content, you can control the size of parts and features by setting the length, width, or other size parameters during their placement.

Part content includes various types of screws, bolts, washers, nuts, and cotter pins. The features you can add to a part include holes, external threads, and slots. The available sizes and shapes for each of these parts and features are based on common industry standards.

Because you are drafting in 2D, you can specify the direction from which you want to view the part or feature while you are placing it in a drawing view. After you have added standard content to a view, you can project the different views of that standard content to other orthographic or auxiliary views of your design.

You can cycle the display of standard content between three different settings to add or remove detail from the display. When you use Mechanical structure, you can control what is displayed as visible and hidden geometry by establishing an associative hide condition between parts in the assembly or geometry in the part. If you are not using Mechanical structure, you can still establish hidden display for a part or feature using 2D hide. This hide calculation method does not update automatically as associative hide does.

In the following illustration, one of the standards has been expanded and the Features standard content has been selected. The preview buttons on the right show the types of features that you can add to your part designs.

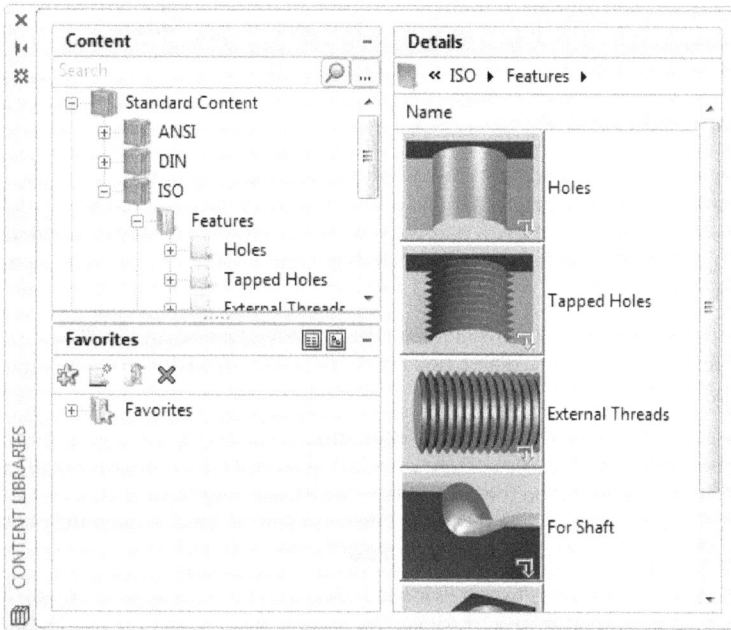

Example of Standard Content

Standard content makes the process of adding geometry to a design easier and quicker than creating the geometry from scratch. In the following illustration, a bolted connection is shown in the assembly with two different appearances. For bolted connections, you can select and place industry standard parts, and set how the geometry should be displayed relative to other geometry in the assembly.

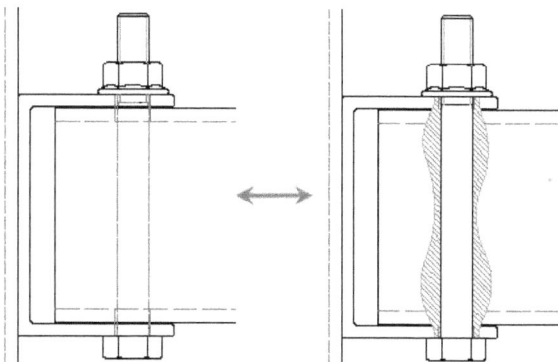

About Standard Features

You can use standard features to add geometry to your drawings. They should meet industry and company drafting standards and can save time and effort. By learning what standard features are, how to select them, how they interact with structure, and how to edit them after they have been added to the drawing, you can achieve these benefits.

Definition of Standard Features

Standard features are an aspect of a part that can be defined based on an industry standard. They are holes, slots, and threads. For holes, you can add blind or through holes, and counterbore, countersunk, and tapped holes. You can draw slots that go part way into the part or all the way through. When adding threads, you can select different types of ends for external threads and different pipe threads for internal and external conditions.

You can insert a standard feature into a drawing using the Content Libraries, or the Ribbon or menus specific to that feature. When you open a dialog box a second time during a drawing session, it returns to the last selected part.

As part of the process of adding a standard feature, you can select the view that you want to insert. You can place front, top, and in some cases bottom views of the features. You can place features at any angle in a drawing. The view is placed on the current layer with the centerline and thread lines placed on the correct layer as defined in the active standard. You can select and manipulate the geometry in the view of a standard feature as though it were a single object.

When you are adding standard features to a drawing in which structure has been enabled, the standard feature is added to the active structure level. The feature displays in the Browser below that level with a unique icon to help identify what the feature is.

In the following illustration, the Through Hole can be selected on the Holes panel in the Ribbon.

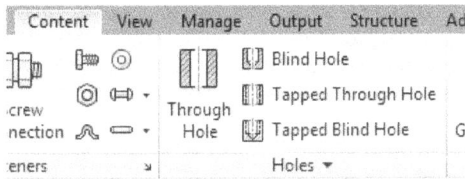

Selecting Feature Sizes

You can insert standard features using fastener information to determine its size, or you can insert user features, such as User Through Holes and User Through Slots. When you insert a user feature, you can the values for the feature's size. Depending on the type of object, you can the diameter, length, depth, countersink diameter, angle, etc. You can use the user features to insert feature sizes that are not of the standard library.

In the following illustration, a threaded blind hole for an ISO 262 regular threaded fastener is in the process of being added to a drawing. The location for the hole has been specified and the nominal diameter is being selected from a list of accepted industry sizes. Because this is a blind hole, the depth of the threads needs to be defined after selecting the diameter.

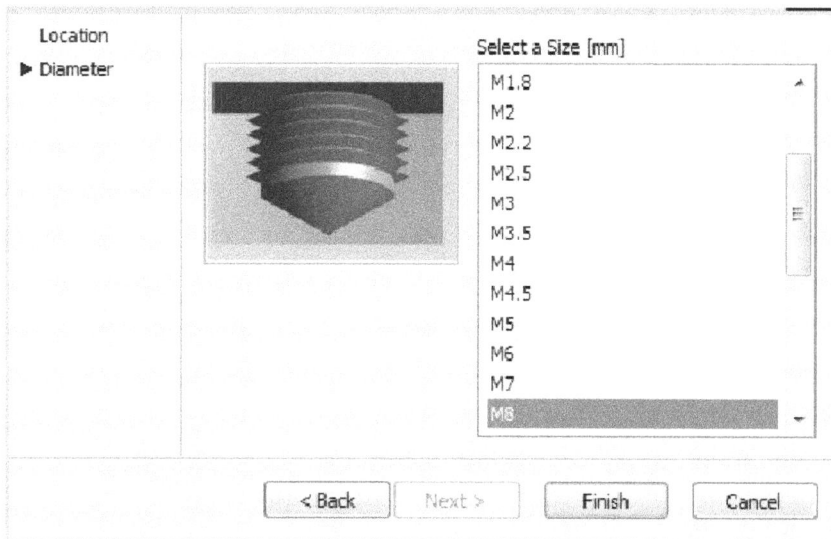

Standard Features and Mechanical Structure

When you add a standard feature to a drawing in which Mechanical structure has been enabled, the feature is added to the structure definition that is currently active. A Browser entry is also added below that component view or folder. The standard feature icon that displays in the Browser is unique to the type of feature added to the drawing and helps identify the feature. The standard feature can be considered a special custom type of folder. If no structure definition is active, the standard feature is added to the top level of the drawing and icons display in the Browser at that level of the structure.

A standard feature added to a drawing automatically applies a hidden line calculation to the geometry within. When a structured feature is added to a drawing with structure, it automatically creates an associative hide condition. However, this hide condition does not display in the Browser. To edit the hide display, right-click on the standard feature and click Edit Hide Situation(s).

If structure is not enabled, a 2D hide situation is created and background objects are automatically broken and hidden with the Hide Invisible Edges command. The default display of hidden lines is set in the Options dialog box on the AM:Standard Parts tab.

In the following illustration, two views of a multiple part drawing and its Browser are shown. The standard features have been added to their corresponding component views. Note the relationship of the standard feature to the component view and their unique icons.

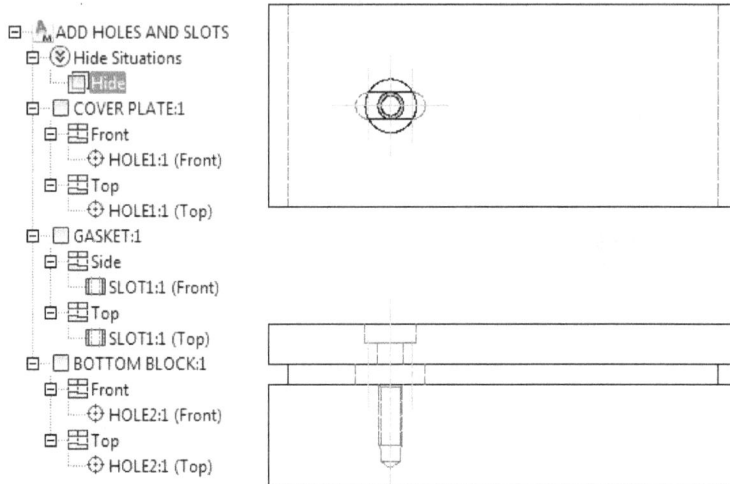

Layering of Standard Features

The geometry within a standard feature depends on the feature being selected for insertion. At a minimum, features consist of lines, circles, or arcs representing the edges of the hole or slot, and lines indicating the center point or axis. If it is a threaded feature, hidden lines or circles are also included to show the depth of the thread cut in the part.

You can place standard features on the three contour layers and on the hidden line layer. The centerlines for features are placed on the centerline layer. If reserved layers, such as text and hatch layers, are active when you place a feature, it is placed on the AM_0 layer.

Editing Existing Features

You can edit any of the AutoCAD Mechanical features by double-clicking on the feature. This opens the dialog box that was initially used to select and define the feature. In the dialog box, you can modify the hole size, length, and other available variables. When you edit a feature, you can access additional variables in some dialog boxes by clicking Back.

Inserting Standard Holes

You can add holes to the design of a part for many different reasons. Most often they are used in the alignment and assembly of parts by having other parts, such as fasteners, pass through or thread into the holes. By knowing how to insert basic through holes, blind holes, tapped holes, counterbore holes, and countersink holes, you can complete your drawing more quickly than by creating the geometry from scratch while simultaneously matching industry-accepted sizes.

Accessing the Commands to Insert Standard Holes

There are seven different hole commands from which you can select to create different types of standard holes. You can add a basic hole, counterbore hole, or countersink hole.

For the basic hole, you can select from holes that go all the way through the part or not and are tapped or not. When inserting counterbore or countersink holes, you can select the size of hole based on standard industry sizes. You can also select the type of screw that you want to insert into the hole. Depending on the selected industry standard, you can also select the hole size so that it is close, normal, or loose relative to the selected screw size.

You can access these commands by clicking *Content* tab > Holes panel. The Blind and Tapped Blind Holes are located in Content > Holes menu.

Access

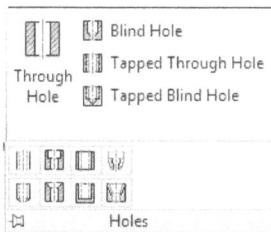

Ribbon: Content tab > Holes panel and expanded Holes panel

Menu: Content > Holes

Description of the Commands to Insert Standard Holes

Icon	Command	Description
	Through Holes	Creates a hole that goes all the way through a part.
	Tapped Through Holes	Creates a tapped hole that goes all the way through a part.
	Blind Holes	Creates a hole to the specified depth.
	Tapped Blind Holes	Creates a tapped hole to the specified depth.
	Counterbored Holes	Creates a counterbored hole that goes all the way through a part. A counterbore hole uses a counterbore diameter, a counterbore depth, and a nominal diameter.
	Countersinks	Creates a countersunk hole that goes all the way through a part. A countersunk hole uses a countersink diameter, a countersink angle, and a nominal diameter.
	Taper Internal Thread	Creates a tapered hole that contains internal threads.

Selecting Standards, Holes, and Views

After you start the command to insert a hole, you can use various dialog boxes to specify which standard, hole, hole view, and standard size to insert. You can select the required standard from the tree view. Under Details, you can specify the view orientation of the hole.

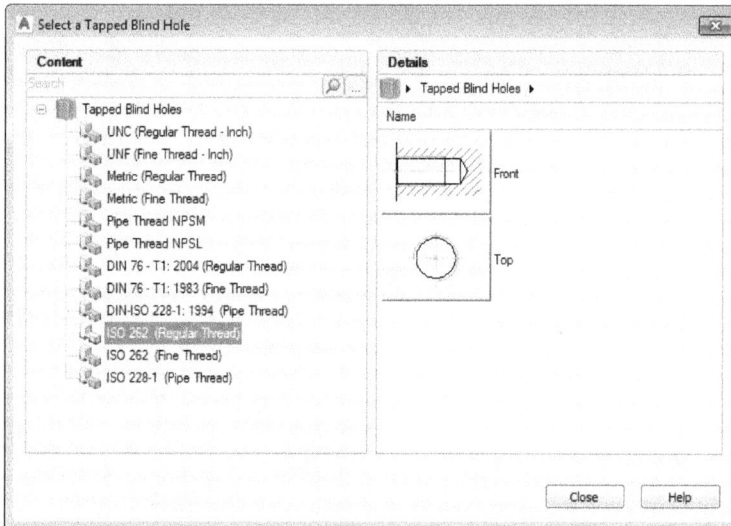

Screw Connection for Counterbore and Countersink Holes

When you select to add a counterbore or countersink hole, you can also select the size of the screw for which you want the hole to be sized in the Screw Connection dialog box. You can also change the type of fastener, add washers to the fastener connection, and select to have those parts automatically added to the drawing when you finish inserting the hole.

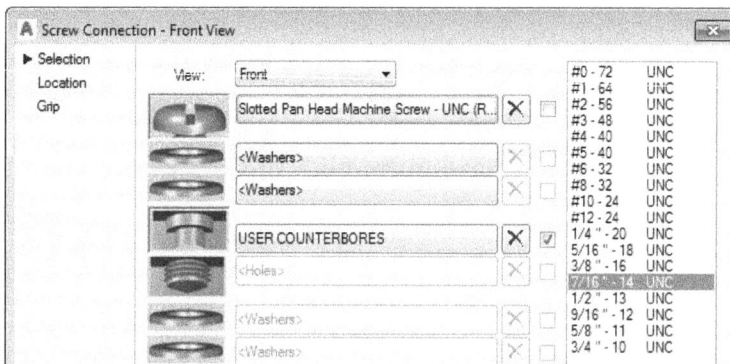

User-Defined Screw Hole Size

When you select to create a counterbore or countersink hole and the hole type for the screw is a user-defined hole, the User Counterbores/Countersinks dialog box opens before the hole is created in the drawing. In this dialog box, you can override the default parameters with custom values that meet your design requirements.

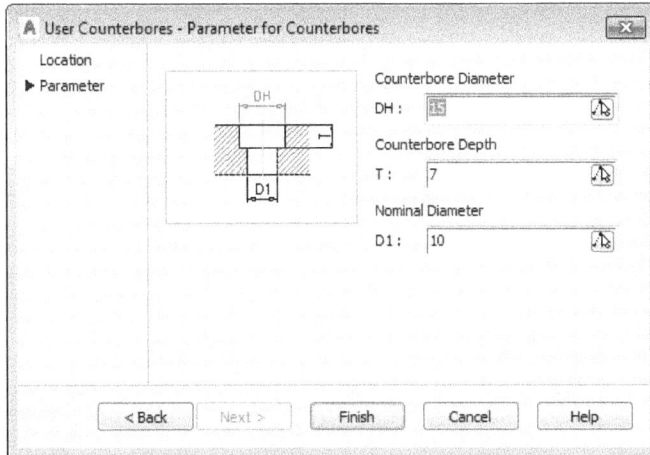

Standard and Fit Defined Screw Hole Size

When you select to create a counterbore or countersink hole and the hole type for the screw is based on a standard hole, the Select Part Size dialog box opens before the hole is created in the drawing. In this dialog box, you can size the hole by selecting a standard that defines how the screw is to fit relative to the hole (close, normal, or loose).

Procedure: Inserting Basic Standard Holes

To insert industry standard holes into a drawing view, complete the following steps:

1. Start the command for the type of hole you want to add.

2. In the dialog box, select the specific type of hole to add.

3. Select the view direction for the hole.

4. In the drawing window, specify the insertion point for the hole.

5. Enter the rotation angle for the hole and its centerlines.

6. In the dialog box, select the hole size from the list of standard industry sizes.

7. If available, specify additional values to define the length of the hole or thread.

Procedure: Inserting Countersink and Counterbore Holes

To insert industry-standard countersink or counterbore holes into a drawing view, complete the following steps:

1. Start the command for the type of hole you want to add.

2. In the dialog box, select the industry standard that you want to follow.

3. Select the direction of view for the hole.

4. Select the type of screw that is to be inserted through the countersink or counterbore hole.

5. Select the direction of view for the screw.

6. In the Screw Connection dialog box, select the screw size from the list of standard sizes.

7. In the Screw Connection dialog box, further define the screw connection if required. You can select the option to have the screw to be added to the drawing when the hole is added, or to add washers to the connection.

8. In the drawing window, specify the start points and endpoints for the hole.

9. In the dialog box, if required, manually adjust the values for the hole's insertion point, insertion angle, and length.

10. In the dialog box, select the display representation for the hole and screw assembly.

11. Specify the oversizing of the hole by selecting the fit condition or entering new values.

12. If you are also adding the screw, drag and specify its length.

Inserting Threaded Features

When your design requires internal or external pipe threads or a threaded stud or shaft, you can add external threads with various ends, tapered external threads, and straight or tapered internal threads to complete the drawing more quickly while following industry standards.

In the following illustration, the part contains external threaded features and an internal tapered thread feature.

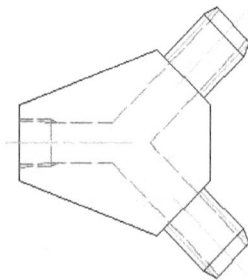

Accessing the Commands to Insert Threaded Features

You can use the commands for threaded features to show where external threads are created on a cylindrical part, or pipe threads that are created externally or internally to the pipe.

You can access these commands on the Content tab > Holes panel, and on the Content menu > Holes drop-down list.

Icon	Command	Description
	External Threads	Creates external threads for the specified length.
	Thread Ends	Creates threaded ends with a choice of standard end styles.
	Taper External Threads	Creates external tapered pipe threads.
	Taper Internal Threads	Creates internal tapered or straight pipe threads to a specified depth. You can create internal taper threads with runout or use a fixed length.

Access

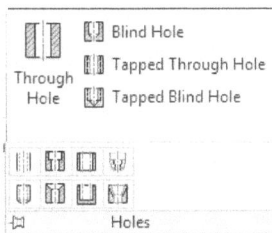

Ribbon: Content tab > Holes panel and expanded Holes panel

Menu: Content > Holes

Procedure: Inserting Threaded Features

To insert threaded features, complete the following steps:

1. Start the command for the type of threaded feature that you want to add.

2. In the dialog box, select the industry standard that you want to follow.

3. Select the direction from which you want to view the threaded feature.

4. In the drawing window, specify the insertion point and rotation angle.

5. In the dialog box, select the thread size from the list of standard size.

Inserting Slot Features

In some design cases, you can add slots to a part instead of holes so that there is built-in compensation for manufacturing variation and incorporated assembly adjustment between parts. You can also add slots that do not go all the way through the part to size and position pockets in the part. To add these slots to your drawing, you need to learn which commands to use and how to use them.

In the following illustration, the middle part has a through slot rather than a hole. With the current alignment of the slot, you can slide the position of the middle part left or right before the bolt is tightened and locked in place.

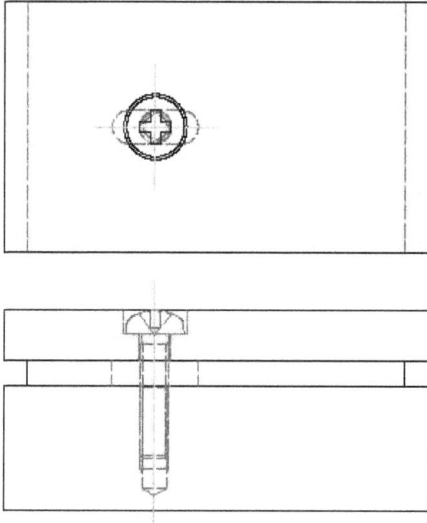

Accessing the Commands to Insert Slot Features

With the slot commands, you can create a slot in your drawing that goes part of the way or all of the way through the part. You can select the slot size by selecting the size of the fastener to pass through the slot and the type of fit between the fastener and the slot. You can select from close, normal, or loose fits.

You can access these commands from the Content tab > expanded Holes panel.

Icon	Command	Description
▯	**Through Slots**	Creates slots that go all the way through a part. You can select a slot size based on the standard sizes for mating fasteners.
▯	**Blind Slots**	Creates slots to the specified depth. You can select a slot size based on the standard sizes for mating fasteners.

Access

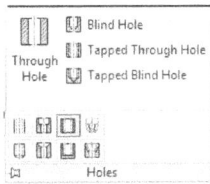

Command Line: AMTSLOT2D

Ribbon: Content tab > expanded Holes panel > Through Slot

Menu Bar: Content > Holes > Through Slots

Access

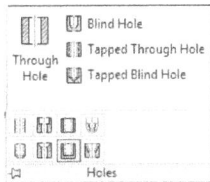

Command Line: AMBSLOT2D

Ribbon: Content tab > expanded Holes panel > Blind Slot

Menu Bar: Content > Holes > Blind Slots

Slot Styles

You can set a slot style to determine the type of insertion point and how the dimension lengths are applied. Slot styles that end in "I" are dimensioned to the outer tangent arcs and the insertion point is at the midpoint of the slot. Slots that end with "II" are dimensioned to the centerlines and the insertion point is at the left center.

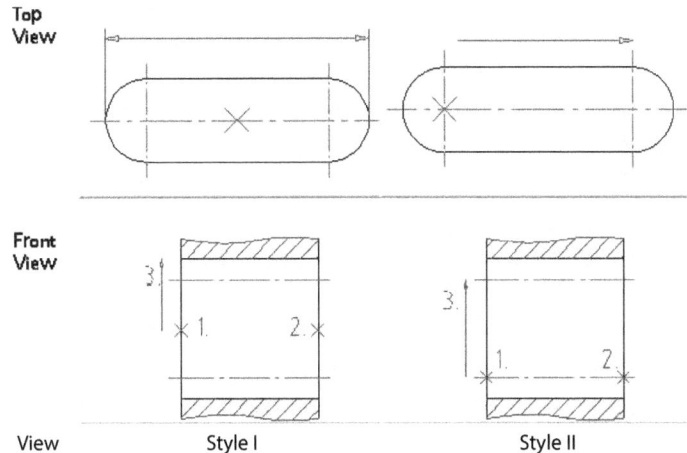

Procedure: Inserting Slot Features

To insert a slot into a drawing view, complete the following steps:

1. Start the command to create a through or blind slot based on your requirements.

2. In the Select a Slot dialog box, under Details, click a standard.

3. Under Details, click the required view direction.

4. Click in the drawing area to locate the insertion point.

5. If you are inserting a top view, enter the rotation angle. If you are inserting a side or front view, specify the depth of the slot.

6. In the dialog box listing the sizes for the selected standard slot, click the size.

7. Click Finish.

8. Drag and specify the depth or length value based on the view you are inserting.

Exercise: Add Holes and Slots

In this exercise, you will add a counterbore hole, slot, and threaded blind hole to different structured parts. You will also use the counterbore hole to create another view without having to specify the sizes again.

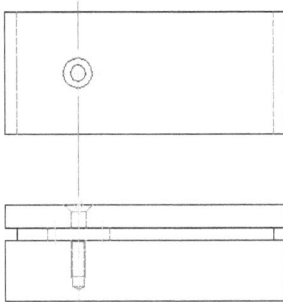

The completed exercise

1. Open *Add Holes and Slots.dwg*.

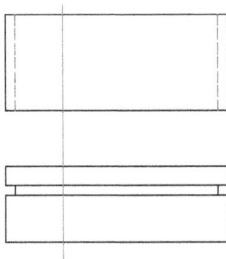

2. Change the current layer to hidden line by clicking Home tab > Layers panel > Mechanical Layers drop-down list > AM_3.

3. Begin to add a counterbore hole for an M6 regular thread bolt:

   - Click Content tab > expanded Holes panel > Countersink.
   - In the Select a Hole Standard dialog box, in the Content pane, expand the Holes folder and click **ISO Countersinks**.
   - On the Details pane for ISO Countersinks, click **Front**.

4. Begin to specify the size of hole based on a selected screw. In the Select a Screw dialog box, in the Details pane, click **ISO 7046-1: 1994 H (Regular Thread)**.

5. To specify the view and size of the screw:

   - In the Select a Screw dialog box, in the Details pane, click Front.
   - In the Details pane, select **ISO 7721 For Metric Threads**.
   - In the Screw Connection dialog box, list of standard sizes, click **M 6**.
   - Click Next.

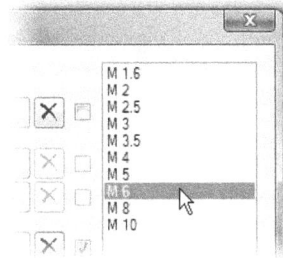

6. For the start and endpoints of the hole, click the intersections of the construction line and cover plate part.

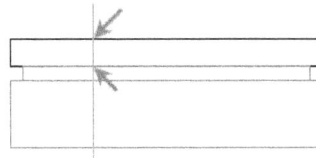

7. To complete the definition of the hole:
   - In the Screw Assembly Location dialog box, click Next.
   - In the Screw Assembly Grip Representation dialog box, click **Hidden**.
   - Click **Finish**.

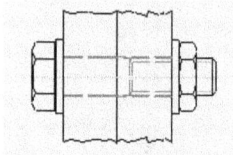

   - The hole should now display as shown:

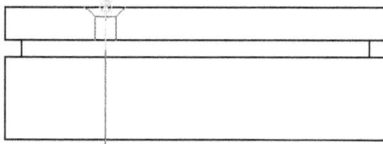

8. Begin to add a slot to this part:
   - Click Content tab > expanded Holes panel > Through Slot.
   - In the Select a Slot dialog box, in the Content pane, expand Slot - Through and click **ISO normal (I)**.
   - On the Details pane, click **Front**.

9. For the start and endpoints of the slot, click the intersections of the construction line and gasket part.

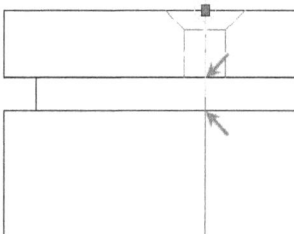

10. In the ISO normal (I) dialog box, in the list of standard sizes, click **M6**. Click **Finish**.

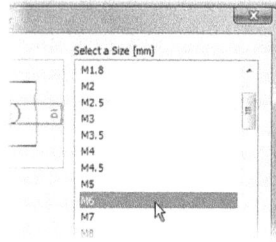

11. When prompted to drag the size of the slot, enter **18**. Press ENTER. The slot should display as shown in the following illustration.

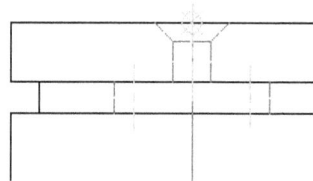

12. Begin to add a tapped hole to this part:
    - Click Content tab > Holes panel > Tapped Blind Hole.
    - In the Select a Tapped Blind Hole dialog box, under Details, click **ISO 262 (Regular Thread)**.
    - On the Details pane, click **Front**.

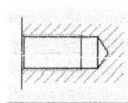

13. To specify the insertion point and rotation angle, click the top intersection of the construction line and bottom block part and then the bottom intersection.

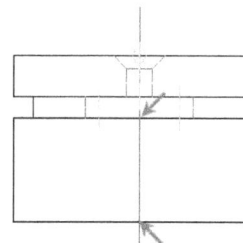

14. In the ISO 262 (Regular Thread) dialog box, in the list of standard sizes, click **M6**. Click **Finish**.

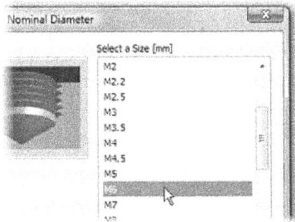

15. In the drawing window, drag the preview down and click when it is the approximate size shown in the following illustration.

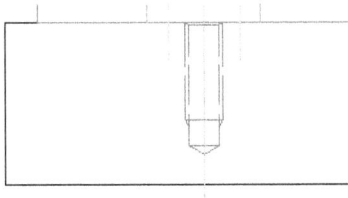

16. Click Home tab > Layers panel > Mechanical Layers drop-down list > Contour to set the Contour (AM_1) layer current.

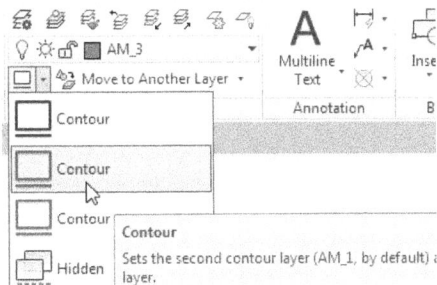

17. Begin to use an existing standard hole to create another view of it in another view of the part.

- Click Content tab > Tools panel > Power View.

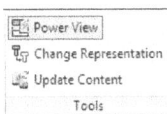

18. To select the hole and view to create:

- In the drawing window, select the counterbore hole.
- In the AutoCAD Mechanical question dialog box, for which the view should be drawn, click **Top**.

19. In the drawing area, insert the top view of the counterbore hole at the intersection of the construction lines and the tracked midpoint of the top view to create the results shown in the following illustration.

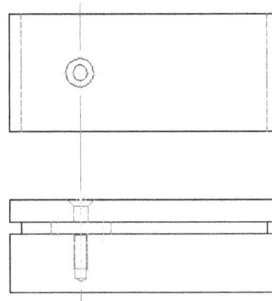

20. Save and close all of the files.

Chapter Summary

In this chapter, you learned about the core mechanical design productivity tools for creating rectangles, hatching, fillets, chamfers, holes, slots, and threads. You also learned about the AutoCAD Mechanical power snap configuration and its use with the geometry creation and editing tools.

Having completed this chapter, you can:

- Create and modify geometry using rectangle, hatch, fillet, chamfer, and the contour finder.
- Configure and activate power snaps.
- Add centerlines, holes with centerlines, and circles with centerlines to a drawing.
- Create, erase, and change the visibility of construction lines.
- Create polylines based on existing contour geometry.
- Add holes, slots, and threads to a drawing.

Tools for Manipulating Geometry

In this chapter, you learn how to edit drawing objects using the AutoCAD® Mechanical editing tools and power commands. You also learn how to modify the display of drawing geometry through the creation of annotation views.

Objectives

After completing this chapter, you will be able to:

- Copy drawing objects, join separate objects into a single object, create breaks in lines, and create multiple offset copies of objects.
- Modify objects in a drawing with power commands, use one command to edit and erase all object types, and create additional views while maintaining an accurate database.
- Create and edit associative hide situations.

Lesson: Editing Tools

Overview

This lesson describes the AutoCAD Mechanical editing tools for modifying objects in a drawing. The editing methods include copying objects, joining separate objects into a single object, creating corners, and creating breaks in lines.

One of the most common tasks in any design environment is editing drawings. To ensure that you are using the most efficient methods in the editing process, you must become familiar with the available editing tools.

In the following illustration, the basic editing tools discussed in this lesson were used to create, modify, and copy objects.

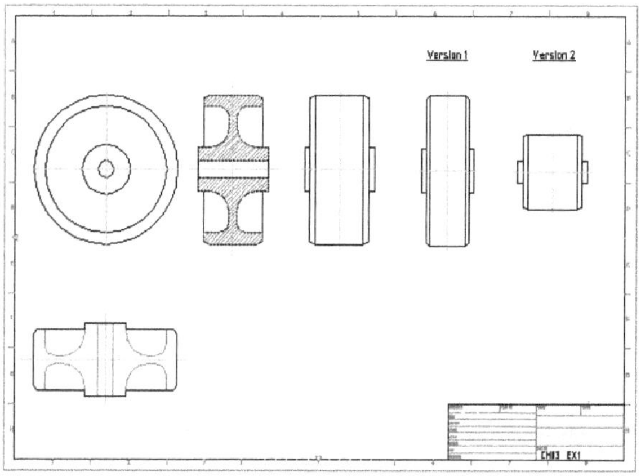

Objectives

After completing this lesson, you will be able to:

- Copy drawing objects.
- Create multiple offset copies of objects.
- Join drawing objects to form corners and single objects.
- Break objects into multiple parts.
- Scale objects with separate values for X and Y direction.

Copying Objects

You can use the AutoCAD® Copy command on standard objects and on intelligent mechanical objects to duplicate objects rather than recreating them. You can make multiple copies of objects and position them relative to the base point. You can also define an insertion point by clicking a point in the drawing window or entering coordinates.

Access

Command Line: COPY

Ribbon: Home tab > Modify panel > Copy drop-down list > Copy

Menu: Modify > Copy

Procedure: Copying Objects

To copy objects, complete the following steps:

1. On the Home tab > Modify panel > Copy drop-down list, click Copy.

2. Select the object to copy and press ENTER.

3. Specify a base point.

4. Move the cursor to the point of displacement to see a preview of the copy.

5. Click to enter a second point for displacement. The new object is placed there.

6. Preview and enter a third point for displacement. The new object is displayed.

7. Press ENTER.

Offsetting Objects

You can use the Offset command to construct objects that are parallel to or concentric with other objects at a specified distance from them. You can offset lines, arcs, circles, 2D polylines, ellipses, elliptical arcs, xlines, rays, and planar splines. Offsetting circles creates larger or smaller circles, depending on the offset side. For example, offsetting a circle to the outside creates a larger circle and offsetting a circle to the inside creates a smaller circle.

> The AMOFFSET command is similar to the AutoCAD Offset command. However, with the AMOFFSET command, you can specify multiple distances.

Access

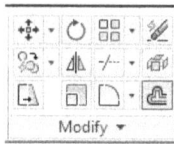

Command Line: AMOFFSET

Ribbon: Home tab > Modify panel > Offset

Menu: Modify > Offset

Options for the Offset Command

Use the following options with the command:

Option	Description
Specify Offset	Use the pointing device to specify the offset distance, or enter one or several values for the offset distance. You must separate multiple distances with the pipe symbol (|).
Through	Instead of specifying a distance, you can click a point through which you want the offset copy to pass.
Mode	Enables you to set the layer of the new objects.
Normal mode	The layer property of the new object is the same as the pattern object.
Current Layer mode	The layer property of the new object is set to the current layer and layer group.

Procedure: Offsetting Objects

To offset objects, complete the following steps:

1. Click Home tab > Modify panel > Offset.

2. Enter the offset distance(s).

3. Select the object to offset.

4. Move the cursor to the side to offset and note the preview of the offset object.

5. Click to place the offset object.

6. Press ENTER.

Joining Entities

You can use the **Join Entities** command to create corners and to combine lines that are colinear. During the construction phase, parts are designed from several line segments. For example, a single edge of a part can consist of three adjacent lines. Therefore, when placing an object that needs to snap to the midpoint of an object's edge, you can only select the midpoint of a section of the edge. You can use the Join Entities command to modify the three lines into a single line.

The following list shows some possible object selections and results.

Object Selection	Results
	Joined into 1 Line
	Lines connected with radius 0
Polyline / Line	
Line / Polyline	Line / Polyline
Line / Polyline	Joined into 1 Polyline
	Arc and Line connected
Using "RETURN" (overlapping arcs)	Arcs merged

You use the Join Entities command to do the following:

- Join disparate objects.
- Connect polylines, arcs, and circles.
- Connect overlapping lines, arcs, and circles.
- Connect separate arcs, forming a circle.
- Extend or shorten nonparallel lines to their intersection point.

Access

Command Line: AMJOIN

Ribbon: Home tab > expanded Modify panel > Join

Menu: Modify > Join Entities

Modify

Procedure: Joining Entities

To join objects where they intersect, complete the following steps:

1. On the Home tab > expanded Modify panel, click Join.
2. Select the first object.
3. Select the second object. The two objects are connected at the point at which they intersect.

> When you are prompted to select the first object, pressing ENTER enables you to select multiple objects. If you select overlapping objects, they are joined as one object.

Breaking Objects into Multiple Parts

Use one of the break commands to split an object into two segments. The Break command is often used to create a space in which to insert a block or text.

Two commands are available to break an object. The Break command is an AutoCAD software command that is available in the AutoCAD Mechanical software. The Break Object at One Point command is an AutoCAD Mechanical software command that automates the Break command.

Access

Command Line: BREAK

Ribbon: Home tab > expanded Modify panel > Break

Menu: Modify > Break > Break

Access

Command Line: AMBREAKATPT

Ribbon: Home tab > expanded Modify panel > Break at one Point

Menu: Modify > Break > Break at one Point

> The Break and AMBREAKATPT commands differ slightly. You should try each method to determine which option works best for you.

Breaking Objects at One Point

Use the **Break at One Point** command to break an object into two segments at a specified point with no space around the break. You can specify a break point location on an object and use the break point to separate lines, traces, circles, arcs, or polylines. If the break point is at the intersection point for several objects, all of the objects at the intersection are broken at that point. Circles are broken into arcs. The Break at One Point command is useful when a portion of a line needs to be changed to a different linetype.

Options for Break at One Point

Use the following options with the Break at One Point command.

Option	Description
Select Entities to Break	Enables you to select the entities that you want to break at the specified point. Use this option with at least two lines.
Return to Break All Highlighted Entities	Breaks all highlighted entities at the specified break point.

> Before using the Break at One Point command, check the object snap settings and specify the correct settings

Procedure: Breaking Objects

To break objects in a drawing, complete the following steps:

1. Click Home tab > expanded Modify panel > Break.

2. In the drawing area, click on the object to break. The break object is highlighted.

3. Click the location of the second break point.

> With the Break command, the location in the drawing area where you click the object is used as the first break point. After selecting the object, you can select a different first break point location using the First Point command-line option.

Procedure: Breaking Objects at One Point

To break an object at a single point, complete the following steps:

1. Click Home tab > expanded Modify panel > Break at one Point.

2. Specify the break point. The break object is highlighted.

3. Press ENTER to cut the highlighted object.

Scaling Objects Along the X and Y Axes

You can use the Scale XY command to scale objects along the X and Y axes. You can scale objects proportionally in length without adding height and proportionally in height without making it longer.

About Scaling Objects Along the X and Y Axes

Values greater than 1 enlarge objects and values smaller than 1 make objects smaller. Negative values mirror the object about the perpendicular axis, relative to the base point.

For example, you can scale a C-shaped arc that is 1 unit high by 1 unit wide and use the center point of the arc shape as the basepoint. You can use an X value of -2 and a Y value of 3 to create a backward-C shape that is 2 units wide and 3 units high and is mirrored across a line parallel to the Y axis and passing through the selected base point.

The Scale XY command prompts you to select the object or objects to be scaled. Select a base point and specify an X scale factor. You can enter a value or reference length. The Y scale factor defaults to the X scale factor. You can select this value or enter a new value. The reference value can be specified with numeric values or by selecting points. After entering a Y scale value, press ENTER and the object or objects are rescaled.

Access

Command Line: AMSCALEXY

Ribbon: N/A

Menu: Modify > Scale > Scale xy

Options for Scale XY

Use the following options with the Scale XY command.

Option	Description
X and Y Scale factor	Specifies the value for the X or Y scale factor.
Reference	Scales the selected objects based on a reference length and a specified new length.

When a polyline is scaled with the Scale XY command, the polyline is broken up into single line segments.

Procedure: Scaling Objects Along the X and Y Axes

To scale objects along the X and Y axes, complete the following steps:

1. Click Modify menu > Scale > Scale XY.

2. Select the object that you want to scale and press ENTER. Specify a base point.

3. Enter the X scale factor and press ENTER. Enter the Y scale factor and press ENTER to scale the object.

Exercise: Basic Editing Tools

In this exercise, you will use the following editing tool commands: Offset, Join Entities, and Scale XY.

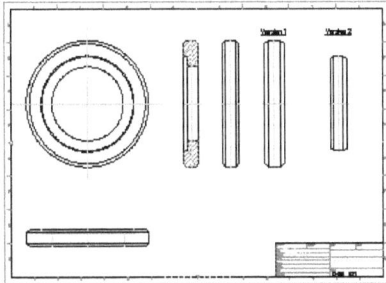

The completed exercise

1. Open *Weld_Flange.dwg*.

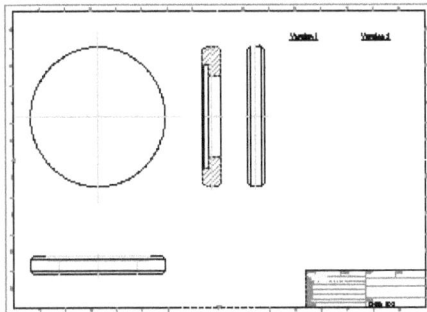

2. To begin offsetting the circle at multiple distances, do the following:

   ▪ Click Home tab > Modify panel > Offset.
   ▪ On the Command Prompt, using the pipe symbol, enter **5|22.5|24|39**. (These are four values for offset separated by pipe symbol.)
   ▪ Press ENTER.

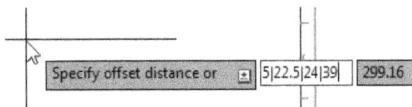

3. To specify what to offset and where, do the following:

   ▪ Select the circle in the front view.
   ▪ When prompted to specify a point, move the cursor inside the circle to see the preview and then click to place the offset circles.
   ▪ Press ENTER to exit the command.

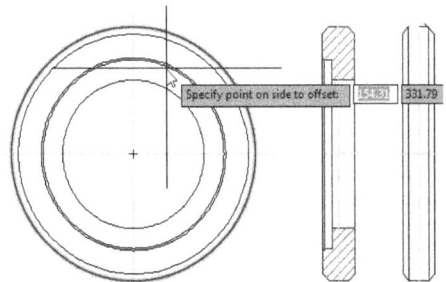

4. Zoom into the incomplete top portion of the geometry on the right side of the offset circles. Click Home tab > expanded Modify panel > Join. Select near point 1 and point 2. The line ends are connected.

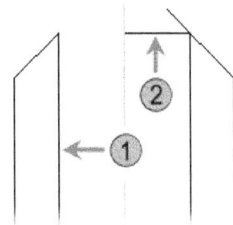

5. Repeat the Join command. Select near point 3 and point 4 to connect the line ends by automatically trimming the extra portion.

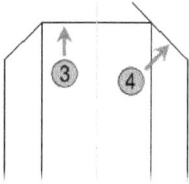

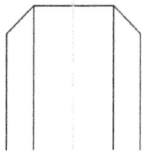

6. Zoom out to view the entire drawing. Toggle on polar tracking.

7. To create additional versions of the Weld Flange:

- Click Home tab > Modify panel > Copy drop-down list > Copy.
- Select the geometry of the right-side view. Press ENTER.
- For the base point, object snap to the midpoint of the top horizontal line of the selected geometry.
- Place copies below Version 1 and Version 2 text.
- Press ENTER to exit the command.

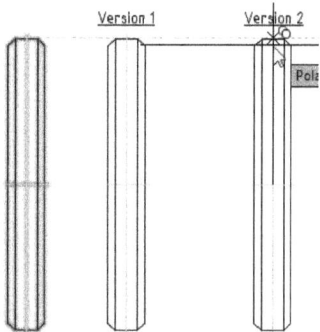

8. To begin scaling one view at different scale factors, do the following:

- On the Command Line, enter **AMSCALEXY** and press ENTER.
- In the drawing area, select the Version 1 geometry.
- Press ENTER.
- Select the midpoint of the vertical center line as the base point.

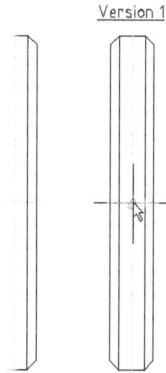

Version 1

9. When prompted for the scale factors, do the following:

- For the x-axis scale factor, enter **1.25**. Press ENTER.
- For the y-axis scale factor, enter **1.00**. Press ENTER.

10. Repeat the previous two steps for Version 2, using the following values:

- For the x-axis scale factor enter **1.00**.
- For the y-axis scale factor enter **0.75**.

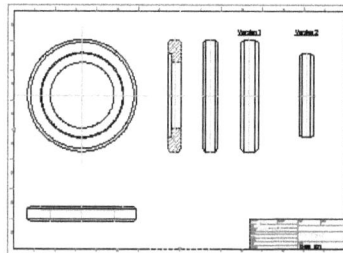

11. Save and close all of the files.

Lesson: Power Commands

Overview

You can use power commands with AutoCAD Mechanical objects, such as borders, part lists, standard parts, dimensions, symbols, and basic objects, including arcs, lines, and circles.

The following illustration shows some of the available power commands.

As with all design disciplines, mechanical design uses drawing objects and techniques that are unique to this discipline. Power tools enable you to quickly perform tasks specific to mechanical design.

Objectives

After completing this lesson, you will be able to:

- Modify objects in a drawing with power commands.
- Edit all of the various object types using one command.
- Erase all of the various object types using one command.
- Create copies of objects.
- Recall commands that were used to create objects.
- Create additional views while maintaining an accurate database.

About Power Commands

Every object knows whether it is a line, arc, or group of related objects, such as a hole, screw connection, or shaft. Information is attached to an object when it is created. Using power commands on intelligent AutoCAD Mechanical objects ensures that the objects are not destroyed when edited, or that all parts of an object are selected when erasing.

Definition of Power Commands

A power object is an object that contains specific information about itself and the command used to edit it. A power command is a universal command that accesses the internal information of an object and opens the appropriate dialog box, depending on the selected object. You can use power commands to edit, copy, and delete both AutoCAD and AutoCAD Mechanical objects.

Example of Using Power Commands

For example, you can insert a standard hole feature into a section view of a plate. After you provide a specific position, the lines or circle for the hole are drawn, the hatch is removed, and a centerline cross is inserted. All of these parameters are saved with the hole.

In this scenario you can use the following power commands:

- Power Edit command to change the hole diameter.
- Power Copy command to create a second hole.
- Power View command to add a top view of the hole.
- Power Erase command to delete the hole.
- Power Recall command to recall the same Hole dialog box that was used to create the original hole.

Modifying Objects

You can edit an object in a drawing with the **Power Edit** command by double-clicking on the object. The appropriate dialog box or function that was used to create that object opens. You only have to start one command to perform edits instead of using a separate command for each object type.

Access

Command Line: AMPOWEREDIT

Ribbon: N/A

Menu: Modify > Power Edit

Deleting Objects

You use the **Power Erase** command to delete any object type. With AutoCAD software objects, the Power Erase command functions such as the AutoCAD software Erase command.

When you use the **Power Erase** command to remove a standard hole feature or screw connection from a drawing, all parts associated with the object are removed and the remaining objects that were affected by that feature's hide situation are updated.

Access

Command Line: AMPOWERERASE

Ribbon: Home tab > Modify panel > Power Erase

Menu: Modify > Power Erase

Power Erase and AutoCAD Mechanical Object Types

The following table lists what happens when Power Erase is used on AutoCAD Mechanical objects.

Object	Action
Drawing Border/ Title	Deletes the border and title and the defined scale area.
Standard Parts and Features	Deletes the standard part or feature with the centerline. Updates the visibility of objects that are behind a hatch and refreshes the hatch.
Symbol	Deletes the symbol with the leader line.
Cross	Deletes the four centerlines that make the cross.
Section Lines	Deletes the section line and text labels.
Part Reference	Deletes the part reference and Bill of Material (BOM) entry.
Dimension	Deletes the selected dimension. If it is included in a base dimension or chain dimension, the other dimensions are rearranged.
Hole Charts	Deletes the hole chart, hole labels, and origin.
Calculations	Deletes charts and related graphics.

Copying Objects

You can use the **Power Copy** command to create single copies of objects. An object created with the AutoCAD Mechanical software knows what object class it belongs to based on the information attached to it when it was created. You can use these objects to create objects of the same class or to create duplicates of the object. Power Copy simplifies the process of creating new objects.

Copies that you create with the **Power Copy** command are intelligent. For example, if you use the Power Copy command on a standard hole feature or screw connection, it copies the screw and all of the information required to correctly hide the background. For an automatic dimension, the Power Copy command enables you to add dimension locations.

Access

Command Line: AMPOWERCOPY

Ribbon: Home tab > Modify panel > Copy drop-down list > Power Copy

Menu: Modify > Power Copy

Power Copy Guidelines

Follow these guidelines as you use Power Copy:

- The procedure for copying objects with the **Power Copy** command varies depending on the type of object that you select.
- Using the Power Copy command to copy standard parts helps keep the bill of materials accurate and hides objects behind the part.

Procedure: Copying Standard Parts

To copy standard parts, complete the following steps:

1. Click Home tab > Modify panel > Copy drop-down list > Power Copy.

2. Select a standard part.

3. Click the new insertion point.

4. Specify the angle and press ENTER.

Recalling Commands

You can select any object in the drawing area and open the command that was used to create the object by using the **Power Recall** command. Power Recall is very effective if you want to copy an object and use different parameters. Power Recall works with AutoCAD Mechanical software objects and with AutoCAD software objects, such as lines, rectangles, hatches, and construction lines.

For example, to create a circle based on an existing circle, select a circle in your drawing. This starts the command for creating a circle. You are prompted to select the creation method, location, and size for the new circle. The software uses the same layer, linetype, and color settings as the selected circle.

Access

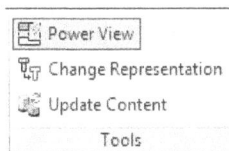

Command Line: AMPOWERRECALL

Ribbon: N/A

Menu: Modify > Power Recall

Creating Views

You can use the **Power View** command on AutoCAD Mechanical software standard parts and standard features to create different orthographic views of the parts or features. You can add side, top, front, or other views while maintaining an accurate list of parts in the drawing database. After you start the Power View command and select an existing standard part or hole, the Select New View dialog box opens with the size and object type information set according to the originally selected view.

Access

▣ Power View	Command Line: AMPOWERVIEW
⬚ Change Representation	Ribbon: Content tab > Tools panel > Power View
⬚ Update Content	Menu: Modify > Power View
Tools	

> If 2D structure is on when you are using the Power View command on standard parts or features, the original view and the new view are associative. Changing the size of one of the views changes the size of the other one as well. If 2D structure is not on, the views are updated independently.

Power View When Using Structure

When you use Power View to create views in a drawing that uses Mechanical structure, the location of the generated view definition is dependent on the active view. If the overall drawing is active, the new component view is added to the view definition of the selected component. If a different component view is active, the new view definition becomes part of that view definition. Because of this, you should activate the component view in which the new view geometry is supposed to be defined before using Power View to create a new view.

In the following illustration, a section of the front and top views of the assembly are shown, along with their Browser information, as an example of the correct relationship and steps for using Power View to create a new view. On the left, the assembly's Front component view is selected to highlight the geometry within that view. At this point, the hexagon socket head bolt only has one view defined. In the middle illustration, you see the assembly's Top component view made active. The illustration on the right shows the assembly after using Power View to create the top view of the bolt. You can tell the bolt's Top component view is part of the assembly's Top component view because the geometry is bold like the rest of the view's geometry.

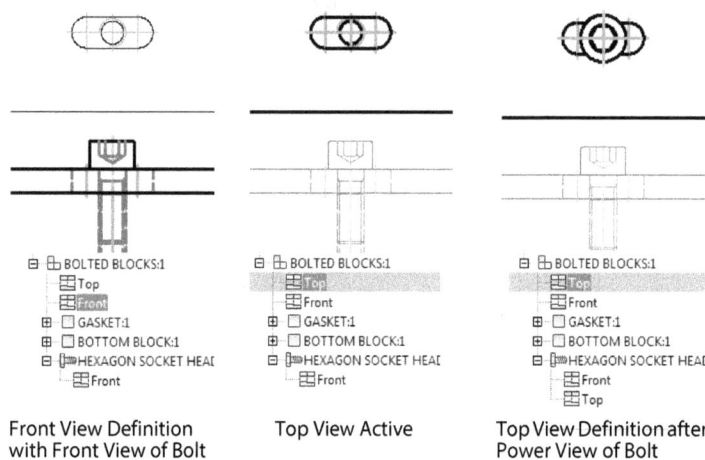

Front View Definition
with Front View of Bolt

Top View Active

Top View Definition after
Power View of Bolt

Exercise: Use Power Commands

In this exercise, you will learn to work with the power commands: Power Edit, Power Recall, Power Copy, and Power Erase. You will use the power commands to edit, copy, or delete intelligent objects. When you work with the power commands, you take full advantage of these objects without damaging them.

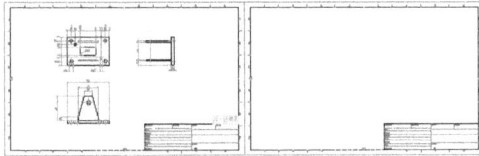

The completed exercise

1. Open *Power_Exercise.dwg*.

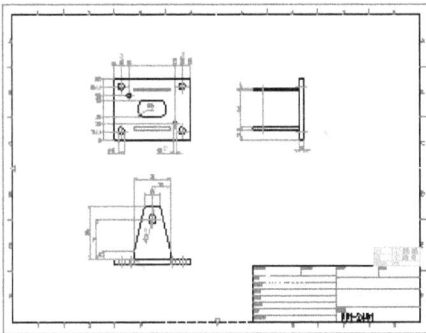

2. Zoom into the title block and note that under DWG NO a - (dash) is displayed.

3. Double-click on the title block to power edit it. The Change Title Block Entry dialog box opens. Do the following:

    ▪ In the Drawing Number box, enter **001-0863**.

    ▪ Click OK to close the dialog box.

    ▪ Note the new DWG NO.

4. Zoom out and double-click on the drawing border to power edit it. The Drawing Borders with Title Block dialog box opens. Do the following:

    ▪ Note the paper format size. You can change the title block, drawing border, and scale of the drawing.

    ▪ Click Cancel to close the dialog box.

5. To Power Edit a dimension do the following:

    ▪ Zoom into the top view and double-click on the 135 dimension.

    ▪ The dimension is converted into an edit box. In the Power Dimensioning contextual Ribbon tab that opens, click Tolerance to toggle off tolerancing (gray).

    ▪ Click Close Editor to close the Power Dimensioning contextual tab.

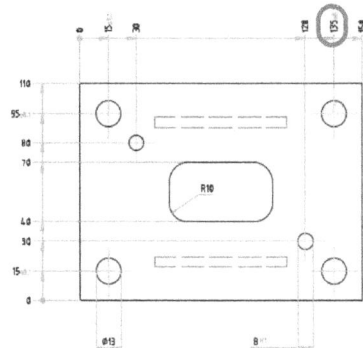

6. Double-click on the R10 fillet geometry (not the dimension).

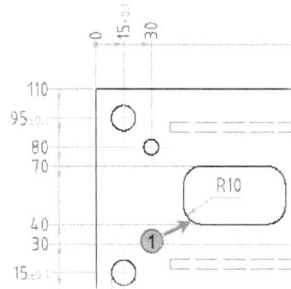

7. The Fillet dialog box opens. Do the following:

- In the Fillet Size drop-down list, select **2.5**.
- Click **OK**.

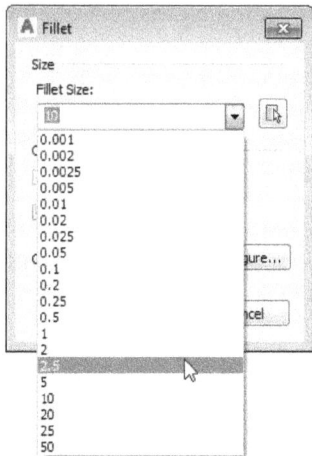

8. The fillet is temporarily removed and the left vertical line where the fillet was is highlighted. To create the new fillet do the following:

- Hover the cursor over the bottom horizontal line to preview the new fillet.
- Click to accept the fillet.

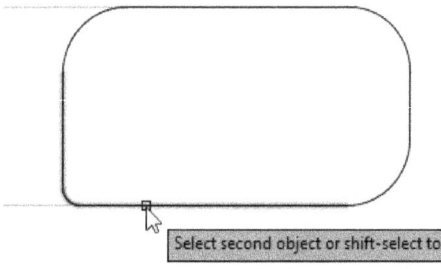

9. Note that the new dimension is dynamically attached to the cursor. Do the following:

- Place the dimension at the same place as the original dimension.
- Click Close Editor to close the Power Dimensioning contextual tab.

10. To apply the same fillet change to the other three corners of the rectangle do the following:

- Select the other three fillets in the following order: top left, top right, and then the bottom right fillet.
- Press ENTER to display the options.
- Click **Accept** in the display options.
- In the Fillet dialog box, select **2.5** as the Fillet Size and then click OK.
- The bottom right fillet is edited. Select the other two fillets and press ENTER.
- Select the top horizontal line and press ENTER to exit the command.

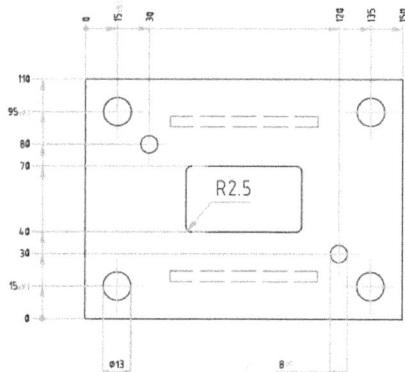

11. On the Command Prompt, enter **AMPOWERRECALL**, and press <Enter>, and do the following:

- Select the outer rectangle in the top view. The Rectangle command is started.
- Press ESC to end the command.

12. Start the **Power Recall** command and do the following:

- Select the 0 ordinate dimension in the top view. The Automatic Dimension command is started and the Multiple Dimensioning dialog box opens.
- Click Cancel to end the command.

13. Click Home tab > Modify panel > Power Erase and do the following:

- In the side view, select the 71 and 35 dimensions.
- Press ENTER.

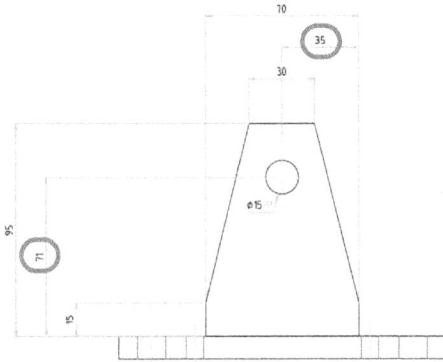

The selected dimensions are erased and the remaining dimensions are reorganized.

14. Start the **Power Erase** command, select the 15 diameter dimension, and press ENTER. The dimension is deleted completely.

15. Click Home tab > Modify panel > Copy drop-down list > Power Copy and do the following:

- Select the 70 dimension.
- Click on the top right endpoint of the base as shown in the following illustration.

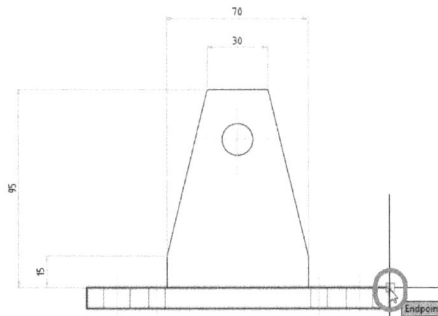

- A new symmetrical dimension is added. Press ENTER.

16. To add dimensions to the dimension set, in the top view do the following:

- Start the **Power Copy** command.
- Select the 0 dimension (1) as shown in the following illustration.
- Select endpoints of both vertical lines (2, 3) as shown in the following illustration.
- Press ENTER.

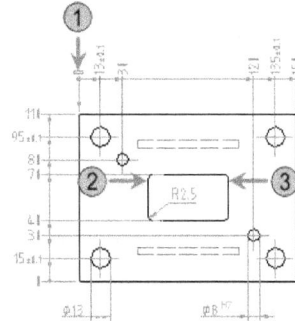

17. Start the **Power Copy** command and do the following:

- Select the drawing border.
- Enter **850,0,0** as the insertion point

A new drawing border is inserted into the drawing. All entries in the current title block are adapted to the new drawing border.

18. Zoom to extents.

19. Save and close all of the files.

Lesson: Associative Hide

Overview

This lesson describes the creation and editing of associative hide situations for structured and non-structured drawing geometry.

When following a traditional workflow, converting geometry to hidden lines can be a time-consuming task. This is because you typically need to break objects into multiple objects to use different linetypes in different areas of the drawing view. As the design evolves, additional time is required if the changes affect areas that are supposed to be visible or hidden. In some cases, geometry that was hidden must now be shown as visible and visible geometry as hidden. Having to change a portion of the geometry makes the task even more time consuming. Knowing how to create and edit associative hide situations makes completing your designs faster and easier.

In the following illustration, this simple design consists of structural members of a frame that overlap. To visually communicate the way the members overlap, the obstructed geometry needs to be hidden from view or needs to display as dashed geometry.

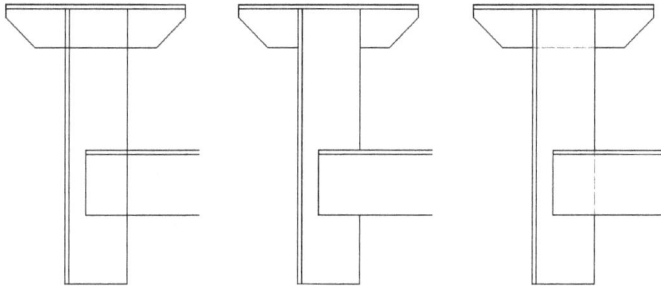

Objectives

After completing this lesson, you will be able to:

- Describe the purpose and benefits of associative hide situations.
- Hide objects by association with other drawing objects.
- Edit associative hidden lines.

About Associative Hides

You can create associative hides to make it easier to complete and modify a design. Before creating and editing associative hide situations, you should understand their purpose and benefits.

Definition of an Associative Hide

You can create associative hide situations to calculate where the visibility of parts is obstructed by other parts and to automatically change the display of the obstructed geometry. Depending on the settings for the associative hide, the obstructed geometry is set to be invisible or set to display with a hidden linetype. A key aspect of the associative hide is that the display change occurs without the geometry being broken into multiple objects. For example, a long line segment obstructed in the middle is still a single line, although it might display with dashed segments in the middle where it is obstructed by another part.

The associative aspect of an associative hide means that as you modify the size, shape, or position of the geometry used in the calculation, the hide situation automatically recalculates and updates the drawing view.

You can use the associative hide command, AMSHIDE, to create associative hides for structured and non-structured geometry. To create an associative hide situation, mechanical structure does not need to be on. If you are creating associative hides of non-structured geometry and the geometry contains blocks, those blocks are recognized by the associative hide and listed as separate entries in the levels.

Each associative hide situation that you create is added as an entry in the Mechanical Browser. Its position in the Browser depends on whether or not Mechanical structure is being used in the drawing. After you have created an associative hide, you can edit it and change its display settings or which geometry to use in the hide calculation.

Example of an Associative Hide

Because every assembly design and almost every part design has some aspect being obstructed from view, there are a multitude of examples for the use of associative hide situations.

In the following illustration, after creating and positioning the different parts in the assembly, the hidden lines were calculated by selecting and specifying which parts are in front of the others.

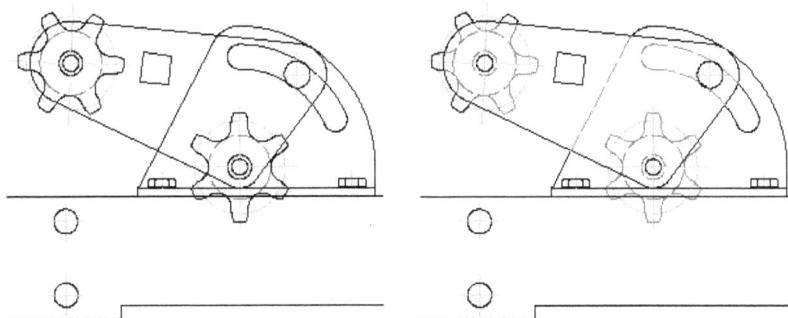

In the following illustration, the design and associative hide were both edited. The bracket and sprocket were rotated to a new position that caused the associative hide to automatically recalculate and update. The associative hide was then edited to toggle off the display of hidden lines and centerlines hidden by the part geometry.

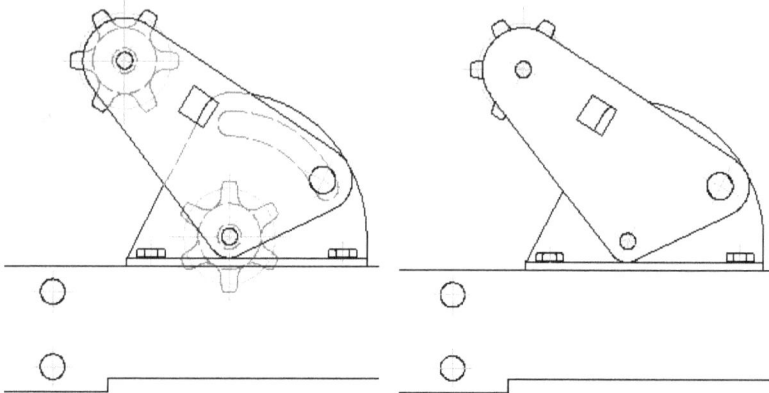

Benefits of Associative Hide

There are many benefits to using the Associative Hide command over other methods that can be used to achieve the same final visual results. Those benefits include:

- Associative hides have all of the aspects of the hide calculation saved as part of the drawing. All of the aspects of the hide calculation can be changed at a later time.
- You can use the same associative hide commands to create and edit hide situations whether or not the drawing uses Mechanical structure. Mechanical structure is not required to be on in the drawing.
- Associative hide does not break lines at the intersections where the lines change to hidden. Instead, it modifies the visibility of objects in the drawing by assigning them to the foreground and background. Background objects are then displayed as hidden or dashed lines.
- You can toggle the display of background hidden lines on and off to match your display requirements.
- Associative hide always updates to display the current hide situation as you move objects or edit structure definitions.
- You can create multiple levels in a hide situation. You can also create multiple hide situations to create complex combinations of geometry display. You can create and edit multiple level hides in an intuitive interface with a tree structure organization.
- Established associative hide conditions are listed in the Browser. This enables you to easily review and edit the hide condition.

Based on these benefits, the associative hide command (AMSHIDE) is the recommended method for creating hide situations in drawing views.

Creating an Associative Hide

Creating an associative hide enables you to quickly change the display of the geometry in a drawing view so that objects behind other objects appear to be hidden. To achieve the required results, you need to understand the process of creating associative hides and the creation options.

In the following illustration, the assembly view is shown before, during, and after the creation of an associative hide.

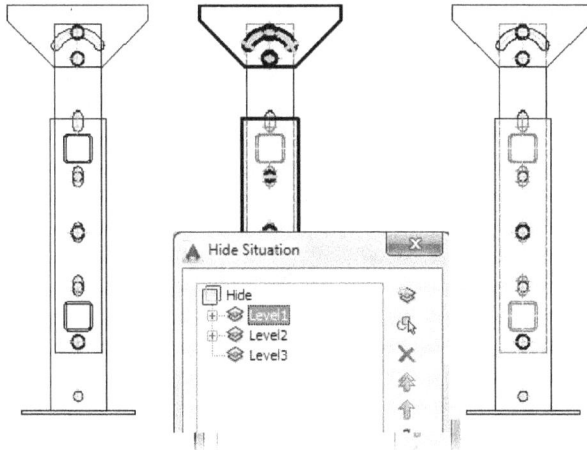

Access

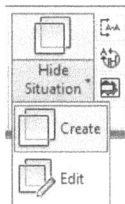

Command Line: AMSHIDE

Ribbon: Home tab > Detail panel > Hide Situation drop-down list > Create

Menu: Modify > Associative Hide > Create Associative Hide Situation

Hide Situation Dialog Box Options

When creating a hide situation, you can set objects to be in the foreground or background. The initial foreground objects are based on your initial selection set. The automatic selection of background objects depends on the current Hide Options settings.

The first level listed in the tree list in the Hide Situation dialog box is the level of foreground objects. The other levels are background objects and each level is calculated behind the objects in the level listed above in the tree. By default, a hide situation only has two levels. You can add more levels to create a more complex multi-tiered hide situation. Changing the order of the levels changes the foreground to background relationship between the levels.

The tools in the vertical toolbar in the Hide Situation dialog box enable you to accomplish the common tasks of adding levels, adding objects to the levels, deleting objects and levels, and changing the order of the levels.

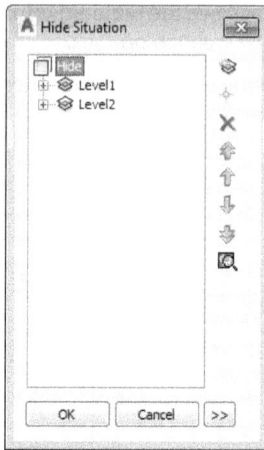

The Hide Situation dialog box defaults to a collapsed view with only the typical tools and options shown. Expand the dialog box to display all of the available advanced options. The information and options displayed in the expanded area of the dialog box depend on what is selected in the tree view. When the dialog box is expanded, click Settings to open the Hide Options dialog box in which you can set what you want as the default for these options.

Other tasks that you can accomplish after selecting the hide situation in the tree list and expanding the dialog box include:

- Entering a unique name for the overall hide situation.
- Assigning where the hide situation should be stored.
- Toggling the display of hidden lines for hidden background geometry on and off.
- Toggling the calculation of only the geometry on specific layers on and off.
- Suppress and unsuppress the hide situations.

The following illustration shows the expanded Hide Situation dialog box and identifies its key areas.

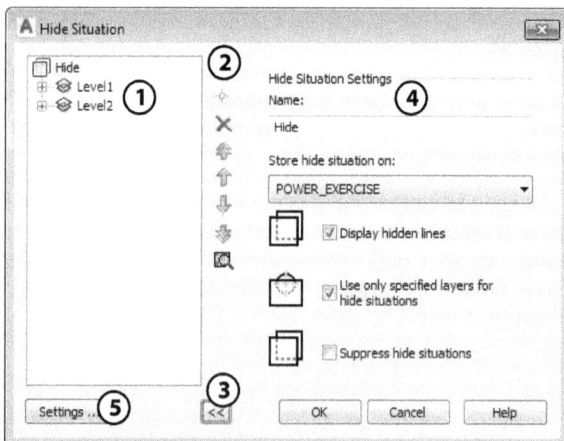

1. Use the tree view to review the levels and its content for the hide situation. Rearrange the levels or selected content by dragging them to a new location in the tree.

2. Use the tools in this vertical toolbar to perform tasks, such as adding levels, adding objects to selected levels, deleting objects or levels, or rearranging the order of levels.

3. Click to expand or collapse the dialog box.

4. Change the settings for the selected item in the tree list. The available options depend on what is selected in the tree.

5. Click to display the Hide Options dialog box to change what should be the default setting in the Hide Situation dialog box.

> Clicking Settings in the Hide Situation dialog box opens the Hide Options dialog box and achieves the same setting results as clicking Hide Options on the AM:Structure tab in the Options dialog box.

Store Locations for Hide Situations

When you create a hide situation, its storage location depends on whether structure is enabled in the drawing. In a non-structure drawing, hide situations are stored at the drawing file level. In a drawing in which structure is enabled, the storage location for the hide situation depends on which component view is active when the hide situation is created.

When you create an associative hide using structured geometry, before creating the associative hide, you should determine the component view in which you want to store the calculated associative hide and set it to be active. By creating the associative hide at the appropriate level, it becomes part of the component view and carries through as you reuse the structured part or assembly. You should store the hide situation in the lowest level component view to which the hide situation is pertinent.

In the following illustration, an example of the storage location for hide situations in a non-structured drawing and a structured drawing are shown. The hide situations for the non-structured drawing are listed in the Browser directly below the top node of the drawing name. In the structured drawing, the hide situations are stored in the component view to which they pertains.

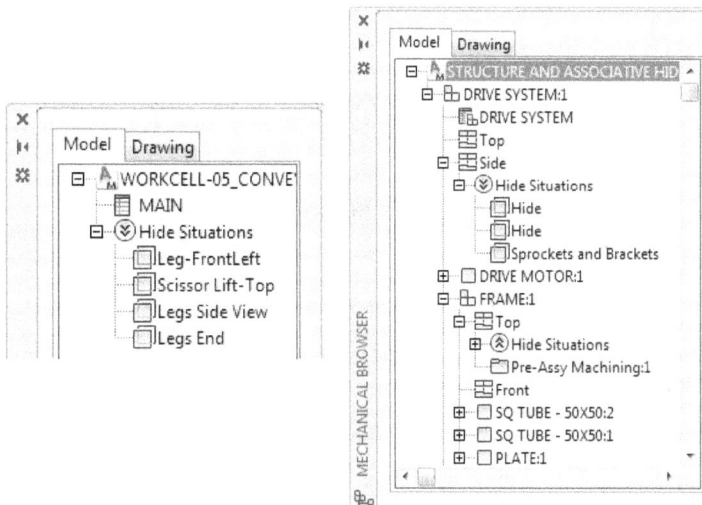

Hide Situation Dialog Box - Levels

When you are creating an associative hide situation and you select a level in the list, the Basic, Advanced, and Object Exclusion tabs display if the dialog box is expanded. These tabs enable you to modify the name of the level and how the hide is calculated and represented.

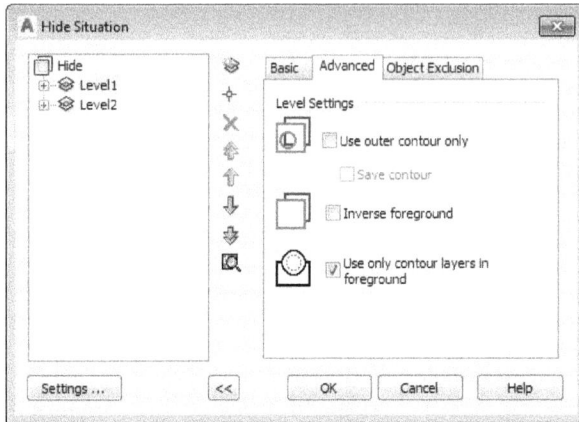

Option	Description
Basic tab	Enter a custom name for the level to make it easier to identify the different levels in a complex multilevel hide situation.
Advanced tab	Set the options to control how islands and boundaries in the foreground geometry are referenced when calculating the visible and hidden areas of the background geometry.
Object Exclusion tab	Set exclusions for foreground and background objects.

> You can create and manage the hide calculation for an area by creating multiple levels in a single hide situation when the hide for an area in a drawing view has multiple levels of parts.

Process: Creating an Associative Hide

An overview of creating an associative hide is shown in the following steps. The first step of activating a component view is only required if you are creating an associative hide for a Mechanically structured design.

1. Activate the assembly component view to which the associative hide pertains.

2. Start the **Associative Hide** command.

3. Select the objects that you see first in that view of the design.

4. In the Hide Situation dialog box, create additional levels and adjust the objects or component views within the levels as required.

5. Select the required hide settings and enter a unique identifying name for the hide situation.

6. Review your results to ensure that they match your requirements.

Editing an Associative Hide

Use the Edit Associative Hide command to control which objects are used in the foreground or background. You can also change the representation style for the background objects, rename the hide situation, change the types of objects to exclude from the hide, and modify the hide contours.

Editing an Associative Hide

There are two ways in which you can edit an existing hide situation. One is to access the Browser shortcut menu options for a hide situation in the Browser and toggle the display of hidden lines or toggle the suppression of the hide situation. The other is to edit the settings and objects in the hide situation using the Edit Associative Hide Situation command. This command opens the same dialog box with the same options that were used to initially create the hide situation.

Access

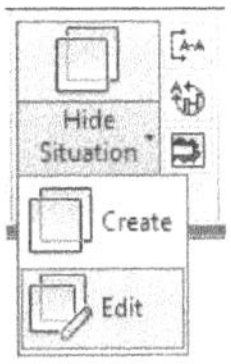

Command Line: AMSHIDEEDIT

Ribbon: Home tab > Detail panel > Hide Situation drop-down list > Edit

Menu: Modify > Associative Hide > Edit Associative Hide Situation

Another way to access the Edit Hide Situation command is in the shortcut menu after selecting an object in the drawing window that is used in a hide situation. If the selected object is used in multiple associative hide situations, you can cycle through them. As you are cycling through each hide situation, the geometry is highlighted and a tooltip lists the name of the hide situation.

Some of the editing options provided in the Hide Situation dialog box can be easily accessed in the Hide Situation drop-down list in the Ribbon as shown in the following illustration. It bypasses the need to access those options through the dialog box.

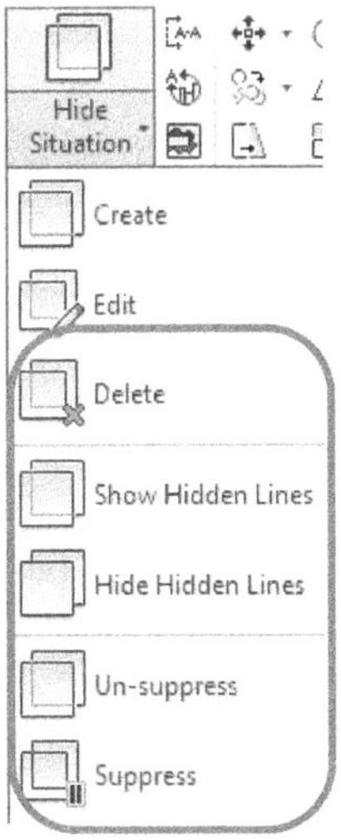

Process: Modifying Associative Hide Situations

An overview of modifying an existing associative hide situation is shown in the following steps:

1. Use one of the access methods to open the Edit Hide Situation dialog box for the associative hide situation that you want to edit.

2. In the Edit Hide Situation dialog box, modify the hide situation by modifying the levels, adding or removing the components or geometry to a level, changing the order of the levels, changing the hide style, renaming the hide situation, or setting the advanced foreground and background relationships. Click the different tree nodes to access the different editing options.

Exercise: Create and Edit Associative Hides

In this exercise, you will create associative hide situations of non-structured geometry that represents both free objects and objects defined within a block definition. Before creating the associative hide situations, you will remove some Mechanical structure content from the drawing file and then toggle Structure off in the drawing.

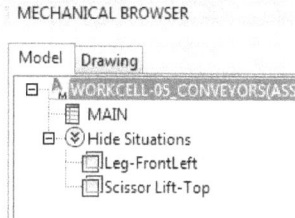

The completed exercise

Create and Edit an Associative Hide

In this section of the exercise, you will create associative hide situations of non-structured geometry of free objects. Before creating the associative hide situations, you will remove some Mechanical structure content from the drawing file and then toggle Structure off in the drawing.

1. Open *WorkCell-05_conveyors(Associative Hide).dwg*.

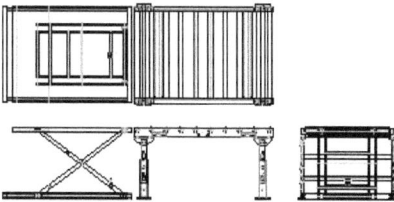

2. On the Status Bar, verify that the Mechanical Structure is On.

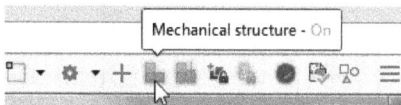

3. On the Status Bar, click Workspace Switching and select Structure if not already selected.

4. In the Mechanical Browser, review the structured definitions that have been added to the drawing. (If the Mechanical Browser is not displayed, select Structure tab>Tools panel>Mechanical Browser.)

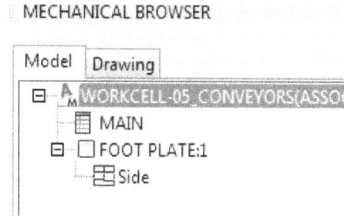

5. To delete and remove the structured content from the drawing, do the following:

   - In the Browser, right-click on FOOT PLATE:1 and click **Delete**.
   - In the message box prompting if you want to remove the definition, click **Yes**.
   - Review the Browser. It now displays as shown in the following illustration.

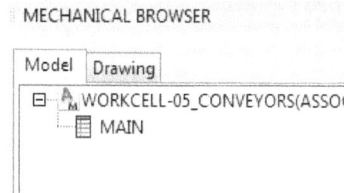

6. On the Status Bar, click Mechanical Structure to toggle it off in this drawing file. The Status Bar now displays as shown in the following illustration.

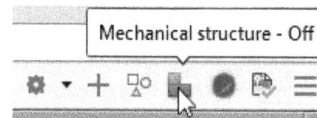

7. Zoom into the left leg in the front view as shown in the following illustration.

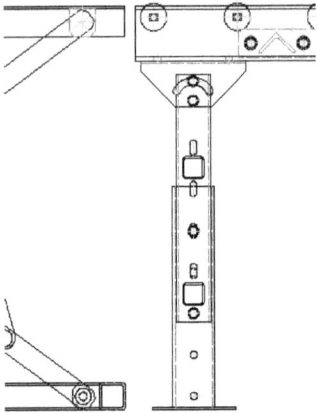

8. To begin creating an associative hide situation for the geometry representing the adjustable leg support, click Structure tab > Hide Situation panel > Create.

9. For the foreground objects, select the rectangle of the lower channel, bolts, washers, and hole as shown in the following illustration. Right-click after selecting the identified objects.

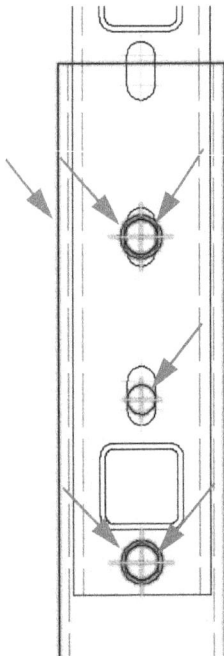

10. To remove the automatically selected objects from Level2, in the Hide Situation dialog box, do the following:

- In the tree view below Level2, click Free Objects.
- Click Remove.

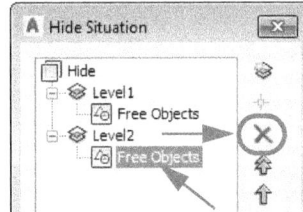

11. To specify the objects that you want to have in Level2:

- In the Hide Situation dialog box, click Select Objects.
- In the drawing window, select the outer lines of the top channel and the four slots as shown in the following illustration.
- Right-click after selecting the identified objects.

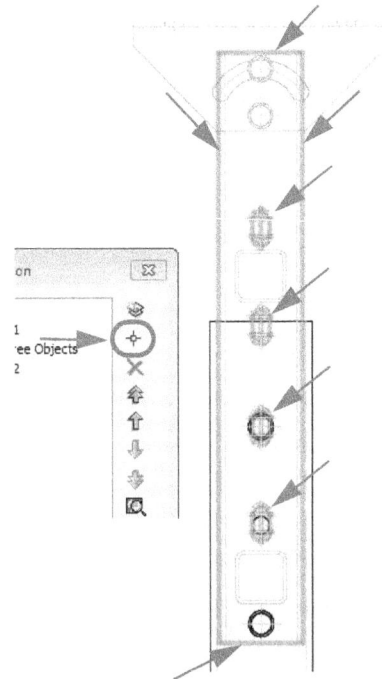

12. To add a third level to the hide calculation, in the Hide Situation dialog box, with Level2 selected, click New Level. The new third level named Level3 is listed in the dialog box.

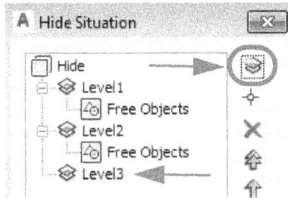

13. To add the square tubing to Level3:

- In the Hide Situation dialog box, click Select Objects.
- In the drawing window, select the two identified square tube parts.
- Right-click after selecting the identified objects.

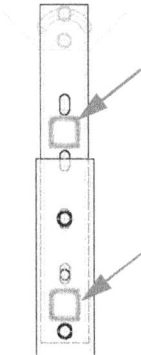

14. To rename the hide situation, in the Hide Situation dialog box do the following:

- Right-click on the top node titled Hide and click Rename.
- Enter **Leg-FrontLeft** as shown in the following illustration.

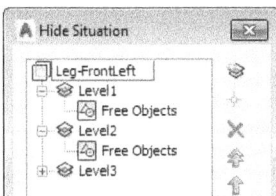

15. In the Hide Situation dialog box, click OK. In the drawing window, review the results of the hide calculation.

16. In the Browser, review the inclusion of the newly created and named hide situation.

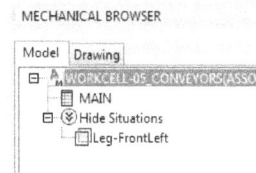

17. On the Status Bar, review the Mechanical Structure setting. Structure remained off even after you created the associative hide situation.

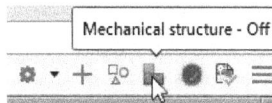

Create an Associative Hide Using Blocks

In this section of the exercise, you will create an associative hide situation of objects defined within a block definition.

1. Pan and zoom the drawing to view the top view of the scissor lift as shown in the following illustration.

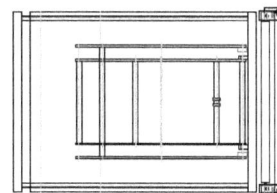

2. To preview that the free objects in this view are part of different block definitions, use the LIST command to view the information for the geometry in the top view of the scissor lift.

3. To begin creating an associative hide situation for the top view of the scissor lift, on the Structure tab > Hide Situation panel, click Create.

4. In the drawing window, select the BASEFRAME_T and PLATFORM_T blocks as shown in the following illustration. Right-click after selecting the identified objects.

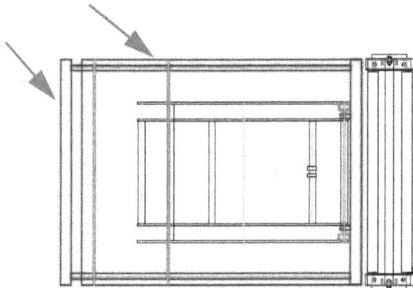

5. In the Hide Situation dialog box, review the list of block objects and the levels to which they were initially assigned.

6. In the Hide Situation dialog box, click and drag the entry for block BASEFRAME_T from Level1 to Level2 to create the results as shown in the following illustration.

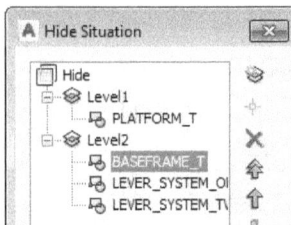

7. To view the advanced settings for the overall hide situation, in the Hide Situation dialog box do the following:
   - Click the expand button to expand the dialog box to the right.
   - In the tree view, click the top node titled Hide.

8. In the Hide Situation Settings area, in the Name field, enter **Scissor Lift-Top**.

9. In the Hide Situation dialog box, click OK. In the drawing window, review the results of the hide calculation.

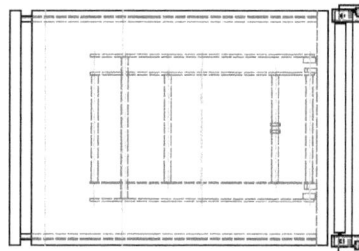

10. In the Browser, review the inclusion of the newly created and named hide situation.

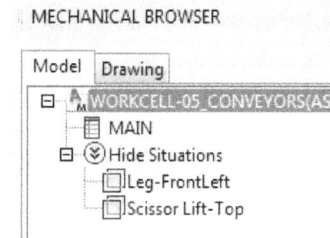

11. Save and close all of the drawings.

Exercise: Create and Edit Associative Hides - When Using Structure

In this exercise, you will create associative hide situations of mechanically structured geometry.

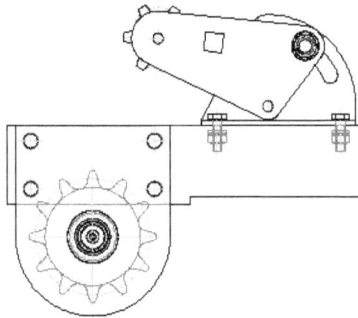

The completed exercise

Note: This exercise assumes that the workspace **Structure** is active and that the structure selection order is set to **Top-down**.

1. Open *Structure and Associative Hides.dwg*.

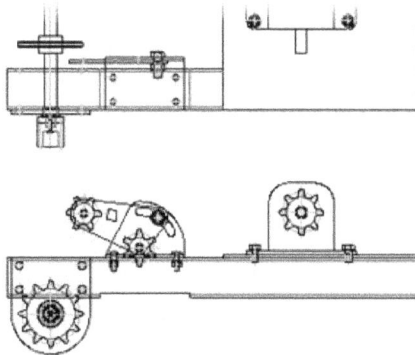

2. To toggle off the display of hidden lines for multiple components, do the following:

   - In the Browser, expand the tree and click FRAME:1.
   - Press and hold CTRL. Click SPROCKET BRACKET-BASE:1.
   - In the Browser, right-click on FRAME:1 and click Property Overrides.

3. To toggle off the hidden line display for these two components, do the following:

   - In the Property Overrides dialog box, select the Override Properties checkbox.
   - Under Visibility, clear the Hidden Lines checkbox.
   - Click OK.

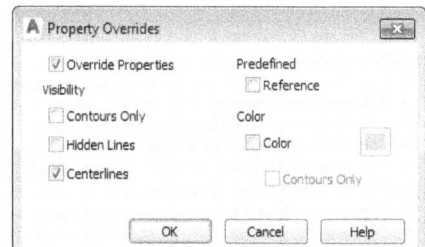

4. In the Browser under DRIVE SYSTEM:1, double-click on the Side component view to set it to be active.

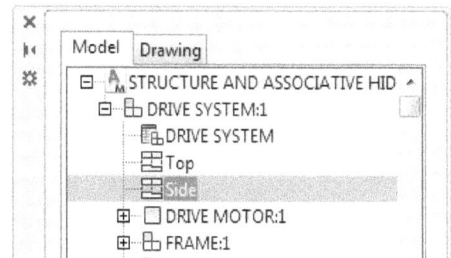

5. To begin creating an associative hide condition between the components, do the following:

- Click Structure tab > Hide Situation panel > Create.
- For the foreground objects, keep on clicking on the geometry, as shown in the following illustration, until you cycle to the component DRIVE AXLE BRACKET:1.
- Press ENTER.

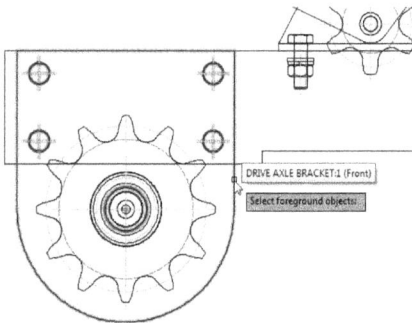

6. In the Hide Situation dialog box, drag SHAFT END DRIVE from Level2 and drop it in Level1. Click OK.

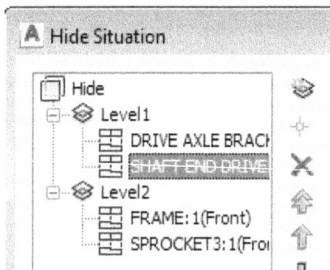

7. To begin creating a multiple level hide condition, do the following:

- Click Structure tab > Hide Situation panel > Create.
- For the foreground objects, in the drawing window, keep on clicking on the geometry, as shown in the following illustration, until you cycle to the component FRAME:1. Press ENTER.

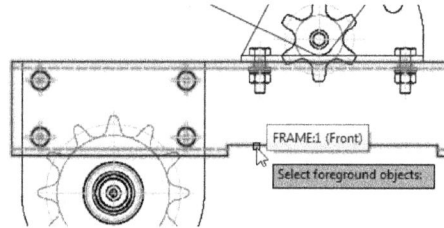

8. In the Hide Situation dialog box, under Level2 select and click Remove to remove all objects except the eight components that start with EX-.

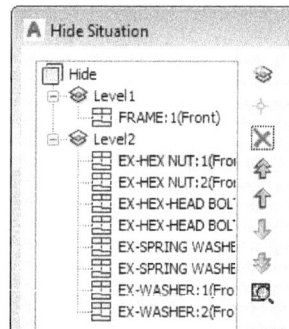

9. To add another level between Level1 and Level2 do the following:

- Click Level1.
- Click New Level.

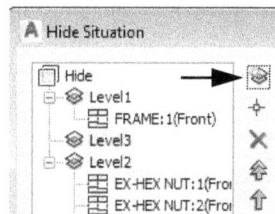

10. To add objects to Level3, in the Hide Situation dialog box, click Select Objects. In the drawing window, click the geometry (as shown in the following illustration) until you cycle to the component LWPOLYLINE. Right-click anywhere in the drawing window.

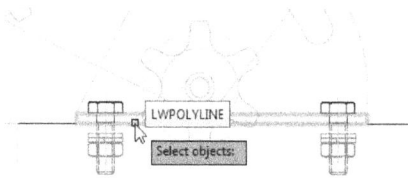

11. In the Hide Situation dialog box, click OK.

12. To begin creating another hide condition for the brackets and sprockets, do the following:

    ▪ Click Structure tab > Hide Situation panel > Create.

    ▪ For the foreground objects, in the drawing window, click SPROCKET BRACKET-PIVOT:1 as shown in the following illustration. Right-click anywhere in the drawing window.

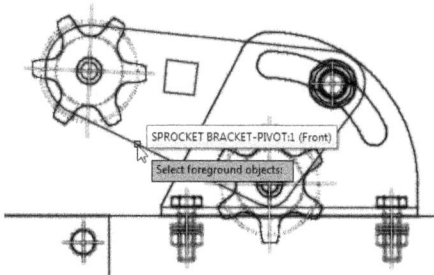

13. In the Hide Situation dialog box, drag SCREW CON1:1 from Level2 and drop it in Level1, above SPROCKET BRACKET-PIVOT.

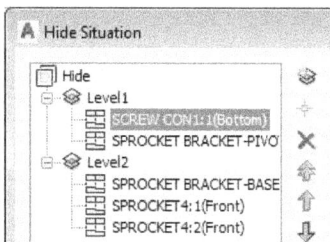

14. To have the hidden lines calculate correctly for the lower sprocket, do the following:

    ▪ In the list, click Level2.

    ▪ On the vertical toolbar, click Select Objects.

    ▪ In the drawing window, select FRAME 1 as shown in the following illustration.

    ▪ Right-click anywhere in the drawing window.

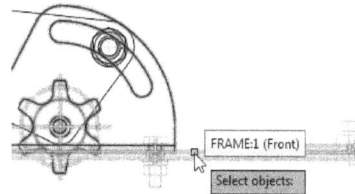

15. In the Hide Situation dialog box, click New Level.

16. In the list of levels, drag both instances of SPROCKET4 to Level3. Click OK.

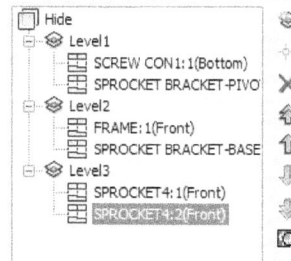

17. Review the graphic results of the hide situations that you just created.

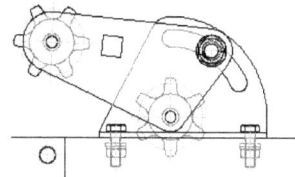

18. To begin editing the associative hide for the sprockets and brackets, in the Browser, for the assembly component DRIVE SYSTEM:1, under the Side > Hide Situations, double-click on the third Hide folder.

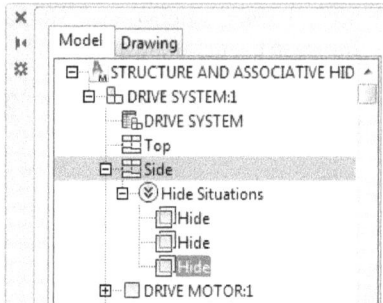

19. In the Hide Situation dialog box, do the following:

- Expand the dialog box if not already expanded.
- For Name, enter **Sprockets and Brackets**.
- Toggle off (clear) Display hidden lines and Use only specified layers for hide situations, as shown in the following illustration.

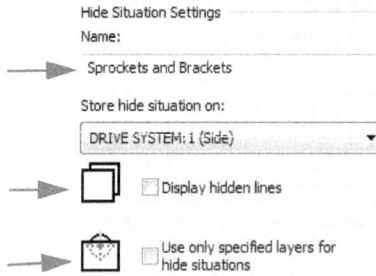

20. In the Hide Situation dialog box, click OK. Note the hidden sprockets and brackets in the drawing window.

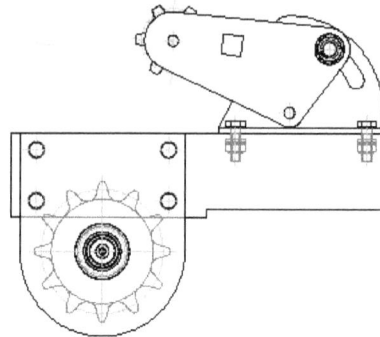

21. In the Browser, double-click on the filename listed at the top of the Browser.

22. Save and close all of the files.

Chapter Summary

In this chapter, you learned how to edit drawing objects using the AutoCAD Mechanical editing tools and power commands. You also learned how to modify the display of drawing geometry through the creation of annotation views.

Having completed this chapter, you can:

- Copy drawing objects, join separate objects into a single object, create breaks in lines, and create multiple offset copies of objects.
- Modify objects in a drawing with power commands, use one command to edit and erase all object types, and create additional views while maintaining an accurate database.
- Create and edit associative hide situations.

Mechanical Part Generators

This chapter describes industry standard parts and how you insert them into your assembly designs. You learn how to use the spring, chains and belts generators and the shaft generator to create rotationally symmetric drawings.

Objectives

After completing this chapter, you will be able to:

- Insert industry standard parts into your assembly designs.
- Add sprockets, pulleys, chains, and belts to a drawing.
- Create complete drawings of cylindrical parts with the Shaft Generator.
- Place standard shaft parts on shaft segments.
- Insert springs into an assembly design.

About Machinery Generators

When designing machinery, you often need to include shafts, shaft parts, springs, sprockets, belt or chain drives, or cams. With the AutoCAD® Mechanical software, you can use its capabilities to create such parts.

In the following illustration, the shaft view was created as it was being designed using the Shaft Generator. The end view was then created from the same shaft design by the Shaft Generator.

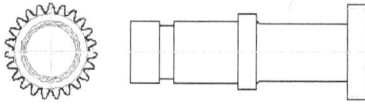

Definition of Machinery Generators

The different commands in AutoCAD Mechanical software that can create and add shafts, shaft parts, springs, sprockets, belt or chain drives, and cams to a design are referred to as machinery generators. During the creation of each of these parts, you can select and sizes and values based on industry standards. For some of the generators, you can also stresses, loads, and other design data to identify the correct part for your design requirements.

In the following illustration, the required design criteria for an extension spring has been specified to determine which springs exist that meet this criteria so that the most appropriate spring can be inserted.

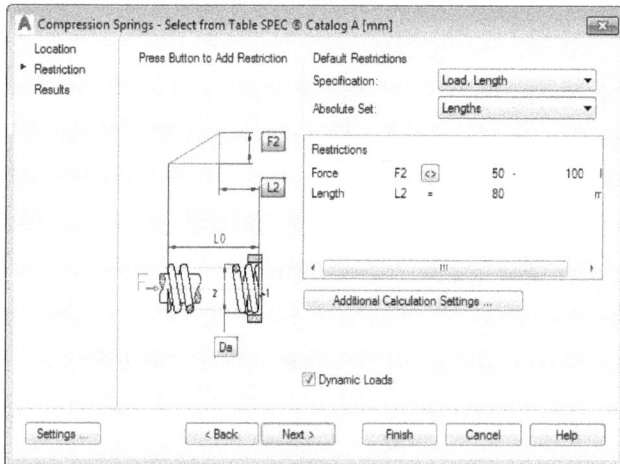

Example of Machinery Generators

The designing of machines typically includes shafts, bearings, gears, cams, belts, and chains. Creating this geometry from scratch or building and manipulating a library of industry-accepted parts is time consuming. In the following illustration, the sprockets, chain, chain length, shafts, bearings, and gears were all added to the drawing after specific criteria in their corresponding generators had been selected or specified. The hidden line calculation and the selection of which hidden lines to display in these views was done using Associative Hide.

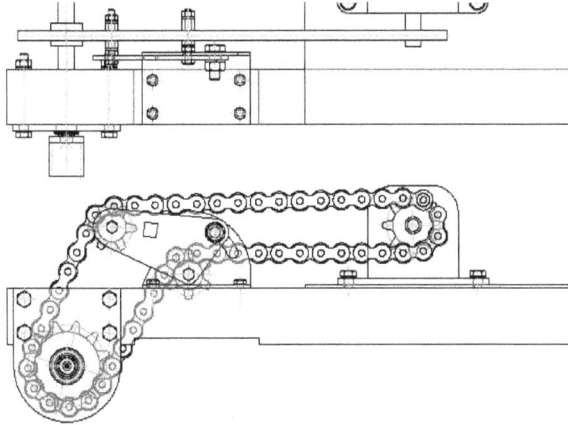

Machinery Generated Parts When Using Structure

In a drawing with structure enabled, the different machinery generators create structured parts. The tools either place standard parts after you select them from a list or create it based on the design values that you specify in the generator. The generated parts display in the Browser and Structure Catalog with a unique icon. This helps identify the part as one that was created by a specific tool while also identifying what type of part it is.

In the following illustration, a chain drive system is in the process of being designed. A number of structured parts were added to this design using specific tools for placing and creating sprockets, bolts, nuts, and washers. In the Browser, these structured parts are clearly identified by their unique icon. This indicates that they were created using a specific tool, and what the part is without requiring you to read or understand the part's name.

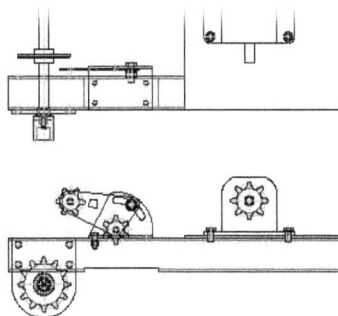

Lesson: Standard Parts

Overview

This lesson describes industry standard parts and how you can insert them into your assembly designs.

You can use industry standard parts in your designs for many reasons. If you find an industry standard part that meets or exceeds the requirements of your design, note that they are cheaper and more readily available than custom parts. Because these parts are purchased parts, you do not want to spend valuable design and documentation time researching available parts and then drawing them. When you insert a part based on an industry standard into your drawing, you save valuable design time and ensure that the component you add is an available standard part.

In the following illustration, a standard bolt, nut, and washers were added to a section view of an assembly by specifying the industry standard to be used, the diameter, and then the start point and endpoint of the bolted connection.

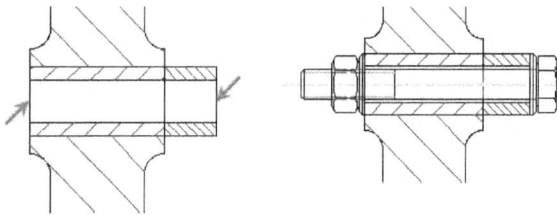

Objectives

After completing this lesson, you will be able to:

- Describe standard parts and their benefits.
- Insert standard parts by accessing them through the parts library.
- Create and edit favorites in the Standard Parts Library palette.
- Insert standard parts by accessing the commands from the toolbar or menus.
- Insert individual screws, nuts, and washers and also insert screw connections of screws, nuts, and washers.
- Create a screw template and insert a screw connection based on a screw template.
- Change standard part representations between symbolic, simplified, and standard.
- Add a note with a leader line to a standard part.

About Standard Parts

With an understanding of what standard parts are, their benefits, and their characteristics in a drawing, you learn why it is important to understand the different methods of inserting standard parts into your drawing.

In the following illustration, the Ribbons and flyout toolbars for inserting specific standard content are shown. As indicated by the icons in the Ribbon, you can select from a number of different types of parts.

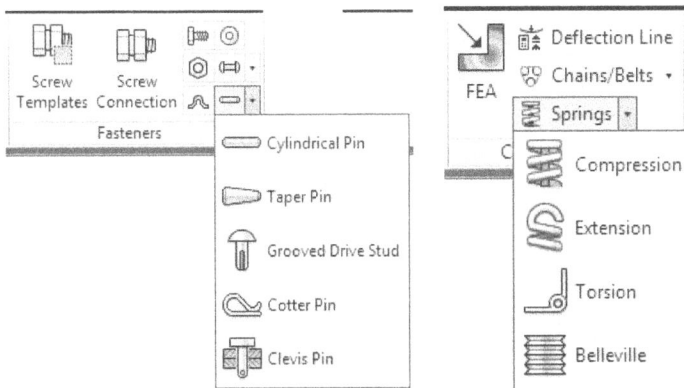

Definition of Standard Parts

A standard part is a commercially available part that has been accepted and identified as a standard part by one of the regulatory industry standard organizations. There is a wide range of standard fastener parts that you can use in your designs ranging from locking parts, such as retaining rings, split pins, rivets, and drill bushings to screw connections of bolts, washers, and nuts.

All of the standard parts are located in the content library. The content library is a single database file that contains all of the installed industry standards and their defined content.

Because of the different types of standard parts, the method of sizing a standard part when you insert it into the drawing can vary. For some parts you can specify all of the sizes in a dialog box and for other parts you are prompted for its length or size in the drawing window.

When you insert a standard part into the drawing, the part is automatically added to the bill of materials (BOM) database. If Mechanical structure is enabled, not only is the part added to the BOM, but the part component definition and its component view are added to the current structure level.

When you place standard parts over other objects, the background objects are automatically hidden. The type of hide situation created depends on whether structure is enabled. If structure is enabled, an associative hide situation is created and the Create Hide Situation dialog box opens. If structure is not enabled, a 2D hide situation is created and background objects are automatically hidden by the Hide Invisible Edges command.

> If mechanical structure is ON when you add standard parts and features to the drawing they are added as mechanical structure content. When mechanical structure is OFF, standard parts and features are added to the drawing as non-structured content.

Industry Standards

Parts in the library are organized by standards that are accepted worldwide. The available standards depend on what was selected during the installation of the software. It also depends on the standards that are selected in the Options dialog box, in the *AM:Standard* Parts tab.

Some of the standards that are available in the AutoCAD Mechanical software are as follows:

- **DIN -** Deutsches Institut fr Normung (German Institute for Standards)
- **ISO -** International Standards Organization
- **ANSI -** American National Standards Institute
- **BSI -** British Standards Institute
- **JIS -** Japanese Industrial Standard
- **GB -** Chinese National Standard

Option Settings

You can modify the default behaviors of standard parts in the Options dialog box, in the *AM:Content* tab. You can specify which database of standard parts to use and the order in which they are displayed. You can modify which parts are available for selection and in what order. You can determine whether a hide situation is automatically added, if centerlines are used, and what the default representation should be.

AM: Content Tab

The *AM:Content* tab in the Options dialog box contains options and settings that are divided into categories of Content Libraries Management, Content Behavior on Insertion, Object Properties Overrides, and Default Representation For Standard Content.

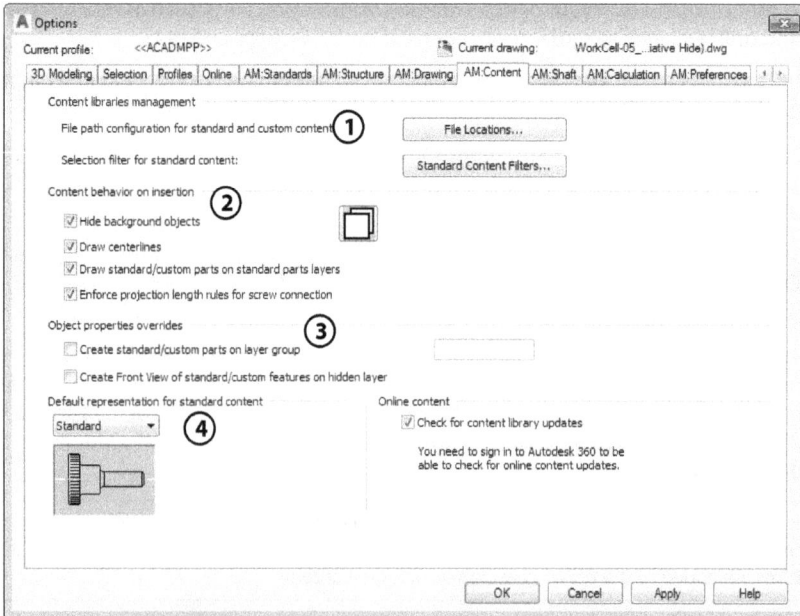

1. In the Database area, you can select and configure the database of standard content and the standards that you want to access.

2. In the Standard Content Behavior area, you can set how the parts and features should display in different conditions and if they are created on the layer that has been assigned to standard parts.

3. In the Object Properties Overrides area, you can specify whether you want standard parts to be placed on a layer group and specify the group. You can also set whether you always want the front view to be placed on the hidden layer.

4. In the Representation area, you can select how you want the standard content to display in the drawing. For 2D you can select Standard, Simplified, or Symbolic. 3D representations are for Mechanical Desktop and have the options of Standard or Detailed.

Content Behavior On Insertion

The layers on which the geometry for standard parts are created depend on the Create Standard Parts On Standard Parts Layer setting in the Content Behavior area and the settings for layers and objects in the active standard.

Draw Standard/Custom Parts On Standard Parts Layer - On

When you add standard parts to your drawing and the Draw Standard/Custom Parts On Standard Parts Layers checkbox is selected, all aspects of the standard part are created on the standard content layers. This includes the definition for the standard part and the geometry that represents the standard part. The default names for standard part layers have the letter N as a suffix (AM_#N).

If you have one of the three contour layers or the hidden layer current when you add standard parts, the definition for that part resides on the corresponding layer name with an N suffix. Therefore, if layer AM_3 is current and you add a standard part, the definition for that part resides on layer AM_3N. If a layer other than a contour or hidden layer is current, the definition is created on layer AM_0N.

The benefit of having this option on is that you can quickly toggle the visibility of all of the inserted standard parts on and off.

Draw Standard/Custom Parts On Standard Parts Layer - Off

When you add standard parts to your drawing and clear the Draw Standard/Custom Parts On Standard Parts Layer checkbox, all aspects of the standard part are created on the layers that have been defined for the objects in the Drafting category. Therefore, instead of a centerline for standard parts being on layer AM_7N, it is located on layer AM_7. The definition of the standard part is located on one of the three contour layers or on the hidden layer depending on which one is current. If a layer other than a contour or hidden layer is current, the definition is created on layer AM_0.

> The previous explanations use the default layer names. If you have renamed the Mechanical layers, those layer names are used as you create the drawings. Additionally, the previous explanations assume that the standard is set to use the default option that enables the AutoCAD Mechanical software to create standard content on contours or hidden layers.

Example of Standard Parts

The most commonly used standard parts in assemblies consist of screws, bolts, nuts, and washers. The ability to quickly insert those parts into your assembly enables you benefit from using the tools to insert standard parts. You can also use the tools when you require standard parts that you do not use frequently to be added to your design. If they were not readily accessible for reuse, you would have to research the available sizes of the parts and how to correctly draft them in the drawing.

In the following illustration, the assembly required the inclusion of a drill bushing. The part also required a new hole to be defined for the bushing to pass through. Using the standard parts Drill Bushings with Hole command, the drill bushing was inserted into the assembly, a hole feature was added to the component view for the part through which the bushing passes, and hidden line calculation was computed. This was all done by selecting the required drill bushing and specifying the start points and endpoints for the hole through which the drill bushing passes.

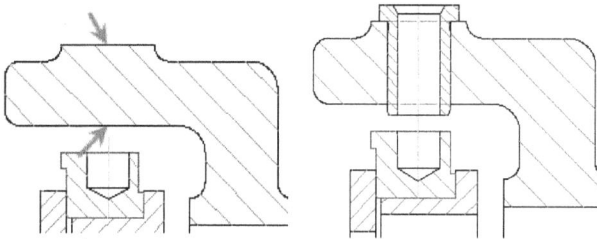

Inserting Standard Parts Using the Parts Library

You can access and insert the parts and features defined in an industry standard using the Content Libraries palette. To insert parts into your drawing from this palette, you need to know which command to use to open the palette and how to navigate through the palette.

Access

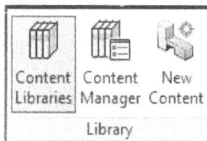

Command Line: AMCONTENTLIB

Ribbon: Content tab > Library panel > Content Libraries

Menu Bar: Content > Content Libraries

Content Libraries

The Content Libraries is a palette that you can position or dock in the location that suits your requirements. As with other palettes, you can set it to automatically hide to conserve screen area and anchor it on the left or right side of the screen.

The Content Libraries palette is composed of three panes: Content, Favorites, and Details. You can collapse the display of the Content or Favorites panes to have more display area for the other pane. To have more display area for the Details pane, click and drag the vertical dividing bar to the left. Dragging the divider all the way to the left, collapses the entire display of both the Content and Favorites panes.

In the Details pane, you can change the size of the images being displayed and select between displaying the content in an icon view or list view.

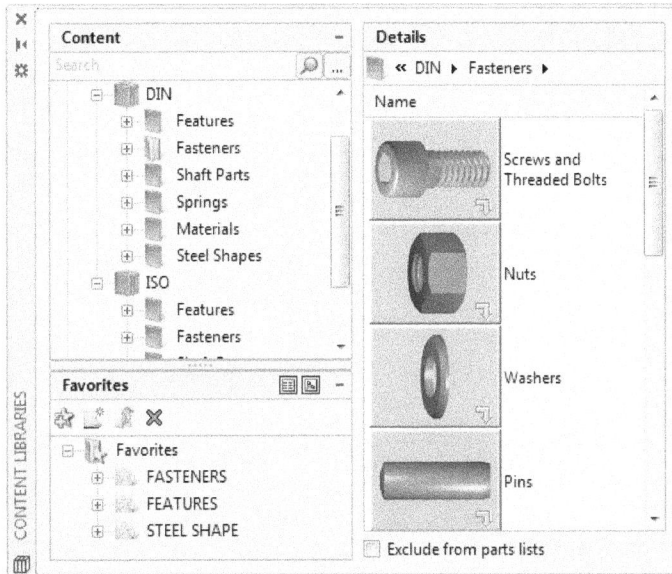

To change the palette settings for anchoring, auto-hiding, etc., right-click on the title bar for the palette and then click the required option in the shortcut menu. You can access the options to change the icons in the Details pane by right-clicking in an open area of the Details pane and then clicking View Options.

Content Use and Navigation

The Content Libraries palette lists the content first by the individual industry standards and then by the categories of parts within those standards.

To reuse standard content from the Content Libraries, select the part or feature and then select the view that you want to insert into the drawing. You can select the standard content in the Content, Favorites, or Details pane and select the view that you want to insert by clicking it in the Detail pane. After clicking the view, you can add it to your drawing after supplying the values and criteria as prompted for that standard content.

In the Content and Favorites panes, you can navigate to the required content using a tree view or list view of the content. You can also use the Details pane to navigate through the Content or Favorites panes. The content that you navigate through depends on which of the two panes had content selected last. To navigate the content shown in the Details pane, you can either click the preview images in the pane or click the level or separator arrows in the navigation bar located below the pane's title bar.

In the following illustration, a DIN standard radial bearing is selected in the Standard Parts tree. The available views that can be selected and inserted are shown in the Details pane.

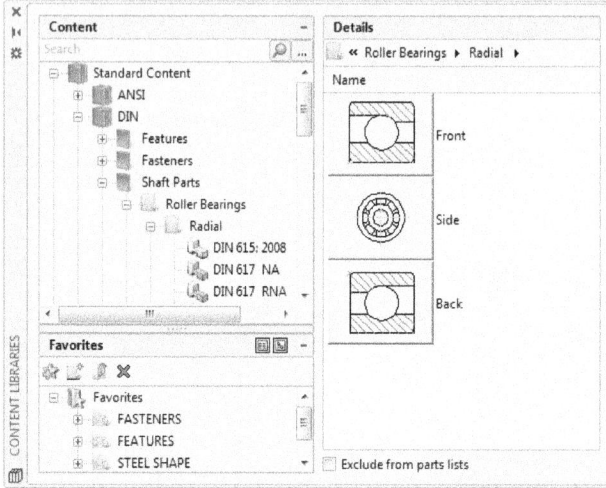

Process: Inserting Standard Parts and Features Using the Contents Libraries

The following illustration shows the common process of inserting standard parts and features by accessing them from the Content Libraries. While the steps to insert the different standard components are very similar, a step for a specific part might vary from those shown.

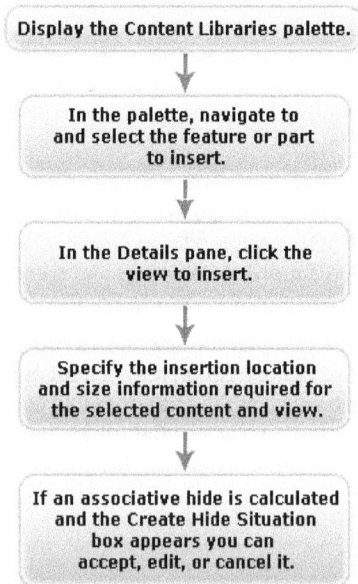

Standard Part Library Favorites

When you use the Standard Part Library palette, you can access and insert standards based parts and features into your designs. Through the configuration and use of the Favorites pane in the Standard Part Library palette, you can reuse the same industry standard content more efficiently and consistently. To achieve these benefits, you must know how to create and edit favorites in the Standard Parts Library palette.

In the following illustration, the DIN 913: 1980 standard fastener was added to the Favorites. The name of the entry for the favorite was changed to better correspond to the terminology used by the user setting up this favorite.

Content Libraries Favorites

To make it more efficient to access the same standard content from the Content Libraries palette, you can add the standard parts and features that you use most often to the Favorites pane.

You can add standard content to the Favorites pane following a workflow going from the top left pane to the bottom left pane. To add a favorite to the Favorites pane, right-click on the feature or part in the Content pane and click Add To Favorites. Because the content in the Favorites pane comes from the Content pane, the Favorites pane becomes a subset of the content.

After you have added the feature or part to your favorites, you can set the favorite entry to insert a specific view and even a set size. To set the view and size properties for a Favorites entry, you must first change the display to List View from the default Tree View.

The options for defining the view and size depend on what is available for that standard content. When you define the size, you can define all aspects of the size or just define the first part of its size. A partially defined size displays with a question mark for the undefined size.

You can organize your favorites by creating folders and nested folders. To list a favorite part or feature in a custom folder, you can add the content directly to the folder or move an existing favorite into the custom folder.

To add a favorite directly to a custom folder, before selecting to add the part or feature, you can select the folder in the Favorites pane. You can move an existing favorite to a different folder in the Favorites pane by dragging and dropping that entry to the required location.

The configuration of your favorites in the Favorites pane is stored in the file *Favorites.gdb*. This file is located at *C:\Users\<username>\AppData\Roaming\Autodesk\AutoCAD Mechanical<version>\<release>\<language>\Acadm\Std Part Favorites* for Windows 7. After you have configured your Favorites content, you can share your *Favorites.gdb* file with other users so that they do not need to configure the same list of favorites.

In the following illustration, the Favorites pane displays the favorites content in both tree view and list view. The corresponding view option icon for that view is also identified.

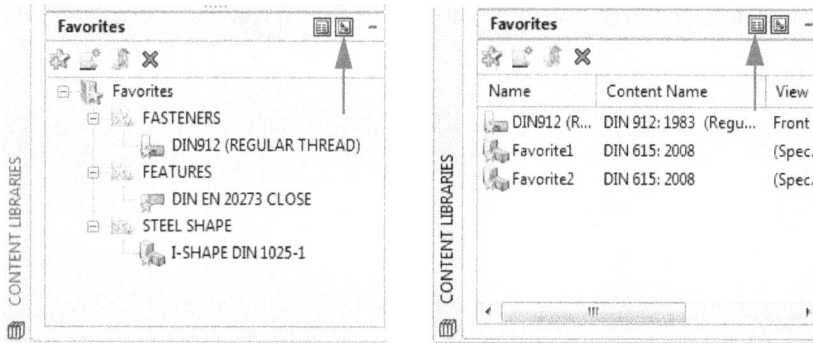

Tree View	List View

Setting Combinations for a Favorite

Each entry of a favorite can have a different setting for the view and size setting. The default setting for a favorite is to specify the view and size during insertion into the drawing.

You can configure a favorite with different combinations of view and size settings. The possible setting combinations for a favorite are as follows:

- The view is set to specify during insertion and the size is set to specify during insertion.
- The view is preset to a defined view and the size is fully or partially defined.
- The view is set to specify during insertion and the size is fully or partially defined.
- The view is preset to a defined view and the size is set to specify during insertion.

In the following illustration, the same standard part was added as a favorite four times. Each entry has different settings for its view and size options to show examples of the different possible combinations.

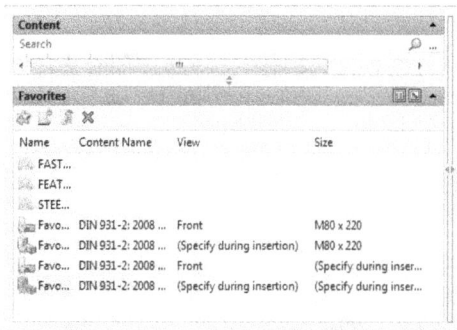

> 💡 If all of the content that you need is defined as favorites, increase the area for the Favorites pane by collapsing the display of the Content pane.

> 💡 To only use the Details pane to insert content from Favorites, select a favorite or folder in the Favorites pane and then drag the vertical divider all the way to the left.

Process: Creating a Standard Part Library Favorite

The following illustration shows the process of adding an entry to the Favorites pane in the Standard Part Library palette.

In the Favorites pane, select the folder where you want the new favorite created.

↓

In the Standard Parts pane, right-click the feature or part you want added as a favorite. Click Add To Favorites.

↓

Enter a name for the new favorite.

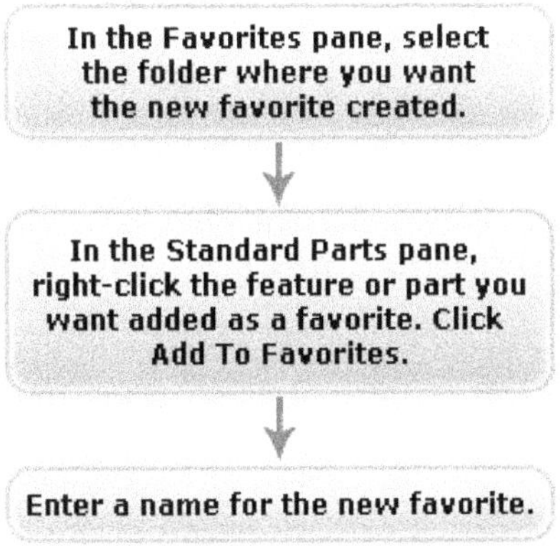

> 💡 You can create a favorite from a standard part or feature that has already been inserted into the model space. To create a favorite from standard content in the drawing, select the content in model space to activate its grip. After selecting the content, right-click and drag and drop to the Favorites pane. The size and view settings for the new favorite match the settings for the content that was selected in the model space.

Process: Preconfiguring Values for a Standard Part Library Favorite

The following illustration shows the process of preconfiguring view and size values for an entry in the Favorites pane in the Standard Part Library palette.

Set the Favorites pane to List View.

↓

For the entry of the favorite, select the view or define the size to insert.

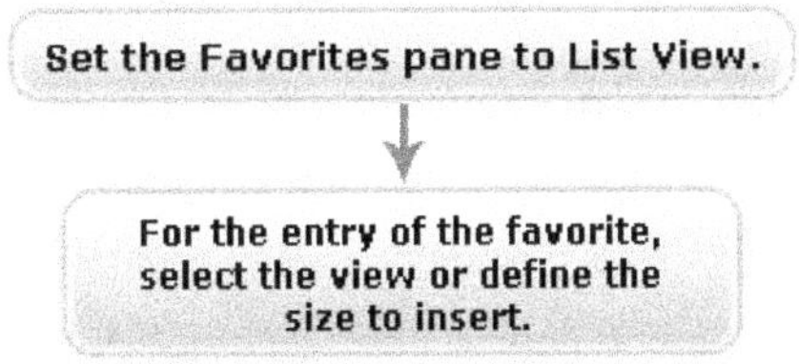

Inserting Standard Parts Using the Ribbon and Menus

You can access and insert specific parts from the content libraries by using individual commands for the different standard part types. To directly access and insert specific part types, you need to learn which standard parts have commands that you can use, where you can access those commands, and the overall steps to insert the components.

Accessing the Commands to Insert Standard Parts

When you access the standard parts through the Content Libraries palette, the parts are initially divided and displayed by the industry standard. To list the components by the type of standard part and then by the standard, start the command for that specific standard part. When you start the command for a specific standard part, the Select dialog box for that component lists all of the available parts for that component. In that listing, the parts are displayed in the order that you have set in the Options dialog box, in the *AM: Content* tab.

You can start the command to select and insert a specific standard part using the *Content* tab on the Ribbon or using the Content menu on the menu bar. The standard part option for steel shapes and fastener type standard parts is accessed directly on the Content tab of the Ribbon while the drill bushing parts are found on the menu bar in the Content menu.

In the following illustration, the Ribbons and flyout toolbars for inserting specific standard content are shown. Note that the icons in the Ribbon indicate that there are a number of different types of parts that you can select and insert into the drawing.

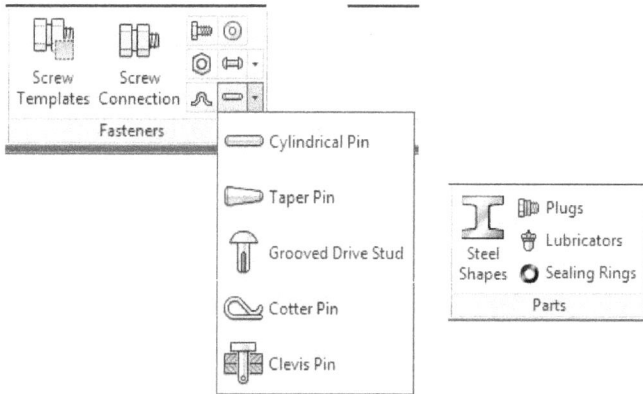

Icon	Command	Description
	Steel Shapes	Enables you to create parts based on common steel shapes, such as I-beams, angle irons, channels, tubes, and solid bar stock.
	Cylindrical Pins	Use to insert solid, tube, split, and threaded pins.
	Taper Pins	Use to insert solid pins that taper their diameter from one end to the other.
	Grooved Drive Studs	Use to insert different shaped studs with grooves.

	Cotter Pins	Use to insert cotter pins.
	Plain Rivets	Use to insert various headed rivets. At least one head of the rivet extends beyond the surface of the material being fastened together.
	Countersunk Rivets	Lists all rivets with at least one head that is countersunk.
	Clevis Pins	Use to insert headed and headless clevis pins.
	Plugs	Use to insert threaded plugs from the DIN standard with fine threads or pipe threads.
	Lubricators	Use to insert fittings for lubricating a mechanism.
	Sealing Rings	Inserts a solid washer-shaped sealing ring.
	Drill Bushings	Use to insert headed and headless drill bushings.
	Drill Bushings with Hole	Use to insert a headed or headless drill bushing and create the hole into which it is inserted. (Not available on the Ribbon).

Procedure: Inserting Standard Parts Using The Ribbon and Menus

To use the common procedure for inserting standard parts after accessing the command from the Ribbon or menu, complete the following steps. While the steps to insert the different standard components are very similar, a step for a specific part might vary from what is listed here.

1. Start the command for the component that you want to select and insert.

2. In the Select dialog box for the component type, in the Content pane or Details pane, click the industry standard and then the specific type of component that you want to insert.

3. In the Details pane, click the view direction that you want to insert into the drawing.

4. In the drawing window, click to specify the insertion point.

5. Specify the length, endpoint, or rotation angle depending on the required input.

6. In the dialog box, select the size to insert from the list of industry sizes.

7. Click Finish.

8. If requested, drag or the size of the component.

9. If an associative hide is calculated and the Create Hide Situation dialog box opens, edit, accept, or cancel its creation.

Inserting Screw Components

You can insert screws, nuts, and washers one at a time as you would insert pins, rivets, or drill bushings. By directly executing the command to insert one of these screw components, you can save time by focusing your selection on a specific type of part. Inserting a screw connection enables you to select multiple screw components and their corresponding holes.

By knowing which command to use to insert individual parts or a collection of screws, nuts, and washers, you can save design time by using easily available industry standard parts. You also benefit by automatically following your configured drafting standards.

In the following illustration, various sized bolts, nuts, and washers were added to the assembly to finish its design.

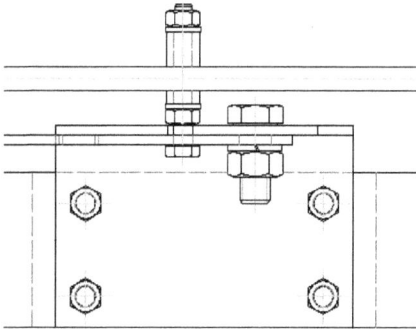

Accessing the Commands to Insert Screw Connection Components

Access

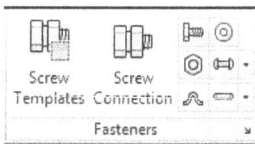

Ribbon: Content tab > Fasteners panel

Menu: Content > Fasteners

You can start the command to select and insert a screw connection, screw, nut, or washer on the Ribbon by selecting the Content tab > Fasteners panel.

Icon	Command	Description
	Screw Connection	Use to specify and insert a combination of fastener parts and holes into your design at one time.
	Screw	Use to insert a single industry standard screw or bolt.
	Nut	Use to insert a single industry standard nut.
	Washer	Use to insert a single industry standard washer.

Screw Connection Dialog Box

When you start the **Screw Connection** command, the Screw Connection dialog box opens. In it, you can select and define the view direction for the parts you are defining, the parts and holes that need to be created, and their sizes.

Screw connections that are added to a drawing in which Mechanical structure has been enabled add the part's component definitions to the active level. If you include holes in your screw connection definition, any holes that are created are automatically added to the part's component view definition that the hole goes through or into.

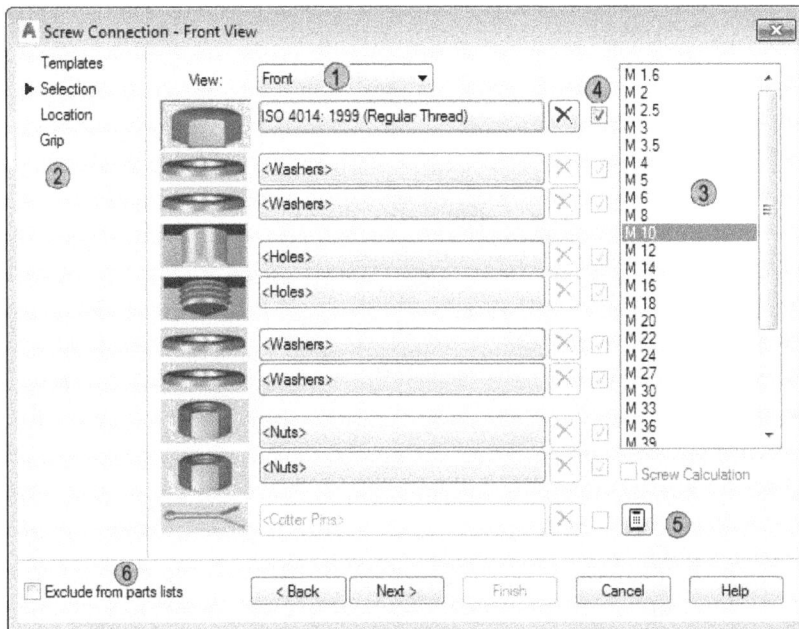

1. Select the view direction that should be inserted for the defined screw connection.

2. Select the parts and hole features that should be added to the drawing when the screw connection is created.

3. Select the industry standard size for the selected part or hole feature.

4. Use to toggle the inclusion of the standard parts on or off. On means the parts are added to the drawing and off means they are not added to the drawing at the time of insertion.

5. Opens the Screw Diameter Estimation dialog box in which you can calculate the minimum and maximum forces for a specific nominal diameter fastener resisting a specified natural load.

6. Selecting this option enables parts to display in the BOM but not to display in any corresponding parts lists.

Screw Connection Representations

You can select from the four representations for the screw assembly in the Screw Assembly Grip Representation dialog box. Click Normal to place a screw assembly view when the material in front of the screw is represented as cutaway, such as with a section view. To only display a cutaway section around the screw assembly, click Sectional. You can click Hidden or No to display the center portion of the screw assembly behind other parts.

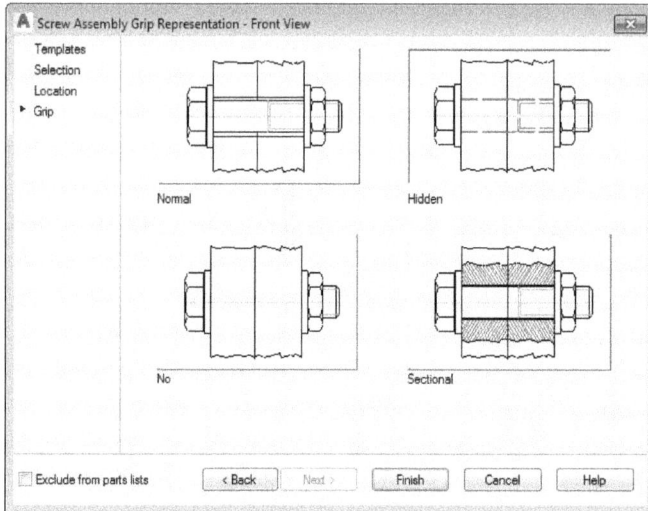

Inserting a Single Screw, Nut, or Washer

When you click to start the command to only insert a screw, nut, or washer, the Select dialog box for that standard part opens. This dialog box is the same as the Content Libraries palette except for the list of parts. In the Select dialog box, only the standard parts for that type are listed. The parts within the categories are listed in the order of industry standards that you set in the Options dialog box, in the AM:Content tab.

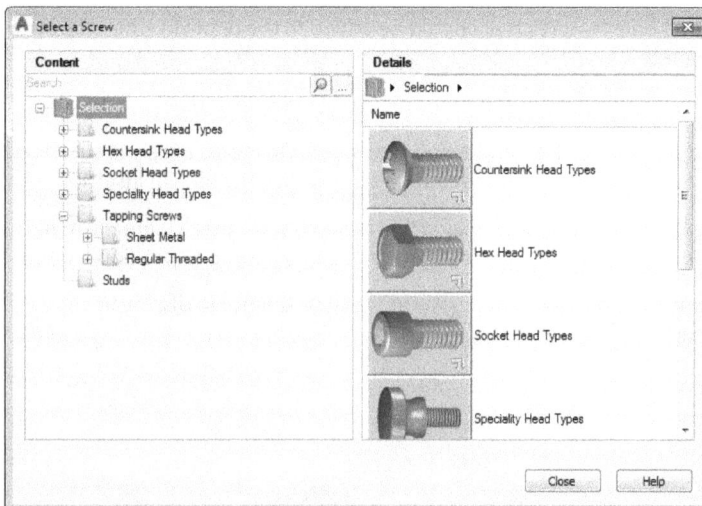

Procedure: Inserting Screw Connections

To define and insert a screw connection into an assembly drawing, complete the following steps:

1. Start the **Screw Connection** command. Note that if you are using Mechanical structure, you need to activate the component view in which you want the standard parts to be inserted.

2. In the Screw Connection dialog box, in the View drop-down list, select a view.

3. In the Screw Connection dialog box, click the screws, washers, holes, nuts, or cotter pin buttons to select the required standard parts and standard hole features.

4. Select the required size from the list of available standard sizes.

5. Click Next.

6. Click in the drawing window to specify the insertion point.

7. Click in the drawing window to specify the endpoint or endpoints depending on the number of holes that you selected to create.

8. In the Screw Assembly Location dialog box, edit any of the values as required.

9. Click Next.

10. Select how you want the bolted connection to display in the assembly and click Finish.

11. In the drawing window, drag the part to the required size and click to accept the size.

Procedure: Inserting Screw Components

To insert a single screw, nut, or washer into an assembly, complete the following steps:

1. Start the Screw, Nut, or Washer command. Note that if you are using Mechanical structure, you need to activate the component view in which you want the standard parts to be inserted before starting the command.

2. In the Select dialog box, select the category for the part that you want to insert.

3. Select the specific standard part that you want to insert.

4. In the Details pane, click the direction of view for the part that you want to insert.

5. In the drawing window, specify the insertion point and rotation angle.

6. In the dialog box, from the list of standard sizes, select the required size.

7. In the drawing window, drag the part to the required size, and click to accept the size.

8. If an associative hide is calculated and the Hide Situation dialog box opens, edit, accept, or cancel its creation.

> If you are adding a number of screw components and their hide calculation conditions reference the same parts in the assembly, either toggle off the Auto Hide Background option or click Cancel in the dialog box. This means you can create a single hide condition for all of the parts at a later time.

Creating and Using Screw Templates

If you often use the same screw connections, you might find it useful to create one template that contains all of the screw connection information. A template stores multiple connections and views that you define when inserting the screw assembly. Instead of selecting each component separately, you can select the saved screw assembly template.

Access

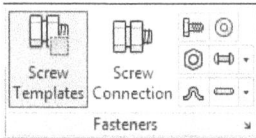

Command Line: AMSCREWMACRO2D

Ribbon: Content tab > Fasteners panel > Screw Templates

Menu: Content > Fasteners > Screw Templates

Screw Assembly Templates Dialog Box

You can create and access predefined screw assemblies in the Screw Assembly Templates dialog box. You can select the template from the list of existing templates in the panel on the right. You can use the tools in the list panel to delete, load, and save templates and you can indicate whether the screw assembly is excluded from the drawing's parts list.

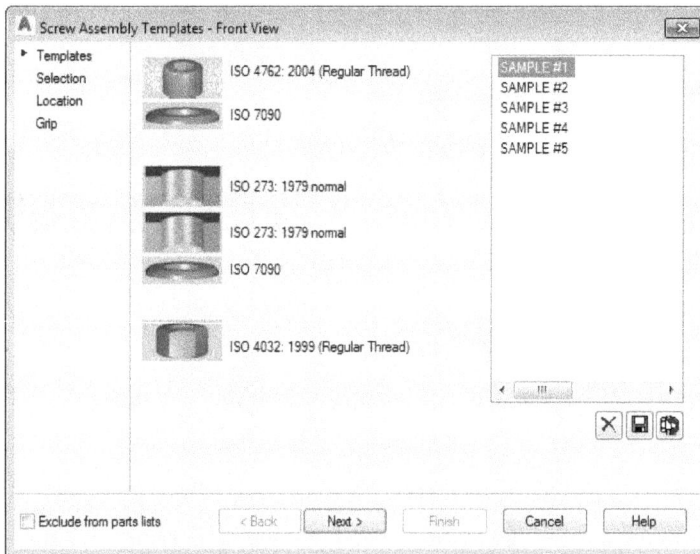

Procedure: Creating Screw Templates

An overview of creating a new screw template for a screw connection is shown in the following steps:

1. Start the **Screw Connection** command.

2. In the Screw Connection dialog box, select the parts and features for the screw connection.

3. Click Back to go to the Screw Assembly Templates page.

4. Click Save The Template.

5. Right-click on the new name in the list and click Rename.

6. Rename the template and press.

Procedure: Using Screw Templates

To access and reuse the information stored in a screw template, complete the following steps:

1. Start the **Screw Template** command.

2. In the Screw Assembly Template dialog box, in the list of templates, double-click on a screw template name.

3. Click Next to specify the insertion point. Follow the procedure for inserting a screw connection.

Changing Part Representations

You might have some standard parts that do not need to be fully represented in the drawing. You can change the representation type for any of the standard parts in a drawing and make changes using the Change Representation command. You can set the default representation of 2D standard parts for all new standard parts that are placed in the drawing in the Options dialog box on the *AM:Standard* tab. Changing the default setting does not affect standard parts that are already placed in the drawing.

In the following illustration, the different part representations are shown for a grooved drive stud.

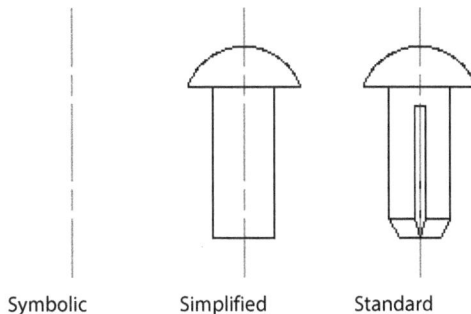

Symbolic   Simplified   Standard

Access

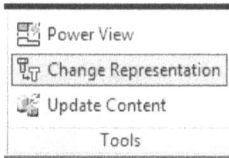

Command Line: AMSTDPREP

Ribbon: Content tab > Tools panel > Change Representation

Menu Bar: Content > Change Representation

🖳 Power View	
🔩 Change Representation	
🔧 Update Content	
Tools	

Switch Representation of Standard Parts Dialog Box

You can select from three different representations in the Switch Representation of Standard Parts dialog box.

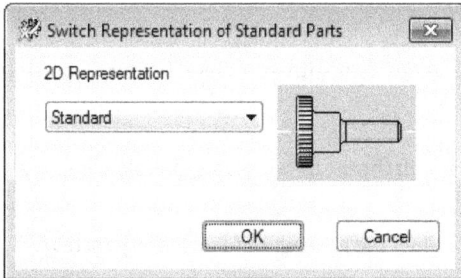

Use the following options with the command:

Option	Description
Symbolic	Displays only a centerline.
Simplified	Displays simplified contours.
Standard	Displays a detailed representation of the part.

Procedure: Changing Part Representations

To change the representation of one or more standard parts, complete the following steps:

1. Start the **Change Representation** command.

2. Select the standard part or parts for which you want to change representation.

3. In the Switch Representation of Standard Parts dialog box, click the required type.

Adding Leader Notes to Standard Parts

You can use the Leader Note command when you want to add text with an associated leader line to your drawing. To add a note with a leader line to a standard part or feature, you need to know how to access the command and how it is used.

In the following illustration, the information in the note was automatically extracted from the selected standard part and formatted based on the selected note template.

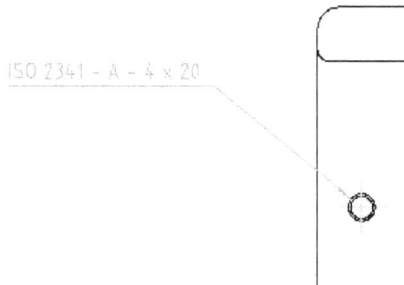

Leader Note Symbols

When you add a leader note, you can select existing drawing geometry so that the leader line points to the selected objects. If you select a Mechanical object, the information for that object is automatically entered into an edit box displayed with the leader line on the screen. The information that is automatically populated and the note's format are both based on a predefined library template configuration for that object type.

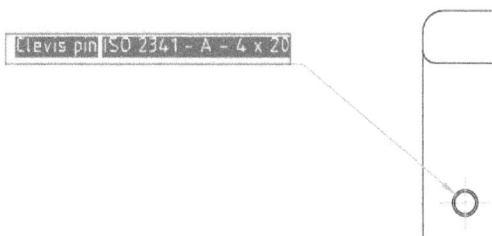

You can create a note template in the *Leader Note* contextual tab in the Ribbon or in the Leader Note Settings dialog box, which you can open through the Options dialog box on the *AM:Standards* tab. You can make a note template with standard text or using formulas and expressions.

Access

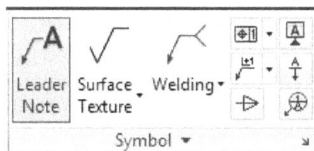

Command Line: AMNOTE

Ribbon: Annotate tab > Symbol panel > Leader Note

Menu Bar: Annotate > Leader Note

Leader Note Contextual Tab

After you click to place the leader note for a standard part or feature, the information for that object is automatically entered into an edit box that is displayed with the leader line on the screen. A Leader Note contextual tab displays in the Ribbon, which enables you to select a defined template and modify the values for the note. To update the note to use a defined template, in the Leader Note contextual tab>Library panel, click Templates and select a template.

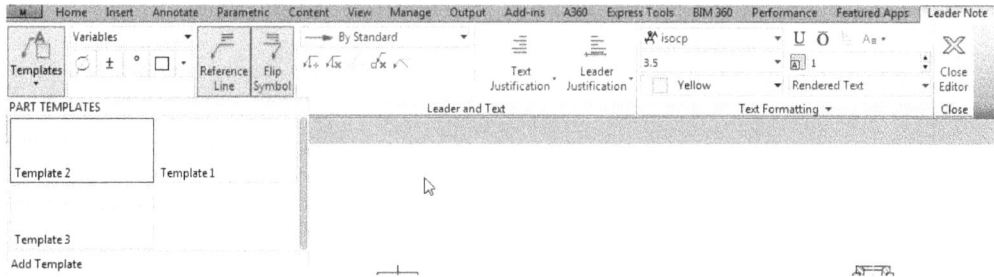

Leader Note Library Templates

The workflow for creating and using note library entries is similar to the workflow for creating and using weld and surface texture symbol library entries. The Library area in the Leader Note Settings dialog box is similar to the Library area in the Weld Symbol and Surface Texture Symbol dialog boxes.

For leader notes, the format of the library in the drawing file always controls the appearance of a leader note added to the drawing. Therefore, if you add one or more note symbols to a drawing and edit that library entry at later, all of the notes in the drawing that are based on that template update to reflect the new configuration. All static text in the note changes to reflect the current configuration while note information based on a variable maintains its value because that value is based on the selected geometry.

The following illustration shows the library area in the Leader Note Settings dialog box.

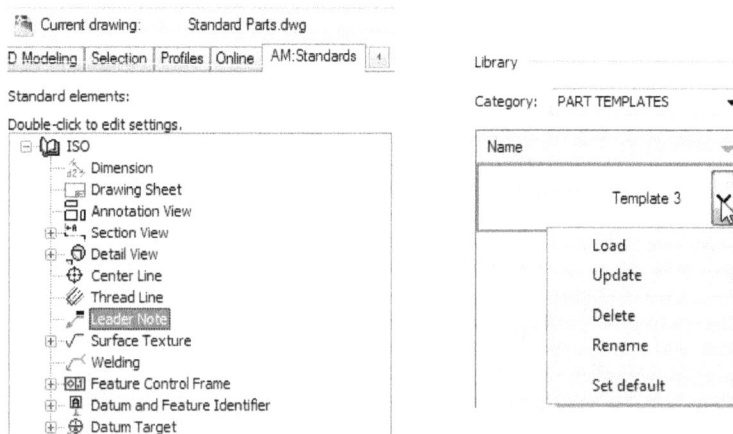

Procedure: Adding Leader Notes to Standard Parts

To add a note with a leader to a standard part, complete the following steps:

1. Start the **Leader Note** command.

2. In the drawing, select the standard part.

3. Specify one or more points for the leader line and press ENTER.

4. In the Leader Note contextual tab, open the list of templates, double-click on the appropriate template for your notation requirements.

5. Edit the note contents as required and click Close Editor.

Exercise: Insert and Notate Standard Parts

In this exercise, you will insert standard parts into a partially finished drawing. You will insert a bushing with hole, a screw connection, and a clevis pin. You will save the screw connection to a template so that it can be easily accessed later. You will also add a note with a leader to a part.

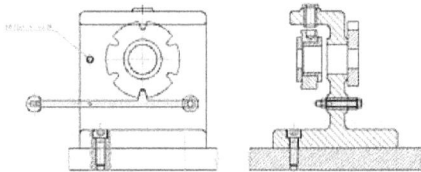

The completed exercise

1. Open *Standard Parts.dwg*.

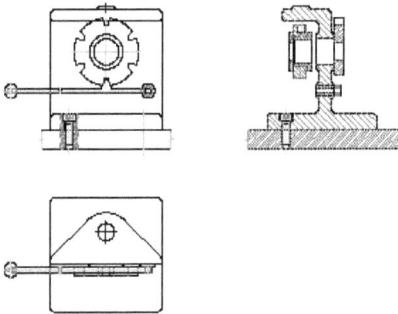

2. Zoom in to the top half of the section view near the upper right area of the drawing window.

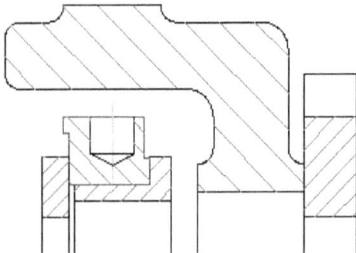

3. On the Status Bar, use the Workspace Switching drop-down list to set the current workspace to **Mechanical**.

4. To begin inserting a drill bushing and new hole in this assembly section view, click the Application Menu and enter **drill** in the search box. Click Drill Bushings With Hole as shown in the following illustration. (Alternatively, you can access it from Content menu > Drill Bushings > Drill Bushing with Hole, or by entering **AMDRBUSHHOLD2D** in the Command Line.

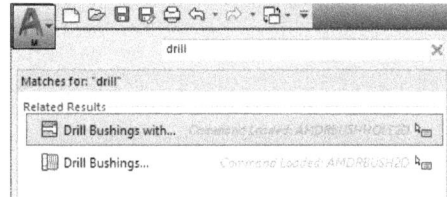

5. In the Select a Drill Bushing with Hole dialog box, in the Details pane:

   - Click Front.
   - Click Headed Type.
   - Click ISO 4247.

6. To specify the insertion point and hole length:

   - Object snap to the midpoint of the top line as shown in the following illustration.
   - Object snap to the midpoint of the bottom line as shown in the following illustration.

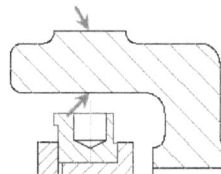

7. In the ISO 4247 - Nominal Diameter dialog box, in the Nominal Diameter, D1 field, enter **8**. Click Finish.

8. In the drawing window, drag the preview down to its maximum size of 20. Click in the drawing window to accept the size of 20.

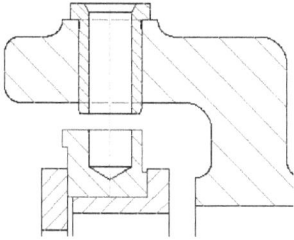

9. Pan down to the lower area of the assembly view.

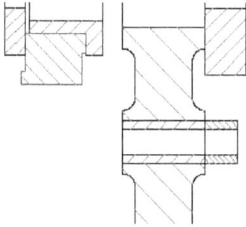

10. To begin defining a screw connection to assemble the lever to the base body:

- Click Content tab > Fasteners panel > Screw Connection.
- In the Screw Connection dialog box, click <SCREWS>.

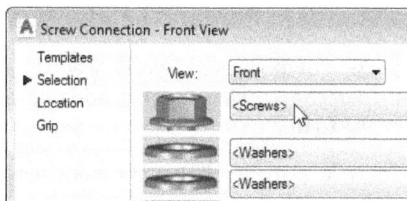

11. To specify the type of screw, in the Select a Screw dialog box, in the Details pane:

- Click Hex Head Types.
- Click ISO 4014: 1999 (Regular Thread).
- Click Front.

12. In the Screw Connection dialog box, click the first <Washers> option.

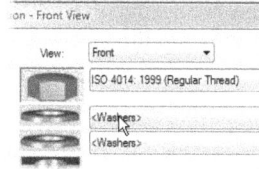

13. To specify the type of washer, in the Select a Washer dialog box, in the Details pane:

- Click Plain.
- Click ISO 7090.

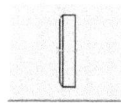

14. To specify the washer on the nut side:

- In the Screw Connection dialog box, click the <Washers> option after <Holes>.
- In the Select a Washer dialog box, click Plain.
- Click ISO 7090.

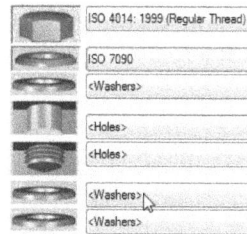

15. To specify the nut:

- In the Screw Connection dialog box, click the first <Nuts> option.
- In the Select a Nut dialog box, click Hex Nuts.
- Click ISO 4032: 1999 (Regular Thread).
- Click Front.

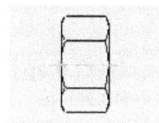

16. In the Screw Connection dialog box, in the list of standard sizes, click **M 5**.

17. Review the screw connection that you have just defined, as shown in the following illustration.

18. To save this configuration as a template:

- Click Back.
- In the Screw Assembly Templates dialog box, under the list of templates, click the Save icon. Note that ISO 4014: 1999 is displayed in the list shown in the following illustration.

19. To insert the screw connection:

- Click Next.
- Click Next again.
- For the insertion point, object snap to the midpoint of the right vertical line.

- For the endpoint of the screw connection, object snap to the midpoint of the left vertical line.

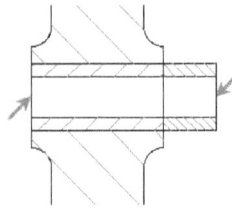

20. In the Screw Assembly Location dialog box, click Next.

21. For the representation, in the Screw Assembly Grip Representation dialog box, click Normal.

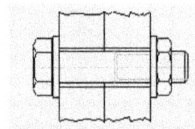

22. Click Finish. The drawing view should now display as shown in the following illustration.

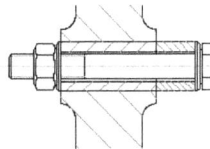

Add a Standard Part and Leader Note

In this section of the exercise, you will add a standard part to a drawing and then add a note with a leader line to that part.

1. Zoom in to the left half of the front view.

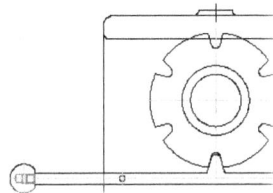

2. To begin adding a clevis pin to the front view, click Content tab > Fasteners panel > Pins drop-down list > Clevis Pin.

3. In the Select a Clevis Pin dialog box:

- Click Headed Type.
- Click ISO 2341: 1986 A.
- Click Left Side.

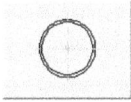

4. To position the clevis pin:

- For the insertion location, object track to the intersection of the centerlines, as shown in the following illustration.
- For the rotation angle, press ENTER.

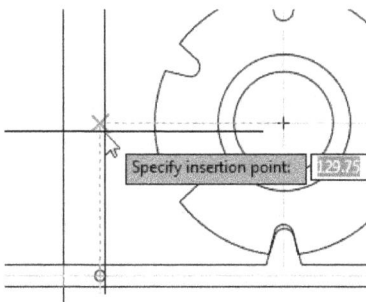

5. In the ISO 2341: 1986 A - Nominal Diameter dialog box, in the Select a Size list for Diameter, click **4**. Click Next.

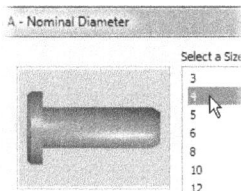

6. In the ISO 2341: 1986 A - Length Selection dialog box, in the Select a Size list for length, click **20**. Click Finish.

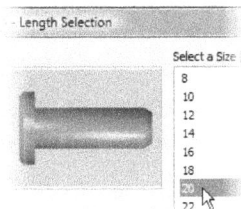

7. A clevis pin is added. To begin adding a leader and note to the clevis pin:

- Click Annotate tab > Symbol panel > Leader Note.
- In the drawing window, select the instance of CLEVIS PIN1.

8. For the points on the leader line:

- Click one point up and to the left of the clevis pin.
- Press ENTER.

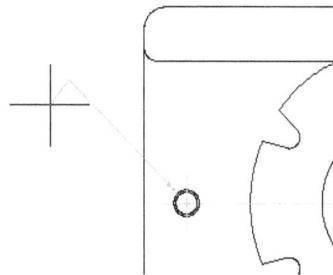

9. To change the leader note settings, do the following:

- In the Leader Note contextual tab > Library panel, click Templates and select Template 3.
- Click Close Editor.

The note color has been changed for printing clarity).

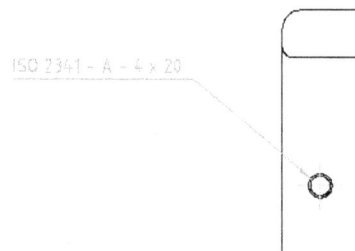

10. Save and close all of the files.

Exercise: Insert from the Content Libraries Palette

In this exercise, you will use the Standard Parts Library palette to insert parts into a design. You will also configure library favorites and then insert parts into the design using those favorites.

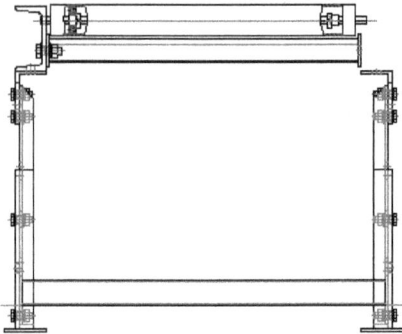

The completed exercise

Content Libraries

In this section of the exercise, you will display the Content Libraries palette, position it for easy access, and insert different content from the library.

1. Open *Standard Parts Library.dwg*.

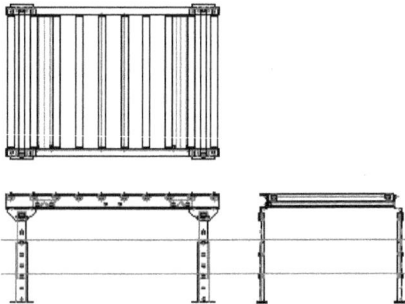

2. To open the Content Libraries, click Content tab > Library panel > Content Libraries.

3. To have the palette anchor to the left side of the screen, right-click on the title bar for the palette and click Anchor Left <.

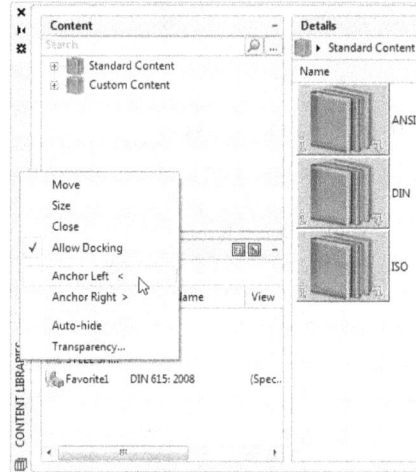

4. Review the display position for the Content Libraries palette. It now displays as a bar along the left side of the drawing window, as shown in the following illustration.

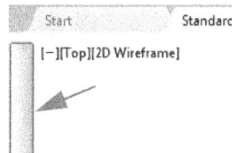

5. Zoom into the top left corner of the right side view as shown in the following illustration.

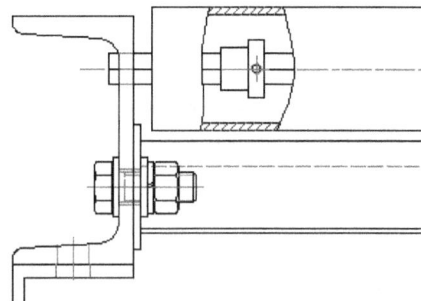

6. To expand the display of the hidden Content Libraries palette, hover the cursor over the palette bar.

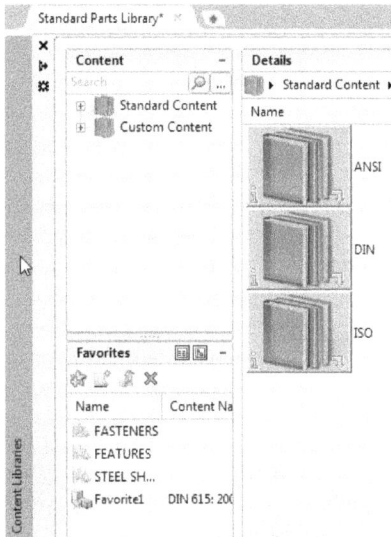

7. To begin inserting a radial bearing into the drawing view, in the Content Libraries palette, do the following:

- In the Content tree, click to expand the categories Standard Content > DIN > Shaft Parts > Roller Bearings > Radial.
- In the tree list, click DIN 615: 2008.
- In the Details pane, click Front.

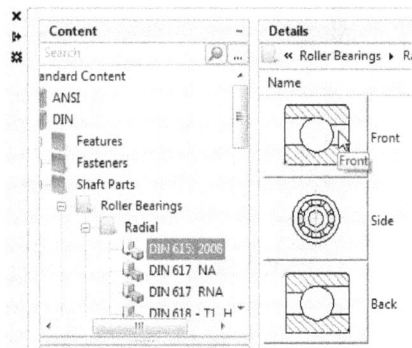

8. For the insertion point, in the drawing window, object snap (click) to the identified intersection location.

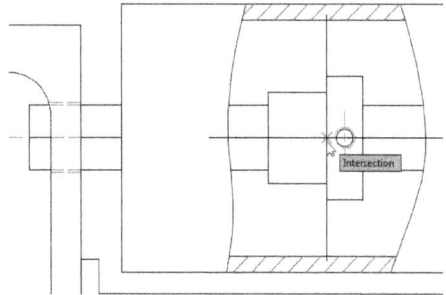

9. Move the cursor left along the centerline and click again to select the centerline as shown in the following illustration.

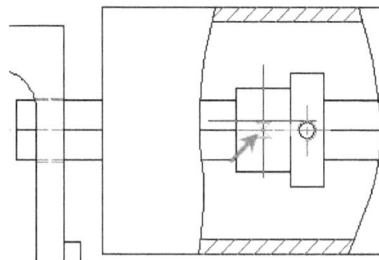

10. In the DIN 615: 2008 dialog box:

- For Inner Diameter, select > = from the drop-down list and then enter **17**, as shown in the illustration.
- For Outer Diameter, select < = from the drop-down list and then enter **44**.

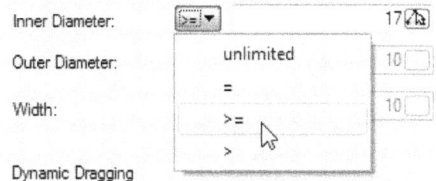

11. In the DIN 615: 2008 dialog box, click Next twice to advance to the Result page.

12. In the DIN 615: 2008 dialog box, in the Result page, do the following:

- Press CTRL and select the three listed results.
- Click Finish.

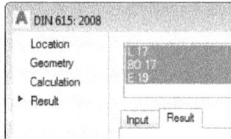

13. To insert the bearing, in the drawing window, move the cursor to the left side and above the top hatching to drag the preview to the largest result size as shown in the following illustration. Click when the largest preview displays.

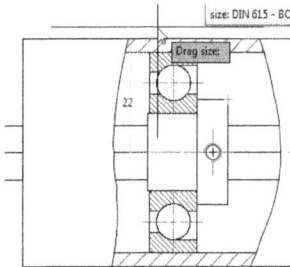

14. To begin adding a piece of rectangular hollow tubing to the design:

- Hover the cursor over the Content Libraries palette title bar.
- In the Standard Content tree, click to expand the categories ISO > Steel Shapes > Square / Rectangular Hollow Section.
- In the tree list, click ISO 4019 -1982 (rectangular).

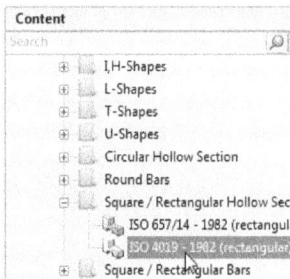

15. In the Details pane, click Right Side.

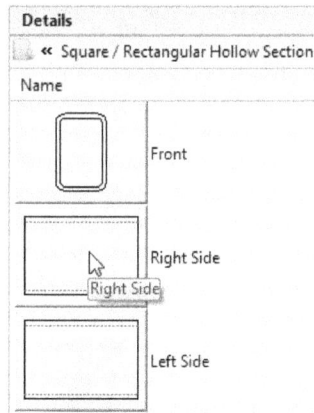

16. To position the steel part:

- For the insertion location, object snap to the intersection of the top construction line with the hidden line as shown in the following illustration.
- When prompted for the rotation angle, press ENTER.

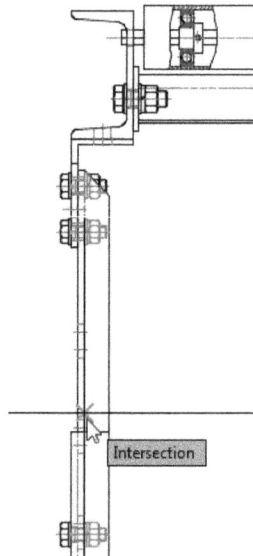

17. In the Size Selection dialog box, in Select a Size list, select 40 x 40 x 2.6. Click Finish.

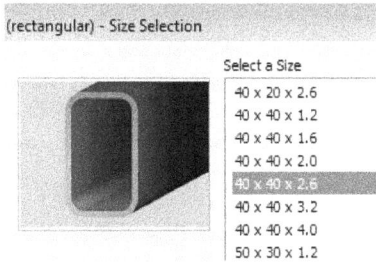

18. To specify the length, object snap to the construction line's intersection on the right hidden line as shown in the following illustration.

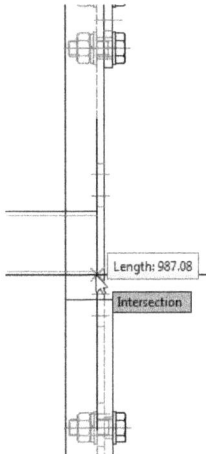

Configure Content Libraries Favorites

In this section of the exercise, you will add standard content to your favorites, organize your favorites by creating a folder, and edit some favorites so that they insert with a set view or size.

1. In the Content Libraries palette, in the Favorites pane, click on Tree view. Expand Favorites and click on Favorites to highlight it.

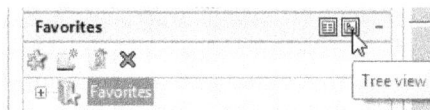

2. To add the rectangular tube to the Favorites pane:

- In the Content tree list, right-click on ISO 4019 -1982 (rectangular) and click Add To Favorites.
- In the Favorites pane for the added favorite (Favorite1), enter **Rectangle Tube** to rename it.

3. In the Content Libraries palette, in the Favorites pane, click Favorites.

4. To add another ISO steel shape to the list of favorites:

- In the Content tree list, under U-Shapes, right-click on ISO 657/11 - 1980 and click Add To Favorites.
- In the Favorites pane for the added favorite, enter **Conveyor Side Rail**.

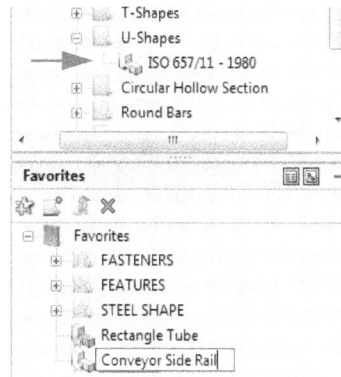

5. To create a custom favorites folder, in the Favorites pane:

- At the top of the tree, right-click on Favorites and click New Folder.
- Rename the new folder to **Conveyor Framework**.

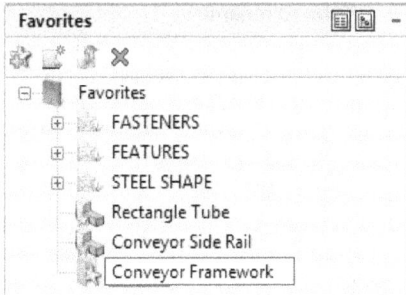

6. Restructure the location of some of the favorites in the Favorites pane by dragging and dropping the favorites Conveyor Side Rail and Rectangle Tube into the folder Conveyor Framework. The favorites are now listed as shown in the following illustration.

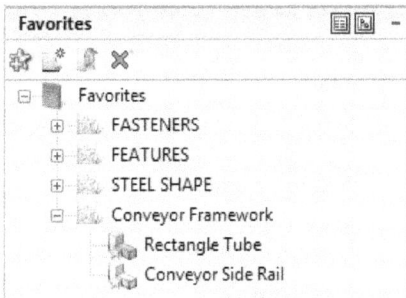

7. To begin adding a DIN set screw directly to the FASTENERS folder in Favorites, in the Favorites pane:

- Expand the FASTENERS folder.
- Click FASTENERS to highlight it.

8. To add the content to favorites:

- In the Standard Content tree, click to expand the categories DIN > Fasteners > Screw and Threaded Bolts > Set Screws.
- Right-click on DIN 913: 1980 (Regular Thread) and click Add To Favorites.
- Enter **Set Screw – 4x5**.

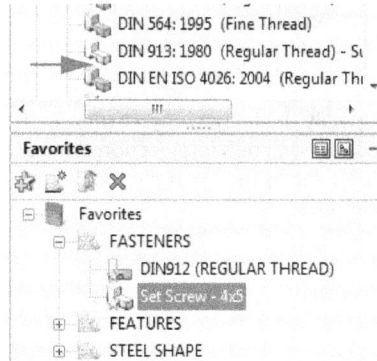

9. To begin setting the size for the set screw, on the Favorites title bar, click List View.

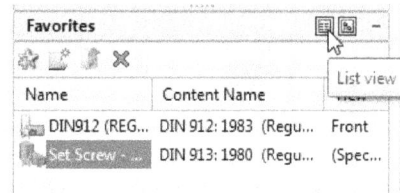

10. In the Size list for Set Screw – 4x5, click on Specify during insertion to open the drop-down list and then select (Define size…).

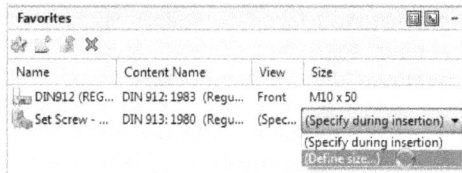

11. In the DIN 913:1980 ---Nominal Diameter dialog box:

- Note in the title bar, DIN 913: 1980 - Superseded by DIN EN ISO 4026: 2004.
- On the Diameter page, click M4. Click Next.
- On the Length page, click 5. Click Finish. In the Contents Library, the size displays as shown in the following illustration.

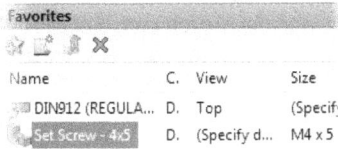

12. To navigate to the Conveyor Framework folder, in the Favorites pane:

- Click Up to go up one folder level.
- Double-click on the Conveyor Framework folder.

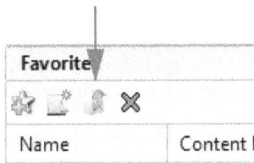

13. In the View list for Rectangle Tube, select Right Side.

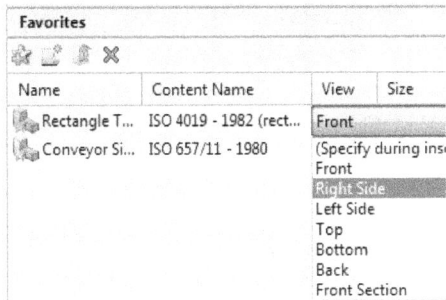

14. To begin adding the bearing directly to the Favorites folder:

- On the Favorites title bar, click Tree view.
- Drag and drop DIN 615: 2008 from the Standard Content >DIN > Shafts Parts > Roller Bearings > Radial to the Favorites folder.

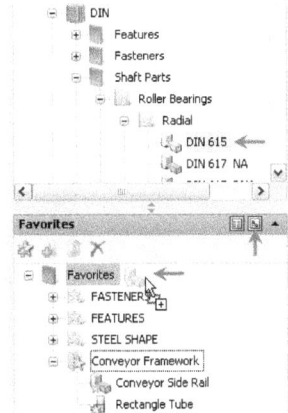

15. Right-click on Favorite1 to rename it to **Bearing-BO 17**.

16. On the Favorites title bar, click List view.

17. To specify the view that you want to insert for the bearing, in the View list, click Front.

18. To begin specifying the insertion size, in the Size list, click (Define size...).

19. In the DIN 615: 2008 dialog box, for each value first set it to =, and then specify the following values:

- In the Inner Diameter field, enter **17**.
- In the Outer Diameter field, enter **44**.
- In the Width field, enter **11**.
- Click Finish.

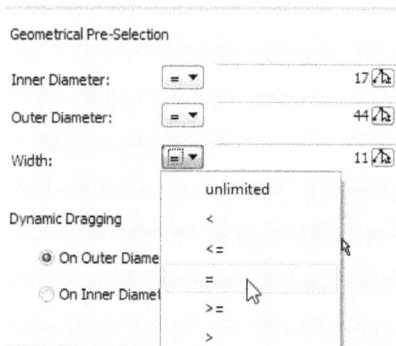

Geometrical Pre-Selection

Inner Diameter:	= ▼	17
Outer Diameter:	= ▼	44
Width:	= ▼	11

unlimited
<
<=
=
>=
>

Dynamic Dragging

◉ On Outer Diame

◯ On Inner Diamet

20. Review the settings for the bearing. They display as shown in the following illustration.

Name	C	View	Size
FASTENERS			
FEATURES			
STEEL SHAPE			
Conveyor Fra...			
Bearing-BO 17	D	Front	BO 17 - 17 x 44 x 11

21. To collapse the Content pane and increase the area for the Favorites pane, on the Content title bar, click the **-** sign on the right, as shown in the following illustration.

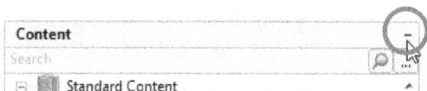

Content

Search

⊟ Standard Content

Insert from Content Libraries Favorites

In this section of the exercise, you will add standard content to your drawing by accessing it from the Favorites pane in the Content Libraries palette.

1. Open *Custom Roller Conveyor.dwg*.

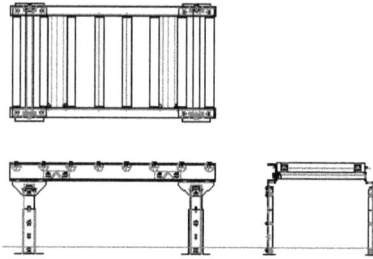

2. Zoom in to the top left corner of the right side view as shown in the following illustration.

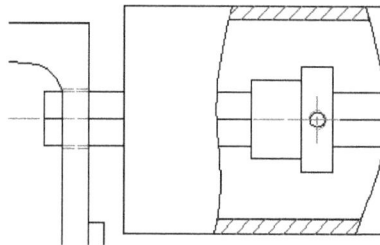

3. To begin inserting the bearing:

- In the Favorites pane, click Bearing-BO 17.
- In the Details pane, click Bearing-BO 17.

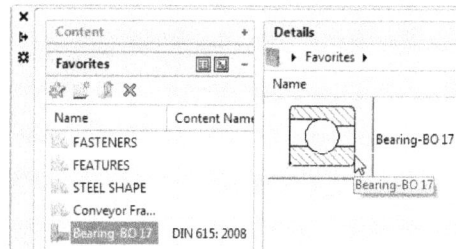

4. Object snap to the identified intersection location.

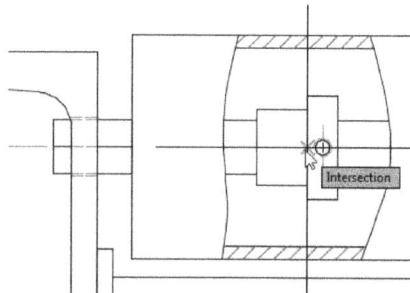

5. Click a point along the centerline as shown in the following illustration.

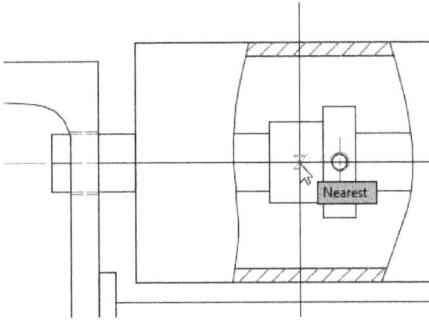

6. To accept the size and position of the bearing:

- In the DIN 615: 2008 dialog box, click Finish.
- Move the cursor to the left of the intersection point and click to place the bearing.

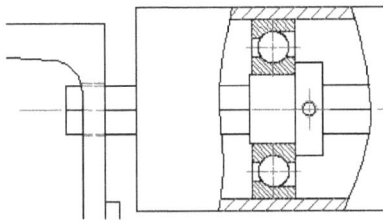

7. To begin adding the set screw to the view:

- In the Favorites pane, double-click on FASTENERS.
- Click Set Screw - 4x5.
- In the Details pane, click Set Screw - 4x5.

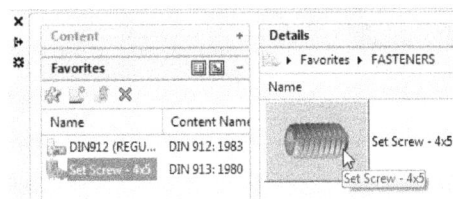

8. In the Select New View dialog box, in the Details pane:

- Click DIN 913:1980 (Regular Thread)-Superseded by DIN EN ISO 4026: 2004.
- Click Top.

9. To position the set screw:

- In the drawing window, object snap to the center of the threaded hole.
- For the rotation angle, press ENTER.

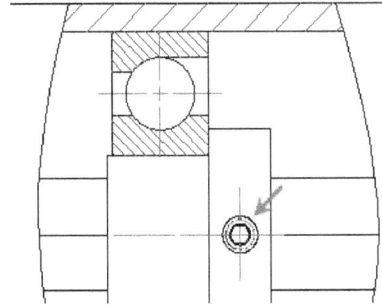

10. Pan and zoom to view the full right side view.

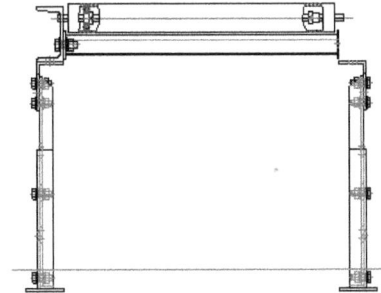

11. To navigate directly to another favorites folder, in the navigation area of the Details pane:

- Click the arrow to the right of Favorites.
- Click Conveyor Framework.

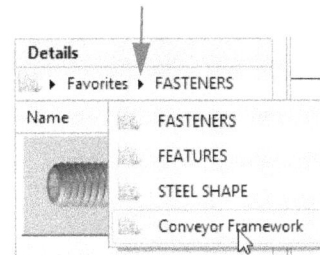

12. In the Details pane, click Rectangle Tube.

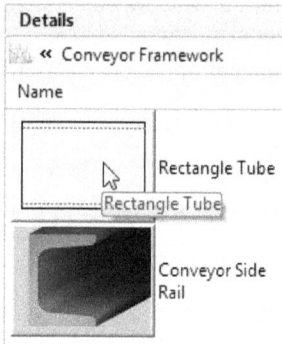

13. To specify the part's insertion and rotation:

- In the drawing window, zoom to the bottom left leg area of the right side view (near the construction line area) and then object snap to the intersection location of the right hidden line and the construction line.

- For the rotation angle, press ENTER.

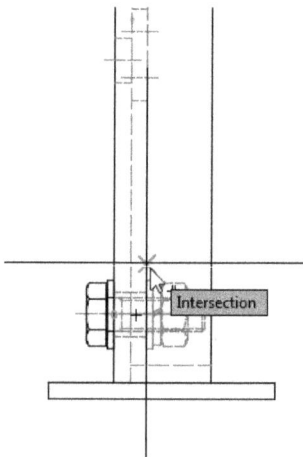

14. In the Size Selection dialog box, list of sizes, select 40 x40 x 2.6. Click Finish.

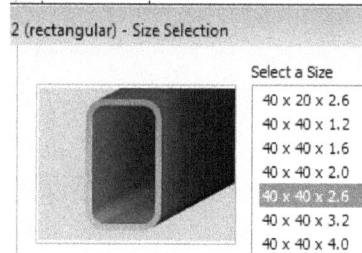

15. To specify the length, object snap to the intersection location of the left hidden line and the construction line in the bottom right leg area.

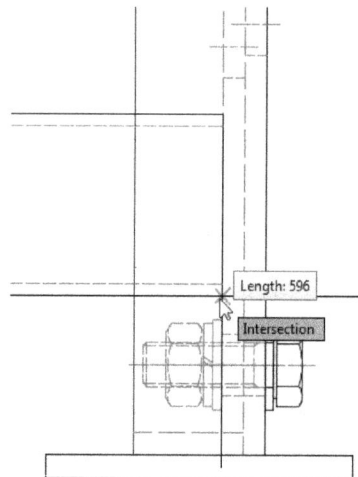

16. Save and close all files.

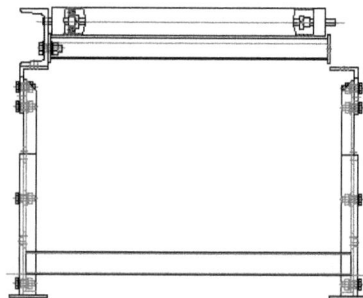

Lesson: Chains and Belts

Overview

This lesson describes how to create custom sprockets and pulleys. You learn how to automatically create chains and belts from a library, how to calculate for length, and how to optimize the chain length.

In the following illustration, the sprockets, chain length, and chain were designed and created using the AutoCAD Mechanical software tools for chains and belts.

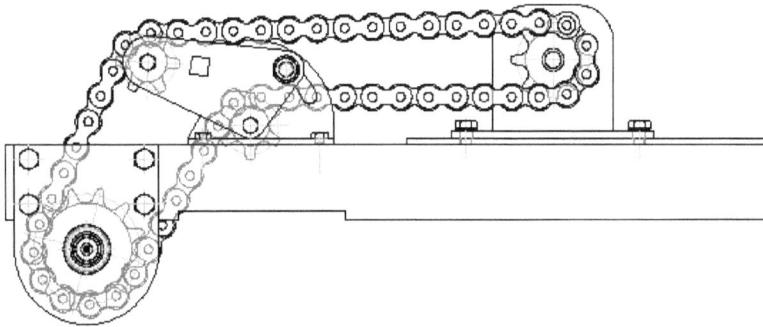

Objectives

After completing this lesson, you will be able to:

- Create sprockets and pulleys for a design.
- Calculate the optimal chain and belt lengths.
- Insert chains and belts into a drawing.

Creating Sprockets and Pulleys

Many machines use belts and pulleys. You can use sprockets to engage a chain and pulleys to engage a belt.

In the following illustration, a sprocket is shown on the left and a pulley for a synchronous belt is shown on the right. Both of these parts were added to the drawing after their standard and size were selected in a dialog box.

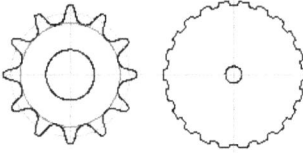

Access

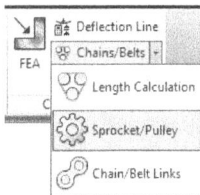

Command Line: AMSPROCKET

Ribbon: Content tab > Calculation panel > Chains/Belts drop-down list > Sprocket/Pulley

Menu: Content > Chains / Belts > Draw Sprocket/Pulley

Procedure: Creating Sprockets and Pulleys

To add a pulley or sprocket to a design, complete the following steps:

1. Start the **Sprocket/Pulley** command.

2. In the Select Pulley and Sprocket dialog box, from the tree view on the left, click the Pulleys or Sprockets category based on your requirements.

3. Under Details, click the type or standard that you want to insert.

4. Specify the center insertion point and rotation angle.

5. Define a chain style.

6. In the dialog box for the size selection, specify the chain size.

7. In the dialog box for geometry, enter the number of teeth for the gear, the number of teeth visible in the drawing, and the shaft diameter.

> To have the sprocket or pulley display with all of its teeth rather than three teeth (the default), the total number of teeth for the selected pulley in the Number of Visible Teeth box.

Calculate Chain and Belt Lengths

With the Belt and Chain Length Calculation command, you can determine the location and length information for belts and chains. You can also set sprocket and pulley locations and the direction in which an idler can be moved. When using the Belt and Chain Length Calculation command, you first create and store intelligent tangencies on sprockets, pulleys, or circles. A red polyline is created around the tangent objects. After the polyline is created, you can do additional calculations and insert a chain or belt along the polyline.

In the following illustration, the highlighted polyline path for the chain was created during the process of calculating its location, tangency, and length. The correct length was established by the calculator when it rotated the tension sprocket and bracket.

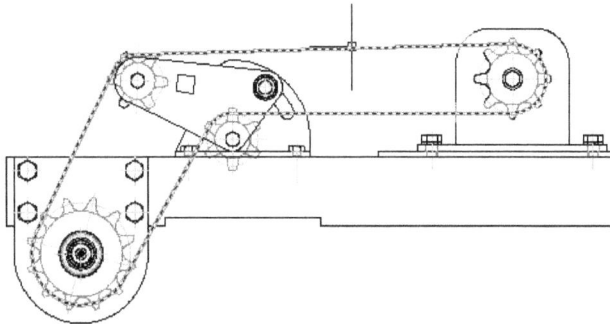

Access

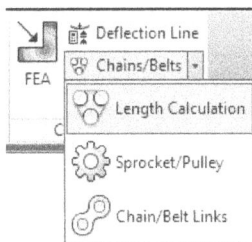

Command Line: AMCHAINLENGTHCAL

Ribbon: Content tab > Calculation panel > Chains/Belts drop-down list > Length Calculation

Menu Bar: Content > Chains / Belts > Length Calculation

Belt and Chain Length Calculation Dialog Box

You can use the Belt and Chain Length Calculation dialog box to conduct multiple calculations. If a tangent polyline between sprockets or pulleys does not exist, the New Tangent Definition Between Sprocket/ Pulley checkbox is automatically selected. If a polyline created with this dialog box already exists, the checkbox is cleared.

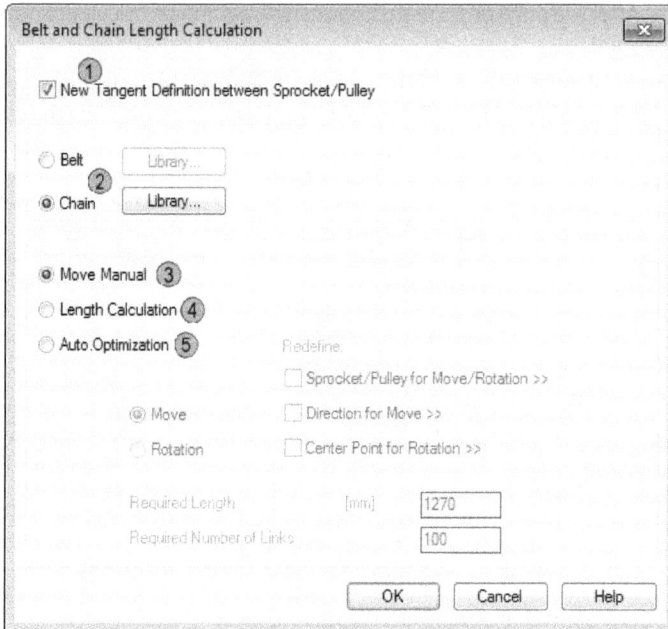

1.   Select this option when you are editing a belt or chain path and want to specify a new tangent path.

2.   Use to select the type of part that you are inserting on the path and its standard and size.

3.   Select to move the pulley, sprocket, or circle manually so that a new length can be calculated.

4.   Use to calculate the total number of chain links required to go around the red polyline. For the results you have the total number of full links and the distance to the next link.

5.   Select to specify a move or rotation condition for the automatic repositioning of the pulley, sprocket, or circle. The sprocket, pulley, or circle is moved in a straight line or along an arc until the property length or number of links is achieved.

Optimizing Error Message

If the optimization fails because too many calculation steps are required, an error message is displayed. To resolve this, you can select Manual and the position of the chain wheel with the cursor to get to the required result. The chain length and number of chain links are displayed on the Command Line so that you can check the result.

Inserting Chains and Belts

You can draw a chain or belt on any drawing that has a closed polyline. When you draw a chain, you need to a point on the polyline so that the AutoCAD Mechanical software knows which line to follow. This point becomes the starting point of the chain. After inserting the first chain link, you are prompted to confirm that the position of the link is correct. If the links are to be inserted in another direction, you can change the direction.

Access

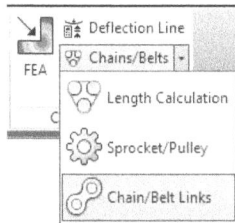

Command Line: AMCHAINDRAW

Ribbon: Content tab > Calculation panel > Chains/Belts drop-down list > Chain/Belt Links

Menu: Content > Chains/Belts > Draw Chain/Belt Links

Inserting Chains and Belts

To insert chains or belts into an assembly design, complete the following steps:

1. Create a closed loop polyline to define the path of the belt or chain. Use the Length Calculation command to create a polyline with the exact length required for the belt or chain.

2. Start the **Chain/Belt Links** command.

3. In the Select Belt and Chain dialog box, under Details, click Belts or Chains based on your requirements.

4. In the Select a Chain dialog box, select a chain style.

5. Select the closed loop polyline.

6. Specify the start point on the polyline for the chain link or belt tooth.

7. If requested, select the standard in the dialog box.

8. In the dialog box for size selection, select the size of the belt or chain.

9. Specify the number or links in the belt or chain that you need to draw.

10. Specify the direction in which the belt or chain is to be created by clicking a point to the left or right of the start point.

11. Specify the side of the polyline that is on the inside of the belt or chain.

12. If an associative hide is calculated and the Create Hide Situation dialog box opens, edit, accept, or cancel its creation.

Exercise: Design Chains and Belts

In this exercise, you will draw a sprocket and chain to provide movement to a design. You will also insert the roller chain.

The completed exercise

1. Open *Chains and Belts.dwg*.

2. Begin to add another sprocket, as follows:

    - Click Content tab > Calculation panel > Chains/Belts drop-down list > Sprocket/ Pulley.
    - In the Select Pulley and Sprocket dialog box, in the Details pane, click Sprockets.

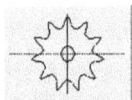

3. To specify the insertion and rotation angle, do the following:

    - For location, enter **0,0**.
    - For rotation angle, press ENTER.

4. In the Select a Chain dialog box, under Details, click ISO 606 Metric.

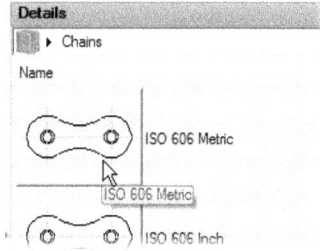

5. In the Sprockets - Size Selection dialog box, in Select a Size list, double-click on ISO 606 - 05B - 1.

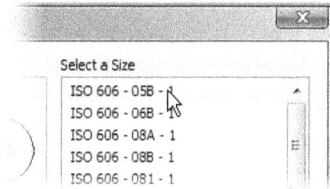

6. In the Sprockets - Geometry dialog box, in the Geometry of Sprocket area, enter the following geometry values:

    - For Number of Teeth, enter **30**.
    - For Number of Visible Teeth, enter **30**.
    - For Shaft Diameter, enter **30**.

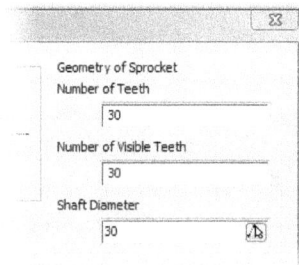

7. Click Finish. The drawing now displays as shown in the following illustration.

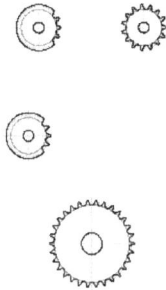

8. Begin to define the location and length of the chain path, as follows:

- Click Content tab > Calculation panel > Chains/Belts drop-down list > Length Calculation.
- In the Belt and Chain Length Calculation dialog box, click Length Calculation.
- Click OK.

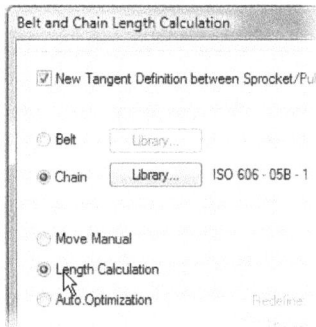

9. To specify the chain path and length, do the following:

- Select the centerline circle of the upper left sprocket at point **1** as the 1st point of tangent.
- Select the centerline circle of the upper right sprocket at point **2** as the 2nd point of tangent.
- Similarly, select the centerline circles of the sprockets by selecting the 1st and 2nd tangent points in the order identified (3 and 4), (5 and 6), and (7 and 8) as shown in the following illustration.

- Press ENTER.
- Select the newly created polyline. Note the number of links (85) and the length reported in the Command Line. (You might need to scroll up in the Command Line.)

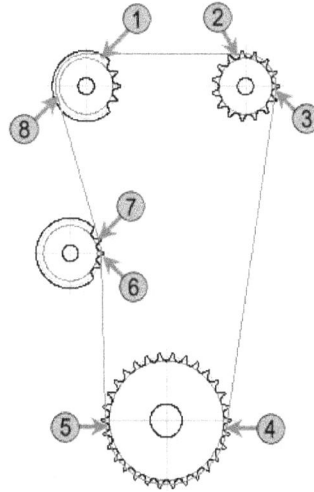

10. Begin to add the chain links to the path, as follows:

- Click Content tab > Calculation panel > Chains/Belts drop-down list > Chain/Belt Links.
- In the Select Belt and Chain dialog box, under Details, click Chains.
- In the drawing window, click the polyline path.
- Object snap to any point along the polyline.

11. To specify the chain link type and number of links, do the following:

- In the Chains - Size Selection dialog box, double-click on ISO 606 - 05B - 1.
- In the Chains - Geometry dialog box, in the Number of Links to Draw box, enter **85**.
- Click Finish.

12. To specify the direction and orientation of the chain, do the following:

- Press ENTER to accept the direction.
- Press ENTER to accept the orientation.

13. In the Hide Situation dialog box, click OK. The drawing now displays as shown in the following illustration.

14. Save and close all of the files.

Lesson: Shaft Generator

Overview

This lesson describes how to use the shaft generator to create rotationally symmetric or cylindrical parts for the shafts, axles, and other round parts. You learn how to create the two types of commonly used shaft segments: cylindrical and conical.

You learn how to draw segments with standard-size wrench geometry, threads, gears, and standard profiles. You learn how to create a break in a shaft segment and how to draw grooves, fillets, and chamfers. Finally, you learn how to enhance the shaft drawing by adding hatching, notes, and end views.

In the following illustration, two views of the shaft were created using the Shaft Generator. This shaft consists of plain cylindrical sections, a wrench section, and two threaded sections, one with an undercut and one without.

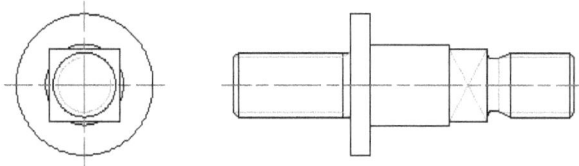

Objectives

After completing this lesson, you will be able to:

- Create cylindrical parts using the shaft generator.
- Add cylinder and conical sections during the creation of a shaft component.
- Place contour features on a shaft.
- Create cylindrical parts by using complex shaft segments.
- Change a shaft display by adding breaks, breakout lines, hatching, and notes.
- Create associative section and end views of a shaft.

Generating Shafts

Shafts are generally composed of consecutively placed segments that are drawn from left to right or right to left. You can insert, delete, or edit segments of the shaft.

You can create internal and external geometry with the Shaft Generator. You can also automatically display the shaft side view or cross-sections for different cutting planes.

In the following illustration, a shaft coupler converter is shown in the two views created by the shaft generator. The information in the leader notes comes from the shaft section that was selected when the note was added.

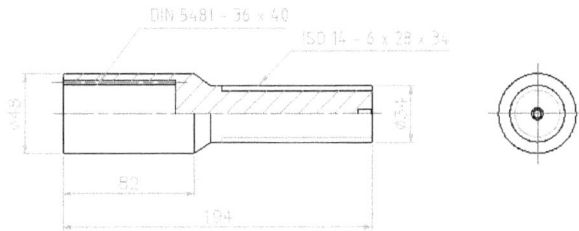

About Structure and the Shaft Generator

When structure is enabled, you must a shaft name during shaft creation and the shaft is added to the bill of materials database. When structure is disabled, you are not prompted for a name and the shaft is not added to the database. When structure is disabled, you can add shafts to the database by adding a part reference or by enabling structure and editing the shaft. Editing the shaft causes it to become a structured part.

Access

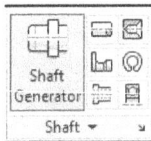

Command Line: AMSHAFT2D

Ribbon: Content tab > Shaft panel > Shaft Generator

Menu: Content > Shaft Generator

Setting the Shaft Angle

When you create a new shaft, you can specify its start point and the alignment of its center axis in the drawing window. The Ortho setting is automatically toggled on when you start this command. To draw a shaft at an angle other than horizontal or vertical, toggle Ortho off.

Shaft Generator Dialog Box

The Shaft Generator dialog box contains three tabs that you can use to draw shaft contours. The dialog box opens with the *Outer Contour* tab active. The *Left Inner Contour* tab and *Right Inner Contour* tab are similar to the *Outer Contour* tab. However, you use the *Left Inner Contour* tab to draw geometry internally from the left end of a shaft, and the *Right Inner Contour* tab to draw geometry internally from the right end of a shaft.

The different options in the Shaft Generator dialog box enable you to:

- Create cylindrical and conical shaped sections.
- Add shaft sections of basic shapes that are defined by industry standards.
- Add contours to control the display of the shaft.
- Add standard parts to the shaft.
- Create associative sections and end views.

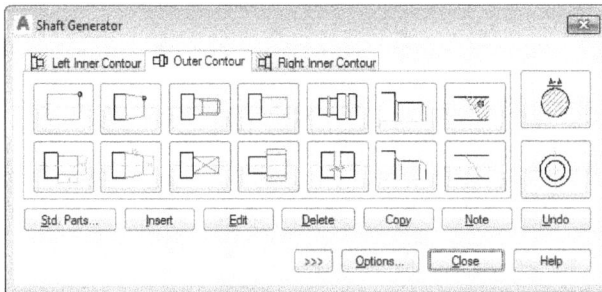

Control Shaft Settings

In the Options dialog box, in the *AM:Shaft* tab, you can control how shafts are created and how they look when created. You can also control how the shaft behaves when it is inserted into the drawing. You can set which end of the shaft remains stationary as you add or delete shaft sections.

You can change the appearance of the shaft centerlines, the different views, and the type of line used for view interruptions. You can change how the front view lines display and the side and sectional view representation. At the bottom of the dialog box, you can set how the standard parts used on the shaft behave when associative hide is used on the shaft.

You can control the settings for how a shaft looks and behaves before creating the shaft. Modifications made to the standards after a shaft has been created might not be reflected on already created shafts.

Procedure: Generating Shafts

To create a cylindrical part using the shaft generator, complete the following steps:

1. Start the **Shaft Generator** command.

2. If structure is enabled, at the Name prompt, a shaft name. Press ENTER.

3. Specify the start point and endpoint or select an existing AutoCAD Mechanical centerline.

4. In the Shaft Generator dialog box, select the shaft segment and its defining values.

5. When you have finished defining the components of the shaft, click Close.

You can use negative values for the shaft length to build shaft sections to the left.

Creating Basic Shaft Sections

You can create many types of cylindrical objects using basic shaft sections, which consist of cylinders and cones.

As sections are added or removed from the shaft, the shaft centerline adjusts to match the shaft length. New shaft segments are added to the end that is not defined as stationary in the standard. To specify an alternate start location for a shaft segment, click Insert.

In the following illustration, the cylindrical part was created using the shaft generator and basic cylinder and conical shapes. Note how the shapes can be used to define both external and internal sections.

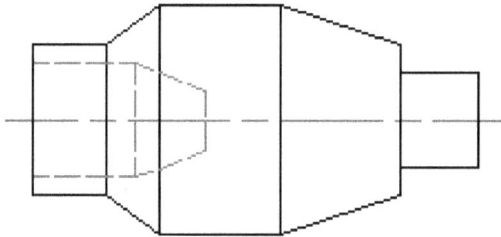

Creating a Cylinder Shaft Section

In the Shaft Generator dialog box, you can define a plain cylindrical section of the shaft in one of two ways. You can size it by specifying the position of its outer edge point or its length and diameter.

 Use to create a cylinder by selecting a single point.

 Use to create cylinders by entering two dimension values.

Procedure: Creating a Cylinder Shaft Section

An overview of adding a cylindrical section to a shaft while in the Shaft Generator command is shown in the following steps:

1. In the Shaft Generator dialog box, click to create a cylinder by a point or dimensions.

2. In the drawing window, set the cylinder size by object snapping to existing geometry or entering the required values.

Creating a Conical Shaft Section

There are two options for creating conical shaft geometry: Slope and Cone. Slope provides greater accuracy control. You can determine the dimensions of conical geometry by using your keyboard to respond to the Command Line prompts. You can open the Shaft Generator - Cone dialog box to use advanced methods of establishing the dimensions of conical geometry.

Use Cone to create a conical section by selecting a single point. The diameter at the starting side is equal to the last shaft segment's diameter.

Use Slope 1:x to create a conical section by entering dimension values of length, diameter, slope, or angle. Select the Dialog option to specify the conical size in the Shaft Generator Cone dialog box.

When using the Slope 1:x option in the Shaft Generator dialog box, you can open and define the size and shape of a cone in the Shaft Generator - Cone dialog box. You can a value or right-click in a field to open the Measure menu. In the Measure menu, in the shortcut menu, you can select different measurement methods that enable you to object snap to points in the drawing and have those values returned.ing a value causes other values to recalculate.

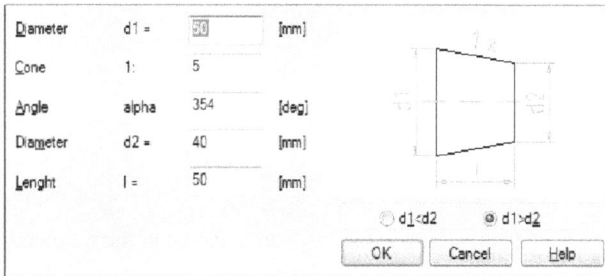

Diameter	d1 =	50	[mm]
Cone	1:	5	
Angle	alpha	354	[deg]
Diameter	d2 =	40	[mm]
Lenght	l =	50	[mm]

○ d1<d2   ◉ d1>d2

OK   Cancel   Help

Procedure: Creating a Conical Shaft Section

An overview of adding a conical section to a shaft while in the Shaft Generator command is shown in the following steps:

1. In the Shaft Generator dialog box, click to create a cone by a point or by its dimensions and slope.

2. In the drawing window, set the cylinder size by object snapping to existing geometry or entering the required values. If you clicked Slope 1:x to create the cone, select the command Dialog option to open the Shaft Generator - Cone dialog box and enter the values.

3. Continue adding segments to the shaft or close it to complete the shaft.

Placing Shaft Contour Features

Shaft contours include tools that change the outer shape of the shaft. Contour features are not available unless there is a shaft on which to place them. Shaft contours include grooves, chamfers, and fillets. The contour features are available for inner and outer contours.

In the following illustration, the cylindrical part created with the shaft generator has some rounded edges and its grooves were cut using contour features.

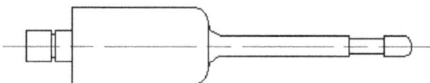

About Placing a Groove

You can insert a groove into a shaft section to remove or add material to the shaft. The groove moves with the shaft segment during editing. When a groove is added, removed, or edited, the length of the original shaft section remains unchanged.

When you a diameter that is less than the diameter of the shaft section into which you are inserting the shaft, the groove feature removes material from the shaft. When the diameter of the shaft is greater than the shaft section's diameter, material is added.

In the following illustration, two grooves were added to the shaft. One groove (1) shows the addition of material to the shaft section because its diameter was larger than that section. The other groove (2) shows the removal of material from the shaft section.

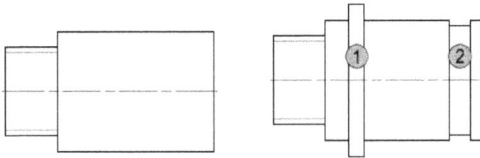

Procedure: Placing a Groove

An overview of adding a groove feature to an existing shaft section is shown in the following steps:

1. In the Shaft Generator dialog box, click Groove.

2. Click the shaft to specify the start point of the groove.

3. Enter a positive or negative value for the groove length and press ENTER.

4. Enter a value for the diameter.

> If the length that you specify creates a groove that is longer than the shaft section length, the groove is created within the shaft section boundaries. If the diameter that you specify is larger than the shaft diameter, the groove is created at the larger diameter. The larger diameter groove indicates that material is added to the shaft.

About Placing a Chamfer

Click Chamfer to add chamfers to shaft sections. You cannot place chamfers on grooves.

Procedure: Placing a Chamfer

An overview of adding a chamfer to sections of a shaft is shown in the following steps:

1. In the Shaft Generator dialog box, click Chamfer.

2. In the drawing window, select the edge of the shaft that you want to chamfer. Red circles display around the corners of the shaft section that is going to be chamfered. The maximum possible value for the chamfer is displayed in the Command Line. The maximum value is based on the location that you select on the shaft.

3. At the length prompt, a value for the chamfer length.

4. At the angle prompt, specify the angle for the chamfer.

> You can define a chamfer with two different distances using the distance option at the angle prompt.

About Placing a Fillet

Use the Fillet option to fillet shaft section edges on both sides of the shaft centerline.

Procedure: Placing a Fillet

An overview of adding a fillet to sections of a shaft is shown in the following steps:

1. In the Shaft Generator dialog box, click [icon] Fillet.

2. In the drawing window, select the edge of the shaft that you want to fillet. Red circles display around the corners of the shaft section that is going to be filleted. The maximum possible value for the fillet is displayed at the Command Line. The maximum value is based on the location that you select.

3. At the radius prompt, the fillet radius.

Creating Complex Shaft Segments

You can use the shaft generator to create complex shaft segments. You can create complex segments as internal or external segments on existing shafts or as stand-alone parts. Complex shaft segments include threads, profiles, wrenches, and gears.

In the following illustration, the two views show a shaft consisting of three complex segments. One segment is a gear, the middle one is a DIN profile, and the third segment is threaded.

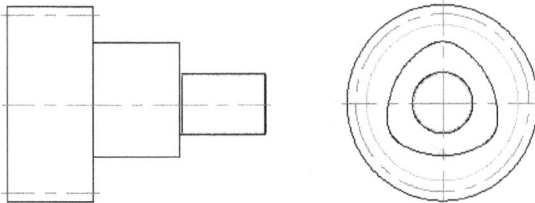

Inserting a Thread Segment

You can click Thread to insert threaded shaft segments using predefined thread standards. After clicking to insert threads, the Thread dialog box opens and you can select the thread standard to use. You can select from the standards for ISO, ANSI, DIN, and shaft lock nuts.

Thread Standard Dialog Box

After you select a thread standard, you can select the nominal thread size from the list of standard sizes. You can highlight the value that you want or use Drag (d) to select the size graphically. You can add any value for the thread length. Select Undercut to set the diameter, radius, and length values for the undercut thread.

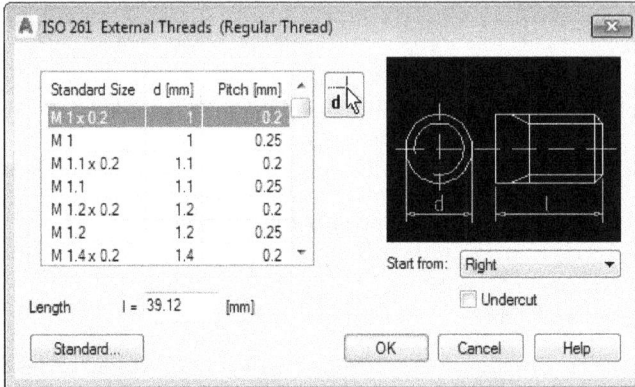

Inserting a Profile Segment

You can click Shaft Generator Profile to insert sectional profiles as shaft sections. Profiles include splined shafts, serrated shafts, involute splined shafts, and polygons. After clicking to insert a profile, the Profile dialog box opens and you can select the industry standard for the required profile.

Profile Dialog Box

You can select the nominal standard size for the profile in the Profile dialog box, which varies depending on the selected profile. the length, tolerance, angles, or other values. You can click Standard to display other profile standards. Clicking Modified Design enables you to modify the values of a selected standard to create a custom profile.

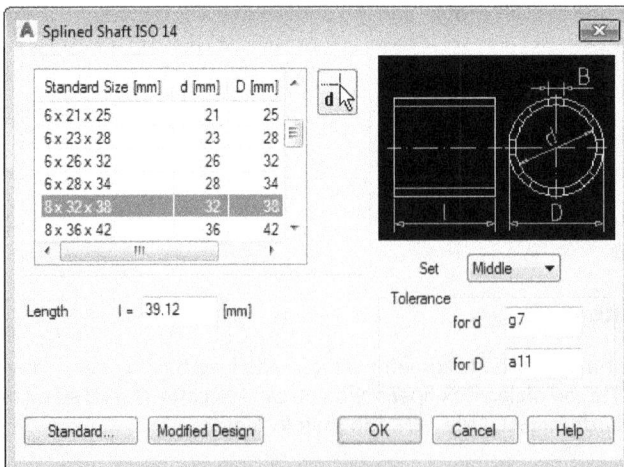

Modifying a Standard Profile

By selecting a profile size from the list of standard sizes and clicking Modified Design, you can create a custom profile. Information displayed in each Profile Standards dialog box is subject to the selected profile type.

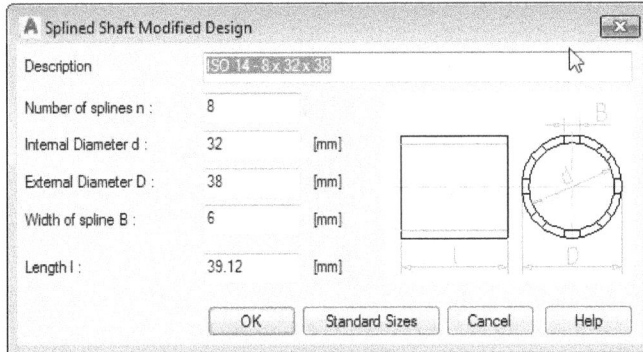

Inserting a Wrench Segment

Click Wrench to insert a segment shaped and sized to standard wrenches. After clicking to insert a wrench segment, the Wrench Opening dialog box opens enabling you to select the industry standard for the required wrench type and shape.

Wrench Dialog Box

After clicking the standard that you want to use for the wrench type and shape, the Wrench dialog box opens, displaying a list of standard sizes from which you can select.

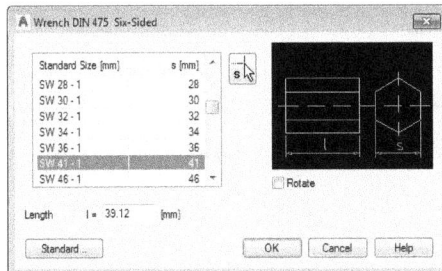

Inserting a Gear Segment

You can click **Gear** to generate gears with involute teeth on a shaft segment.

Gear Dialog Box

After you click to insert a gear segment, the Gear dialog box opens. You can select from DIN and ANSI industry standards and any required values.

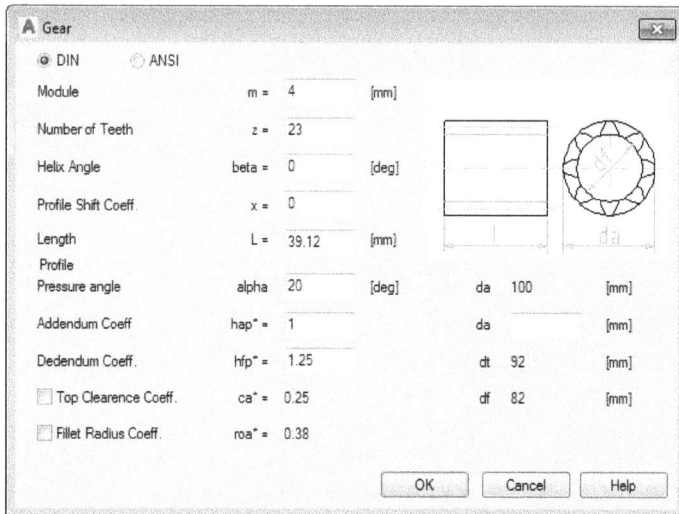

Procedure: Creating Complex Shaft Segments

To add a complex shaft segment of a thread, profile, wrench, or gear to a shaft, complete the following steps:

1.   In the Shaft Generator dialog box, select the shaft segment type.

2.   If you selected thread, profile, or wrench segments, select the standard on which to base this segment.

3.   In the dialog box for the type of segment, select sizes and set values to suit your requirements.

4.   Click OK to create the shaft segment and return to the Shaft Generator dialog box.

Inserting Shaft Display Features

You can set the shaft to best display its sections and features. You can add shaft breaks, break lines, hatches, section views, and end views to fully communicate the shaft design.

About Shaft Breaks

You can add a shaft break to a section of shaft that is long or not critical to the current display. The Break button inserts a shaft break into any segment of a shaft. The shaft break places two break lines on the shaft perpendicular to the shaft centerline. The shaft lines between the two break lines are removed. You can display shaft breaks with zigzag, freehand, or hatch lines.

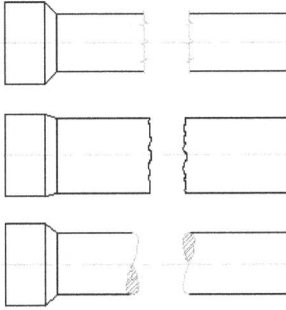

Procedure: Adding a Shaft Break

An overview of removing a section of a shaft by inserting a break is shown in the following steps:

1. In the Shaft Generator dialog box, click Break.

2. At the Specify Point prompt, click the point on the shaft segment at which you want to insert the break.

3. At the Specify Length prompt, a value, or in the drawing window, click to define the break endpoint.

> The shaft break style depends on the drawing standard. You can modify the break line style by clicking Options in the Shaft Generator dialog box and setting the View of Interrupt. If the shaft break is already placed, you can change the break style by closing the Shaft Generator dialog box and double-clicking on the break.

About Break Lines

You can use break lines to define a hatch boundary to create a breakout area on a shaft. You can use a break line to remove the front material from the shaft and display internal contours. A hatch is then placed on the broken section of the shaft.

Procedure: Adding a Break Line

An overview of adding a break line that is going to be used to show a boundary area for a breakout drawing view is shown in the following steps:

1. In the Shaft Generator dialog box, click Break Line.

2. At the Specify Starting Point prompt, click a point on the shaft contour at which you want the break line to start.

3. At the Specify Next prompt, click additional supporting points. Click the last point on the shaft contour.

4. After the points have been selected, press to create the smoothed break line.

The shaft's hidden lines, representing the inner contour, continue to display as hidden lines until the hatch area is applied to the breakout section.

About Hatch

You can click Hatch to insert half or full sections of hatch. In the following illustration, different types of hatching are shown.

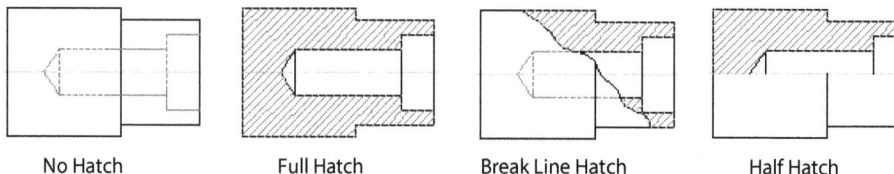

No Hatch   Full Hatch   Break Line Hatch   Half Hatch

Procedure: Adding Full Hatch or Break Line Hatch

An overview of adding a hatch to an entire shaft part created by the shaft generator, or to an area partially defined with a break line is shown in the following steps:

1. In the Shaft Generator dialog box, click Hatch.

2. At the Specify Internal Point prompt, click inside the shaft contour or inside the break line to define the hatch boundaries.

3. In the Hatch Parameter dialog box, click Full Section. Click OK to place a symbol at the point at which you want the hatch to be applied.

4. Close the Shaft Generator dialog box after you have completed your shaft creation and editing tasks so that you can display the hatch in the drawing view.

About Shaft Notes

You can add notes to the shaft in the drawing to identify the shaft features. The notes in the Shaft dialog box display the size of the shaft sections and contour features. When you modify the shaft, the shaft information in the notes updates.

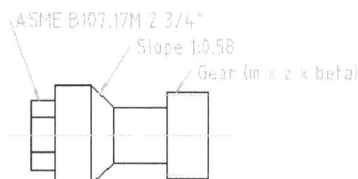

Procedure: Adding Shaft Notes

An overview of adding a note to a section of the shaft is shown in the following steps:

1. In the Shaft Generator dialog box, click Note.

2. Click the shaft section that you want to annotate.

3. Click a point on the shaft segment that specifies the arrow point location.

4. Specify one or more points for the leader line and press ENTER.

5. In the Note Symbol dialog box, in the Symbol tab, under Requirements, click to expand the Variables list.

6. Click the + symbol to expand SHAFT and click DESC.

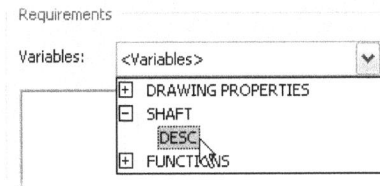

7. Edit the note contents if required. Click OK.

> You can create the same dynamic note using the Leader Note command.

Creating Associative Shaft Views

You can automatically generate shaft side and detail views from the shaft using tools in the Shaft Generator dialog box. You can place the views anywhere in a drawing. Views are associative to the shaft. When changes are made to the shaft, the end and section views are automatically updated.

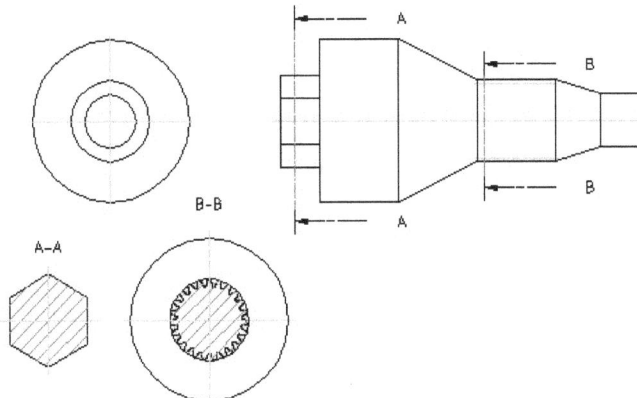

Creating Side Views

You can create side views of the shaft end with Side View. When you click Side View, the Side View From dialog box opens.

Side View From Dialog Box

To create the required view, in the Side View From dialog box, click Right or Left. After clicking the direction of view on which the new drawing is based, in the drawing window, click to position the center of the shaft view.

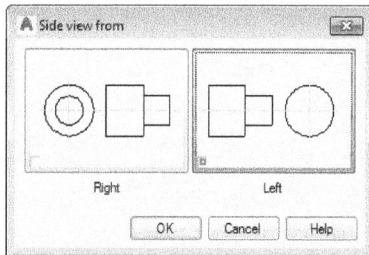

About Section Views

You can create as many section views as required to fully describe and communicate the shaft. With Section, you can create an end view of a shaft that is cut at a specific point. The section view displays a profile of the cut location with the hatch area applied. A section line is placed on the shaft at the same point.

Procedure: Creating a Shaft Section View

To create a section view of a shaft, complete the following steps:

1. In the Shaft Generator dialog box, click **Section**.

2. Click on the shaft position that you want to section.

3. Click in the drawing area above the shaft to place the start point of the section line.

4. Click in the drawing area below the shaft to place the end point of the section line.

5. In the Hatch Parameters dialog box, specify the hatch angle and whether the other hatch properties are set automatically or manually.

6. At the Letter for Sectional View <default> prompt, press ENTER.

7. Click in the drawing area to indicate the view side of the cutting plane.

8. Click in the drawing area to place the section view.

Exercise: Place a Shaft in an Assembly

In this exercise, you will add a shaft to a partially finished assembly drawing.

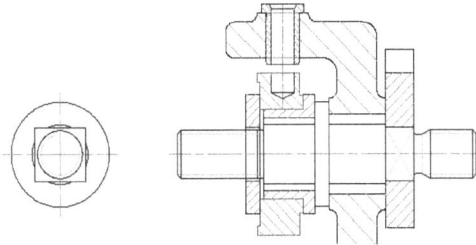

The completed exercise

1. Open *Shaft Generator.dwg*.

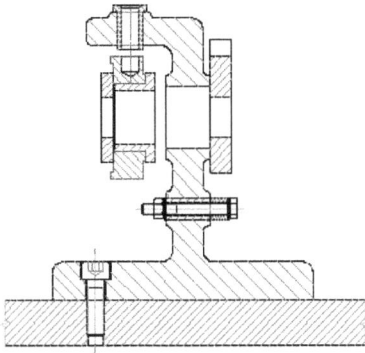

2. To begin adding a shaft component to the assembly do the following:

   - Click Content tab > Shaft panel > Shaft Generator.
   - Object snap to the midpoint of the support part.
   - Click any point to the right of the last entered point.

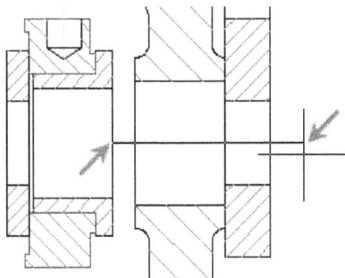

3. To add the first shaft section:

   - In the Shaft Generator dialog box, click the bottom Cylinder button.
   - For length, enter **5**.
   - For diameter, enter **35**.

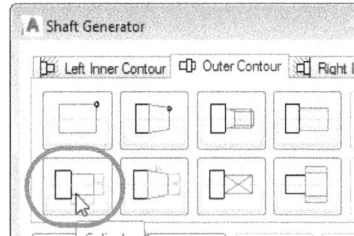

4. To add the second shaft section:

   - In the Shaft Generator dialog box, click the bottom Cylinder button again.
   - For length, object snap to the intersection as indicated in the following illustration.
   - For diameter, enter **20**.

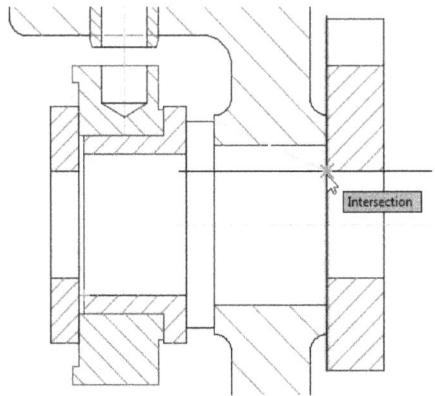

5. To begin adding a third section with a wrench shape:

   - In the Shaft Generator dialog box,

     click [ ] Wrench.

   - In the Wrench Opening dialog box, in the Details pane, click DIN 475 Four-Sided.

---

6. To define the wrench size, in the Wrench dialog box:

- In the list of standard sizes, click SW 18 - 1.
- In the Length field, enter **10**.
- Click OK.

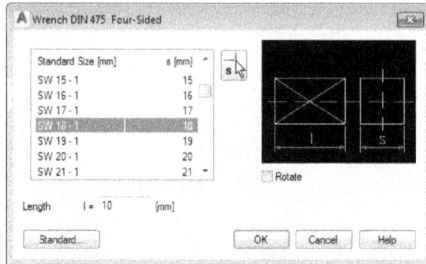

7. To begin adding a fourth section with threads:

- In the Shaft Generator dialog box, click Thread.
- In the Thread dialog box, click ISO 261 External Threads (Regular Thread).

8. To define the thread size and length:

- In the ISO 261 External Threads dialog box, list of standard sizes, click M 16.
- In the Length field, enter **22**.

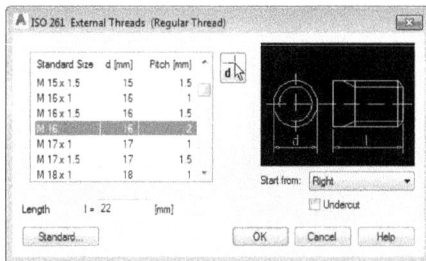

9. To create the thread with an undercut:

- Click the Undercut checkbox.
- In the field g2, enter **6**.
- Click OK.

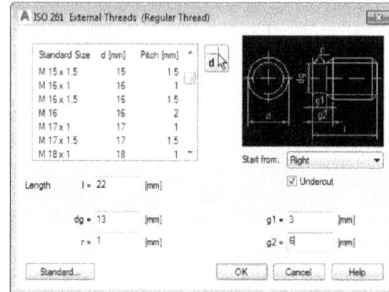

10. Begin to create a right-side view of the currently defined shaft.

- In the Shaft Generator dialog box, click Side View.
- In the Side view from dialog box, click Right.
- Click OK.

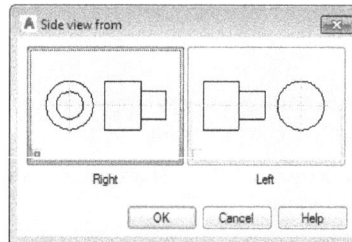

11. To position and create the view, click to place the end view to the left of the shaft part as shown in the following illustration.

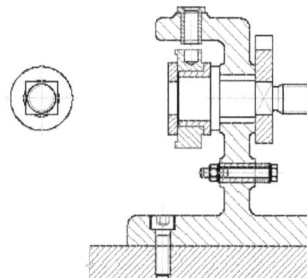

12. To change the direction from which the segments are added to the shaft:

- In the Shaft Generator dialog box, click Options.
- In the Shaft Generator - Configuration dialog box, in the Stationary Shaft End area, click Right.
- Click OK.

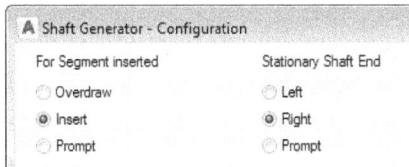

13. To define a new starting point:

- In the Shaft Generator dialog box, click Insert.
- In the drawing window, object snap to the intersection of the centerline and the vertical line as shown in the following illustration.

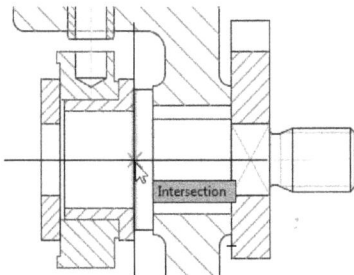

14. To add a cylinder section to the left:

- In the Shaft Generator dialog box, click the bottom Cylinder button.
- For length, enter -**18**.
- For diameter, enter **20**.

15. To add a threaded section to the left:

- In the Shaft Generator dialog box, click Thread.
- In the Thread dialog box, click ISO 261 External Threads (Regular Thread).

16. To define the thread size and length:

- In the ISO 261 External Threads dialog box, list of standard sizes, click M 16.
- In the Length field, enter -**30**.
- Click OK.

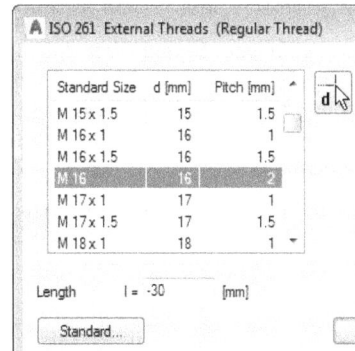

17. In the Shaft Generator dialog box, click Close. When prompted to update the side view, click Yes. The shaft views now display as shown in the following illustration.

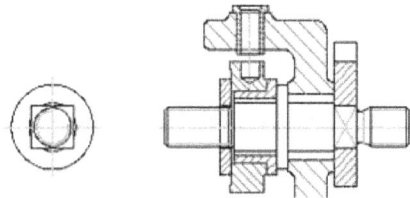

18. Save and close all of the files.

Lesson: Standard Shaft Parts

Overview

You can insert standard shaft parts into an assembly that contains a shaft part.

To complete your design when it includes a shaft part, you often require standard parts, such as bearings, keys, and seals to accompany the shaft. In this lesson, you learn to insert keys, rings, seals, nuts, and bearings on a shaft. You also learn about placing cut features and inserting shaft ends and how to access and insert these items from the Shaft Generator dialog box and from individual commands.

In the following illustration, roller bearings and a parallel key were added to the assembly and design of the shaft.

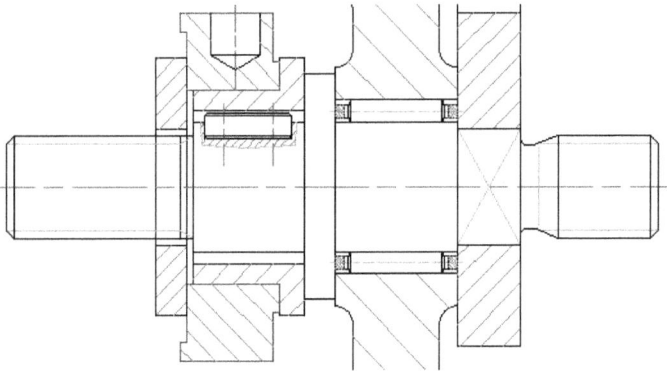

Objectives

After completing this lesson, you will be able to:

- Insert standard shaft parts from the Shaft Generator dialog box.
- Insert standard shaft parts from the Ribbon or menu.

Inserting from the Shaft Generator

As you create a shaft component, you can add related standard shaft parts to the assembly by accessing them from the Shaft Generator dialog box. When you use standard shaft parts and access them from the Shaft Generator dialog box, you can reusing existing content and information.

About Standard Shaft Parts and Features

You can place standard parts and features on shafts created with the AutoCAD Mechanical software's Shaft Generator or onto lines, arcs, or circles that represent shafts. Standard parts are added to the bill of materials database, display in end views, and can be ballooned. Many of the standard parts change the shaft contour. As you place common standard parts on the shaft, the part is drawn and the shaft segment is edited for the part.

You can place cut features to modify the shaft contour by removing material from the shaft. When you place a cut feature, you are prompted to add a drawing detail. Adding a detail of the cut feature creates a named detail with dimensions. The detail default settings follow the drawing standards.

During the process of inserting standard parts for the shaft, a preview of each available size is displayed in the drawing area as you move the cursor. A tooltip indicates the current size being previewed. To select the required size, move the cursor to adjust the preview size, and then click to accept the current preview size.

If background hiding and structure are both enabled, the Create Hide Situation dialog box opens when you place some of the shaft standard parts. When the Create Hide Situation dialog box opens, you can accept, edit, or cancel the calculated hide condition.

Standard Parts from the Shaft Generator

When the Shaft Generator dialog box is open, you can access the standard shaft parts by clicking the Std. Parts option. When you click this option, a new dialog box opens. You can use this dialog box to navigate to and select the standard shaft part that you want to insert into your assembly.

This new active dialog box displays the information that you last accessed. Click Selection at the top of the tree in the Standard Parts pane to display buttons for all categories. You can then select parts from the Details pane.

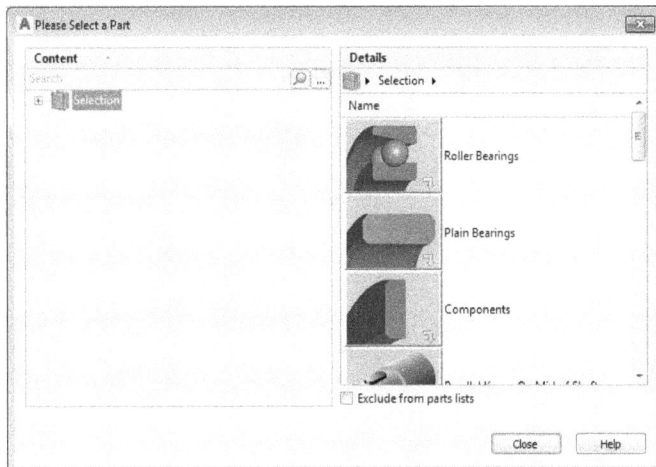

Procedure: Inserting Standard Shaft Parts using the Shaft Generator

An overview of inserting standard shaft parts into an assembly by accessing the standard parts from within the Shaft Generator dialog box is shown in the following steps:

1. In the Shaft Generator dialog box, click Std. Parts.

2. In the active dialog box, select a standard part, determine the direction of view, and specify the standard.

3. Specify the insertion point on the shaft contour.

4. Select the centerline. Enter the direction if prompted.

5. If prompted for a size, select one in the dialog box or drag the preview until the required size is displayed. Click anywhere in the drawing window.

6. If an associative hide is calculated and the Create Hide Situation dialog box opens, edit, accept, or cancel its creation.

Inserting from Other Locations

To make it easier to directly access and insert specific shaft parts from the standard parts library, you can use individual commands for the different standard shaft part types. To directly access and insert specific shaft part types, you need to learn which standard shaft parts include commands, where you can access those commands, and what the overall steps are for inserting the components.

The following illustration shows the Shaft panel expanded to access the tools for inserting specific shaft parts. The panel was pinned open for continued quick access.

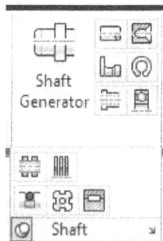

Access

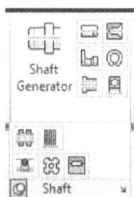

Ribbon: Content tab > Shaft panel and extended Shaft panel

Menu Bar: Content > Shaft Components

Accessing the Commands to Insert Standard Shaft Parts

You can start the command to select and insert a specific standard shaft part by clicking on the Ribbon Content tab > Shaft panel and extended Shaft panel, or by clicking Content menu > Shaft Components.

Icon	Command	Description
	Parallel/ Woodruff Key	You can insert a parallel or woodruff key to establish a positive locking shaft-hub connection for transferring a torque.
	Retaining Ring/Circlip	Retaining rings and circular clips are used as locking elements that prevent pins or other components from moving. Circlips are available for shafts and bores.
	Seal	You can use seals to prevent leakage of lubricants to other areas (e.g., shafts and housing).
	Adjusting Ring	Insert adjusting rings to set a distance between a standard part and a contour.
	Centerhole	Center holes are used to clamp a shaft centric to a lathe. You can place center holes with or without thread. Center holes are drilled into the center of the shaft end. When you place a center hole with the Shaft Generator, the end view is automatically updated with the hole.
	Undercut	You can insert undercuts at the ends of treated surfaces. For example, you can place an undercut before placing threads or ground cylinders.
	Shaft End	You can place shaft breaks on a shaft to indicate that the shaft continues beyond what is shown. You can create shaft breaks on any line in the drawing. A shaft break does not have to be placed on a shaft created with the Shaft Generator. The shaft break is placed perpendicular to the line selected for the centerline and through the second point selected.
	Roller Bearing	Roller bearings permit shafts to rotate. You can select a nominal size bearing from the standards. If the selected size does not match the size of the existing shaft, an AutoCAD Question dialog box opens, prompting you to accept the automatic resizing of the shaft diameter.
	Plain Bearing	Plain bearings permit shafts to move rotationally or longitudinally, as the result of a low coefficient of friction of the bearing material.
	Shaft Lock Nut	You can insert shaft lock nuts on a threaded cylinder to fix a part on the shaft (e.g., a bearing).
	Shim Ring	Shim rings provide the exact positioning of machine elements on shafts in the axial direction.

Shaft Bearing Dialog Box

You can values in the Shaft Bearing dialog box to narrow the selection of the bearing. Dynamic dragging can be set to graphically select the required bearing from the selection results.

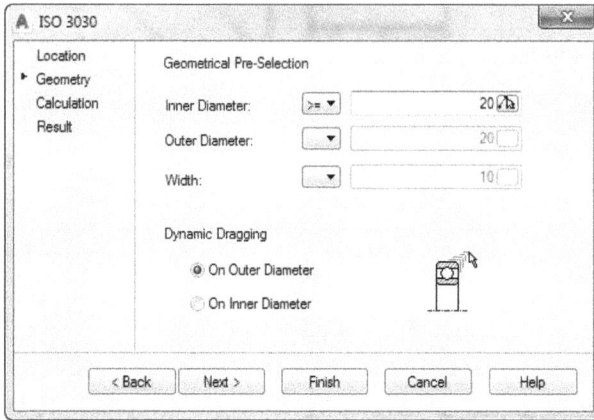

Clicking = in the size lists limits the available bearings.

Select a Shaft End Dialog Box

When you add a break to the end of a shaft, you can select from three different shaft breaks: zigzag, freehand, or hatch. Select the centerline and then the point that you want the shaft break to go through. You can access the Break options by entering AMSHAFTEND at the Command Line or clicking Content menu > Shaft Components > Shaft Ends.

You can place both right-side and left-side shaft ends by changing where you click the contour. After you select the centerline, click the contour above the centerline for the right-side ends. Click the contour below the centerline for left-side ends.

Procedure: Inserting Standard Shaft Parts Using Toolbars and Menus

To use the common procedure for inserting standard shaft parts after accessing the command from the Ribbon or menu, complete the following steps. Although the steps to insert the different standard components are very similar, a step for a specific part might vary from what is listed here.

1. Start the individual command to insert a standard shaft part.

2. In the Details pane, click the standard from which you want to select.

3. In the Details pane, click the view direction for the part that you want to create.

4. Specify the insertion criteria for that standard part.

5. Select the standard size that you require from the dialog box or dynamically drag the size in the drawing window.

6. If an associative hide is calculated and the Create Hide Situation dialog box opens, edit, accept, or cancel its creation.

Exercise: Insert Standard Shaft Parts

In this exercise, you will add a bearing and parallel key to the assembly.

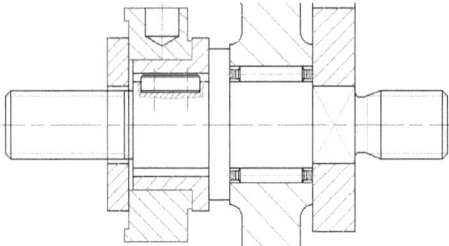

The completed exercise

1. Open *Standard Shaft Parts.dwg*.

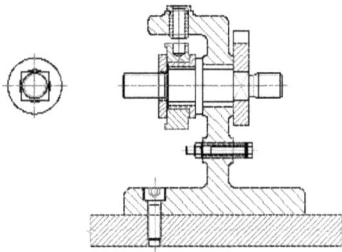

2. Begin to insert a radial roller bearing, as follows:

    ▪ Click Content tab > Shaft panel > Roller Bearing.

    ▪ In the Select a Roller Bearing dialog box, in Details pane, click Radial.

3. To specify the standard and view direction, do the following:

    ▪ In Details pane, scroll down and click ISO 3030.

    ▪ In Details pane, click Front.

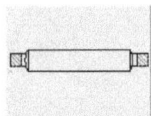

4. To specify the insertion point and direction of the bearing, in the drawing window, do the following:

    ▪ Object snap to the endpoint as shown in the following illustration.

    ▪ Click the shaft centerline to the right of the insertion point that you just clicked.

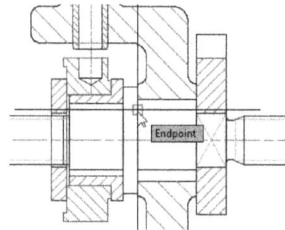

5. In the ISO 3030 dialog box, in Geometrical Pre-Selection area, click = for the Inner Diameter and unlimited for Width. Click Finish.

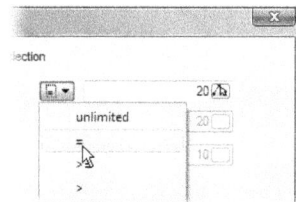

6. In the drawing window, drag the standard part to the right and slightly up (endpoint) until you reach the size ISO 3030 24C. Click the point as shown in the following illustration to insert the bearing.

    ▪ In the Hide Situation dialog box, click OK.

    ▪ When prompted to update side and sectional views, click No.

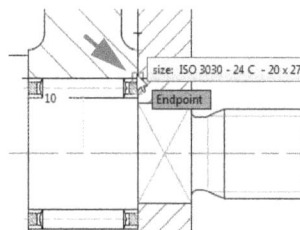

7. Begin to insert a parallel key, as follows:
    - Click Content tab > expanded Shaft panel > Parallel/Woodruff Key.
    - In the Select a Key or Hub dialog box, under Details, click Parallel Keys - On Mid of Shaft.
    - Click Front.
    - Under Details, click ISO 2491 - A.

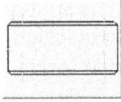

8. To set the insertion point for the key, do the following:
    - In the drawing window, press CTRL+right-click and click Reference From.
    - Object snap to the endpoint shown in the following illustration.
    - Move the cursor to the right and enter **2**.

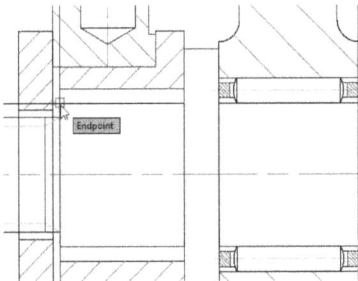

9. To complete the insertion of the key, do the following:
    - Click the centerline of the shaft.
    - In the ISO 2491 - A dialog box, click Finish.
    - Dynamically drag the part to the size A 6 x 4 x 14. Ensure that no object snap is displayed (you can toggle off OSnap in the Status Bar). Click to accept.

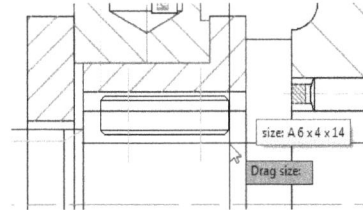

10. When prompted to update the side view, click Yes. The assembly should now display as shown in the following illustration.

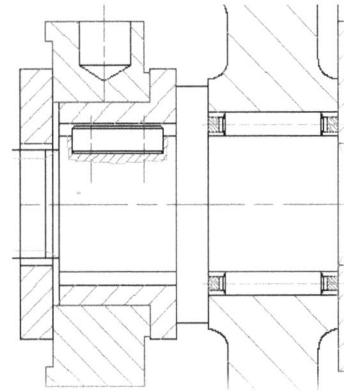

11. Save and close all of the files.

Lesson: Springs

Overview

You can use the spring generator to automate spring design and insertion into an assembly. In this lesson you learn how to insert springs from catalogs and apply additional calculations during spring selection.

Designing or finding the correct spring for a design can be a time-consuming task. The Spring Generator in the AutoCAD Mechanical software can help you perform this task more quickly and easily. You can select industry standards and your design criteria to locate an available spring or design a custom spring.

In the following illustration, an extension spring was added to the assembly to complete the drawing view. Using the Spring Generator, the spring was quickly added to the assembly and a standard spring was used.

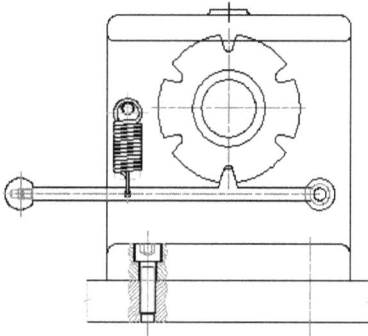

Objectives

After completing this lesson, you will be able to:

- Describe how to insert springs and the different categories you can use to insert them.
- Insert springs into a drawing from an industry standards catalog.
- Insert a custom spring that uses industry standard material and meets specified load conditions.
- Insert springs into a drawing by only defining the geometry.

Process of Adding Springs to Your Assembly Design

To learn how to insert specific types of springs into your designs and methods of designing and selecting the springs, you need to learn the overall process of inserting springs. You also need to learn the types of springs and the categories you need to select to define the type of spring you want to insert.

The following illustration shows examples of each of the types of springs you can insert.

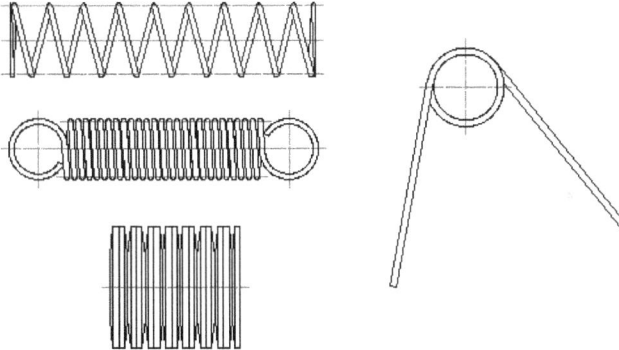

About Spring Design in AutoCAD Mechanical

You can use the spring calculation function in the AutoCAD Mechanical software to automate the design and insertion of different types of springs. You can insert compression, extension, torsion, and Belleville springs.

To begin inserting a spring, start the command for the specific type of spring that you want to insert. The Select dialog box opens listing three categories that you can use to define the specifics for the required spring type. Each of these categories has different capabilities and characteristics for defining and selecting a spring. The three categories and their characteristics are as follows:

Category	Characteristics
Standards	Select an industry catalog, specify the spring's restrictions for use, and select a spring from the results of catalog springs that meet the specified restrictions.
Modified Design	Select an industry standard wire, specify the spring's restrictions for use, and specify the geometry size requirements for the spring.
Only Draw	Select to draw a spring based only on geometry size requirements and no industry standards.

In the following illustration, the Select dialog box for compression springs is shown with the three categories being identified. For the Standards and Modified Design categories, you must click one of the standards below to be able to select a view in the Details pane.

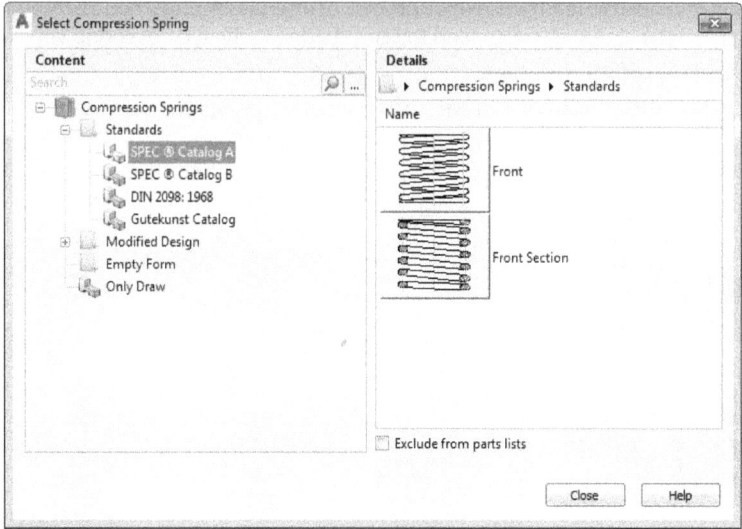

Access

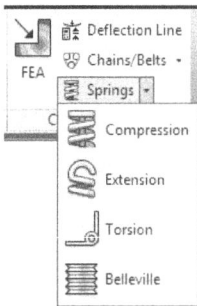

Ribbon: Content tab > Calculation panel > Springs drop-down list

Menu Bar: Content > Springs

Accessing the Commands to Insert Springs

Icon	Command	Description
	Compression	Use to insert a single compression spring common in industry or custom to your design.
	Extension	Use to insert a single extension spring common in industry or custom to your design.
	Torsion	Use to insert a single torsion spring common in industry or custom to your design.
	Belleville	Use to insert Belleville spring washers common in industry or custom to your design.

Spring Length

To set the length of a spring in the drawing window, drag the preview to change its size. After the preview shows the required size, click to insert the drawing of the spring at that length.

Spring Report Forms

If you are inserting a spring by selecting or modifying an industry-standard spring, you can also insert a form that contains the data and calculations for that spring. You can insert this form by clicking Settings in the dialog box when specifying the restrictions and geometry, or by selecting the results.

Process: Adding Springs to Your Designs

1. Start the command to insert a specific type of spring: compression, extension, torsion, or Belleville.

2. In the Select dialog box for that spring type, select the type of category that you want to use to define the spring.

3. Based on the selected spring and category of definition, specify the spring criteria.

4. Insert the spring and if that spring wraps around a rod, select the rod so that the hidden line calculation is done.

Inserting Springs from a Standard

You can insert springs from existing standards by specifying what you require in a spring and then selecting the spring to insert from the resulting list of springs that meet your requirements.

The dialog box pages of Location, Restriction, and Results are similar for each type of spring. Any variation is specific to the definition and selection of that spring type.

Select the Category and Standard

To insert an industry-standard spring into your design, start the command for the type of spring you want to insert. Select the catalog of the standard under the Standards category for that spring type. With the catalog selected, click the direction and type of drawing view that you want to insert into the drawing.

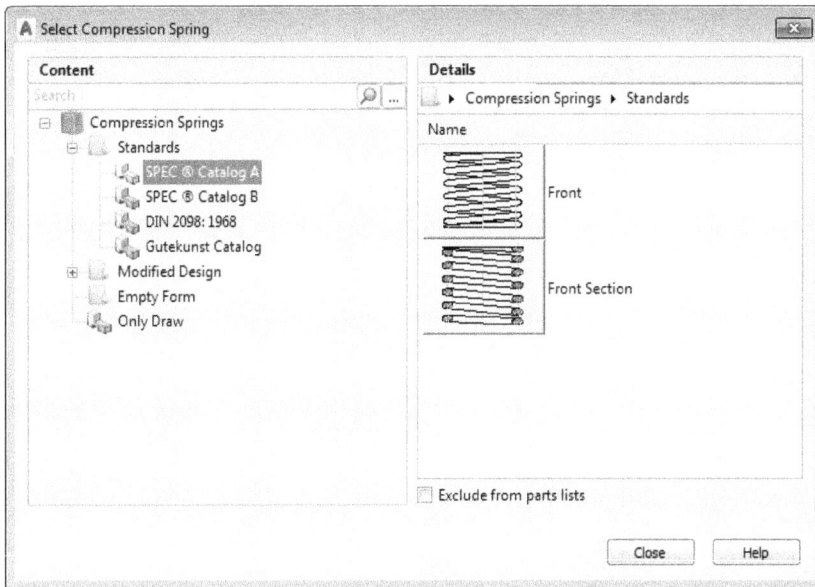

Spring by Standard - Define Restrictions

After you click a view for a standard and specify the insertion location and direction of the spring, the dialog box for that spring type opens to the Restrictions page. On this page, you set the restrictions for spring selection. These restrictions focus the search through the standard so that only springs that meet these restrictions are returned.

Under Default Restrictions, you can set the category by which you want to define your restrictions. You can further modify those restrictions in the Press Button to Add Restriction area. By clicking a button in this preview area, you can add or remove that restriction field from the list on the right.

You can modify the calculation settings by clicking the Additional Calculation Settings, Dynamic Loads, or Settings buttons.

Click Back to confirm the spring's angle and location. Click Finish to accept all of the springs meeting the criteria. Click Next to display the calculation results.

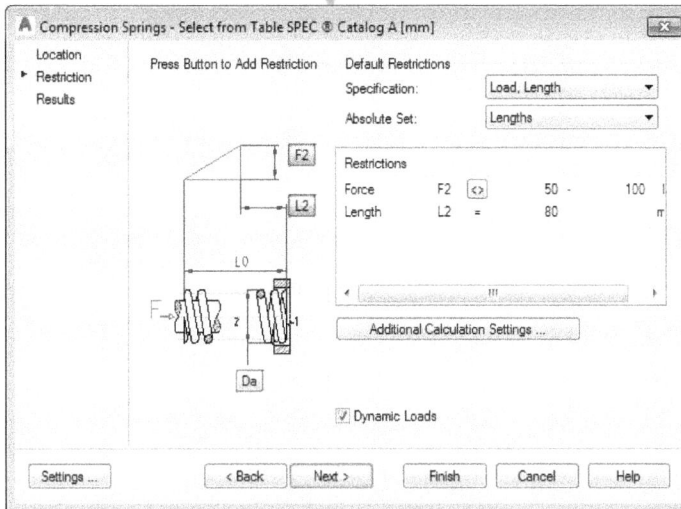

Springs by Standard - Select Results

On the Results page, a list of springs is displayed that meet the restrictions provided on the previous page of the dialog box. You can highlight a row in the spring list to display the calculated results for the selected spring. The results are located on the three tabs at the bottom of the dialog box.

You can select the required spring from the list to place in the drawing. You can pick multiple springs by holding CTRL or SHIFT. After selecting multiple springs, you can make the final selection in the drawing area by dynamically dragging the cursor.

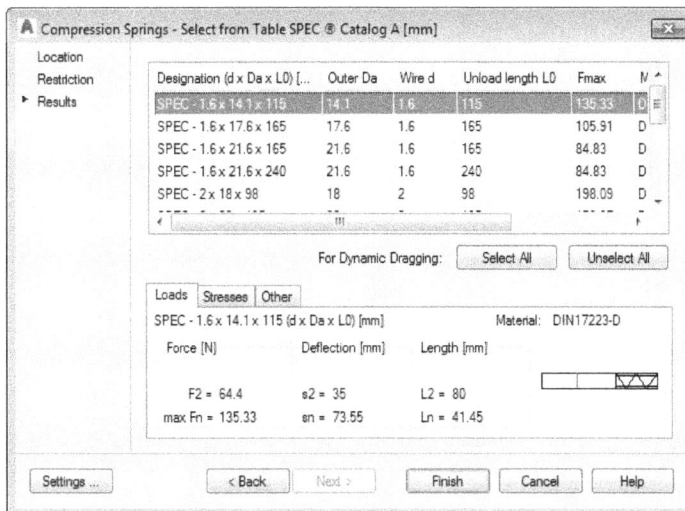

The Results page contains three tabs with additional information about the selected spring in the list.

Tab	Description
Loads	Displays the calculated results for force, maximum force, deflection, maximum allowed deflection, and the length of the spring caused by corresponding forces.
Stresses	Displays the stress in the spring calculated according to allowable stress, the safeties as a ratio between stresses and allowed stress, and the length of spring caused by the corresponding forces. The number of displayed forces depends on your specifications.
Other	Displays information, such as the natural frequency of the spring and the permitted number of stress cycles. If you defined inputs in the Additional Calculation dialog box, this tab displays information about the spring safety against buckling and against influences of shear load.

Procedure: Inserting Springs from a Standard

An overview of inserting a spring from an industry catalog is shown in the following steps:

1. Start the command for the type of spring that you want to insert.

2. In the dialog box for the spring type, in the Standard Parts pane, select the type of standard to use.

3. In the Details pane, select the required view direction and type.

4. In the drawing area, click a point to specify the start point of the spring.

5. Specify the direction of the spring.

6. On the Restrictions page in the dialog box, set the restrictions on the spring to match your requirements.

7. Click Next to review the available springs from the standard that are within the specified restrictions.

8. In the list of results, select one or more springs. Click Finish.

9. In the drawing area, move the cursor until the preview and tooltip information identify the required part, and then click to create the part based on that preview.

10. If a shaft passes through the opening of the spring, select the shaft component. Otherwise, press ENTER to display the spring in the drawing.

Inserting Modified Designed Springs

When you click to create a spring based on a modified design, you select an industry-standard material and define its loads and geometry. By using this method, you know that this custom spring is going to suit your requirements.

The Location, Load, Geometry, and Results pages in the dialog box are very similar for each type of spring. Any variation is specific for the definition and selection of that spring type.

Selecting the Category and Standard

To insert a custom spring that uses industry-standard material and meets specified load conditions, start the command for the type of spring that you want to insert. Select the industry standard material that you want to use on the Standard Parts pane, under Modified Design. On the Details pane, click the direction and type of drawing view to insert into the drawing.

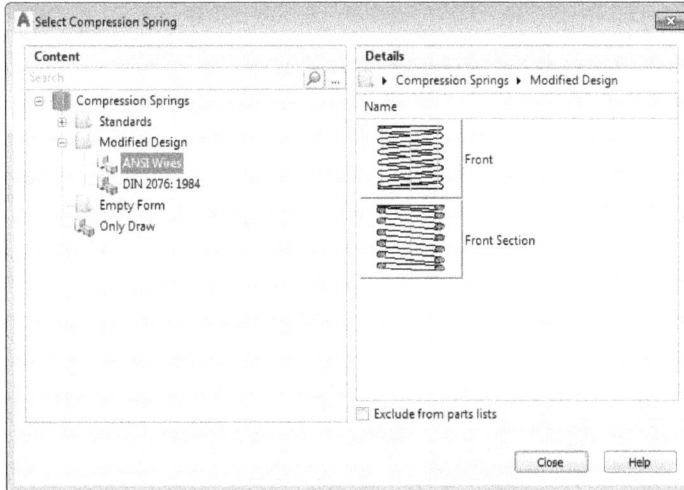

Spring by Modification - Define Load

After you click a view for the selected spring material and specify its insertion location and direction, the dialog box for that spring type opens to the Load page. On this page, you can set the force and calculation criteria that this custom spring must meet. The restrictions that are specified here are used in conjunction with the geometry values that you specify on the next page.

All of the options for defining a load on this page are the same as those available on the Restrictions tab for standard catalog springs.

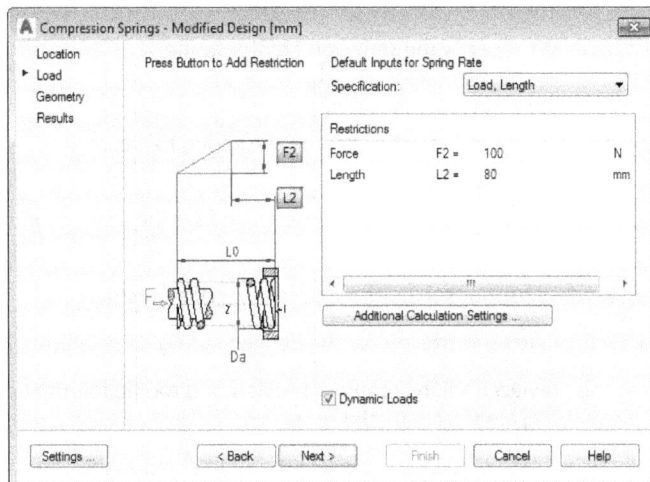

Spring by Modification - Define Geometry

You can further define the custom spring on the Geometry page by selecting its material and wire diameter, and setting its other geometry values.

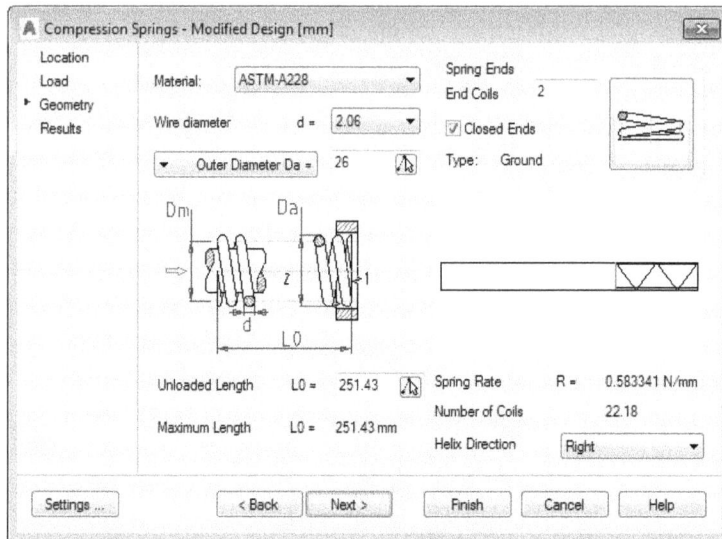

Procedure: Inserting Custom Springs Using a Standard Material

An overview of inserting a custom spring by selecting an industry material, defining loads, and specifying other geometry requirements is shown in the following steps:

1.   Start the command for the type of spring that you want to insert.

2.   In the dialog box for the spring type, under the Modified Design category in the Standard Parts pane, select the material standard.

3.   In the Details pane, select the required view direction and type.

4.   In the drawing area, click a point to specify the start point of the spring.

5.   Specify the direction of the spring.

6.   On the Load page of the dialog box, set the restrictions on the spring to match your requirements.

7.   On the Geometry page, select the material and wire diameter, and set the other geometry values.

8.   Click Next to review the standard's springs that are within the specified restrictions.

9.   In the list of results, review the loads and stresses for the defined spring. Click Finish.

10. In the drawing area, drag the preview until the required preview and tooltip information are displayed, and click in the drawing area to create the spring.

11. If a shaft passes through the opening of the spring, select the shaft component. The spring is displayed in the drawing.

Inserting Springs By Only Drawing the Geometry

When you want to insert a spring into your design and it does not have to meet specified design restrictions for loads or follow a specified standard, you can create the spring by selecting the Only Draw category. Using this method, you need to specify specific geometry restrictions for your custom spring to be ready to be inserted into the drawing.

The Location and Restrictions pages in the dialog box are similar for each type of spring. Any variation is specific for the definition and selection of that spring type.

Select to Only Draw the Spring

To insert a custom spring that does not use industry standards, start the command for the type of spring that you want to insert, and then select the Only Draw category. With this category selected, click the direction and type of drawing view to insert into the drawing.

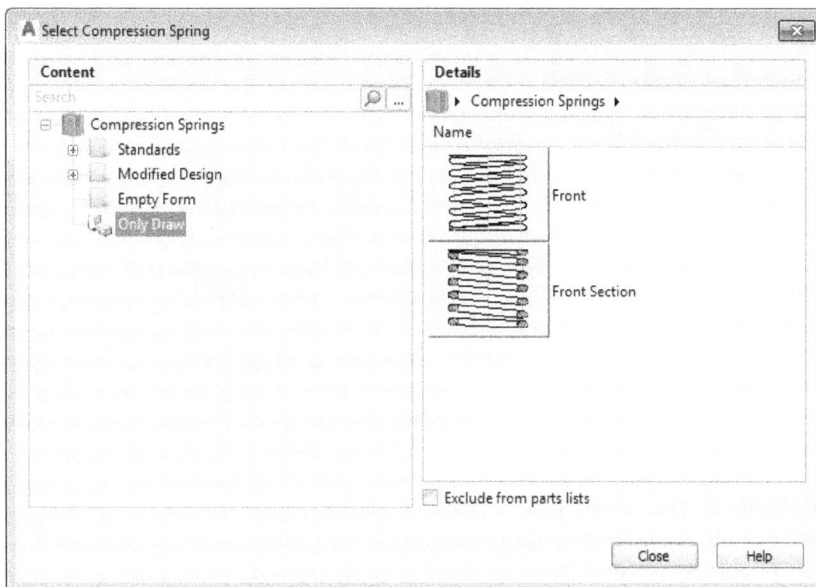

Spring by Only Draw - Define Restrictions

You can define the custom spring on the Restrictions page by selecting anding its defining geometry values. The options on this page are similar to the options that are available on the Geometry page when you are creating a custom spring based on an industry material.

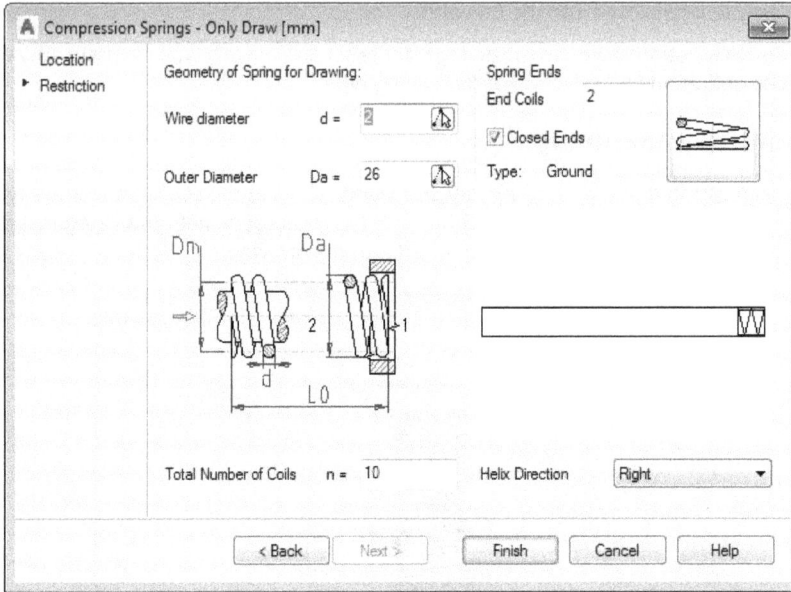

Procedure: Inserting Springs by Only Drawing the Geometry

An overview of inserting a custom spring by specifying the geometry restrictions and no industry standards is shown in the following steps:

1. Start the command for the type of spring that you want to insert.

2. In the dialog box for the spring type, in the Standard Parts pane, click Only Draw.

3. In the Details pane, click the required view direction and type.

4. In the drawing area, click a point to specify the start point of the spring.

5. Specify the direction of the spring.

6. On the Restriction page in the dialog box, select and enter the geometry restriction values so that the spring meets your requirements.

7. Click Finish.

8. In the drawing area, drag the preview until the preview and tooltip information are as required, and then click in the drawing area to create the spring.

9. If a shaft passes through the opening of the spring, select the shaft component. The spring is displayed in the drawing.

Exercise: Insert a Spring

In this exercise, you will make the assembly operative by inserting an extension spring at the lever and the base body. You will also place a spring form in the drawing with detailed information about the spring specifications.

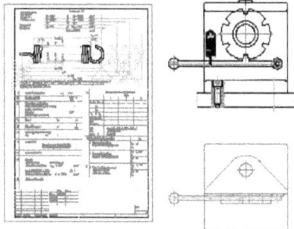

The completed exercise

1. Open *Spring Generator.dwg*.

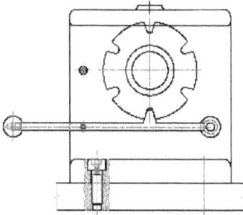

2. To begin adding an extension spring to the front view, on the Content tab > Calculation panel > Spring drop-down list, click Extension.

3. In the Select an Extension Spring dialog box:

   ▪ Content pane, expand Extension Springs and Standards categories.

   ▪ Click Gutekunst Catalog.

   ▪ In the Details pane, click Front.

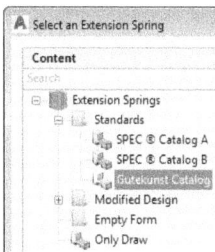

4. To specify the insertion point and direction of the spring, do the following:

   ▪ In the drawing window, object snap to the top quadrant location of the outer circle of the pin as shown in the following illustration.

   ▪ Drag the cursor down so that it polar tracks at 270 degrees. Click to specify that direction.

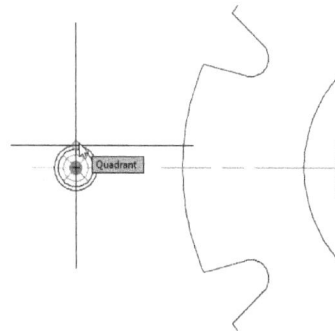

5. On the Restriction page of the Extension Springs dialog box, for the Length value, enter **65**. Click Next.

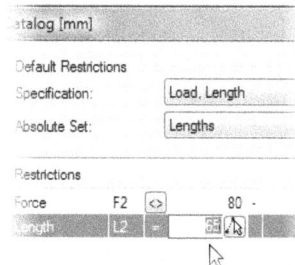

6. On the Results page, in the list of springs, click Gutekunst - 1.6 x 14.1 x 38.2X.

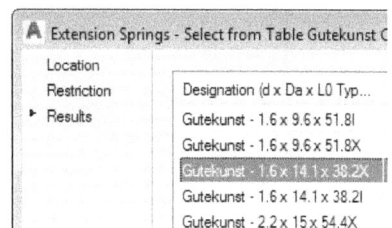

7. To insert a properties form for the selected spring, do the following:

- In the lower-left corner of the Extension Springs dialog box, click Settings.
- In the Additional Settings dialog box, select the Draw Form Together with Spring checkbox.
- Click OK.

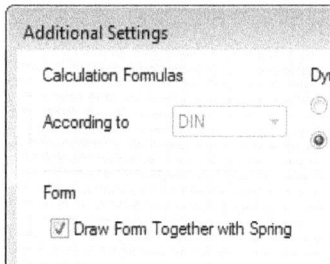

8. To set the topical length, do the following:

- Click Finish.
- In the drawing window, drag the cursor down and object snap to the intersection of the vertical centerline and the top of the circle in the lever as shown in the following illustration.

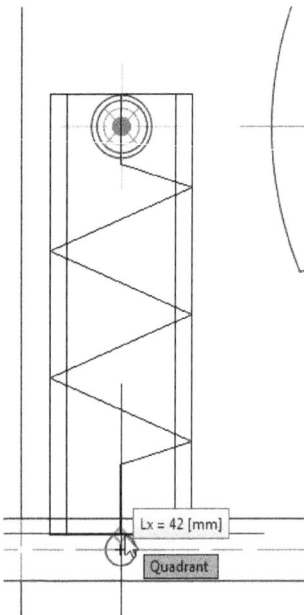

9. In the Angle of View for Drawing dialog box, with the first option selected, click Next.

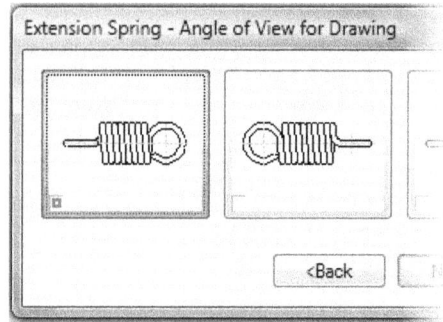

10. To finish the insertion of the spring, when prompted to select a rod, press ENTER.

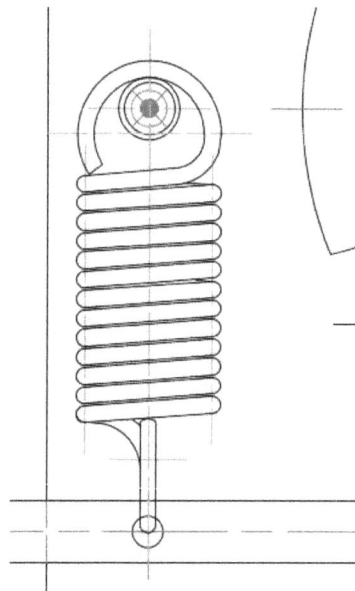

11. In the drawing window, pan and zoom to the left of the drawing views and click to insert the report form as shown in the following illustration. Review the contents of the form.

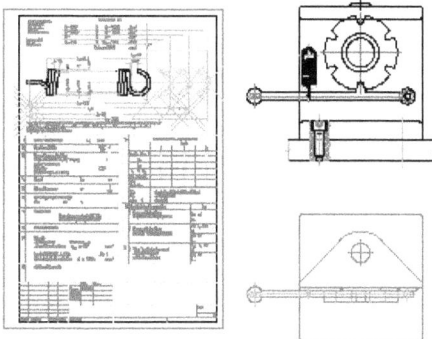

12. Save and close all files.

Chapter Summary

You have learned how to use the spring, chains and belts generators, and the Shaft Generator to create rotationally symmetric drawings.

Having completed this chapter, you can:

- Insert industry standard parts into your assembly designs.
- Add sprockets, pulleys, chains, and belts to a drawing.
- Create complete drawings of cylindrical parts with the Shaft Generator.
- Place standard shaft parts on shaft segments.
- Insert springs into an assembly design.

Creating Drawing Sheets

In this chapter, you learn how to create layout views of model space geometry and how to insert title blocks and borders into layouts and model space. You also learn how to create production-ready drawing sheets of parts or assemblies in model space and how to create annotation views of mechanically structured geometry.

Objectives

After completing this chapter, you will be able to:

- Create layout views of model space geometry.
- Create production-ready drawing sheets in model space.
- Create and edit annotation views of structured geometry.
- Insert title blocks and drawing borders.

Lesson: Model Space Views in Layouts

Overview

You can create layout views of model space geometry. By learning how to create layout views of the geometry you have drawn in model space and how to set the scale of those views, you can create production-ready drawing sheets of your part and assembly designs.

In the following illustration, production drawings for a design are shown in the process of being created. The full scale model space geometry is shown on the left and one of the layouts showing some of the model space geometry is shown on the right.

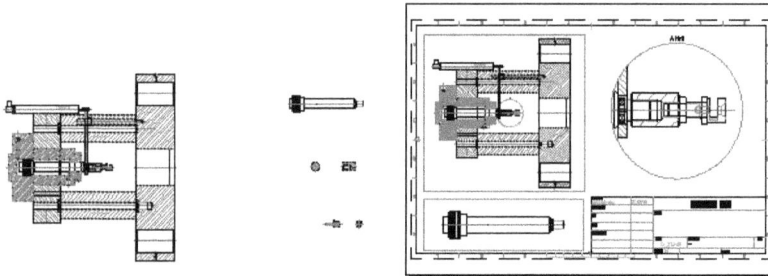

Objectives

After completing this lesson, you will be able to:

- Create viewports in a layout to show model space geometry.
- Create detail views of model space geometry in a layout.
- Create scale areas in model space.
- Create viewports from scale areas.
- Zoom all viewports simultaneously according to their scale factor.
- Toggle the visibility of viewports on and off.

Creating Model Views in Layouts

You can create drawings so that you can check that the design is working correctly and communicate your ideas to other users. You can use layouts and viewports to organize your design for communication by distributing it as a printed document or electronic media. To communicate your part or assembly designs in this way, you need to understand layouts and how to create viewports on those layouts.

In the following illustration, two different layouts have viewports that only display a portion of the geometry drawn in model space.

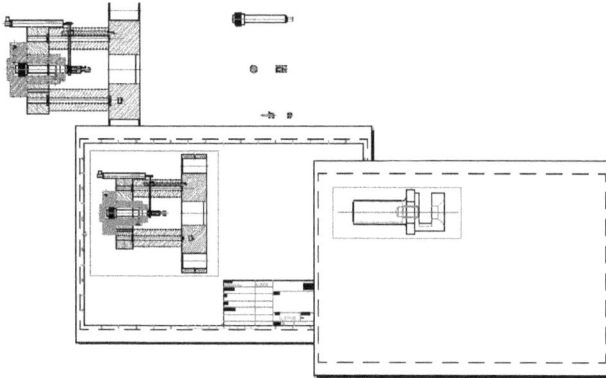

About Layouts

Layouts are an environment that is used to output your drawing data. You can use layouts to create production-ready drawings of your part or assembly designs.

In a layout, you can select the paper size on which you want to plot and set its scale to full scale (1:1). You can then create viewports on the layout to view different model space geometry at specified scale factors. You can then add additional geometry and information to the layout to enhance that plotted sheet.

By selecting and keeping the paper size at full scale and then scaling the views of the part or assembly up or down to fit on the paper, you can follow the logical and consistent approach that has been used in traditional manual drafting.

In the following illustration, the sheet on the left has the front and section views shown at full scale. The sheet on the right has those views shown at half scale (1:2). Although the views fit on the sheet at full scale, not much room is left on the sheet for supporting information. By having the views set to a smaller scale, information is presented correctly and there is additional room on the sheet for supporting information.

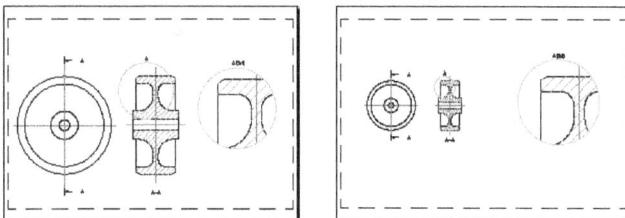

About Layout Viewport Creation

A number of commands and methods are available for creating viewports in a layout. While you can use the standard AutoCAD® viewport creation commands, the AutoCAD® Mechanical **Viewport** command enables you to create and configure your layout viewports at the same time. This command also has options and capabilities that are not available in the traditional viewport creation commands.

Each time you create a viewport, an entry is added to the Browser's Drawing tab. When you right-click on the viewport in the Browser, different shortcut menu options are available, including Edit. If you right-click on the layout name in the Browser, you can click New Viewport in the shortcut menu to start the **Viewport** command.

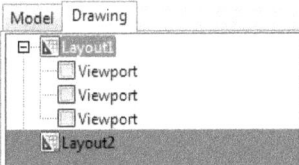

If you are using Mechanical structure, instead of creating viewports to view the model space geometry, you typically create the views directly in the layout through creating Annotation Views. If you create the annotation views in model space instead of in a layout, you can create viewports showing the model space annotation views as you would you create viewports of non-structured geometry.

Access

Command Line: AMVPORT (in Layout mode)

Ribbon: Layout tab > Viewports panel > Viewport

Options for Viewport

After you start the Viewport command, instead of creating a rectangular viewport, you can create a viewport in a different shape or slightly different procedure.

Option	Description
Circle	Creates a circular border for the viewport.
Border	Enables you to select a scale area in model space and create a viewport of that scale area.
Object	Enables you to use different predefined objects (for example, polyline or ellipse) as the border for the viewport.

View Dialog Box

You can use the View dialog box during the creation or editing of a layout viewport to set its display scale factor and other properties. The dialog box automatically opens when you are creating a new viewport using the Viewport command and after you have specified the viewport's size and location in the layout.

To open this dialog box to edit an existing viewport, in the drawing window, double-click on the viewport that you want to edit. Alternatively, in the Mechanical Browser, in the Drawing tab, right-click on the viewport and click Edit.

1. Sets the zoom magnification of the viewport to have its geometry display at the selected or entered scale relative to the layout on which the viewport is drawn.

2. Use to select a model space point that aligns with the middle of the viewport. You can think of it as the point on which you focus a camera on an object when taking a picture.

3. With this selected, the viewport display zooms in or out to match the set scale factor. If you specified a midpoint, the viewport pans the view so that the point is in the middle of the viewport.

4. Click New to redefine the viewport size and location or click Move to reposition the viewport.

5. Toggles the display of all of the viewport geometry on and off.

Creating Detail Views in a Layout

When you create a detail view, you can draw a specific area of an existing drawing view at a larger scale. You can create detail views to show enlarged areas of geometry that are not clearly displayed or dimensioned in another view. To create detail views of model space geometry in a layout, you need to know which command to use, the options for creating a detail view, and the procedure to follow.

In the following illustration, the single layout has one view of the model space design geometry and two detail views. One detail view uses the default circular boundary shape and the other one uses a closed loop object. In this case, the closed loop object is an ellipse.

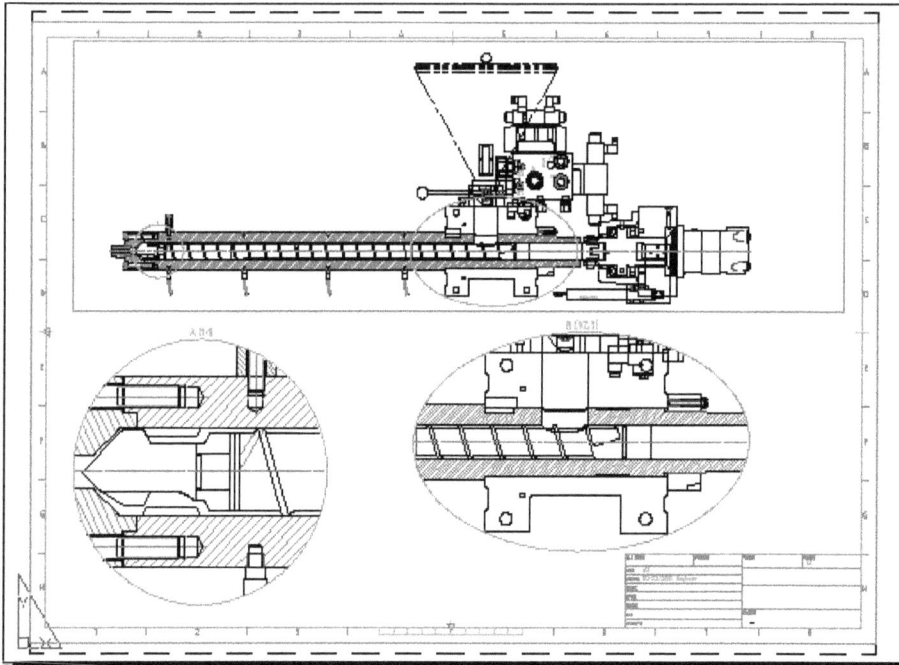

About Detail Views in a Layout

You can use the **Detail** command to create detail views in model space and on a layout tab. You can initiate the creation of a detail view from within model space or a layout. To use the **Detail** command in a layout environment, there must be an existing viewport in the layout.

When you use the **Detail** command, you can define the detailed area by creating a circular or rectangular fence area or by selecting an existing closed loop object. The closed loop object can be a polyline or ellipse. All geometry contained within the detail view rectangle or circle is included in the detail view.

The detail view magnifies the area of the drawing and is created in model space or in a layout depending on the settings that you use. The drawing view from which the detail view originates is referred to as the base view to that detail view.

Although the view is scaled, as is true of other scaled views, when you place dimensions on geometry within the view using the Power Dimensioning command, the dimensions reflect the actual geometry size.

In the following illustration, two views of the same area of a part are shown. The one view is a detail of the area and is drawn at a different scale factor. Even through the scale factors are different, the dimensions added to either view using the **Power Dimension** command display the correct dimension value for the size of the geometry.

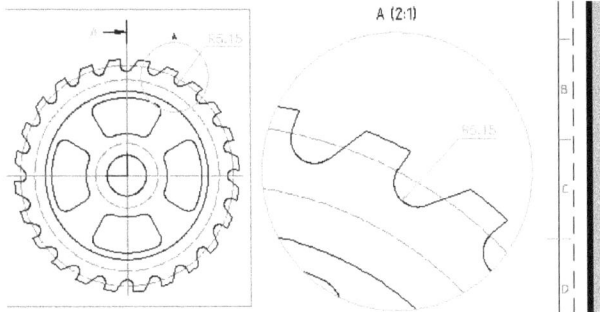

Access

Command Line: AMDETAIL

Ribbon: Home tab > Detail panel > Detail View

Menu: Draw > Detail

Detail View Creation Options

After you start the **Detail** command and specify the area to receive the detail, the Detail dialog box opens. Because the detail view's text, border, and label properties are controlled by the active standard's current settings, the name of the active standard is shown as part of the dialog box name. You can change the settings for the active standard in the Options dialog box, in the *AM:Standards* tab, with the Detail View standard element.

When you are creating a detail view, you can specify the scale factor at which to have the geometry drawn, where the detail view is going to be created, the label information for the view, which view name to use, and if there should be a leader from the view name to the boundary in the base view. If you are creating a detail view of an annotation view in a layout, you can only place the detail view in the layout and the detail view is always going to be associative to the base view.

To define the scale, you can select or a ratio in the absolute scale list or a multiplication factor in the factor field after clicking Specify By Factor.

In the Detail View area, you can specify which information to display in the view label and where and how the detail view information should be created or referenced. You can specify the view label information by entering the text to be displayed or by selecting the default fields to include.

You can specify where and how to create or reference the detail view geometry by selecting one of three options. The characteristics and use of the options are as follows:

Option	Definition
Current Space	Use this option when you want to create a detail view in the same space as the base geometry. For drawings that do not use Mechanical Structure, a copy of the detail view geometry is created in model space. The new detail view DOES NOT automatically have a viewport created in the active layout even when the command is started. If you are using Mechanical Structure, a new special associative annotation detail view is created in the layout.
Layout	Use this to create a viewport in the current or specified layout that displays the boundary area of the base view. Boundary geometry and a view name are added to the base view but no new view geometry is created with this option.
Model space and layout	This option is similar to the Detail In Current Space option except that when you have finished, a viewport is automatically created in the layout to display the new detail view geometry in model space.

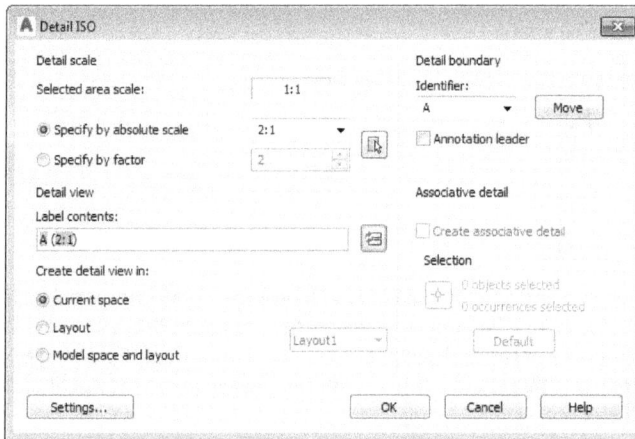

To update a detail view that is a copy in model space, after adding or modifying the geometry in the base view within the boundary area, double-click on the boundary in the base view in model space and click OK in the Detail dialog box. The detail view based on that boundary updates to reflect the current geometry in that boundary.

Procedure: Creating Detail Views in a Layout

An overview of creating a detail view in a layout using the Viewport of Original in Layout option is shown in the following steps:

1.   Select a layout with one existing viewport.

2.   On the Ribbon, click Home tab > Detail panel > Detail View.

3.   Click in the viewport to specify the center point (or first point) for the detail border.

4.   Click in the viewport to specify the size for the detail border.

5. In the Detail dialog box, in the Specify By Absolute Scale list, select or a scale factor.

6. Select the Viewport of Original in Layout option.

7. Click OK. A preview of the detail displays, attached to the cursor.

8. Click in the drawing window to place the new detail view.

Creating Scale Areas in Model Space

When you create a CAD drawing, you normally draw the geometry in its full-scale size. Creating the geometry in full size is useful as you work on your design. Outputting the geometry to paper or an electronic file at full scale is not always possible. If you cannot output the geometry at full size, you must scale it up or down to create the output.

When you create viewports on a layout you scale the display while the geometry remains at the same size. However, any text notation that you might have added to the drawing view in model space now appears to be too large or too small. By creating a scale area in model space, you can set the scale and have the text rescaled accordingly. The rescaled text then displays at the correct height in the layout.

If you need to draw the geometry in model space larger or smaller than it actually is, you can define the area around that geometry as a scale area and set the area to compensate any dimension added to it. Because the distance the dimension is measuring between is larger or smaller than its true size, the dimension values are automatically adjusted to show the true size value for that distance.

Model Space Scale Areas

You can use the Scale Area command to define one or more scale areas in model space.

Access

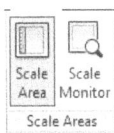

Command Line: AMSCAREA (in Model Space)

Ribbon: View tab > Scale Areas panel > Scale Area

Scale Area Dialog Box

After you start the **Viewport/Scale Area** command, you can define the area in model space that you want to set with a scale and scaling method. You can define the area by drawing a rectangle or circle or selecting a closed polyline or ellipse. With the scale area specified, the Scale Area dialog box opens enabling you to set the scale and type of scaling.

If you click the Length Scaling option, the values of the dimensions in this area are increased or decreased based on the scale factor. When Text Scaling is clicked, the text in this area can be selected for automatic scaling.

Selecting Automatic View Creation In enables you to create a viewport of this area in the selected layout when creating the model space scale area.

Procedure: Creating Scale Areas in Model Space

An overview of how to define a scale area in model space is shown in the following steps:

1.   On the Ribbon, click View tab > Scale Areas panel > Scale Area.

2.   Define the scale area as a rectangle, circle, closed polyline, or ellipse shaped area.

3.   In the Scale Area dialog box, set the scale factor and select the type of scaling.

4.   If required, select existing objects in the scale area that require rescaling.

Creating Viewports from Scale Areas

You can use the Viewport Auto Create command when you have created one or more scale areas in a drawing and want to place them in the same layout. You can generate viewports in a layout from all of the scale areas that have not been assigned to a viewport.

Access

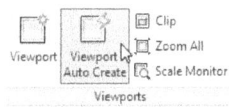

Command Line: AMVPORTAUTO

Ribbon: Layout tab > Viewports panel > Viewport Auto Create

Menu: View > Viewports > Viewport Auto Create

Procedure: Creating Viewports with the Viewport Auto Create Command in Layouts

To create one or more viewports in the active layout based on scale areas in model space, complete the following steps:

1.   On the Ribbon, click Layout tab > Viewports panel > Viewport Auto Create.

2.   Select the target position or positions, or press ENTER to accept the default position in the current layout.

3.   The viewport or viewports are created and zoomed according to the predefined scale factor.

Zooming All Viewport to Defined Scales

Use the Zoom All Viewports command to zoom all viewports simultaneously according to the assigned scale factor. Viewport scales are assigned using AutoCAD Mechanical tools that create viewports. You can use the Zoom All Viewports command to compare the scale factor of each viewport and the current zoom ratio of each viewport in the current layout. If the assigned scale and actual scale differ, all viewports in the current layout are adjusted according to the assigned scale. If the viewport has a midpoint value set, the viewport has that point at its center.

Access

Command Line: AMVPZOOMALL

Ribbon: Layout tab > Viewports panel > Zoom All

Menu: View > Viewports > Zoom all Viewports

Procedure: Adjusting Viewports with Zoom All Viewports

An overview of having all viewports zoom to their set mechanical scale is shown in the following steps:

1. Select a layout.

2. On the Ribbon, click Layout tab> Viewports panel > Zoom All.

Viewport Layer On/Off

You can control the visibility of the viewport layer (AM_VIEWS) with the **Viewport Layer On/Off** command. For this command to work, the viewport must be created on the AM_VIEWS layer. Using the command decreases the need to know all of the layer names.

Access

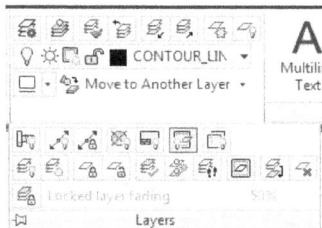

Ribbon: Home tab > expanded Layers panel > Viewport Layer On/Off

Menu: Format > Layer Tools > Viewport Layer On/Off

Exercise: Create Viewports and Details in Layouts

In this exercise, you will create multiple views on different layouts to show the drawing view geometry of an assembly and parts drawn in model space.

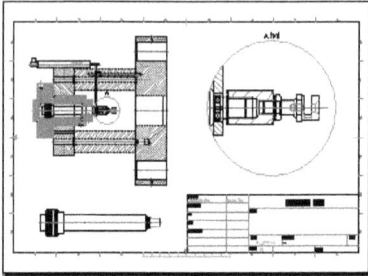

The completed exercise

Create Layout Viewports to Display Model Space Geometry

In this section of the exercise, you will use different methods and workflows to create viewports in layouts to display model space geometry.

1. Open *Create Views in Layouts.dwg*.

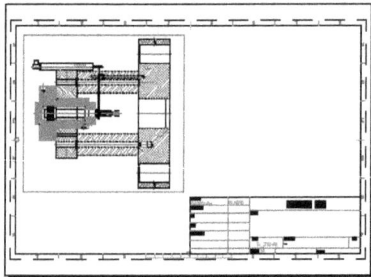

2. You are required to be in the Structure workspace (Status Bar>Workspace Switching>Structure). In the Mechanical Browser, click on the *Drawing* tab and note that the layouts are displayed. Note the information displayed on the current layout.

3. In the Mechanical Browser, click on the *Model* tab and note the number of additional views in model space.

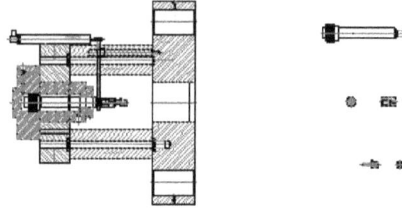

4. In the Mechanical Browser, click on the *Drawing* tab to open the layouts and verify that Layout1 is selected.

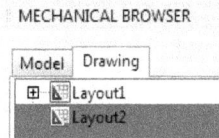

5. To begin creating a viewport to show a part in model space, in the Ribbon, click on Layout tab > Viewports panel > Viewport.

6. In the drawing window, below the layout view and along the left side of the title block, click to define a rectangular viewport as shown in the following illustration.

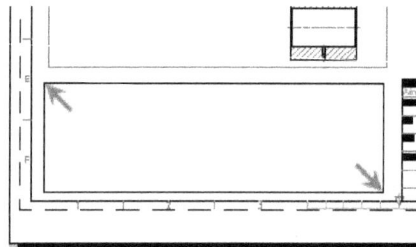

7. In the View dialog box, in the Scale list, select **1:2.5**.

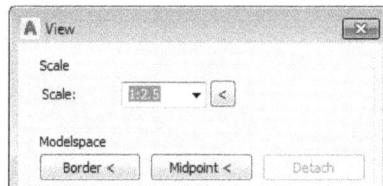

8. To set the geometry to display in the viewport:

- In the View dialog box, in the Modelspace area, click Midpoint.

- In the drawing window, click the midpoint of the part as shown in the following illustration.

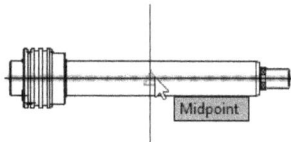

9. In the View dialog box, click OK. Review the results of the viewport creation.

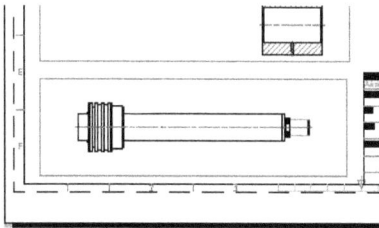

10. In the Mechanical Browser, in the *Drawing* tab, double-click on Layout2 to open it.

11. To create a viewport based on an existing model space scale area:

- Click on Layout tab > Viewports panel > Viewport.

- Right-click in the drawing window and click Border.

- In model space, select the scale area rectangle.

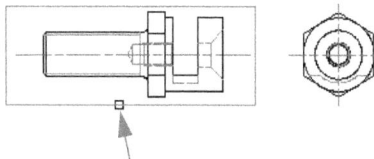

12. To position and create the viewport:

- Click in the upper left corner of the layout.

- In the View dialog box, click OK.

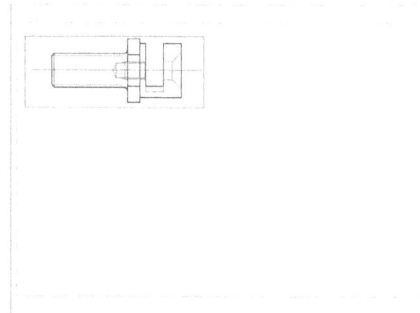

13. In the Mechanical Browser, select the Model tab to set it to be current.

14. To begin creating a scale area in model space around the end view of the same part and a viewport of the scale area in a layout, click on View tab > Scale Areas panel > Scale Area.

15. In the drawing window, define a rectangular scale area around the view as shown in the following illustration.

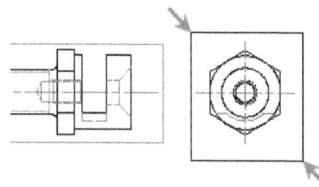

16. In the Scale Area dialog box:

- In the Scale drop-down list, select 2:1.
- Place a checkmark in the box next to the Automatic view creation in option.
- Clear the Perform rescaling checkbox.
- Click OK.

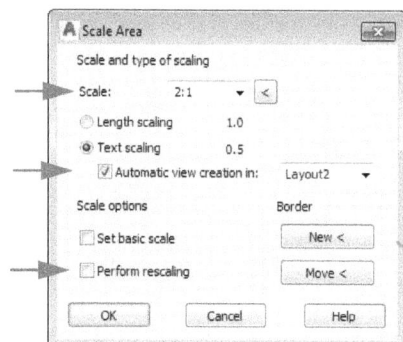

17. Click to position the viewport as shown in the following illustration.

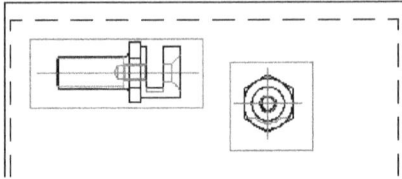

18. To align the two views, start the Move command, select the last created viewport, set the base point by object snapping to the endpoint of the horizontal centerline, and object track from the horizontal centerline in the front view.

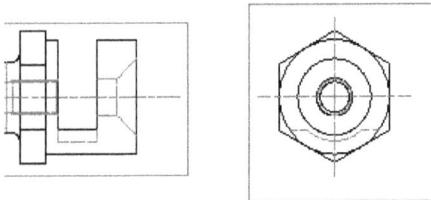

Create a Detail View

In this section of the exercise, you will create a detail view and create a scale area around the base view to have the annotation label sized correctly.

1. In the Drawing tab, double-click on Layout1 to make it active.

2. In the Mechanical Browser, select the Model tab to make it current.

3. To begin creating a detail view of an area in the assembly and have a viewport created, on the Home tab, in the Detail panel, click Detail View.

4. In the drawing window, specify the detail view area by defining a circular area similar to the one shown in the following illustration.

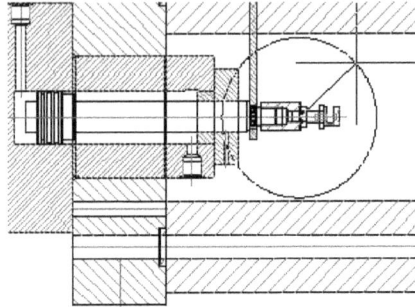

5. In the Detail ISO dialog box:
- In the Detail scale area, click Specify by factor.
- In the Scale by factor field, enter **1**.

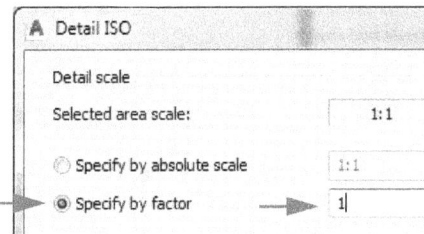

6. In the Detail view area, select the Model space and layout option, and verify that the drop-down list is set to Layout1. Click OK.

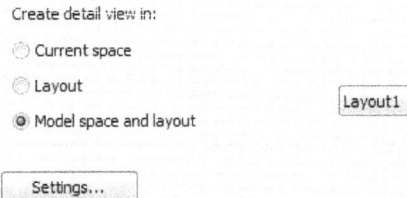

7. In the drawing window, click to position the copy above the base view.

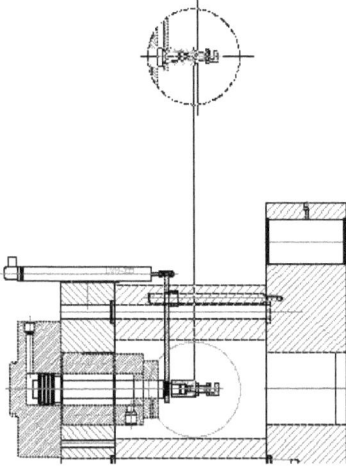

8. Click to position the view in the open area of the viewport as shown in the following illustration.

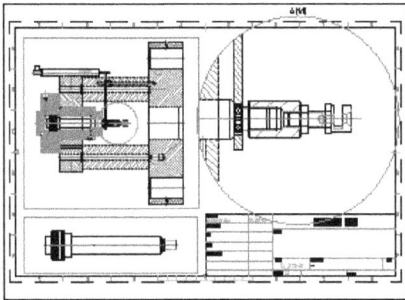

9. In the Mechanical Browser, select the *Model* tab to make it current.

10. Grip edit the size of the detail view boundary circle to make it smaller and call out a smaller area as shown in the following illustration.

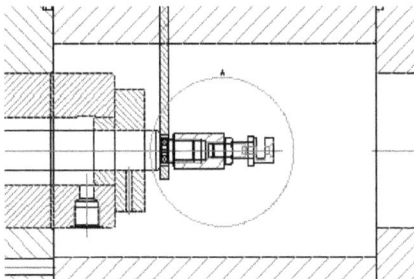

11. To update the separate detail view:

- Double-click on the detail view boundary circle.
- In the Detail dialog box, click OK.
- Press ENTER twice to set the detail views to their current position.

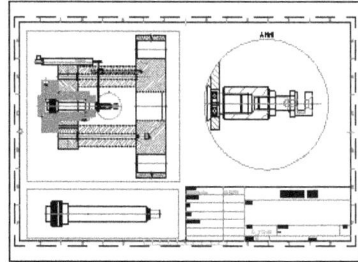

12. To begin creating a scale area in model space to have the label for the detail view boundary display the correct height:

- In the Mechanical Browser, select the *Model* tab to set it current.
- Click on View tab > Scale Areas panel > Scale Area.

13. In the drawing window, define a rectangular scale area around the view as shown in the following illustration.

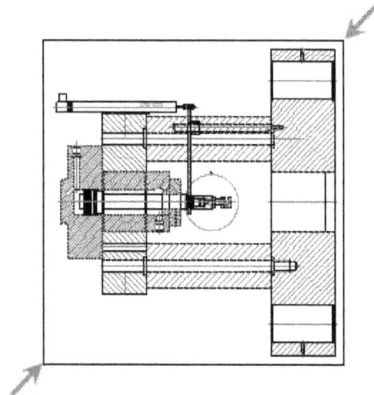

14. In the Scale Area dialog box:

   - In the Scale list, select 1:5.
   - In the Scale options area, ensure that the Perform rescaling checkbox is selected.
   - Click OK.

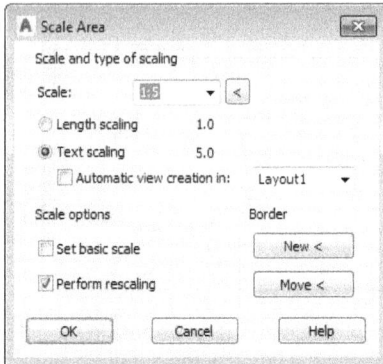

15. In the drawing window, select the label for the detail view boundary circle. Press ENTER.

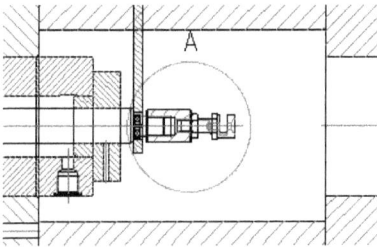

16. In the Mechanical Browser, select the Drawing tab and ensure that Layout1 is the current view. Review the display of the annotation in the layout.

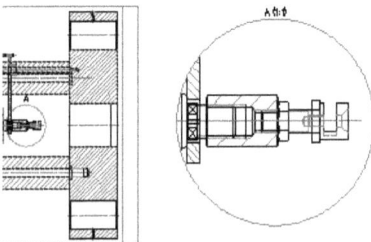

17. Save and close all of the files.

Lesson: Creating Drawing Sheets in Model Space

Overview

This lesson describes creating production-ready drawing sheets in model space of parts or assemblies in model space.

If you decide not to use layouts as the method for creating production-ready drawings, you need to learn about using scale areas and detail views to add the required information to the model space drawing.

In the following illustration, multiple drawing sheets of an assembly and its parts are being prepared for output from the model space.

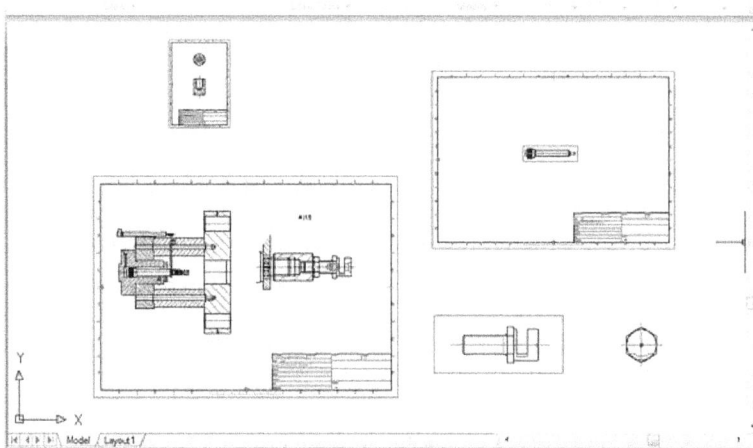

Objectives

After completing this lesson, you will be able to:

- Describe how to establish multiple drawing sheets to plot from model space.
- Determine the scale assigned to a scale area or viewport.
- Create enlarged detail views of geometry in model space.

Process of Plotting from Model Space

When creating production-ready drawings entirely in model space you follow a different workflow than if you were plotting from layouts. Because your drawings typically require plotting geometry at a scale other than full scale, you need to learn about the flow and importance of scale areas that are defined by an inserted border or detail view.

In the following illustration, the same drawing view is shown at two different scales. The view on the left is at 1:1 and the view on the right is at 1:5. By plotting the drawing on the right five times smaller, the text displays at the same height as shown in the view on the left. If the view on the left were scaled down five times, the text would become very difficult to read.

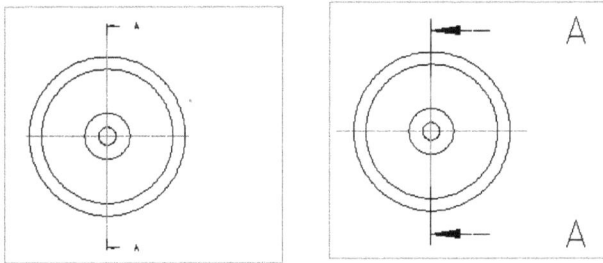

Plotting from Model Space

When you plot from model space, you insert the border and scale it up or down the inverse of the scale at which you plan to plot the drawing sheet. For example, a sheet to be plotted at half scale (1:2) has a border scaled up by a factor of 2. Therefore, when it is plotted, the border is the correct final size.

The same scaling needs to occur for any annotation symbols or text that are placed within the border. You can use scale areas to help set the correct sizes for annotation symbols and text. When you insert a border, the area in the border is automatically set as a scale area with that border's scale factor. After the scale area has been defined, any annotation symbols that you add within that area are automatically scaled up or down based on the scale factor.

You can also use scale areas in model space to specify the factor by which the geometry in the area is larger or smaller than its true full-scale size. This factor is pertinent when you are adding length dimensions to the geometry. If the geometry is drawn larger than it actually is, the dimension value must be made smaller by the scale factor for the value to be correct. When you use the detail command to create an enlarged view, the length scale factor is set correctly for the detail area.

Process: Configuring Drawing Sheets to Plot from Model Space

An overview of plotting drawing sheets from model space is shown in the following steps:

1. Create the part and assembly geometry in model space.

2. Create detail views as required to show your design with greater clarity.

3. Insert border and title blocks around the geometry for each required plotted sheet and set the correct scale values.

4. Define additional scale areas around the geometry if the scale differs from the border scale.

5. Add the required annotation to the view geometry and within the border.

6. Review and adjust the scale values for the different scale areas.

7. Plot the drawing sheets by specifying a plot window around the border.

Determining Scale Overrides

You can use the Scale Monitor tool to determine the scale assigned to an area or viewport in the drawing. You can also use this tool to quickly edit the scale or zoom to a scale area or viewport. To edit the scale area in model space, it must have been defined using the Viewport/Scale Area command. The scale monitor information displayed in the dialog box is based on the location of the crosshair.

In the following illustration, the Scale Monitor dialog box shows the scale, length scale factor, and text scale factor for the highlighted border in the drawing below.

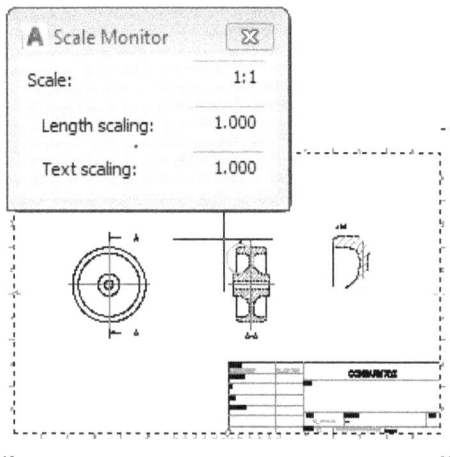

Access

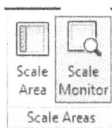

Command Line: AMSCMONITOR

Ribbon: View tab > Scale Areas panel > Scale Monitor

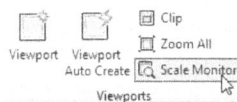

Ribbon: Layout tab > Viewports panel > Scale Monitor

Menu: View > Viewports > Scale Monitor

Scale Monitor Dialog Box

The Scale Monitor dialog box displays the scale of the area behind the cursor. It also displays the length scale and text scale of the area. Length scaling changes the value displayed when you add a dimension within the area. Text scaling changes the font size of the text and scales other AutoCAD Mechanical software annotation.

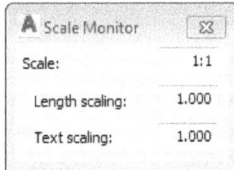

Procedure: Determining Scale Overrides

An overview of determining the length and text scale value for different areas of the model geometry is shown in the following steps:

1. Start the **Scale Monitor** command.

2. Hover the cursor over the areas of the drawing to display their scale settings in the dialog box. To zoom extents to that scale area, double-click in the area.

Creating Detail Views in Model Space

You can use the Detail View command to define and create a scaled detail view of selected geometry, parts, or subassemblies in model space as you would create them in a layout. You can create circular, rectangular, or free defined detail areas.

Unlike when you create a detail view in a layout, when you create detail views for plotting from model space, you only use the Detail in Current Space option. In a model space detail view the geometry is at a larger scale, and also defines the area of the detail view as a scaled area with a length scale factor.

If you are using Mechanical structure, you can create the detail view to be automatically associative to the component view shown in the detail view. The associative setting automatically updates the detail view when the component view definition changes.

In the following illustration, a detail view of the full section was added to the right of the section view. By using the scale monitor and hovering over the detail view, the length scaling factor is set so that any length dimensions added to this view display the correct values.

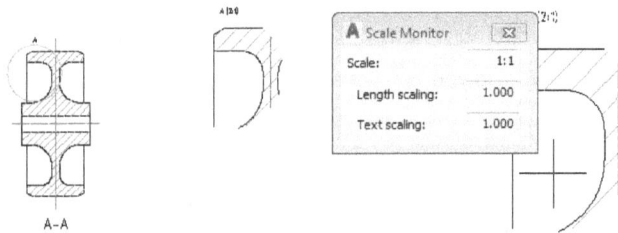

Access

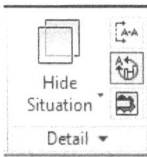

Command Line: AMDETAIL

Ribbon: Home tab > Detail panel > Detail View

Menu: Draw > Detail

Procedure: Creating Detail Views in Model Space

An overview of creating detail views in model space is shown in the following steps:

1. Start the **Detail View** command.

2. In the drawing area, specify the area that you want to display at a larger scale.

3. In the Detail dialog box, set the scale factor for the detail view.

4. Specify the location in model space at which to place the detail view.

Exercise: Create Drawing Sheets in Model Space

In this exercise, you will review the scale values for different scale areas in model space, insert a detail view to define a new scale area and new geometry, define a scale area around existing geometry, and change the scale set for an existing border.

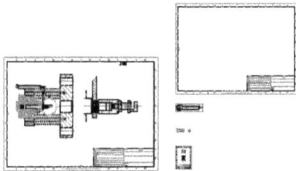

The completed exercise

1. Open *Drawing Sheets in Model Space.dwg*.

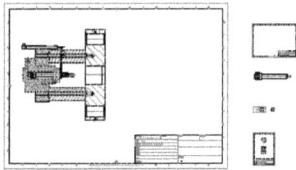

2. To review the existing scaling values in the drawing, do the following:

   ▪ In the View tab>Scale Areas panel, click Scale Monitor.

   ▪ Hover the cursor over the different title blocks and drawing geometry. Review the values in the Scale Monitor dialog box. The scale area in the larger title block has a scale of 1:5 with a length scale factor of 1 and a text scaling factor of 5 times.

   ▪ Press ENTER.

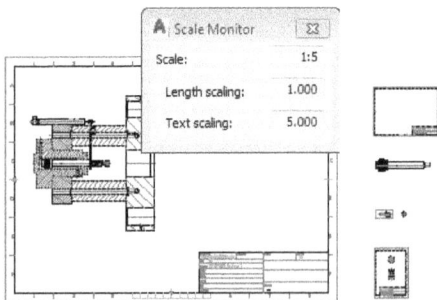

3. Zoom in to the center area of the section view of the assembly view.

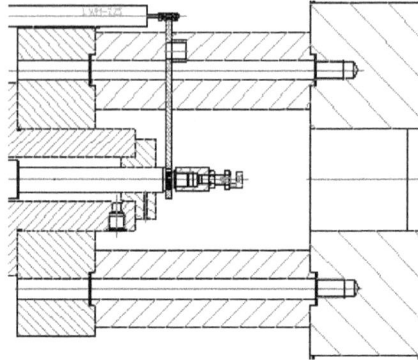

4. To begin creating a detail view of an area of the assembly:

   ▪ Click Home tab > Detail panel > Detail View.

   ▪ In the drawing area, specify the detail view area by defining a circular area similar to the one shown in the following illustration.

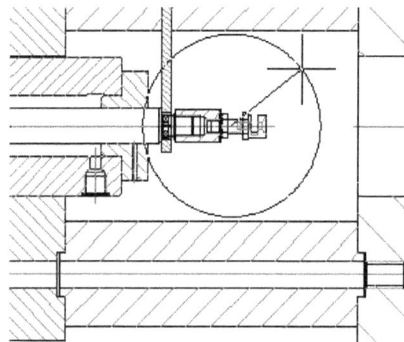

5. In the Detail ISO dialog box:

- In the Detail Scale area, click Specify by factor.
- In the Scale factor field, enter **5**.
- Click OK.

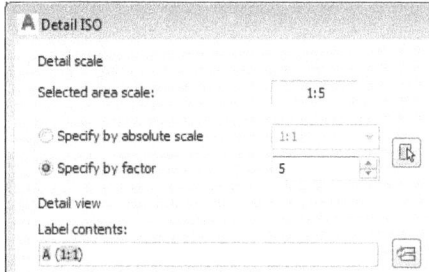

6. In the drawing area, click to position the copy to the right of the base view and within the border.

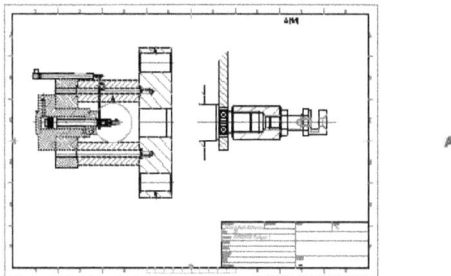

7. Click View tab > Scale Areas panel > Scale Monitor. Hover the cursor over the detail view to review its scale and scale factors. Note that the Length scaling is 0.2 and the Text scaling is 5.0 while the full section has a scale of 1:1. Press ENTER.

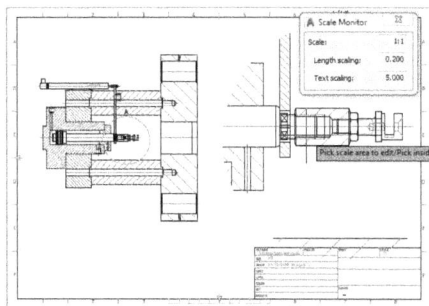

8. To begin defining a scale area around the piston shaft drawing geometry:

- Zoom in to the piston shaft.
- Click View tab > Scale Areas panel > Scale Area.
- In the drawing area, draw a rectangular scale area around the piston shaft as shown in the following illustration.

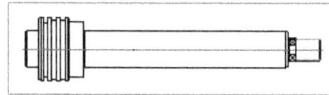

9. In the Scale Area dialog box:

- In the Scale drop-down list, select 1:2.
- In the Scale options area, clear the Perform rescaling checkbox.
- Click OK.

10. Click View tab > Scale Areas panel > Scale Monitor. Hover the cursor over the scale area and the title block directly above the scale area to review their scale and scale factors. Press ENTER.

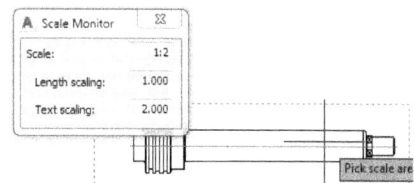

11. To change the scale factor of the empty title block:

   - In the drawing area, double-click on the outer line on the title block.
   - In the Drawing Borders with Title Block dialog box, in the Scale drop-down list, select 1:4.
   - Click OK.
   - Press ENTER twice.

12. Click View tab > Scale Areas panel > Scale Monitor. Hover the cursor over the title block to review its scale and scale factors. Press ENTER.

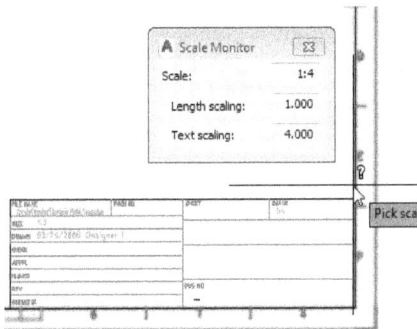

13. Save and close all of the files.

Lesson: Annotation Views When Using Structure

Overview

This lesson describes the creation and editing of annotation views.

When you follow a workflow of creating a structured part or subassembly in the context of an overall assembly drawing file, you need to document the part or subassembly by itself and not as it would display in the overall assembly with modified linetypes or hidden lines. You typically need separate documentation of the part or subassembly component for manufacturing the part or subassembly. To create separate views without affecting the quantity count in the assembly, you need to learn about annotation views and how to create and edit them.

In the following illustration, the component views in model space are shown on the left and an annotation view of the assembly component is shown on the right. The annotation view enables the order of the component views to be displayed differently than in the original design and with different notation information.

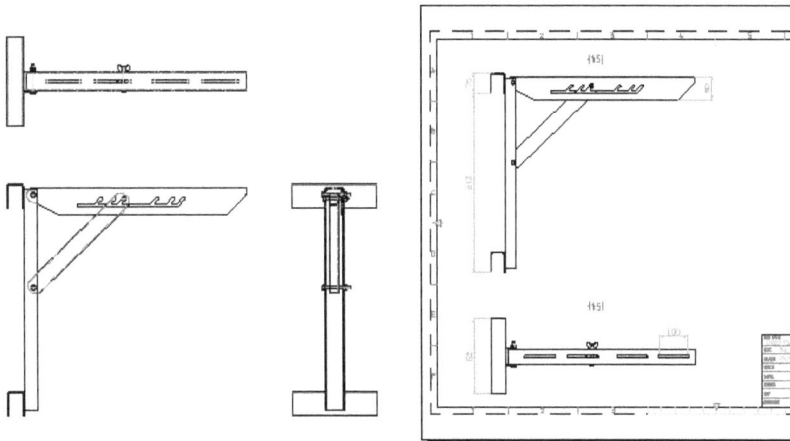

Objectives

After completing this lesson, you will be able to:

- Describe the purpose of annotation views and where they are created.
- Create an annotation view of a part or assembly component.
- Edit annotation views of a part or assembly component.

About Annotation Views

To achieve a greater benefit from creating mechanically structured designs, you should use annotation views to document the design. Before learning how to create and edit annotation views, you should learn the purpose of annotation views and where they can be created. With this understanding, it is easier to learn and understand how to create and edit annotation views.

In the following illustration, a drawing sheet to show the progressive steps for assembly is being created in a layout. In this case a single annotation view of an assembly contains multiple views of the same structured component. The two views on the left were edited to only display some of the components in the assembly. An additional component view is being added to the annotation view.

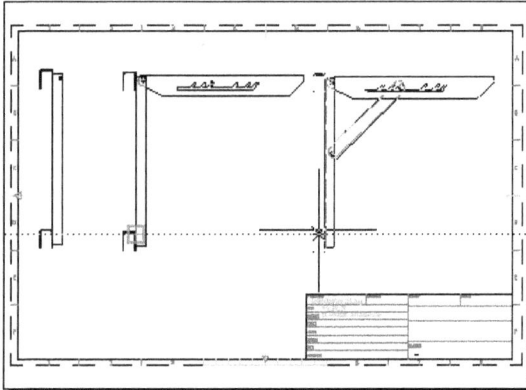

Definition of Annotation Views

Annotation views are inserted component views of a defined part or assembly component. You can create annotation views to display component view definitions in their true form for the purpose of fully documenting that separate part or assembly. You can create and insert an annotation view in model space or directly into a layout. You can also externally reference an annotation view and insert it into the current drawing.

An annotation view only pertains to a single assembly or part component definition. After you select the component to which the annotation view pertains, you can insert the required views from that component. The component view then always displays the current information for that component and view. Any changes made to the design are automatically reflected in the views in the annotation view. Within the annotation view, you can add any of the component's views multiple times or not at all. You can add the same view multiple times to an annotation view when you have different documentation requirements of the same view.

The component views inserted with an annotation view do not increase the quantity count of that component in the assembly's bill of materials. The annotation view and its information are only there for display reference. The annotation view can be used to specify the parts that are listed in a parts list. For example, if you want to document a subassembly in the same drawing as an overall assembly while having different parts lists for each, you can create separate annotation views and then create the parts list based on the separate annotation views.

When you insert an annotation view into model space, it is listed in the Browser between the drawing filename and the first component. An annotation view inserted into a layout causes the annotation view to display in the Browser below that layout name.

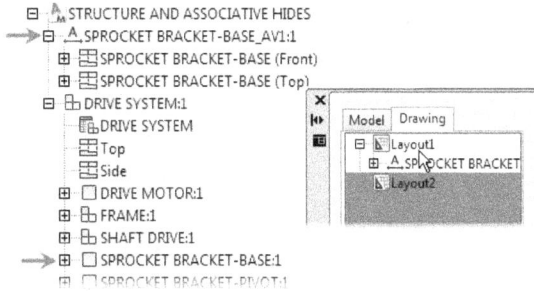

After you create an annotation view, you can edit it to add additional geometry, symbols, or notation. When you add information to the active annotation view, it becomes part of the annotation view definition. Therefore, if you use the annotation view again in the active drawing or reference it into another drawing, the information is automatically included. You can also override the annotation view's display settings to have it display differently from the primary design.

Along with creating and adding annotation views in the current drawing, you can also externally reference annotation views from other drawings. Reasons for externally referencing annotation views might include needing to create a drawing set that documents all of the parts and subassemblies in a design or needing to show how another part or assembly relates to this design without including the part or assembly in this assembly design. A primary benefit of externally referencing annotation views is that the annotation view displays the most current information for that view while also providing flexibility in what is displayed in the annotation view.

Example of Using Annotation Views

Because the assembly design shown in the following illustration was created using structured components and associative hides, an annotation view of the bracket was easily created on a layout that shows all of the edge geometry for that part. The annotation view of the bracket shows the line geometry, although some of it is not viewable in the assembly view.

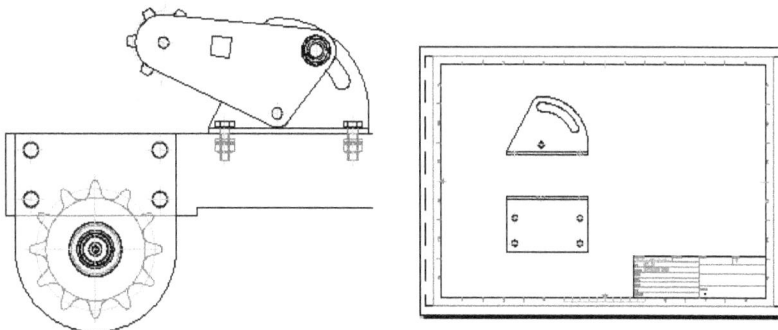

Key Points of Annotation Views

Note the following key points when using or creating annotation views:

- Used specifically with Mechanical Structure.
- Used to document and annotate your designs.
- Enable you to document a design and reuse the design geometry at the same time.
- Can be created in model space or layouts.
- Can be externally referenced from other drawings.
- Can have a different display to the primary design.
- Can have drawing geometry and notation added within the defined annotation view.
- Does not increase the component's quantity count in the assembly's bill of materials.

Creating Annotation Views

You can create annotation views of your mechanically structured designs when creating production drawings. To create drawing views for documentation, you need to know how to start creating annotation views, the procedure to follow, and the options available for creating annotation views.

In the following illustration, the Browser and drawing area are shown with three annotation views that have been partially dimensioned. The first two annotation views only have one component view displayed while the third annotation view has two component views displayed.

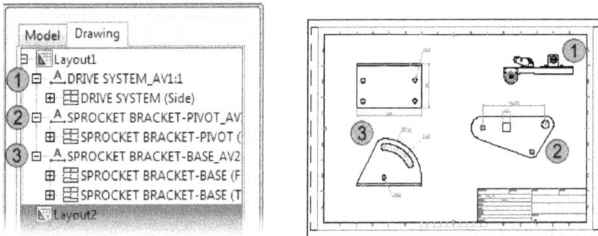

Access

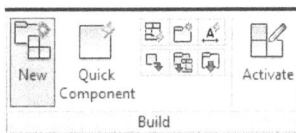

Command Line: AMSNEW

Ribbon: Structure tab > Build panel > New

You can use the **New Structure** command to create an annotation view of a part or assembly component or right-click on the component in the Browser and click New > Annotation View in the shortcut menu. The annotation view's name defaults to the name of the selected component and a suffix of (AV). You can a new name for the annotation view while it is being created. You can also set a new default suffix by changing it in the Options dialog box on the AM:Structure tab.

New Dialog Box - Annotation View Tab

When you use the New Structure command to create a new annotation view, the New dialog box opens. With the *Annotation View* tab active, you can set the component to insert as an annotation view, specify where it is going to be placed, and toggle on or off the inclusion of view labels. If you start the New Structure command when a layout is active, only the Annotation View tab is shown in the dialog box.

1.   When creating a new annotation view, select a component from the list and a name for the annotation view. When adding instances of a component view or adding views to an annotation view, select the appropriate view from the list.

2.   Specify where the annotation view is going to be inserted.

3.   Use to calculate an appropriate drawing scale for the annotation view. Select a paper size to have it automatically calculate a scale value or select a specific view scale that matches your requirements. **Note:** The paper size setting does not change the paper size of a selected layout.

4.   Set the insertion basepoint for the annotation view definition. The annotation view basepoint can be redefined using the procedure that is used to redefine a component view's basepoint.

5.   Select to have a label positioned for the component views within the annotation view. The appearance and information in the label is initially based on the configuration in the active standard.

Externally Referenced Annotation Views

You can use the Structure Catalog to create an external reference to an annotation view in another drawing. You can create the external reference by dragging and dropping the annotation view from the Details pane to the drawing area. After dropping the referenced annotation view into the drawing area, you are prompted to specify the scale for the views, the insertion point, and rotation angle. The referenced view's scale value can be a completely different scale than its original scale.

In the following illustration, an annotation view is being created in the current drawing by externally referencing it from another drawing as shown on the left. After the insertion location and scale were specified, the new annotation view listed in the Browser as shown in the middle. The annotation view and component views display a blue triangle on their icons to indicate they are externally referenced as shown on the right.

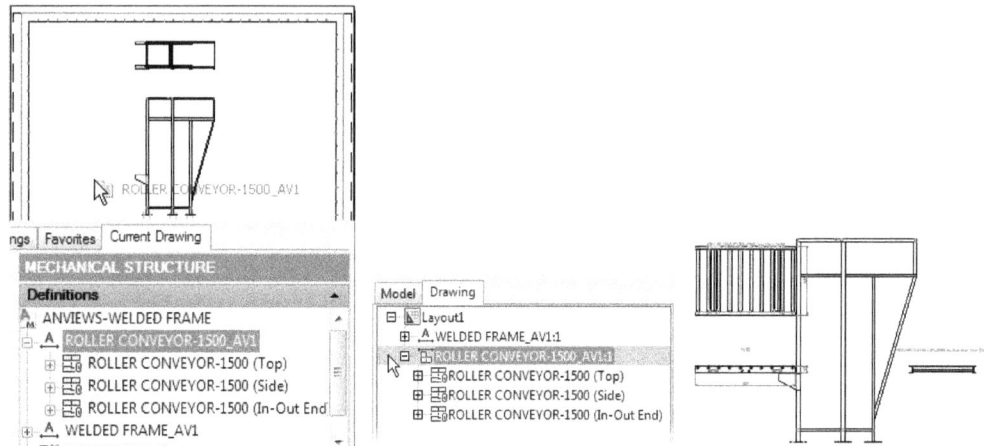

Standards Settings for the Annotation View Label

Each component view in an annotation view can display a label for which information is automatically populated. The information is based on the Annotation View configuration in the standard and the information unique for that component view. Automatic label information can be the component name, view name, and scale. You can also add your own text to the label for each individual component view or by editing the standards element Annotation View.

You can configure the settings for the view label in the Annotation View Settings dialog box. You can open this dialog box from the Options dialog box, in the *AM:Standards* tab by double-clicking on the standards element Annotation View.

Under Label, you can select or the text that should be displayed and whether it is positioned above or below the annotation view. Under Text, you can select the style, color, and height properties for the text.

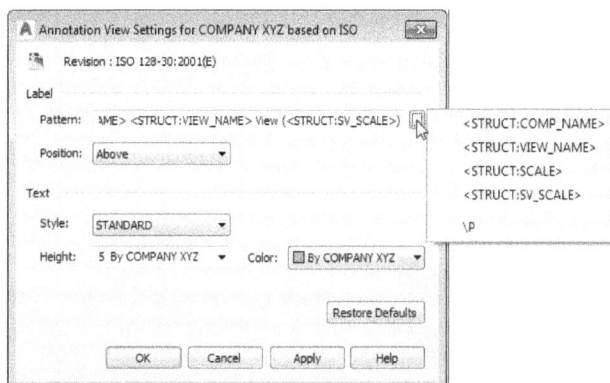

Procedure: Creating an Annotation View

An overview of using the New Structure command to create a new annotation view for a part or assembly component in a layout is shown in the following steps:

1. On the Ribbon, click Structure tab > Build panel > New.

2. In the New dialog box, select and set the component, placement, and label options to match your requirements, as follows:
   - Select the component from the list of components and edit the annotation view name if required.
   - Click the Layout option. In the list of layouts, select the name of the layout in which you want to insert the new annotation view.
   - Select or a specific scale if the automatically calculated scale for the selected paper size does not match your requirements.
   - Specify the insertion basepoint for the annotation view.
   - Select or clear the option for inserting a label for all subviews.

3. In the drawing window, specify the insertion point for the component view.

4. Specify the rotation angle for the component view.

5. Continue specifying insertion locations and rotation angles for other component views of the component or the same component view if required.

6. Right-click when the annotation view contains the required views.

Editing Annotation Views

After you create annotation views, you need to add to the annotation view and modify what it contains or how it displays. To create the final results, you need to know about the types of edits you can make to the annotation views of a part or assembly component and how to initiate those edits.

In the following illustration, the Browser is shown with an active annotation view and a portion of a layout with the same annotation view and added dimensions. The dimensions were added directly to the annotation view so that they always display where the annotation view is inserted. The dimension values are the correct ones for the design, although the annotation view is displayed at a scale smaller than full size.

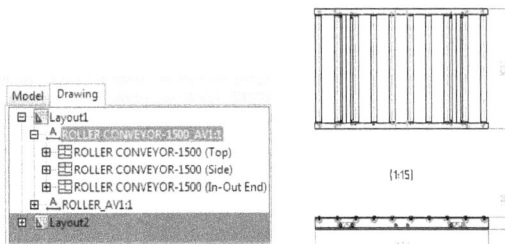

Editing Annotation Views

You can use the Browser to initiate an edit of an annotation view. When you want to edit an annotation view, you can activate it before making the modifications or select a shortcut menu option to make a specific type of edit. To activate an annotation view for an edit, double-click on the annotation view in the Browser. You can access the shortcut menu options by right-clicking on the annotation view in the Browser.

When the annotation view is active, you can add geometry, notation, or symbols to the annotation view. You can also modify any added geometry or delete component views from the annotation view. However, you cannot modify the geometry in a component view when editing the annotation view. You can add dimensions, geometry, or other notation to an active annotation view when you want that information to carry forward with the annotation view if additional instances of it are created in the same or other drawings. If you add dimensions, geometry, or other notations when the annotation view is not active, that information does not carry forward with any additional instances of the annotation view.

Edits to an annotation view can include:

- Activating the view to add geometry, notation, or symbols directly in the view.
- Deleting component views from the annotation view.
- Adding more views of the component to the annotation view.
- Overriding the properties of a component view or all of the views in the annotation view.
- Toggling the visibility of component views.
- Changing the insertion basepoint.
- Editing the scale for the views.

> When you add power dimensions to an annotation view, regardless of whether it is active or not, the values for the dimensions automatically display the correct value, although the geometry in the annotation view might be larger or smaller than its true full scale size.

Localizing Externally Referenced Annotation Views

A variation for externally referenced annotation views is to have the annotation view that is local with the component views within the annotation view externally referenced. You can create this type of variation by localizing an annotation view that was initially externally referenced. With this annotation view configuration variation, you can modify or add to the annotation view while also having the component view always display the current and most up-to-date information. After making changes, you can write the annotation view back to the drawing file from which it was initially referenced. When you write the annotation view back, you add it to that drawing file and establish the annotation view as an external reference.

You can localize an externally referenced annotation view by right-clicking on the view in the Browser and clicking Localize Annotation View in the shortcut menu. If you have changed the annotation view and want to write it back to the original drawing, right-click on the annotation view in the Browser and click Externalize To <drawing name>.

In the following illustration, the Browser is shown before and after localizing the annotation view. While the annotation view is local, the component views within the annotation view are still externally referenced as indicated by the paper clip in their Browser icons.

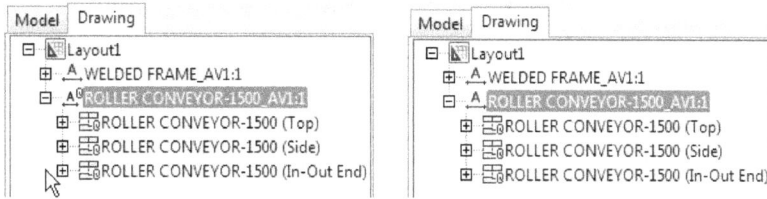

Process: Editing Annotation Views

The following diagram shows the process and options for editing annotation views.

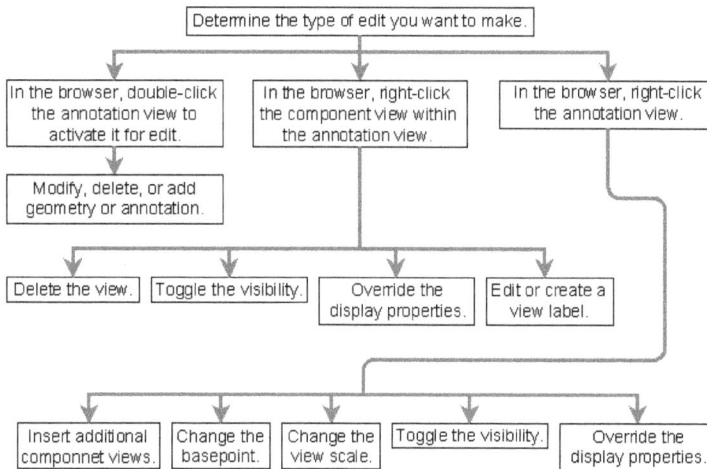

Exercise: Create and Edit Annotation Views

In this exercise, you will create annotation views of structured content, edit the annotation views to add content to the view, and externally reference an annotation view.

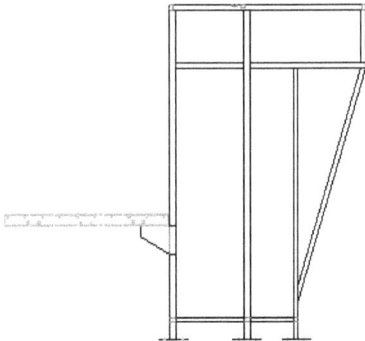

The completed exercise

Create Annotation Views

In this section of the exercise, you will create annotation views of different structured components.

1. Open *AnViews-Roller Conveyor-1500.dwg*.

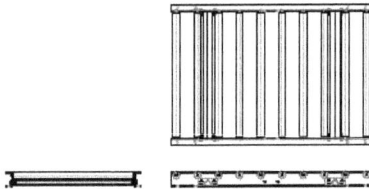

2. Verify that the Workspace is set as Structure. (Status Bar>Workspace Switching> Structure).

3. On the Structure tab > Build panel, click New.

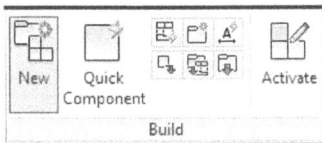

4. To set the component for which to create an annotation view, in the New dialog box, in the *Annotation View* tab, under Component, in the Create annotation view of list, select ROLLER CONVEYOR-1500.

5. To specify the placement location and include labels:

   - In the Placement area, click Layout.
   - In the Label area, click the Create labels for all subviews checkbox.
   - Click OK.

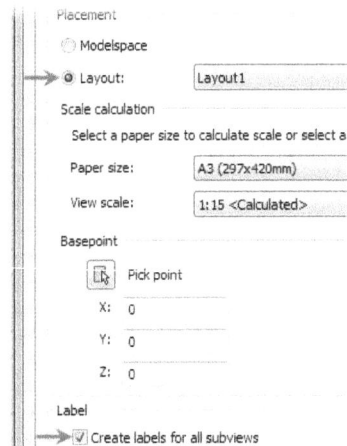

6. To add the first view in the annotation view to Layout1, do the following:

   - In the drawing window, click to position the view on the sheet approximately where shown in the following illustration.
   - For the rotation angle, press ENTER.

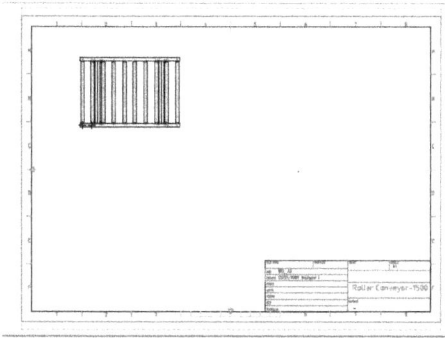

7. Continuing with the same command, position two more views approximately as shown in the following illustration and press ENTER when prompted for the rotation angle after positioning the view. Press ENTER to end the command after setting the second view. The labels are placed automatically once you end the command.

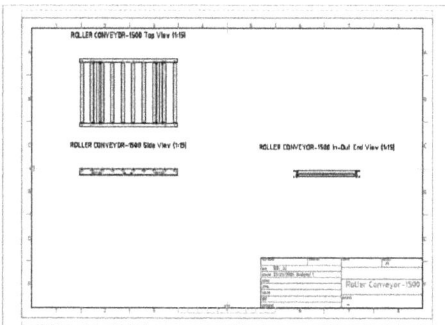

8. To begin adding another annotation view of another component to the same layout:

- On the Structure tab > Build panel, click New.
- In the New dialog box, in the Create annotation view of list, select ROLLER (ROLLER.dwg).
- In the Scale calculation area, in the View scale list, select 1:5.
- Click OK.

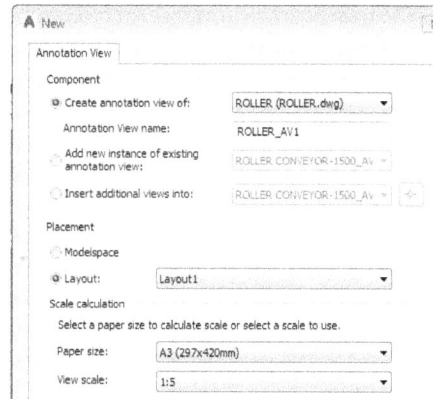

9. In the drawing area, click to position the two views of the component as shown in the following illustration. Press ENTER when prompted for the rotation angle. Press ENTER to end the command after setting the second view.

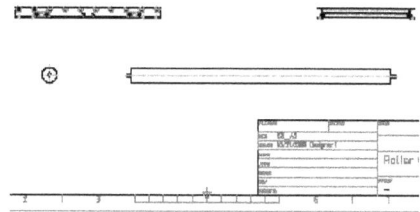

10. In the Browser, double-click on Layout2 to set it to be active.

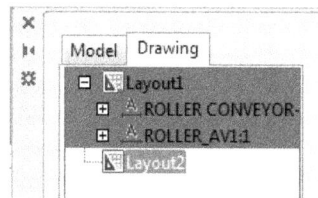

11. To begin creating another annotation view of the overall assembly with only one view:

- On the Structure tab > Build panel, click New.
- In the New dialog box, in the Create annotation view of list, select ROLLER CONVEYOR-1500.
- In the Scale calculation area, in the View scale list, select 1:5.
- Click OK.

12. To cycle to the end view of the assembly:

- Enter **V**.
- Enter **V** again.

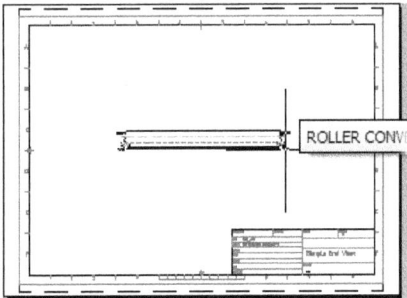

13. In the drawing area, click to position the view. Press ENTER when prompted for the rotation angle. Press ENTER to end the command after setting the view.

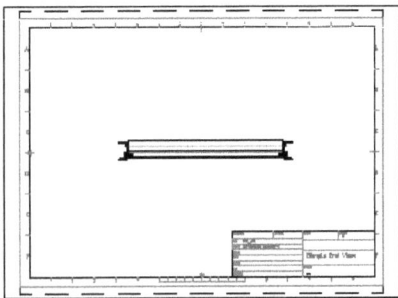

Edit Annotation Views

In this section of the exercise, you will edit annotation views by adding dimensions, editing view labels, and changing the display settings of a view.

1. In the Browser, expand Layout2 and then right-click on ROLLER CONVEYOR-1500_AV2:1 and click Property Overrides.

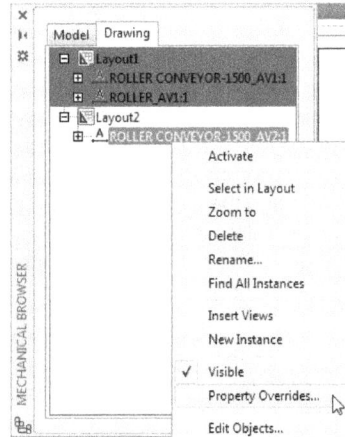

2. In the Property Overrides dialog box:

- Select the Override Properties checkbox.
- Clear the Centerlines checkbox.

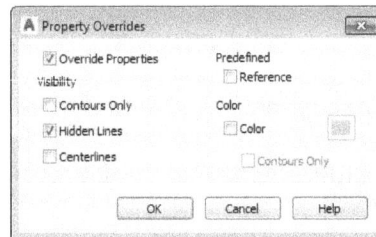

3. Click OK and review the changes to the drawing view. Note that the centerline is not displayed.

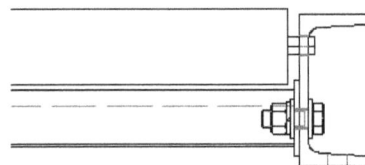

4. In the Browser, double-click on Layout1 to set it to be active.

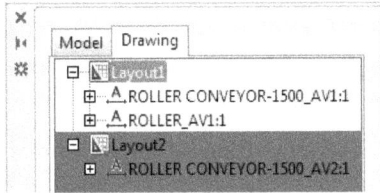

5. To begin editing the text in a view label, in the drawing area, double-click on the text ROLLER CONVEYOR-1500 Side View (1:15).

6. In the View Label dialog box:

- In the Pattern field, delete all of the text except = (**<STRUCT:SV_SCALE>**).
- Click OK. The view label displays as shown in the following illustration.

(1:15)

7. In the Browser, expand and then double-click on ROLLER CONVEYOR-1500_AV:1 to activate the view so that you can edit a view label's location and add dimensions to the annotation view.

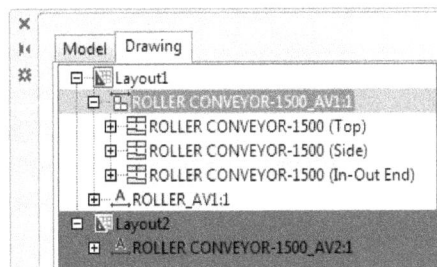

8. Start the Move command and move the top view label closer to the view as shown in the following illustration.

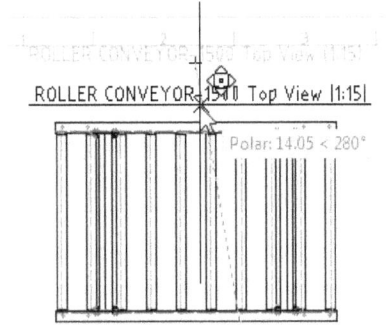

9. To add dimensions to the top and front views:

- On the Annotate tab > Dimension panel, click Power Dimension.
- Object snap to the bottom far left and right endpoints on the front view.
- Move the cursor down and click to place the dimension.
- Press ENTER to accept the dimension.

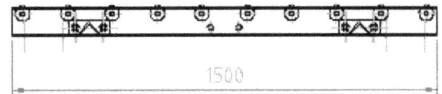

10. Add two more dimensions to the views as shown in the following illustration. Press ESC after positioning the second vertical dimension.

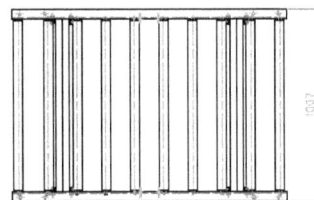

(1:15)

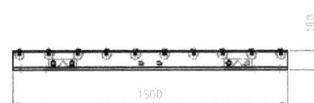

11. To activate the overall layout, in the Browser, double-click on Layout1.

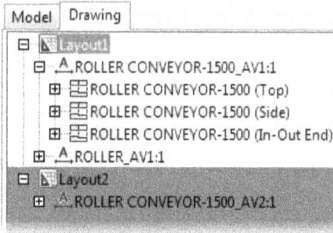

12. To add a view label to the roller, in the Browser under ROLLER_AV1:1, right-click on ROLLER (Front) and click Create Label.

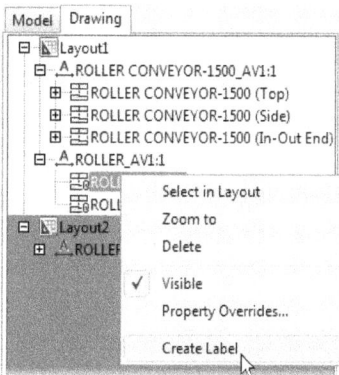

13. In the View Label dialog box, click OK.

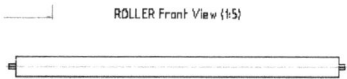

14. To reset an insertion basepoint, in the Browser, right-click on ROLLER CONVEYOR-1500_AV1:1 and click Change Basepoint.

15. In the drawing area, object snap to the endpoint as shown in the following illustration.

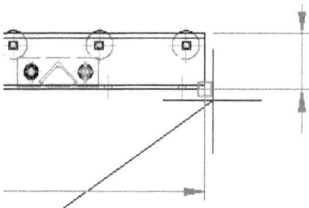

16. Save the files. If you are prompted to upgrade the external files to the new version, click Yes. The saved file is used in the next section. Close the file.

Externally Reference Annotation Views

In this section of the exercise, you will reference an annotation view from one file into the current design. You will then localize the annotation view to edit what is being displayed while keeping the individual views externally referenced.

1. Open *AnViews-Welded Frame.dwg*.

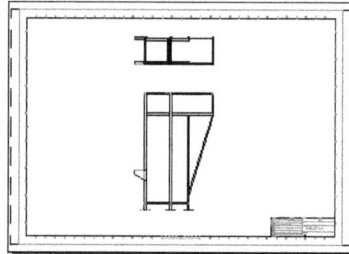

2. On the Structure tab > Tools panel, click Structure Catalog, if it is not already open.

3. To begin creating an external reference to the annotation view of the roller conveyor, in the Structure Catalog, in the *External Drawings* tab, in the Files pane, navigate to and select *AnViews-Roller Conveyor-1500.dwg*.

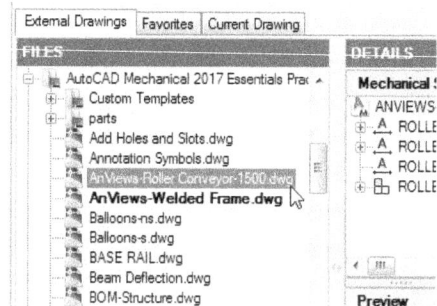

4. In the Details pane, click and drag ROLLER CONVEYOR-1500_AV1 and drop it in the drawing area.

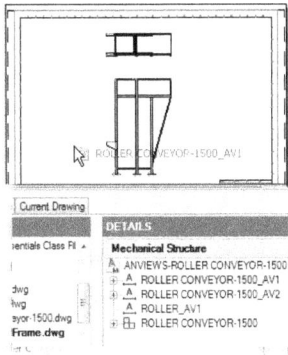

5. To set the scale and insertion position:
- For the scale, enter **1:10**.
- For the insertion point, object snap to the required intersection as shown in the following illustration.
- For the rotation angle, press ENTER.

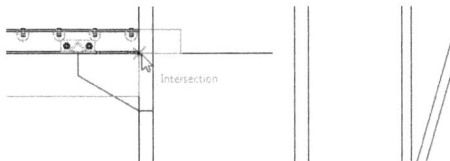

6. Review the referenced annotation view.
- In the Mechanical Browser, expand ROLLER CONVEYOR-1500_AV1:1 and review the items that are externally referenced.
- In the drawing area, review the geometry being displayed in this annotation view.

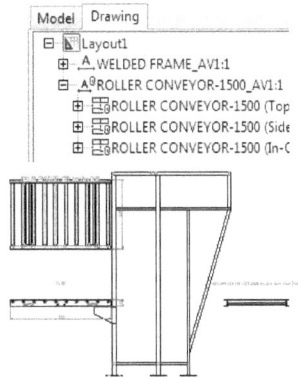

7. In the Browser, right-click on ROLLER CONVEYOR-1500_AV1:1 and click Localize Annotation View.

8. In the Browser, double-click on ROLLER CONVEYOR-1500_AV1:1.

9. Delete the top and right views, view labels, and dimensions to create the results shown in the following illustration.

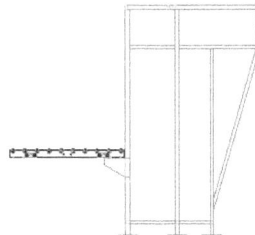

10. In the Browser, double-click on Layout1.

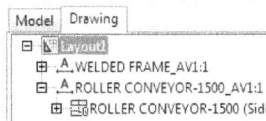

11. To begin overriding the display properties of the conveyor annotation view, in the Browser, right-click on ROLLER CONVEYOR-1500_AV1:1 and click Property Overrides.

12. In the Property Overrides dialog box:

- Select the Override Properties checkbox.
- In the Predefined area, select the Reference checkbox.
- Click OK.

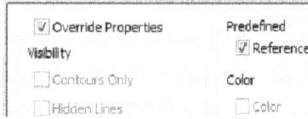

13. Review the changes to this annotation view:

- In the Browser note that the annotation view is locally defined and that its single view is externally referenced.
- The geometry for the view displays in the drawing as reference geometry relative to the primary design.

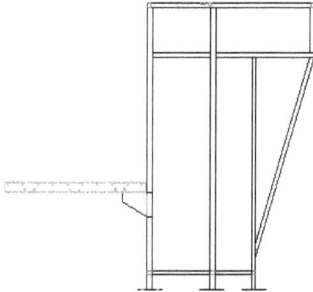

14. Save and close all of the files.

Lesson: Title Blocks and Drawing Borders

Overview

This lesson describes the insertion of title blocks and borders into layouts and model space.

You can use a drawing border and title block to make the drawing a professional-looking presentation of information. The title block also enables you to organize and present additional data about the drawing.

In the following illustration, the drawing in the layout is one step closer to being complete after the border and title block were inserted.

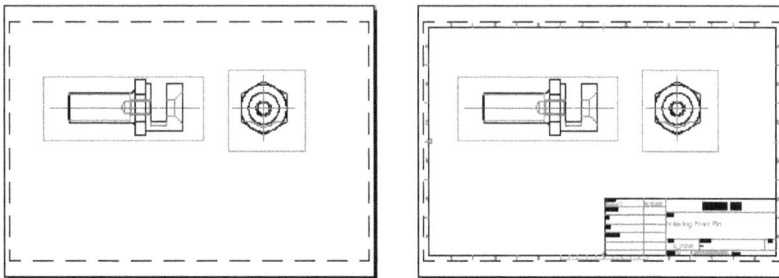

Objectives

After completing this lesson, you will be able to:

- Insert title blocks and borders into a drawing.
- Replace an inserted title block or border with a different title block or border.
- Edit the attribute values of an inserted title block.
- State where the list of title blocks and borders are configured.
- Toggle on and off the display of borders and title blocks.

Inserting Drawing Title Blocks and Borders

You can insert a drawing title block and border to define the boundary of a drawing, add general information in the title block, set the drawing scale, and scale existing annotation.

About Plotting Philosophies

There are two ways to plot your final, production-ready drawing. One is to plot from model space and the other is to plot from layouts.

When you plot from model space, all of the geometry is located in the model space environment and the border and title block are scaled up or down based on the plot scale that you are going to use. To create multiple different sheets, you can add multiple borders and title blocks to model space. Each time you plot a different sheet, you need to select a different window area to plot or specify a different defined view.

When you plot from layouts, you can select the required paper size and set the plot scale to 1:1. Because the paper is at full scale, you can add the title block and border to the layout at a scale of 1:1. You can then create viewports within the border area and scale the display in the viewport. To create multiple different sheets, you can add and configure multiple layouts. To plot the different layouts you can make each one active or select multiple layout tabs and publish them.

In the following illustration, the image on the left shows a model space environment with multiple title blocks and borders inserted and scaled up around the geometry to plot. The image on the right shows multiple layouts configured to present and communicate the design. These layouts have the page size set at full scale with the title block and border inserted into the layout. Viewports are used to display the different model space geometry.

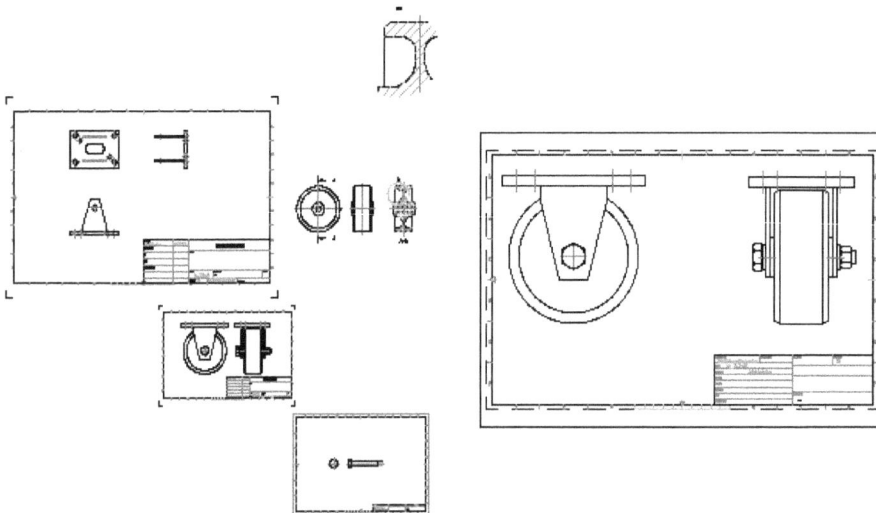

About Title Blocks and Drawing Borders

You can use the Title Border command to insert both the title block and the drawing border. The title block and border are two distinct blocks that come from two distinct drawing files. This enables you to use a single title block with different drawing borders. If you have multiple title blocks and borders that are used on different drawings, keeping them separate enables you to create multiple combinations without having to preconfigure all of the title block and border combinations.

When you insert a title block or border that was supplied with the AutoCAD Mechanical software or one that is customized to follow similar automation, some of the attribute data is automatically populated to save time.

Because you insert title blocks and borders into the layouts at full scale (1:1), when you insert the border, you select one that is drawn to fit the required page size. You do not need to rescale text or move objects.

If you are inserting title blocks and borders into model space, there are a number of options to select and set that automatically assist you during title block and border insertion. Those settings and automatic actions are as follows:

- Scale the title block and border to fit around the drawing objects based on the selected scale.
- Populate the values in the title block based on drawing information, part references, or assembly properties.
- Move the drawing objects inside the border.
- Rescale any existing objects, including text, dimensions, hatch, symbols, balloons, tables, details, leaders, and other annotation objects.
- Modify drawing settings according to the border location and scale. Settings that change include snap, grid, limits, linetype scale, and the drawing standard scale.
- Create a named view of the area defined by the border.
- Zoom to the extents of the inserted border.

Access

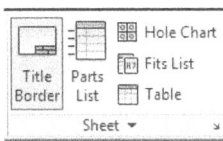

Command Line: AMTITLE

Ribbon: Annotate tab > Sheet panel > Title Border

Ribbon: Layout tab > Sheet panel > Title Border

Menu: Annotate > Drawing Title and Revision > Drawing Title/Borders

Drawing Borders with Title Block Dialog Box

You can set the default settings for inserting a drawing border and title block in the Drawing Borders With Title Block dialog box. Select your paper format and title block and set the required scale. When inserting into model space, you can use Calculate to calculate a recommended scale factor. The calculated scale factor is then shown in the Scale box.

If you are inserting into model space, select the options for setting the scale factor in the drawing, rescaling existing text and other symbols, and moving objects within the border area.

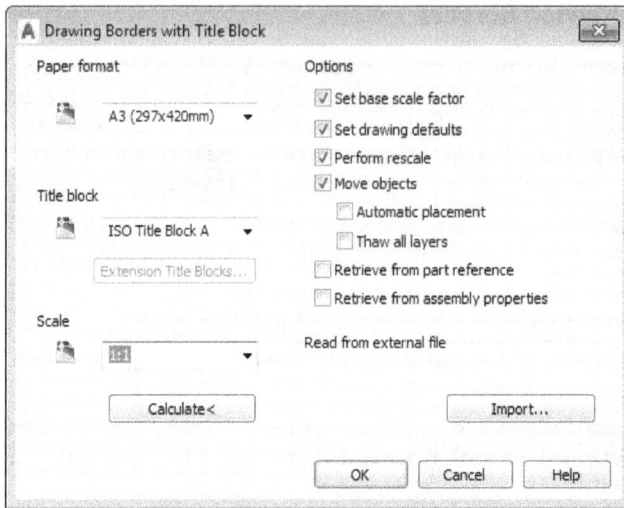

> If you select the Move Objects option, select the Thaw All Layer option as well. If it is not selected, you might leave behind important drawing objects that require cleanup.

Procedure: Inserting a Border and Title Block into a Layout

An overview of inserting a border and title block into an active layout is shown in the following steps:

1. Start the **Title Border** command.

2. In the Drawing Borders with Title Block dialog box, select the paper format for the layout page size.

3. Select the title block.

4. Select a scale of 1:1.

5. Under Options, clear the checkboxes.

6. Click OK.

7. In the Page Setup Manager, click Close.

8. Enter **0,0** for the insertion point.

9. Enter or change the title block attribute data.

Procedure: Inserting the First Border and Title Block into Model Space

An overview of inserting a border and title block into model space when no other border and title blocks have yet been inserted is shown in the following steps:

1. Start the **Title Border** command.

2. In the Drawing Borders with Title Block dialog box, select the paper format for the size of paper to which you want to output.

3. Select the title block.

4. Select or calculate the scale.

5. Select the required options.

6. Click OK.

7. Specify the insertion point.

8. Based on the previously selected options, complete the tasks as prompted.

9. Enter or change the title block attribute data.

10. Based on the previously selected options, complete the tasks as prompted.

Procedure: Inserting Additional Borders and Title Blocks into Model Space

The following steps describe how to add a border and title block to model space when at least one border and title block have already been inserted.

1. Start the **Title Border** command.

2. In the Edit Drawing Border/Title Block dialog box, select New Drawing Border/Title Block. Click OK.

3. With the Drawing Borders with Title Block dialog box open, follow the steps that are used when inserting the first border and title block into model space.

Replacing Inserted Title Blocks or Borders

You can replace a title block or border that has already been inserted into a drawing with a different title block or border. When you replace a title block, the attribute information that was previously entered automatically transfers to the new inserted title block. Along with replacing a title block or border, you can also change the scale factor at which the border and title block were inserted into the drawing.

In the following illustration, the drawing shown at the top initially had the title block inserted with a border. It was later replaced by the custom title block shown at the bottom. Because they used the same attribute definitions, the values that were previously entered were not lost during replacement.

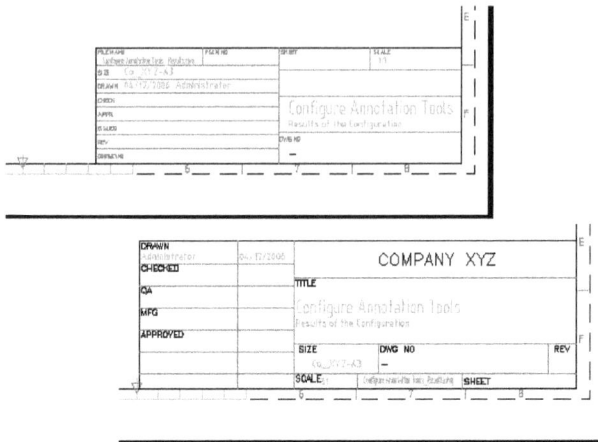

Replacement Access

You can replace an inserted title block or border or change its insertion scale using either of the following methods:

- In the drawing window, double-click on the border.
- Start the Title Border command in a drawing that already contains a drawing border and title block. When an existing border and title block definition is found, the Edit Drawing Border/ Title Block dialog box opens.

Edit Drawing Border/Title Block Dialog Box

The Edit Drawing Border/Title Block dialog box opens after you start the Title Border command and if a drawing border already exists. You can select options in this dialog box to insert a new drawing border and title block or to change or modify an existing border and title block. Your edit options are based on what the options that are selected in the dialog box. If you do not select an option to change, that field is not selectable in the Drawing Borders With Title Block dialog box.

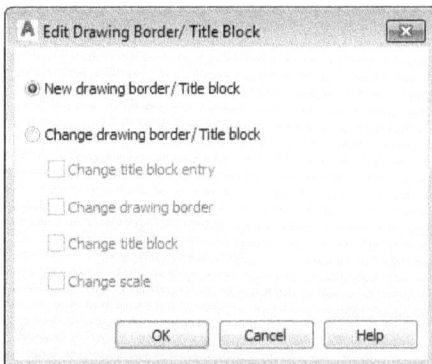

Procedure: Changing an Existing Border, Title Block, or Scale

To change from an existing border, title block, or scale to a new one, complete the following steps:

1. In the drawing window, double-click on the drawing border.

2. In the Drawing Borders with Title Block dialog box, select a new paper format, title block, or scale.

Editing Title Block Attribute Values

You can add or edit the data in the title block by changing the attribute values defined within the title block. By editing the attribute values, the text is already configured to be inserted at the correct location and display in the correct manner. This helps you to the information more quickly while conforming to the drafting standards.

In the following illustration, the values in a title block are shown in the process of being edited.

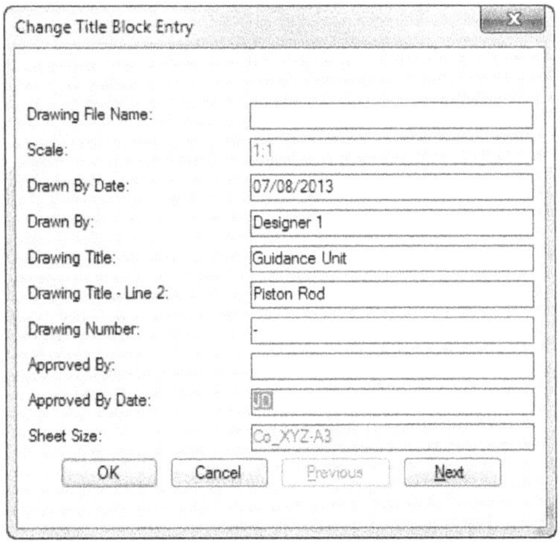

Accessing Title Block Attribute Values

You can open the Change Title Block Entry dialog box to edit the attribute values of an inserted title block by using either of the following methods:

- In the drawing window, double-click on the title block.
- Start the Title Border command in a drawing that already contains a title block. When an existing border and title block definition are found, the Edit Drawing Border/Title Block dialog box opens. In the Edit Drawing Border/Title Block dialog box, select the Change Title Block Entry option.

Procedure: Editing Title Block Attribute Values

To edit the attribute values in an inserted title block, complete the following steps:

1. In the drawing window, double-click on the title block.

2. In the Change Title Block Entry dialog box, change the values to meet your requirements.

Drawing Sheet Settings

The list of available borders and title blocks is based on the current standard in the drawing. You can change the listing of borders and title blocks and other settings by editing the current standard. You can access the current standard in the Options dialog box, in the AM:Standard tab. You can access the drawing sheet settings by double-clicking on the standard element Drawing Sheet.

Drawing Sheet Settings

The Drawing Sheet Settings dialog box controls the settings that are available for inserting title blocks and borders. You can use Browse [...] to add custom paper formats and title blocks. In the Scale Change Settings area, you can set manual or automatic object selection for objects to be rescaled. You can set defaults for creating named views and defining the drawing limits.

Title Block Layer On/Off

You can control the title block visibility with the Title Block Layer On/Off command. It toggles the title block and border layer on or off. For this command to work, the title block must be located on the layer defined for borders and title blocks, as set in the current standard.

Access

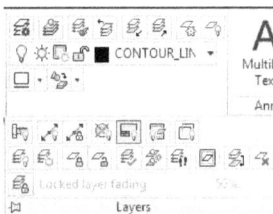

Command Line: AMLAYTIBLO

Ribbon: Home tab > expanded Layers panel > Title Block Layer On/Off

Menu: Format > Layer Tools > Title Block Layer On/Off

Exercise: Insert Title Blocks and Borders

In this exercise, you will insert a title block and border on an existing layout, add information to the title block on another layout, and replace that title block with another title block.

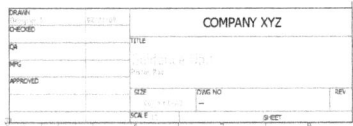

The completed exercise

1. Open *Title Blocks-Borders.dwg*.

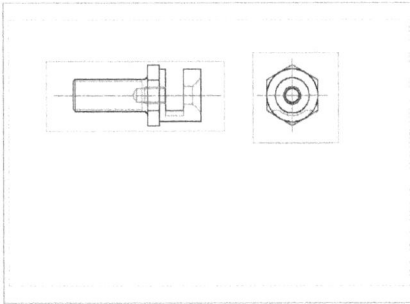

2. To begin inserting a title block and border to the active layout, click Annotate tab > Sheet panel > Title Border.

3. In the Drawing Borders with Title Block dialog box, do the following:

    - In the Paper format drop-down list, select Co_XYZ-A3.
    - In the Title block drop-down list, select Co_XYZ-titleblock1.
    - In the Scale drop-down list, select 1:1.
    - In the Options area, clear all of the checkboxes.
    - Click OK.

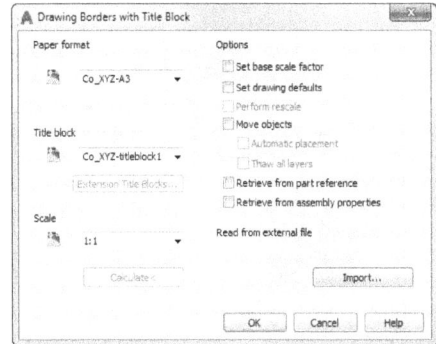

4. In the Page Setup Manager dialog box, click Close.

5. For the boundary insertion point, enter **0,0**.

6. In the Change Title Block Entry dialog box, for Drawing Title, enter **Indexing Pivot Pin**. Click OK.

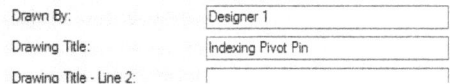

7. Review the geometry and title block text that were just inserted.

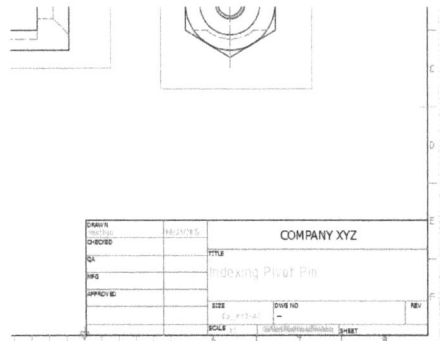

8. In the Mechanical Browser, double-click on Layout1 to make it active.

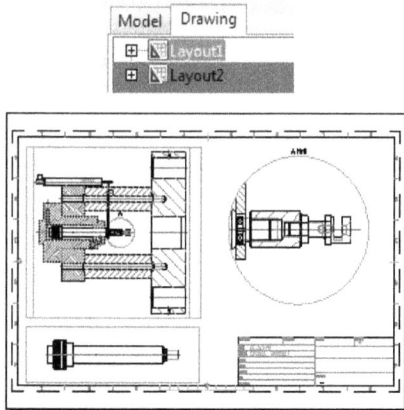

9. To add information to the title block, do the following:

- In the drawing area, double-click on the title block.
- In the Change Title Block Entry dialog box, for Drawing Title, enter **Guidance Unit**.
- For Drawing Subtitle, enter **Piston Rod**.

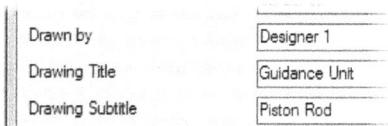

Drawn by	Designer 1
Drawing Title	Guidance Unit
Drawing Subtitle	Piston Rod

10. Click OK to add the text and review your changes.

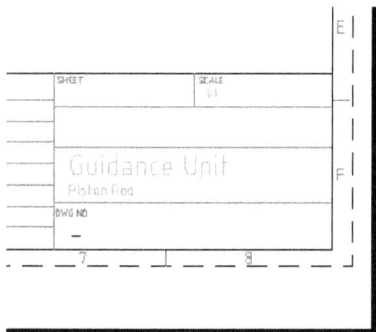

11. To replace the title block with a custom title block, do the following:

- In the drawing area, double-click on the border.
- In the Drawing Borders with Title Block dialog box, in the Title block drop-down list, select Co_XYZ-titleblock1.

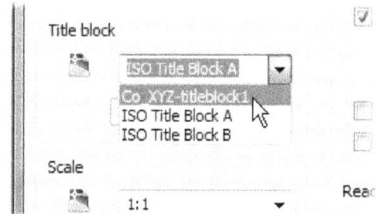

12. In the Options area, clear all of the checkboxes. Click OK. Review the change and the contents of the new title block.

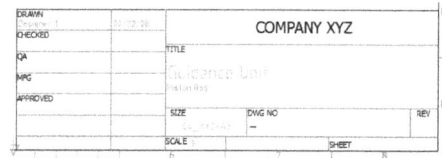

13. Save and close all of the files.

Chapter Summary

In this chapter, you learned how to create layout views of model space geometry and how to insert title blocks and borders into layouts and model space. You also learned how to create production-ready drawing sheets of parts or assemblies in model space and how to create annotation views of mechanically structured geometry.

Having completed this chapter, you can:

- Create layout views of model space geometry.
- Create production-ready drawing sheets in model space.
- Create and edit annotation views of structured geometry.
- Insert title blocks and drawing borders.

Dimensioning and Annotating Drawings

In this chapter, you learn how to add design information to a drawing in the form of mechanical symbols and text, including symbols for surface texture, welds, and geometric dimensioning and tolerancing. You then learn about the power dimensioning and automatic dimensioning tools that you can use to add dimensions to your drawings. Along with creating dimensions, you learn how to edit, stretch, arrange, align, join, and break dimensions. You also learn about hole charts and fits lists and how to insert them into your drawings.

Objectives

After completing this chapter, you will be able to:

- Add symbols for surface texture, welds, and geometric dimensioning and tolerancing.
- Add dimensions that automatically follow a drawing's standards.
- Edit dimensions using different methods to change their display and positions.
- Place hole charts and fits lists into a drawing.
- Insert a revision list into a drawing and add additional revision lines.

About Dimensions and Annotation

An important but time-consuming task when completing a design is the adding of dimensions and other annotations. By learning about the benefits of using the AutoCAD® Mechanical software commands to add dimensions and annotation, you can understand using those commands to decrease the time required to dimension and annotate your designs.

In the following illustration, the different views of the part were dimensioned using Mechanical specific dimensioning commands.

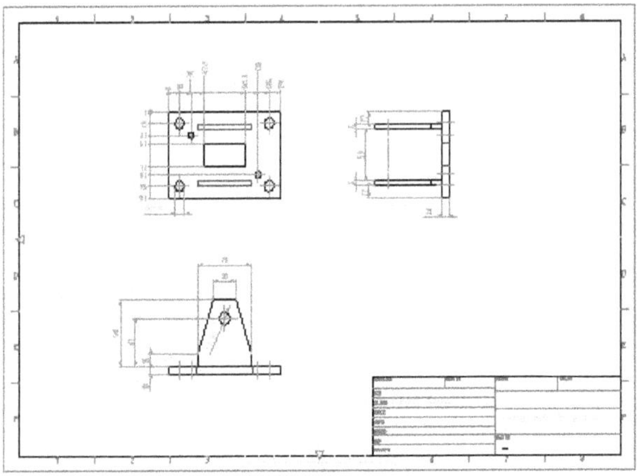

Definition of Dimensions and Annotation

The dimension and annotation commands follow industry standards for defining their configuration, contents, and appearance. The layer on which the dimension or annotation are located after they have been created automatically follows the settings in the active standard regardless of which layer might be active before the command is used. The size of the symbols and text is based on the model scale factor set in the standard.

When you use the power dimensioning command, the type of dimension that you create is based on the selected geometry. This enables you to add various dimension types while using a single dimension command. For each dimension that you create, you can quickly add special characters, such as square, countersink, centerline, depth, and tolerance or fit values.

The different dimension and annotation commands also enable you to add a set of baseline, chain, ordinate, symmetrical, and shaft diameter dimensions. You can also notate the position and size of holes by adding hole charts and lists to a drawing sheet. Feature control frames, datum identifiers, weld symbols, and surface texture symbols are a few of the other types of annotations that you can add to your drawing. The display of each of these symbols is also controlled by the active standard.

By using one of the three text tools, you can create the text using one of three set heights that automatically scale in the model space based on the standard's model scale factor value.

Example of Dimensions and Annotation

In the following illustration, a drawing view of a cylindrical connecting part is shown with dimensions and other notations. The dimensions in this view specify the size of the part and location of some of the features. Some of the notations for the dimensions were modified from their defaults during their creation and others were modified after they were placed. The size of the text under the view was set using two of the three text tools provided for sizing and creating text.

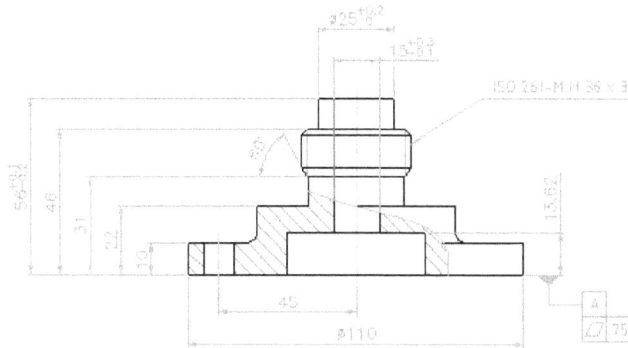

UNLESS OTHERWISE SPECIFIED:
±0.5 TOLERANCE ON MACHINING DIMS
±1.0 TOLERANCE ON CASTING DIMS

Lesson: Annotation and Annotation Symbols

Overview

You can add design information to a drawing in the form of mechanical symbols and text including symbols for surface texture, welds, and geometric dimensioning and tolerancing.

You can add this annotation information to your drawings to communicate important manufacturing information to others in text and symbol form. By knowing how to use the tools to add the required annotation, you can add it quickly while easily following industry and company standards.

In the following illustration, the drawing sheet contains annotation in the form of standard text and in special symbols and text that communicate critical or unique final characteristics for the part.

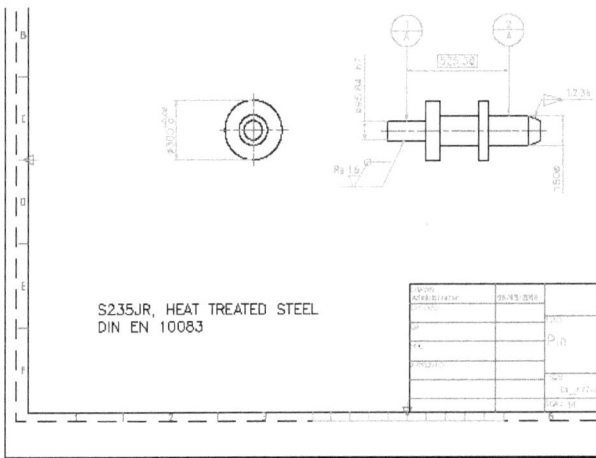

Objectives

After completing this lesson, you will be able to:

- Insert text annotations of different sizes in drawings.
- Insert surface texture to define the material finish.
- Insert a welding symbol in a drawing to convey complete welding information.
- Insert feature control frames to add dimensioning and tolerancing information.
- Insert edge symbols to annotate a drawing.
- State the purpose of the symbol libraries.
- Insert simple weld symbols to represent the physical weld material in an assembly.
- Insert a datum identifier symbol to annotate a drawing.
- Insert a feature identifier symbol to annotate a drawing.
- Insert a datum target symbol to annotate a drawing.
- Insert a taper or slope symbol on a part.
- Locate where the default settings are configured for the different annotation tools.

Insert Text

In addition to the standard AutoCAD® text commands, you can annotate your drawing with text by selecting from one of three preset text tools. As you place text, the text size in the drawing is based on the preset text size multiplied by the drawing scale. As you modify the drawing scale, the text size updates. By using the AutoCAD Mechanical text commands, you can consistently place the text on the layer specified in the active standard without having to change layers.

Insert Text

You can access the three preset text commands by clicking Annotate tab > Text panel > Multiline Text flyout. These preset text commands automatically set the display properties based on the scale of the area in which the text is inserted and the object property settings in the active standard.

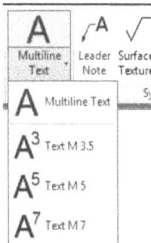

Text Tool	Object Descriptions	Default Settings
Text M3.5	Medium Text	Light blue at 3.5 mm or .120 inches at full scale.
Text M5	Text Large	White or black text at 5 mm or .175 inches at full scale.
Text M7	Text Very Large	Orange text at 7 mm or .24 inches at full scale.

Each of these text commands uses the standard AutoCAD MTEXT command as the basis for creating the text. Because these text tools use the standard MTEXT command and automatically set the layer and properties of the text, you can use any of the formatting tools, including bullets, numbering, tabbed indents, and fields. You can use the shortcut menu to add symbols and apply opaque backgrounds. You can also toggle on AutoCAPS to automatically toggle on Caps Lock when you open the text editor.

In the following illustration, the **Text M7** command is being used to add text to a drawing area set at full scale. The Text Editor tab on the Ribbon shows the property settings that were automatically set when the command was started.

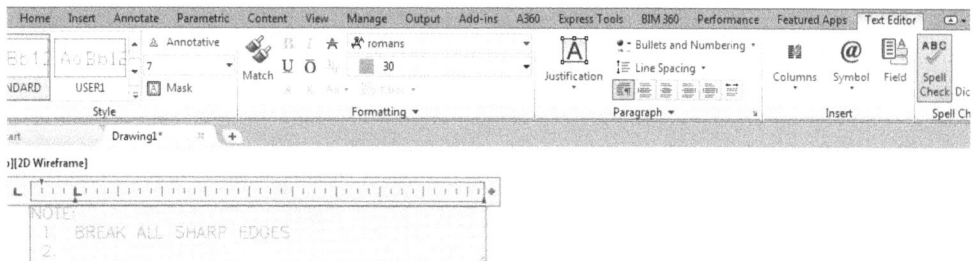

Inserting Surface Textures

You can add the surface texture symbols to define the material finish on the face of a part when the finish is important to the performance or appearance of the design. Surface texture is associated with the type of manufacturing methods used to create the part.

You can insert surface textures according to the current mechanical standard. Surface textures are placed on the AM_5 layer and displayed at the current drawing scale. You can attach the surface texture symbol to geometry. If you move the geometry, the surface texture symbol moves as well. You can use grip editing to reposition the symbol after it has been inserted.

In the following illustration, a surface texture symbol indicates that material has to be removed to achieve a specific roughness average.

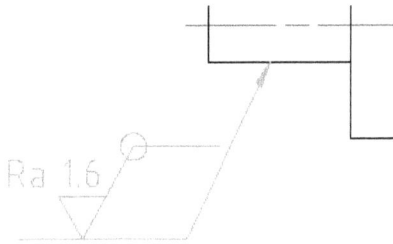

Access

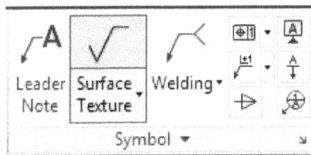

Command Line: AMSURFSYM

Ribbon: Annotate tab > Symbol panel > Surface Texture

Menu: Annotate > Symbols > Surface Texture

Surface Texture Terminology

You can define a finish by setting the roughness average (Ra), which is defined as the average value of all absolute distances of the roughness profile from the centerline. The smaller the number used, the finer the finish. For example, a 32 Ra finish is smoother than a 125 Ra finish. Use the Rz for an average that is based on the sum of the height of the highest peak and the lowest valley. Rz is generally used for ISO and DIN documents to indicate the roughness surface texture.

Surface Texture Dialog Box - Symbol Tab

In the Surface Texture dialog box, on the *Symbol* tab, you can specify the surface type and its associated properties. Based on the active standard and the selected surface type, the values, notations, and miscellaneous settings for the surface texture symbol vary. This dialog box opens during the process of inserting a surface texture symbol and after you double-click on an existing symbol to edit it.

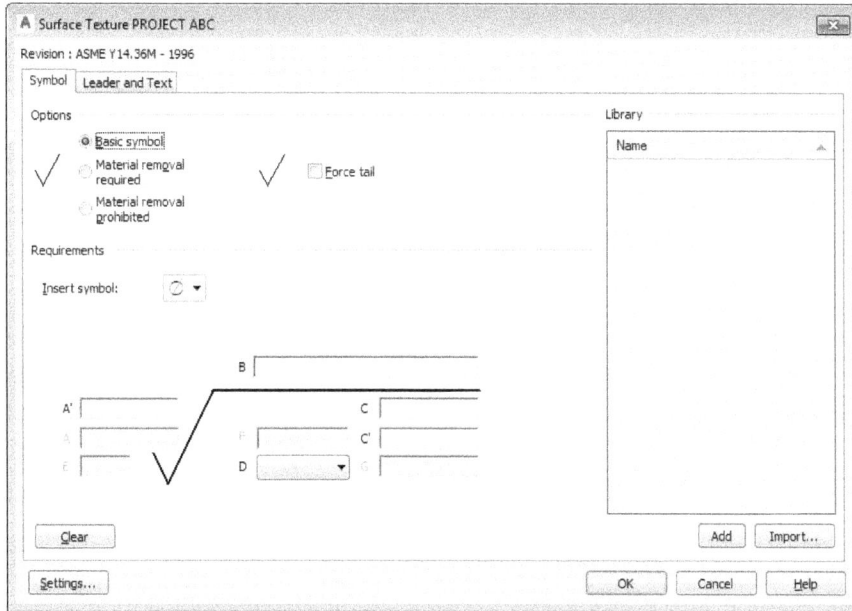

Surface Texture Dialog Box - Leader and Text Tab

In the Surface Texture dialog box, on the *Leader and Text* tab, you can remove or add leader segments. You can also attach or detach the symbol from the object. When you detach the symbol, it no longer moves with the object.

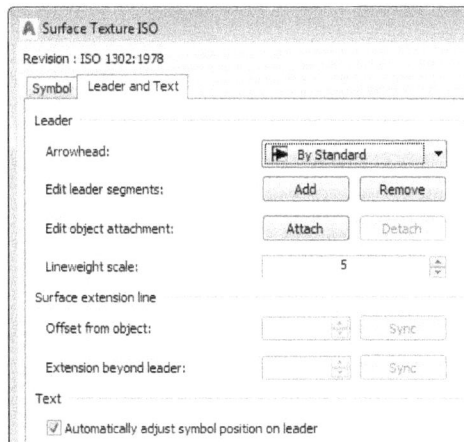

Procedure: Inserting a Surface Texture Symbol

An overview of notating the surface texture of a part by inserting a surface texture symbol is shown in the following steps:

1. Start the **Surface Texture** command.

2. In the drawing area, click the geometry to which the surface texture symbol should attach.

3. Click to locate the surface texture symbol along the selected geometry.

4. Press ENTER to place the symbol on the geometry. You can also click to create leader segments from the geometry to the symbol.

5. In the Surface Texture dialog box, select a surface type style and additional specifications.

Inserting Weld Symbols

You can place a welding symbol in a drawing to convey the complete welding information about a design. A welding symbol comprises many parts, including a reference line with weld symbols above and below, weld dimensions, contour symbols, and tail specifications.

You can place welding symbols according to the current mechanical standard. The welding symbol is placed on the AM_5 layer and displayed at the current drawing scale. Welding symbols are attached to geometry and change position as the geometry is changed. You can use grip editing to reposition the weld symbol after it has been inserted.

In the following illustration, the fillet weld symbol defines the type and size of weld that should be created for the symbol weld to which it is pointing.

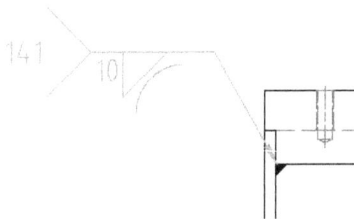

Access

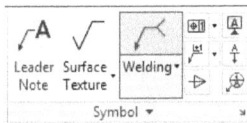

Command Line: AMWELDSYM

Ribbon: Annotate tab > Symbol panel > Welding

Menu: Annotate > Symbols > Welding

Weld Symbol Dialog Box - Symbol Tab

You can use the Weld Symbol dialog box to define the information about a weld. The dialog box opens when you initially insert the weld symbol and when you edit an existing weld symbol by double- clicking on it. The exact options and settings in the dialog box depend on the industry drafting standard that is currently active.

When you define a weld symbol, you can specify the type of weld on both the arrow side and other side by clicking the icons in the weld preview in the Requirements area in the Weld Symbol dialog box. You can then the required weld values in the fields after selecting a specific weld type. If the arrow side and other side weld information were specified on the incorrect side of the weld symbol reference line, select the Flip Sides checkbox in the Options area to have the weld information automatically switch from above the reference line to below and from below to above.

Along with the specific weld type and size information, you can select the flag button to indicate that the weld is completed in the field and you can specify the weld to go all the way around the joint. Process information can be added by entering it in the text field on the right end of the symbol or by clicking Add process and selecting the common weld note in the Process List dialog box.

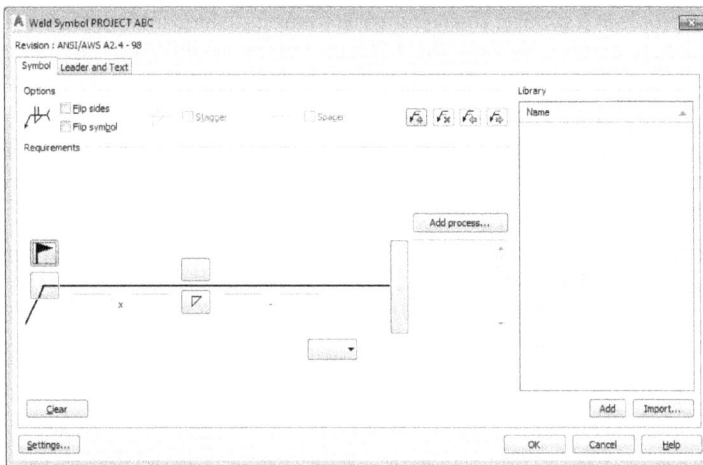

Leader and Text Tab

You can add and remove leader segments as the design changes. You can click to attach or detach the weld symbol to geometry. You can also change the text justification and arrowhead type.

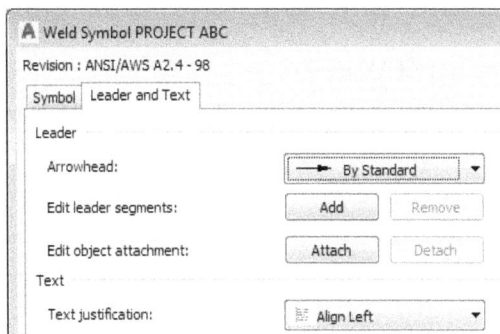

Procedure: Inserting a Welding Symbol

To notate a weld location by inserting a weld symbol, complete the following steps:

1. Start the **Welding Symbol** command.

2. Select the geometry to which to attach the symbol.

3. Click to locate the welding symbol along the selected geometry.

4. Click to create leader segments from the geometry to the symbol.

5. In the Weld Symbol dialog box, select and values to meet your specifications.

Inserting Feature Control Frames

Feature control frames help you to precisely define the precise permitted variation in size and shape of a part. You can use feature frames to define information, such as the position, runout, cylindricity, flatness, angularity, and profile of a surface. The rectangular frame is divided into multiple sections to display the control symbol, tolerances, and datums. You can attach the feature control frame to objects and edges in the drawing. Feature control frames are part of geometric dimensioning and tolerancing (GD&T).

You can add feature control frames according to the current mechanical standard. They are placed on the AM_5 layer and displayed at the current drawing scale. Feature control frame symbols are attached to geometry and change position as the geometry is changed.

In the following illustration, the feature control frame indicates that the center axis of the hole has to be within .10 of perpendicular to datum A.

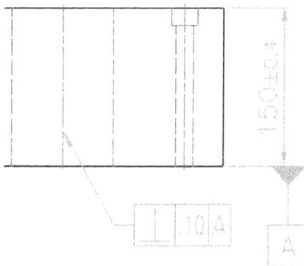

Access

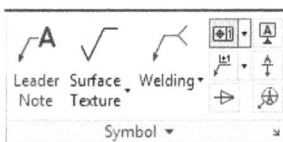

Command Line: AMFCFRAME

Ribbon: Annotate tab > Symbol panel > Feature Control Frame

Menu: Annotate > Symbols > Feature Control Frame

Feature Control Frame Dialog Box

In the Feature Control Frame dialog box, you can enter notes to be placed above and below the symbol. Use this dialog box to describe the permitted variation from nominal geometry.

On the Leader and Text tab, you can set the arrowhead style for the leader line, remove or add additional leader segments, and attach or detach the symbol from the object. When you detach it, the symbol no longer moves with the object.

You can click Settings when you want to directly access and edit the settings in the active standard. Setting changes include modifying the end padding style, modifying the merge options, and changing the availability of symbols for general characteristics or for the material removal modifier.

This dialog box opens during the process of inserting a feature control frame and after double-clicking an existing symbol to edit it.

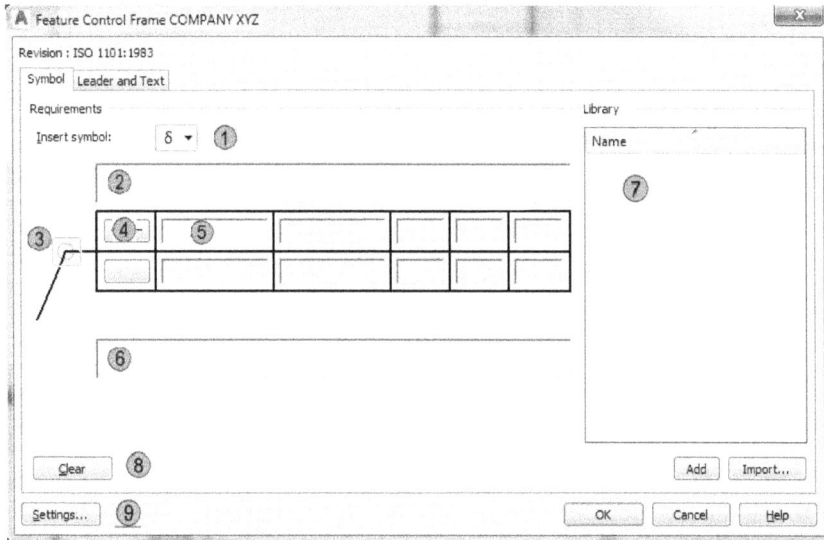

1. Displays a palette enabling you to insert a special character at the current cursor position. The preview in the drawing area displays the special character while the dialog box displays the corresponding control key sequence.

2. Specifies text that must display above the feature control frame. In the drawing area, the notes and feature control frame move together as a single entity.

3. Adds all around indication to the symbol. This option is not available for the GOST standard.

4. Displays a list of symbols that enable you to specify the geometric characteristic to which you are defining the tolerance. The symbols on this list depend on the current standard.

5. The larger edit boxes specify the primary and secondary tolerance data. Use the Insert Symbol list to insert special characters, such as the diameter symbol or the maximum material condition symbol. The secondary tolerance option is only available for the ANSI standard. The smaller edit boxes specify the primary, secondary, and tertiary datum.

6. Specifies text that must display below the feature control frame. In the drawing area, the notes and feature control frame move together as a single entity.

7. Lists all of the feature control frame symbols in the symbol library for the current drafting standard. The Add button saves current settings to the symbol library as a new item in the library. A prompt enables you to name the new item. The Import button imports the feature control frame symbols from the symbol library of another drawing. You can import symbols of the same standard and revision as the feature control frame symbol that you are editing.

8. Clears all of the data and returns the dialog box options to their default values.

9. Opens the Feature Control Frame Settings dialog box so that you can edit the default settings for the current drafting standard.

Procedure: Inserting a Feature Control Frame

To add GD&T notation to a drawing by inserting a feature control frame, complete the following steps:

1. Start the **Feature Control Frame** command.

2. In the drawing area, click the geometry to attach the feature control frame.

3. Click to locate the feature control frame symbol along the selected geometry.

4. Press ENTER to place the symbol on the geometry. You can also click to create leader segments from the geometry to the symbol.

5. In the Feature Control Frame dialog box, enter the text, symbols, tolerances, and datum information to match your notation requirements.

Inserting Edge Symbols

You can use an edge symbol to represent the edge of a part. The information in the edge symbol describes how the edge is finished.

The option to add edge symbols depends on the current drawing standard and whether or not that standard supports edge symbols. DIN, ISO, GB, and JIS are standards that support edge symbols. Edge symbols are placed on the AM_5 layer and displayed at the current drawing scale. Edge symbols are attached to geometry and change position as the geometry is moved.

In the following illustration, an edge symbol was added to the drawing view to provide specific information about the identified edge.

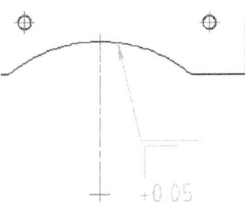

Access

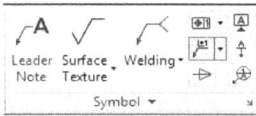

Command Line: AMEDGESYM

Ribbon: Annotate tab > Symbol panel > Edge Symbol

Menu: Annotate > Symbols > Edge

Edge Symbol Dialog Box

In the Edge Symbol dialog box, you can define the edge conditions and values. This includes specifying whether this symbol is placed as a majority symbol, size values, and other requirements. When specifying the size, you can select an existing value from the list or a unique value. On the Leader tab you can change the arrowhead style for the leader line, remove or add additional leader segments, and attach or detach the symbol from the object. When you detach the symbol it no longer moves with the object. You can click Settings when you want to directly access and edit the settings in the active standard. The dialog box opens during the process of inserting an edge symbol and after double-clicking on an existing symbol that you want to edit.

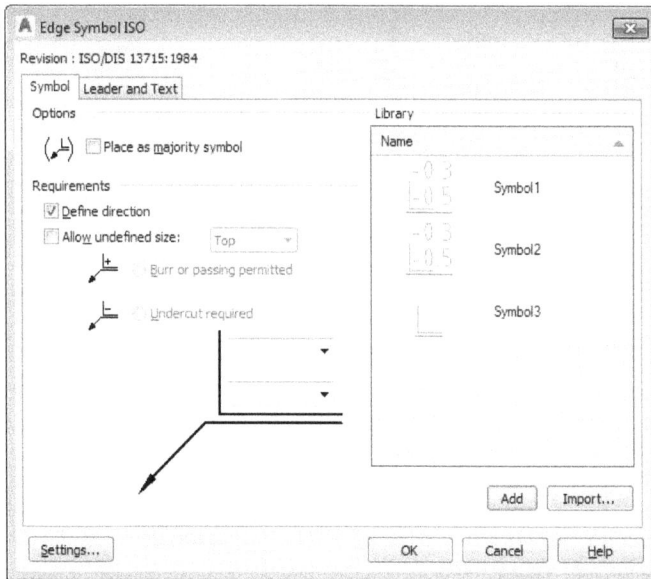

Procedure: Placing an Edge Symbol

To insert an edge symbol on a part, complete the following steps:

1. Start the **Edge Symbol** command.

2. In the drawing area, select the geometry to which to attach the edge symbol.

3. Click to locate the start point of the leader along the selected geometry.

4. Click to specify the next point of the leader.

5. In the Edge Symbol dialog box, enter the values that match your design requirements.

Symbol Libraries

To make it quicker and easier to add the same surface texture or weld symbol notation to your drawing, you can add and reuse library entries from the Library lists in the Surface Texture Symbol, Edge Symbol, Feature Control Frame Symbol, and Weld Symbol dialog boxes. You can add frequently used symbols to these symbol libraries and use them directly from the Ribbon. Since the symbols in the library are fully configured, the AutoCAD Mechanical software does not open a dialog box when you place them in the drawing. This can lead to significant time savings when compared with inserting the raw symbol and then specifying the geometric tolerances. To benefits from using symbol libraries, you need to understand how they are created, where they are stored, and how to use them.

In the following illustration, the library area of the Weld Symbol and Surface Texture Symbols dialog boxes is shown with an example listing of library entries for each of those symbols.

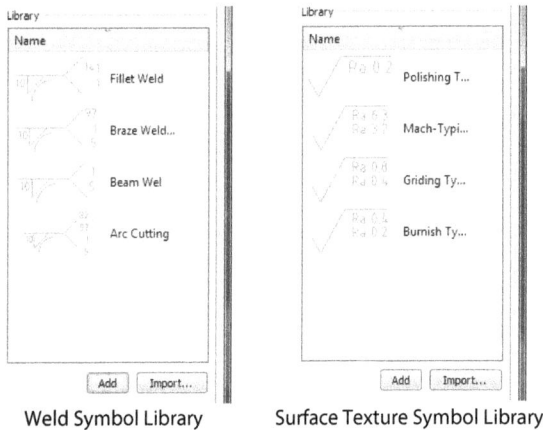

Weld Symbol Library   Surface Texture Symbol Library

Use of Symbol Library Entries

You use the surface texture symbol and weld symbol libraries to save and reuse common symbols. You can create and access symbol library entries within the dialog box for that symbol object. You can add, delete, rename, and update library entries. You can also set a library entry to be the default configuration for that symbol. To help locate a library entry, you can sort the library in forward or reverse numeric and alphabetic order. You can change the sort order by clicking the heading Name at the top of the library list. Hovering the cursor over a library entry causes a tooltip to display, listing the specific settings and options for that library entry.

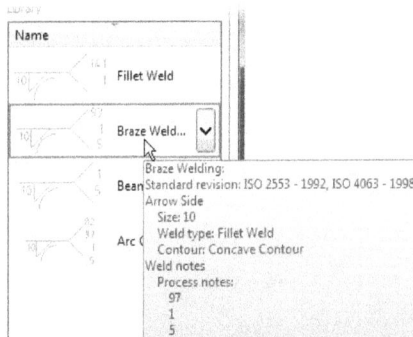

The list of library entries for a symbol is based on the active drafting standard and what is configured in the current drawing. The relationship of the active standard to the symbol library is important for weld and surface texture symbols because their options and appearance are dictated by the drafting standard. For easy reuse in drawings in which your library entries are not initially listed, you can import the library entries from another drawing or drawing template file.

To reuse a library entry and have it display as notation in your drawing, you can load its settings into the active symbol being created or edited. You can load a library entry's settings by double-clicking on the symbol in the Library list or selecting the Load option after clicking the down arrow for that library option. You can also directly create the library symbol or note by creating a custom macro that starts the creation command and automatically loads the library template entry.

Accessing Symbol Libraries From The Ribbon

The symbol libraries are readily accessible from the Ribbon by selecting the drop-down menu on each symbol library button. You can create frequently used symbols directly from the Ribbon. It is much faster than displaying the symbol dialog box and loading the symbols from the library.

Since the symbols in the library are fully configured, the AutoCAD Mechanical software does not open a dialog box when you place them in the drawing. This can lead to significant time savings when compared with inserting the raw symbol and then specifying the geometric tolerances.

The illustration below shows the Weld Symbol library being accessed from the Ribbon.

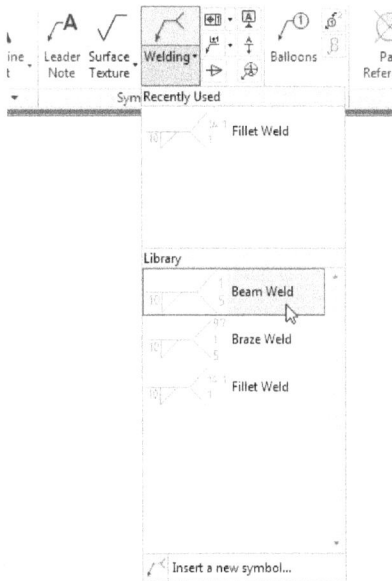

Add and Edit Library Entries

As you add or edit a weld symbol, surface texture symbol, edge symbol, or feature control frame symbol you can add its current configuration to the library. To add to the library, in the Weld Symbol, Edge Symbol, Feature Control Frame Symbol, or Surface Texture dialog boxes, after all of the properties for the symbol have been specified, click Add. After clicking Add, in the Library list, enter an appropriate name for the new symbol library entry.

You can access the editing options for a library entry by selecting the library entry in the Library list and clicking the down arrow for that entry. You can then select the Load, Update, Delete, Rename, or Set Default options.

When you select the Update option for a library entry, the current symbol values overwrite the previous settings for the library entry. Only symbols that you create after that point using this library entry have the properties that are set in the library. Symbols that exist in the drawing do not update if the template that was used to create the symbol is updated.

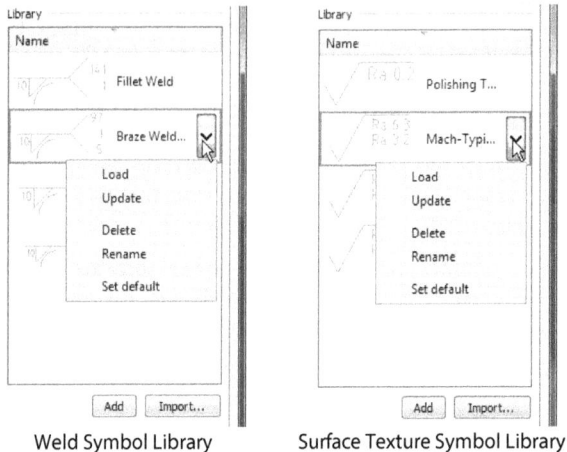

Weld Symbol Library   Surface Texture Symbol Library

If you are using the ANSI drafting standard and define a weld symbol that contains notation for a sequence of multiple weld operations, you can only add separate library entries for each of the weld reference lines. Clicking Add causes the active weld reference line to be added to the library. To add the other reference lines, navigate up or down to activate that reference line and click to add it as a separate library entry.

Importing Library Entries

To import library entries for a symbol into the active drawing, in the dialog box for that symbol in the Library area, click Import. After clicking Import, select a drawing file (DWG) or drawing template file (DWT) from which to import symbols.

Only the library entries for that symbol type and corresponding drafting standard are imported into the current drawing. If the drawing being imported contain libraries for other symbols or other drafting standards, those other symbols are ignored during this import.

Therefore, to be able to import symbol library entries from another drawing, the active drafting standard and standard version in the drawing being imported must match the active drafting standard and version in the active drawing. If custom standards have been defined, the industry drafting standards on which the custom standards are based must match.

If you import symbol library entries into a drawing that already contains library entries for that symbol, the Library - Import dialog box opens prompting you to specify how the library entries from the other drawing should be imported.

The options that are selected when importing library entries into a drawing that already contains library entries are Append, Overwrite, and Replace.

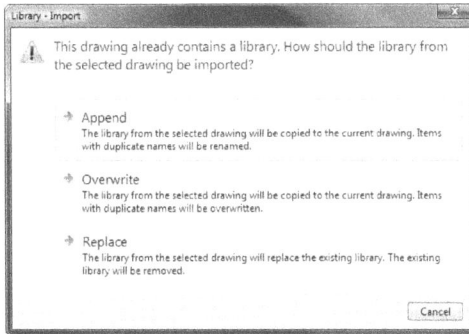

Inserting Weld Representations

You can place a simple weld symbol to represent the weld material in the front or side view of the weld. You can place the front fillet welds along a line from right to left to place the weld above the line. You can place the weld from left to right to place the weld below the line. You can switch the side the weld is on before accepting it. You can place front welds on a circle by selecting the start points and endpoints, going counterclockwise around the circle.

You can edit the size and location of inserted simple welds after double-clicking on them.

In the following illustration, the top view of the V-butt weld is represented along the butted miter seam with a series of arcs.

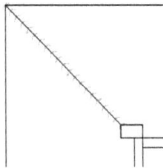

Access

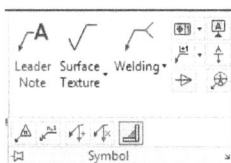

Command Line: AMSIMPLEWELD

Ribbon: Annotate tab > expanded Symbol panel > Weld Representation

Ribbon: Home tab > expanded Detail panel > Weld Representation

Menu: Annotate > Symbols > Weld Representation

Weld Representation Dialog Box

You can select the weld type in the Weld Representation dialog box. You can select the front view or side view of a single V-butt or fillet weld to represent the weld when you are looking down on it or from the end.

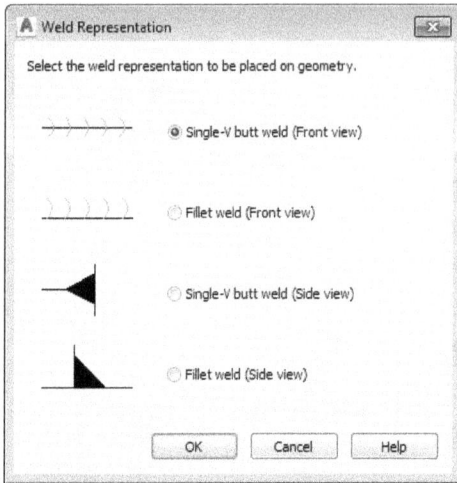

Procedure: Inserting Weld Representations

To insert a front and side view weld representation of a single V-butt or fillet weld, complete the following steps:

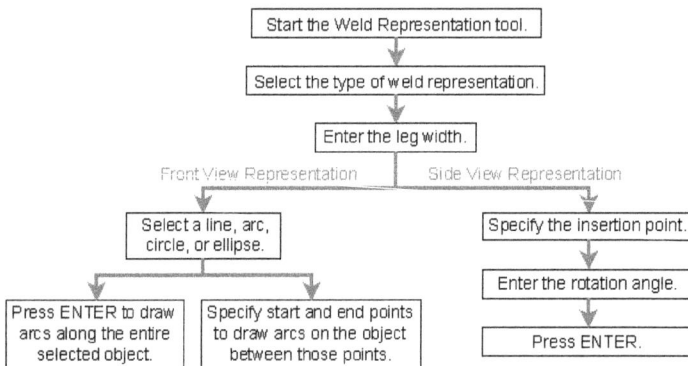

Inserting Datum Identifiers

You can use the datum identifier to reference actual part surfaces or features so that you can establish datums in your drawing. You can place the datum identifier by itself or attach it to geometry in the drawing. When you attach datum identifier symbols to geometry, the datum identifier changes position as the geometry is moved.

You can assign a different letter for each datum. After exhausting single letters, you can use two characters. Most standards do not use hyphens in the character name. However, you can identify datums with hyphens (e.g., -A-) by modifying the drawing standard in the Options dialog box, on the AM:Standards tab. Set the Datum and Feature identifiers to the ANSI standard, ASME Y14.5M 1982 R(1988).

You can add datum identifiers according to the current mechanical standard. They are placed on the AM_5 layer and displayed at the current drawing scale.

In the following illustration, datum A was added to the extension line coming from the bottom line for the part. This shows that the bottom face of the part is datum A.

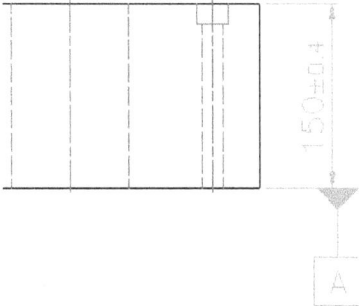

Access

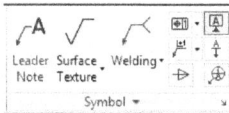

Command Line: AMDATUMID

Ribbon: Annotate tab > Symbol panel > Datum Identifier

Menu: Annotate > Symbol > Datum Identifier

Datum Identifier Dialog Box

You can the identifying name for the datum in the Datum Identifier dialog box. When you have drawn a leader line with the symbol, you can override the arrowhead used with the leader line. You can attach or detach the symbol to an object. When it is attached, the symbol moves with the object. When it is detached, it is a freestanding object. The dialog box opens during the process of inserting a datum identifier and after double-clicking on an existing symbol to edit it.

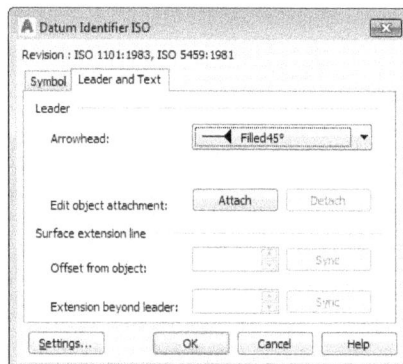

Procedure: Inserting Datum Identifiers

To add GD&T notation to your drawing by inserting a datum identifier, complete the following steps:

1. Start the **Datum Identifier** command.

2. In the drawing area, click the geometry to which you want to attach the datum identifier.

3. Click to locate the datum identifier symbol along the selected geometry.

4. Press ENTER to place the symbol on the geometry. You can also click to create leader segments from the geometry to the symbol.

5. In the Datum Identifier dialog box, enter the datum identifier text and set the arrowhead style.

Inserting Feature Identifiers

You can use the feature identifier when you need to call out a specific feature for tolerancing. You can use feature identifiers for ISO, DIN, BSI, CSN, JIS, and similar drawing standards. Feature identifiers are not supported in the ANSI standard.

In the following illustration, the feature identifier helps to identify the square notch in the part.

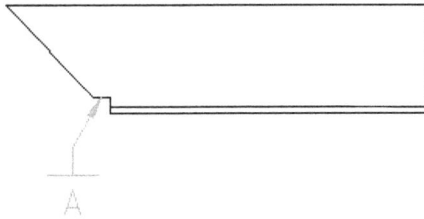

Access

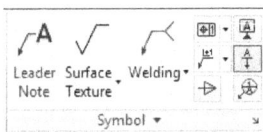

Command Line: AMFEATID

Ribbon: Annotate tab > Symbol panel > Feature Identifier

Menu: Annotate > Symbols > Feature Identifier

Feature Identifier Dialog Box

You can enter an identifying name for a feature in the Feature Identifier dialog box and assign a different letter for each feature. After exhausting single letters, you can use two characters. Selecting a different arrowhead style changes the arrowhead used with the leader line and overrides the current setting in the standard. You can attach or detach the symbol to an object. When it is attached, the symbol moves with the object. When it is detached, it is a freestanding object. The dialog box opens during the process of inserting a feature identifier and after double-clicking on an existing symbol to edit it.

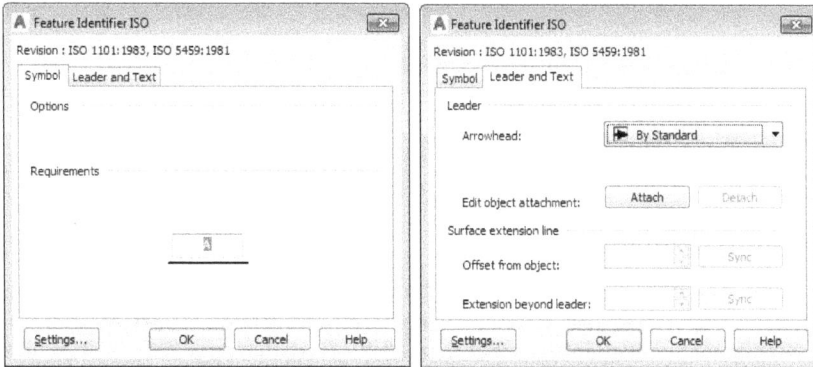

Procedure: Inserting a Feature Identifier

To add a feature identifier to a drawing, complete the following steps:

1. Start the **Feature Identifier** command.

2. In the drawing area, click the geometry to attach the feature identifier.

3. Click to locate the feature identifier along the selected geometry.

4. Click to create leader segments from the geometry to the symbol.

5. In the Feature Identifier dialog box, enter the feature identifier text.

Inserting Datum Targets

You can use datum targets to establish the datum plane and part orientation. You can use datum targets on irregular contours, such as forgings, castings, and sheet metal. A datum target establishes a theoretically exact plane, line, or profile. You can use datum targets on points, lines, or faces of a part.

You can insert datum targets according to the current mechanical standard. Datum targets are placed on the AM_5 layer and displayed at the current drawing scale. Datum target symbols are attached to geometry and change position as the geometry is moved. The following illustration shows the different styles of datum targets placed into a drawing.

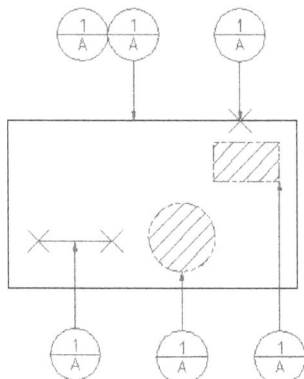

Access

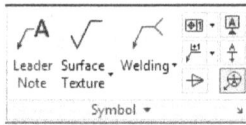

Command Line: AMDATUMTGT

Ribbon: Annotate tab > Symbol panel > Datum Target

Menu: Modify > Define

Datum Target Termination Types

After you start the **Datum Target** command, the Termination Type dialog box opens and you can select the type of datum target that you are defining. In the Termination Type dialog box, you can select from six different termination types that are available for datum targets. The datum termination type is placed at the arrow on the end of the leader.

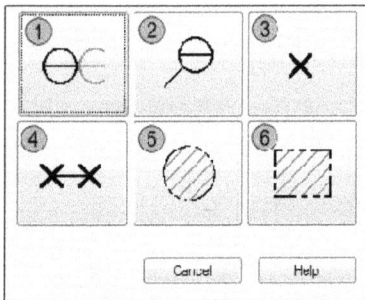

	Option	Definition
1.	**Attached to Another**	Datum target attached to another datum target.
2.	**None**	Datum target without any datum termination.
3.	**Point**	Datum target with a point termination.
4.	**Line**	Datum target with a line termination or a line with points on each end. The datum target is tied to the middle of the line.
5.	**Circle**	Datum target with a hatched circle to specify the Datum Target area.
6.	**Rectangle**	Datum target with a hatched rectangle to specify the Datum Target area.

Datum Target Dialog Box

In the Datum Target dialog box, you can enter the target dimension value and the datum value. Click Settings to modify the drawing standard default settings for the target point size, hatch style, arrowhead usage, and linetype. On the Leader and Text tab, you can modify the linetype, change the type of arrowhead, or detach the datum target from the selected geometry. This dialog box opens during the process of inserting a datum target and after double-clicking on an existing symbol to edit it.

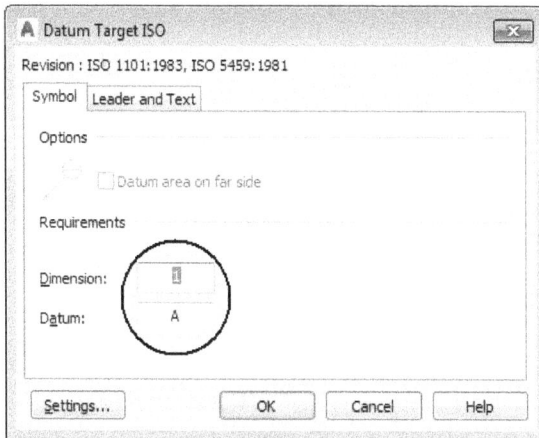

Procedure: Inserting Datum Targets

To insert a datum target notation, complete the following steps:

1. Start the **Datum Target** command.

2. In the Termination Type dialog box, click the required termination type.

3. In the drawing area, select the geometry to which you want to attach the datum target.

4. Click to locate the datum target.

5. Click to create leader segments from the geometry to the symbol.

6. In the Datum Target dialog box, enter the dimension and datum values.

Inserting Taper and Slope Symbols

You can use the taper and slope symbols to notate the amount of taper contained by a symmetrical or conical part or how much slope is along a part's edge. The initial shape and contents of a taper or slope symbol depend on the active standard when the symbol is created.

In the following illustration, a taper symbol was added to indicate how the end of the cylinder transitions from the defined diameter.

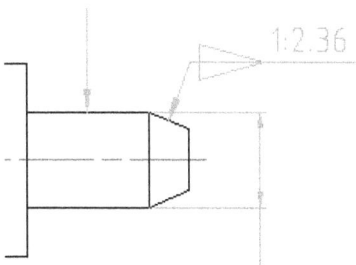

Access

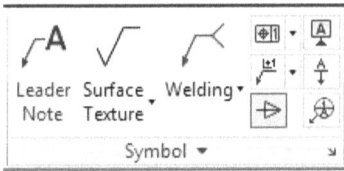

Command Line: AMTAPERSYM

Ribbon: Annotate tab > Symbol panel > Taper and Slope Symbol

Menu: Annotate > Symbols > Taper and Slope

Taper and Slope Symbol Dialog Box

In the Taper and Slope Symbol dialog box, you can select between defining a taper or slope, the direction the symbol should display, and the value that should be shown. On the *Leader and Text* tab, you can select to detach the symbol from the selected object or to change the type of arrowhead displayed at the end of the leader line. Click Settings when you want to directly access and edit the settings in the active standard. The dialog box opens during the process of inserting a taper and slope symbol and after double-clicking on an existing symbol to edit it.

If you select a baseline in addition to selecting the taper/slope object, the AutoCAD Mechanical software measures the slope/taper rate and uses that value as the default dimension text. Additionally, it determines whether the attached object is a taper or slope, automatically adjusts the orientation of the symbol, and aligns the reference line of the symbol to the baseline as you place it in the drawing area.

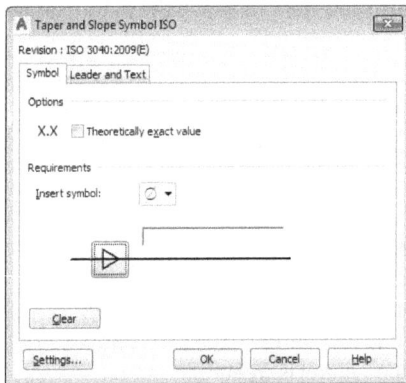

Procedure: Inserting Taper and Slope Symbols

To insert and attach a taper or slope symbol notation to a part, complete the following steps:

1. Start the **Taper and Slope** command.

2. In the drawing area, click the geometry to which to attach the symbol.

3. Click to locate the symbol location along the selected geometry.

4. Press ENTER to place the symbol on the geometry. You can also click to create leader segments from the geometry to the symbol.

5. In the Taper and Slope Symbol dialog box, select the appropriate type of taper of slope symbol and enter its values.

Standards Symbol Settings

The initial options and settings of all of the annotation symbols are based on the configuration of the active standard. Although you can override the initial settings for each symbol that you add, the standard should be configured in your template file so that you can accept the configured settings. This saves time and enables you to maintain consistency between your drawings.

Options Dialog Box - AM:Standards Tab

You can configure each symbol type in the Options dialog box, in the *AM:Standards* tab. You can access the configuration options by double-clicking on the element in the list of standard elements. The available options can vary depending on which standard is active. The text for the symbols is based on the overall text settings for the active standard.

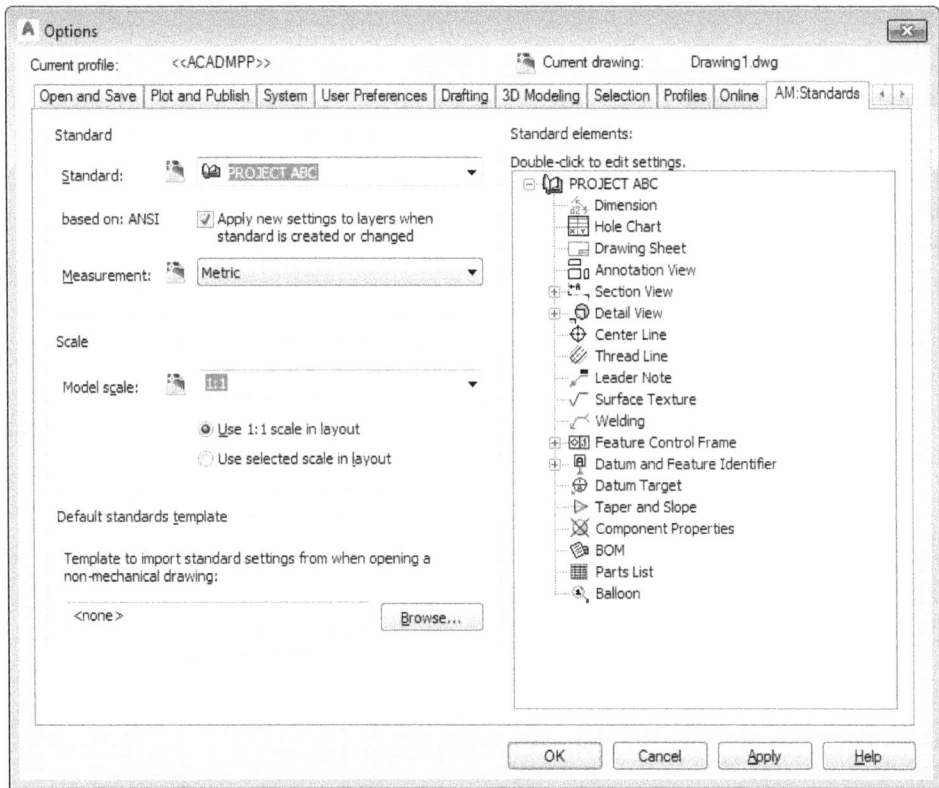

Exercise: Annotate Parts and Subassemblies

In this exercise, you will add different annotation symbols to different drawing sheets of different parts and subassemblies. This includes datum identifiers, datum targets, feature control frames, text, simple welds, and weld symbols.

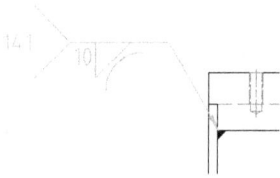

The completed exercise

Add Annotation Symbols

In this section of the exercise, you will add a datum identifier, a feature control frame, datum targets, and text to a drawing. You will also edit an existing dimension to change its display.

1. Open *Annotation Symbols.dwg*.

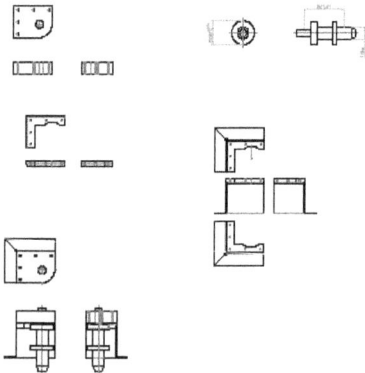

2. In the Mechanical Browser, in the *Drawing* tab, double-click on Block to make it active.

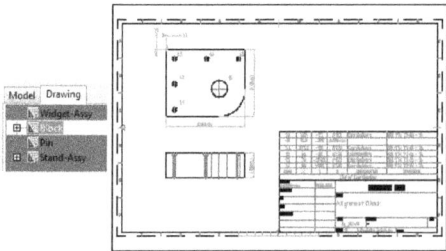

3. To begin adding a datum identifier, zoom into the lower view, click Annotate tab > Symbol panel > Datum Identifier.

4. In the drawing area:

   - Click the lower horizontal extension line to the dimension.
   - Move the cursor so that the preview is at the far right end of the extension line.
   - Click to set the leader start point.

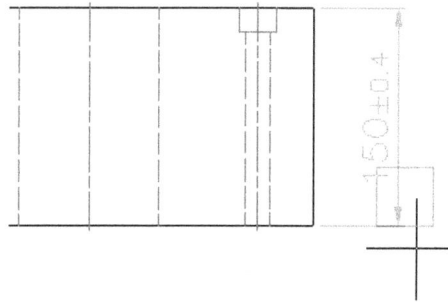

5. To complete the creation of the datum identifier, do the following:

   - Click a point below the extension line.
   - Press ENTER.
   - In the Datum Identifier dialog box, click OK to accept the letter A.

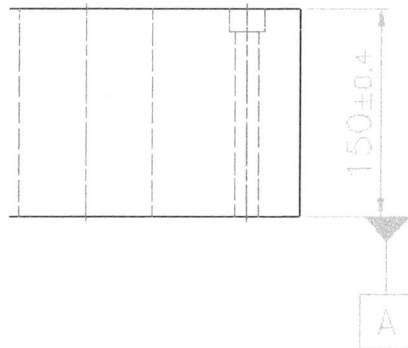

6. To define the centerline perpendicularity for the large hole, do the following:

- Click Annotate tab > Symbol panel > Feature Control Frame.
- Click the centerline for the large hole.
- Click a point on the lower half of the centerline.
- Click a point to the right.
- Click a point down and to the right.
- Press ENTER to create the leader segment.

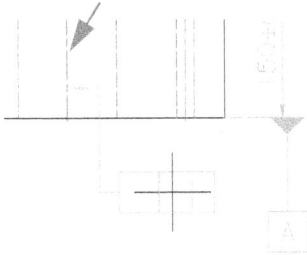

7. To specify the feature control information, in the Feature Control Frame dialog box, do the following:

- Click the top geometric symbol. Click Perpendicularity.
- In the Tolerance 1 box, enter **0.10**.
- In the Datum 1 box, enter **A**.

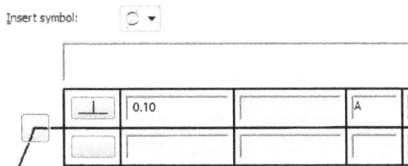

8. Click OK. The symbol is created as shown in the following illustration.

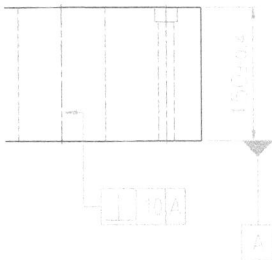

9. In the Mechanical Browser, click the *Model* tab to activate it.

10. Begin to add datum targets to the side view of the pin, as follows:

- Zoom into the shaft located near the top right of the drawing.
- Click Annotate tab > Symbol panel > Datum Target.
- In the Termination Type dialog box, click the None type.

11. To position the datum target, do the following:

- Select the top left horizontal line of the shaft.
- Object snap to the midpoint of the line as shown in the following illustration.
- Click to place the symbol above the extension line.
- Press ENTER.

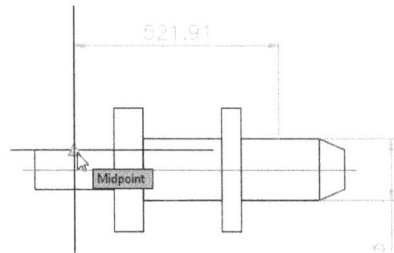

12. In the Datum Target dialog box, click OK to accept the default of dimension 1 and datum A.

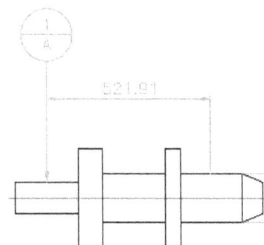

13. Follow the same process to add a datum target using the midpoint of the top right horizontal line of the shaft. Place the datum target above the right extension line with a dimension value of 2.

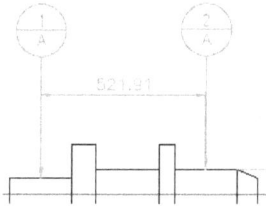

14. Double-click on the dimension 521.91. On the Power Dimensioning contextual tab > Representation panel, click Theoretically Exact. Press ENTER.

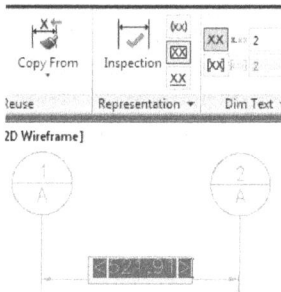

15. In the Mechanical Browser, in the *Drawing* tab, double-click on Pin to make it active.

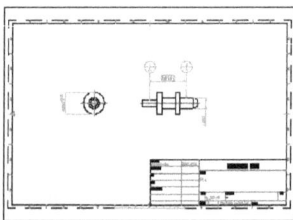

16. To begin adding a text note to the layout, do the following:

- Click Annotate tab > Text panel > Multiline Text drop-down list > Text M 5.
- In the open area to the left of the title block, define the text paragraph area.

17. Enter **S235JR, HEAT TREATED STEEL DIN EN 10083**.

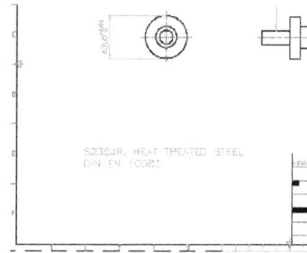

18. Click in the open drawing area.

Add Welding Information

In this section of the exercise you will add welding symbols and notes to communicate the location, type, and size of welds.

1. In the Mechanical Browser, click the *Model* tab to activate it.

2. Zoom in to the miter joint in the top view of this assembly annotation view.

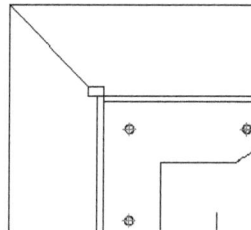

3. To begin adding a top view of a simple V-butt weld, do the following:

- Click Annotate tab > expanded Symbol panel > Weld Representation.
- In the Weld Representation dialog box, verify that Single-V butt weld (Front view) is selected.
- Click OK.

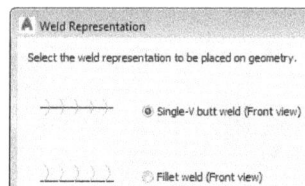

4. For the size and location of the simple weld symbol, do the following:

- For the leg width, enter **10**.
- In the drawing window, select the diagonal line.
- Press ENTER.

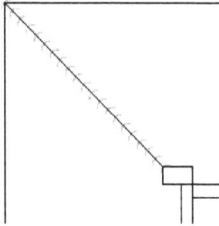

5. To begin adding a side view of a simple fillet weld to the front view of the assembly view, do the following:

- Click Annotate tab > expanded Symbol panel > Weld Representation.
- In the Weld Representation dialog box, click Fillet weld (Side view).
- Click OK.

6. To specify the size and location of the fillet weld symbol, do the following:

- For the leg width, enter **10**.
- In the drawing area, object snap to the intersection of the side and top part as shown in the following illustration.
- For the angle, move the cursor down and click.
- Press ENTER.

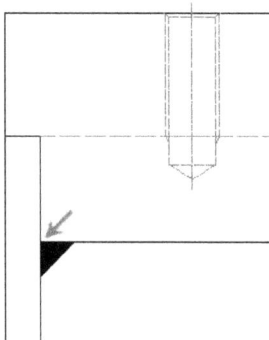

7. To add a weld symbol in the front view with the fillet weld, do the following:

- Click Annotate tab > Symbol panel > Welding.
- In the drawing area, click near the top left corner of the fillet weld that you just created.
- Press Enter to accept an option.
- In the drawing area, click close to the same location again (near the top left corner of the fillet).
- For the next leader line point, click up and to the left.
- Press ENTER.

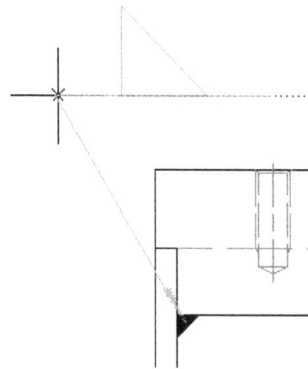

8. In the Weld Symbol dialog box, in the Options area:

- Select the Flip sides checkbox to set the weld type information to the arrow side.
- Select the Flip symbol checkbox to have the symbol's tail on the left.

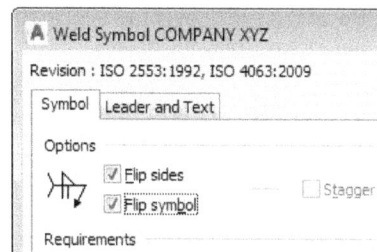

9. To add information to the symbol notation:

- In the Requirements area, click Add process.
- In the Process List dialog box, click 141 Tungsten inert gas arc welding; TIG welding. Click Insert.
- Click Close. The process note displays as shown in the following illustration.

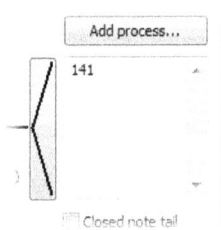

10. Add the following notation to the weld:

- In the size field, enter **10**.
- From the contour list, select the concave symbol.

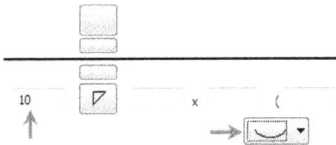

11. To add this symbol to the library, do the following:

- Click Add.
- Enter **Fillet-10-Concave-141**.
- Hover the cursor over this fillet in the library to display the details.

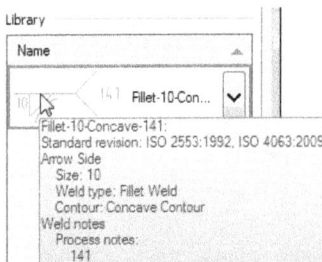

12. Click OK. The weld symbol is created as shown in the following illustration.

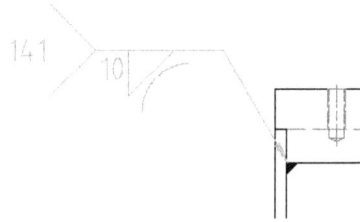

13. Save and close all of the files.

Lesson: Creating Dimensions

Overview

This lesson describes the power dimensioning and multiple automatic dimensioning tools that can be used to add dimensions to your drawings. This lesson explores the various command options, contextual Ribbon tabs, and dialog boxes associated with the AutoCAD Mechanical dimensioning functions.

When adding dimensions to your drawings, you can adjust the dimension to display tolerances and fits. The AutoCAD Mechanical dimensioning tools save time by placing the dimensions on the correct layer, at the correct size, and with the correct spacing.

In the following illustration, the Power Dimension tool was used to add the three different types of dimensions and annotation.

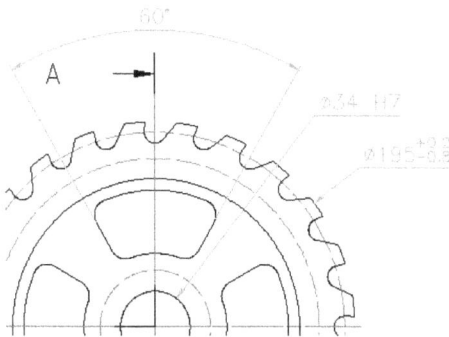

Objectives

After completing this lesson, you will be able to:

- Place dimensions using the Power Dimension command.
- Describe the options and settings that can be set for a dimension on the Power Dimensioning
- contextual Ribbon tab.
- State how to directly create chamfer dimensions.
- State the purpose and capabilities of the Dimension Overdrawn dialog box.
- Add multiple dimensions to a drawing at the same time.
- Make a dimension style active and state where changes to a dimension style are made.

Placing Power Dimensions

Dimensions play a crucial role in communicating your design to others. They specify the size of the part and its features or the part's location in an assembly. By using the Power Dimension command to generate angular, linear, radial, and diameter dimensions, you have a lot of flexibility in defining the appearance and content of the dimension.

In the following illustration, two views of a part have been partially dimensioned using the **Power Dimension** command.

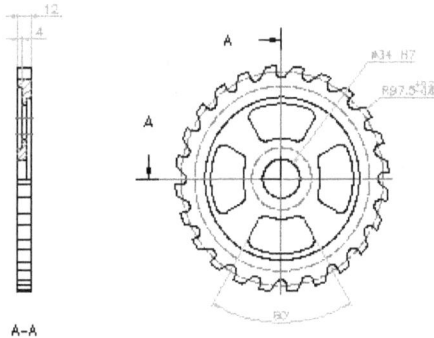

About Power Dimensions

The **Power Dimension** command enables you to create multiple types of dimensions using the same command. You can use it to place linear, angular, radial, diameter, baseline, and chain dimensions. To select the geometry to dimension instead of object snapping to locations, press to activate the Select Command Line option.

Power dimensions can be added in model space or in a layout while referencing the geometry in model space. Power dimensions added to a scaled area in model space automatically adjust based on that area's scale factors. Dimensions added to a layout also automatically adjust their linear scale based on the points or geometry selected.

When placing the dimension, you can locate the dimension from the drawing geometry or another dimension based on spacing set in the mechanical standard. The dimension is displayed in red when the cursor is located at a distance from the object contour. You can modify the type of dimension that is being placed. For example, when placing a radial dimension you can change it to a diameter dimension or change a diameter dimension to a radial dimension.

You can confirm or modify the style and appearance of the dimension on the Power Dimensioning contextual Ribbon tab. You can control the look, style, and behavior of power dimensions in the mechanical standards in the Options dialog box. The dimensions are placed on the AM_5 layer and are scaled appropriately.

When you double-click on any existing AutoCAD Mechanical software or AutoCAD software dimension, the Power Dimensioning contextual tab displays, enabling you to make modifications.

Dimensioning Workflows

After you initiate the Power Dimension command, the AutoCAD Mechanical software defaults to creating a linear dimension based on two points that you pick. After defining two dimension points, you can place the linear dimension in the horizontal or vertical direction, aligned to selected points, or aligned to any line at the selected points. Within the top level of the command, before picking two points you can also create a specific main type of dimension. The top-level dimension type options are Angular, Baseline, Chain, Linear, and Radial.

Instead of starting the Power Dimension command and selecting a suboption to create a specific type of dimension, you can execute a separate command to directly initiate the Power Dimension command for that suboption. You can directly create horizontal, vertical, aligned, rotated, radial, diameter, angular, chamfer, jogged radius, arc length, baseline, or chained dimensions.

To help identify the type of dimension you are creating, an icon displays next to the cursor and indicates the dimension type.

When using the Power Dimension command, you can open the Power Dimension Options and Placement Options dialog boxes. In these dialog boxes, you can preset the representation of the dimension value and assign fits or tolerance information to the dimension.

Access

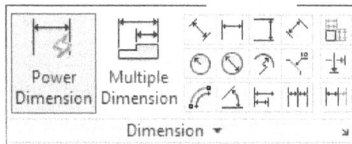

Command Line: AMPOWERDIM

Ribbon: Annotate tab > Dimension panel > Power Dimension

Menu: Annotate > Power Dimensioning

You can access and start specific Power Dimension commands in different ways and from different locations. The dimension creation tools are located on the Annotate tab > Dimension panel. You can also access the dimension tools on the Annotate menu in the Menu Bar.

Power Dimension Commands

You can directly initiate and create specific power dimensions using the following Command Line commands or Ribbon icons.

Command	Icon	Description
AMPowerDim_Hor		Create linear horizontal dimensions.
AMPowerDim_Ver		Create linear vertical dimensions.
AMPowerDim_Ali		Create linear aligned dimensions.
AMPowerDim_Rot		Create linear dimensions with extension lines slanted at a rotation angle relative to the two points being dimensioned.
AMPowerDim_Rad		Create radius dimensions for arcs or circles.

AMPowerDim_Dia		Create diameter dimensions for arcs and circles.
AMPowerDim_Jog		Create a radius dimension with a jog in the dimension line that does not extend from the center of the arc or circle.
AMPowerDim_Cham		Directly create a chamfer dimension for the selected chamfer. You are required to select the chamfer line and then the first and second extension lines.
AMPowerDim_Arclen		Directly create an angle style dimension that dimensions the length of the arc.
AMPowerDim_Ang		Creates an angular dimension for the selected object.
AMPowerDim_Bas		Create a number of linear or angular dimensions originating from a single base extension line.
AMPowerDim_Chain		Create a number of linear or angular dimensions, each one dimensioning from the extension line of the previous dimension.

Power Dimension Visual Aids

To help identify which type of dimension you are in the process of creating, an icon indicating the dimension type displays next to the cursor.

After starting the Power Dimension command and pressing ENTER to initiate the Select Objects option, the icon displayed next to the cursor changes based on the geometry that the cursor hovers over. The icon dynamically changes between linear, radial, and diameter dimension types.

When you directly initiate a specific power dimension command, only the icon for that dimension type displays next to the cursor.

The following table shows the different icons that display near the cursor when you are creating power dimensions.

Icon	Dimension Type	Icon	Dimension Type	Icon	Dimension Type
	Point Power Dimension		Horizontal		Vertical
	Aligned		Rotated		Angular
	Radius		Jogged Radius		Diameter
	Arc Length		Chamfer		

Power Dimensioning Contextual Ribbon Tab

After you start any of the power dimensioning commands, the Power Dimensioning contextual Ribbon tab displays. Within it you can set how you want the dimensions to be represented and whether the dimension should include fits or tolerance information.

On the Representation panel, select how you want the dimension to be displayed. Your representation options include Dimension Not to Scale, Theoretically Exact, Inspection Dimension, and Reference Dimension. The representation option that you select is only applied to the dimensions that you create during that power dimension command. The next time you start a power dimension command, all of the representation options are cleared.

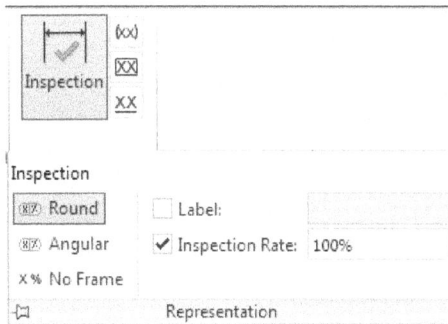

On the Fit/Tolerance panel, select whether or not to include fit or tolerance information with the dimension, and then select whether or not to include the information as either fit or tolerance. After you click Fit or Tolerance, specify the required notation information. The fit or tolerance information is then added to all dimensions during the use of that power dimension command and all subsequent power dimension uses until you reopen the Power Dimensioning contextual tab and change the setting or toggle it off.

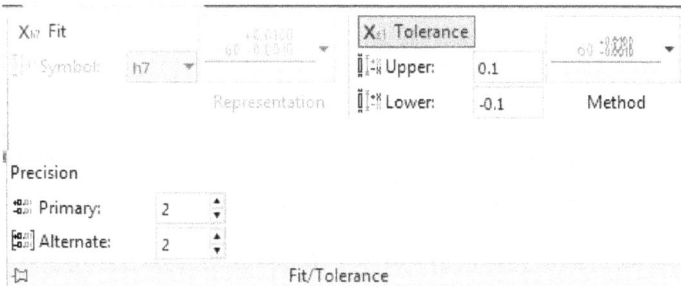

Radius and Diameter Representation Options

When you are adding a radius or diameter power dimension, after selecting the arc or circle, selecting the Option suboption enables you to override the default representation settings for that dimension. The dialog boxes for radius and diameter dimensions have the same options and format as the dimension element settings.

The Radius Dimension Options dialog box opens when you add a radius dimension after selecting the arc or circle, and before clicking to place the dimension using the Options suboption. When the dialog box opens, the changes you make are temporary overrides to the default settings in the Dimension standard element. The next time you add a radius power dimension, the appearance of the dimension matches the active settings in the Dimension element.

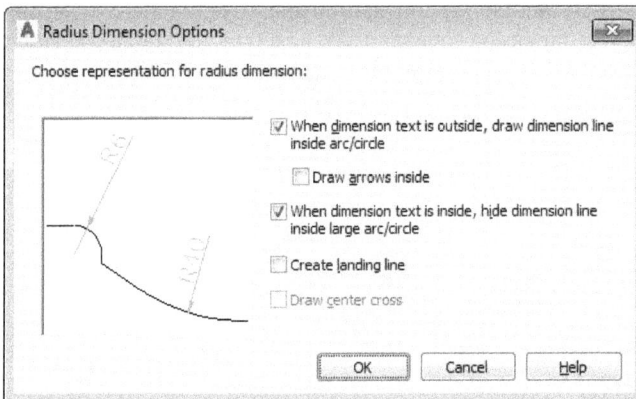

The Diameter Dimension Options dialog box opens when you add a diameter dimension after selecting the arc or circle and before clicking to place the dimension using the Options suboption. When the dialog box opens, the changes you make are temporary overrides to the default settings in the Dimension standard element. The next time you add a diameter power dimension, the appearance of the dimension matches the active settings in the Dimension element.

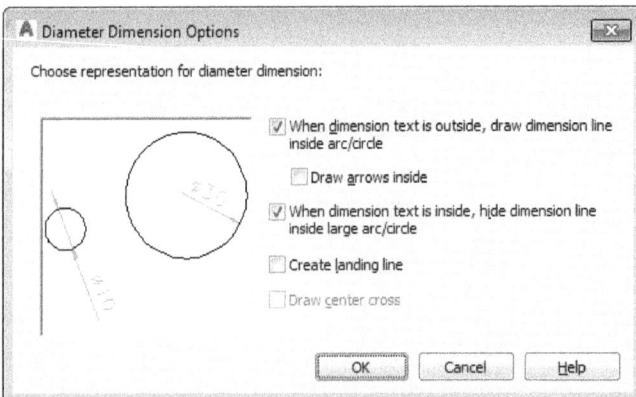

Process: Placing Power Dimensions

The following diagram shows the process of placing dimensions in a drawing when using the power dimensioning commands.

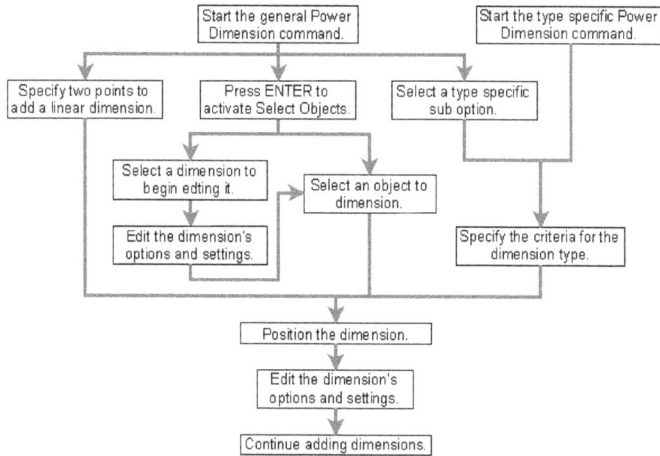

Power Dimensioning Options and Settings

During the placement of a dimension in a drawing or when editing an existing dimension, the Power Dimensioning contextual tab displays, enabling you to change the dimension's display options and settings. To have dimensions display with the information and in the format that you require, you need to learn about the options and settings that are available for selection in the Power Dimensioning contextual tab.

In the following illustration, the same dimensioning schema is shown with different settings and configuration options for the dimensions. Based on the differences in the settings, the same dimensions have a slightly different meanings for manufacturing this part.

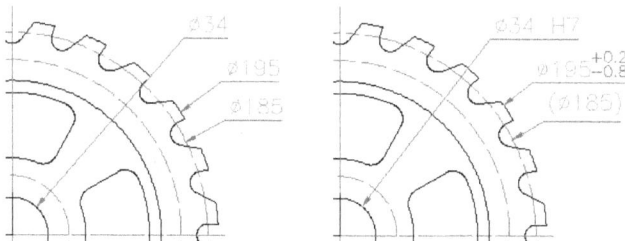

Power Dimensioning Contextual Tab

You can use the options and settings on the Power Dimension contextual tab to define the dimension text and geometry. The default standard settings are displayed on the Power Dimensioning contextual tab after you start a Power Dimension command. Each time you access the Power Dimension command thereafter, any dimensions you add are displayed with the same settings. If you change the dimension settings in the Power Dimensioning contextual tab, any dimensions that you add are displayed with those settings. Some options for the dimension text are only available if the in-place editor is active.

Power Dimensioning Contextual Tab - Reuse Panel

The Reuse panel enables you to reuse dimension settings. The Predefined Text drop-down list contains a list of stock dimension text templates to apply to a selected dimension. The Import/Export drop-down list, contains the option of importing (Copy From) properties from another dimension, or exporting (Apply To) properties to another dimension.

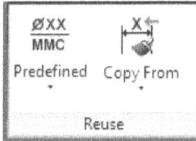

Power Dimensioning Contextual Tab - Representation Panel

The options on the Representation panel enable you to adjust the dimension notation. Selecting Inspection enables you to specify the inspection shape (including Round, Angular, or No Frame) for a dimension, and the option to include an additional Label or Inspection Rate. Additional options include whether to display the dimension with parenthesis (Reference), with a box around it (Theoretically Exact), or underlined (Not to Scale).

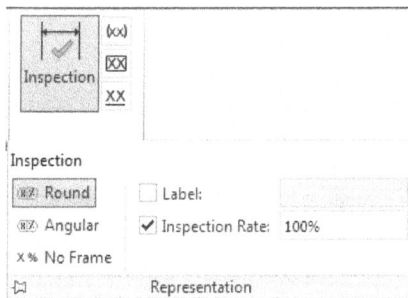

Power Dimensioning Contextual Tab - Dim Text Panel

On the Dim Text panel, you can toggle the dimension text for either the Primary or Alternate units on or off, and set its number of decimal places. You can change the type of unit used for the dimension, round off the dimension value, and modify the linear scale values to multiply the dimension value when the geometry is not drawn to scale. The linear scale value automatically adjusts to the correct value when adding a dimension in a scale area in model space or to geometry displayed in a layout viewport.

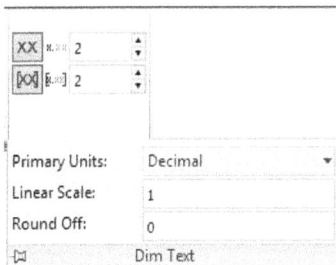

Power Dimensioning Contextual Tab - Insert Panel

The Insert panel includes the option of inserting a symbol from the Symbol Gallery into the dimension text, or inserting a dimension line break character so that additional text is displayed below the dimension line.

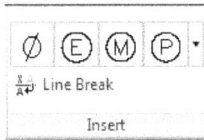

Power Dimensioning Contextual Tab - Fit/Tolerance Panel

You can display fit or tolerance information on the dimension, but not both. Toggling one on, automatically toggles the other one off.

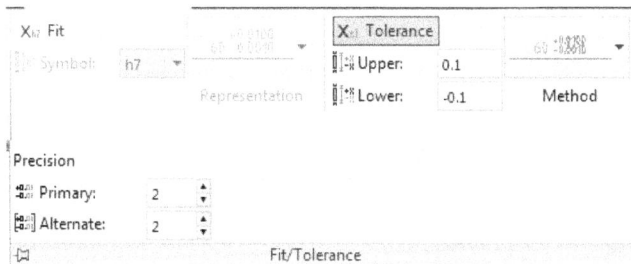

Click Fit to display a fit notation. In the Fit Symbol drop-down list, select Fit Dialog Box to open the Fits dialog box in which you can manually fit values or select them from lists of standard fits for a hole or shaft. You can preview the fit results in this dialog box.

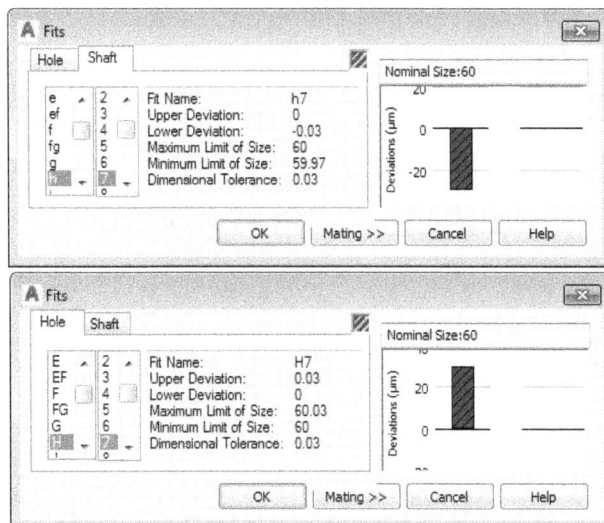

Expand the Fit Representation drop-down list to select the appearance method for the fit dimension notation.

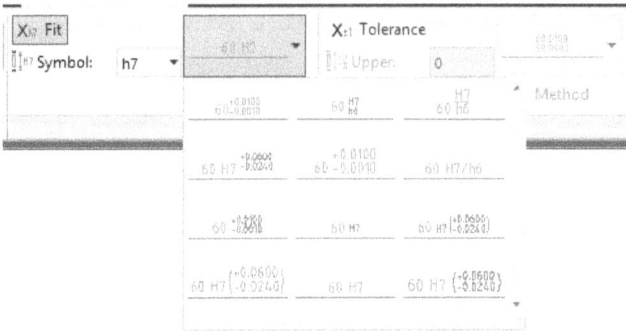

Click Tolerance to display a tolerance notation. Specify the Upper and Lower values for the difference between the nominal dimension value and the maximum and minimum limits. You can also specify the precision for the tolerance's primary and alternate units. Expand the Tolerance Representation drop-down list to select the appearance method for the tolerance dimension notation.

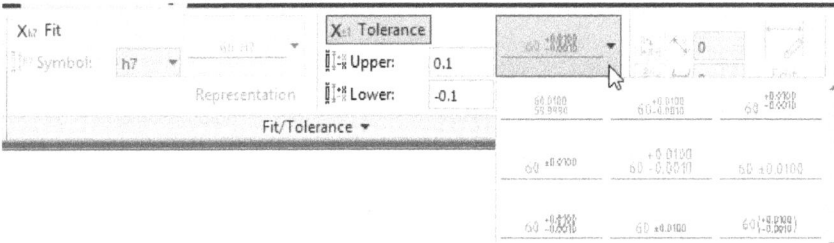

Power Dimensioning Contextual Tab - Format Panel

The Format panel includes options for formatting selected dimension text. It includes options for rotating dimension text by a specified angle (or rotating it back to its default position), converting a dimension into one that indicates symmetry, or slanting extension lines by a specified angle. The options on the expanded panel enable you to adjust how to arrange arrows and dimension text when space is limited, how dimension text behaves when moved, and (for radial dimension text outside the circle or arc) where the arrow is displayed and whether a landing line is displayed.

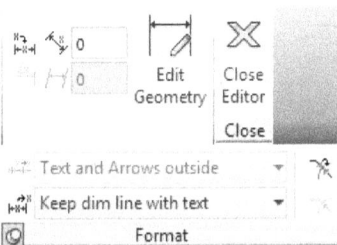

The Edit Geometry button opens the Power Dimensioning - Edit Geometry dialog box enabling you to modify the dimension geometry. You can click the geometry in the selection window to toggle the visibility on/off and click the arrowhead to change its style. You can modify the gap size between the text and dimension lines by entering an offset value.

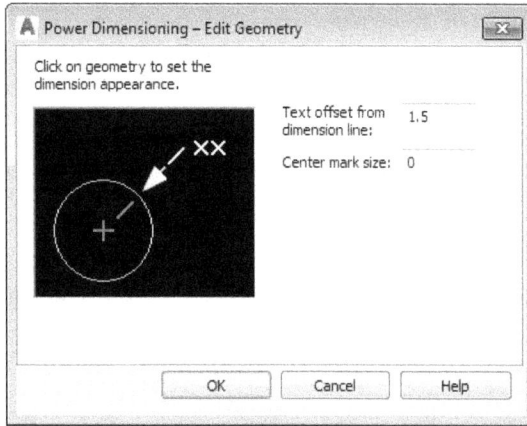

Chamfer Dimensions

The method used to dimension a chamfer is typically consistent from one chamfer to another. To add the notation for the chamfer to the drawing as quickly as possible while adhering to your drafting standards, you need to learn which command to use to directly create chamfer dimensions.

The following illustration shows the same chamfer on a part using different chamfer notation methods.

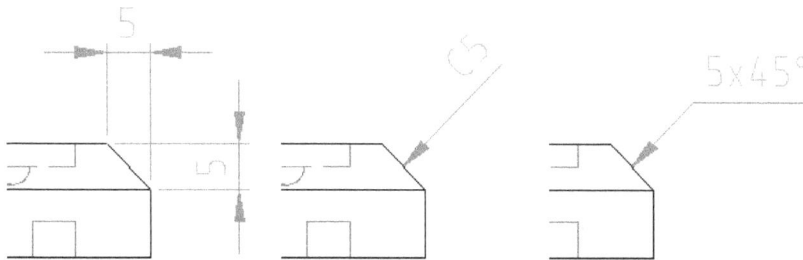

Chamfer Dimension

The **AMPOWERDIM_CHAM** command enables you to directly dimension any existing chamfer. You can use this dimensioning command to dimension any line geometry that represents a chamfer. The chamfer does not have to have been initially created with the AutoCAD Mechanical Chamfer command.

The dimensioning method or representation is automatically based on the default representations setting in the dimension setting for the active standard.

This command supersedes the AMCHAM2D_DIM command provided in the earlier version of the software and is provided for backward compatibility.

Access

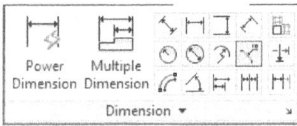

Command Line: AMPOWERDIM_CHAM

Ribbon: Annotate tab > Chamfer

Menu: Annotate > Chamfer

Overdrawn Dimensions

When you place a dimension on top of another dimension, the Dimension Overdrawn dialog box opens. With the options in this dialog box, you can select how you want to make room for the additional dimension.

In the following illustration, a new linear dimension was placed on top of an existing dimension. This caused the Dimension Overdrawn dialog box to open. After selecting the Move Away option, the dimensions display on the part correctly to meet standard drafting practices.

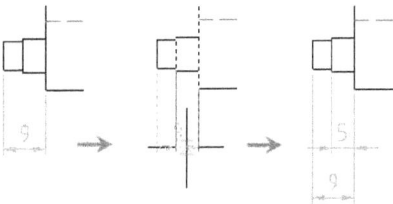

Dimension Overdrawn Dialog Box

The Dimension Overdrawn dialog box automatically opens after you click to position a power dimension that is drawn over the top of an existing dimension. The options in this dialog box enable you to select the method that you want to use to correct the notation problem. The images to the left of the option help clarify the correction by showing how the current dimension is going to change relative to the new dimension.

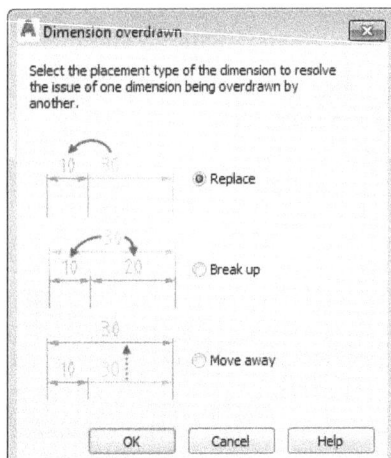

Placing Multiple Dimensions

Dimensioning a drawing can be time-consuming when you need to add many dimensions to fully communicate a view. When the multiple dimensions share a common format, such as baseline or continuous dimension format, you can save a lot of time by knowing how to add multiple dimensions to a drawing at the same time.

In the following illustration, multiple vertical dimensions were added to the drawing view after the geometry was selected and the identified point for the baseline dimensions was specified.

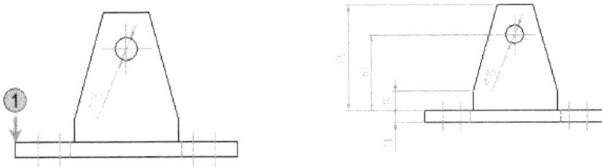

About Adding Multiple Dimensions Automatically

The multiple dimensions that you add at same time are added according to the current dimension style and specific style type selected in the Automatic Dimensioning dialog box. You can use the Multiple Dimension command to place a group of multiple parallel, ordinate, shaft, and symmetric dimensions. You can place multiple dimensions for both horizontal and vertical dimensions at the same time.

The multiple automatic dimensions follow your current mechanical drawing standards. When you use the Multiple Dimension command, the dimensions are placed on the AM_5 layer and displayed at the current drawing scale. The Multiple Dimension command only selects the standard objects and linetypes that require dimensions. Filtering is automatically toggled on to prevent you from dimensioning to hidden lines, auxiliary lines, text, phantom lines, section lines, hatch, or other dimension lines. If an additional dimension location is required, you can add it manually.

As you specify the criteria for adding multiple dimensions, you can enable the rearranging of existing dimensions. When the Rearrange option is selected, when you select the geometry to dimension, if your selection set includes an existing dimension, that dimension is recreated as part of the new multiple automatic dimensions.

When adding multiple dimensions, you can also set the Power Dimensioning dialog box to open for each of the dimensions that are automatically created so that you can change the dimensions' options and settings.

Access

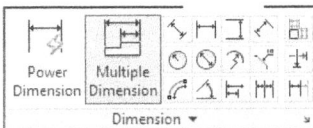

Command Line: AMAUTODIM

Ribbon: Annotate tab > Dimension panel > Multiple Dimension

Menu: Annotate > Multiple Dimensioning

Multiple Parallel Dimensions

When you create multiple parallel dimensions, they are either created in a continuous chain or reference the same baseline. You can select the type of parallel dimensions to create by selecting Baseline or Chain in the Type list or by clicking the preview image to cycle the type.

For parallel dimension creation, you can add multiple parallel dimensions in one axis direction for selected geometry and dimension in both axes.

If you create parallel baseline dimensions, you can set how the dimensions should align with each other when dimensions are created on each side of the base extension line. When the Alignment option is set to Inside Out, the dimensions on each side begin aligning near the start point of the base extension line. This location is also closest to the geometry being dimensioned. An Alignment option setting of Outside In causes the dimensions on each side of the base extension line to begin aligning near the end point of the base extension line, which would also be the farthest location from the geometry being dimensioned.

After you have the options set to match your requirements, click OK to select the geometry to dimension and then position the dimensions in the drawing.

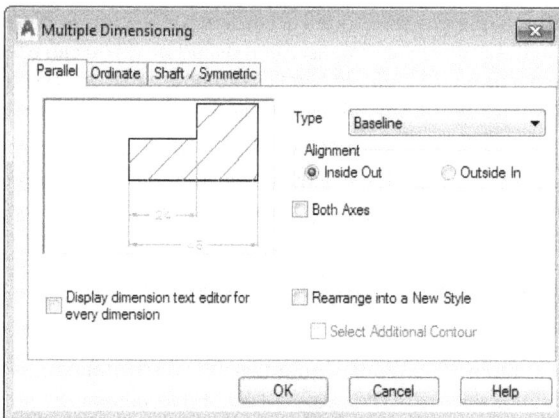

In the following illustration, multiple parallel dimensions were added using the Inside Out alignment as shown on the left, while dimensions shown on the right were added using the Outside In alignment.

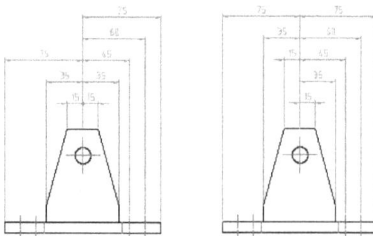

Multiple Ordinate Dimensions

When you create multiple ordinate dimensions, you need to select one of the three types of ordinate dimensions. You can select between Current Standard (ISO for example), Equal Leader Length, or Center Cross on Edge. You can select the type of ordinate dimension to add by selecting that type in the Type list or clicking the preview image to cycle through the types.

By selecting the option to dimension both axes, you can add ordinate dimensions in the horizontal and vertical directions.

For further control of the display of the ordinate dimensions, you can select to have the text rotate so that it aligns with the dimension line rather than the extension line or to have the dimension lines drawn as short segments. When using the Center Cross On Edge type, you also have the option of centering the text at the dimensioned point.

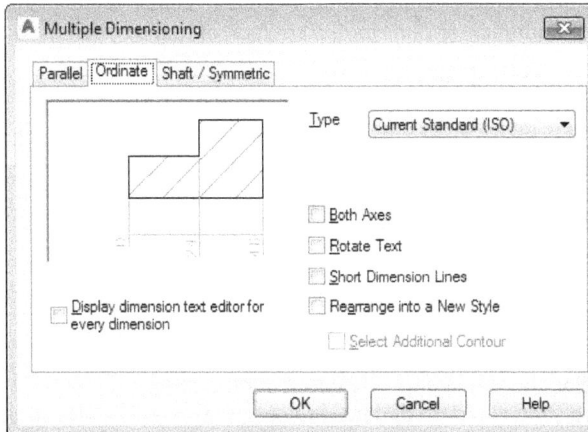

Multiple Shaft or Symmetric Dimensions

To add multiple linear diametric dimensions or linear dimensions symmetric to a centerline, you can select the required type in the Type list or click the preview image to cycle through the options.

When you have a cylindrical part to which you want to add multiple linear diametric dimensions, you can use the Shaft (Front View) or Shaft (Side View) dimension type. Special configuration options for multiple shaft dimensions include selecting to draw only one extension line for each dimension and to have the dimensions positioned within the contours being dimensioned or outside of the contours.

If the part is not cylindrical but symmetric about a centerline, you can select the Symmetric dimension type to add multiple linear dimensions centered about a selected centerline or point.

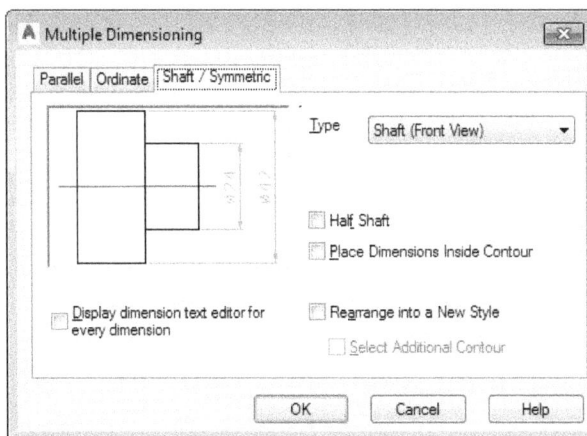

Process: Placing Multiple Dimensions Automatically

The following steps describe how to place multiple dimensions in a drawing automatically based on the selected geometry.

1. On the Ribbon, click Annotate tab > Dimension panel > Multiple Dimension.

2. Select the type of dimension that you want to create.

3. Set any special creation or configuration options for the creation of that dimension type.

4. Select the geometry that you want to dimension.

5. If required for the type of dimensions being added, specify any origin or centerline location.

6. Position the dimensions.

7. Click to add additional individual dimensions to the set if required.

Control Dimension Standards

There are many options for controlling the appearance and information displayed in a dimension. You can configure the overall dimension style, standard dimension notes, snap distance, and many other dimension settings. To add dimensions to a drawing that conform to your standards, you need to know how to activate an existing dimension style in the drawing or to configure the active dimension style.

Dimension Configuration in the Standard

You can preconfigure your dimension settings in the Dimension Settings dialog box. You can open the dialog box from the Options dialog box, in the *AM:Standards* tab, by double-clicking on the Dimension standards element.

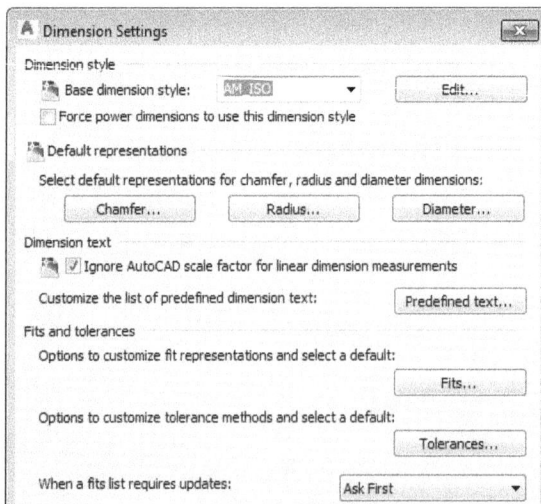

Within the Dimension Settings dialog box, you can:

- Click and configure the dimension style.
- Set the default dimension representation for chamfers, radiuses, and diameters.
- Set the dimensions to follow or ignore the AutoCAD linear scale factor (DIMLFAC) variable value.
- Predefine the dimension text arrangement and information.
- Choose the default representation for fits and tolerance information and customize the fit representations or tolerance methods.
- Set the values for various dimension placement options including whether the Power Dimensioning dialog box should display during the placement of dimensions.

When a new drawing standard is created, a new dimension style is also automatically created with the same name as the newly created drawing standard. This new dimension style is also made active in the standard. The dimension style that is listed in the Base Dimension Style field is the active dimension style. Selecting a new style in the list makes it the active standard. Selecting a different style to make it the active style in the standard only affects the dimensions that you are about to create, not the dimensions that have already been created. If you change the settings within a standard, any dimensions that you have created with the style update and reflect the new settings.

Exercise: Use the Power Dimension Command

In this exercise, you will add dimensions to two different layout views of a part using the Power Dimension command.

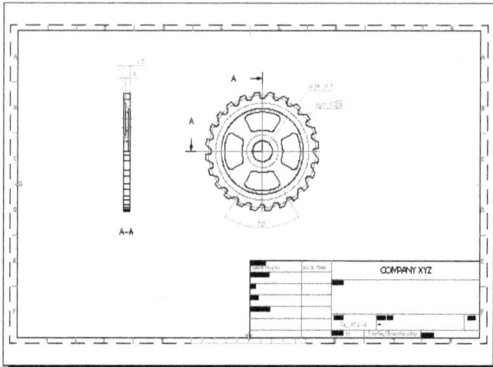

The completed exercise

1. Open *Power_Dimension.dwg*.

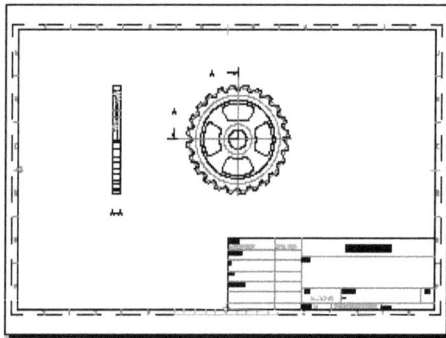

2. On the Annotate tab > Dimension panel, click Power Dimension.

3. To add a linear dimension to the half section view to show the part's thickness, do the following:

- Object snap to the top two corners.
- Move the cursor up and click to place the dimension when the preview is displayed in red.
- Press ENTER to continue.

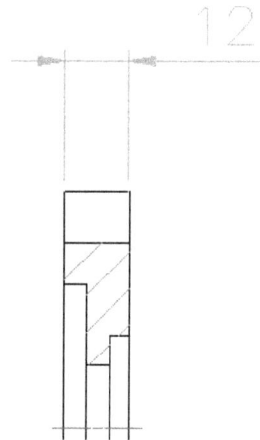

4. Add another dimension from the top left outside corner to the first recessed corner. Click on the horizontal dimension line of the previously placed dimension (12) to place the new dimension on top of it.

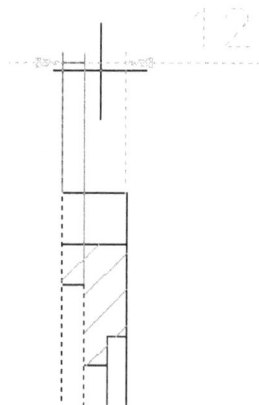

5. In the Dimension Overdrawn dialog box, click Move away. Click OK to create the dimensions as shown in the following illustration.

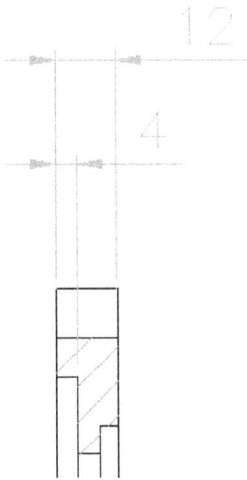

6. While still in the Power Dimension command, switch to dimensioning the angles. Right-click anywhere in the drawing window and click Angular.

7. In the front view, click the diagonal lines and place the angular dimension as shown in the following illustration.

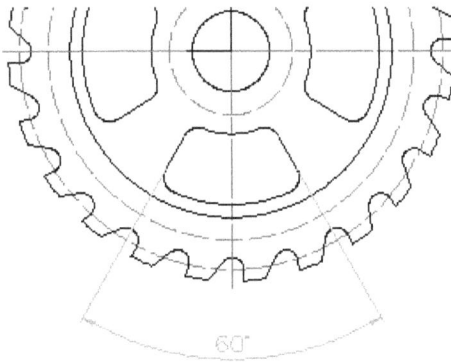

8. To switch to dimensioning based on selected objects, do the following:

- Right-click in the drawing window and click eXit in the menu.
- Right-click in the drawing window and click Enter in the menu.

9. Click an outermost arc of the part and click to place the dimension.

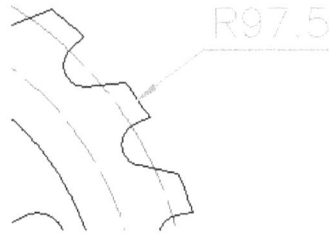

10. To begin configuring the dimension notation to have fit tolerance information, do the following:

- On the Power Dimensioning contextual tab > Fit/Tolerance panel, click Fit.
- On the Power Dimensioning contextual tab > Fit/Tolerance panel > Fit Symbol drop-down, click Fit Dialog Box.

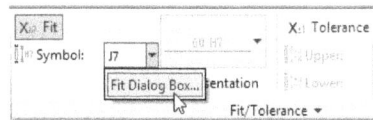

11. In the Fits dialog box, do the following:

- On the Hole tab, in the fit definition lists, click H and 7.
- Click OK.

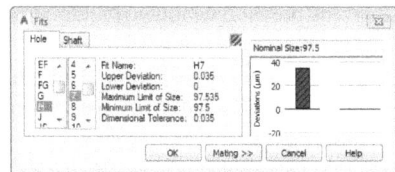

12. To create and position the diameter dimension, do the following:

- Press ENTER to accept the Select Object default option.
- Select the innermost circle and position the dimension up and to the right of the part as shown in the following illustration.
- Press ESC.

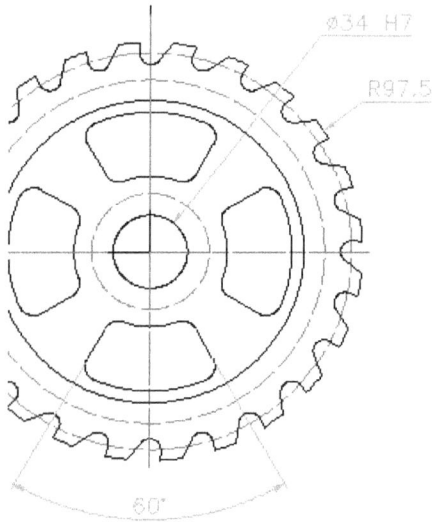

13. To add a tolerance value to the radius dimension that you previously created, do the following:

- In the drawing window, double-click on the radius dimension value.
- In the Power Dimensioning contextual tab > Fit/Tolerance panel, click Tolerance.
- Press ENTER.

14. Review the drawing and note the different types of dimensions that you just created using the same dimensioning command.

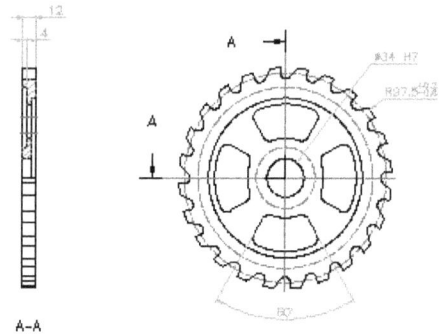

A-A

15. Save and close all of the files.

Exercise: Add Different Power Dimensions

In this exercise, you will add power dimensions by starting the commands in different ways and modifying some of the settings in the standard for dimensions.

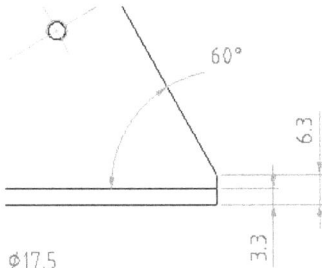

The completed exercise

1. Open *Mounting Bracket-C5.dwg*.

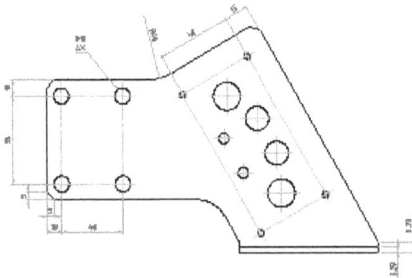

2. To begin adding power dimensions based on selected geometry, do the following:

   - On the Annotate tab > Dimension panel, click Power Dimension.
   - Press ENTER.

3. To display the different preview icons for the dimension types, hover the cursor over different pieces of drawing geometry as shown in the following illustration.

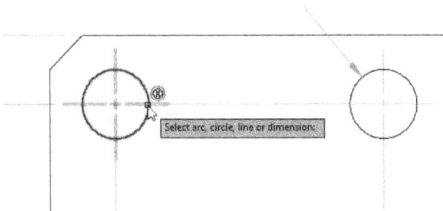

4. Near the bottom right portion of the drawing, click on the large hole and position the dimension as shown in the following illustration. Press ENTER.

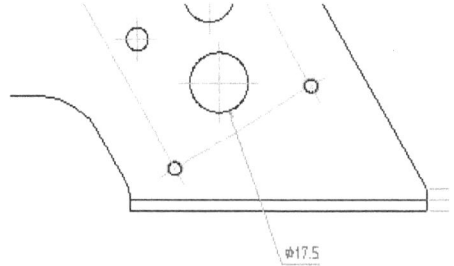

5. To begin creating only radial power dimensions, do the following:

   - Enter **R** for the Radial option.
   - Press ENTER.
   - Select the Radius option.

6. In the drawing window, select the large arc and position the dimension as shown in the following illustration. Click to accept the position. Press ESC to end the dimension command.

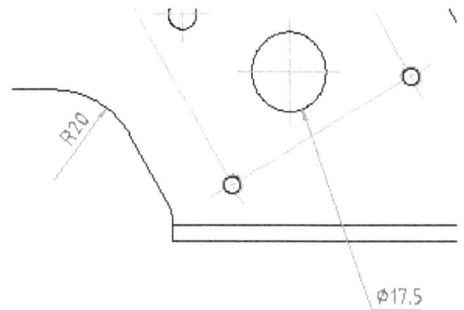

7. To begin editing the standards settings for dimensions, do the following:

- Right-click in an open area of the drawing window and click Options.
- In the Options dialog box, in the *AM:Standards* tab, in the Standard elements list, double-click on Dimension.

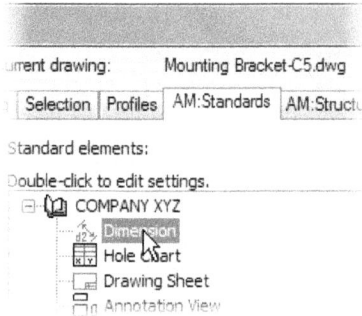

urrent drawing:	Mounting Bracket-C5.dwg

Selection | Profiles | AM:Standards | AM:Structu

Standard elements:

Double-click to edit settings.

- COMPANY XYZ
  - Dimension
  - Hole Chart
  - Drawing Sheet
  - Annotation View

8. In the Dimension Settings dialog box, in the Dimension style area, click Edit.

9. In the Edit Dimension Style dialog box, in the Dimension Style list, select Linear. Click Modify.

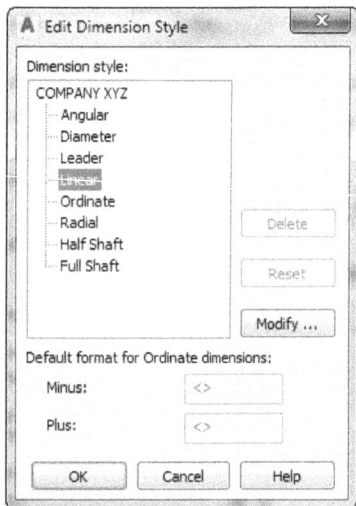

10. In the Modify Dimension Style dialog box, in the *Primary Units* tab, in the Linear dimensions area, in the Precision list, select a precision of 0.0. Click OK.

11. In the Edit Dimension Style dialog box, do the following:

- Note that the text for the Linear dimension style is bold, indicating that overrides exist.
- Hover the cursor over Linear to display the override differences between the overall dimension style and this substyle.
- Click OK.

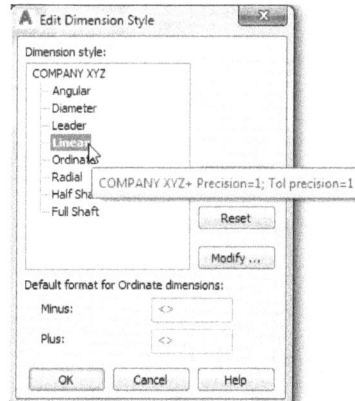

12. In the Dimension Settings dialog box, in the *Default representations* area, select Radius.

13. In the Radius Representation dialog box, do the following:

- Clear the checkbox for the top option and verify that its sub-option is cleared as well.
- Select the When Dimension text is inside and the Create landing line checkboxes as shown in the following illustration to toggle on these display options.
- Click OK.

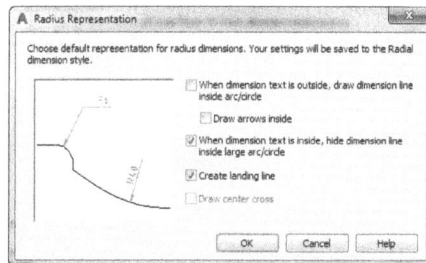

14. In the Dimension Settings dialog box, in the *Default representation* area, select Chamfer.

15. In the Chamfer Representation dialog box, do the following:

- In the drop-down list of representations, click the preview image for 10x10 located in the second row all the way to the left as shown in the following illustration.
- Click OK.

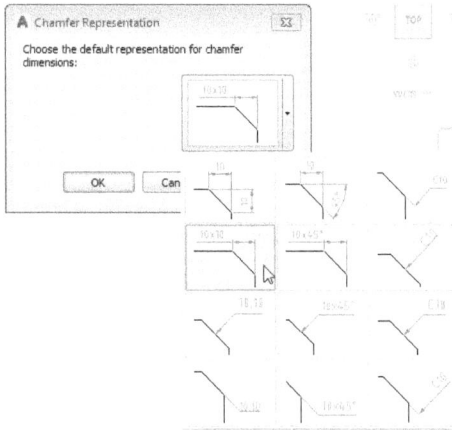

16. In the Dimension Settings dialog box, in the *Placement options* area, in the Display dimension text editor drop-down list, select Only on Demand.

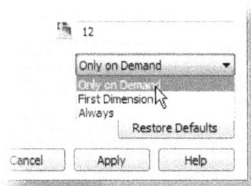

17. To save these changes and return to the drawing, do the following:

- In the Dimension Settings dialog box, click OK.
- In the Options dialog box, click OK.

18. To add a radius dimension to the arc below the radius dimension that you previously added, do the following:

- On the Annotate tab > Dimension panel, click Radius.
- In the drawing window, select the arc and click to position the dimension as shown in the following illustration.
- Press ESC.

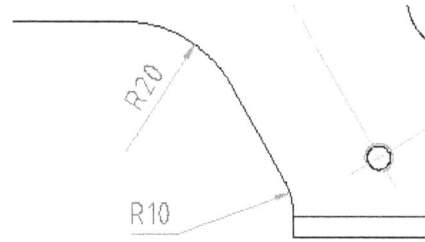

19. To add an aligned dimension to indicate the distance between one set of holes, do the following:

- On the Annotate tab > Dimension panel, click Aligned.
- In the drawing window, object snap to the endpoints of the centerlines and position the dimension as shown in the following illustration.
- Press ESC.

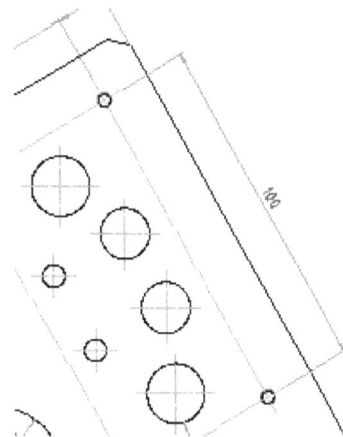

20. To begin adding dimensions to a chamfer, on the Annotate tab > Dimension panel, click Chamfer.

21. To create and position the chamfer dimension, in the drawing window, do the following:

- Select the chamfer line (1).
- Select the first line that connects to the chamfer line (2).
- Select the second line that connects to the chamfer line (3).
- Press ESC.

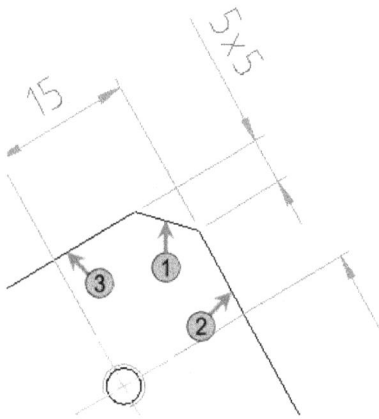

22. To begin adding an angular dimension to one quadrant area with the text in another, on the Annotate tab > Dimension panel, click Angular.

23. In the drawing window, select the identified horizontal line and then select the identified angled line.

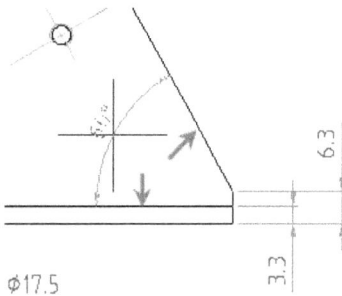

24. To specify which quadrant to dimension, do the following:

- Right-click in the drawing window and select Quadrant.
- Click in the drawing window when the dimension preview displays between the two selected lines.

25. To position the dimension text, click when the dimension text preview is similar to that shown in the following illustration. Press ESC.

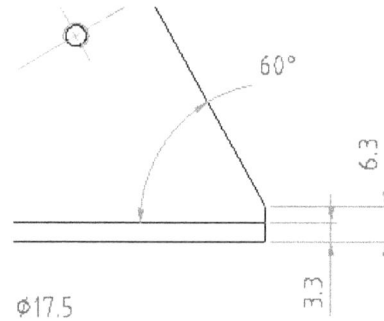

26. Save and close all of the files.

Exercise: Place Multiple Dimensions Automatically

In this exercise, you will add multiple dimensions at the same time using the Multiple Dimension command.

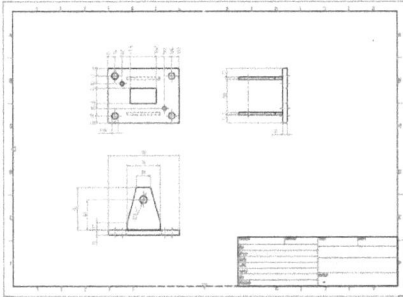

The completed exercise

1. Open *Multiple_Dimensions.dwg*.

2. On the Annotate tab > Dimension panel, click Multiple Dimension. In the Multiple Dimension dialog box, do the following:

   - On the *Parallel* tab, under Type, select Baseline if not already selected.
   - Verify that the Alignment is set to Inside Out.
   - Click OK.

3. To add baseline dimensions to the lower left view:

   - In the drawing window, select all of the geometry in the lower left view and press ENTER.
   - Select the origin at point 1.

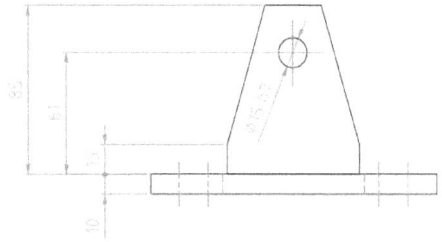

4. Move the cursor to the left until the dimensions are displayed in red and snap into place.

   - Click to place the dimensions.
   - Press ESC to end the command.

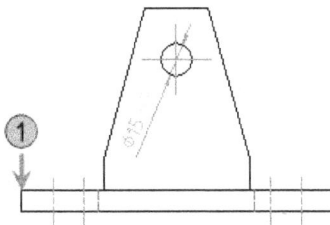

5. To begin adding a set of symmetric dimensions, on the Annotate tab > Dimension panel, click Multiple Dimension.

6. To set the type and select the geometry:

   - In the Multiple Dimension dialog box, click the *Shaft/Symmetric* tab. Set the Type to Symmetric.
   - Click OK.
   - Select the contour object at point 1. (The red lines shown in the illustration are created as you select other points in the next step.)
   - Press ENTER.

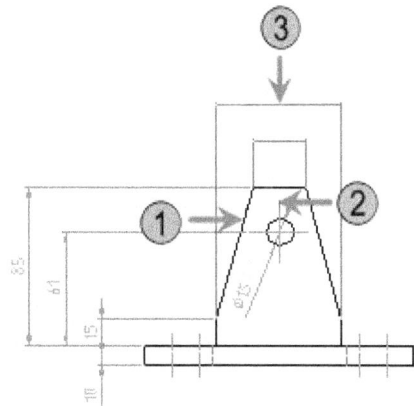

7. To specify the point of symmetry and position the dimensions, refer to points in the previous illustration:

- Select the centerline at point 2.
- Move the cursor until the dimensions display as horizontal and red. Select near point 3.

8. To add an additional dimension to the set of symmetrical dimensions, object snap to the identified point 1. Press ENTER to end the command.

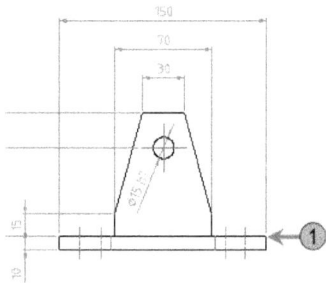

9. Zoom to the view in the top left of the drawing.

10. To begin adding ordinate dimensions to this view, on the Annotate tab > Dimension panel, click Multiple Dimension.

11. In the Multiple Dimensioning dialog box, in the *Ordinate* tab:

- In the Type list, select Current Standard (ISO), if required.
- Select the Both Axes checkbox.
- Click OK.

12. Window-select the entire top left view. Press ENTER.

13. Select point 1 for the origin. Press ENTER.

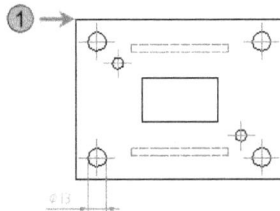

14. Move the cursor above the view until the first ordinate dimension is displayed in red.

- Click to place the dimension.
- Press ENTER.

15. Move the cursor left until the dimensions on the left side display in red.

- Click to place the dimensions.
- Press ENTER.

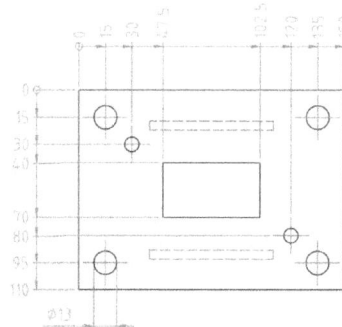

16. Save and close all of the files.

Lesson: Editing Dimensions

Overview

In this lesson, you learn to edit, stretch, arrange, align, join, and break dimensions. You also learn to highlight and edit overridden dimensions and move existing dimensions to make room for new ones.

In general, when working in a 2D design environment, you a lot of time is spent placing or editing dimensions. These objects are among the most important parts of a 2D drawing because it would be impossible to validate and manufacture the design without them. Because of the importance of these objects, you must present them in a clear and accurate manner each time. The commands discussed in this lesson enable you to validate and modify the dimensions in your drawing.

In the following illustration, the dimensions in this view have been arranged with the **Arrange** command.

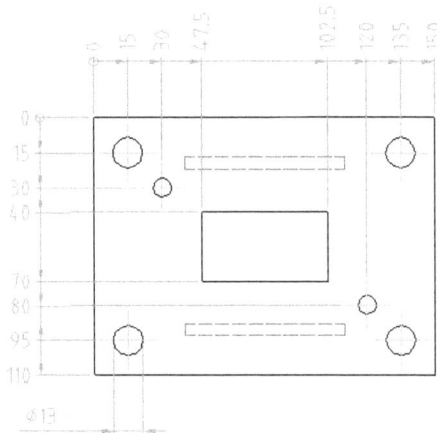

Objectives

After completing this lesson, you will be able to:

- Modify dimensions by double-clicking.
- Edit multiple dimensions simultaneously.
- Stretch objects by changing the dimensions.
- Rearrange dimension locations around a contour.
- Align dimensions to a continuous dimension style.
- Join multiple dimensions into a single dimension.
- Split one dimension into two dimensions.
- Add breaks to dimension lines.
- Check dimensions for text overrides.

Modifying Dimensions with Power Edit

Introduction to Modifying Dimensions with Power Edit

You can use the Power Edit command to modify dimensions. Using Power Edit it the same as double-clicking on the dimension. You can double-click on the different locations of some dimensions to get different editing tools. You can double-click on the following two locations of a dimension:

- **Double-click on text -** The Power Dimensioning contextual tab is displayed. From this contextual tab, you can change the dimension text, the number of decimals that are displayed, and add or change tolerance and fit values for the selected dimension.
- **Double-click on the extension line of multiple dimensions -** The Multiple Dimensioning dialog box opens. In it, you can rearrange selected dimensions in a new style.

About Dimension Overrides

When you use Power Edit on dimensions placed with the Multiple Dimensioning command you can rearrange the dimensions. When you select Rearrange into a New Style, the existing dimensions are deleted and replaced with new dimensions. Any overrides, fits, or tolerances that were added manually are removed.

The changes that are set in the Power Dimensioning contextual tab do not change the dimension standard settings. You can change the default standard in the Options dialog box on the AM:Standards tab.

Editing Multiple Dimensions

You can modify multiple dimensions simultaneously with the **Edit Multiple** command. You can create a selection set of dimensions and edit them together. A fit, tolerance, special character, or format can be included or edited in one step in all dimensions. This function is very helpful because tolerances and fits are often inserted at the end of the design phase.

Access

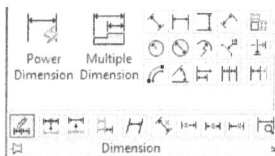

Command Line: AMDIMMEDIT

Ribbon: Annotate tab > expanded Dimension panel > Edit Multiple

Menu: Annotate > Edit Dimensions > Multi Edit

Procedure: Editing Multiple Dimensions

To edit multiple dimensions simultaneously, complete the following steps:

1. On the Ribbon, click Annotate tab > expanded Dimension panel > Edit Multiple.

2. Select two or more dimensions to edit.

3. On the Power Dimensioning contextual tab, change or add fits.

4. Click OK. The changes are displayed.

Stretching Objects with Dimensions

You can use the **Linear/Symmetric Stretch** command when you need to modify the length or position of dimensioned objects. The length or position of the objects are modified after you a new value for a selected dimension and after selecting the objects that you want to stretch. You can use the Linear/Symmetric Stretch command at any angle at which linear dimensions are placed.

Access

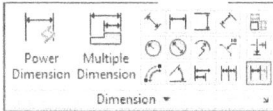

Command Line: AMDIMSTRETCH

Ribbon: Annotate tab > Dimension panel > Linear/Symmetric Stretch

Menu: Annotate > Edit Dimensions > Linear/Symmetric Stretch

You can use the following options with the Linear/Symmetric command.

Option	Definition
Linear	Stretches or shortens a linear dimension. Stretches the selection set in one direction. The stretched amount is based on the end value provided.
Symmetric	Stretches or shortens a symmetric dimension. Stretches the selection set in two directions on either side of a centerline by equal amounts. The total stretched amount is based on the end value provided.
Select Dimension Text	Selects the dimension text.
Specify Current and New Distance	Enters the current distance and the new distance.

Procedure: Stretching Linear Dimensions

To stretch geometry in a linear direction using dimensions, complete the following steps:

1. Click Annotate tab > Dimension panel > Linear/Symmetric Stretch.

2. Press ENTER for Linear.

3. Select the dimension text.

4. Enter the new dimension text value.

5. Specify the first corner for the selection crossing.

6. Specify the second corner for the selection crossing. Include at least one dimension definition point and one object. The object with the dimension is stretched to the new value.

7. Make additional selection sets to stretch additional areas as required.

8. Press ENTER when finished.

Procedure: Stretching Symmetric Dimensions

To perform the symmetric stretching of geometry using dimensions, complete the following steps:

1.   Click Annotate tab > Dimension panel > Linear/Symmetric Stretch.

2.   Enter **S**. Press ENTER for Symmetric.

3.   Select the dimension text.

4.   Enter the new dimension text.

5.   Select the centerline.

6.   Specify the first corner for crossing.

7.   Specify the second corner for crossing. Include at least one dimension definition point and one object. The object with the dimension is stretched to the new value.

8.   Make additional select sets as required.

9.   Press ENTER when you are finished.

Procedure: Stretching Linear Dimensions at an Angle

1.   Click Annotate tab > Dimension panel > Linear/Symmetric Stretch.

2.   Press ENTER for Linear.

3.   Enter **S**. Press ENTER for Stretch.

4.   Select the first point for the selection set.

5.   Select the second point for the selection set. The stretch initial distance and direction are defined. A temporary UCS shows the current angle being used.

6.   Enter a new dimension text value.

7.   Specify the first corner for crossing.

8.   Specify the second corner for crossing. Include at least one dimension definition point and one object. The object with the dimension is stretched to the new value.

9.   Make additional selections to stretch as required.

10.   Press ENTER when you are finished.

Arranging Dimensions

You can use the **Arrange** command to rearrange both linear dimensions and coordinate dimensions. The dimension is not replaced; the position is rearranged and all fit and tolerance overrides are maintained. You can select the dimensions of both axes with a window. After you press, the outer contour of the object is recognized automatically and the dimensions are arranged according to the standard. You can select a point on any contour to reference the dimension placement.

Access

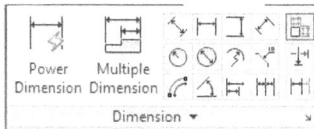

Command Line: AMDIMARRANGE

Ribbon: Annotate tab > Dimension panel > Arrange

Menu: Annotate > Edit Dimensions > Arrange Dimensions

Procedure: Arranging Dimensions

To arrange dimensions, complete the following steps:

1. Click Annotate tab > Dimension panel > Arrange.

2. Window-select the dimensions.

3. Select a point on the contour.

4. Press ENTER. All of the dimensions are arranged.

Aligning Dimensions

You can align the dimension lines, arrowheads, and text for a group of dimensions with the **Align** command. When you use the Align command, the dimensions are arranged as continuous dimensions. You can align both angular and linear dimensions.

The first dimension that you select is the one to which all other dimensions are going to align. To align linear dimensions, the dimension lines must be similar in type and their planes must be parallel.

Access

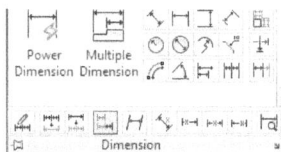

Command Line: AMDIMALIGN

Ribbon: Annotate tab > expanded Dimension panel > Align

Menu: Annotate > Edit Dimensions > Align Dimensions

Procedure: Aligning Dimensions

To align dimensions, complete the following steps:

1. Click Annotate tab > expanded Dimension panel > Align.

2. Select the base dimension.

3. Select the dimensions that you want to align. Press ENTER. The dimensions are aligned to the base dimension.

Joining Dimensions

You can combine multiple dimensions into a single dimension using the **Join** command. You can join linear, aligned, and angular dimensions.

Access

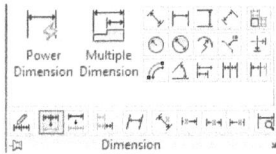

Command Line: AMDIMJOIN

Ribbon: Annotate tab > expanded Dimension panel > Join

Menu: Annotate > Edit Dimensions > Join Dimensions

Procedure: Joining Dimensions

To join two dimensions, complete the following steps:

1. Click Annotate tab > expanded Dimension panel > Join.

2. Select the base dimension.

3. Select the dimension to join. Press ENTER. The dimensions are joined into one dimension.

> The base dimension determines the type of dimension to join. The AutoCAD Mechanical software ignores dimensions that do not match the base dimension type. In an angular dimension, the direction of the join is determined by bisecting the dimension and using the half where the extension line was initially selected. If you select a set of dimensions that includes dimension lines inside and outside the extension lines, and if the dimension line arrowheads overlap, use the UNDO command or adjust the dimensions individually with AMDIMJOIN command.

Splitting Dimensions

You can split a dimension into two dimensions with the Insert command.

The **Insert Dimension** command changes a two-line dimension to a three-point dimension and an aligned dimension to a rotated dimension.

Access

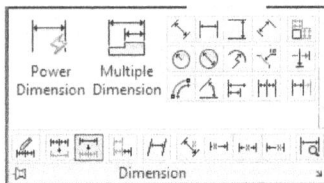

Command Line: AMDIMINSERT

Ribbon: Annotate tab > expanded Dimension panel > Insert

Menu: Annotate > Edit Dimensions > Insert Dimension

Procedure: Inserting New Dimensions

To split dimensions, complete the following steps:

1. Click Annotate tab > expanded Dimension panel > Insert.

2. Select the base dimension.

3. Specify the extension line origin where the dimension is to be split.

Breaking Dimension Lines

When dimension lines cross other dimension lines, you can create breaks in one of the dimension lines at the point at which they cross. With the **Break** command, you can create breaks in existing dimensions or extension lines. Dimensions are not exploded and the break can be associative to the dimension crossing the break.

You can use the Multiple option to apply breaks to multiple dimensions. You can select the crossing objects or use the Automatic option to place breaks where it crosses other dimensions. The break is associative to the object crossing it. This means the break follows the other dimension as it is being moved and the break is removed if the other dimension is deleted.

If you use the default method of selecting the extension line and clicking a point on the line, the break is not associative because a crossing object was not selected.

Access

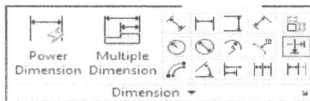

Command Line: AMDIMBREAK

Ribbon: Annotate tab > Dimension panel > Break

Menu: Annotate > Edit Dimensions > Break Dimension

Procedure: Breaking Dimensions

To break dimension extension lines, complete the following steps:

1. Click Annotate tab > Dimension panel > Break.

2. Select the dimension or extension line that you want to break.

3. Press ENTER for Automatic.

Checking Dimensions

You might not want to have overridden dimensions your drawing. You can use the **Check** command to highlight and check for dimensions with overridden text and set the overridden dimensions to remain highlighted until they have been edited. You can use the Check command to walk through each overridden dimension and make your changes on the Power Dimensioning contextual tab.

Access

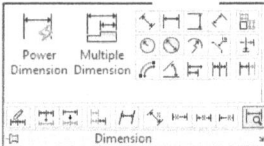

Command Line: AMCHECKDIM

Ribbon: Annotate tab > expanded Dimension panel > Check

Menu: Annotate > Edit Dimensions > Check Dimensions

Check Command Options

You are provided with the following two options with the **Check** command.

Option	Definition
Highlight	Overridden dimensions remain highlighted and the command ends. The dimensions remain highlighted until the command is modified. Use REGEN to remove the highlighting.
Edit	Opens the Power Dimensioning contextual tab for each overridden dimension.

You can press ENTER to end the command.

Procedure: Checking Dimensions

An overview of locating dimensions with overridden values and replacing their overridden value with the actual dimension value is shown in the following steps:

1. Click Annotate tab > expanded Dimension panel > Check.

2. With one or more dimensions identified with text overrides, select the Edit option.

3. On the Power Dimensioning contextual tab > Reuse panel, Predefined Text drop-down list, select the required dimension text template.

4. Make any other required adjustments.

5. Press ENTER to accept the changes and cycle to the next dimension with an override value or finish the command.

Exercise: Edit Dimensions

In this exercise, you will find overridden dimensions and stretch dimensions with Linear/Symmetric Stretch. You will also edit, modify, rearrange and align existing dimensions.

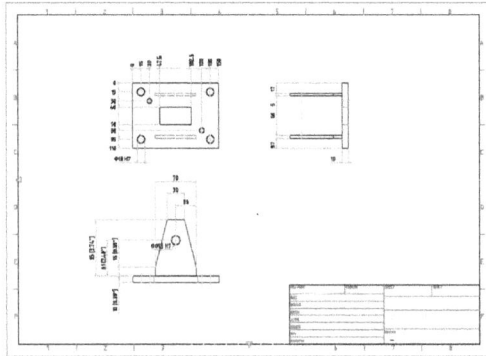

The completed exercise

1. Open *Edit_Dimension_Exercise.dwg*.

2. To check for overridden dimensions, do the following:

   - On the Annotate tab > expanded Dimension panel, click Check. Note that the overridden dimensions are highlighted.
   - Enter **E**.
   - Press ENTER. The dimension 90 displays in the edit box.

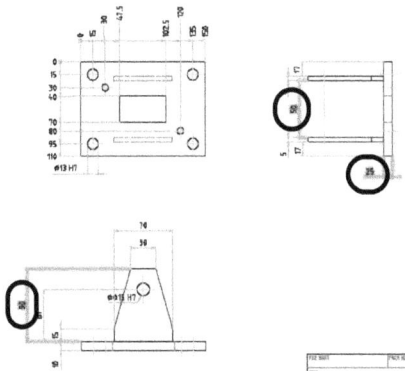

3. To edit the dimension:

   - On the Power Dimensioning contextual tab > Reuse panel > Predefined Text drop-down list, click the first Default Value button < >.
   - Press ENTER.

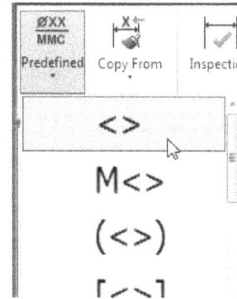

4. The next overridden dimension is displayed in an edit box and its Power Dimensioning contextual tab is displayed. Continue to replace the remaining overridden dimension values with their default values until all of the overridden dimension values have been replaced.

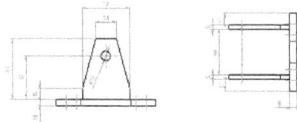

5. Zoom in to the front view.

6. On the Annotate tab > expanded Dimension panel, click Edit Multiple. Do the following:

- Select the four vertical dimensions.
- Press ENTER.

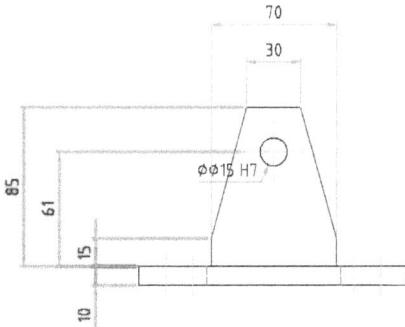

7. On the Power Dimensioning contextual tab > Dim Text panel, click Alternate Text. Press ENTER. Alternate text is added to the selected dimensions as shown in the following illustration.

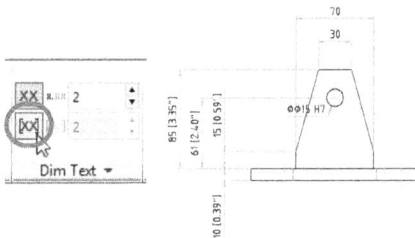

8. On the Annotate tab > Dimension panel, click Power Dimension. Select point 1, and then select point 2 and point 3 to place the dimension.

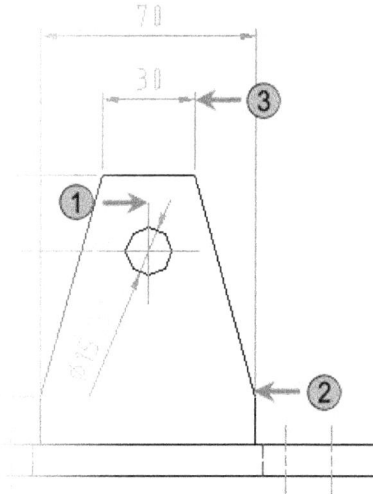

9. To resolve the overdrawn dimension placement problem:

- In the Dimension overdrawn dialog box, click Move away.
- Click OK.

10. Press ENTER twice to exit the command. Note that dimension 35 is added horizontally, and the other two dimensions are moved up.

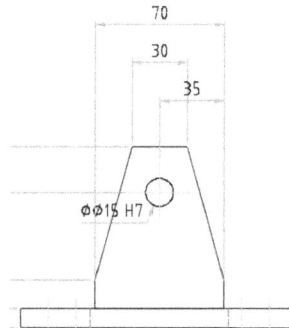

11. On the Annotate tab > Dimension panel, click Linear/Symmetric Stretch. Do the following:

- Press ENTER to select Linear.
- Select the vertical dimension 85 [3.35"].
- On the Command Prompt, enter the new dimension **95**.
- Press ENTER.
- Select the dimensions and objects using the two corners for crossing as shown in the following illustration.
- Press ENTER.
- Press ENTER again to end the command.

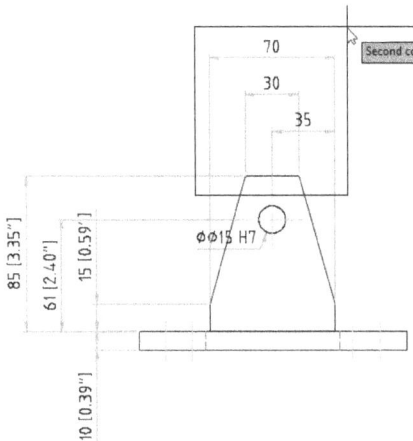

12. On the Annotate tab > Dimension panel, click Break. Do the following to create a break in the overlapping dimension lines:

- Press ENTER to select Multiple.
- Using Window option, select all of the dimensions in the front view.
- Press ENTER.
- Press ENTER again to end the command.

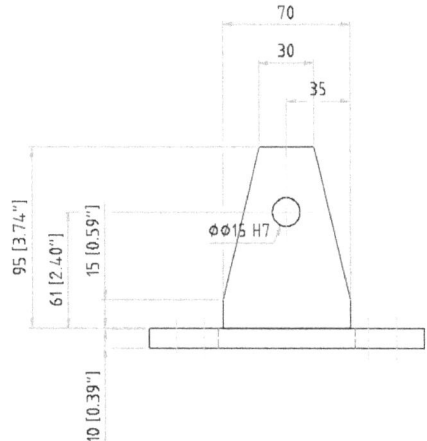

13. On the Annotate tab > Dimension panel, click Arrange. Select all of the dimensions in the top view. Press ENTER to arrange the dimensions.

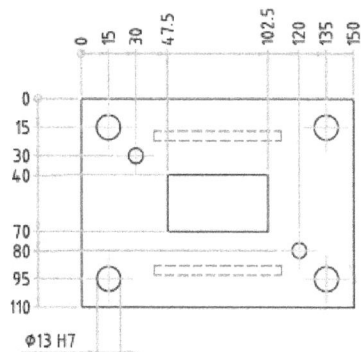

14. On the Annotate tab > expanded Dimension panel, click Align. Do the following:

    ■ Select either of the two vertical dimensions with a value of five (5).
    ■ Select the remaining vertical dimensions.
    ■ Press ENTER to align all the other dimensions with the dimension 5.

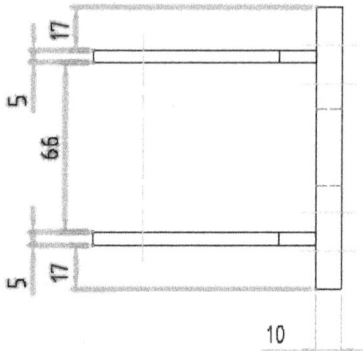

15. Zoom Extents.

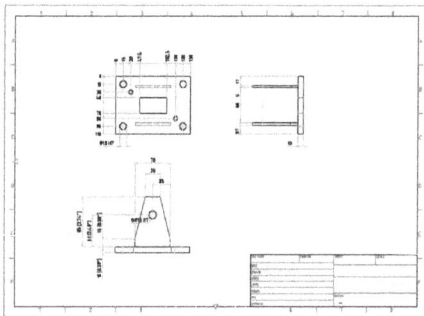

16. Save and close all of the files.

Lesson: Hole Charts and Fits Lists

Overview

This lesson describes hole charts and fits lists and how to insert them into your drawing.

Charts and lists are often used in place of dimensions. They can keep a drawing from becoming cluttered and difficult to read. Many manufacturers prefer charts and lists because of how the information is used.

In the following illustration, two different hole charts were added to the drawing to identify the holes for different manufacturing operations. A fits list was also added for easy referencing.

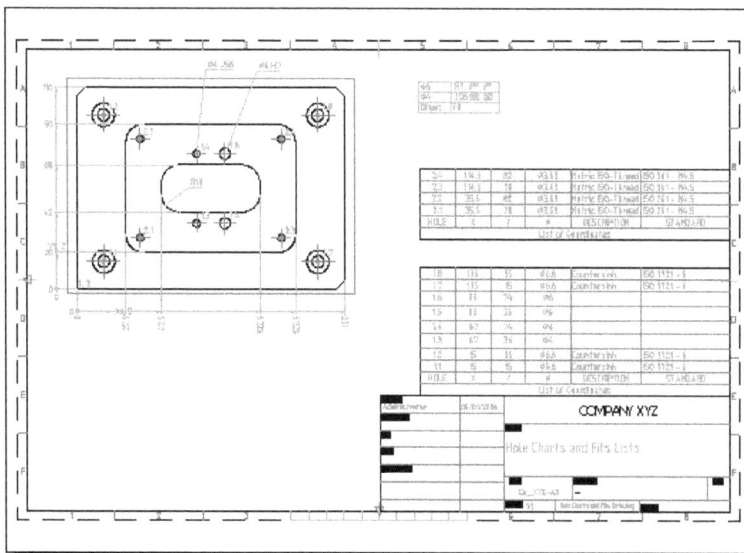

Objectives

After completing this lesson, you will be able to:

- Create hole charts to call out the location, size, and description of holes.
- Locate the settings that control the appearance of hole charts.
- Place a fits list that contains all of the dimension fits in a drawing.

Creating Hole Charts

You can use hole charts to communicate the size and position of multiple holes in a table format. To benefit from hole charts, you must learn what they are and how to insert them into your drawing.

In the following illustration, a Cartesian hole chart is shown on the left and a polar hole chart is shown on the right.

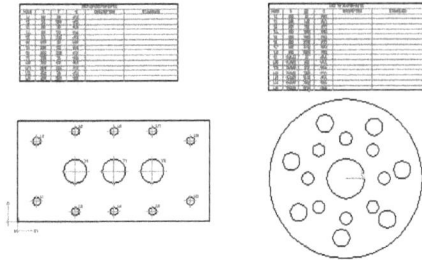

About Hole Charts

You can use hole charts to add dimensional annotation about holes to a drawing using a chart. When you insert a hole chart, each hole is labeled and the corresponding value is placed in the chart. You can use the hole's label name in the hole chart to determine its location, size, and description. You can also place a hole chart for holes created as circles or as hole features from the standard library.

There are two styles of hole charts: Cartesian or Polar. The difference between the two is how the location dimension is defined with respect to a predefined point of origin on the work piece. The Cartesian hole chart displays location values in X, Y coordinates from the origin. The Polar hole chart displays location values as their distance and angle from the origin. You can place one or two charts in a drawing for hole charts depending on the current standard.

Holes that are deleted from the drawing are removed from the hole chart. Labels associated with the holes are also deleted. However, you can retain each hole's numbering as the holes are deleted. The hole chart updates to reflect any size changes that are made to the holes. You can add new holes to the hole chart by copying existing holes with their hole chart label or by using the tools available in the Hole Chart dialog box.

You can split a single hole chart into multiple hole charts. This results in each chart listing specific types of holes or holes that meet specific criteria while using the same origin indicator.

Access

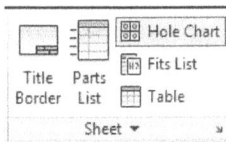

Command Line: AMHOLECHART

Ribbon: Annotate tab > Sheet panel > Hole Chart

Ribbon: Layout tab > Sheet panel > Hole Chart

Menu: Annotate > Hole Chart

Hole Chart Dialog Box

During the placement of a hole chart or after inserting one, you can open the Hole Chart dialog box to split the hole chart into multiple charts or override the settings in the active standard.

The Hole Chart dialog box opens when you select the Dialog option before clicking the insertion point for the hole chart, or when you double-click on any inserted hole chart.

Within the Hole Chart dialog box, you can adjust the information that is displayed and split the selected holes into multiple charts. To split the holes into multiple tables, you can create a custom filter using the properties of the holes, or create a filter based on selected holes.

The options and settings along the top of the Hole Chart dialog box are the same as those used to configure the hole chart for the standard. The difference is that the setting changes you make here only apply to the hole chart inserted into the drawing and not to all new hole charts created with the standard. The top row also includes an option to export the contents of the chart to a spreadsheet or text file.

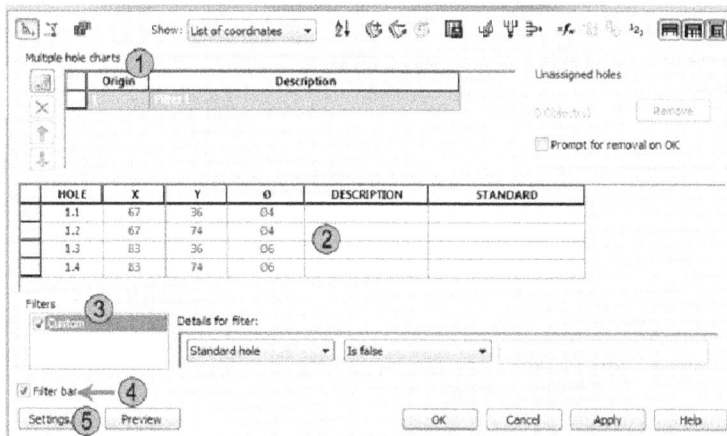

1. Inserts additional hole charts for any unassigned holes that were in the original selection set, deletes the charts selected in the list, changes the order of the charts, adds a description to a chart, or removes unassigned holes from the selection set.

2. Reviews the contents of the hole chart ands data in the editable fields.

3. Creates and defines filters for the hole chart selected in the list in area 1. Click Apply to assign the filter to the hole chart and then select another hole chart for editing.

4. Toggles the display of the Filter list and values on and off.

5. Click to open the Hole Chart Settings dialog box to override chart properties for attachment point, text height, text color, and gap.

Add Hole Charts and Hole Chart Filters

When you create a hole chart, all of the selected holes are listed in a single chart. To set a condition on which holes are displayed in a chart, you can define a filter. Only the holes from the selection set that meet that filter condition display in the hole chart. Any hole in the initial selection set that is not listed in a hole chart is an unassigned hole. An unassigned hole displays a question mark in the drawing. By clicking Add Hole Chart under Multiple Hole Charts, a new hole chart is created and lists the unassigned holes.

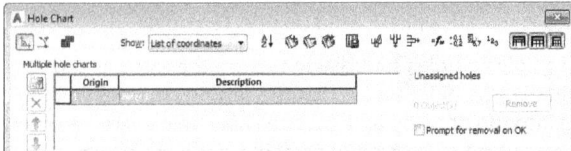

You can apply a filter in the Hole Chart dialog box to the currently selected hole chart in the Multiple Hole Charts list. To apply a filter to the selected hole chart, you must first toggle on the display of the filter bar by clicking the Filter Bar checkbox. With the filter bar displayed, you can add filters by right-clicking on the Filters list and clicking Add Custom Filter or Add Hole Selection Filter. If you click Add Hole Selection Filter, under Details for Filter, you can click Select to select the holes that you want to include in the active chart.

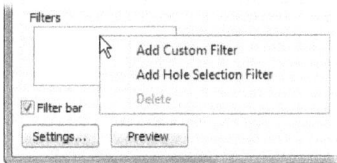

Under Filters, if you select Custom, you can specify the filter criteria under Details for Filter by selecting a parameter, condition, and value for the condition (if required).

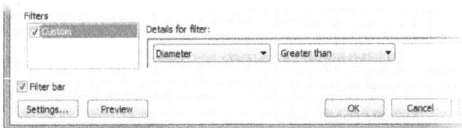

Procedure: Inserting Cartesian Hole Charts

To insert a hole chart using the default linear Cartesian coordinates, complete the following steps:

1. Start the **Hole** command.

2. Specify the insertion point for the origin block.

3. Specify the rotation angle for the origin.

4. Specify the name of the origin.

5. Select the holes.

6. Specify the insertion point for the list of coordinates. You can also select the Dialog Command Line option to open the Hole Chart dialog box and modify the hole chart or split it into multiple hole charts before specifying the insertion point.

Procedure: Inserting Polar Hole Charts

To insert a hole chart using the option to identify hole positions using polar coordinates, complete the following steps:

1. Start the **Hole Chart** command.

2. Enter **P** for Polar.

3. Specify the insertion point for the origin.

4. Specify the rotation angle for the origin.

5. Specify the name of the origin.

6. Select the holes.

7. Specify the insertion point for the list of coordinates. You can also select the Dialog option to open the Hole Chart dialog box and modify the hole chart or split it into multiple hole charts before specifying the insertion point.

Procedure: Adding Holes to a Hole Chart

To add holes to an existing hole chart, complete the following steps:

1. Double-click on the inserted hole chart to which you want to add one or more holes.

2. In the Hole Chart dialog box, click Add Holes.

3. In the drawing window, select the holes that you want to add to the chart.

4. Click OK to close the dialog box.

Hole Chart Settings

There are many options for controlling the information that displays in a hole chart and its appearance. You can configure which columns of information are displayed, how wide each column is, its insertion point, and its text height and colors. You can also control whether you only insert a List of Coordinates table or also insert a Hole table for the selected holes.

To configure these items before inserting the hole chart, you need to be able to locate the settings that control the appearance of hole charts so that you can modify them as required.

Hole Chart Settings Dialog Box

The initial look and configuration of an inserted hole chart is based on the settings in the active standard. To configure the hole chart settings, you can open the Hole Chart Settings dialog box from the Options dialog box, in the AM:Standards tab, by double-clicking on the element Hole Chart.

Within the Hole Chart Settings dialog box, you can set the method of locating holes, the type of charts that you want to be able to create, the columns to display in those charts, and the text's display characteristics.

To maintain consistency and conformance to your requirements, you should configure the hole chart in the standard and save it in the template file that you use to create your new drawings.

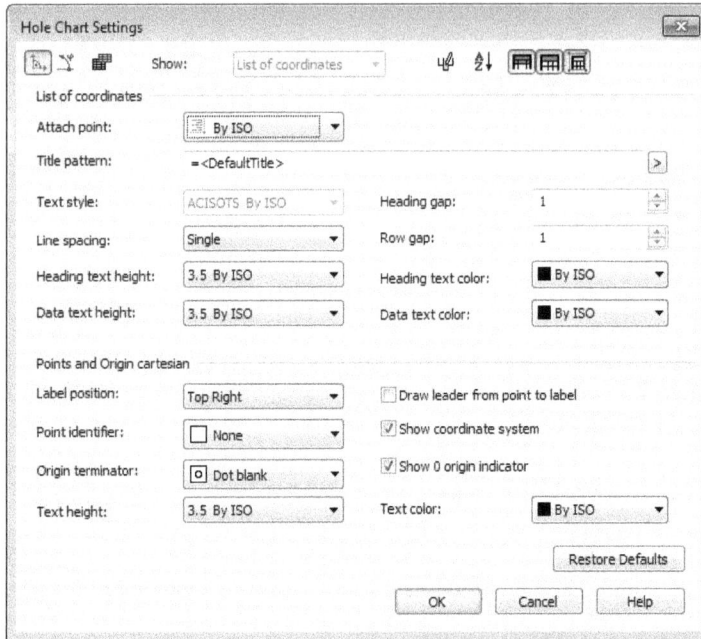

> When you modify hole chart settings in the Mechanical standards, the changes are only applied to hole charts that you create after the modifications have been made.

Placing a Fits List

You can use the Fits List command to place a summary list of all of the dimension fits that are in the drawing. You can insert the list at any location in your drawing. As you add and remove dimension fits, you can regenerate the list to reflect the change. You can control the insertion point and other properties of a fits list in the mechanical standards.

In the following illustration, a fits notation has been added to two hole dimensions. The fits list that was added to the drawing lists the diameters of those holes, their fit condition, and their corresponding tolerance values.

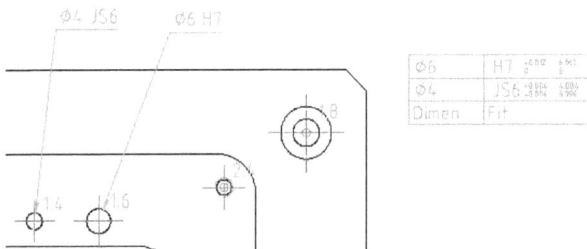

Access

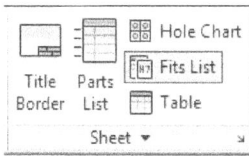

Command Line: AMFITSLIST

Ribbon: Annotate tab > Sheet panel > Fits List

Ribbon: Layout tab > Sheet panel > Fits List

Menu: Annotate > Fits List

Command Line Options

After you start the Fits List command, there are different options in the Command Line for creating, updating, and displaying the fits list table.

Option	Description
Update All	Automatically updates parts and fits lists and the Block Editor when a drawing is saved or when a working session is terminated. Use this option instead of the Power Edit command.
Order	Sorts the fits list by value or fit.
New	Inserts a new fits list. You are prompted for the insertion point of the list in your drawing. At the same time, the new fits list is displayed dynamically at the location of the cursor and can be placed in the drawing.

Procedure: Inserting Fits Lists

To insert a new fits list into a drawing, complete the following steps:

1. Start the **Fits List** command.

2. Press ENTER to create a new list.

3. Specify the insertion point of the list.

Exercise: Add Hole Charts and Fits Lists

In this exercise, you will add two hole charts to call out holes created in two different manufacturing operations and then add a fits list.

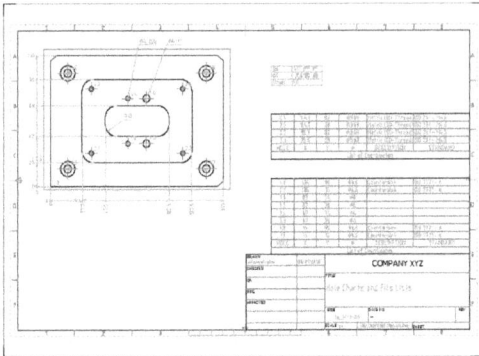

The completed exercise

1. Open *Hole Charts and Fits Lists.dwg*.

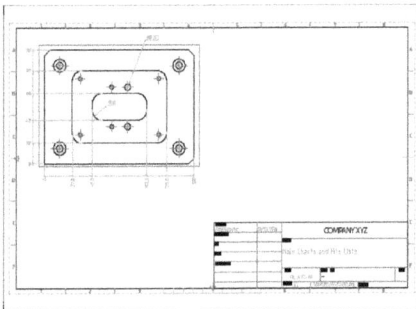

2. Begin to add a List of Coordinates hole chart. Click Annotate tab > Sheet panel > Hole Chart.

3. To specify the origin point and its orientation, do the following:

- In the drawing window, object snap to the lower left corner of the part as shown in the following illustration.
- For the rotation angle, press ENTER.
- For the origin label, press ENTER.

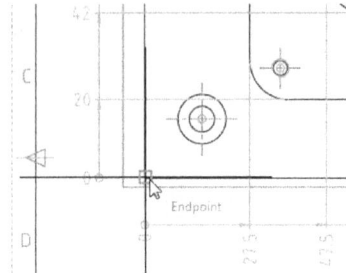

4. Use a window and enclose all the objects that in turn selects all of the holes in the view. Press ENTER.

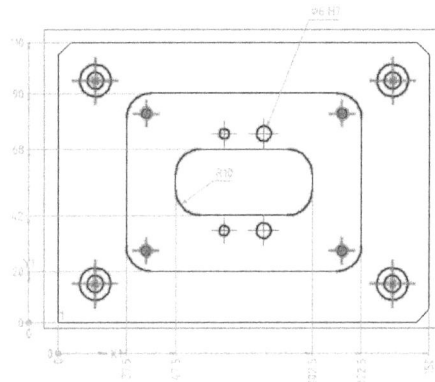

5. Insert the chart just above the title block.

6. Begin to split the hole chart into two charts based on manufacturing operations. In the drawing window, double-click on the table with the title List of Coordinates that you just inserted.

7. In the Hole Chart dialog box, select the Filter bar checkbox.

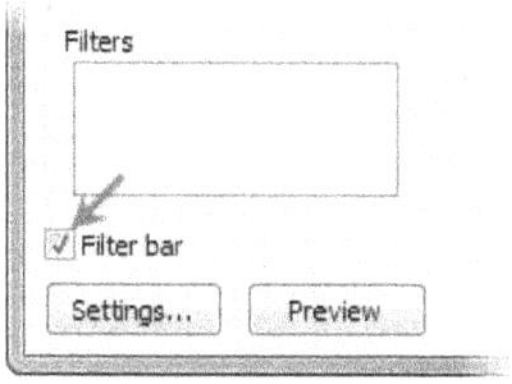

8. To define a filter to exclude all of the tapped holes, do the following:

- Right-click on the blank Filters field and click Add Custom Filter.
- From the Details for filter list, select Tapped.
- Click Apply.

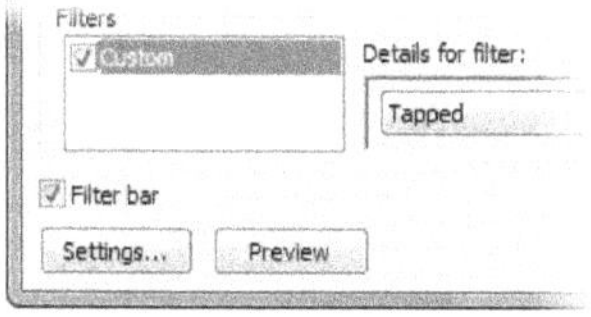

9. Begin to add a List of Coordinates hole chart for the tapped holes as follows:

- Under Multiple hole charts, click Add Hole Chart icon.
- In the drawing window, click to place the chart above the existing chart.

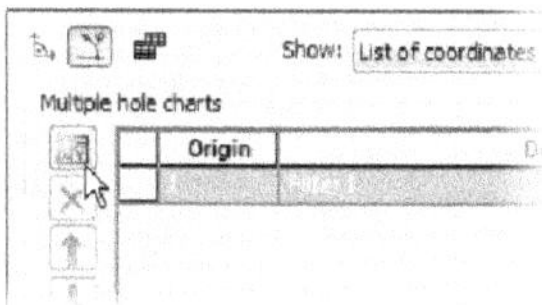

10. In the Hole Chart dialog box, click OK.

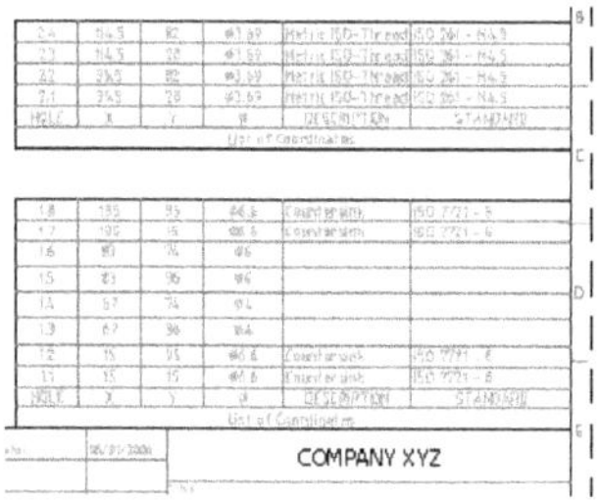

11. To add a fits list, do the following:

- Click Annotate tab > Sheet panel > Fits List.
- Press ENTER to create a new list.
- For the insertion point, click above the recently placed List of Coordinates hole chart.

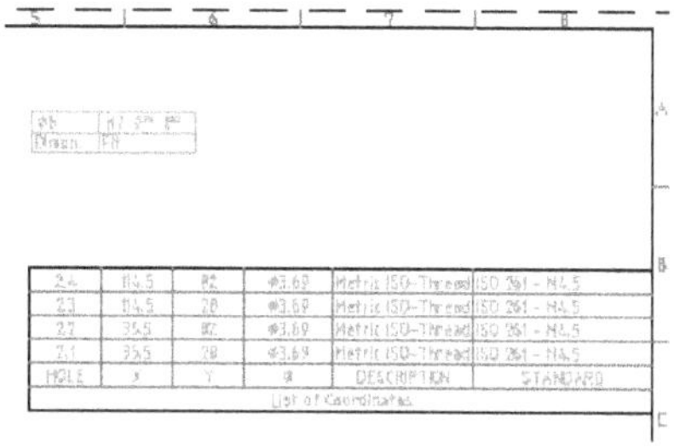

12. To add another dimension with a fits notation, do the following:

- Click Annotate tab > Dimension panel > Power Dimension.

13. To specify a different fit, do the following:

- On the Power Dimensioning contextual tab > Fit/Tolerance panel, click Fit.
- On the Power Dimensioning contextual tab > Fit/Tolerance panel > Fit Symbol drop-down list, click Fit Dialog Box.
- In the Fits dialog box, from the Hole tab lists, select JS and 6.
- Click OK.

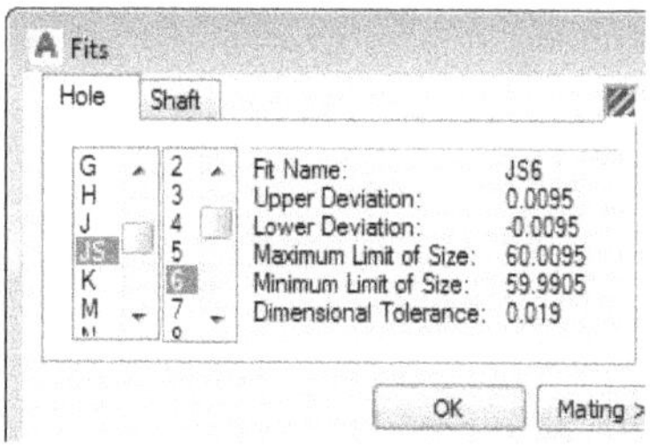

14. To add the dimension with the fits notation, do the following:

- Press ENTER.
- Select the smaller circle. Click to place the dimension as shown in the following illustration.

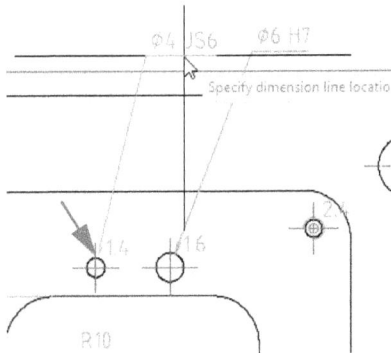

15. Press ENTER twice to finish power dimensioning.

16. Double-click on the fits list to update it.

Ø6	H7	-0.012	6.012
		0	6
Ø4	JS6	+0.004	4.004
		-0.004	3.996
Dimen.	Fit		

17. Save and close all of the files.

Lesson: Revision Lists

This lesson describes the functionality and use of revision lists. Typically, a revision list includes notes and information describing changes that have been made to the design, who made the changes, and when those changes were made. However, revision lists can also contain any information pertinent to the change.

Design changes resulting from customer requests, new manufacturing capabilities, or testing feedback must be documented in the drawing because they might directly impact other designs. Revision lists are used to document these changes throughout the life of a design. The ability to create, manage, and edit revision lists is a critical element in the overall process of documenting a design.

In the following illustration, a revision list is used to track engineering changes to the design.

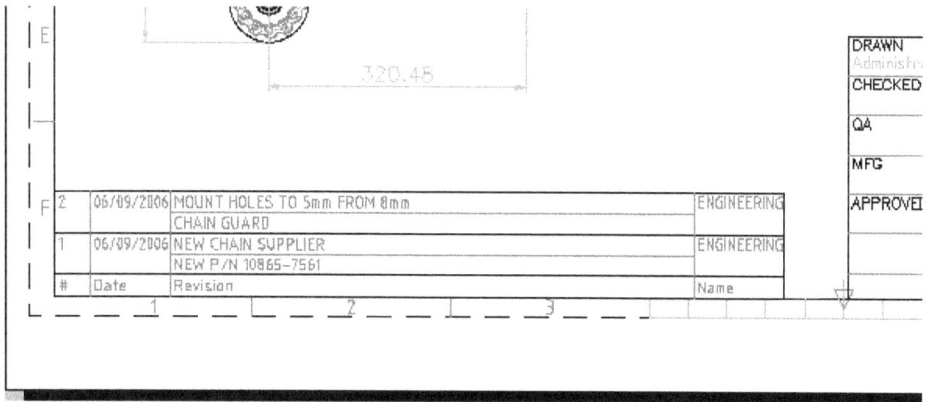

Objectives

After completing this lesson, you will be able to:

- Create and edit revision lists and add revision lines to a revision list.
- Toggle revisions on and off to enable or disable the automatic insertion of revision lines when an externally referenced file is edited.
- Update a revision block after toggling revisions back on.

Inserting Revision Lines in Drawings

You can use the **Revision Line** command to manually add a revision line to a revision block in a drawing. If a revision block does not already exist, it is created when you create the revision line. If a revision block is present, the new revision line is added to the existing revision block. A revision line can be added to a drawing at any time during the design process, and placed anywhere in the drawing.

The configuration of the revision line and its initial insertion point is based on the settings in the standards element Drawing Border.

In the following illustration, information describing an engineering change is used into the Edit Revision Attributes dialog box and is about to be added to the existing Revision List.

Access

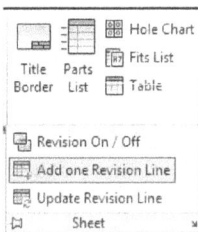

Command Line: AMREVLINE

Ribbon: Annotate tab > expanded Sheet panel > Add one Revision Line

Ribbon: Layout tab > expanded Sheet panel > Add one Revision Line

Menu: Annotate > Drawing Title and Revision > Add one Revision Line

Procedure: Adding a Revision Line

An overview of adding a revision line to a drawing is shown in the following steps:

1. Start the **Revision Line** command.

2. Select a drawing border to associate the revision line to the border or press ENTER to have it relate to the drawing file in general.

3. In the Edit Revision Attributes dialog box, the revision data.

4. Click OK. Place the revision line.

A	06/01/2006	Revised Hole Size Was ⌀10mm	Administrator
#	Date	Revision	Name

Edit Revision Line Values

After one or more revision lines have been added to the drawing, you can edit the values of a revision line by double-clicking on the revision line that you need to change. You can also use the Power Edit command and select the revision line that you want to edit. Editing a revision line opens the Edit Revision Attributes dialog box that was used when the revision line was created.

Inserting Automatic Revision List

You can automatically insert revision lists if the drawing hosts external reference files. After you create an assembly drawing, any in-place editing to the external reference file can automatically add revision lines to your drawing.

After you finish the design work on the assembly drawing, you can use the Revision List tool to document your changes to the drawing. You must toggle on the Revision On/Off command for the automatic revision lists to be available.

A revision list is automatically updated in the following situations:

- If the revision command is on and you close an assembly drawing to work on an external file, you are prompted to add changes to the revision list when you return to the assembly.
- If an external reference is modified with the In-place Xref and Block Edit command, the Edit Revision Attribute dialog box opens when the changes to the external reference are saved.

Access

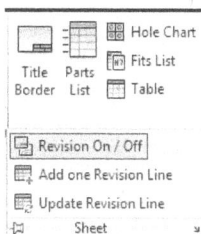

Command Line: AMREV

Ribbon: Annotate tab > expanded Sheet panel > Revision On/Off

Ribbon: Layout tab > expanded Sheet panel > Revision On/Off

Menu: Annotate > Drawing Title and Revision > Revision On/Off

Procedure: Inserting Revision Lists Automatically

An overview of inserting a revision list into the drawing automatically is shown in the following steps:

1. Open a drawing that has external reference files.

2. Verify that revisions are toggled on.

3. Use in-place xref editing to edit an external reference. Save the changes. The Edit Revision Attributes dialog box opens.

4. Enter the required information in the Edit Revision Attributes dialog box. Click OK. The AutoCAD software Question dialog box opens.

5. In the AutoCAD software Question dialog box, click Yes.

6. The revision information is added to an existing revision list, or if a revision list does not exist, a new list is created.

#	DESCRIPTION	DATE	APPROVED
1	Release for Prototype	05/18/2006	Engineering
		Drive System	
2	Revised Material	06/01/2006	Engineering
		Coupling	
3	Decrease Shaft Diameter	06/05/2006	Engineering
		Drive Shaft	

Updating Revision List

You can use the **Update Revision Line** command when multiple changes were made to a drawing, such as with an xref, while the revision list function was not set to On. The **Update Revision Line** command automatically updates the revision list with additional rows. You can make changes to this revision line with the Power Edit tool, or double-click on the revision line to open the Edit Revision Attributes dialog box.

Access

Command Line: AMREVUPDATE

Ribbon: Annotate tab > expanded Sheet panel > Update Revision Line

Ribbon: Layout tab > expanded Sheet panel > Update Revision Line

Menu: Annotate > Drawing Title and Revision > Update Revision Line

Procedure: Updating Revision Lists Automatically

An overview of how to have a revision list update automatically is shown in the following steps:

1.   Open a file with external references.

2.   Verify that the revisions are toggled off.

3.   Use in-place xref editing to edit multiple external references. Save the changes. The Edit Revision Attribute dialog box opens after each edit. Enter the required information in this dialog box.

4.   When the edits are complete, start the **Update Revision Line** command.

5.   The updated revision lines are added to the revision list.

#	DESCRIPTION	DATE	APPROVED
1	Release for Prototype	05/18/2006 Drive System	Engineering
2	Revised Material	06/01/2006 Coupling	Engineering
3	Decrease Shaft Diameter	06/05/2006 Drive Shaft	Engineering
4	Change Bearing to Match New Shaft	06/05/2006	Engineering
5	Update Gear Selection for Smaller Shaft	06/05/2006	Engineering

Exercise: Create a Revision List

In this exercise, you will create a revision list to document a supplier and part number change. You will then edit the drawing and add a revision line to the revision list.

The completed exercise

1. Open *Revision List-ns.dwg*.

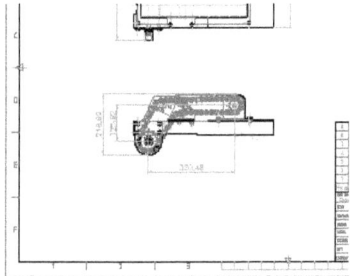

2. To begin adding a revision title and line to the drawing, do the following:

   - Click Annotate tab > expanded Sheet panel > Add one Revision Line.
   - When prompted to select a drawing border, select anywhere on the drawing border.

3. In the Edit Revision Attributes dialog box, the following information for the identified fields:

   - For #, enter **1**.
   - For Revision 1st line, enter **NEW CHAIN SUPPLIER**.
   - For Revision 2nd line, enter **NEW P/N 10865-7561**.
   - For name enter **ENGINEERING**.

4. To insert the revision line, do the following:

   - In the Edit Revision Attributes dialog box, click OK.
   - In the drawing window, object snap to the lower left corner of the inside border as shown in the following illustration.

5. To change the diameter of the hole in the top view of the chain guard, do the following:

   - In the drawing window, double-click on the identified hole on the left end of the chain guard part.
   - In the list of sizes in the dialog box, double-click on M5.

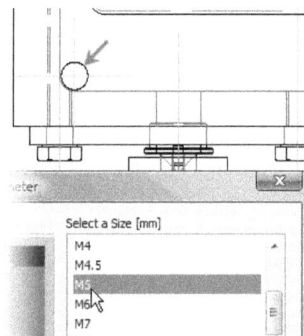

6. Repeat the previous step to change the hole size on the right end of the chain guard part.

7. To begin adding another revision line for these changes:

- Click Annotate tab > expanded Sheet panel > Add one Revision Line.
- When prompted to select a drawing border, select anywhere on the drawing border.

8. In the Edit Revision Attributes dialog box, the following information:

- For #, enter **2**.
- For Revision 1st line, enter **MOUNT HOLES TO 5mm FROM 8mm**.
- For Revision 2nd line, enter **CHAIN GUARD**.

9. Click OK to have the revision line added to the existing inserted revision block.

F	2	09/01/2016	MOUNT HOLES TO 5mm FROM 8mm
			CHAIN GUARD
	1	09/01/2016	NEW CHAIN SUPPLIER
			NEW P/N 10865-7561
	#	Date	Revision

10. Save and close all of the files.

Chapter Summary

In this chapter you learned how to add design information to a drawing in the form of mechanical symbols and text, including symbols for surface texture, welds, and geometric dimensioning and tolerancing. You then learned about the power dimensioning and automatic dimensioning tools that you can use to add dimensions to your drawings. Along with creating dimensions, you learned how to edit, stretch, arrange, align, join, and break dimensions. You also learned about hole charts and fits lists and how to insert them into your drawings.

Having completed this chapter, you can:

- Add symbols for surface texture, welds, and geometric dimensioning and tolerancing.
- Add dimensions that automatically follow a drawing's standards.
- Edit dimensions using different methods to change their display and positions.
- Place hole charts and fits lists into a drawing.
- Insert a revision list into a drawing and add additional revision lines.

Bill of Materials, Parts Lists, and Balloons

In this chapter, you learn about part references, how to create and edit the bill of materials (BOM) in an assembly drawing, and how to insert and edit a parts list. You also learn how to add balloons to an assembly drawing to identify the parts and subassemblies.

Objectives

After completing this chapter, you will be able to:

- Describe, create, and edit part reference objects in the drawing.
- Create and edit a bill of materials in an assembly drawing.
- Insert and edit a parts list on a drawing sheet.
- Add balloons to parts in an assembly drawing.

About Production Drawing Creation

To complete your design and create production-ready drawings, you often need to add balloons to parts in an assembly and add a parts list relating to those balloons. By having an understanding of how the AutoCAD® Mechanical software assists you in these tasks, you identify the importance of learning more about the commands and options so that you can use them to complete your production-ready drawings.

In the following illustration, a completed drawing sheet shows multiple drawing views of an assembly, a detail view for greater clarity, part balloons, and a parts list. The numbers in the balloons were automatically populated based on the selected parts. The item numbers in the parts list automatically match the balloon numbers.

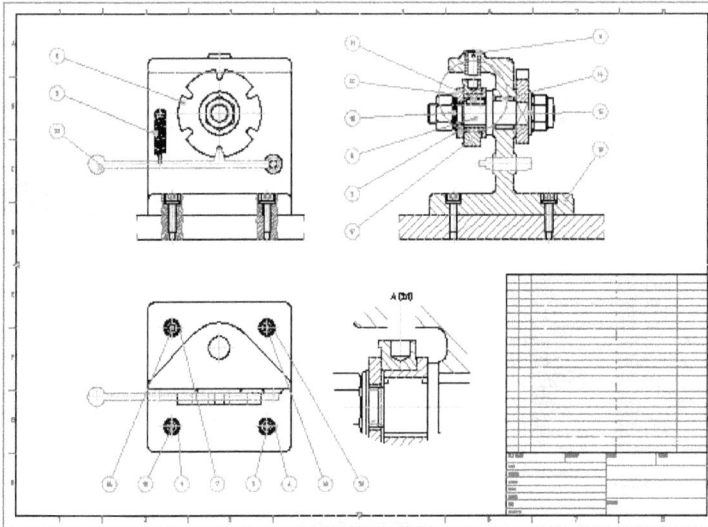

About Production Drawings and Bill of Materials, Parts Lists, and Balloons

When you create an assembly, you typically need to list the parts and subassemblies, their quantities, and their specific properties in a table or chart format. The table you place on the drawing that displays this information is referred to as a parts list. To identify the different items in the drawing views, you can add balloons with item numbers that match the item numbers in the parts list. The information for the balloons and parts lists come from a bill of materials (BOM) that is stored in the assembly file. The BOM often contains more information than you want to display on the drawing sheet. The BOM then becomes a central location for entering and editing data and can be exported for use in other software applications.

There are three methods for populating data in the BOM. One method is to enter all of the data for the entire assembly manually. A second method is to enter the data associated with a part or subassembly into part references. The third method involves entering values into the component properties for mechanically structured parts and subassemblies.

The second and third methods of populating BOM data are similar. In each of these methods, you enter the properties for each unique part or subassembly and the BOM is automatically populated with that information. By entering the data in the part reference or structured component properties, you can enter the data once and reuse it in multiple assemblies. For all of the assemblies where the part or assembly is used, the BOM is automatically populated with that information. The quantity value in the BOM is then based on the number of instances of a part or subassembly in the overall assembly.

Example of Production Drawing Creation

Drawings used in the production of a design can vary based on the purpose of the drawing. In the following illustration, part of a drawing sheet shows two views of an assembly with some ballooned parts and a section of the parts list. After the drawing is completed, this type of drawing is useful for users that need to identify the parts for assembly or to order replacement parts.

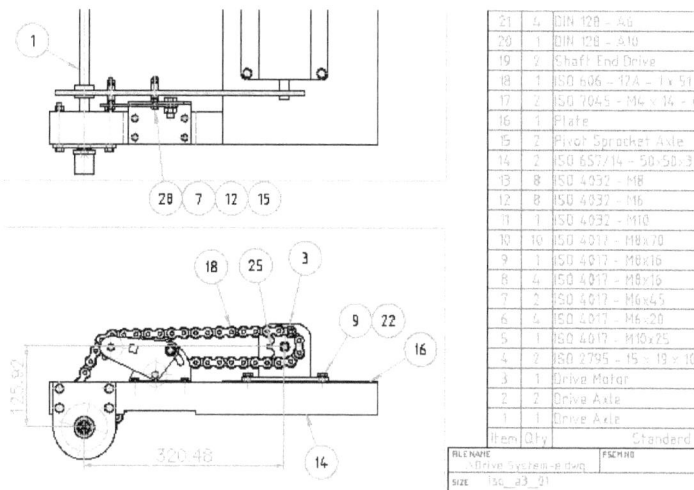

Lesson: Part References

Overview

This lesson describes part references and how you can enhance your parts by adding textual information that can be used in parts lists, bills of materials, and balloons.

Geometry creation is only part of any typical design process. All designs require some type of annotation and documentation. For mechanical designs, parts lists, bills of materials, and balloons are a critical part of final documentation. Part references enable you to attach textual information to geometry for use in these types of documentation objects.

In the following illustration, a simple mechanical assembly is shown with balloons and a parts list. Part reference objects are the source of the information used in the balloons and parts list.

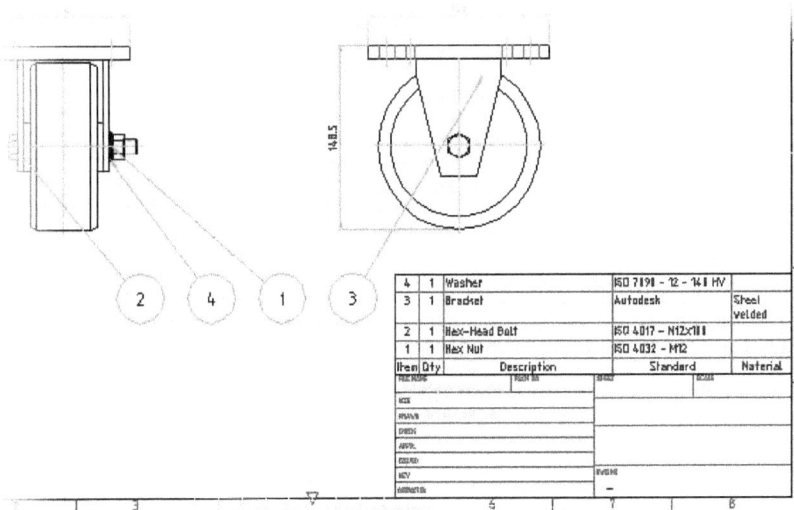

Objectives

After completing this lesson, you will be able to:

- Describe part references and how they can be used.
- Add part references and part reference information.
- Edit part reference information.

About Part References

You can store part information about parts by creating a part reference for each part. The part reference information can be used in balloons and parts lists and is associative. If the data changes in the part reference, the changes are automatically reflected in the balloons, parts list, and BOM.

In the following illustration, a part reference object stores textual information for a custom part.

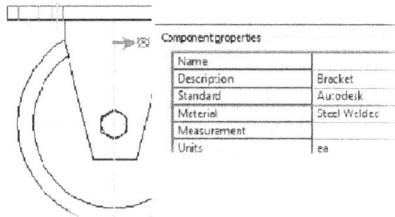

Definition of Part References

A part reference is a special attribute block that stores information that you have added about the part and displays information in the bill of materials (BOM) database. Once created, a part reference displays as a node object. If you double-click on the object, you can edit part reference information.

Standard parts, such as bolts, already have attached part reference nodes, while other custom objects require that you create part references if you want the objects to be referenced in the BOM.

You can attach part reference nodes to any type of object, such as lines, circles, and blocks. When you move the object to which the part reference is attached, the part reference remains attached and automatically moves with the geometry.

When you copy or delete a part reference, the quantity in the bill of materials for that part reference adjusts automatically. For part references identifying that the same part is used multiple times in a design, if the data in any of the part references changes, those changes are reflected in all instances of the part reference for that part.

In the following illustration, the part references for a bolt, nut, and washer are visible. The part reference information for the bolt is displayed in the Part Reference dialog box.

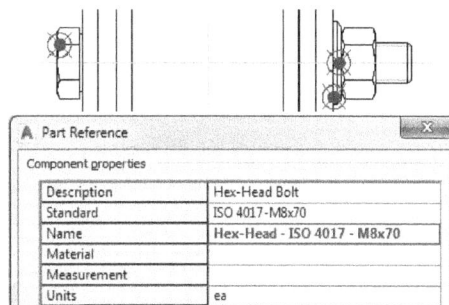

Example of Part Reference Information

You have created a 2D assembly that consists of both standard and custom parts. You need to create and maintain an associative BOM, parts lists, and balloons for all of the parts in the assembly. You can use part references to store the information about standard parts and custom parts.

Adding Part References

You can add part references to your drawings to help in populating the data in the bill of materials and to identify the parts in an assembly with balloon callouts.

When you are using the Part Reference command to add a part reference, you can select a point in the drawing, select a block, or copy or reference an existing part reference. Selecting a point on an object creates a part reference that is associated to that object. A part reference that is created by selecting a point in an open area of the drawing creates an unassociated part reference.

In the following illustration, the part reference associated with geometry in the drawing displays with a filled-in circle at its center (1). The unassociated part reference displays without the filled-in circle at its center (2).

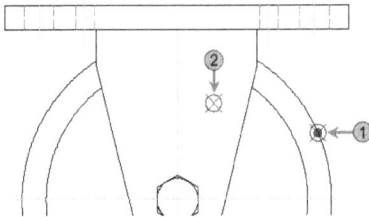

Access

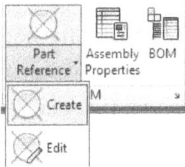

Command Line: AMPARTREF

Ribbon: Annotate tab > BOM panel > Part Reference drop-down list > Create Part Reference

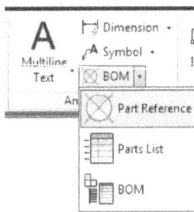

Ribbon: Home tab > Annotation panel > BOM drop-down list > Create Part Reference

Menu: Annotate > Part Reference

Command Line Options

Use the following options with the command.

Option	Definition
Select Point	Select a point to create the part reference node.
Block	Use to create and attach a part reference to an inserted block. Additional instances of the block in the same file automatically contain the part reference. Exploding an instance of the block deletes the part reference for that instance. The part reference created using this option is not included with the block definition if the block is written out to its own drawing file.

Copy	Create a copy of a part reference node and its data. The new part reference becomes a new item in the BOM.
Reference	Create an additional instance of the selected part reference. This additional instance increments the quantity value for the part reference. It does not add a new item row to the BOM.

Part Reference Dialog Box

You can add information about parts in the Part Reference dialog box. The list of component properties for which you can enter data is based on the settings in the active standard for the standards element Component Properties.

1. Enter the values for the component properties.

2. Use Settings to open the BOM Settings dialog box for the standard. You can edit the list or value of the component properties.

3. The incremental value that is used to calculate the total quantity in the assembly each time the part reference is placed. Enter the total quantity for this part when you are not adding a part reference each time the part is used in the assembly.

4. Select this option to prevent the information from displaying in the parts list.

5. Available when editing a part reference that was created using the Block suboption. Connect adds another part reference instance to another block. Disconnect removes the part reference from the block.

6. Attach or detach the BOM data from an external file. When attached, only the BOM data from the selected file is externally referenced.

Process: Adding Part References

An overview of adding part references to a drawing is shown in the following steps:

1. Start the **Part Reference** command.

2. Specify the location of the part reference in the drawing.

3. In the Part Reference dialog box, the values for the listed component properties.

Editing Part References

You can change part reference information at any time after a part reference has been placed. You can change values or modify the object to which the part reference is connected, and control whether the part reference is excluded from the part list.

To edit a part reference, you can toggle the part reference visibility on and then double-click on the part reference node, or use another method to start the AMPARTREFEDIT command. When you have finished editing the part references, you can toggle off the visibility of the part reference.

In the following illustration, the changes made in the Part Reference dialog box are automatically reflected in the parts list.

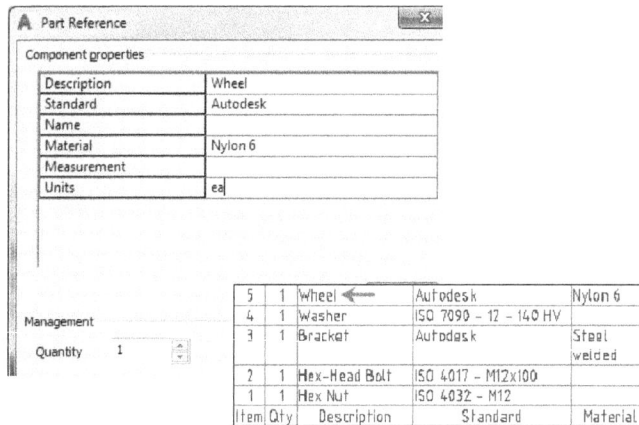

Access

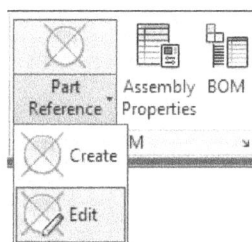

Command Line: AMPARTREFEDIT

Ribbon: Annotate tab > BOM panel > Part Reference drop-down list > Edit Part Reference

Menu: Annotate > Part Reference Edit

You can also use the **Power Edit** command or double-click on the part reference that you want to edit.

Access

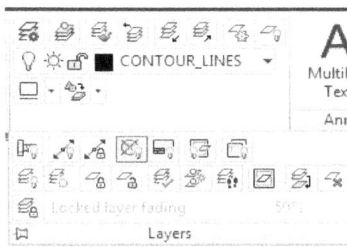

Command Line: AMLAYPARTREFO

Ribbon: Home tab > expanded Layers panel > Part Reference
Layer On/Off

Menu: Format > Layer Tools > Part Reference Layer On/Off

Editing Part Reference Values and Settings

When you edit part reference information, the dialog box that was initially use to create the part reference opens. Any locked component property that you cannot edit displays its value in gray text.

Click in the value cell for a component property to enter a new value or select a new value from a list if the component property has a predefined list of values.

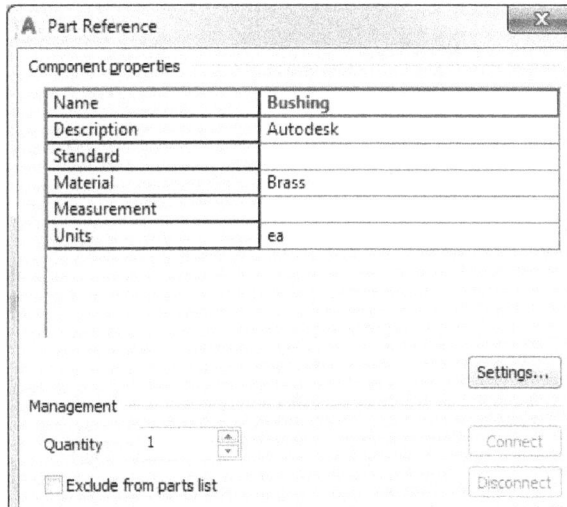

Procedure: Editing Existing Part References

An overview of editing existing part references is shown in the following steps:

1. Verify that the Part Reference layer is on.

2. Double-click on a part reference node.

3. In the Part Reference dialog box, edit the information and values as required. Click OK.

Exercise: Create Part References

In this exercise, you will add part references to store part information and add balloons.

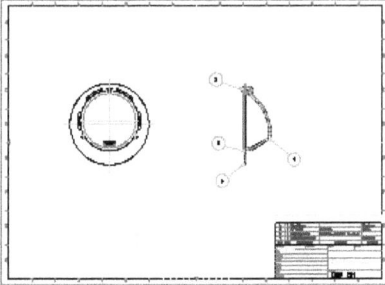

The completed exercise

1. Open *Part_Ref-Exercise.dwg*. Some part references have already been added to the drawing.

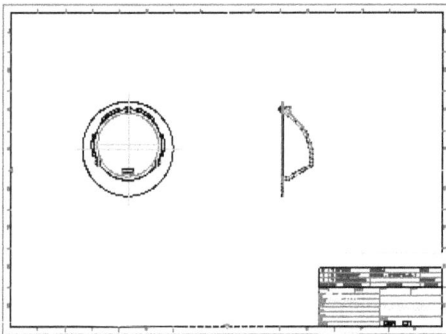

2. To create a part reference, do the following:

- Click Annotate tab > BOM panel > Part Reference drop-down list > Create Part Reference.
- Right-click anywhere in the graphics window and select Copy.
- Select the part reference node as shown in the following illustration.

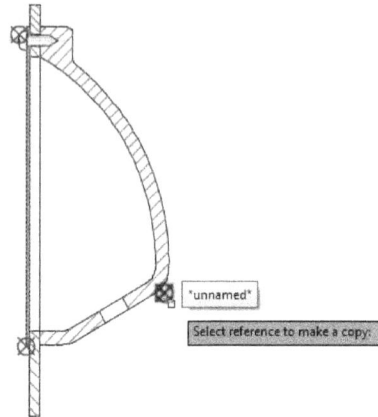

3. Select the bottom edge of the part as shown in the following illustration and press ENTER to accept.

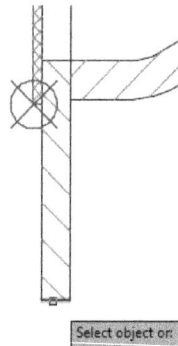

4. In the Part Reference dialog box, do the following:

- For Description, to change it, click on it and enter **Cover**.
- Note that the Material is complete from the previous Part Reference.
- Click OK.

5. Review the parts list and note that the new item was automatically added to the list.

4	1	Cover ←	
3	1	UV Filter	Autodesk
2	3	Tapping Screw	ISO 7049 - ST
1	1	Reflective Housing	
Item	Qty	Description	St
FILE NAME		FSCM NO	SHEET

6. To display the part reference node objects as shown in the following illustration, click Home tab > expanded Layers panel > Part Reference Layer On/Off.

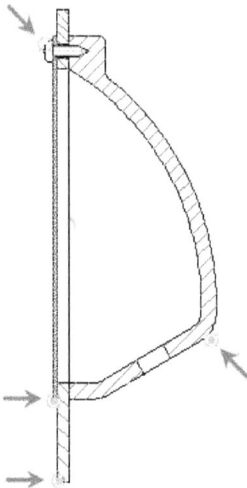

7. To edit the part reference, do the following:

- Double-click on the part reference that you previously created (node at the bottom edge).
- In the Part Reference dialog box, for Description, enter **Vent Cover**.
- Click OK. The parts list automatically updates to reflect the change.

4	1	Vent Cover ←
3	1	UV Filter
2	3	Tapping Screw
1	1	Reflective Housing
Item	Qty	Description
FILE NAME		FSCM NO

8. To add a balloon, do the following:

- Click Annotate tab > Balloon panel > Balloons.
- Select the new part reference.
- Select a second point for the balloon as shown in the following illustration.
- Press ENTER to place the balloon.

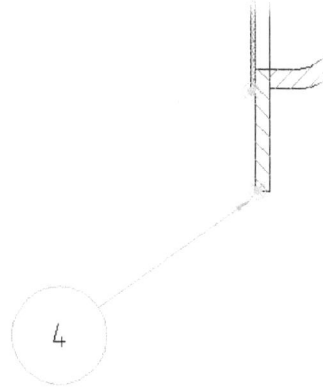

9. Continue to add balloons to the remaining part reference objects.

10. To hide the part reference objects, click Home tab > expanded Layers panel > Part Reference Layer On/Off.

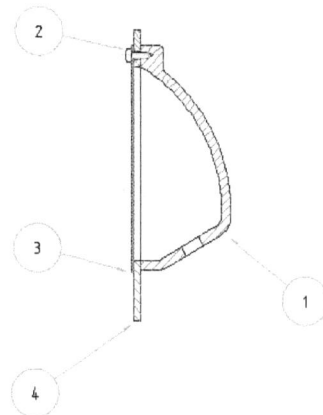

11. Save and close all of the files.

Lesson: Bill of Materials

Overview

This lesson describes how to create and edit a bill of materials (BOM) in an assembly drawing.

The BOM is the central access location for all part and subassembly component information in the assembly. By understanding how to create and edit a BOM so that it displays the required information, you can export this information for use in other software applications or use it to further annotate and complete your drawings.

In the following illustration, the main BOM for the assembly drawing of a drive system is listing all of the parts and subassemblies that define it. In this example, Mechanical structure is not being used.

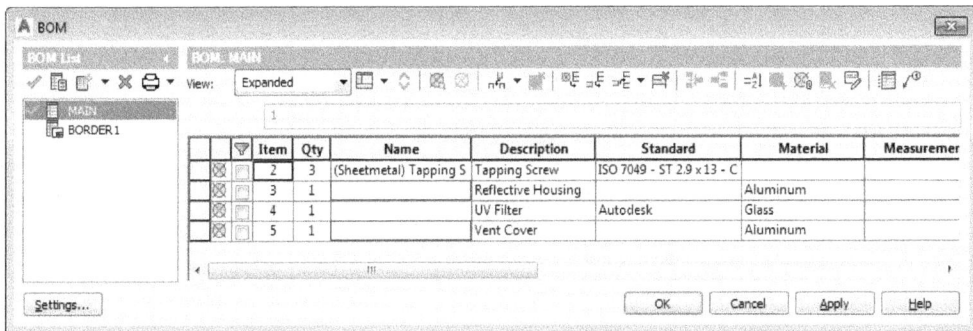

Objectives

After completing this lesson, you will be able to:

- Create and view a bill of materials for a drawing.
- Describe how structured components and an assembly BOM interact.
- Expand database subassemblies to display components at varying levels.
- Sort the data in the BOM based on specified criteria.
- Renumber parts in the bill of materials.
- Identify where the initial bill of material properties are configured.

Creating Bill of Materials

To use the bill of materials correctly, you need to understand its purpose and how you create it and populate its data.

In the following illustration, the attribute data for the part component is shown in the dialog box for editing the part attributes and in a section of the BOM for the assembly.

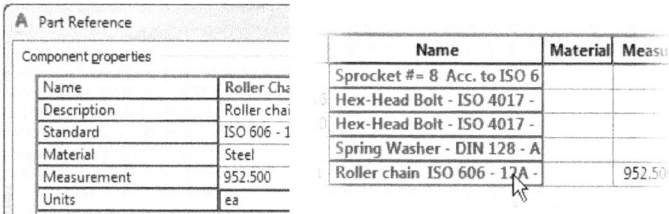

About Bill of Materials

The BOM is a database stored within an assembly file that stores, organizes, and makes available the attribute values of all of the parts and subassemblies inserted into the assembly design. More than one BOM can be defined in a drawing.

You can view and edit the BOM information in the BOM dialog box. It displays the part and subassembly information in a row and column table similar to a spreadsheet's row and column format. You can edit any of the values in cells that do not display their data in light gray by clicking the cell and entering a new value. Values displayed in light gray are not manually editable.

There are three ways in which the BOM can be populated with data. You can manually add rows to the BOM and values in each row, add part references to a drawing that is not using mechanical structure, or add instances of mechanically structured parts and assemblies into an assembly design that is using Mechanical structure.

Items added as a new row are only defined in the BOM. To increase or decrease the count of that item, you must enter a new quantity value. By copying or deleting part references or structured components, the quantity value for that item automatically changes.

When using part references or structured components, the data in the BOM for an item stays up to date with the data entered for the part reference or structured component properties. The part reference or structured component properties also stay up to date with any changes made in the BOM. Therefore, if you change the values in the BOM, when you edit the attribute values for the part definition, the current value reflects that change. A change in the attribute values at the part level is automatically reflected in the BOM the next time it is opened.

After you have created the BOM, you can export the values for use in other software applications, insert parts lists into a drawing to display some of the BOM data, and insert balloons pointing to the parts. BOMs added to a structured assembly display in the Browser directly below the assembly component name.

Access

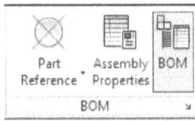

Command Line: AMBOM

Ribbon: Annotate tab > BOM panel > BOM

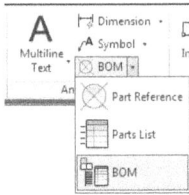

Ribbon: Home tab > Annotation panel > BOM drop-down list > BOM

Menu: Annotate > BOM Database

Shortcut Menu: In the Browser, right-click on an open area and click Create BOM.

Shortcut Menu: In the Browser, right-click on an assembly component and click Create Assembly BOM.

BOM Dialog Box

You can add or delete parts and edit bill of materials information in the BOM dialog box. When more than one BOM is available in a drawing file, you can select which BOM information you want to view and edit. A green checkmark indicates that the selected BOM is the current BOM and displays its contents within the BOM panel. A drawing that does not use Mechanical structure and has not created another BOM based on an inserted title block only lists the BOM Main.

The top row of buttons in the BOM dialog box enable you to print or delete the current BOM information or export it to another file format. You can also add or remove columns or rows of information, change the order in which the information is displayed, and insert parts lists or balloons into the drawing.

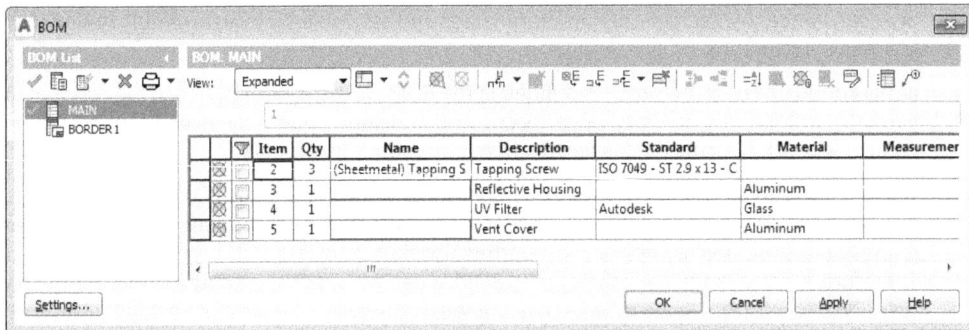

Procedure: Creating a BOM Database Specific to a Drawing Border

An overview of how to create a BOM based on the components or part references within a border inserted in model space is shown in the following steps:

1. Start the **BOM** command.

2. In the drawing area, click along any edge of the AutoCAD Mechanical software border.

3. In the BOM dialog box, adjust the display or data as required.

4. In the BOM dialog box, click OK.

Procedure: Creating a BOM for a Structured Assembly Component

An overview of how to create a BOM for an assembly or subassembly in a Mechanical structure assembly file is shown in the following steps:

1. In the Browser, expand the structure display to make the assembly or subassembly visible in the Browser.
2. In the Browser, right-click on the assembly or subassembly component. Click Create Assembly BOM.
3. In the BOM dialog box, adjust the display or data as required.
4. In the BOM dialog box, click OK to have the BOM created and added to the Browser below the assembly icon.

Structured Components and the BOM

Creating a BOM can be a tedious and time-consuming process of documenting an assembly. When you use structure, the BOM and its information are automatically created. To have the BOM reflect the required structure information, you need to learn how and where to and set the information for a component so that the BOM correctly represents the assembly.

In the following illustration, the BOM for the mechanical structured assembly DRIVE SYSTEM lists all of the parts and subassemblies that define it. The bill of materials for the subassemblies is also available for viewing within the same dialog box.

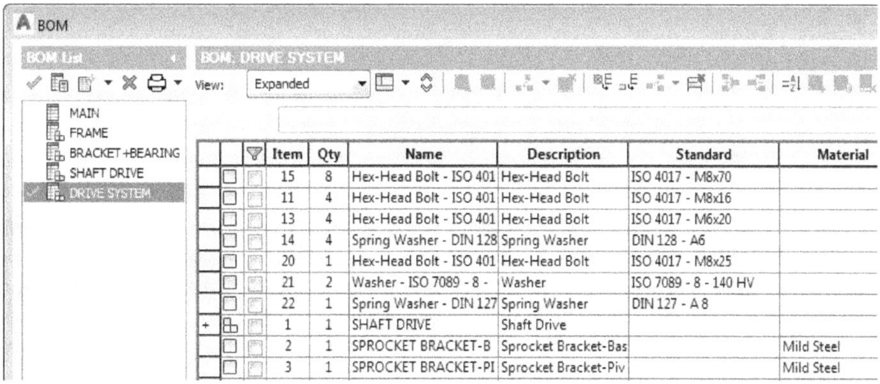

Item	Qty	Name	Description	Standard	Material
15	8	Hex-Head Bolt - ISO 401	Hex-Head Bolt	ISO 4017 - M8x70	
11	4	Hex-Head Bolt - ISO 401	Hex-Head Bolt	ISO 4017 - M8x16	
13	4	Hex-Head Bolt - ISO 401	Hex-Head Bolt	ISO 4017 - M6x20	
14	4	Spring Washer - DIN 128	Spring Washer	DIN 128 - A6	
20	1	Hex-Head Bolt - ISO 401	Hex-Head Bolt	ISO 4017 - M8x25	
21	2	Washer - ISO 7089 - 8 -	Washer	ISO 7089 - 8 - 140 HV	
22	1	Spring Washer - DIN 127	Spring Washer	DIN 127 - A 8	
1	1	SHAFT DRIVE	Shaft Drive		
2	1	SPROCKET BRACKET-B	Sprocket Bracket-Bas		Mild Steel
3	1	SPROCKET BRACKET-PI	Sprocket Bracket-Piv		Mild Steel

About Structured Components and the BOM

You can create a BOM for any assembly component or drawing file. By default, the BOM for the overall drawing file is titled MAIN. Although you do not have to have structure enabled to create a BOM, the automatic population of data in the BOM is very useful when using structure.

For each component that you instance into the assembly, a line item of that component and its properties is added to the BOM. When you add multiple instances of a component to the assembly, the quantity value for that item in the BOM increases to match.

You can selectively remove component instances from the BOM if and when your designs require that structure change. You can also add levels of structure to your designs through the creation of an organizing assembly component for the purpose of making it easier to place and manipulate multiple related components. You can then change the assembly properties for that organizing assembly structure so it does not display in the BOM but its components do display.

In the following illustration, multiple BOMs have been created and defined within the drawing file. The top one, MAIN, is the BOM for the overall drawing and the next one, DRIVE SYSTEM, is the BOM for the assembly DRIVE SYSTEM and contains the information of the part and assembly components in that assembly. The FRAME BOM only lists the components within that subassembly.

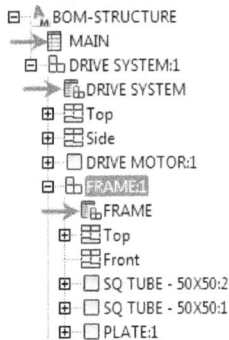

BOM Data and Component Attribute Data

The properties displayed in the BOM for a component are the same as the component's attribute values. Therefore, when you edit an attribute value for a component, the information in the BOM also changes. When you edit the property data for a component in the BOM dialog box, the attribute data for the component changes. The initial list of attribute fields for which you can enter information is based on the current BOM configuration in the current standard. You can set the standard in the Options dialog box on the AM:Standards tab.

Although you can use the BOM to edit a component's attribute values, the actual values are stored within the component definition. By entering the attribute values for a component, each time you insert that component in another drawing, the property data you entered once automatically populates the BOM wherever it is inserted. This method helps save time and prevent possible mistakes due to data reentry.

In the following illustration, the Properties dialog box for the selected component lists the BOM fields that were selected in the active standard. You can open this dialog box to change the attribute values or reference quantity, or exclude the component from the parts list that is placed on the drawing sheet. To open it, in the Browser, right-click on the component instance for which you want to change the values. Click Properties.

Reference Setting

To assist in creating your design, you might have situations in which you want to add parts to your design to help you visualize or size what you are designing in relation to that component. However, at the same time you do not want the BOM to list the component you are using as a reference. To achieve both of these points, you need to select the Reference option for the component.

You can set any component to be a reference component. To toggle Reference on and off, in the Browser, right-click on the component for which you want to change the reference setting and click Reference. The Browser icon for a reference component then displays with an image of a book.

Normal and Phantom Setting

Sometimes when you are working on a design, there are parts that relate to each other but are not put together into an assembly. For manufacturing purposes, those parts need to be separate line items and independent in the overall assembly BOM. To make placement and manipulation of such related parts easier in the drawing, while also maintaining the integrity of the BOM, you can place the parts in an assembly component and set that assembly component to Phantom.

An assembly component that is set to Phantom does not display in the BOM. Instead, the components within the assembly are listed as individual line items in the BOM. You can create phantom assemblies to organize components together for the sake of making the design and drafting tasks with these components easier.

You can set the assembly component to be Normal or Phantom from the Structure Catalog. In the Structure Catalog, Current Drawing tab, Definitions pane, right-click on the component and click Normal, Phantom, or Phantom in Current Drawing. An assembly component that is set as a phantom assembly displays in the Browser with a red X in its upper right corner.

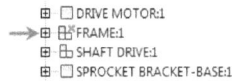

```
⊞  ☐ DRIVE MOTOR:1
⊞  🗗ˣ FRAME:1
⊞  🗗 SHAFT DRIVE:1
⊞  ☐ SPROCKET BRACKET-BASE:1
```

Example of Structured Components and the BOM

In the following illustration, the quantity and data in the BOM was automatically populated based on the number of times a component was instanced in the assembly and the component's attribute data. In the BOM shown on the left, item number 4 (CYLINDER ASSEMBLY) was expanded to display the components that are defined within that assembly. The image on the right shows the same BOM after item number4 assembly was set to be a phantom assembly. This caused the components within that assembly to display at the same level as the overall assembly and the item4 (CYLINDER ASSEMBLY) entry to disappear from the BOM.

		Item	Qty	Name	
☐		1	1	CLAMP	CL
☐		2	1	LEVER	LE
☐		3	1	JOINT	JO
☐	🗗	4	1	CYLINDER ASSEMBLY	
☐		5	1	STROKE	ST
☐		6	1	CYLINDER	C

		Item	Qty	Name	
☐		1	1	CLAMP	CL
☐		2	1	LEVER	LE
☐		3	1	JOINT	JO
☐		4	1	STROKE	ST
☐		5	1	CYLINDER	C

Expanding Subassembly Information

The display of subassembly data varies depending on the type of design and your company standards. A subassembly can list as a single line item in the BOM and none of the parts within the subassembly are listed. The subassembly is ignored in the BOM and the parts within it are elevated and listed as if they are parts directly in the overall assembly. Alternatively, the subassembly is listed and the parts within the subassembly are listed.

You can control how you want to list the subassembly and its parts by changing the BOM representation. When you change the representation, you can have the components take the next incremental item number or display with a prefix value and separator.

In the following illustration, the subassembly has been expanded to display its parts in two different ways. The BOM on the left shows the subassembly expanded and the BOM on the right shows the subassembly structured with a separator.

		Item	Qty	Descr
☐	🗗	1	1	Frame
☐		28	2	Hot Finished Hollow
☐		29	1	Plate
☐		2	1	Drive Motor

		Item	Qty	Descr
☐	🗗	1	1	Frame
☐		1-1	2	Hot Finished Hollow
☐		1-2	1	Plate
☐		2	1	Drive Motor

BOM Representation

To expand the display of the subassembly information, in the BOM dialog box, in the top toolbar, expand the View drop-down list.

When you click in the BOM dialog box to display the parts within a subassembly, they display in Expanded representation by default. By clicking Structured in the View drop-down list, the parts within the subassembly display the item number of the subassembly with the separator that you specify in the Separator box.

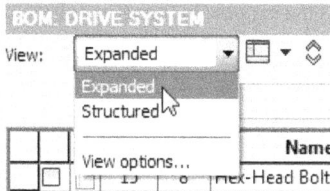

Select View options in the View drop-down list to open the View Options dialog box.

You can use the View Options dialog box to specify the type of character to use as the separator. The separator is only used when the view is set to Structured.

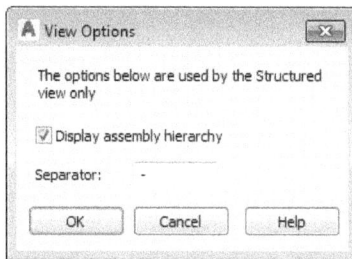

Procedure: Changing BOM Representation

An overview of setting the parts within subassemblies to display with structured item numbers is shown in the following steps:

1. In the BOM dialog box, click the View drop-down list.

2. In the View drop-down list, click Structured.

3. To change the separator, click View options in the View drop-down list. Enter the separator that you want to use.

4. Click OK to return to the BOM dialog box.

Sorting BOM Data

The order in which the data is initially displayed in the BOM is not always the way that you want to display it in parts lists on the drawing or in exported files. You can change the order in which items are displayed by clicking and dragging their rows to new locations or sorting multiple rows based on specific criteria.

Sort

To sort the order in which BOM data is displayed, in the BOM dialog box, in the top toolbar, click Sort.

Icon	Option	Description
≡ᵃ↓	Sort	Use to display the Sort dialog box.

You can sort the rows of BOM data based on the values in the selected columns. You can select up to three key columns to use for sorting the data. For each key, you can set the values to sort in ascending or descending order.

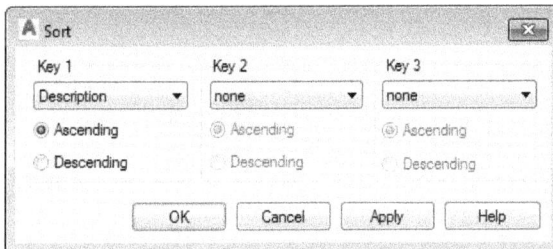

Procedure: Sorting BOM Data

An overview of sorting the rows of data in a BOM based on the values in one to three columns is shown in the following steps:

1. In the BOM dialog box, select the rows of information that you want to sort.

2. Click Sort.

3. In the Sort dialog box, select the BOM column for the keys on which to sort.

4. Click Ascending or Descending for the sort direction.

> To only select some of the rows of data in the BOM, press and hold CTRL to randomly select rows, or press and hold SHIFT to select a contiguous range of rows.

Renumbering BOM Entries

If you reorder or sort the rows of data, the item numbers are no longer shown in sequential order. This can make it difficult to find an item when you are looking up a part based on its item number. If you want the item numbers to match the current order of the BOM rows, you can select the Set Values option. You can also use this option to change multiple fields of BOM data to have the same value.

Set Values

To set the values of a single column for multiple rows, in the BOM dialog box, in the top toolbar, click Set Values.

Icon	Option	Description
☑	**Set values**	Use to display the Set Value dialog box.

You can use the Set Value dialog box to change the values in a column of multiple selected rows of data. If you click the cells in the BOM table, by default the column that you are editing is the column of the last cell that you selected. The option to increment or add values based on a stepping value is dependent on the column of data being edited.

Procedure: Renumbering BOM Entries

An overview of renumbering the BOM entries in sequential order based on their current order in the BOM is shown in the following steps:

1. Click the Item column header to select the entire column.

2. Click Set Values.

3. In the Set Value dialog box, change the starting value or stepping value if required for your design.

4. Click OK to make the change and return to the BOM dialog box.

5. In the BOM dialog box, click Apply or OK to write the changes to the BOM.

Bill of Material Standards

The initial list of attribute columns and their configurations are based on the settings in the active standard. While you can override these initial settings in the BOM dialog box, your standard should be configured in your template file so that you can save time by using what you have configured. This also helps to maintain consistency between your drawings.

BOM Settings

The default BOM columns and their attributes are configured on the BOM tab in the BOM Settings dialog box for the active standard. You can open the BOM Settings dialog box from the Options dialog box, in the AM:Standards tab, by double-clicking on Component Properties, BOM, Parts List, or Balloon in the Standard Element list. Double-clicking on BOM opens the BOM Settings dialog box and sets the BOM tab to be active.

Within this dialog box, you can change the caption of the column headers, change the width of the column, change the alignment of the text, toggle the visibility of the column on or off, change the data type, or set the value to be calculated from a formula. You can also add columns to the BOM list by adding them from the Available Component Properties list. You can add your own custom property to the Available Component Properties list and then add that to the BOM.

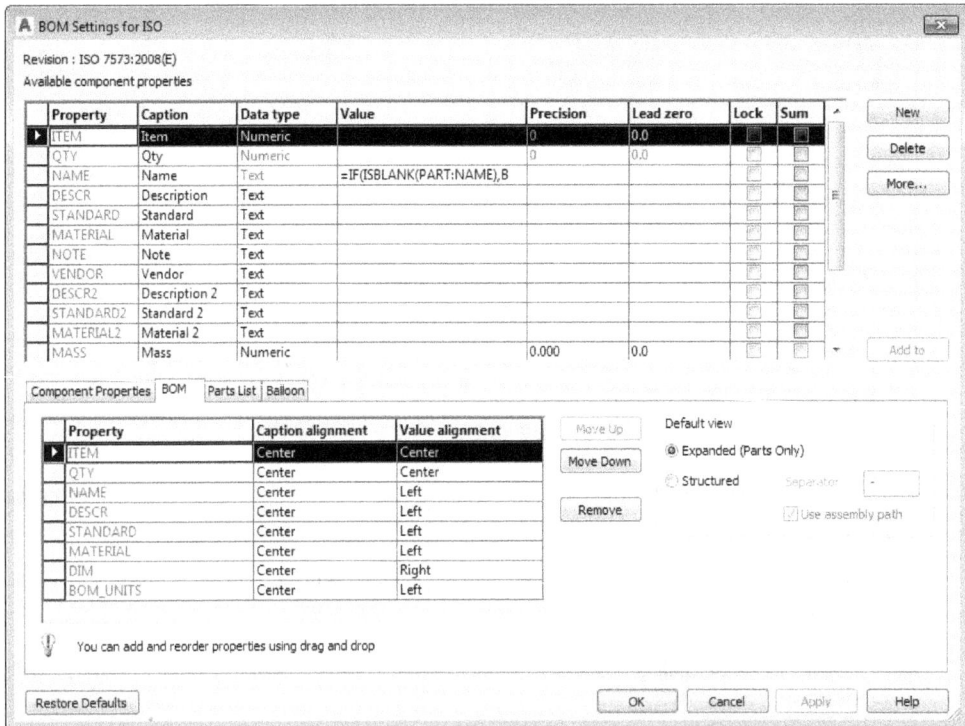

Exercise: Create and Edit a Bill of Materials

In this exercise, you will create and edit a bill of materials for an assembly. You will change the way the data is displayed and change values for the items in the BOM.

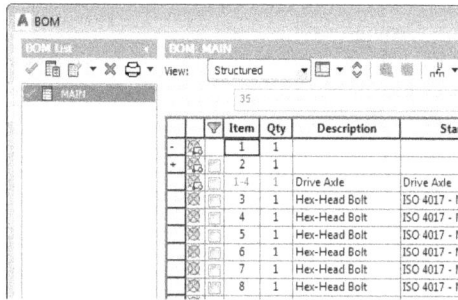

The completed exercise

1. Open *BOM.dwg*.

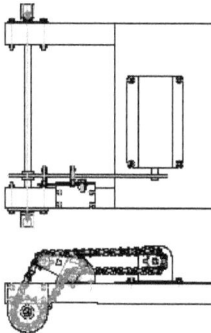

2. To display the BOM dialog box, click Annotate tab > BOM panel > BOM. Press ENTER.

3. In the BOM dialog box, review the listed bill of materials information.

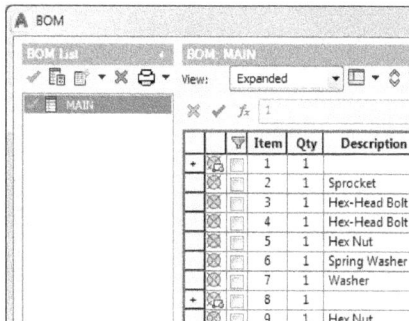

4. Click the plus sign (+) for items 1 and 8 to review the list of components in that subassembly.

5. To change the numbering system for subassembly components, in the BOM dialog box, click the View drop-down list and select Structured.

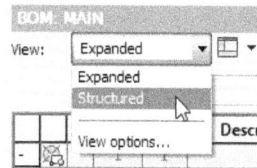

6. Review the changes to the BOM display.

7. To add a material value for the component SPROCKET BRACKET-BASE, do the following:

- Click in the Material cell for SPROCKET BRACKET-BASE.
- Enter **Steel**.
- Click OK.

Standard	Name	Material
ISO 606 - 12A - 1	Roller chain ISO 606	
Sprocket #= 12	Sprocket #= 12 Acc.	
Sprocket #= 6	Sprocket #= 6 Acc. t	
Sprocket #= 6	Sprocket #= 6 Acc. t	
ISO 4017 - M8x16	Hex-Head Bolt - ISO	
	SPROCKET BRACKET	Steel

8. To review the attribute values for the SPROCKET BRACKET-BASE part, do the following:

- In the drawing, double-click on the part reference for SPROCKET BRACKET-BASE as shown in the following illustration (1).
- In the Part Reference dialog box, in the Material field, enter **Mild Steel** (2).
- Click OK.

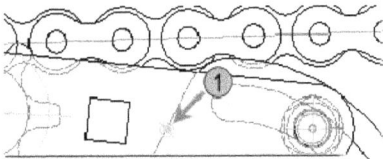

Component properties	
Description	Sprocket Brack
Standard	
Name	SPROCKET BR
Material	Mild Steel
Measurement	
Units	②

9. Click Annotate tab > BOM panel > BOM. Press ENTER. Review the Material column for the Sprocket Bracket-Base and now that it is now Mild Steel.

Sprocket #= 12 Acc. to ISO 6	
Sprocket #= 6 Acc. to ISO 60	
Sprocket #= 6 Acc. to ISO 60	
Hex-Head Bolt - ISO 4017 -	
SPROCKET BRACKET-BASE	Mild Steel

10. To reorder the contents of the BOM, do the following:

- In the BOM dialog box, select the top left corner cell to highlight the entire BOM.
- In the top toolbar of the dialog box, click Sort.
- In the Sort dialog box, for Key 1, select Description.
- Click OK.

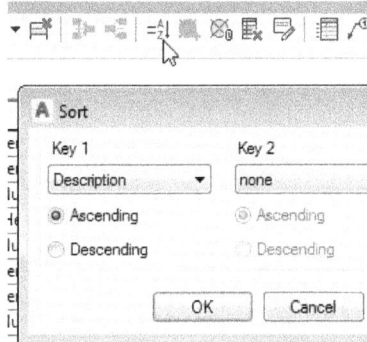

A Sort	
Key 1	Key 2
Description ▼	none
⦿ Ascending	◉ Ascending
○ Descending	○ Descending
OK	Cancel

11. To begin changing the item numbers to go in the new sort order:

- Click a cell in the Item column.
- Click the Item column header.

		▽	Item	Qty	Description
-			1	1	
+		☐	8	1	
		☐	1-4	1	Drive Axle
		☐	3	1	Hex-Head Bolt
		☐	4	1	Hex-Head Bolt
		☐	10	1	Hex-Head Bolt

12. To change the numbers, do the following:

- In the BOM dialog box, in the buttons in the top toolbar, click Set values.
- In the Set Value dialog box, click OK to accept the default values.

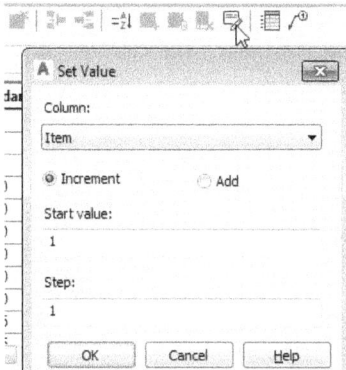

13. Review the changes made to the BOM item values. Click OK.

			Item	Qty	Description
-			1	1	
-			2	1	
			1-4	1	Drive Axle
			3	1	Hex-Head Bolt
			4	1	Hex-Head Bolt
			5	1	Hex-Head Bolt
			6	1	Hex-Head Bolt
			7	1	Hex-Head Bolt
			8	1	Hex-Head Bolt

14. Save and close all of the files.

Exercise: Create and Edit a Bill of Materials - When Using Structure

In this exercise, you will create and edit bill of materials for an assembly that is using Mechanical structure. You will change the way the data is displayed and change values for the items in the BOM.

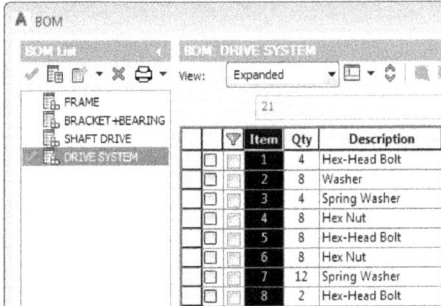

The completed exercise

1. Open *BOM-Structure.dwg*.

    - On the Status Bar, click Workspace Switching. In the list of workspaces, select Structure to make it current.

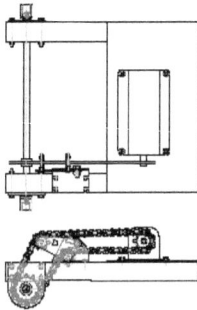

2. In the Browser, expand the assembly DRIVE SYSTEM:1.

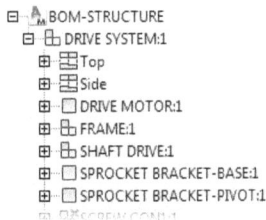

3. In the Browser, right-click on DRIVE SYSTEM:1 and select Create Assembly BOM.

4. In the BOM dialog box, review the listed bill of materials and information for the actively selected BOM.

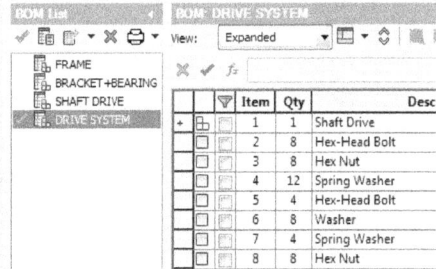

5. In the list of available BOMs, double-click on SHAFT DRIVE and review the list of components in that subassembly.

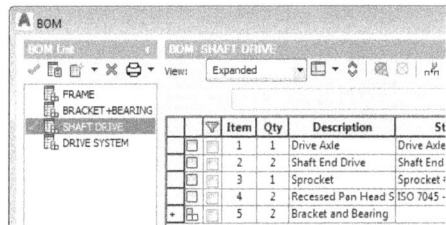

6. Click the plus (+) icon to the left of item 5 to expand that subassembly and note that item 6 and 7 display.

7. To change the numbering system for subassembly components, in the BOM dialog box, expand the View drop-down list and click Structured.

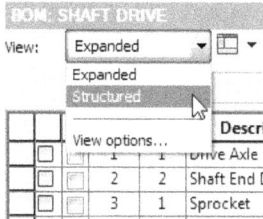

8. Review the 5-1 and 5-2 changes to the BOM display.

9. In the list of available BOMs, double-click on DRIVE SYSTEM to make it active again.

10. To enter a material value for the component SPROCKET BRACKET-BASE:

   - Click in the Material cell for SPROCKET BRACKET-BASE.
   - Enter **Steel**.
   - Click OK.

11. To review the attribute values for the SPROCKET BRACKET-BASE part:

   - In the Browser, right-click on SPROCKET BRACKET-BASE:1 and click Properties.
   - In the Properties dialog box, in the Material field, enter **Mild Steel**.
   - Click OK.

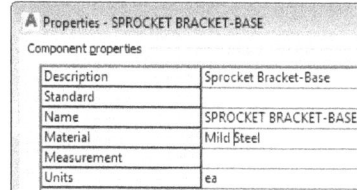

12. In the Browser, under DRIVE SYSTEM:1, double-click on DRIVE SYSTEM to open the BOM.

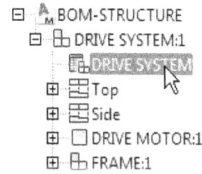

13. In the BOM dialog box, review the material for the SPROCKET BRACKET-BASE.

Name	Material
Hex-Head Bolt - ISO 4017 -	
PIVOT SPROCKET AXLE	
Roller chain ISO 606 - 12A -	
Sprocket #= 8 Acc. to ISO 60	
Hex-Head Bolt - ISO 4017 -	
SPROCKET BRACKET-BASE	Mild Steel
SPROCKET BRACKET-PIVOT	
Hex Nut - ISO 4032 - M10	

14. To reorder the contents of the BOM:

   - In the BOM dialog box, select the top left corner to highlight the entire BOM.
   - In the top toolbar of the dialog box, click Sort.
   - In the Sort dialog box, for Key 1, select Description.
   - Click OK.

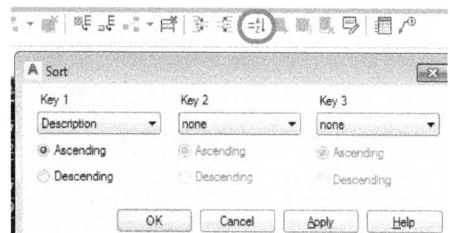

15. Note that the Description is alphabetical.

	Item	Qty	Description
	20	1	Drive Motor
+	21	1	Frame
	2	8	Hex-Head Bolt
	5	4	Hex-Head Bolt
	10	4	Hex-Head Bolt
	13	1	Hex-Head Bolt
	18	2	Hex-Head Bolt
	3	8	Hex Nut

16. Save and close all of the files.

Lesson: Inserting Parts Lists

Overview

This lesson describes how to insert and edit a parts list, how a parts list receives its information, and where the parts list is preconfigured.

You can insert parts lists to provide an accurate detailed text list of all the components in an assembly. The unique item number assigned to each row in the list is used to help identify the parts in the assembly drawing.

In the following illustration, a parts list was added to a drawing layout to list and identify the parts in the assembly shown on the same sheet.

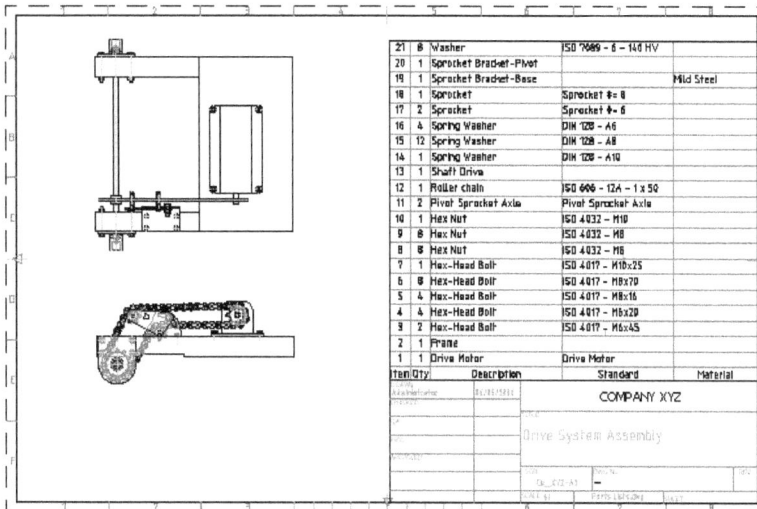

Objectives

After completing this lesson, you will be able to:

- Insert a parts list that displays data from the BOM.
- Edit a parts list in a drawing.
- Identify where the initial parts list properties are configured.

Inserting a Parts List

You can insert a list of parts that presents information from the assembly's BOM to provide an accurate and detailed list of drawing components in that assembly. The parts list uses or excludes component attribute information in the bill of materials. Changes to any setting or to the information in the BOM are automatically reflected in the parts list.

In the following illustration, different border areas contain different parts lists based on the main assembly design, a filtered list of the main assembly, and the parts in the subassemblies drawn in separate drawing borders.

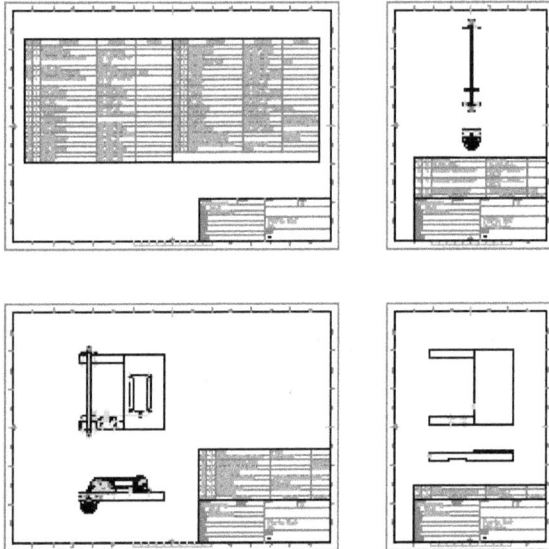

About Inserting a Parts List

The method you use to insert a parts list into your drawing depends on the characteristics of the drawing and where you are inserting the parts list. How you access the command and the steps you follow depends on whether you are using Mechanical structure in the drawing, whether you are inserting the parts list into model space or a layout, and whether the assembly has multiple BOMs.

The initial list of parts in a parts list is based on a defined BOM in the drawing. When you create a drawing that does not use Mechanical structure, in addition to the main BOM that lists all of the parts in the drawing, you can create multiple BOMs based on the parts within a drawing border in model space. When you create a Mechanical structure assembly with subassemblies, individual BOMs are automatically available for the assembly and subassemblies.

You can insert a parts list by doing the following:

- Using the **Parts List** command and entering the name of the BOM, selecting a model space drawing border, or selecting an annotation view.
- Opening the BOM dialog box, activating the BOM from which you want to create a parts list, and then clicking Insert Parts List.
- Right-clicking on an annotation view in the Browser in a layout and then clicking Create Parts List.

Access

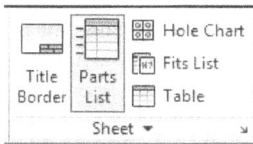

Command Line: AMPARTLIST

Ribbon: Annotate tab > Sheet panel > Parts List

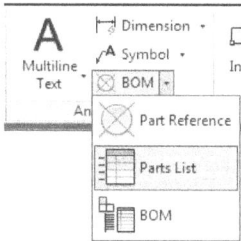

Ribbon: Home tab > Annotation panel > BOM drop-down list > Parts List

Menu: Annotate > Parts List

Procedure: Inserting a Parts List

An overview of inserting a parts list into a drawing is shown in the following steps:

1. Click Annotate tab > Sheet panel > Parts List.

2. Specify the list of parts for which you want to create a parts list by entering the name of an existing BOM, selecting a model space drawing border, or selecting an annotation view.

3. In the Parts List dialog box, adjust the parts list settings if required.

4. In the drawing window, click to specify the insertion point of the parts list.

Editing a Parts List

You can edit parts lists to overwrite the default style set by the active standard. You can insert columns, sort items, add filters, and split the parts list into multiple columns. You can also print the list of parts, export the list of parts, and import other lists of parts.

You can edit the settings, options, and values in a parts list while inserting it into a drawing or after it has been inserted into the drawing. In either case, you can interact with the Parts List dialog box. To edit an inserted parts list in the Parts List dialog box, use the Edit command for parts lists and balloons and select the parts list, or double-click on the parts list. If you want to change the column widths of the parts list, you can also grip edit the interior columns of the inserted parts list.

Access

Command Line: AMEDIT

Shortcut menu: Select the parts list, right-click, and click Edit Parts List symbol.

Power Edit: Double-click on the parts list.

Parts List Dialog Box

When you edit a parts list by changing options and values in the Parts List dialog box, you are typically revising the information that you see in the parts list and how you see it by overriding the default settings in the standard. You are also editing the property values of one or more parts.

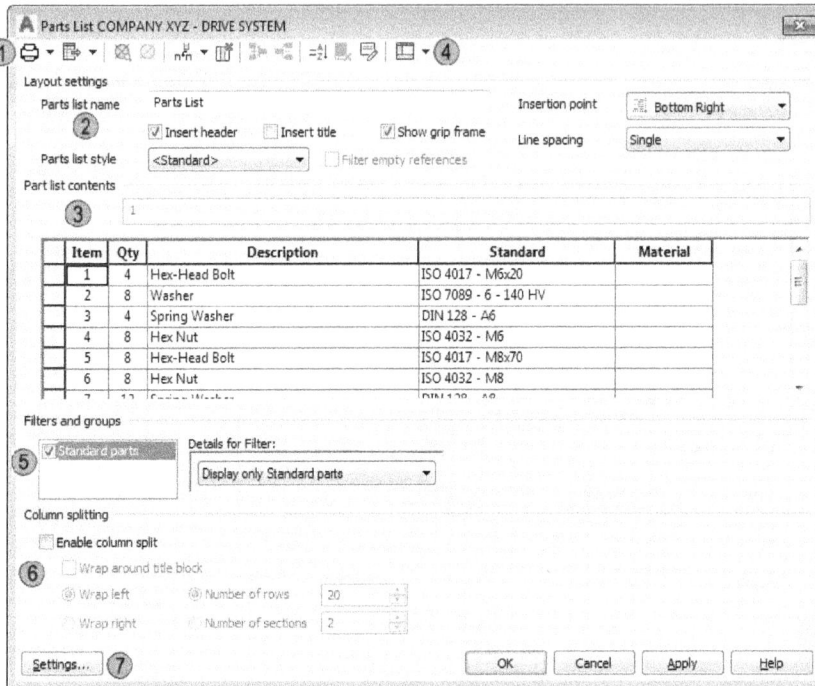

1. Prints, adds, or removes columns, sorts items, sets values, and imports or exports a parts list.

2. Modifies the default format of the parts list for the headers and titles, line spacing, and insertion point.

3. Edits the value in the BOM and subsequently the attribute for the part.

4. Toggle on or off the visibility of the results bar and a formula bar by using the Show/Hide drop-down list. Selecting the Formula bar displays an area below the toolbar (the formula bar), in which you can enter and edit formulas. A checkmark next to the menu item indicates that the formula bar is displayed. Selecting the Results bar displays a row at the bottom of the list of parts (the results bar) to show the totals of the properties configured to be summed. A check mark next to the menu item indicates that the results bar is displayed.

5. Organizes or focuses the parts to display in the parts list. You can create and define filters and groups by right-clicking on the Filters and Groups box.

6. Splits the parts list to decrease its overall height by continuing the listed items in another set of parts list columns. Set this to split in a set number of sections or after so many rows. Also set this to have the additional columns continue to the left or right of the beginning of the parts list.

7. Directly accesses and edits the settings in the active standard.

Accessing and changing the standards settings using the Settings button causes any layout or column splitting overrides that you might have previously set to be reset to match the settings in the standard.

To quickly access the standards settings when you are creating documentation drawings in a layout, right-click on the layout name in the Browser, and click Standards Settings. You can then double-click on the standards element that you need to modify.

Procedure: Editing Parts Lists

To edit a parts list that has been inserted into a drawing, complete the following steps:

1. In the drawing window, double-click on the parts list.

2. In the Parts List dialog box, make your changes. Click OK.

Parts List Standards

You can define the default display characteristics of the parts list in the drawing standard. You can set all of the available columns and column properties for a parts list. When placing a parts list, the settings in the drawing standard are used as the default values. However, you can override the settings for each parts list that you place.

Parts List Settings

You can determine the appearance of your parts list and the information that it displays on the Parts List tab in the BOM Settings dialog box. To configure the default standard, you can open the BOM Settings dialog box with the Parts List tab active in the Options dialog box, in the AM:Standards tab, by double-clicking on Parts List in the Standard Element list.

If you have created a setting to use a parts list based on industry standards, when you click Parts List Settings under Default Style, the Parts List Settings dialog box opens. In it, you can set the insertion point, text properties, internal margin values, and general layout of the parts list, and split the parts list into multiple columns.

To override the current standard when you are inserting or editing the parts list, you can open the Parts List Settings dialog box by clicking Properties in the Parts List dialog box.

You can add and remove columns of properties in the parts list. You can add properties to the parts list by selecting them in the Available Component Properties list above the Parts List tab. You can also change the order of the column properties in the parts list by dragging the column name up or down the list.

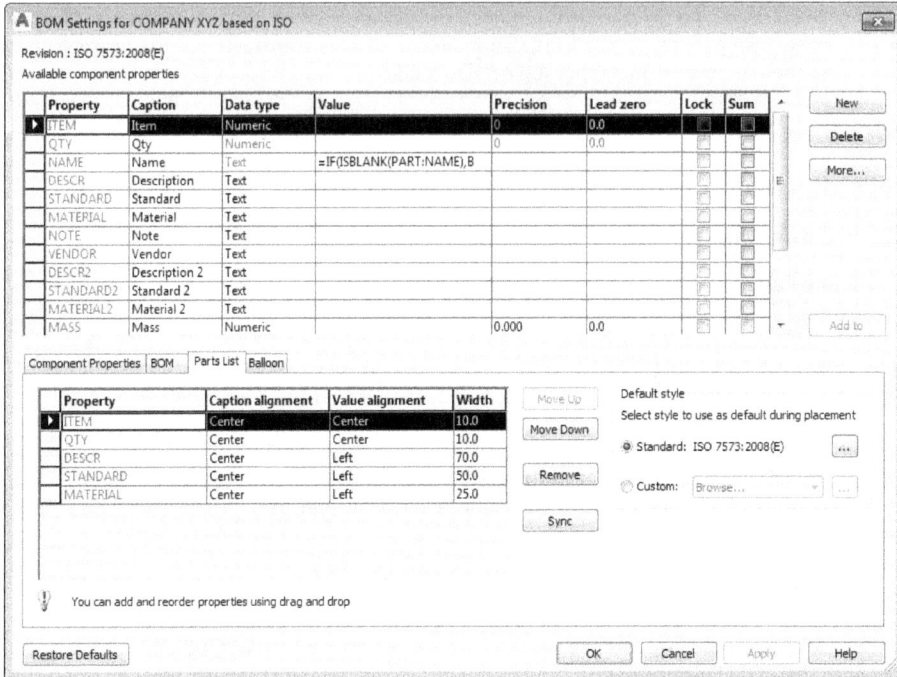

Exercise: Insert and Edit Parts Lists

In this exercise, you will insert parts lists in drawings. You will edit the parts lists to wrap them into multiple columns, adjust the column widths, apply a filter to limit the parts that are displayed, and adjust the margin spacing around the text in the parts list table.

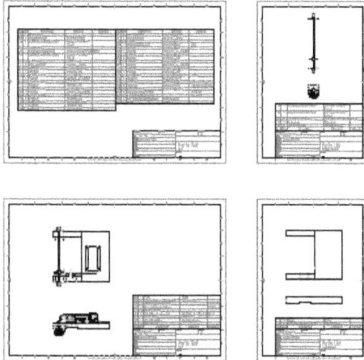

The completed exercise

1. Open *Parts List-ns.dwg*.

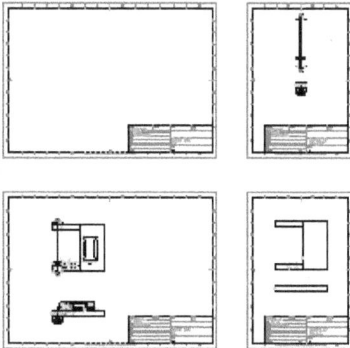

2. To begin adding the entire parts list for the entire assembly to the upper left border, do the following:

   - Click Annotate tab > Sheet panel > Parts List.
   - When prompted to specify the BOM, press ENTER.

3. In the Parts List dialog box, do the following:

   - In the *Column splitting* area, select the Enable column split checkbox.
   - Click the Number of sections option.
   - Click OK.

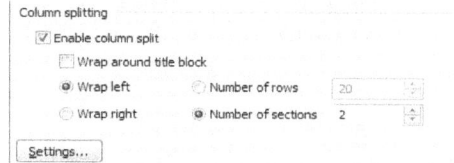

4. In the drawing window, in the top left border, click to position the parts list preview in the approximate center of the border area.

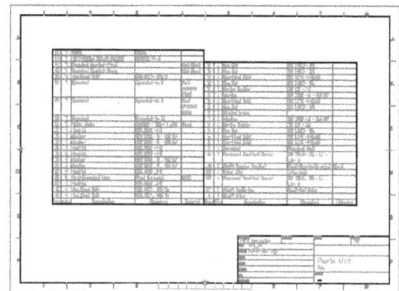

5. To change the direction in which the parts are listed and to change the wrapping direction, in the drawing window, double-click on the newly inserted parts list.

6. In the Parts List dialog box, in the *Layout settings* area, from the Insertion point drop-down list, select Top Left.

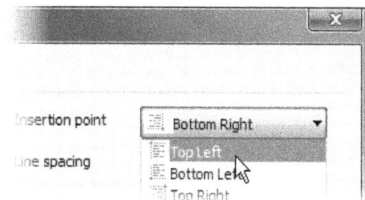

7. In the *Column splitting* area, click the Wrap right option, and then click OK.

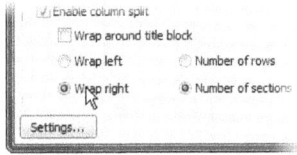

8. Using grips, move the table so that it is placed in the open area of the title block and border.

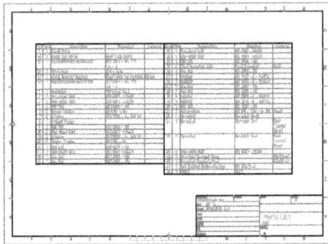

9. To resize the Material column so that the text does not wrap to multiple lines, do the following:

- In the drawing window, click the parts list to activate its grips.
- Click the top center grip.
- Move the cursor to the right, and enter **100**.
- Press ESC to clear the Parts List.
- If required, move the complete table back inside the border.

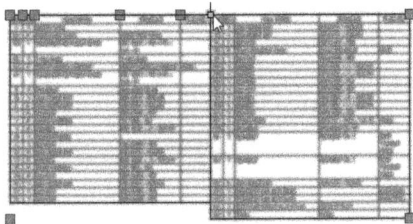

10. To begin adding a main parts list that only lists nonstandard parts, do the following:

- Click Annotate tab > Sheet panel > Parts List.
- When prompted to specify the BOM, press ENTER.

11. In the Parts List dialog box, under Filters and groups, do the following:

- Right-click in the empty Filters and groups list area and click Add filter.
- In the List of filters dialog box, click Standard parts. Click OK.
- In the Parts List dialog box, from the Details for Filter list, select Display all parts except Standard parts.

12. To insert the new parts list, do the following:

- Click OK.
- In the lower left border, object snap to the top right corner of the title block.

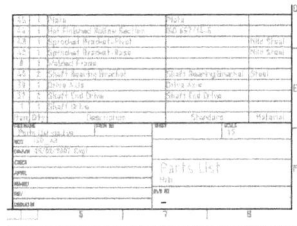

13. To begin adding spacing between the table lines and the value text, do the following:

- In the drawing window, double-click on the parts list that you inserted in the lower left border.
- In the Parts List dialog box, click Settings.

14. In the Parts List Settings dialog box, do the following:

- In the *Internal margins* area, for the Left Data value, enter **3**.
- Click OK.

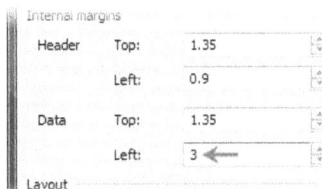

15. In the Parts List dialog box, click OK.

16. To begin inserting a parts list other than Main, and to insert it from the BOM dialog box, do the following:

- Click Annotate tab > BOM panel > BOM.
- When prompted to specify the BOM, press ENTER.

17. In the BOM dialog box, in the list of BOMs, double-click on BORDER1.

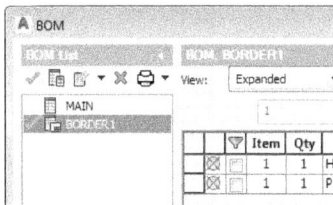

18. In the BOM dialog box, click Parts list.

19. To insert the new parts list, do the following:

- In the Parts List dialog box, click OK.
- In the lower right border, object snap to the top right corner of the title block.
- In the BOM dialog box, click OK.

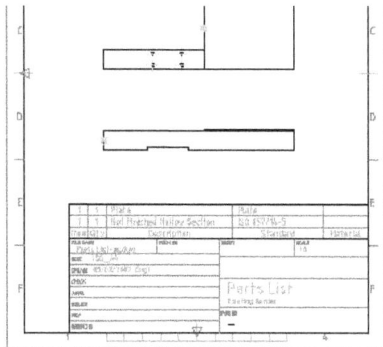

20. To begin creating a new parts list based on the top right border, do the following:

- Click Annotate tab > Sheet panel > Parts List.
- In the drawing window, click the top right border.

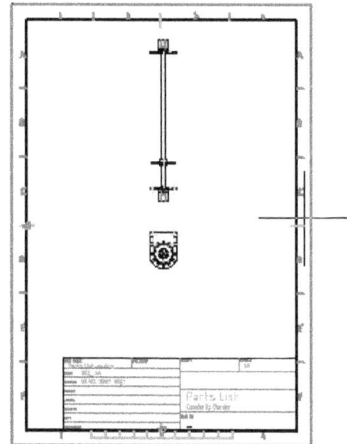

21. To insert the new parts list, do the following:

- In the Parts List dialog box, click OK.
- In the top right border, object snap to the top right corner of the title block.

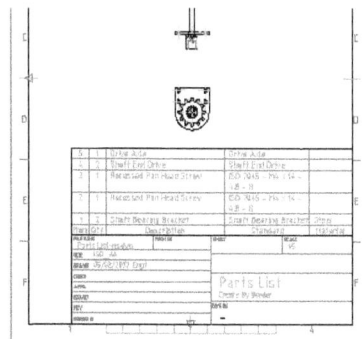

22. Save and close all of the files.

Exercise: Insert and Edit Parts Lists When Using Structure

In this exercise, you will insert parts lists in drawings that use Mechanical structure.

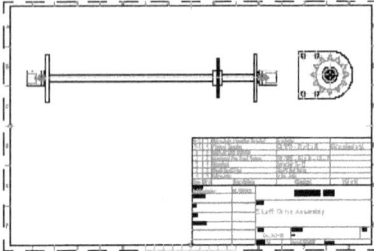

The completed exercise

1. Open *Parts List-s.dwg*.

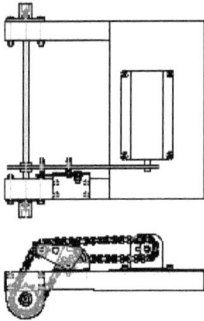

2. On the Status toolbar, click Workspace Switching and ensure that Structure is selected.

3. To review the BOM data for this design, do the following:

    - In the Mechanical Browser, double-click on the Main to open the Main BOM.
    - In the BOM dialog box, click the different listed BOMs and review their listed components.
    - Click Cancel.

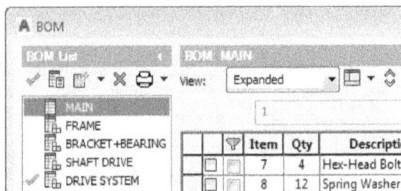

4. In the Browser, click the *Drawing* tab.

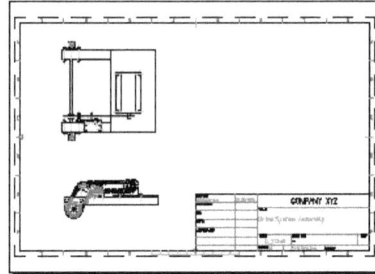

5. To begin inserting a parts list for the annotation view on this layout, in the Browser, expand Drive System Assy, right-click on DRIVE SYSTEM_AV1:1 and click Create Parts List.

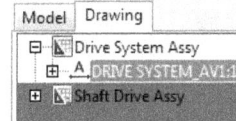

6. To insert the new parts list, do the following:

    - In the Parts List dialog box, click OK.
    - Object snap to the top right corner of the title block.

7. In the Browser, double-click on Shaft Drive Assy to make that layout active. Expand Shaft Drive Assy.

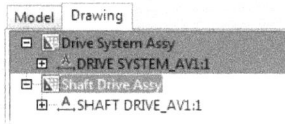

8. To insert a parts list for the annotation view on this layout, do the following:

- In the Browser, right-click on SHAFT DRIVE_AV1:1 and click Create Parts List.
- In the Parts List dialog box, click OK.
- Object snap to the top right corner of the title block.

9. Save and close all of the files.

Lesson: Balloning Parts

Overview

This lesson describes adding balloons to an assembly drawing for the purpose of identifying the parts and subassemblies in the drawing and in the parts list.

Adding balloons to an assembly drawing is an important part of tying your work together and communicating the design to others. With the parts list item number in the balloon and the balloon leader line pointing to the part, anyone who reviews a row of information in the parts list can identify which part it is in the drawing and where it is located in the assembly.

In the following illustration, balloons have been added to the assembly views to help identify the parts and subassemblies in the design. Based on the number in the balloon, you can find the part information in the parts list located on the drawing sheet. For parts that relate to each other and are in a single location, a collection of multiple balloons with a single leader line identifies the parts and their location instead of having multiple leader lines point to the same vicinity. Balloons added in the top and front view for the same part have the same item number which is correct because they are the same part.

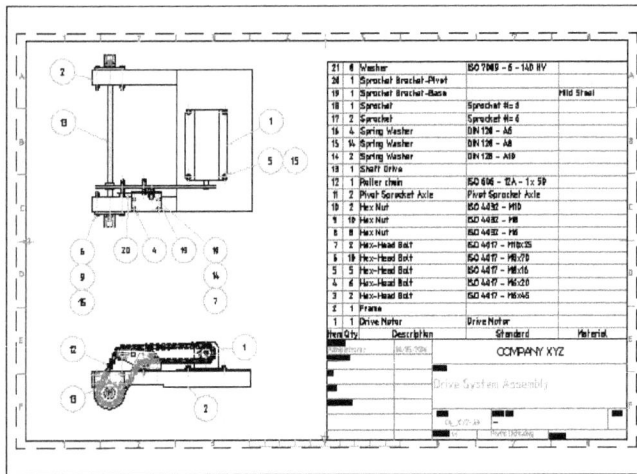

Objectives

After completing this lesson, you will be able to:

- Add balloon callouts to your drawing.
- Edit the properties and values of balloons that have been placed in the drawing.
- Identify where the initial balloon properties are configured.

Adding Balloons

To efficiently add balloons to your drawings, you should know where and how to add balloons and the options for adding them.

In the following illustration, a balloon is being added to the drawing after the structured component has been selected at the location of the leader preview.

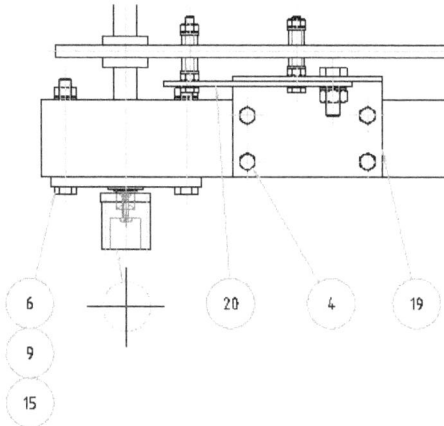

About Adding Balloons

You can add balloons to your drawings by selecting Mechanical structure components or part references. These balloons are then associative to the information in the BOM for the selected component or part reference. This associative relationship means that if the information is changed in the balloon, parts list, or BOM, all of the others display the same changes.

The initial appearance of a balloon and the value it displays are based on the configuration settings in the active standard. You can configure the balloon to insert a standard balloon that displays drawing or BOM attribute values, or configure it to insert a custom block.

You can add one balloon at a time or add multiple balloons at the same time. When you place multiple balloons, you can set their alignment to match the required positioning. The distance at which the balloons are automatically spaced is based on the current settings in the active standard. You can also collect multiple balloons and attach them to the same leader line.

When an assembly has multiple subassemblies and multiple BOMs, the BOM that the balloons refer to must be active before the balloons are added. You can preset the active BOM or set it to be active when you initiate the command to add balloons. The corresponding BOM is automatically set to active when you select to add a balloon in model space within a drawing border or when you select an annotation view.

Balloon Drawings With or Without Mechanical Structured Components

The method for initiating the command to balloon a drawing and the procedures that you follow depends on whether the drawing uses Mechanical structured components or not.

If you are not using Mechanical structure, you must create part references to locate and identify the parts in your design. You can create these part references before adding a balloon or during the process of adding balloons.

For assembly designs that use Mechanical structure, all of the parts and subassemblies are ready to be ballooned. To add a balloon to a drawing view of a structured design, you can select the structured component or the part reference that is automatically created for that structured component. When you balloon a component in different views, the same balloon number is shown for the different component views because the views are for the same part. This saves time and avoids mistakes.

Access

You can use the balloon command to add balloons to a drawing regardless of that drawing's use of Mechanical structure. After you initiate the command, a number of Command Line options can be used when creating and editing balloons.

Access

Command Line: AMBALLOON

Ribbon: Annotate tab > Balloon panel > Balloons

Menu: Annotate > Balloons

Create Balloons Access

When you are ballooning a drawing view that is an annotation view of a structured design, you can initiate the Balloon command by right-clicking on the annotation view in the Browser and clicking Create Balloons. By using this access method, the BOM associated to the annotation view is automatically set to active.

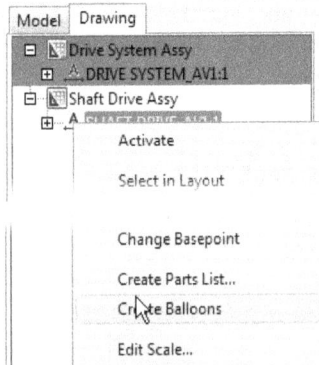

Command Line Options for Balloon Placement

You can use the following options with the Balloon command:

Option	Description
Auto	Creates balloons for selected part references. Select from the alignment options of Angle, Horizontal, Vertical, or Standalone. The first three position the balloons based on a direction. Standalone inserts the balloons on top of the part reference.
AutoAll	Creates balloons for all of the selected part references (part references that are already ballooned are omitted).
Set BOM	Sets the BOM to be current so that the balloon associates to the correct item number. When ballooning an annotation view in a layout, you must use this option each time you initiate the command, otherwise the balloon is based on the Main BOM.
Collect	Creates a collection of balloons that are connected to a single leader or attaches new balloons to an existing balloon.
Manual	Creates a new part reference and adds a balloon for it at the same time. The part reference is added to the Main BOM unless the part reference is added to model space and within a border. In those cases, the part reference is added to the BOM for that border.
Annotation View	Selects the annotation view to balloon. The BOM associated with that view is automatically set to active. This option is the same as accessing the balloon command by right-clicking on the annotation view in the Browser and clicking Create Balloons.

Process: Adding Balloons

An overview of adding balloons to an assembly drawing is shown in the following illustration:

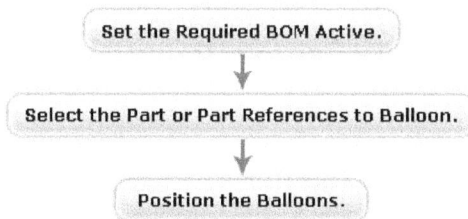

Set the Required BOM Active.

Select the Part or Part References to Balloon.

Position the Balloons.

Editing Balloons

After you have added a balloon to a drawing, there are multiple ways in which you can edit them. You can edit balloons through their grips, modify them after executing the **Balloon** command and selecting one of the command's options, or edit the properties or values of the balloons. To make any required edits to existing balloons, you need to learn about your editing options and how to access those options.

Grip Edits

You can reposition the balloon or the start of its leader line by adjusting its grips as you would adjust grip edits on the ends of a line. In the following illustration, the image on the left shows the end of the balloon leader being repositioned. The balloon leader is being moved from pointing at the part reference for the part to the outer edge of the part. The results of the edit are shown on the right.

Editing Using the Balloon Command

Not only does the ballooning command enable you to add balloons to a drawing, but some of the options enable you to modify existing balloons.

Option	Description
Collect	Use to select multiple individual balloons with separate leader lines and consolidate them into a single leader line.
Renumber	Use to renumber the item number in a balloon. You can set the starting number and the increment value.
Reorganize	Select when you have a number of balloons that you want to reposition on the drawing.

Editing Properties and Values

To modify an existing balloon's appearance or the value it displays, you can use the Power Edit command or the AMEDIT command for parts lists and balloons. You can quickly initiate a power edit of a balloon by double-clicking on the balloon in the drawing window. The Balloon dialog box opens, listing the current properties and values for that balloon or collection of balloons. You can then change the balloon's properties or values.

You can access additional balloon editing tools by selecting a balloon and right-clicking anywhere in the drawing window. The Edit, Standard, Add Leader, Remove Leader, and Reorganize options are then available in the shortcut menu.

Access

Command Line: AMEDIT

Ribbon: N/A

Menu: N/A

Shortcut menu: Right-click on a balloon and click an edit option.

Balloon Dialog Box

You can modify the appearances of a balloon and the property values associated with that ballooned part in the Balloon dialog box.

You can change the leader line, balloon style and type, arrow type, and balloon collection. You can add or remove leader segments and collect, delete, or attach balloons. In the Balloon Style list, you can set the balloon's appearance to be based on a standard balloon or custom block. The custom block displays in the list if it has already been defined in the drawing and contains attributes. With the option selected in the list, you can click the Balloon Type icon and use a balloon that displays differently from the default in the active standard. You can also use a different arrow type from the one set as the default.

Under Balloon Contents, you can new values for the part. Changing the values in the cells in this table is the same as changing the values in the BOM, Parts List, Part Reference, or Properties dialog boxes. Values that are displayed in gray cannot be modified.

Clicking Settings enables you to directly access and change the settings for the active standard.

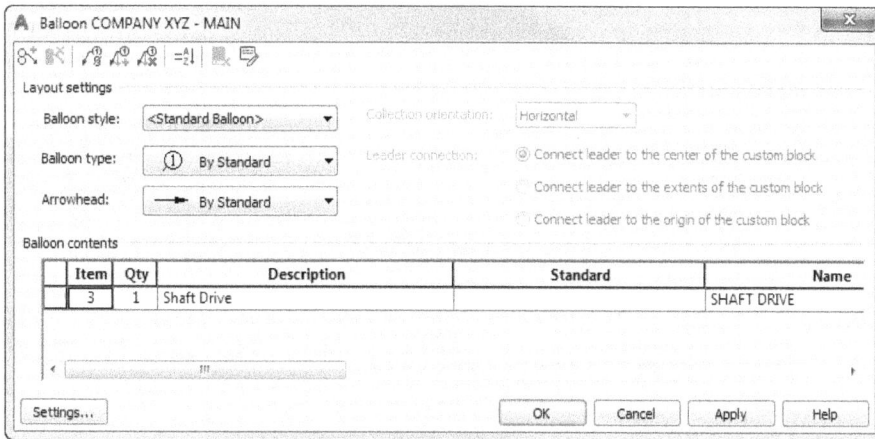

Procedure: Editing Balloons

To edit an existing balloon, complete the following steps:

1. In the drawing window, double-click on the balloon.

2. In the Balloon dialog box, select a new property setting or enter your changes. Click OK.

Balloon Standards

You can define the default properties and which attribute value is displayed in the balloon by configuring the drawing standard. After you insert a balloon, you can override its settings to create a unique balloon notation. Although you can override these initial settings, you should configure your standard in your template file to save time by using the configured settings. This also helps you to maintain consistency between your drawings.

In the following illustration, the balloons are shown using two different standard balloons. The drawing view on the right lists the balloon's item number for the part in the top half of the balloon and the quantity of parts in the bottom half. The quantity values are based on the values in the BOM and automatically stay in sync with the BOM quantity values.

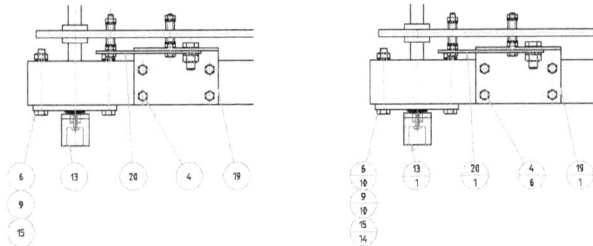

Balloon Settings

You can determine the default appearance of balloons and the information that they display on the Balloon tab in the BOM Settings dialog box. To configure the default standard, you can open the BOM Settings dialog box in the Balloon tab, in the Options dialog box, in the AM:Standards tab, by double-clicking on Balloon in the Standard Element list.

To set the appearance and shape of the balloon, you can select from balloons defined in the standard or a custom block defined with the appropriate attributes. You can set the balloon style under Default Style. If you use a balloon based on industry standards, when you click Balloon Settings under Default Style, the Balloon Settings dialog box opens, and you can set the balloon type, size factor, and spacing when placing multiple balloons. You can also set the arrow type, text height, and text color.

After configuring the balloon settings, in the Expression box, enter the values that should display in the balloon. To define an expression, you can select different component properties, drawing properties, or expression functions by selecting the appropriate category followed by the listed item.

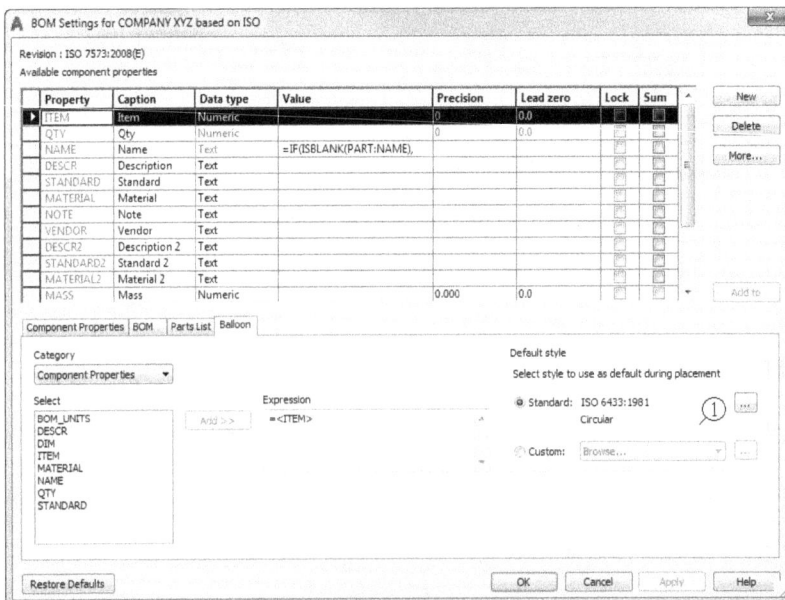

Exercise: Add Balloons to Assembly Drawings

In this exercise, you will add and modify balloons in an assembly drawing that only uses part references. You will also add and modify balloons in an assembly drawing that is based on mechanically structured components.

The completed exercise

Add Balloons to a Non-Mechanical Structure Assembly

In this section of the exercise, you will add balloons to an assembly drawing that uses part references to identify individual parts but does not use mechanically structured components. You will then manipulate the balloons by repositioning them, collecting multiple balloons to the same leader line, and changing their item numbers.

1. Open *Balloons-ns.dwg*.

    ▪ Review the drawing sheet. Balloons with item numbers are needed on the drawing views to identify the parts listed in the parts list.

2. This exercise section assumes that the Mechanical workspace is active. Set Mechanical by clicking Status Bar>Workspace Switching>Mechanical.

3. Click Annotate tab > Balloon panel > Balloons.

4. To automatically create a balloon for a number of selected parts in the assembly, do the following:

- Right-click anywhere in the drawing window and select auTo.
- Use a selection window to select the part reference symbols for the parts as shown in the following illustration.
- Press ENTER.

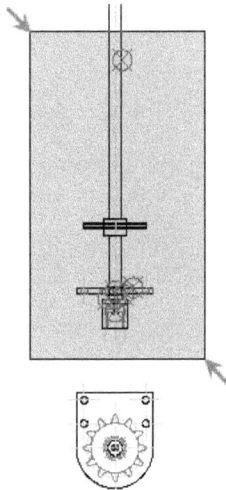

5. The balloon preview is attached with the cursor in horizontal alignment. To change the alignment of the balloons to vertical, right-click anywhere in the drawing window and click Vertical. The preview should now display as shown in the following illustration.

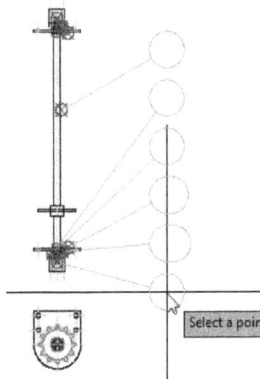

6. Click to the right of the view to place the balloons. The balloon numbers might be placed differently than shown in the following illustration.

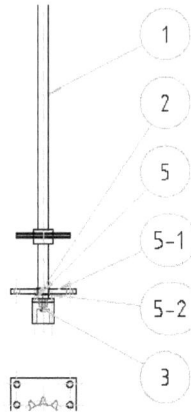

7. Click Annotate tab > Balloon panel > Balloons.

8. To begin adding a single balloon to the other view, do the following:

- Right-click anywhere in the drawing window and select One.
- In the drawing window, select the part reference (Sprocket) in the end view.
- Press ENTER to accept the selection of the part reference.

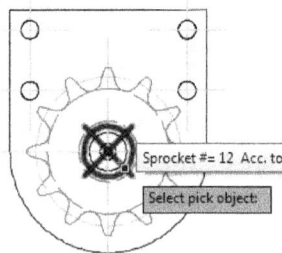

9. To position the balloon, do the following:

   ▪ Object snap to the left side of the sprocket.

   ▪ Click to the left of the view.

   ▪ Press ENTER to complete the creation of the leader line.

   ▪ Press ENTER to finish adding balloons.

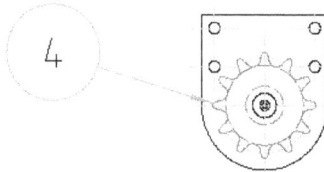

10. To begin rearranging multiple balloons at the same time, do the following:

    ▪ Click Annotate tab > Balloon panel > Balloons.

    ▪ Right-click anywhere in the drawing window and select rEorganize.

    ▪ Select the three balloons that contain a number 5.

    ▪ Press ENTER after selecting the three balloons.

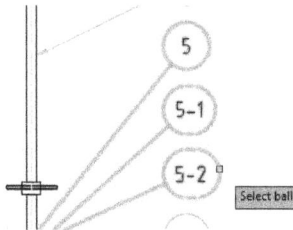

11. The preview of the selected balloons is attached with the cursor in horizontal alignment.To set the alignment and position of the selected balloons, do the following:

    ▪ Right-click anywhere in the drawing window and select Vertical.

    ▪ Click on the left side to position the balloons as shown in the following illustration.

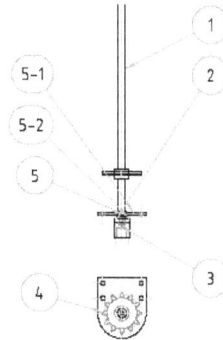

12. To change the balloon type for balloon 5, do the following:

    ▪ In the drawing window, double-click on balloon 5.

13. To begin adding balloons 5-1 and 5-2 to the leader line for balloon 5, in the Balloon dialog box, click Collect Balloons.

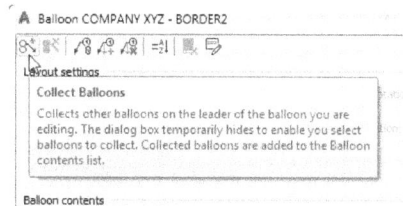

14. To collect the balloons, do the following:

    ▪ In the drawing window, select balloon 5-1 and 5-2.

    ▪ Press ENTER.

    ▪ Move the cursor to the left and click to have the horizontal orientation as shown in the following illustration.

    ▪ In the Balloon dialog box, click OK.

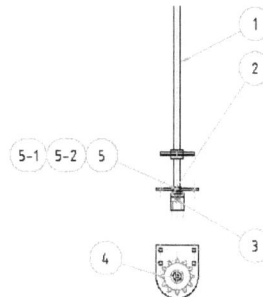

15. To change the item number in a balloon, do the following:

- In the drawing window, double-click on balloon 4.
- In the Balloon dialog box, in the Item field, enter **40**.
- Click OK.

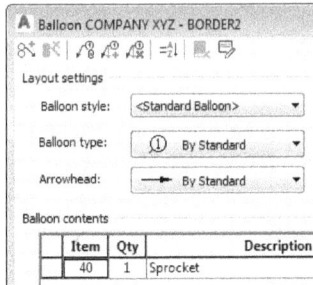

16. Review the impact of changing the balloon item number in the parts list.

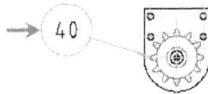

17. To begin renumbering multiple balloons, do the following:

- Click Annotate tab > Balloon panel > Balloons.
- Right-click anywhere in the drawing window and select Renumber.
- For the starting item number, press ENTER to accept the default of 1.
- For the increment, press ENTER to accept the default of 1.

18. To specify which balloons to renumber, do the following:

- In the drawing window, select each of the single balloons starting with balloon 40 and going counterclockwise. Note that the balloons are renumbered as you click on them.
- Press ENTER.

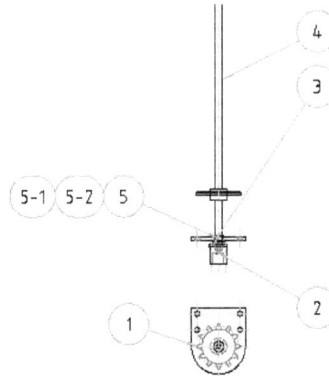

19. Save and close all of the files.

Add Balloons to an Annotation View

In this section of the exercise, you will add balloons to an annotation view of an assembly drawing that uses mechanically structured components.

1. Open *Balloon-s.dwg*.

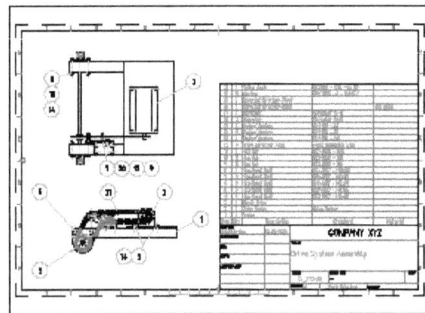

2. Set Structure to be the active workspace by clicking Status Bar>Workspace Switching> Structure.

3. To review the BOMs for this design, do the following:

- In the Browser, below the filename, double-click on the BOM titled MAIN.
- In the BOM dialog box, click the different listed BOMs and review the number of parts listed for each BOM.
- Click Cancel.

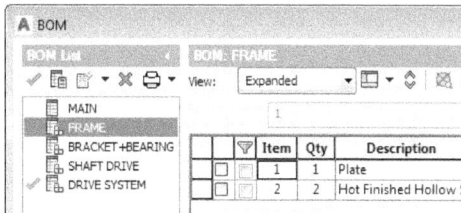

4. In the Browser, click the *Drawing* tab.

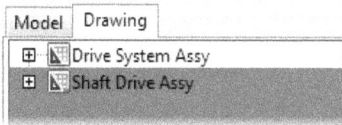

5. In the Browser, double-click on the layout Shaft Drive Assy to make it the active layout. Click to expand the tree.

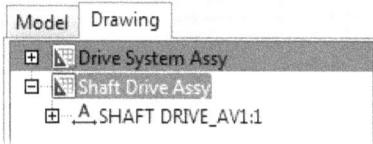

6. To add multiple balloons to the drawing view, do the following:

- In the Browser, right-click on SHAFT DRIVE_AV1:1 and select Create Balloons.
- In the drawing window, use a selection window to select the part references for the parts as shown in the following illustration.
- Press ENTER.

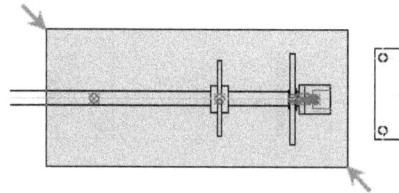

7. Move the cursor up and to the left so that the balloon preview displays above the view and the leftmost balloon is vertically above its reference. Click to create the balloons in a position similar to the one shown in the following illustration.

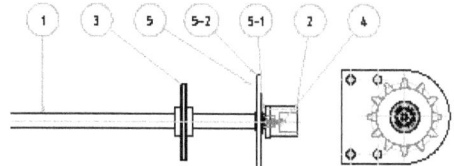

8. To begin adding one balloon at a time to a specifically selected part, and to set the correct BOM, do the following:

- Click Annotate tab > Balloon panel > Balloons.
- Right-click anywhere in the drawing window and select set Bom.
- Enter **shaft drive**.

9. To specify the part and position of the balloon, do the following:

   - In the drawing window, select the sprocket in the end view on the right.
   - Click the second point of the leader line up and to the right of the view as shown in the following illustration.
   - Press ENTER.

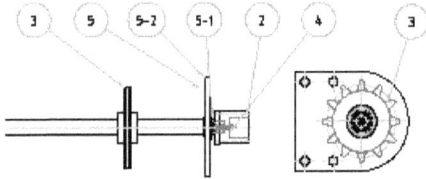

10. To add another balloon based on a selected part, do the following:

    - Select the bottom line of the bracket.
    - Click the second point of the leader line down and to the right of the view as shown in the following illustration.
    - Press ENTER twice to complete the command and create the balloons.

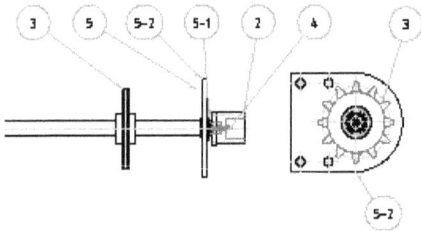

11. Save and close all of the files.

Chapter Summary

In this chapter, you learned about part references, how to create and edit the BOM in an assembly drawing, and how to insert and edit a parts list. You also learned how to add balloons to an assembly drawing to identify parts and subassemblies.

Having completed this chapter, you can:

- Describe, create, and edit part reference objects in the drawing.
- Create and edit a bill of materials in an assembly drawing.
- Insert and edit a parts list on a drawing sheet.
- Add balloons to parts in an assembly drawing.

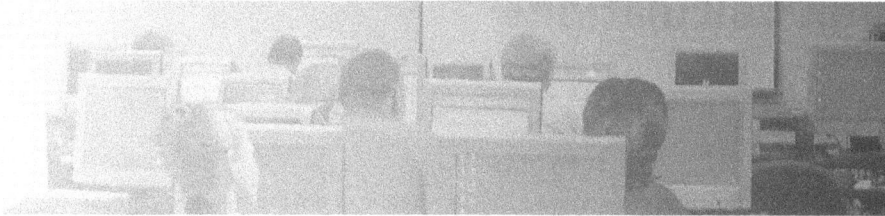

Design Calculations

In this chapter, you learn to perform calculations to validate designs. You learn to calculate beam deflection designs using the Moment of Inertia and Deflection Line commands. You then learn to analyze shafts and perform a Finite Element Analysis (FEA).

Objectives

After completing this chapter, you will be able to:

- Perform design calculations to validate designs.

Lesson: Design Calculations

Overview

This lesson describes some basic tools that you can use to verify whether or not the standard parts or custom parts within your design meet or exceed the requirements for operational use within an assembly.

In this lesson, you learn to calculate the moment of inertia from drawing geometry or from predefined profiles. You learn to calculate the deflection line for a beam or another cross member using the moment of inertia calculations and deflection tools. You learn to calculate cylindrical designs for shaft or axial stresses. You also learn to perform 2D finite element analysis (FEA) stress analysis on a cross section of a design to predict where stresses exist and determine a safety factor.

Objectives

After completing this lesson, you will be able to:

- Describe how the calculation tools assist you when creating a design.
- Calculate the moment of inertia for any cross section.
- Calculate the moment of inertia for rectangular or round cross sections.
- Calculate the deflection line of a beam.
- Calculate shaft stresses.
- Calculate finite element analysis (FEA).

About the Calculation Tools

When creating a design, you might not be sure which size of standard content should be used, or need to calculate and report the results of different scenarios for your design. With an understanding of the available calculation tools, you can identify the situations in which a calculation tool can help you to accomplish these tasks.

In the following illustration, different finite element analysis (FEA) results show and report what happens to this part when it is restrained in a certain way and specific forces are applied.

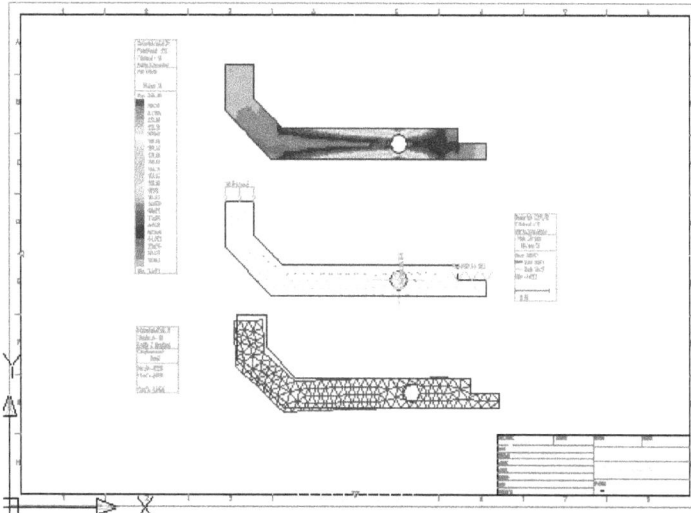

Definition of the Calculation Tools

You can use the calculation tools in two ways. One way is within the standard content and machinery generator commands to help select parts that meet your design criteria. The other way is to a design scenario to calculate results and generate a report. Both uses of the calculation tools apply accepted engineering formulas when calculating the results.

You can calculate results and generate reports for the following areas:

- Finite Element Analysis
- Screw Calculation
- Shaft Calculator
- Moment of Inertia for irregular shapes and predefined cross sections.
- Moments and Deflection of a Beam.
- Bearing Calculator

Example of the Screw Calculation Tool

As you create your designs, you might need to fasten different parts together using screws or bolts. To ensure that you have selected a fastener that meets specific requirements, you can calculate various factors using Screw Calculation. In the following illustration, the calculated results were added to the drawing for future reference. In this way, part of the design knowledge and intent is being captured with the design to be readily available in the future.

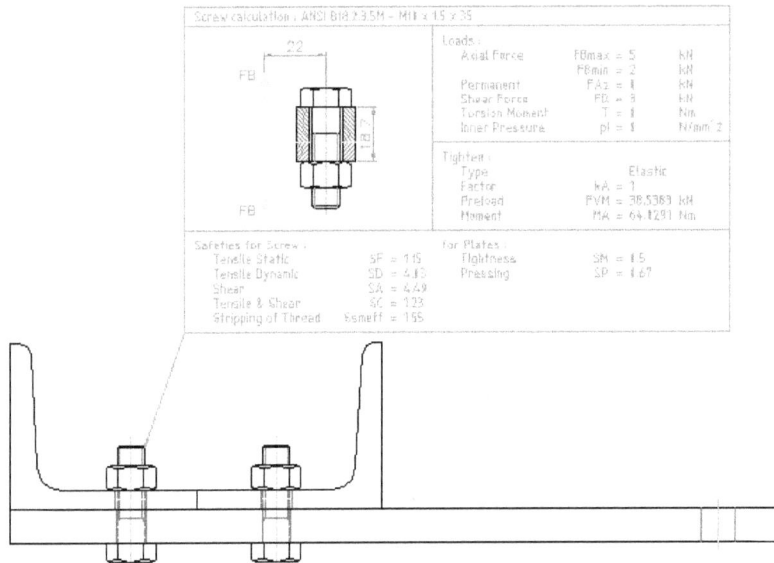

Calculating Moment of Inertia

You can perform moment of inertia calculations to analyze deflection and bending moments. You can determine the moment of inertia for a plane area on cross sections of beams or on other objects that can be represented as closed contours. When calculating, note the mathematical values for areas that depend on the location of the reference axes. You can manually calculate the moment of inertia by multiplying elementary sections of an area by the squares of their distances from the reference axes. You can use the Moment of Inertia command to calculate these values automatically.

About the Moment of Inertia Command

When you use the Moment of Inertia command, you can determine the center of gravity for a cross section and calculate the moment of inertia for each of the main axes. You can also select a load direction for a cross section and determine the angle of deflection for that load.

Defining Direction of the Load

If you move the cursor around the coordinate system before defining the direction of the load, the length of the (s) arrow indicates the bending amount (only relatively, not in real size). The arrow length also shows the bending direction, which depends on the load direction. The direction in which you place the load vector affects the result of the deflection line calculation.

About Moment of Inertia Symbols and Values

The following illustration shows the results of a moment of inertia calculation on two cross sections.

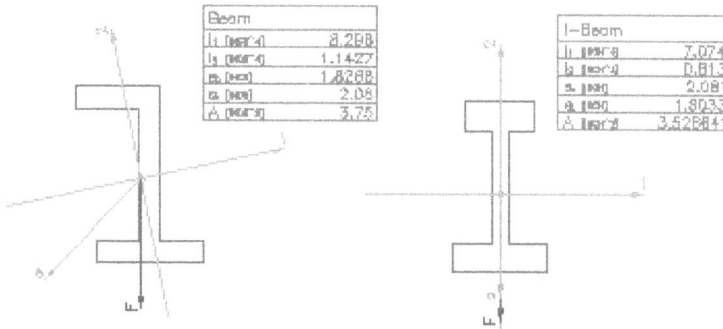

The two main axes (1 and 2) extend out from the center of gravity point. You can use the two vectors to represent the load direction (F) and the deflection (s) directions.

The following illustration shows the value table that is generated for a cross section.

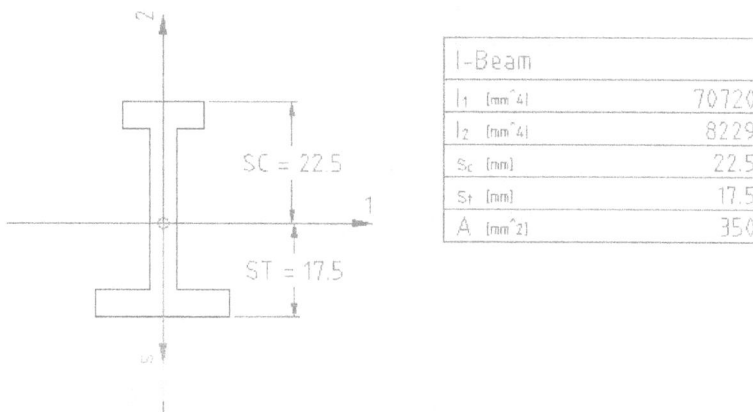

I-Beam	
I_1 [mm^4]	70720
I_2 [mm^4]	8229
S_c [mm]	22.5
S_t [mm]	17.5
A [mm^2]	350

You can use the values for I1 and I2 as the moment of inertia values for the two main axes. You can use the Sc value as the maximum border distance at the compression side and the St value as the maximum border distance on the extension side. You can use the A value as the area of the cross section.

Calculation Results in the Text Window

When you use the Moment of Inertia command, the following values display in the AutoCAD® software's text window:

- X and Y values for the center of gravity with respect to the AutoCAD software's world coordinate system (WCS).
- Rotation angle for the main axis of inertia.
- Effective moment of inertia for the load direction.
- Angle for the deflection.

Access

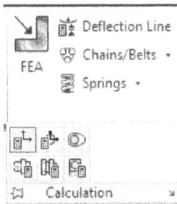

Command Line: AMINERTIA

Ribbon: Content tab > expanded Calculation panel > Moment of Inertia

Menu: Content > Calculations > Moment of Inertia

Procedure: Performing Moment Calculations

An overview of calculating the moment of inertia for each of the main axes of a closed area and inserting a table with the calculated results is shown in the following steps:

1. Start the **Moment of Inertia** command.

2. In the drawing area, click an interior point of a cross section. If the selected object is closed, a magenta boundary is created. You can select additional areas to fully define the cross section.

3. Press ENTER to finish selecting objects. If the selected object is not closed, no selection is made and the command is ended. If the selected object is closed, the area is displayed as filled and you are asked whether the filled area represents the area that you want to analyze.

4. If the area is filled correctly, press ENTER. If the area is not filled correctly, enter **N**. Press ENTER. The X and Y coordinates for the center of gravity of the cross section are determined. The main axes are drawn as they extend out from the center of gravity point.

5. In the drawing area, click to specify the direction of the load forces.

6. In the Command Line, enter a description. Press ENTER.

7. In the drawing area, click to specify an insertion point for the results table.

Calculating Moment of Inertia with Predefined Profiles

You can determine the moment of inertia for cross sections that are rectangular or round using the Predefined Profile Sections command. You can only determine moment of inertia values for the main axes when you use the Predefined Profile Sections dialog box. You do not need to have a graphical representation of the cross section to use predefined profiles.

Access

Command Line: AMINERTIAPROF

Ribbon: Content tab > expanded Calculation panel > Predefined Profile Sections

Menu: Content > Calculations > Predefined Profile Sections

Predefined Profile Sections Dialog Box

In the Predefined Profile Sections dialog box, you can select a cross section of a rectangular prism, hollow rectangular prism, cylinder, or hollow cylinder.

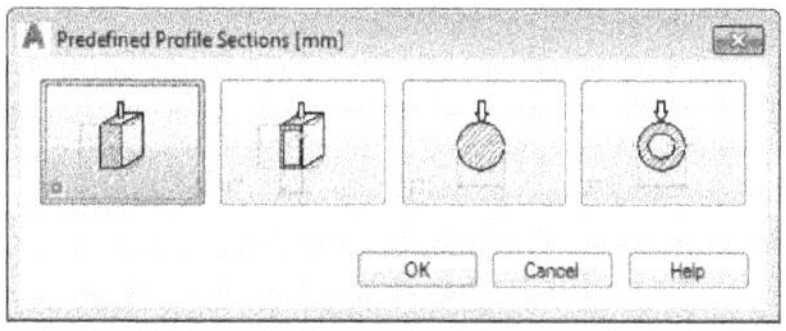

Procedure: Performing Moment Calculations with Predefined Profiles

An overview of inserting a moment of inertia value table based on a selected predefined profile and specified dimensions is shown in the following steps:

1. Start the **Predefined Profile Sections** command.

2. In the Predefined Profile Sections dialog box, click the profile that you want to analyze. Click OK.

3. In the Command Line, enter the dimension values that define the type of profile that you selected.

4. Click in the drawing to place the moment of inertia value table.

Calculating Deflection Line

When you calculate a deflection line, you are determining the sum of the loads and forces along a line to calculate the reaction of a beam. You can determine the reactions because the algebraic sum of the moments must equal zero.

With the **Deflection Line** command, you can calculate values automatically by selecting the moment of inertia table, placing loads and supports, and selecting which graphics to draw. Because calculation is done quickly, you can calculate for many scenarios by using the Deflection Line command.

The following illustration shows the tabulated results of a deflection line analysis.

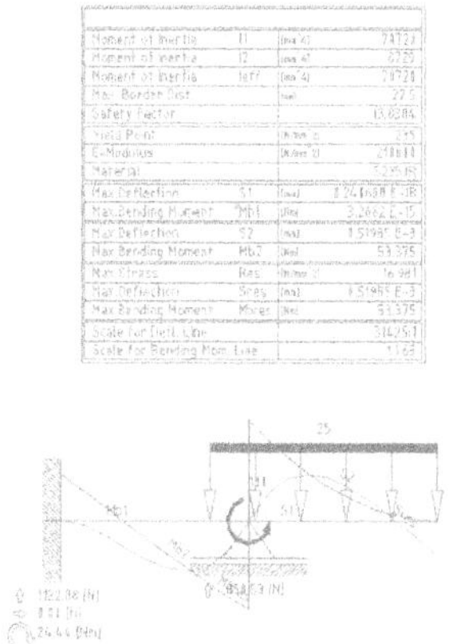

Access

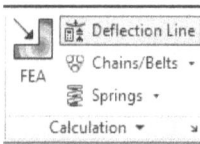

Command Line: AMDEFLINE

Ribbon: Content tab > Calculation panel > Deflection Line

Menu: Content > Calculations > Deflection Line

Beam Calculation Dialog Box

In the Beam Calculation dialog box, you can define supports, loads, materials, and types of graphics that are drawn. The Beam Calculation dialog box opens after selecting the moment of inertia table.

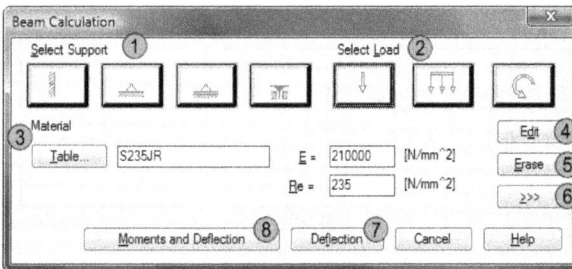

1. Select and insert the structure support type: cantilever, fixed, movable, or guided. After selecting the support type, you can select an insertion point along the beam.

2. Select from three icons for inserting different load forces. Point forces require an insertion point and a rotation angle. For distributed forces, you can enter an insertion point and an endpoint. For deflection moments, you can enter an insertion point. All three types of loads require a force value.

3. Click Table to open the Material dialog box, which contains the E-Modulus, Stretch Limit, Poisson constant, and Brittleness values. You can override values for material E-Modulus and the Stretch Limit (Re).

4. Use to edit the value of supports added to the calculation.

5. Use to erase supports or loads added to the calculation.

6. Select to activate the drawing window to enable you to pan or zoom the drawing while in the command.

7. Use to calculate and graphically represent the deflection line.

8. Use to include the bending moment line with your calculation and graphic results.

Performing Calculations

You can generate graphical results in the Beam Calculation dialog box by clicking Deflection or Moments and Deflection. The Select Graph dialog box opens.

You can draw three types of curves using the Direction of Main Axis 1, Direction of Main Axis 2, and Result checkboxes under Graph Draw In. Under Resolution of Resultant Curve, you can enter the number of segments to divide, or select the Automatically checkbox to have the value determined for you.

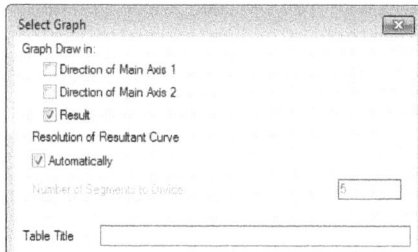

Editing a Deflection Line Calculation

When you double-click on a deflection line calculation, you must select the moment of inertia table to be used in the deflection line calculation. You can select an alternate table and keep all of the original supports and loads. The information is recalculated based on the moment of inertia. You can use this method to test different scenarios for a beam design.

Procedure: Calculating Deflection Lines

To calculate and insert deflection line tables and graphs based on an existing moment of inertia calculation, complete the following steps:

1. Use the **Moment of Inertia** command to calculate the cross section.

2. Start the **Deflection Line** command.

3. In the drawing window, select the Moment of Inertia table.

4. Click the start point of the beam.

5. Click the endpoint of the beam.

6. In the Beam Calculation dialog box, select a material. Place supports and loads.

7. Click Deflection or Moments and Deflection.

8. In the Select Graph dialog box, select which graphs to draw. Enter the table name.

9. Press ENTER twice to accept default scales.

10. In the drawing area, click to place the deflection line table.

Calculating Shaft Stresses

Shafts and axles are typically designed to rotate and transmit torque. Along with the forces of rotation to transmit torque, a shaft also carries and transmits forces from other parts, such as gears, bearings, and hubs. To calculate and identify the varying stresses within a shaft part design, you need to understand how to access and use the Shaft Calculation tool.

In the following illustration, during the process of calculating stresses for the shaft design, a profile of the shaft was automatically created so that the supports and forces could be applied and represented in the drawing.

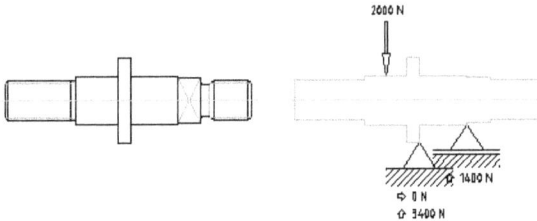

Shaft Calculations

Using the Shaft Calculation tool, after specifying the supports and forces required for your design, you can calculate results for the following calculations:

- Deflection line
- Bending moment
- Torsion moment
- Supporting force
- Torque rotation angle
- Equivalent tension
- Safety factors according to DIN 743 or to the ANSI standard.

After selecting which calculations to run, you can insert corresponding diagrams and a chart into the drawing that show the calculation results that you can then review.

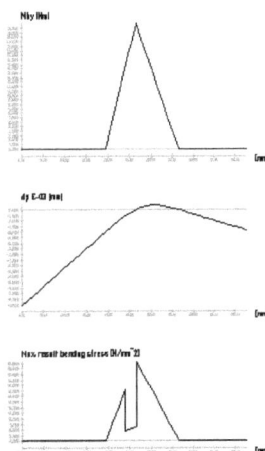

Calculated Values		
Yield Point	[N/mm^2]	235
E-Modulus	[N/mm^2]	210000
Material		S235JR
Max. Res. Deflection	[mm]	8.5851 E-03
at Position	[mm]	0
Max. Res. Bending Moment	[Nm]	28.0
at Position	[mm]	53.0
Max. Torsion Moment	[Nm]	0
at Position	[mm]	0
Max. Torque Rotation Angle	[deg]	0
at Position	[mm]	0
Max. Torsion stress	[N/mm^2]	0
at Position	[mm]	0
Max. axial stress	[N/mm^2]	0
at Position	[mm]	0
Max. result bending stress	[N/mm^2]	35.6507
at Position	[mm]	53.0
Max. Von Mises stress	[N/mm^2]	35.6507
at Position	[mm]	53.0
Maximal values of stresses are calculated without reflection of notches.		

Access

Command Line: AMSHAFTCALC

Ribbon: Content tab > expanded Calculation panel > Shaft Calculation

Menu: Content > Calculations > Shaft Calculation

Shaft Calculation Dialog Box

In the Shaft Calculation dialog box, you can indicate whether the selected object is a shaft or an axle. The calculation method changes according to the selection. You can determine whether a shaft rotates clockwise or counterclockwise. You can define shaft supports and loads and insert a gear load by using the last icon under Select Load. You can select material using Edit under Material. You can click Config to control calculation resolution in the Configuration dialog box.

By clicking Strength, you can modify notch geometry information, set minimum and maximum loads and stresses, and modify fatigue and yield factors for specific locations on the shaft. You can define notch geometry information by selecting from the following categories: Keys, Joints, Shaft, Notches, Undercuts, and Cross Holes.

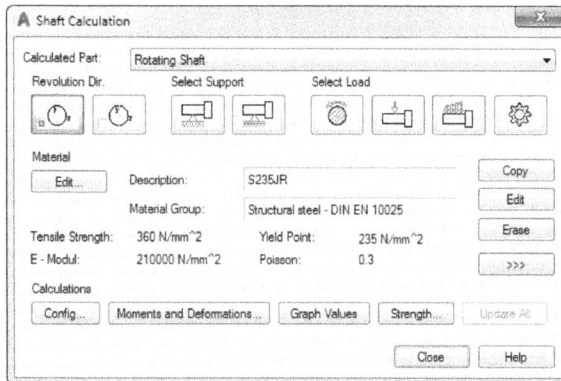

Procedure: Calculating Shafts

An overview of calculating the stresses in an existing shaft design based on loads and supports is shown in the following steps:

1. Start the **Shaft Calculation** command.

2. In the drawing area, select the shaft part.

3. In the drawing area, click to specify the position of the new shaft contour.

4. In the Shaft Calculation dialog box, from the Calculated Part list, select the shaft or axle type.

5. Define two or more supports.

6. Define the loads and the material.

7. Click Moments and Deformations. Select which graphs to draw.

8. In the drawing area, click to place the resulting table.

Calculating the Finite Element Analysis

You can use the FEA function to get an idea of the stress and deformation distributions. The information can be used to determine design changes to a cross section of a part. FEA can be used to help determine the material used to create the part, where to add materials to strengthen the part, and where to remove unnecessary materials to make the part lighter.

About FEA Calculations

You can calculate stress and deformation in a plane for plates with a given thickness using the FEA tool. You can also calculate stress and deformation on a cross section with individual forces and stretching loads that have fixed or movable supports. FEA is a powerful tool, but is not designed for solving all special FEA tasks.

For FEA calculation, you can select a closed cross section outline in which a number of internal outlines and contours can be found. The following preconditions are required:

- The contour has to be drawn before starting the FEA routine.
- The internal and external contours cannot touch one another.
- The contour or cross section has to create a closed surface.

If you modify the contour, a new FEA task has to be solved.

You can place an image and a chart for each of the results, read the results for the isolines and the isoareas in the table, and reference the color in the image. The colors of the result table make it easier for you to find the appropriate sections in the construction drawing. The highest stress is displayed in red. For some calculations, the red areas are within the acceptable stress range of the yield point. You must compare and evaluate the colors and their assigned numeric values to validate a design.

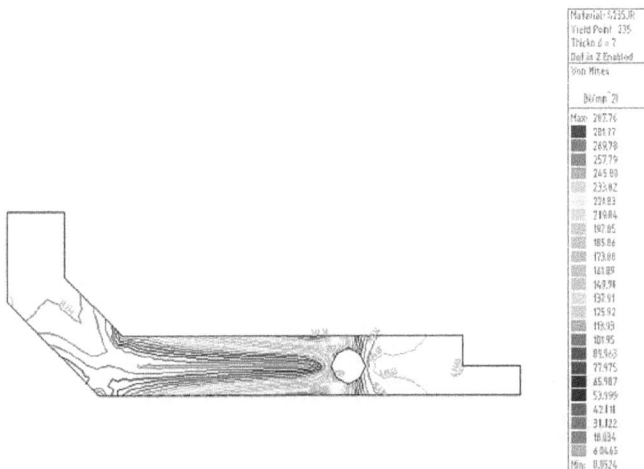

Access

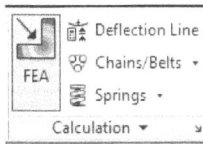

Command Line: AMFEA2D

Ribbon: Content tab > Calculation panel > FEA

Menu: Content > Calculations > FEA

FEA 2D - Calculation Dialog Box

You can use the FEA 2D - Calculation dialog box to define conditions for a cross section calculation. You can place load on a point or over an area and define supports at a point or over an area.

You can set supports to be fixed or movable. Loads and supports that expand over an area are placed counterclockwise from the first point. You can edit the values, angles, and locations of the loads and supports and select the material from the material table and add value overrides as required.

A default thickness is required. You can set whether stress is calculated in the Z direction. A default mesh is provided in the mesh box. Reducing the value improves accuracy but lengthens calculation time. You can refine the mesh to be more precise for a specified area and send the results to a file or place graphical results in the drawing area.

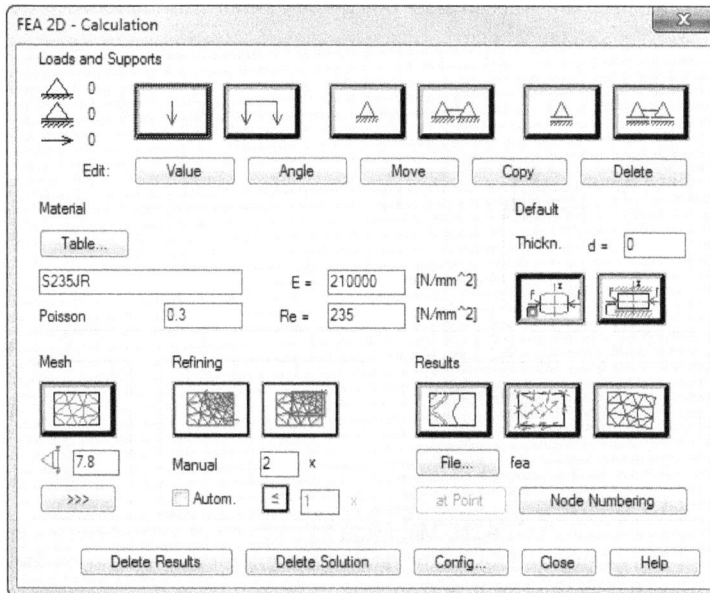

Calculation Result Types

In the FEA 2D - Calculation dialog box, under Results, you can select different ways of representing and communicating the calculated results.

Icon	Option	Description
	Isolines and Isoareas	Represents the internal stress and force using either colored lines or shaded areas. Opens the FEA 2D - Isolines (Isoareas) dialog box.
	Main Stress Lines	Shows the direction and force of stress at each node of the calculated mesh. The length, color, and arrow direction of the vectors indicate the stress and direction. Opens the FEA 2D - Main Stress dialog box.
	Deformed Mesh	Creates a mesh of the area that accentuates the part deforms due to the forces exerted on the part. Opens the FEA 2D - Displacements dialog box.

Isolines and Isoareas

In the FEA 2D - Isolines (Isoareas) dialog box, you can set the type of results that you want to have inserted in the drawing area. You can set the graphics representation to lines or areas. If you select lines for the graphic representation, you can click a precise point along the line to place a text note of the exact stress at a specified location. You can place one graphic in the drawing for each type of result.

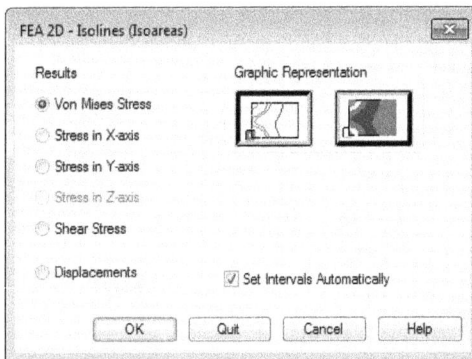

Main Stress Lines

You can set the node spacing ratio in the FEA 2D - Main Stress dialog box. Modifying the node spacing ratio affects the graphics. The graphics represent the ratio coefficient for the main stress lines. The stress is graphically represented by line length and angle.

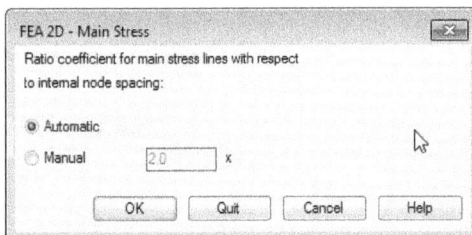

Deformed Mesh

You can place a graphical representation of the material displacement. The displacement is multiplied for visible representation.

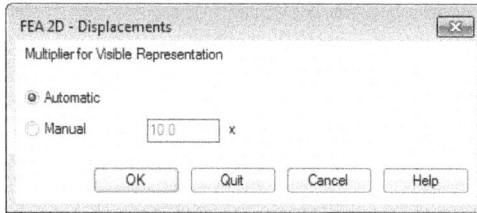

Procedure: Calculating FEA

An overview of how to conduct a finite element analysis on a 2D closed boundary and how to insert the graphical results is shown in the following steps:

1. Start the **FEA** command.

2. In the drawing window, click a point inside a closed boundary.

3. In the FEA 2D Calculations dialog box, add loads and supports.

4. Define material and thickness.

5. Set the mesh size. Refine the mesh in the areas if required.

6. Under Results, click the result type that you want to calculate.

7. Click the required results for the previously selected result type.

8. In the drawing window, position the results. Press ENTER to have the results positioned over the profile being analyzed, or click a base point and click an insertion point at a different location in the drawing.

9. In the drawing window, click a point to place the table.

10. Add additional calculation results as required.

Exercise: Calculate Moments of Inertia

In this exercise, you will calculate moments of inertia for several user-defined profiles and a predefined shape. The moment of inertia results are displayed in value tables with all of the required calculation information. You will later use the calculations to analyze the deflection and bending moment for the different beam design options.

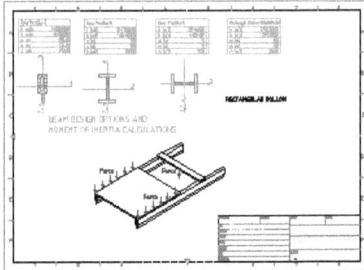

The completed exercise

1. Open the file *Moment of Inertia.dwg*.

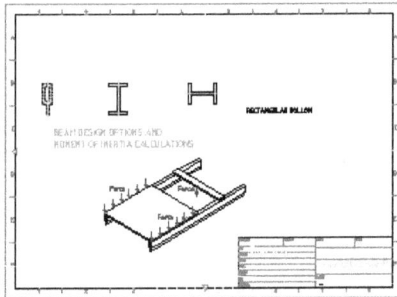

2. Zoom in to the top left section.

3. To begin calculating the moment of inertia for this cross section, do the following:
   - Click Content tab > expanded Calculation panel > Moment of Inertia.
   - In the drawing area, click within the hatch area of the section.
   - Press ENTER.
   - When prompted about the correctly filled area, press ENTER.

4. To set the direction of load forces as -90, in the drawing window, object snap to the bottom endpoint of the vertical line, as shown in the following illustration.

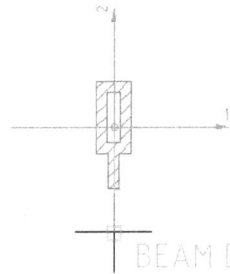

5. To title and insert the table, do the following:
   - For description, **User Profile-1**. Press ENTER.
   - In the drawing window, click to place the table above the section view.

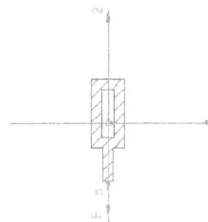

   - Note that the color of the table has been changed for printing clarity.

---

6. To begin calculating the moment of inertia for the middle cross section view, follow the same process as the first cross section, but click on an interior point in all three areas of the section view to create a filled area as shown in the following illustration.

7. For the force direction, description, and table location, do the following:

- Click a point to define the direction of the force as -90.
- For the description, enter **User Profile-2**.
- In the drawing window, click to place the table above the section view.

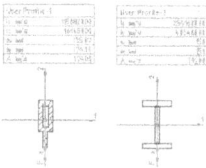

8. Calculate the moment of inertia for the third cross section as follows:

- Click an interior point in all three areas of the section view.
- Click a point to define the direction of the force as -90.
- For the description, enter **User Profile-3**.
- Place the table above the section view.

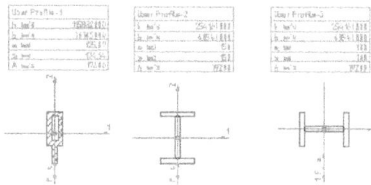

9. To begin calculating the moment of inertia of a predefined rectangular tube cross section, do the following:

- Click Content tab > expanded Calculation panel > Predefined Profile Sections.
- In the Predefined Profile Sections dialog box, click the second rectangular tube (with the c-channel).
- Click OK.

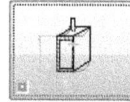

10. For the dimensions of the profile section, use the following values:

- For X-Length, enter **100**.
- For Y-Height, enter **300**.
- For Thickness, enter **30**.

11. For the table insertion point, click to the right and in alignment with the three other tables.

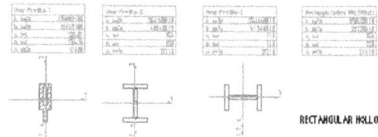

12. Save and close all of the files.

Exercise: Calculate the Deflection Line

In this exercise, you will calculate for beam deflection to determine the properties for different beam designs. You will determine beam deflection for the design and place tables into the drawing area that show the calculated values.

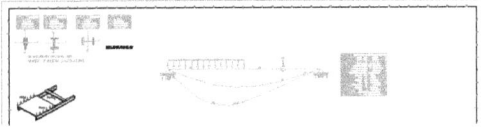

The completed exercise

1. Open *Beam Deflection.dwg*.

2. To begin calculating the deflection line for the moment of inertia block User Profile-1, do the following:

   - Click Content tab > Calculation panel > Deflection Line.
   - In the drawing window, click the moment of inertia block (table) titled User Profile-1.

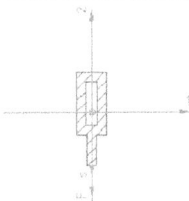

3. To specify the start points and endpoints of the beam, object snap to the endpoints of the top horizontal line as shown in the following illustration.

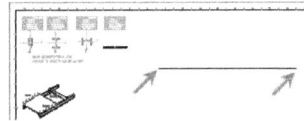

4. To insert a fixed support at the left endpoint, do the following:

   - In the Beam Calculation dialog box, under Select Support, click (Fixed Support) (Second icon).
   - In the drawing window, object snap to the left endpoint of the line.

5. To insert a moveable support at the right endpoint, do the following:

   - In the Beam Calculation dialog box, under Select Support, click (Movable Support) (Third icon).
   - In the drawing window, object snap to the right endpoint of the line.

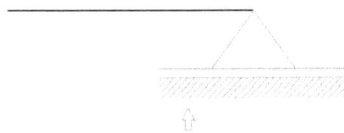

6. To insert a distributed force from the left endpoint to the middle of the beam, do the following:

- In the Beam Calculation dialog box, under Select Load, click ⊡ (Distributed Force).
- In the drawing window, object snap to the left endpoint and then to the midpoint of the horizontal line.
- For the line load, enter **40**.

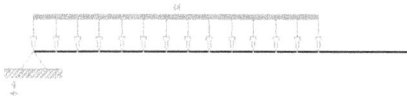

7. To insert a point load to the left of the right endpoint, do the following:

- In the Beam Calculation dialog box, under Select Load, click ⊡ (Point Force).
- In the drawing window, object track from the right endpoint to the left, a distance of 1000.
- For the rotation angle, press ENTER.
- For the force, enter **1000**.

8. To insert a deflection moment at the same location as the single force, do the following:

- In the Beam Calculation dialog box, under Select Load, click ⊡ (Deflection Moment).
- In the drawing window, object snap to the endpoint of the single force arrow point.
- For the bending moment, enter **10**.

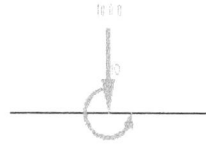

9. In the Beam Calculation dialog box, click Moments and Deflection.

10. In the Select Graph dialog box, do the following:

- Select all of the checkbox options.
- For the table title, enter **Original Beam**.
- Click OK.

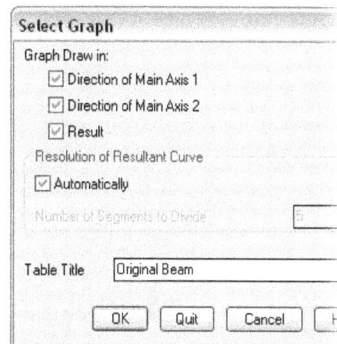

11. To specify the scale and insert the table, do the following:

- Press ENTER twice to accept the default scale values for the bending moment line and deflection.
- In the drawing window, click to place the table on the right side of the graph as shown in the following illustration.

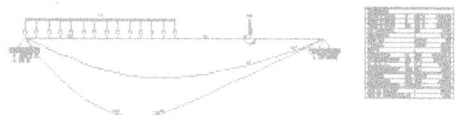

12. Save and close all of the files.

Exercise: Calculate Shaft Strength

In this exercise, you will calculate the expected deformation of a mechanical shaft and set it up to be printed on a drawing sheet.

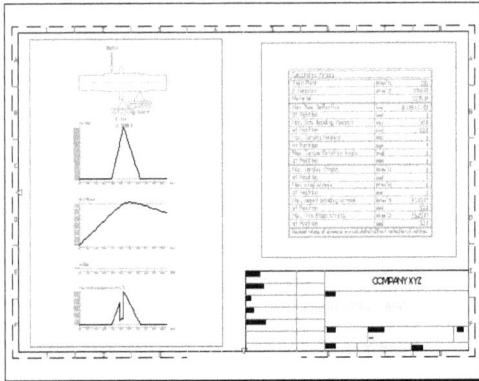

The completed exercise

1. Open *Shaft Calculation.dwg*.

2. Click Content tab > expanded Calculation panel > Shaft Calculation.

3. To begin calculating the shaft deformation for the existing shaft, do the following:

   ▪ In the drawing window, click the centerline in the side view of the shaft.

   ▪ Click to position the outer contour of the shaft below the original shaft.

4. To insert a fixed support, do the following:

   ▪ In the Shaft Calculation dialog box, under Select Support, click Fixed Support.

   ▪ In the drawing window, object snap to the right endpoint of the bottom portion of the outer contour to place the support as shown in the following illustration.

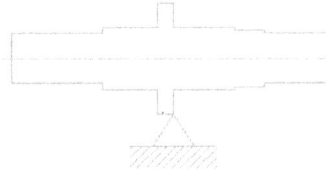

5. To insert a movable support, do the following:

   ▪ In the Shaft Calculation dialog box, under Select Support, click Movable Support.

   ▪ In the drawing window, object snap to another endpoint of the outer contour to place the support as shown in the following illustration.

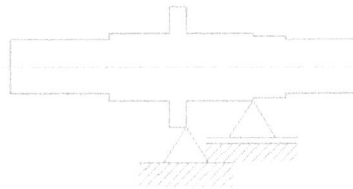

6. To add a single point load, do the following:

- In the Shaft Calculation dialog box, under Select Load, click Point Load.
- In the drawing window, object snap to the midpoint of the shaft segment as shown in the following illustration.
- For the rotation angle, press ENTER.

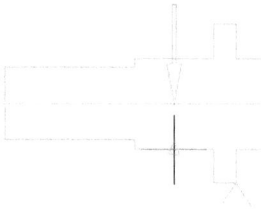

7. In the Point Load dialog box, do the following:

- Click the *Resultant* tab.
- In the Point Load field, enter **2000**.
- Click OK.

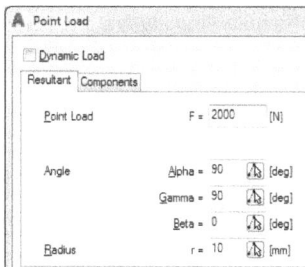

8. In the Shaft Calculation dialog box, click Moments and Deformations.

9. In the Select Graph dialog box, do the following:

- Click the *Torsion* tab.
- Clear the Torsion Moment in X - Direction checkbox.
- Click OK.

10. To insert the table and complete the shaft calculation, do the following:

- In the drawing window, click to place the table to the right of the outer contour of the shaft.
- In the Shaft Calculation dialog box, click Close.

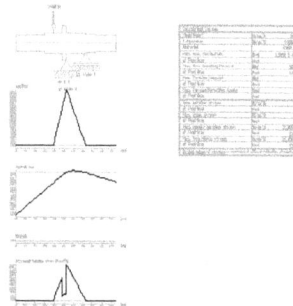

11. Below the Command Line, in the Layout tabs, click Calculations to switch to the Calculations layout.

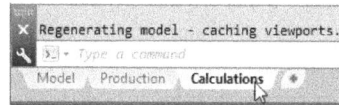

12. Grip edit the viewports to crop the model space geometry to only show the graphs and calculation table. Activate the viewport for the graphs and change the zoom magnification to view all of the graph information if required.

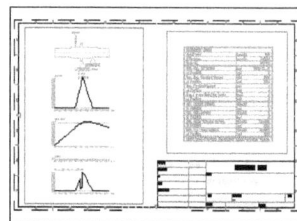

13. Save and close all of the files.

Exercise: Calculate FEA Stresses

In this exercise, you will learn how to optimize the stability and durability of a pedal using the FEA calculation. You will test for high stress areas, main stresses, and estimated deformation of a design and determine whether the part is expected to work or fail under certain conditions. You will save this information as a text file so that it can be studied and permanently record design validation.

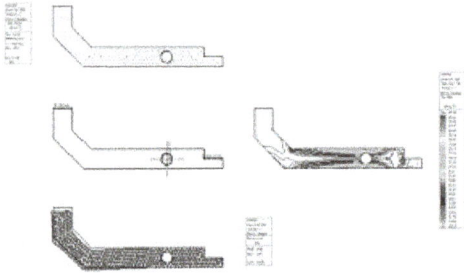

The completed exercise

1. Open *FEA.dwg*.

2. Open the Options dialog box, in the *AM:Standards* tab, verify that the DIN and ANSI standards are currently loaded. If not, add them before continuing with the exercise.

3. To begin analyzing the side view of the pedal, do the following:

   - Click Content tab > Calculation panel > FEA.
   - In the drawing window, click a point inside the contour.

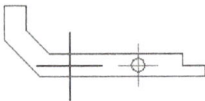

4. To change the scale factor for symbols, do the following:

   - In the FEA 2D - Calculation dialog box, click Config.
   - In the FEA Configuration dialog box > Scale Factor for Symbols field, enter **0.1**.
   - In the FEA Configuration dialog box, click OK.

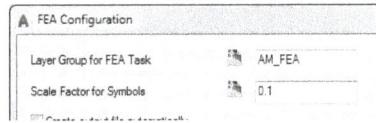

5. To begin inserting a movable line support to the hole, in the FEA 2D - Calculation dialog box, under Loads and Supports, click (Movable Line Support) (the rightmost icon).

6. In the drawing window, select the circle as shown in the following illustration. Press ENTER.

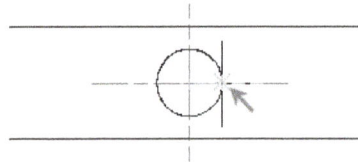

7. To add another movable line support to the top edge of the notch, do the following:

   - In the FEA 2D - Calculation dialog box, under Loads and Supports, click (Movable Line Support).
   - In the drawing window, object snap to the identified endpoints.
   - For the side from endpoint, click a point above the line.

8. To begin adding a line force to the left side of the part, in the FEA 2D - Calculation dialog box, under Loads and Supports, click (Line Force).

9. To specify the force location and value, do the following:

- In the drawing window, object snap to the identified endpoints.
- For the side from endpoint, click a point above the line.
- For the force value, enter **70**.

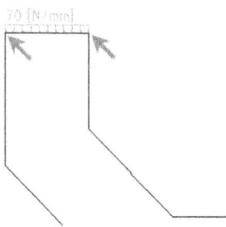

10. To specify a different material by selecting it from the table of standard materials, do the following:

- In the FEA 2D - Calculation dialog box, under Material, click Table.
- In the Select Standard for Material dialog box, click ANSI Material.
- In the Select Material Type dialog box, select **Steel SAE 1025**. Click OK.

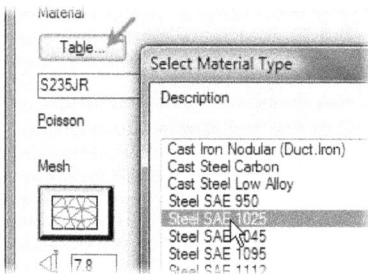

11. To set the material thickness, in the FEA 2D - Calculation dialog box, under Default, in the *Thickn. d=* field, enter **7**.

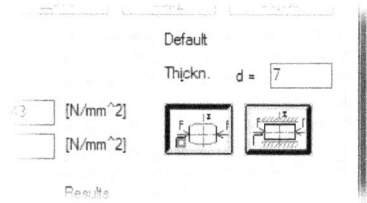

12. To calculate and display the mesh for the part, do the following:

- In the FEA 2D - Calculation dialog box, under Mesh, click Mesh.
- Press ENTER.

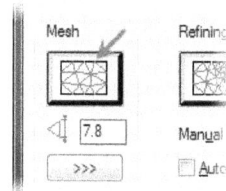

13. To have the mesh calculated with smaller triangle side lengths, do the following:

- In the FEA 2D - Calculation dialog box, under Mesh, enter **5**.
- Click Mesh.
- Press ENTER.

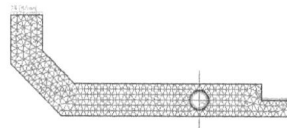

14. To begin inserting the calculated results, do the following:

- In the FEA 2D - Calculation dialog box, under Results, click (Isolines and Isoareas).
- In the FEA 2D - Isolines (Isoareas) dialog box, click OK to accept Von Mises Stress.

15. To position the calculated results and the table in the drawing, do the following:

- In the drawing window, click a point toward the lower left corner of the part.
- Click to place the isoline results to the right of the part.
- Click to place the table to the right of the isoline results.

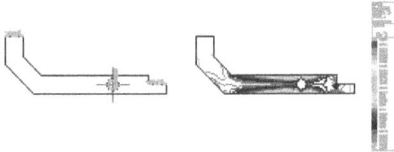

16. To add isoline description labels, do the following:

- Zoom in to the area around the hole of the isoline results.
- Click some of the isolines to attach value labels.
- Press ENTER.

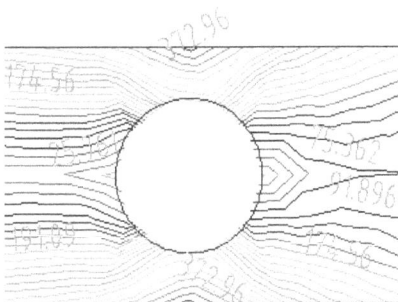

17. To add calculation results showing the main stresses, do the following:

- In the FEA 2D - Calculation dialog box, under Results, click (Main Stress Lines).
- In the FEA 2D - Main Stress dialog box, click OK.

18. To position the calculated results and the table in the drawing, do the following:

- In the drawing window, click a point toward the lower left corner of the part.
- Click to place the main stress results above the part.
- Click to place the table to the left of the main stress results.
- Press ENTER.

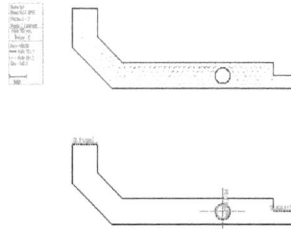

19. To add calculation results showing the displacement, do the following:

- In the FEA 2D - Calculation dialog box, under Results, click (Displacements).
- In the FEA 2D - Displacements dialog box, click OK.

20. To position the calculated results and the table in the drawing, do the following:

- In the drawing window, click a point toward the lower left corner of the part.
- Click to place the displacement results below the part.
- Click to place the table to the right of the displacement results.

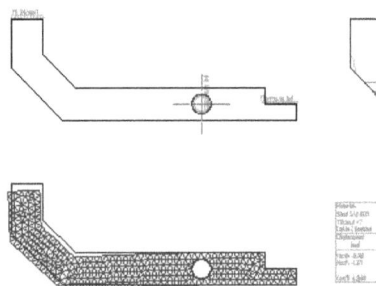

21. Press ENTER to return to the FEA 2D - Calculation dialog box. Click Close to complete the creation of the analysis.

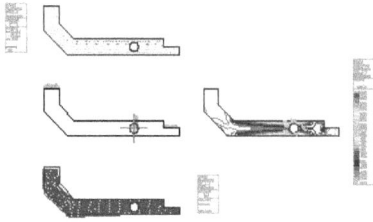

22. Save and close all of the files.

Chapter Summary

In this chapter, you learned to perform calculations to validate designs. You also learned to calculate beam deflection designs using the Moment of Inertia and Deflection Line commands. Finally, you learned to analyze shafts and perform a finite element analysis (FEA).

Having completed this chapter, you can:

- Perform design calculations to validate designs.

Leveraging Your Existing Data

In this chapter, you learn how design data can be exchanged to and from the AutoCAD®
Mechanical software. You learn how to identify Mechanical DWG files and exchange data in the
form of IGES files. You also learn to create 2D associated Model Documentation drawing views in
an AutoCAD Mechanical drawing file of external Autodesk® Inventor® 3D models.

Objectives

After completing this chapter, you will be able to:

- Identify Mechanical DWG files and state how Mechanical DWG files can be used by someone
  using only the AutoCAD software.
- Import and export IGES files.
- Use Inventor Link to create and document Autodesk Inventor software models.

Lesson: DWG Files

Overview

This lesson describes the use of Mechanical DWG files in the AutoCAD® software, and removing AutoCAD Mechanical software objects from drawings.

When you work in an environment in which AutoCAD software and AutoCAD Mechanical DWG files are created, you might need to deliver your designs to other users as AutoCAD software geometry only. You need to know how to manipulate your AutoCAD Mechanical software drawings to keep the information while delivering the required file.

In the following illustration, the same Mechanical drawing content is shown open in the AutoCAD software. On the left, the rollover tooltip lists the identified object as a proxy entity. On the right, the Mechanical drawing was saved as a Mechanical software drawing file or AutoCAD software drawing file to have the object list as a block reference.

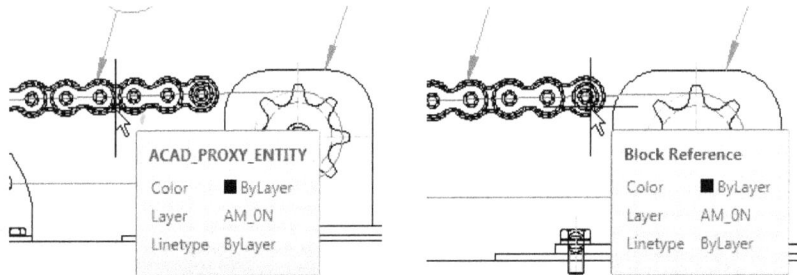

Objectives

After completing this lesson, you will be able to:

- Explain how Mechanical files are handled when opened in the standard AutoCAD software.
- Remove Mechanical object definitions and structure from a DWG file while keeping the geometry in the drawing.

Mechanical Drawing Files in AutoCAD

It might be necessary to exchange AutoCAD Mechanical software drawings with other users using the AutoCAD software. Since the AutoCAD software does not contain the tools found in the AutoCAD Mechanical software, you cannot edit AutoCAD Mechanical software objects as you would in the AutoCAD Mechanical software. However, you can edit these drawings in the AutoCAD software and preserve the AutoCAD Mechanical software objects.

In the following illustration, an AutoCAD Mechanical software drawing with mechanical standard parts was opened in the AutoCAD software. The rollover tooltip lists the mechanical chain as an ACAD_PROXY_ENTITY.

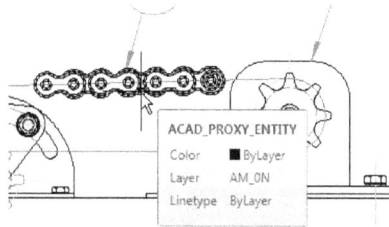

Mechanical Proxy Objects in AutoCAD

As you create a mechanical design using the AutoCAD Mechanical software tools, some of the created geometry might be unique objects specific to the AutoCAD Mechanical software. When someone with the standard AutoCAD software opens an AutoCAD Mechanical software drawing, it is important that they also see the unique mechanical objects.

To have custom objects display in a drawing opened in the standard AutoCAD software, the custom objects display as proxy objects. This means the graphics of those objects are displayed although the AutoCAD software does not contain the tools to create or edit those objects. The objects are just visible in the drawing window.

The AutoCAD Mechanical software is identified by the AutoCAD software as an acceptable creator of proxy objects. Therefore, when a drawing file with recognized AutoCAD Mechanical software file properties is selected to be opened, the drawing automatically opens without prompting you about the existence of any proxy objects that might be in the drawing file.

An AutoCAD Mechanical software drawing opened in the AutoCAD software can have additional geometry added to the drawing and nonproxy objects, such as text that can be edited. To correctly edit Mechanical-specific objects, the drawing should be opened in the AutoCAD Mechanical software so that the correct tools can be used.

Drawing files that contain custom objects created by third-party applications are not identified as acceptable creators of proxy objects. In these cases, a dialog box opens prompting you that the drawing contains custom objects. You can control the automatic notification in the AutoCAD software's Options. Note that because the AutoCAD Mechanical software is identified as an acceptable creator of proxy objects, notification does not occur regardless of the settings that might be set for proxy information on the Open and Save tab in the Options dialog box

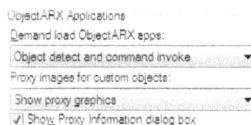

Structured Geometry in AutoCAD

Proxy objects only display in the AutoCAD software for custom Mechanical objects in the drawing. If the drawing uses Mechanical structure, the lines, arcs, and circles that are in a structure definition are not identified in the AutoCAD software as being part of a structured definition.

When you modify the geometry associated with a structure definition in the AutoCAD software, those modifications are lost when you open the drawing in the AutoCAD Mechanical software. The changes are lost because the AutoCAD Mechanical software reverts the geometry back to match how it is defined within the Mechanical definition. When you open a mechanically structured drawing that was last saved outside the AutoCAD Mechanical software, a dialog box opens prompting you that all of the mechanical structured objects are going to revert to their previously defined states. In this dialog box you can select options to continue opening the drawing or to discontinue the open.

While changes in the AutoCAD software to geometry associated to a structure definition revert back to what is defined in the definition when it is opened in the AutoCAD Mechanical software, any geometry you add to the drawing and any changes made to nonstructured geometry are maintained.

Removing Mechanical Objects & Structure from the DWG File

If you need to remove structure from a drawing to enable other users to edit the drawing using the AutoCAD Mechanical software or need to remove all of the mechanical objects to edit the file using only the AutoCAD software, you need to know the process of removing the objects from a drawing.

In the following illustration, a drawing in which mechanical standard parts are defined as structured parts has been saved as a Mechanical software drawing file. When opened in the AutoCAD software, the standard parts that were Mechanical structure definitions are now defined as block references. The rollover tooltip lists the sprocket part as a block reference.

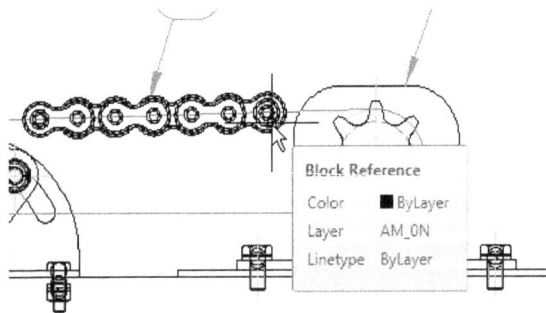

Removing Mechanical Objects and Structure

There are two primary workflows that you can follow to remove mechanical objects or structure from a drawing file. The workflow you use depends on what you are trying to achieve and how you are going to work with the resulting data. One workflow enables you to remove structure definitions while preserving mechanical symbols. The other workflow enables you to remove all of the mechanical objects, symbols, and structure definitions.

If you have a drawing that contains Mechanical structure definitions and do not want it to contain structure definitions, you can save the drawing as an AutoCAD Mechanical software drawing using Save As. After you save the drawing, you need to close and reopen the saved drawing to reload the newly created objects in the drawing. When you save a structured drawing in a Mechanical software file format, the geometry within the drawing is maintained but the structure definitions are removed. Any mechanical standard parts that were defined as structured parts are then defined within a block definition. All mechanical symbols are maintained as mechanical symbol objects unless the standard for a symbol is not supported in the AutoCAD Mechanical software. If a symbol standard is not supported in the AutoCAD Mechanical software, the symbol is converted to a block definition.

If you need to deliver a drawing that does not contain any structure definitions or mechanical symbols, you can save it as an AutoCAD <version> software drawing file using Save As. All of the standard parts and mechanical symbols in the new drawing are converted to block definitions. If the drawing contained structure definitions, all of the definitions are removed while their geometry is maintained in the drawing.

Removing Structure from AutoCAD Mechanical Drawings

An overview of removing mechanical structure definitions from an AutoCAD Mechanical software drawing is shown in the following steps:

1. Open the drawing file in the AutoCAD Mechanical software.

2. Click Application menu > Save As.

3. In the Save Drawing As dialog box:
   - In the Files of Type list, select AutoCAD Mechanical 6 Drawing.
   - Enter a name for the new drawing file, and then click Save.

4. Close the currently open drawing without saving.

5. Open the newly saved drawing.

Removing AutoCAD Mechanical Objects from Drawings

An overview of creating a new drawing from which all of the AutoCAD Mechanical software objects have been removed is shown in the following steps:

1. Open the drawing file that contains Mechanical objects in the AutoCAD Mechanical software.

2. Click Application menu > Save As.

3. In the Save Drawing As dialog box:
   - In the Files of Type list, select AutoCAD <version> Drawing.
   - Enter a name for the new drawing file.
   - Click Save.

4. Close the current open drawing without saving.

5. In the AutoCAD software, open the newly saved drawing.

Exercise: Remove Mechanical Content from a Drawing

In this exercise, you will remove Mechanical content from a drawing. You will save a drawing to remove its Mechanical structure definitions and save another drawing to remove the custom mechanical symbol from the drawing.

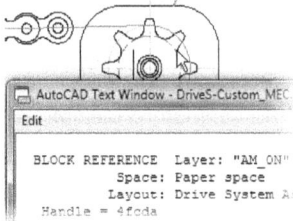

The completed exercise

Remove Mechanical Structure

In this section of the exercise, you will review the types of objects in a drawing and then save the drawing to convert Mechanical structure definitions to standard AutoCAD software block definitions while maintaining the design information and other mechanical objects.

1. In the AutoCAD software, open *DriveS-Custom.dwg*.

2. To review the Mechanical objects in the AutoCAD software:

   - Hover the cursor over the gear as shown in the following illustration.
   - Note the ACAD_PROXY_ENTITY notice.

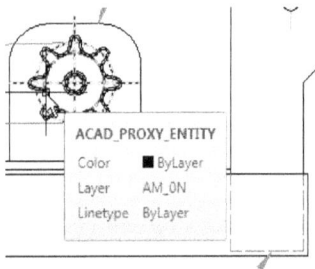

3. Hover the cursor over the weld symbol to review its object properties. Note that the AutoCAD software also identifies the weld symbol object as a proxy object.

4. Close *DriveS-Custom.dwg*.

5. In the AutoCAD Mechanical software, open *DriveS-Custom.dwg*. To set Structure as the current workspace, do the following:

   - In the Status Bar > Workspace Switching, select Structure.

6. To review the structure definitions in the drawing:

   - If the Structure Catalog palette is not displayed, click Structure tab > Tools panel > Structure Catalog.
   - In the Structure Catalog palette, in the *Current Drawing* tab, in the Mechanical Structure pane, review the list of definitions.

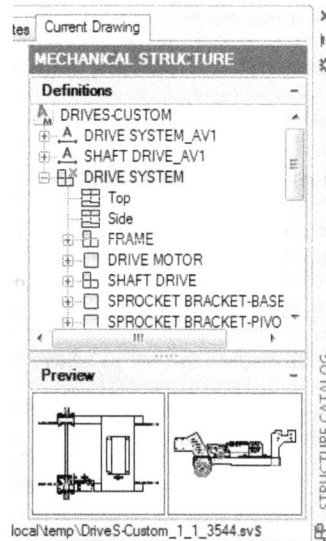

7. To create a new drawing file of this design from which the structured data has been removed:

   - Click Application menu > Save As.
   - In the Save Drawing As dialog box, for Files of type, select AutoCAD Mechanical 6 Drawing.
   - For the File name, enter **DriveS-Custom_ MECH6.dwg**.
   - Click Save.

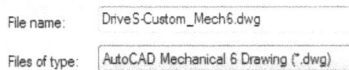

File name:	DriveS-Custom_Mech6.dwg
Files of type:	AutoCAD Mechanical 6 Drawing (*.dwg)

8. Close the newly saved drawing.

9. Open *DriveS-Custom_MECH6.dwg*.

10. In the Structure Catalog, review the lack of structure definitions, indicating that the new drawing does not contain structured content.

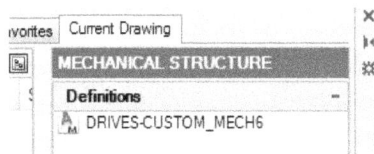

11. Select and right-click on the gear symbol and then select Quick Properties in the shortcut menu. Note that it is listed as a Block Reference object. Open the Quick Properties for the hex bolt symbol and note that it is a Content Library Item.

Remove Mechanical Objects

In this section of the exercise, you will convert all of the AutoCAD Mechanical software objects to standard AutoCAD software block definitions.

1. In the AutoCAD Mechanical software, open *DriveS-Custom.dwg*.

2. To create a new drawing file of this design in which all of the AutoCAD Mechanical software objects have been converted to block references:

   - Click Application menu > Save As.
   - In the Save Drawing As dialog box, for Files of Type, select AutoCAD *<latest version>* Drawing.
   - For the File name, enter **DriveS-Custom_ ACAD.dwg**.
   - Click Save.

3. Close the newly saved drawing.

4. Open *DriveS-Custom_ACAD.dwg*.

5. Review the current setting for the Structure Catalog information for the current drawing.

6. Open the Quick Properties for the gear and hex bolt symbol. Note that both of them list as Block Reference objects.

7. Save and close all of the drawings.

Lesson: IGES Files

Overview

This lesson describes the exchange of data between CAD systems in the form of IGES files.

Because the CAD data you create might need to be opened by other users in different CAD systems or some of the data required in your AutoCAD Mechanical software designs might not be native AutoCAD software geometry, you must learn the options and capabilities of getting different data to other users and into your drawings using the IGES file format.

Objectives

After completing this lesson, you will be able to:

- Identify how IGES files are imported.
- Identify how IGES files are exported.
- Import and export IGES data.

IGES In

You can import IGES data to use design data created in different CAD software. To successfully import an IGES file and use its contents, you need to learn which command to use and how to access the import options. When you import IGES data, it is inserted into the active drawing file. By importing into a new empty drawing (rather than into the drawing containing your design), you can review the data and select the geometry that is required for your design. The command opens the IGESIN translation dialog box to import the drawing.

Access

Command Line: IGESIN

Ribbon: Insert tab > Import panel > IGES

Menu: Insert > External File > IGES

IGES Out

You can translate your design geometry to the neutral IGES format so that users of different CAD software can use the geometry. To create an IGES file of only the design data that you want to export, you need to know which command to use and how to access the export options. When you export your drawing to a neutral IGES file, you export all of the displayed geometry in the model space and layouts, and the configured information in the active drawing file. To only export a portion of the drawing, you can either:

- Freeze the layers that you do not want to export, or
- Copy the geometry that you want to export into a new drawing file, and then export that data from the new file.

The command opens the IGESOUT translation dialog box to expert the drawing as an IGES format.

Access

Command Line: IGESOUT

Ribbon: N/A

Menu: File > Export > IGES

Application Menu: Export > IGES

Lesson: Model Documentation

Overview

This lesson describes Model Documentation and the use of drawing views in an AutoCAD Mechanical software drawing file.

Model Documentation can be used as part of your company's workflow for creating and documenting designs or used to document a design that you received from another user. As a vendor, you might receive Autodesk® Inventor® software part or assembly files from which you need to create drawing views for quoting purposes. Model Documentation enables you to do that.

In the following illustration, an Autodesk Inventor 3D part model was documented in the AutoCAD Mechanical software.

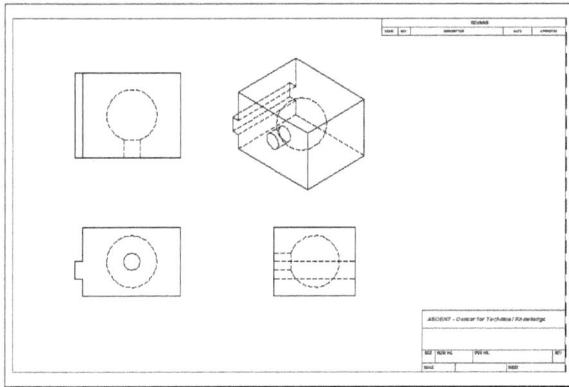

Objectives

After completing this lesson, you will be able to:

- Explain the purpose of Model Documentation.
- Describe how to use Model Documentation to create associative 2D drawing views in the AutoCAD Mechanical software of Autodesk Inventor software 3D models.
- Describe the process for creating projected drawing views from a base view.
- Edit drawing views.

About Model Documentation

If you receive Autodesk Inventor software models and want to create drawing views of them and annotate those views in the AutoCAD Mechanical software, you need to learn about Model Documentation.

In the following illustration, a dimension and hole note have been added to a drawing view created from an associated Autodesk Inventor software model. Because this information comes from the model, if the Autodesk Inventor software model is changed, this information can automatically update.

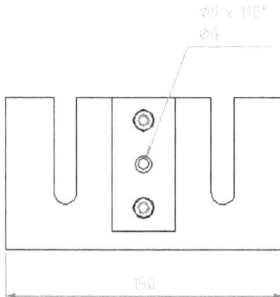

Definition of Model Documentation

Model Documentation enables you to associate the 3D models in an Autodesk Inventor software assembly or part file to an AutoCAD Mechanical software drawing file. This association can be established using the AutoCAD Mechanical software and does not require an Autodesk Inventor software license. This association is made by first creating a base view of the Autodesk Inventor 3D model, in the AutoCAD Mechanical drawing file. You can then use other tools in the AutoCAD Mechanical software to create additional drawing views in the layout based on the base view.

Because the relationship between the Autodesk Inventor software file and the AutoCAD Mechanical software file is a link, the AutoCAD Mechanical software file drawing views can be updated when a change is made in the Autodesk Inventor software part or assembly file. A notification displays indicating that an associated model has changed and that drawing views are no longer up to date. Selecting the option in the notification bubble to update the drawing views, will update the drawing views and its annotation.

Using Model Documentation

When you use Model Documentation, you first create a base view of the Autodesk Inventor 3D model in the layout of an AutoCAD Mechanical drawing file. You can then create additional drawing views which are the projected views, created by projecting orthographic and isometric views from the initial base view. You can use the annotation tools to dimension and annotate the views. When a change occurs in the Autodesk Inventor software model file, a balloon notification displays to prompt you that the model has changed and the drawing views are no longer up to date. You can then select to have the drawing views updated.

Base View

To create drawing views in an AutoCAD Mechanical drawing, switch to a layout tab in Paper Space. The first drawing view must always be a Base view. Additional views can be added or modified as required. To create the base view, start the Base View from an Autodesk Inventor command and select the Autodesk Inventor model you want to associate.

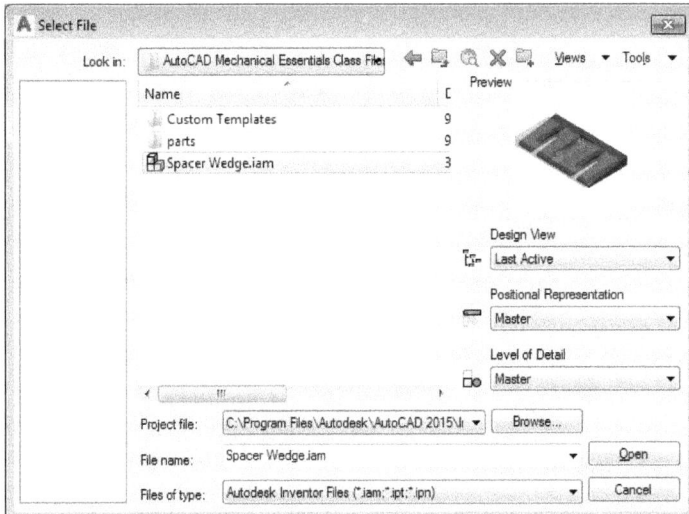

Once the model has been selected, a scaled preview of the model is attached to the cursor, where you can move the cursor to the required location and click on the Paper Space to place the Base view.

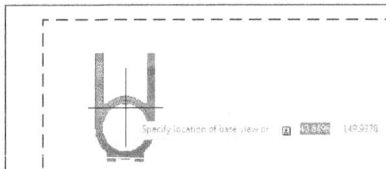

Once the model has been selected, the Drawing View Creation contextual tab displays in the Ribbon. Before you select its location on the layout, you can adjust its orientation and appearance, including its scale along with other options and settings.

- **Orientation -** Sets the base view orientation: Top, Bottom, Left, Right, Front, Back, or one of four Isometric views. The preview updates based on the selected orientation.

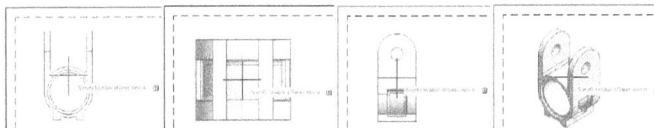

- **Type (at Command Prompt only) -** Controls whether to place the Base view only, or enables you to place and create projected views immediately after placing the Base view.

Other settings include Scale, View Style, and Object Visibility, and Autodesk Inventor Representation. There are also options to move the Base view prior to creating it.

After you select a location for the Base view, press <Enter> to continue, or you can click (OK) on the Create panel.

Access

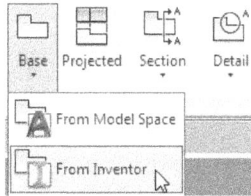

Command Line: VIEWBASE

Ribbon: Layout tab > Create View panel > Base View drop-down list > Base View From Inventor

Process: Adding a Base View from Autodesk Inventor

An overview of using Model Documentation to add a base view in the AutoCAD Mechanical software of Autodesk Inventor software parts or assemblies is shown in the following steps:

1. Have an Autodesk Inventor 3D model created and ready.

2. In Paper Space, switch to the Layout tab.

3. In the Layout tab > Create View panel > Base View drop-down list, click From Inventor.

4. Select the Autodesk Inventor 3D model.

5. Make any Orientation or Appearance modifications.

6. Click on a location in Paper Space to place the Base view.

7. Press ENTER to complete the command and continue.

Projected View

A Projected view is created by projecting off of a Base view in one of eight possible directions: four orthographic and four isometric.

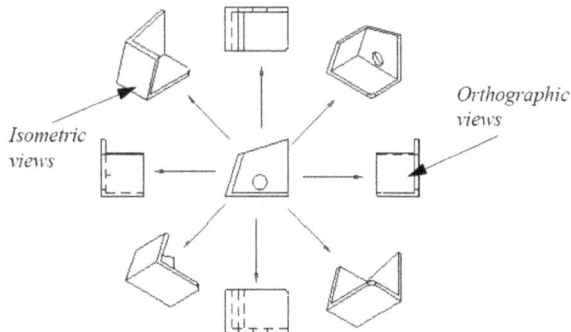

The orthographic views are the top, bottom, and side views. These views align with the Base view and are dependent on that view. The isometric views are the diagonal views. These views are not dependent on the location of the Base view. Projected views are drawn using the Base view's projection angle (first angle or third angle).

There are two ways to place a Projected view: continue and automatically place it after placing a Base view, or at any later time through the **Projected View** command.

To place a Projected view, start the **Projected View** command and select a parent view to project around. Then drag the cursor to the required location around the parent view, and when the preview is acceptable, click at the location. Continue to place additional Projected views as required. Press ENTER when done. You can add more views later.

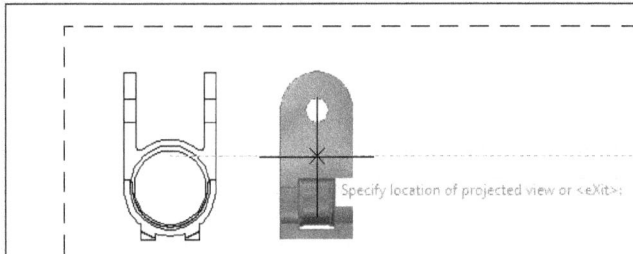

When the command is complete, the views take their final form based on the appearance settings.

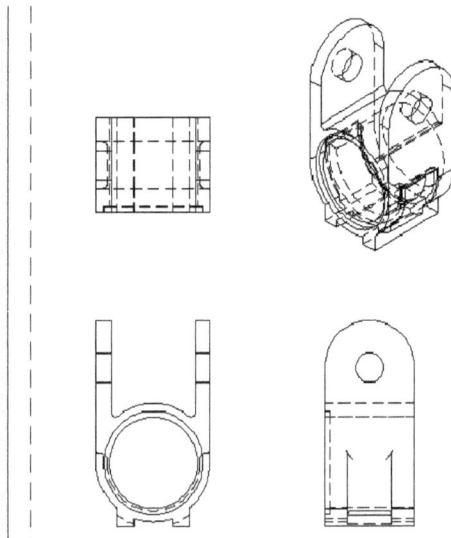

During the creation of projected views, a parent/child relationship is formed between the selected view and the projected views. If, when placing a Base view, its Type is set to Base and Projected, you can immediately place Projected views after the Base view is placed.

Each view created is a new Drawing View object. This object includes a non-printing boundary similar to a viewport and its properties can be modified in the Properties palette.

There are also commands to create various styles of Section Views or Detail Views, projected from any other existing drawing view.

Access

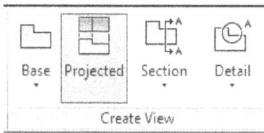

Command Line: VIEWPROJ

Ribbon: Layout tab > Create View panel > Projected View

Process: Adding a Projected View

An overview of adding a projected view from an existing drawing view is shown in the following steps:

1. Place a drawing view in Paper Space.

2. In the *Layout* tab > Create View panel, click Projected View.

3. Select a parent view to project off of.

4. Specify location of the projected view around the parent view.

5. Add as many projected views as required.

6. Press ENTER to complete the command and continue.

Editing Drawing Views

There are several ways to edit Drawing views. Selecting a view displays a single square multifunctional grip at its center, and a Scale drop-down list arrow grip next to it. You can click and drag the square grip to move the Drawing view. You can click on the Scale drop-down list arrow grip and select a different scale for the drawing view.

Double-clicking on a Drawing view (or selecting the **Edit View** command on the *Drawing View* contextual tab that displays when you select a Drawing view), displays the *Drawing View Editor* contextual tab. The *Drawing View Editor* contextual tab enables you to modify the Drawing views appearance and Autodesk Inventor representation.

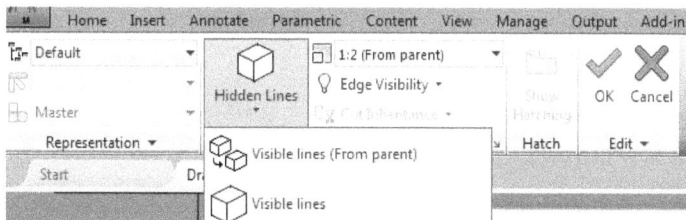

When you edit a parent view, the changes are applied to the parent and all children views.

When the source Autodesk Inventor 3D model gets modified, a bubble notification displays. Click the link in the bubble to update the drawing views. If you choose not to update the drawing views at that time, you can select a drawing view at a later time, and click the Update View command on the *Drawing View contextual* tab.

Exercise: Create Views Associated to an Autodesk Inventor 3D Model

In this exercise, you will create drawing views, including a base view and projected view that link to an Autodesk Inventor 3D model file in a layout tab. You will then edit the appearance of the model in one of the drawing views.

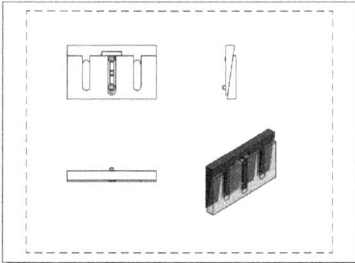

The completed exercise

Place Associated Base and Projected Drawing Views

In this section of the exercise, you will link an Inventor assembly and created drawing views of the linked assembly.

1. Start a new drawing based on the *acadiso.dwt* template file in the Custom Templates folder, and save it.

2. Ensure that the Mechanical workspace is the active workspace. Switch to the Layout1 layout tab.

3. In the Layout tab > Create View panel > Base View drop-down list, click From Inventor.

4. In the Select File dialog box, do the following:
   - Navigate to the location in which you installed the Practice Files.
   - In the Select File dialog box, the Files of Type has been set to Autodesk Inventor Files (*.IAM, .*IPT, .*IPN).
   - Select *Spacer Wedge.iam*. Click Open.

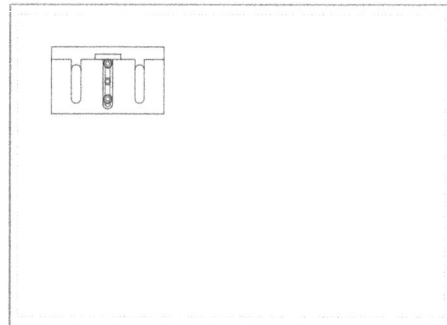

5. To set the option to place only the Base view during this command operation, do the following:
   - At the Specify location of base view, press ENTER to select the **Type** option.
   - At the a view creation option, select the **Base only** option.

6. To set a specific orientation and scale, do the following:
   - In the *Drawing View Creation* contextual tab > Orientation panel, verify that **Front** is selected.
   - In the *Drawing View Creation* contextual tab > Appearance panel, verify that **1:2** is selected in the Scale drop-down list.

7. To position the view on the layout, do the following:
   - Click to position the view near the upper left corner as shown in the following illustration.
   - Press ENTER to accept the location and exit the command. You are not given the option to continue to add Projected views because you selected Base only as the Type.

8. To add Projected views, do the following:

   - In the *Layout* tab > Create View panel, click Projected View
   - For the Select parent view, select the Base view you just added.
   - Click to the right side of the Base view to place a side orthographic projected view.

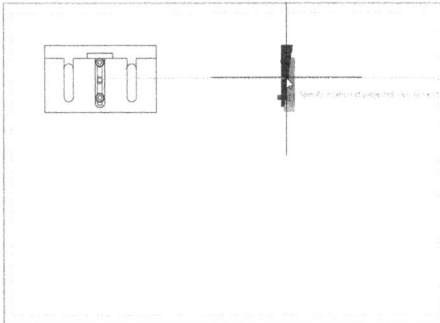

9. Continue to place a bottom orthographic projected view as shown in the following illustration.

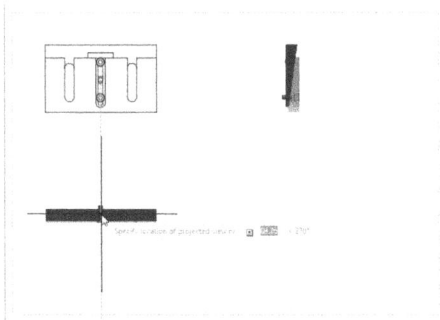

10. Continue to place an isometric projected view as shown in the following illustration.

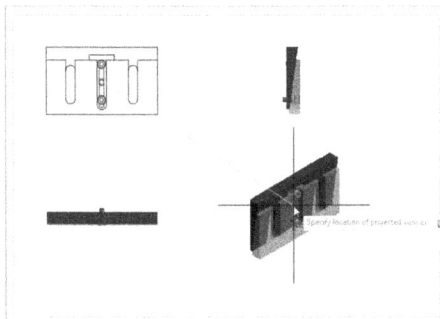

11. Press ENTER to complete the placement of all the projected views, and exit the command.

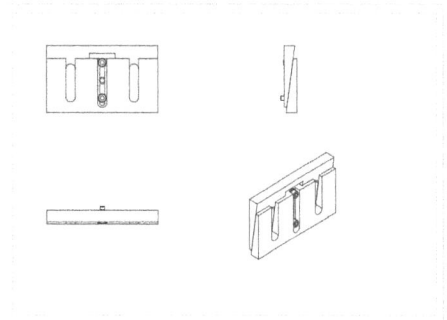

12. To edit the appearance of the isometric projected view, do the following:

   - Select the isometric projected view.
   - In the Drawing View contextual tab > Edit panel, select Edit View.
   - In the Click Drawing View Editor contextual tab > Appearance panel > Display Style drop-down list, select Shaded with visible lines.
   - Press ENTER to complete the modification and exit the command.

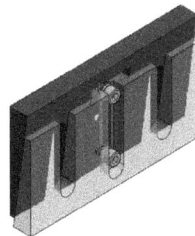

13. Save and close the file.

Chapter Summary

In this chapter, you learned how design data can be exchanged to and from the AutoCAD Mechanical software. You learned how to identify Mechanical DWG files, exchange data in the form of IGES files, and create associated Model Documentation drawing views in an AutoCAD Mechanical software drawing file of external Autodesk Inventor 3D models.

Having completed this chapter, you can:

- Identify Mechanical DWG files and state how Mechanical DWG files can be opened by a user is only using the AutoCAD software.
- Import and export IGES files.
- Use Model Documentation to create 2D drawing views and to document Autodesk Inventor software 3D models.

Mechanical Options
for the CAD Manager

In this chapter, you learn how to create a custom standard and how to configure layer, text, and symbol properties within a standard. You learn how to configure the BOM, parts list, and balloon elements of a standard within a drawing or template file and to describe the configuration of the elements of a standard that relate to various annotation tools.

Objectives

After completing this chapter, you will be able to:

- Create and activate standards and set a default standards template.
- Configure layer, text, and object properties within a standard.
- Configure the elements of a standard within a drawing or template file that relate to annotation tools.
- Configure the component properties, BOM, parts list, and balloon standards within a drawing or template file.

543

Lesson: Standards-Based Design

Overview

This lesson describes what standards mean in the AutoCAD® Mechanical software, how to create a custom standard, and how to have the standards that are saved in a template file imported into drawing files as you open them.

Standards play a crucial role in controlling how geometry displays in a drawing and the options that are available for the creation of geometry. Before learning about all of the elements within a standard, you need to know how to create a custom standard and understand the impact of setting a unit of measure and model scale. By knowing how and why you set a default standard template, you can save time for configuring standards in drawings that were not created in the AutoCAD Mechanical software.

In the following illustration, the initial design of a shaft converter coupling is shown as a half-section drawing view. The tools used to create this view use and follow industry standards for geometry creation and notation.

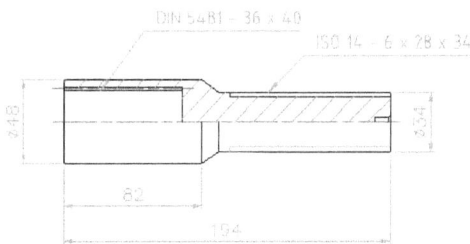

Objectives

After completing this lesson, you will be able to:

- Explain how mechanical standards impact the creation of drawing geometry.
- Select a standard for use in a drawing and create a new standard.
- Change the model scale factor and explain the impact of the change.
- Explain how and why you set a default standards template.

Introduction to Standards-Based Design

To assist in the communication of design data, different standards have been established by different industry organizations. By learning how to configure and use the AutoCAD Mechanical software, your drawings conform to the standards and any variations specified by your company.

In the following illustration, the custom standard called COMPANY STANDARDS is being selected to make it the active standard. This custom standard is initially based on one of the industry standards.

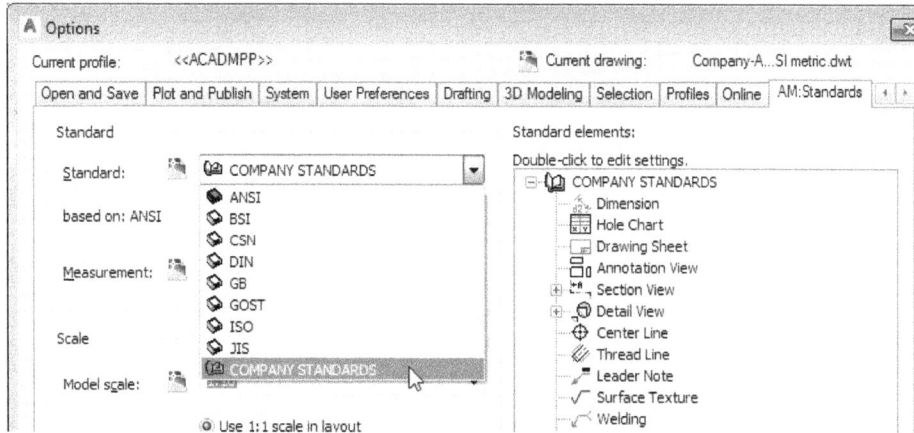

Definition of Standards-Based Design

Standards-based design means you can create geometry and annotation that meets industry accepted standards, such as ANSI, ISO, and DIN. It also means meeting any company-specific variation of those industry standards. Within a standard, there are multiple elements that you can edit to achieve the settings specific to your requirements. Customizing an existing standard can include, but is not limited to, changing the assigned layer geometry, changing how dimensions are to display, selecting the welding symbols that can be added to the drawing, and defining the information that is stored in the bill of materials. You can activate or modify a standard on the *AM:Standards* tab in the Options dialog box.

To create design data that meets these standards, you can use the AutoCAD Mechanical software tools in place of the AutoCAD® software drawing and modifying tools. You can apply your drawing standards to all of the new drawings that you create in the AutoCAD Mechanical software and to previously existing AutoCAD software drawing (DWG) files that are opened in the AutoCAD Mechanical software.

In the following illustration, the Object Property Settings dialog box is shown with the Drafting category selected. The different objects in the Drafting category and their configured properties are listed on the right. The different objects are configured to automatically be created on specific layers. By configuring these objects so that their properties meet your company standards, you can focus on creating the design geometry and not on the layer on which the geometry is being created.

Category:	Show properties for Drafting:					Group by:	Objects
Annotation View	Object	Layer	Color	Linety...	Linew...	Usa...	
Balloon	Auxiliary Line	AM_4	☐ BYL...	ByLayer	ByLayer	Bac...	
BOM	Break Line Long (Zig Zag)	AM_4	☐ BYL...	Amzig...	ByLayer	Bac...	
Calculation	Break Line Short	AM_4	☐ BYL...	ByLayer	ByLayer	Bac...	
Detail View	Break Out Line	AM_4	☐ BYL...	ByLayer	ByLayer	Bac...	
Dimensioning	Contour 1	AM_0	■ BYL...	ByLayer	ByLayer	Acc...	
Drafting	Diagonal Cross for Planes	AM_5	☐ BYL...	ByLayer	ByLayer	Ign...	
Hide	Hatch	AM_8	☐ BYL...	ByLayer	ByLayer	Bac...	
Hole Chart	Reference Circle for Gear ...	AM_7	☐ BYL...	ByLayer	ByLayer	Ign...	
Mechanical Symbols	Thread Contour	AM_0	■ BYL...	ByLayer	ByLayer	Acc...	
Non Plottable	Thread End at Usable Len...	AM_0	■ BYL...	ByLayer	ByLayer	Acc...	
Part List	Thread Line	AM_4	☐ BYL...	ByLayer	ByLayer	Bac...	
Section View	Transition Line	AM_4	☐ BYL...	ByLayer	ByLayer	Bac...	
Standard Features	Centerline	AM_7	☐ BYL...	ByLayer	ByLayer	Ign...	
Standard Parts	Centerline, narrow	AM_7	☐ BYL...	AM_I...	ByLayer	Ign...	
Text	Construction Line	AM_CL	☐ BYL...	ByLayer	ByLayer	Ign...	
Title Border/Revision	Contour 2	AM_1	■ BYL...	ByLayer	ByLayer	A...	

Example of Standards-Based Design

Using the standards-based drafting and design tools of the AutoCAD Mechanical software, the two views of a spacer plate for planting corn seed were created following both industry standards for notation and company standards for layer settings and use.

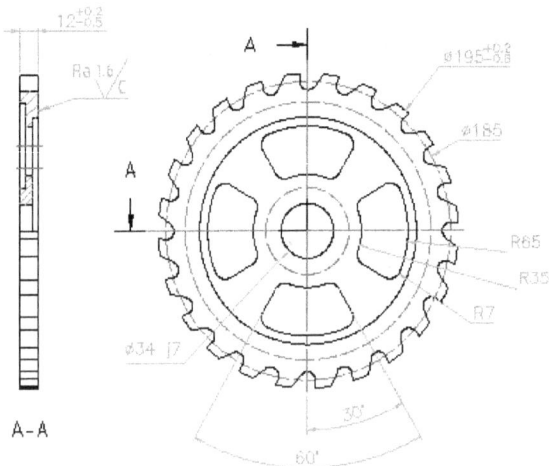

Selecting a Standard and Creating a Custom Standard

Because the creation and display of geometry and symbols is guided by standards, you must know how to select and activate a standard for use in a drawing and how to create a new standard. By knowing this information, you can configure your drawings to include and make active the required standards.

Access

Command Line: OPTIONS

Command Line: AMOPTIONS

Ribbon: N/A

Menu: Tools > Options

Shortcut Menu: Options

Application Menu: Options

Options Dialog Box - Standards

You can select, configure, and create new standards on the *AM:Standards* tab in the Options dialog box. The active standard is shown in the Standard list with an open book icon to its left.

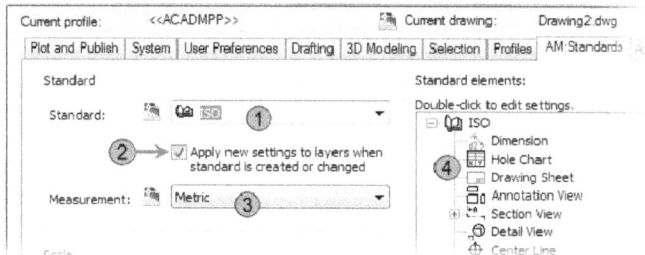

1. Use to select the industry standard to initiate the settings for the elements of the standard. You can also enter the name for a new standard in this field, press ENTER, and select the industry standard on which you want to base the new standard.

2. Use to have the settings in the newly activated standard update the properties of existing drawing layers of the same name.

3. Use to select the unit of measurement for the standard. Select between metric and English (inches and feet). Changing this setting automatically changes the values used by the elements for sizes and distances to be appropriate for the selected unit (e.g., text height and arrow size).

4. Use to view and access the configurable elements within the standard.

Procedure: Selecting a Standard and Creating a Custom Standard

An overview of activating a standard and establishing the initial factors for the standard is shown in the following steps:

1.   Open the Options dialog box. Click the *AM:Standards* tab.

2.   Activate the required standard by selecting it in the list. You can also enter a new standard name in the Standard field, press ENTER, and select the industry standard to be used as the basis for the new standard.

3.   Select or clear the Apply New Settings To Layers When Standard Is Created Or Changed checkbox.

4.   Select the measurement system used in the drawing.

Setting the Model Scale

Setting the scale factor for symbols and their text is important when having the symbols display in the required size. To set the scale factor, you need to know where to set this value and must understand its options and impact.

In the following illustration, the same drawing view is shown with two different model scale factor settings. Note how all of the symbols adjust in size up or down based on the scale factor value.

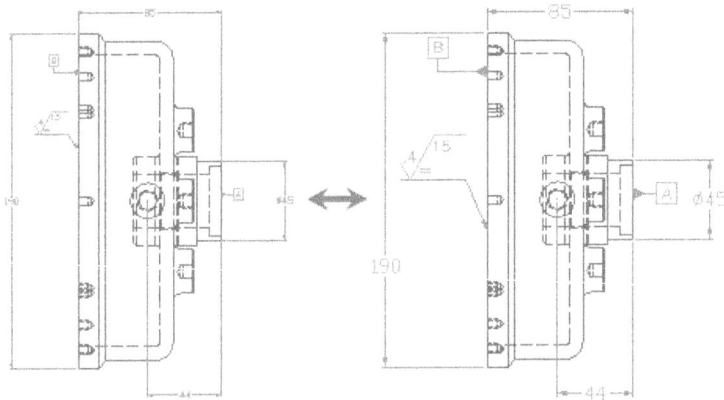

Model Scale Options

You can access the Scale area in the Options dialog box, in the AM:Standards tab. Within this area, two items need to be set. The first thing you set is the scale factor for model space. This sets the scale factor for symbols, such as balloons, parts lists, weld symbols, leader notes, dimensions, etc., and their text. When you change the scale factor and close the dialog box, you can select existing symbols to have them scale based on the new factor. All new symbols added to the drawing are initially created and sized based on the scale factor that is currently set. You can also set the initial plot scale factor for a newly created layout. You can either select the option to make a new layout's plot scale 1:1 or to use the scale factor that is set in the Model Scale box.

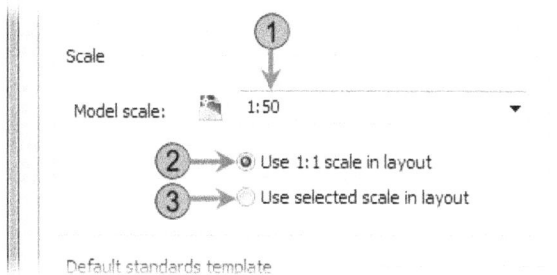

1. Use to select a scale factor from the list or to a factor in the field.

2. Use to set all newly created layouts to have their plot scales set to 1:1.

3. Use to set all newly created layouts to have their plot scales set to the scale that is set in the Model Scale box.

> If a border has been inserted into model space that contains a defined scale factor, all symbol sizes and text within the border are only controlled by the scale factor set for the border. Changing the scale factor on the *AM:Standards* tab does not affect the display of the geometry within that border area.

Procedure: Setting the Model Scale

An overview of setting the model scale factor for mechanical symbols and their text is shown in the following steps:

1. Open the Options dialog box. Click the *AM:Standards* tab.

2. Set the model scale factor by selecting it from the list or entering it into the field.

3. Set the option for the plot scale factor for newly created layouts as required.

Setting a Default Standards Template

It is a good practice to establish a template file to use as a start point for new drawings. The template file that you use to start a new drawing contains all of the unique settings and configurations that are specific to your requirements. They can include a custom standard with settings that vary from its base standard. By making the template available to everyone when starting all new drawings, you establish a consistency between users while making it easier for them to follow the company standards.

An established template file typically only assists the user when they create new drawings. However, by setting a default standards template in the AutoCAD Mechanical software, you can open a non-AutoCAD Mechanical software drawing and have the active standard in the template drawing added and set to be active in the drawing that is being opened.

Default Standards Template

In the Options dialog box, on the *AM:Standards* tab, under Default standards template, you can set the standard to be imported into non-AutoCAD Mechanical software drawings when they are opened. Select a DWT template file that has the standard that you want to automatically import as its active standard. The automatic standards import occurs if the file being opened has the same measurement system assigned to it as the template file. If the measurement systems do not match, the default template is ignored and the file is opened without importing the standards. The default standards template is also ignored when you open a drawing file that has already been saved as an AutoCAD Mechanical software drawing.

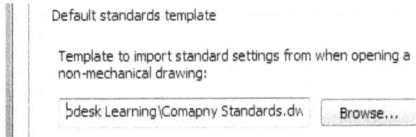

The comparison of measurement systems between drawing files and template files is based on the setting for the MEASUREMENT system variable. The possible settings are Imperial or Metric.

Initially this setting is set in the Template Description dialog box during the creation of the template file. By setting this option when creating the template drawing to match the setting for non-AutoCAD Mechanical software drawings, the active standard in the default drawing template automatically imports when you open those non-AutoCAD Mechanical software drawings.

Because the MEASUREMENT variable is a system variable that is stored in the drawing file, you can change a drawing (DWG) or template (DWT) file's measurement setting at any time by entering the required value for this variable.

Procedure: Setting a Default Standards Template

An overview of how to establish a template file to be used for importing standards into non-AutoCAD Mechanical software drawing files when they are opened is shown in the following steps:

1.	Create a drawing template file (DWT) in which the required standard is active and which contains the required setting for the MEASUREMENT variable.

2.	Display the Options dialog box. Click the *AM:Standards* tab.

3.	Under Default Standards Template, click Browse. Navigate to and select the DWT file.

Exercise: Create and Set a Default Standard Template

In this exercise, you will create a custom standard and save it and the measurement system and model scale factor to a template file. You will then set the template file as the default standard template and open different drawings to review its impact on them.

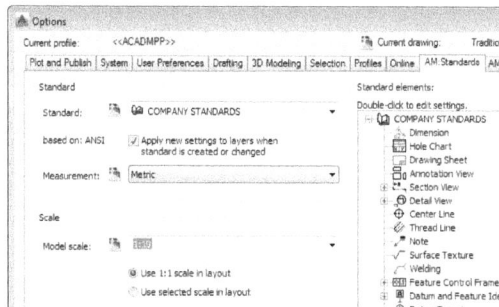

The completed exercise

1. To create a new drawing based on an existing template:

   - Click Application menu > New.
   - In the Select template dialog box, select the software default template, *acad.dwt*. (This is the default template, usually available at C:\Users <*user name*>\AppData\Local\Autodesk\ AutoCAD Mechanical <*Version*>\ <*Revision*>\ <*language*>\Acadm\ Template)
   - Click Open.

2. Click Application menu > Options or right-click anywhere in the drawing window and click Options to open the Options dialog box. Click the *AM:Standards* tab if it is not the active tab.

3. In the Standard list field, enter **Company Standards**. Press ENTER.

4. In the Selection dialog box, verify that ANSI is listed as the base standard. Click OK to accept ANSI as the basis for the new standard.

5. In the *Standard* area, in the Measurement drop-down list, select Metric.

6. In the *Scale* area, in the Model scale drop-down list, select 1:10.

7. With the options set as shown in the following illustration, click OK.

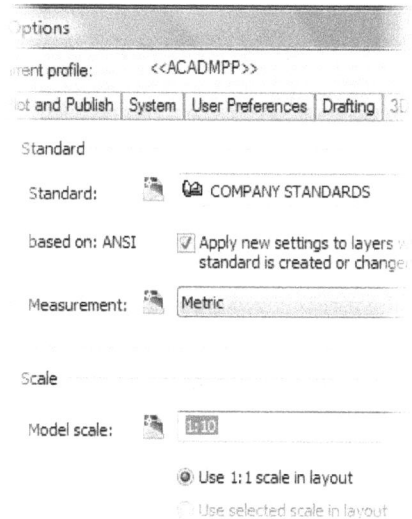

8. In the Scale Changed dialog box, click No.

9. To save this file as a template file:

   - Click Application menu > Save As.
   - In the Save Drawing As dialog box, in the Files of type drop-down list, select AutoCAD Mechanical Drawing Template (*.dwt).
   - In the File name box, enter **Company-ANSI metric**.
   - Click Save.

10. In the Template Options dialog box:

- Clear the contents of the Description box.
- Ensure that Measurement is set to Metric.
- Click OK.

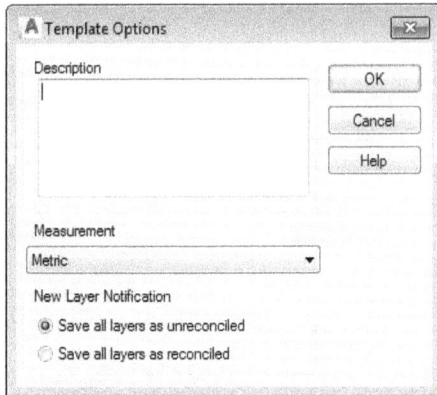

11. Right-click anywhere in the drawing window and select Options.

12. To set the template as the default standards template:

- On the *AM:Standards* tab, under Default standards template, click Browse.
- In the Open dialog box, select *Company-ANSI metric.dwt*. Click Open.
- The file is listed as the default standard template in the Options dialog box. Click OK.

13. Close all of the open drawings.

14. Open *Traditional AutoCAD-English.dwg*.

15. Click Application menu > Options.

16. Review the available standards in the drawing. Note that the COMPANY STANDARDS standard did not import.

17. Open *Traditional AutoCAD-Metric.dwg*.

18. Click Application menu > Options.

19. Review the available standards in the drawing. Note that the COMPANY STANDARDS standard did import. Click Cancel.

20. Close all of the files and do not save.

Lesson: Configure Layer, Text, and Object Properties

Overview

This lesson describes the configuration of layer, text, and object properties within a standard.

A key part of drafting in a CAD system is separating the data and geometry that you create and controlling how the geometry is displayed. Using layers you can do both. Because the AutoCAD Mechanical software manages the placement of geometry onto layers automatically and bases the layer creation and geometry placement on the settings of in the active standard, you must learn how to create and configure layers in a standard so that the standard meets your company's requirements. You must also learn how to set the properties for text and symbols in the standard so that when they are added to a drawing, they also match your requirements.

In the following illustration, the default layer names are shown on the left. On the right, the layers are shown after they have been renamed to match the company standards. In this example, only the first layer (AM_0/CONTOUR_LINES) is actually created in the drawing. The other layers are only defined in the standard and are ready to be added.

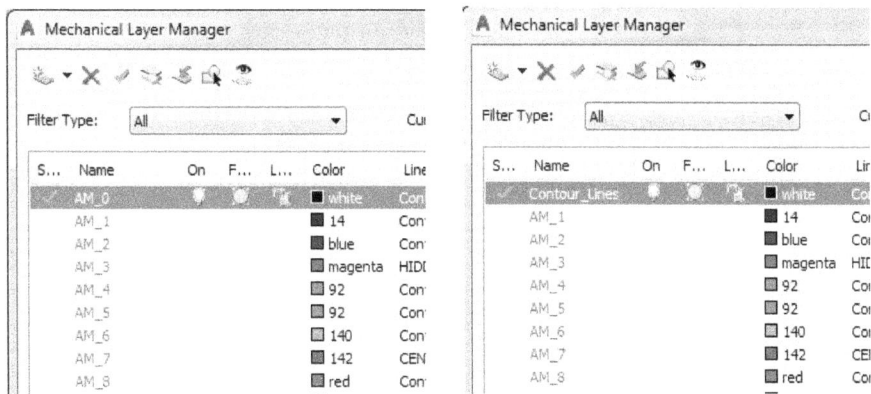

Objectives

After completing this lesson, you will be able to:

- Create new layers and configure layer properties.
- Explain what standard elements are and how to access their settings for editing.
- Edit the properties of a standard.

Configuring Layers

To use the automatic layer management functionality in the AutoCAD Mechanical software and have it meet your requirements, you need to know how to configure layers in the active standard. This includes changing the name and properties of existing layers and adding new layers.

In the following illustration, the same drawing view is shown with the default layer colors and linetype settings on the left and with changes to the standard so that the geometry is displayed according to the company's layer standards on the right.

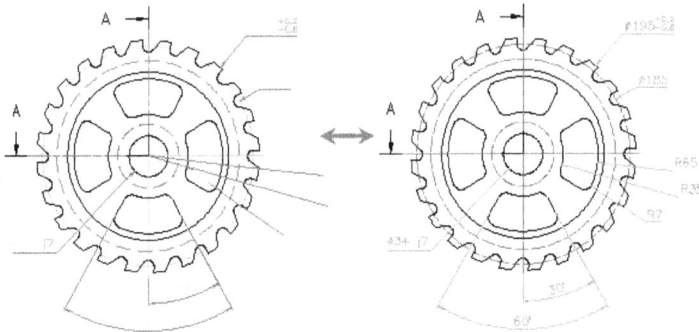

Mechanical Layer Manager

From within the Mechanical Layer Manager, you can:

- Create and edit AutoCAD software and AutoCAD Mechanical software layers and properties.
- Convert AutoCAD software layers to AutoCAD Mechanical software layers.
- Import layer information and settings.
- Set a layer definition to be the current layer and have the predefined layer added to the drawing file.
- Map Lineweights for the layers and colors.

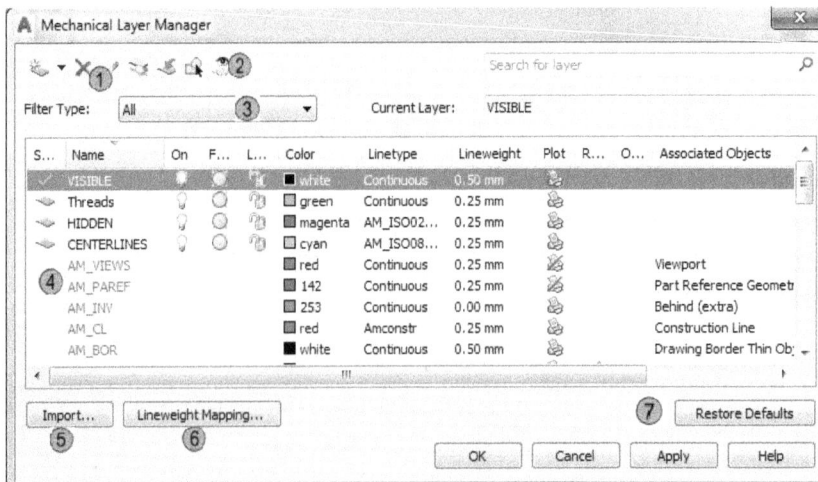

1. Use these toolbar buttons to create and work with the geometry on the layers.

2. The Show/Hide Layer Definitions toggle. Use it to display and hide any AutoCAD Mechanical software layers that have been defined in the drawing but not yet created. Layer definitions that have not yet been created display in gray text without any icons in the On, Freeze, and Lock property columns.

3. Select from the list of defined filters to narrow the list of layers to those that meet the filter criteria.

4. The list of created and defined layers in the drawing and their properties. Use this area to review and change the properties of existing layers and to create new layers.

5. Use to import the configuration for layers and object settings from another file. The import adds unique layers to the drawing and changes the properties of common layers and objects.

6. Use to set the default lineweight for a specific color. In the Lineweight Mapping dialog box, there is a checkbox titled Apply To Existing Layers. When this checkbox is cleared, any changes made to lineweight mapping only apply to newly created layers. When the checkbox is selected, the lineweight mapping changes update all of the existing layers.

7. Use to restore the layer and object settings back to factory defaults. Unique layer names are maintained. However, if they were AutoCAD Mechanical software layers they are converted to AutoCAD software layers.

Mechanical Layer Manager and Associated Objects

The Associated Objects field for a layer lists all of the objects that are currently configured in the standard to automatically be created on that layer. This information helps you to understand the impact on your drawing geometry if you modify the properties of the layer. In the following illustration, when the cursor hovered over the Associated Objects field for the Mechanical layer DIMENSIONS, a tooltip displayed listing all of the geometry that is mapped to that layer. For example, for the layer name HIDDEN, no mechanical geometry is not going automatically be created on this layer because the field for the layer is blank.

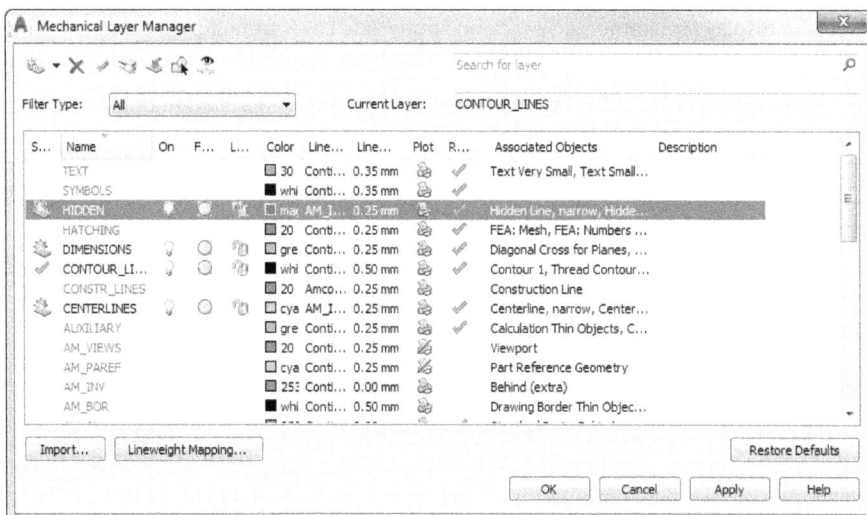

Defined Layers in the Mechanical Layer Manager

The Mechanical Layer Manager also contains a list of defined layers that have not yet been created and used in the drawing. You can toggle the display of these layer definitions on and off by clicking Show/ Hide Layer Definition. When you select the option to show layer definitions, their names display in gray text and the icons for the On, Freeze, and Lock properties are not displayed. You can display the layer definitions so that you can modify their names and properties. By changing the definitions and saving them as part of your drawing template file, the AutoCAD Mechanical software layers that are automatically created by the AutoCAD Mechanical software contain the required names and properties for your standard. To add a new layer definition to the list, click the down arrow for the new layer and click New Layer Definition.

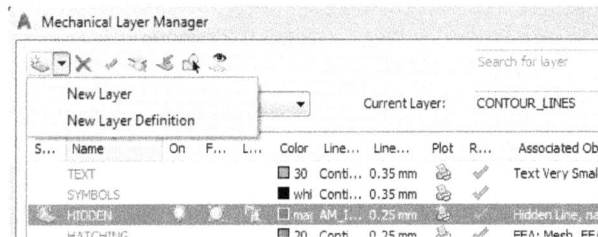

> Because all of the AutoCAD Mechanical software layer definition names can be modified to meet your company standards, you need to rename the default layers so that they match your standards before adding any custom Mechanical Standards. This saves time when configuring the object settings later.

Procedure: Configuring Layers

An overview of configuring layers for automatic property management is shown in the following steps:

1. Open the Mechanical Layer Manager.

2. Set your display requirements by clicking Show/Hide Layer Definitions to toggle the listing of all of the layer definitions or only the layers that have already been created in the drawing.

3. Change the properties of the layers to meet your requirements. If additional layers are required, add and set their properties.

About Standard Elements and Accessing Their Settings

To configure a standard to meet your company's requirements, you need to understand the standard's elements and how to access the standard's properties.

Definition of Standard Elements and Accessing their Settings

When you select a standard from the list of standards, the tree view on the right displays all of the different elements for that standard. The name of the selected standard is listed as the top element. Each element in the standard controls the definition and creation of geometry and is either a logical grouping of settings or specific settings associated with an industry-based standard.

You can change the settings of an element by double-clicking on that element in the tree view. Alternatively, you can right-click on the element and click Settings. You edit the settings of the elements below the listing of the standard and also change the settings of the standard element itself.

When you access the settings for a standard element, a settings dialog box opens for that element.

In the following illustration, the DIN standard has been selected as the active standard so that the top element in the list is DIN. All of the elements below it contain the specific properties for the standard.

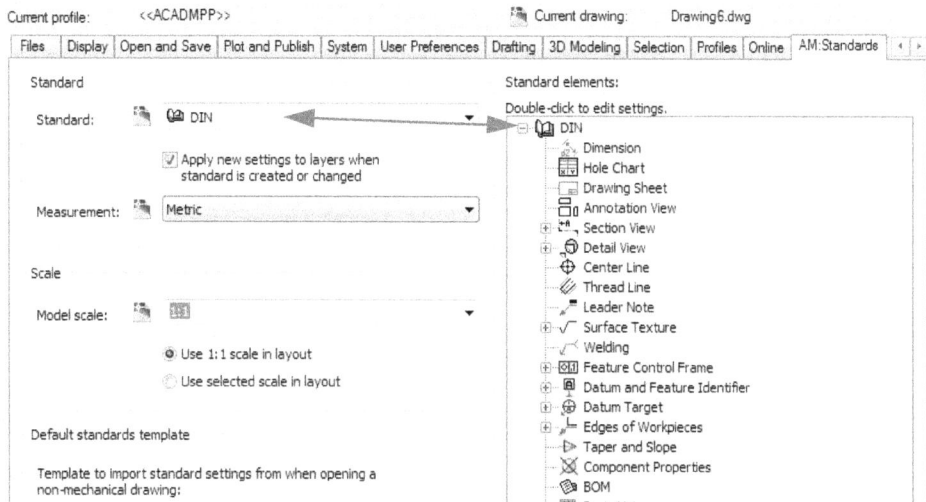

Example of Standard Elements and Accessing their Settings

As shown in the following illustration, the Hole Chart Settings dialog box opens after you double-click on the Hole Chart element name in the Standard elements tree view for the active standard. The setting changes for the hole chart only apply to the standard.

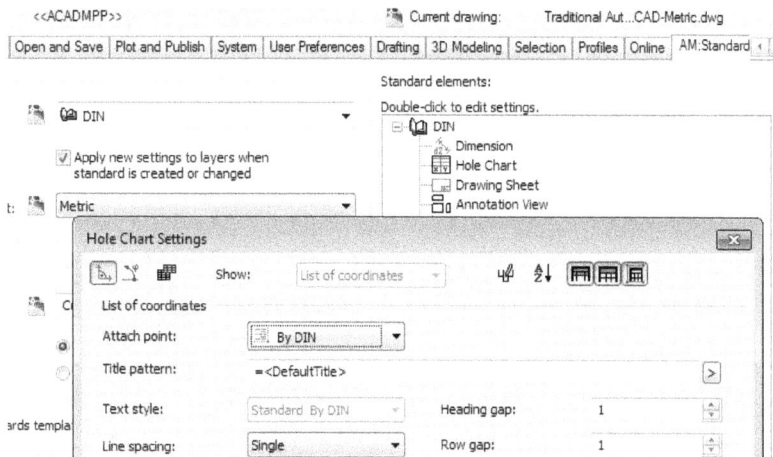

Configuring Standard Properties

As part of the process of configuring a standard, you need to configure the global properties for the standard. These properties include the settings for symbol properties, insertion points for lists, and orthographic projection types.

Accessing the Master Settings

The master settings for a standard are set in the Standard Settings dialog box when that standard is the active standard. You can open this dialog box by double-clicking on the top node of the active standard in the Options dialog box, in the *AM:Standards* tab. These settings in the top node for the active standard are important when configuring the drawing and all of the elements in the standard.

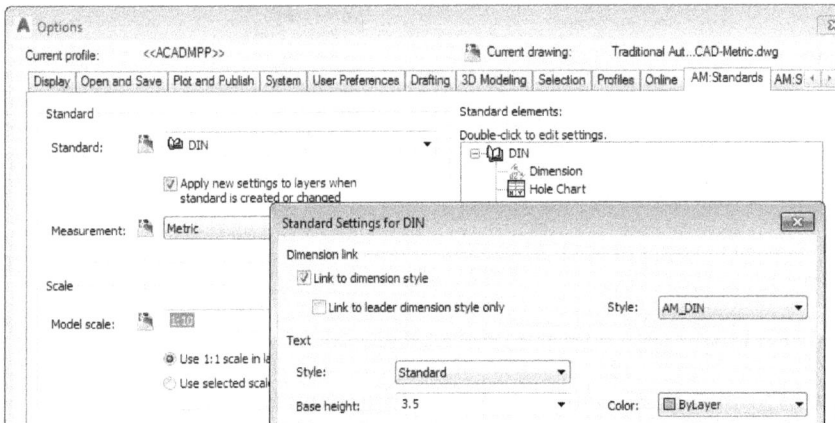

Standard Settings

With the Standard Settings dialog box displayed, you can change the settings and properties for text, arrowheads on leader lines, and symbols. You can select the option to have the properties of a dimension style change as you make these changes. You can also enable and configure automatic property management and set the required orthographic projection angle. These settings are set in the dialog box in a top-down flow for an easy understanding of what can be configured in each area.

When you change a setting or property in the Standard Settings dialog box, that change is also applied to other elements in the standard. Therefore, if you enter a new text height here, the text heights for all of the other elements are changed as well. For some elements the text equals this value and for others it is one size larger.

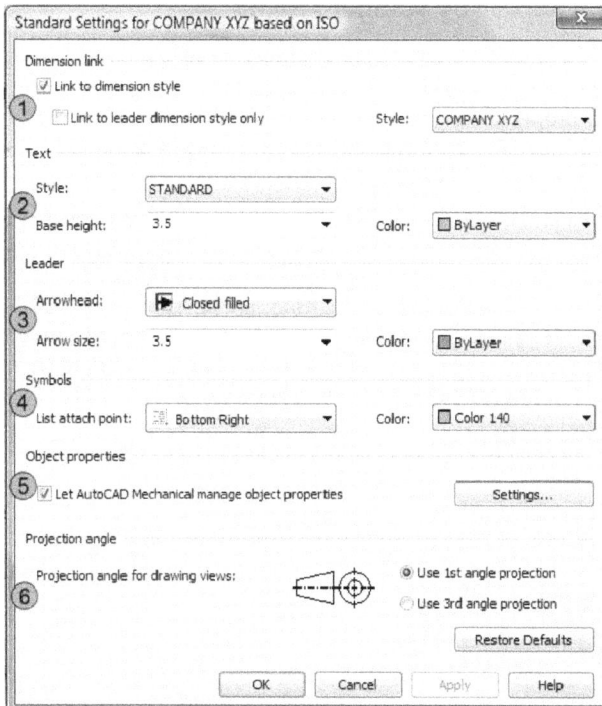

1. Select the Link to Dimension Style checkbox to link the current symbol property settings to the selected dimension style. Select the Link To Leader Dimension Style Only checkbox to only have the properties set for the leader dimension subtype.

2. Use to set the style, size, and color for all of the mechanical objects that contain text.

3. Use to set the style, size, and color of leader lines and arrows for all of the mechanical symbols.

4. Set which corner of a list to use as the insertion point during the placement of the list and also set its display color.

5. Enables the automatic object property and layer management functionality. Click Settings to open the Object Property Settings dialog box.

6. Set the required orthographic projection method for new views.

When you select the Let AutoCAD Mechanical manage object properties option, the AutoCAD Mechanical software uses the current object property settings to create geometry that is on the correct layers and with the correct property settings. If you clear this option, you cannot create Mechanical layers or layer groups. If you use mechanical tools to create mechanical objects, such as bolts or weld symbols, the geometry is placed on the current layer. It is strongly recommended that you keep this option on and configure the object property settings to meet your requirements.

Master Settings When Elements Use By Standard Name

When you set a property in the Standard Settings dialog box, it is set for all of the elements in the standard. The only way a change in the master setting does not update an individual element is if that element has a unique value set for property. A unique property value is any value other than By Standard Name. A unique setting in an element always takes precedence over any setting changes in the master standard settings.

In the following illustration, the Text and Leader areas of the Standard Settings and the Welding Settings dialog boxes for the ISO standard are shown. When you compare the global settings for the standard in the Standard Settings dialog box to the settings for welding symbols in the Welding Settings dialog box, note that the text settings for the weld settings are not set to By ISO as the leader settings are set. In this example, text height and color changes made in the Standard Settings dialog box now apply to welding symbols because they have a setting other than By Standard Name. The leader properties match the settings in the Standard Settings dialog box.

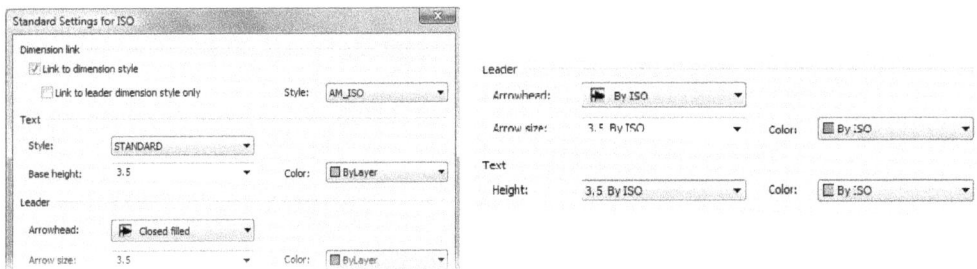

Procedure: Changing the Global Standard Settings

An overview of configuring the global settings for a standard is shown in the following steps:

1.   Open the Options dialog box. Click the *AM:Standards* tab.

2.   Activate the standard that you want to configure.

3.   In the list of Standard Elements, double-click on the name of the active standard.

4.   Change the properties and settings to match your requirements.

Exercise: Configure Layers and Object Properties

In this exercise, you will configure layer and object properties in a drawing that was originally created in the AutoCAD software. In addition to changing settings in that drawing, you will import the settings from an already configured drawing.

The completed exercise

Layer and Object Properties

In this section of the exercise, you will migrate an AutoCAD software layer into an AutoCAD Mechanical software layer, change the master color setting for mechanical text, and change the layer on which mechanical objects are to be created.

1. Open *Conveyor Legs-ACAD.dwg*.

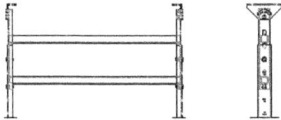

2. Click Home tab > Layers panel > Mechanical Layer Manager.

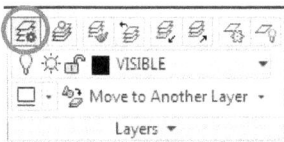

3. If not already set, toggle on Show/Hide Layer Definitions in the Mechanical Layer Manager dialog box. In the Mechanical Layer Manager, review the list of layers that are currently created in the drawing and the status icon associated with each layer.

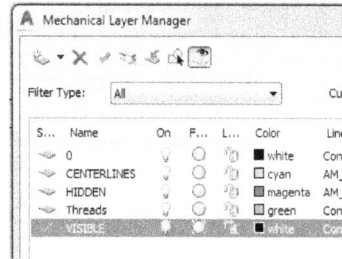

4. To review the entire list of all of the defined Mechanical layers, in the Mechanical Layer Manager dialog box, click Show/Hide Layer Definitions to toggle it off.

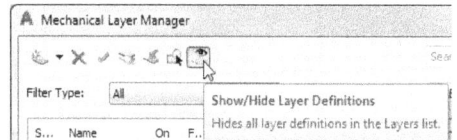

5. Scroll down the list to review the names of the defined Mechanical layers and their properties and to view the layers that exist in the drawing.

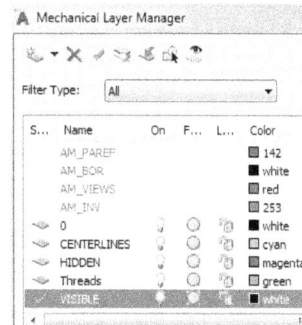

6. To convert the CENTERLINES layer from an AutoCAD layer to an AutoCAD Mechanical layer, right-click on CENTERLINES and select Convert To Mechanical Layer. The Status icon for the layer now displays as shown in the following illustration.

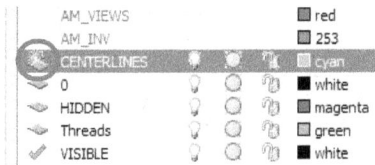

7. To change the name of a defined Mechanical layer and not create it in the drawing yet:

- Right-click on the layer name AM_BOR and select Rename Layer.
- Enter **Border**.

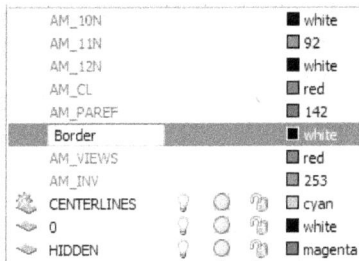

8. Double-click on the layer Border to add the defined layer to the drawing and have it set to be current layer.

9. Double-click on the layer VISIBLE to set it to be current. The layer list now displays as shown in the following illustration.

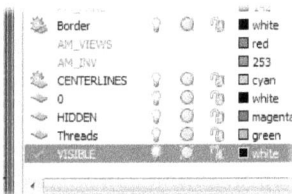

10. To switch the layer list back to only displaying layers that exist in the drawing, click Show/Hide Layer Definitions. The layer list now displays as shown in the following illustration.

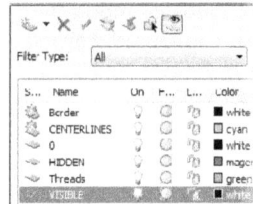

11. Review the information in the Associated Objects column for the layers. Note how only the Border layer currently has objects assigned to be created on that layer. The CENTERLINES layer is a Mechanical layer but no objects have been assigned to be created on that layer.

12. In the Mechanical Layer Manager, click OK.

13. To begin setting the overall properties of mechanical objects, including which layer they should be created on:

- Right-click in an open area of the drawing window and select Options.
- In the Options dialog box, click the *AM:Standards* tab.

14. To open the Standard Settings dialog box, in the list of elements in the active standard, double-click on the top node (COMPANY STANDARDS) as shown in the following illustration.

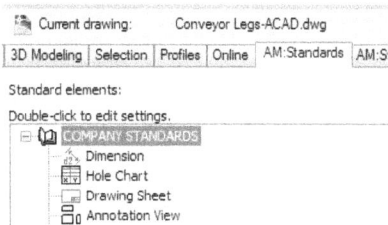

15. To set the text color for all of the elements in the standard, in the *Text* area, in the Color list, select Blue.

16. To open the Object Property Settings dialog box to configure the properties of the Mechanical objects, in the *Object properties* area, click Settings.

17. To begin changing the properties of centerline objects so that they are created on the newly migrated CENTERLINES Mechanical layer, in the Object Property Settings dialog box, in the Category list, click Drafting.

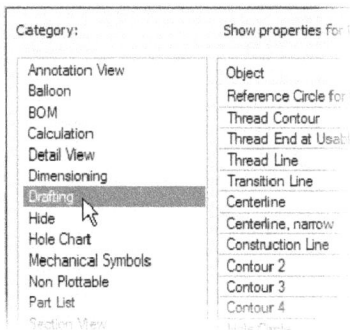

18. In the Show properties for Drafting list:

- In the Layer column, click the layer field for the Centerline object.
- In the Object Property Settings dialog box, select CENTERLINES. Click OK. The Layer is changed to CENTERLINES, as shown in the following illustration.

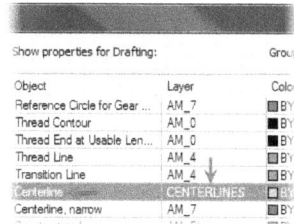

19. In the Show properties for Drafting list:

- Click the object Centerline, narrow.
- Read the information text for this object.

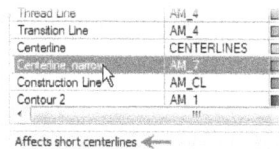

20. Select the Highlight all categories that use the selected object checkbox to have categories that also use this object highlight in the Category list in light blue.

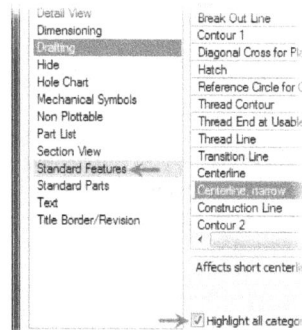

21. In the Show properties for Drafting list, select CENTERLINES in the Layer field for the object Centerline, narrow. When prompted about changes for Centerline, narrow affecting the properties for the Standard Features, click Change property.

Transition Line	AM_4	
Centerline	CENTERLINES	
Centerline, narrow	CENTERLINES	
Construction Line	AM_CL	
Contour 2	AM_1	

22. To save these changes and return to the drawing:

- In the Object Property Settings dialog box, click OK.
- In the Standard Settings dialog box, click OK.
- In the Options dialog box, click OK.

23. Click Home tab > Layers panel > Mechanical Layer Manager.

- In the Associated Objects column, for the layer CENTERLINES, review the Mechanical objects that are now associated to the layer.
- Click OK.

S...	Name	On	F...	...et...	Lin...	P...	R...	O	Associated Objects
	Border	√	○	...tin...	0.50 ...				Drawing Border Thin Objects,...
	CENTERLINES	√	○	...IS...	0.25 ...		√		Centerline, narrow, Centerline
	0	√	○	...tin...	Default				
	HIDDEN	√	○	...IS...	0.25 ...				
	Threads	√	○	...tin...	0.25 ...				
	VISIBLE				0.50				

24. Do not close the drawing.

Import Layer and Object Settings

In this section of the exercise, you will review the settings in a Mechanical drawing and then import those layer and object settings into another drawing.

1. Open *Pre-Configured Properties.dwg*.

2. Click Home tab > Layers panel > Mechanical Layer Manager.

3. To display the list of all of the defined Mechanical layers, in the Mechanical Layer Manager, click Show/Hide Layer Definitions.

4. Review the list of defined layer names and objects that are associated to each layer. Click OK when you have finished reviewing the layer properties.

S...	Name	On	F...	L...	C...	Li...	L...	P..	R.	Associated Objects
	Visible				whi	Cont...	0.5...			Contour 1, Contour 2,
	AM_1				14	Cont...	0.5...			
	AM_2				blue	Cont...	0.5...			FEA: Deformation Mesh
	Hidden				mag	AM_...	0.2...			Hidden Line, narrow, Hi
	Threads				92	Cont...	0.2...			Calculation Thin Objects
	Dimensions				92	Cont...	0.2...			Diagonal Cross for Plan
	Text				140	Cont...	0.3...			Text Very Small, Text S
	Centerlines				142	AM_...	0.2...			Centerline, narrow, Cer
	Hatch				red	Cont...	0.2...			FEA: Mesh, FEA: Numbe
	AM_9				253	Cont...	0.0...			Behind

5. To begin reviewing the property settings for mechanical objects:

- Right-click in an open area of the drawing window and select Options.
- In the Options dialog box, click the *AM:Standards* tab.
- In the list of Standard elements, double-click on the standard name (ISO) at the top node.
- In the Standard Settings dialog box, in the *Object properties* area, click Settings.

6. In the Object Property Settings dialog box:

- In the Category list, verify that Drafting is still selected.
- In the Show properties for Drafting list, review the layers on which the different objects will be created.

Show properties for Drafting:		G
Object	Layer	C
Reference Circle for Gear ...	Centerlines	
Thread Contour	Visible	
Thread End at Usable Len...	Visible	
Thread Line	Threads	
Transition Line	Threads	
Centerline	Centerlines	
Centerline, narrow	Centerlines	
Construction Line	Constr_Lines	
Contour 2	Visible	
Contour 3	Visible	
Contour 4	Visible	

7. After reviewing the settings, click Cancel in the open dialog boxes to close all of them.

8. Close *Pre-Configured Properties.dwg* without saving.

9. To begin importing the layer and object settings into *Conveyor Legs-ACAD.dwg* from *Pre-Configured Properties.dwg*, with the *Conveyor Legs-ACAD.dwg* active, click Home tab > Layers panel > Mechanical Layer Manager.

10. In the Mechanical Layer Manager dialog box, review the list of layer names again.

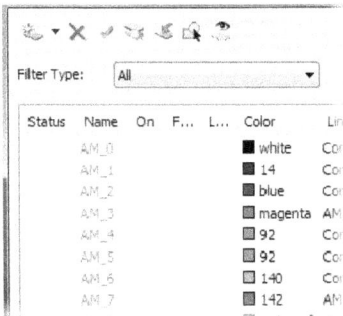

11. Click Import. In the Warning message dialog box, click Import settings.

12. In the Open dialog box:

- Select *Pre-Configured Properties.dwg* from your practice files folder.
- Click Open.

13. Review the updated list of configured Mechanical layers and the objects that are associated to those layers.

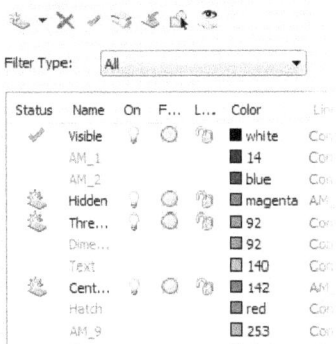

14. In the Mechanical Layer Manager dialog box, click OK.

15. To begin reviewing the imported property settings for mechanical objects:

- Right-click in an open area of the drawing window and click Options.
- In the Options dialog box, click the *AM:Standards* tab.
- In the list of Standard elements, double-click on the standard name (Company Standards) at the top node.
- In the Standard Settings dialog box, in the *Object properties* area, click Settings.

16. In the Object Property Settings dialog box:

- In the Category list, ensure that Drafting is selected.
- In the properties table listing the drafting objects, review the layers on which the different objects will be created.

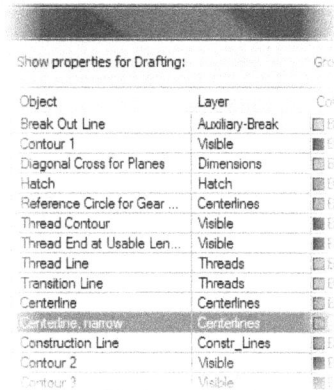

17. After reviewing the settings, click Cancel in the open dialog boxes to close them all.

18. Save and close the drawing.

Lesson: Configure the Annotation Tools

Overview

This lesson describes how to configure the elements of a standard that relate to various annotation tools. This includes but is not limited to the standard elements for dimensions, hole charts, drawing sheets, notes, and welding symbols.

Drafting standards are defined in an industry and in a company to help ensure that the information contained on the drawing is communicated consistently to others. By configuring the elements of the standard that control the initial appearance of various annotation types, you help ensure that the annotation is consistent between drawings by making it easy to conform to and follow your company standards.

In the following illustration, the annotation objects added to the drawing are automatically displayed as shown because their properties were previously configured in the active standard.

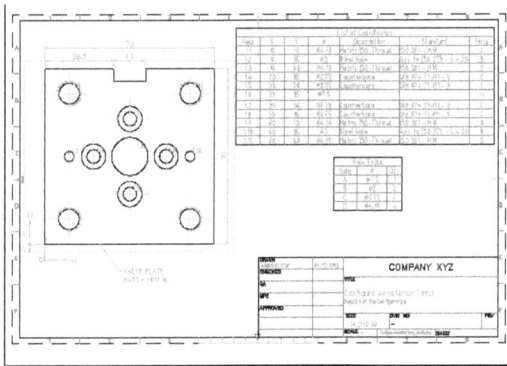

Objectives

After completing this lesson, you will be able to:

- Describe the benefits of using AutoCAD Mechanical software commands to add dimensions and annotation to your designs.
- Configure the dimension style settings within the active standard.
- Configure the hole chart settings within the active standard.
- Configure the drawing sheet settings within the active standard.
- Configure the notes settings within the active standard.
- List other types of annotation symbols and state where they are initially configured.

About Dimensions and Annotation

An important but time-consuming task when completing a design is adding dimensions and other annotations. By learning about the benefits of using the AutoCAD Mechanical software commands to add dimensions and annotation, you can understand the importance of learning how to use those commands to decrease the time required to dimension and annotate your designs.

In the following illustration, the different views of the part were dimensioned using Mechanical specific dimensioning commands.

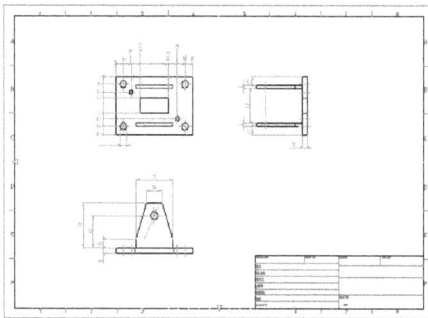

Definition of Dimensions and Annotation

The dimension and annotation commands follow industry standards for defining their configuration, contents, and appearance. The layer on which the dimension or annotation is located after it has been automatically created follows the settings in the active standard regardless of which layer might be active before the command was launched. The size of the symbols and text is based on the model scale factor that was set in the standard.

When you use the power dimensioning commands, the type of dimension that you create is based on the selected geometry. This enables you to add various dimension types while using a single dimension command. For each dimension that is created, you can quickly add special characters, such as square, countersink, centerline, depth, and tolerance or fit values.

The different dimension and annotation commands also enable you to add a set of baseline, chain, ordinate, symmetrical, and shaft diameter dimensions. You can also notate the position and size of holes by adding hole charts and lists to a drawing sheet. Feature control frames, datum identifiers, weld symbols, and surface texture symbols are a few of the other types of annotations that you can add to your drawing. The display of each of these symbols is also controlled by the active standard.

By using one of the three text tools, you can create the text using one of three set heights that automatically scale in the model space based on the standard's model scale factor value.

Example of Dimensions and Annotation

In the following illustration, a drawing view of a cylindrical connecting part is shown with dimensions and other notations. The dimensions in this view specify the size of the part and location of some of the features. Some of the notations for the dimensions were modified from their defaults during their creation and others were modified after they were placed. The size of the text under the view was set using two of the three text tools for sizing and creating text.

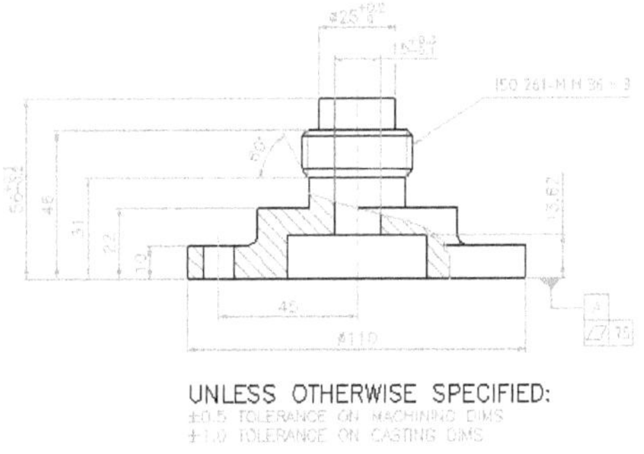

UNLESS OTHERWISE SPECIFIED:

Configuring Dimension Styles

To annotate a drawing with dimensions and have them display so that they match your standards, you might need to change a number of dimension settings. If each user had to configure the dimension settings for each new drawing, a lot of time would be wasted and the settings might vary from drawing to drawing. By configuring the dimensions in the standard and saving it as part of your template, using the standards become easier and more automatic.

In the following illustration, the same overall dimension style was used to annotate the drawing with dimensions. The dimensions' different appearances occurred automatically because of the different settings made between the overall dimension style and the substyle for diameter dimensions.

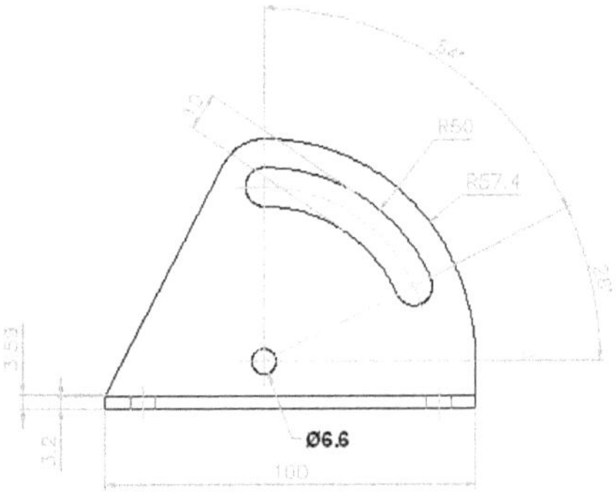

Ø6.6

Dimension Configuration in the Standard

You can preconfigure your dimension settings in the Dimension Settings dialog box. You can open this dialog box from the Options dialog box, in the AM:Standards tab, by double-clicking on the Dimension standards element.

Within the Dimension Settings dialog box, you can:

- Set the base dimension style to be active or create a new one.
- Configure the dimension style.
- Set the default dimension representation for chamfers, radii, and diameters.
- Set the dimensions to either follow or ignore the AutoCAD software's linear scale factor (DIMLFAC) variable value.
- Predefine dimension text arrangement and information.
- Choose the default representation for fits and tolerance information and customize the fit representations or tolerance methods.
- Set the values for various dimension placement options, including whether the Power Dimensioning dialog box should open during the placement of dimensions.

When a new drawing standard is created, a new dimension style is also automatically created with the same name as the newly created drawing standard. This new dimension style is also made active in the standard. The dimension style that is listed in the Base Dimension Style field is the active dimension style. Selecting a new style from the list makes it the active standard. Selecting a different style to make it the active style in the standard only affects the dimensions that you are about to create, not the dimensions that have already been created. If you change the settings within a standard, any dimensions that you have created with the style update and reflect those new settings.

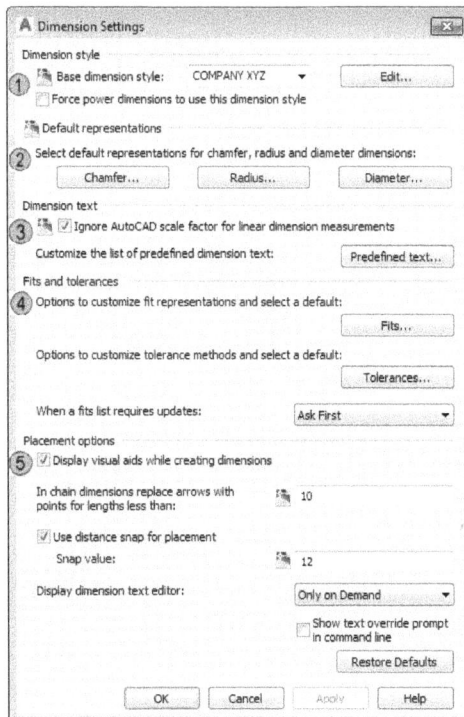

1. Use these settings and options to create a new dimension style by entering text into the list field, set the active dimension style, open the Edit Dimension Style dialog box to configure the settings of the dimension style and substyles, and to use the base dimension style regardless of whether the DIMSTYLE command was used by a user to set a different dimension style current.

2. Click the options to open the corresponding dialog boxes to configure the default representations for chamfers, radii, and diameter dimensions.

3. Set the value of the dimension text to ignore or honor the DIMLFAC setting in the drawing. Click Predefined Text to preconfigure different formats for dimension text and information.

4. Set the default representation and documentation method for fits and tolerances. You can also set when and how an existing fits list updates when a dimension's fit value is edited.

5. Use these settings and options to control visual feedback when creating dimensions, set the distance when chain dimensions display with dots instead of arrows, and set the distance at which the dimensions are to be placed offset from the part or assembly drawing geometry. You can also set when the Power Dimensioning dialog box should open.

Edit Dimension Style Dialog Box

When you click to edit the dimension style, only the active base dimension style can be edited, as selected in the Base Dimension Style list. After clicking Edit in the Dimension Settings dialog box, the Edit Dimension Style dialog box opens listing the base dimension style and the individual dimension types within that base style. In the Edit Dimension Style dialog box, you can set whether to change the dimension settings for the overall dimension style or whether you want to configure a substyle to display differently from the overall style. To change the settings for the overall dimension style, you can select the base name of the dimension style in the list and click Modify. To configure some unique settings for a substyle, select that substyle in the list and click Modify. Changes made to the overall dimension style are applied to the substyles unless the substyle has a unique configuration for that setting.

When you click Modify in the Dimension Styles dialog box, the Modify Dimension Style dialog box opens. In this dialog box, you can configure the specific settings for the selected dimension style or substyle. The options in this dialog box are identical to the options in the Dimension Style Manager dialog box that opens when you use the traditional AutoCAD Dimstyle command.

Although you can change dimension settings using the Dimstyle command, it is recommended that you configure the dimension settings in the standard using the procedure in this training guide. One key reason to configure the dimension style and substyles in the standard is because these dimension styles are not added to the drawing unless a dimension that uses the style or substyle is added to the drawing. Therefore, these dimension styles are only stored in the standard and are ready to be added to the drawing if they are required. This helps decrease the amount of definition information created and stored in the drawing.

The following illustration displays the Modify Dimension Style dialog box.

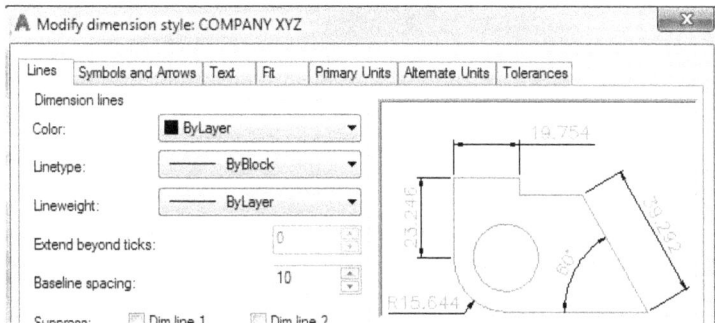

For the different dimension member types to display in accordance with an industry drafting standard, the AutoCAD Mechanical software automatically overrides some of the dimension settings in an individual dimension type. When you hover the cursor over a dimension type in the dimension style list, a tooltip displays listing the overrides that the AutoCAD Mechanical software has automatically applied to that member.

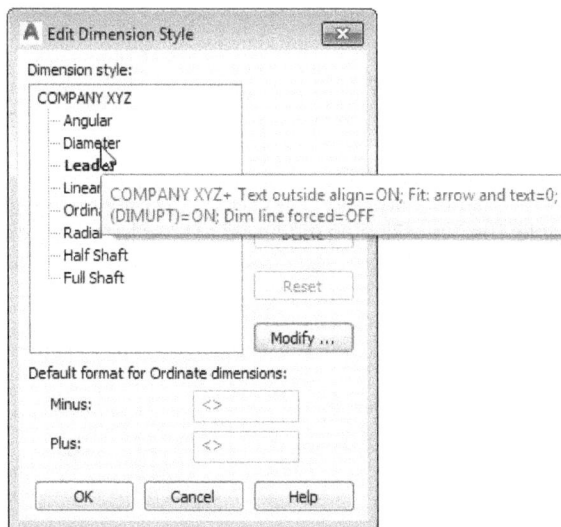

If you select an individual dimension type and modify any of its dimension style settings, that dimension type displays in bold text in the list. Because the dimension type displays in bold text, it clearly indicates that the dimension type currently has dimension settings that override the base dimension style or industry standard overrides. Hovering the cursor over the dimension type displays a tooltip listing all of the overrides that have been applied to that dimension type. You can clear the custom overrides and return the dimension type to its default configuration by selecting the dimension type from the list and clicking Reset.

If any dimension style settings are changed by entering the dimension variable at the Command Line anding a new value, the Edit Dimension Style dialog box includes an entry titled <style overrides>.

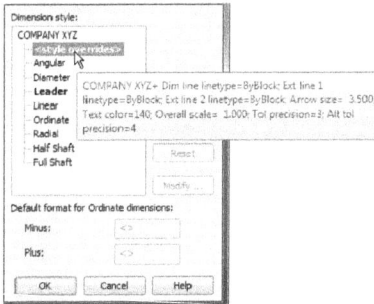

Default Representations

You can set the default representation for chamfer dimensions by clicking the preview image and selecting the required option in the table. The dimensioning method that is set here is the default dimensioning method that is used by the AutoCAD Mechanical **Chamfer** command and **Chamfer Dimension** command.

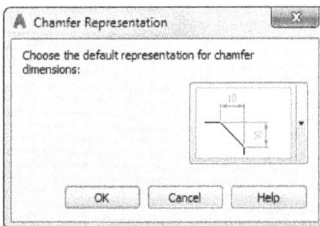

You can configure how radius dimensions should be formatted by selecting or clearing the checkboxes in the Radius Representation dialog box. Changing the settings in this dialog box updates the settings in the current dimension style. If you change the settings in the dimension style, these settings are overwritten.

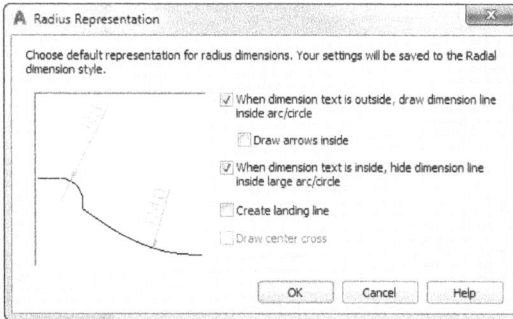

You can configure how the diameter dimensions should be formatted by selecting or clearing the checkboxes in the Diameter Representation dialog box. Changing the settings in this dialog box updates the settings in the current dimension style. If you change the settings in the dimension style, these settings are overwritten.

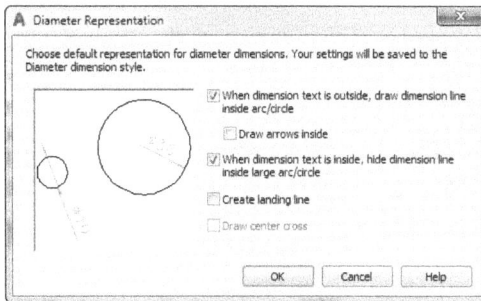

Predefined Dimension Text

To save time formatting and adding text to dimensions and to help maintain consistency between dimensions, you can define a list of predefined dimension text strings and formats. You can add to the list and can edit existing entries. The predefined text can consist of dynamic fields and static symbols or text. You can also format the text string in the Text Editor area. The list of predefined text strings is then available in the Power Dimensioning dialog box.

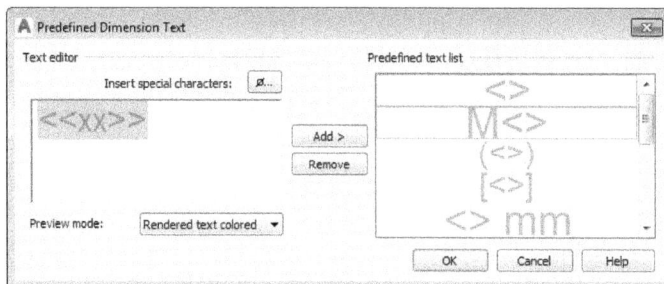

Fits and Tolerances

You can set the default values and formatting for fit and tolerances in their respective dialog boxes. You can set the default fit representation or tolerance method by clicking the preview image and then selecting the required option from the table. Click System Editor to open the System Editor dialog box with only the fits or tolerance keys to customize a predefined option.

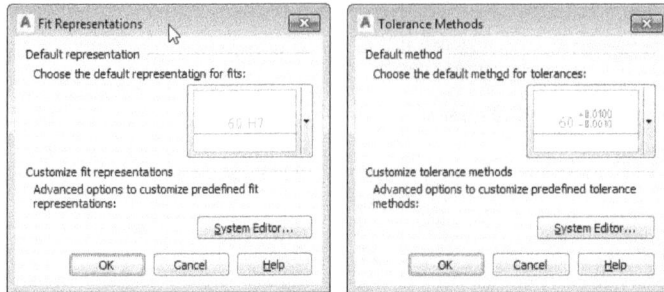

Procedure: Creating and Modifying Dimension Styles

An overview of configuring the dimension style settings in the active mechanical standard is shown in the following steps:

1. Open the Options dialog box. Click the *AM:Standards* tab.

2. Double-click on the standard Dimension element.

3. In the Dimensioning Settings dialog box, select the base dimension style for which you want to configure the settings. You can also enter a new name to create a new base dimension style.

4. Click Edit to open the Edit Dimension Style dialog box.

5. Modify the base standard and its substyles as required.

6. Repeat the previous two steps for each dimension style that might be used in a drawing.

7. Set the dimension style active that you want to use initially when adding dimensions.

8. Change the remaining settings in the Dimensioning Settings dialog box as required.

Configuring Hole Charts

Hole charts are an efficient way of calling out the location and properties of multiple holes. To maintain consistency and conformance to your standards, you should configure the standard as required and set it to be saved in the template file in the appropriate standard. To configure the hole charts as required, you need to understand which settings are available in the standard and how to configure them.

In the following illustration, the configuration of a hole chart was changed to include the Hole Index column of information.

Hole	X	Y	Ø	Description	Standard	Hole Index
1.1	10	10	Ø4.19	Metric ISO-Thread	ISO 261 - M10	D
1.2	10	35	Ø2	Blind Hole	Acc. to ISO 273 - 4 x 20	B
1.3	10	60	Ø4.19	Metric ISO-Thread	ISO 261 - M10	D
1.4	20	35	Ø2.75	Counterbore	DIN 974 T1-R1 - 5	C
1.5	35	20	Ø2.75	Counterbore	DIN 974 T1-R1 - 5	C
1.6	35	35	Ø7.5			A
1.7	35	50	Ø2.75	Counterbore	DIN 974 T1-R1 - 5	C
1.8	50	35	Ø2.75	Counterbore	DIN 974 T1-R1 - 5	C
1.9	60	10	Ø4.19	Metric ISO-Thread	ISO 261 - M10	D
1.10	60	35	Ø2	Blind Hole	Acc. to ISO 273 - 4 x 20	B
1.11	60	60	Ø4.19	Metric ISO-Thread	ISO 261 - M10	D

Hole Chart Settings Dialog Box

You can configure the hole charts for the List of Coordinates and the Hole Table by changing the settings in the Hole Chart Settings, Hole Chart Columns, and Sort dialog boxes. You can open the Hole Chart Columns dialog box and Sort dialog box from the Hole Chart Settings dialog box. You can open the Hole Chart Settings dialog box from the Options dialog box, in the AM:Standards tab, by double-clicking on the Hole Chart element.

In the Hole Chart Settings dialog box, you can set the method of locating the holes, the type of charts that you want to be able to create, the columns to display in those charts, and the text's display characteristics.

1. Use to select the method of calculating and representing the position of the holes: Cartesian Coordinates or Polar Coordinates.

2. Toggle on or off the option for the user to add a Hole Table chart to the drawing after they have placed the List of Coordinates chart. Selecting this option activates the list in Item 3.

3. Use to select the type of chart that you want to configure. The setting changes in Items 4, 5, 6, and 7 apply to the type that you have selected in this list. Select the chart type before making any changes.

4. Click to open the Hole Chart Columns dialog box for configuring which columns to display in the List of Coordinates chart or Hole Table chart.

5. Click to open the Sort dialog box to configure the order and method of sorting the data in the chart.

6. Use to toggle on or off the display of the chart's header, titles, or grips.

7. Use the options in this area to control the text appearance in the table, title, and direction of the information displayed in the table.

8. Use the options under Points and Origin to control the label position and appearance on the drawing view. The application of the settings in this area depend on the method selected for the hole position.

Hole Chart Columns Dialog Box

In the Hole Chart Columns dialog box, you can select which columns to display in the chart and configure the format for those columns. To change the format of a column, you can select the row in which column name is located and change the settings under Format Columns at the bottom of the dialog box. The list of available columns depends on the chart type that was selected before the dialog box was opened. Click the expand button in the lower right corner of the dialog box to display a list of additionally defined columns that you can select and add to the table list of columns.

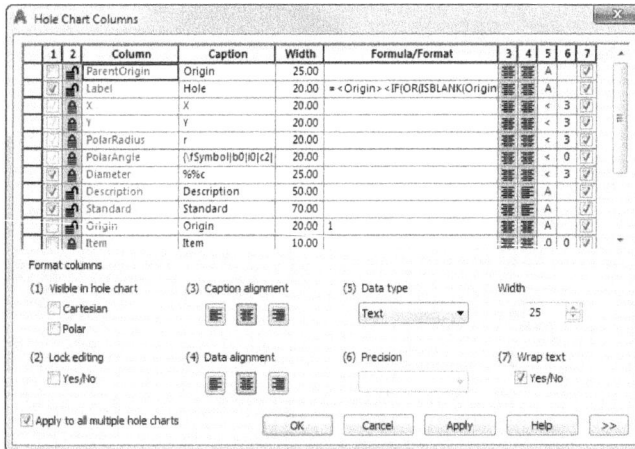

Sort Dialog Box

In the Sort dialog box, you can configure how the hole data should be ordered for display in the different charts. The Sorting Style area in the Sort dialog box is only available if you are configuring the sort order for the List of Coordinates chart. Hole Table charts only have the Sorting Criteria area available for configuration.

When you are configuring the sort using the options under Sorting Criteria, you can add chart column names to the sorting criteria, move the columns up or down the Sort Key list, and change the order in which data is sorted.

Procedure: Configuring Hole Charts

An overview of configuring hole chart settings in the active mechanical standard is shown in the following steps:

1. Open the Options dialog box. Click the *AM:Standards* tab.

2. Double-click on the standard Hole Chart element.

3. In the Hole Chart Settings dialog box, select the coordinate method to be configured.

4. Toggle on or off the option that enables the user to place a hole table with the List of Coordinates table.

5. Change the settings, column properties, and sort criteria for the selected coordinate method and chart type as required.

6. If you selected the option to make the Hole Table chart available for placement, select the other type of chart that is not yet configured. Change its settings, column properties, and sort criteria as required.

Configuring Drawing Sheets

The drawing border, title block, and revision list contain global information about the design. The drawing border helps frame the design data and present it in a professional manner. For ease of use and consistency between drawing sheets, you need to configure the Drawing Sheet element in the standard to include the required border, title block, and revision list formats. To configure these formats, you need to understand what you configure and how to configure them.

In the following illustration, the same lower left corner of the same drawing sheet is shown with two different title blocks positioned on the sheet. The top one uses the default title block configuration ISO Title Block A, and the bottom one uses a custom title block that was added to the standard and was available for selection.

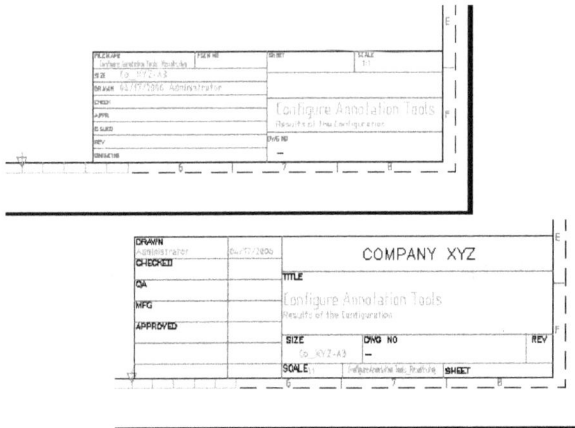

Drawing Sheet Settings

You can configure the drawing borders, title blocks, and revision lists that are available for insertion and other associated properties by changing the settings in the Drawing Sheet Settings dialog box. You can open the Drawing Sheet Settings dialog box from the Options dialog box, in the *AM:Standards* tab, by double-clicking on the Drawing Sheet element.

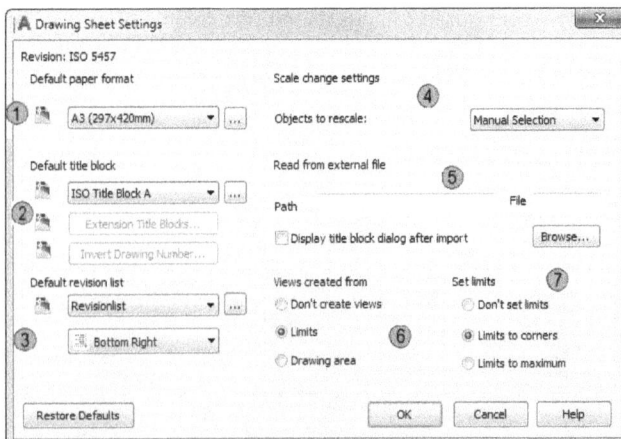

1. Use to set the default page format. Click Browse to navigate to and select a drawing to include as a block in the standard. The default formats have special attribute tags that are defined to assist in the automation of their use.

2. Use to set the default title block for insertion. Click Browse to navigate to and select a drawing to include as a block in the standard. The default title blocks have special attribute tags defined that are used to assist in their automatic positioning and the entry of data. If using the GOST standard, select up to two additional title block extensions.

3. Use to set the default revision list for insertion and where that insertion control point is located. Click Browse to navigate to and select a drawing to include as a block in the standard. As with title blocks, the default revision lists contain special attribute tags.

4. Use to set the workflow for scaling annotation symbols that reside within the area of the border. Keep this set to Manual Selection if you are inserting the border and title block into a layout at a scale of 1:1.

5. Use to specify a default ASCII text file that can be used to determine the paper format, scale, and title block attribute values while a user is placing a drawing border and title block.

6. Use to have six named views automatically created based on the border. Limits specifies the outside of the border to determine how far out to define the views. Selecting Drawing Area enables the named views to zoom to areas inside the border. The user can then use the named views to restore viewing locations in the drawing. These named views are also available for activation if a DWF file is created from the drawing.

7. Use to have the limits area of the model space automatically set after inserting a border into model space. Limits to Corners sets the limits to the outside corners of the last inserted border. Limits to Maximum sets the limits to a calculated bounding value that encompasses all of the geometry in the model space. When the border and title block are added to a layout, these settings are ignored.

Edit List of Scale Values

You can set the default scales for inserting the title block and border in the System Editor dialog box. You can open the dialog box in the Options dialog box, in the *AM:Preferences* tab, by clicking System. After the dialog box opens, expand the Acad/M tree and click Title to display the list of available scale factors. There are two lists for the title scale: ScaleList%M for drawings that use metric and ScaleList%I for drawings that use inches. You can modify the value list after double-clicking on the listed name. Remove or add the required scale, using a comma to separate the values.

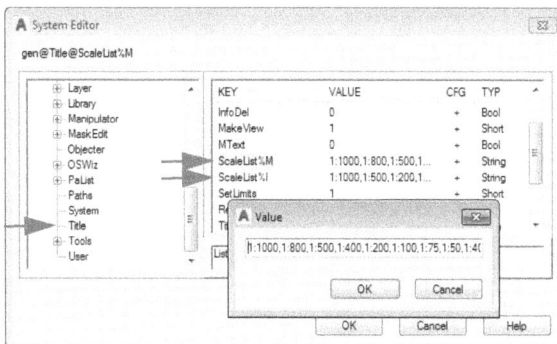

Procedure: Configuring Drawing Sheets

An overview of configuring the drawing sheet settings in the active mechanical standard is shown in the following steps:

1. Open the Options dialog box. Click the *AM:Standards* tab.

2. Double-click on the standard Drawing Sheet element.

3. Select the paper format that you want to use as the initial default format. Click Additional to add custom page and border formats.

4. Select the title block that you want to use as the initial default title block. Click Additional to add custom title blocks.

5. Select the revision list and insertion location that you want to use as the initial default. Click Additional to add custom revision lists.

6. Change the object rescaling and named view creation and then limit settings to match your workflow and requirements.

Configuring Notes

Adding note callouts to a drawing and ensuring that their content is correct can be time-consuming. To make this process more efficient, you can use note templates to pull data from the properties and attributes that are defined in the drawing. You can define additional note templates to enable you to notate the drawing with the required results. By configuring the note templates in the standard and saving them as part of the drawing template file, you improve productivity and help ensure consistency between drawings. To configure the note templates as required, you need to understand which settings are available in the standard and how to configure them.

In the following illustration, different notes were added to the drawing view. The structure of the notes is based on the template selected during the placement of the note. The data in the note was based on text defined in the template and the variables in the template. In this case, all of the numeric values were automatically taken from the drawing when the note was placed. If the values in the drawing are changed later, they automatically update to display the current value.

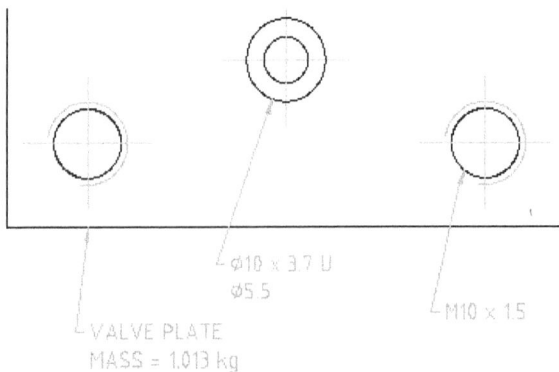

Leader Note Templates

The workflow for creating and using note library entries is similar to the workflow for creating and using weld and surface texture symbol library entries. The library area for notes is almost the same as the library area for weld symbols and surface texture symbols. The differences are that the library template entries for notes do not have a preview of the notation symbol and you can select different categories of note templates.

The library options for adding, importing, loading, updating, deleting, renaming, and setting the default template are the same for as the other symbol libraries. You can configure leader note library templates in the active drafting standard or when adding or editing a note in the drawing. You can configure the note library templates in the active standard in the Note Settings dialog box. The Note Settings dialog box can be opened from the Options dialog box, in the *AM:Standards* tab, by double-clicking on the Leader Note element.

For leader notes, the format of the library in the drawing file always controls the appearance of a leader note added to the drawing. Therefore if you add one or more note symbols to a drawing and edit that library entry later, all of the notes in the drawing based on that template update to reflect the new configuration. All of the static text in the note changes to reflect the current configuration while note information based on a variable maintains its value because that value is based on the selected geometry.

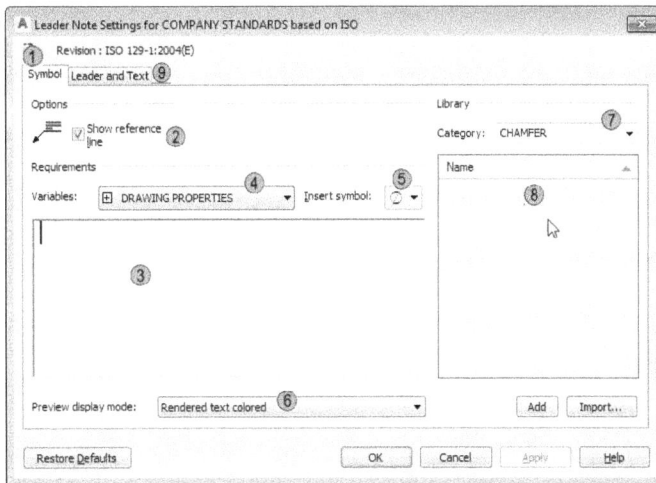

1. With this tab active, review and configure the content of note templates.

2. Select to add a shoulder or underline to the leader line that meets the active industry drafting standard.

3. Use to review and text and symbols for the active note template. You can also formulas for use with the property or attribute tags that are added to the note template from the variables list (4).

4. Use to select defined variables of properties, attributes, and formula functions and add them to the note. These variables automatically populate with a value when the note is added to the drawing. They also automatically update as the drawing changes. You can select variables from the list categories: Drawing Properties, Hole, Part Data, STDP, BOM Attributes, and Functions.

5. Use to display and insert different symbols into the note string.

6. Use to change the preview display of the note text as identified in Item 3.

7. Select the category of note templates that you want to review or edit.

8. Lists the available templates for the selected category. Use the options for an entry to load its settings into the note field (3), update the template to reflect the current note settings, delete or rename the entry, or make the entry the default.

9. Activate this tab to set the properties for the leader line arrowhead, the properties for the text, and the location at which the leader line connects to the note string.

Procedure: Configuring Note Templates

An overview of configuring note templates in the active mechanical standard is shown in the following steps:

1. Open the Options dialog box. Click the *AM:Standards* tab.

2. Double-click on the standard Leader Note element.

3. In the Category list, select the category that you want to add or edit in a note template.

4. In the text field in the Symbol tab, configure a new note with the symbols and drawing properties or attribute values that you want to display in the note. You can also load an existing template's information and then configure the note information.

5. Click Add to add and name the note as a new library template. You can also select an existing library entry and select the option to update it to match the current note configuration.

6. On the Leader and Text tab, select and set the arrow and text properties and justification method for the leader line to the note text.

Other Annotation Symbols and Their Settings

When you are configuring a drafting standard, you can change the initial default settings for many types of annotation symbols that you can add to a drawing. For most of these annotation symbols, the setting options consist of selecting one setting over another or selecting the options that are available to a user.

By learning how to configure an annotation symbol, you can configure these symbols to match your requirements. Making the changes to the standard in the template drawing ensures that all of the newly created drawings based on the template match your requirements.

Arrow and Text Settings

The majority of symbols that you configure include options for setting the properties for arrowheads and text. To set the property to be based on the global settings for the standard, the setting should be set to By <standard name>. When you set an option to have a unique property, it always has that property regardless of what is set globally for the standard.

In the following illustration, all of the arrowhead and text properties are set to use the settings in the standard COMPANY XYZ, except the arrowhead size and color. Those settings have a specific custom property override.

Leader			
Arrowhead:	By COMPANY XYZ		
Arrow size:	5	Color:	Red
Text			
Height:	4 By COMPANY X'	Color:	By COMPANY XY2
Leader justification:	To Reference Line		

Center Line Settings Dialog Box

You can configure the calculation method for determining the distance that the centerlines extend past the selected objects by changing the settings in the Center Line Settings dialog box. You can open this dialog box from the Options dialog box, in the *AM:Standards* tab, by double-clicking on the Center Line element.

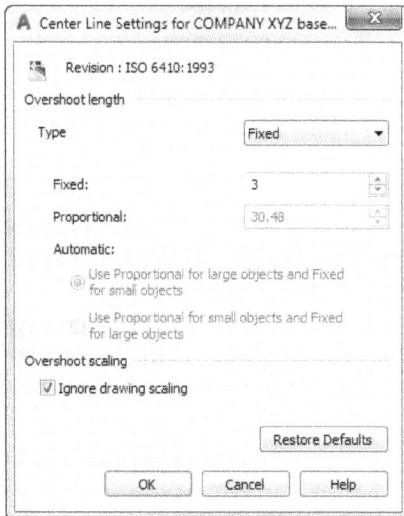

Center Line Settings for COMPANY XYZ base...

Revision : ISO 6410: 1993

Overshoot length

Type	Fixed

Fixed:	3
Proportional:	30.48

Automatic:

- Use Proportional for large objects and Fixed for small objects
- Use Proportional for small objects and Fixed for large objects

Overshoot scaling

☑ Ignore drawing scaling

Restore Defaults

OK   Cancel   Help

Section View Settings

In the Section View Settings dialog box, you can configure the text and line properties associated with the annotation of section views. You can open this dialog box from the Options dialog box, in the *AM:Standards* tab, by double-clicking on the Section View element.

Some industry standards might list multiple section view standards below the Section View element. Right-click on the listed standard to insert or remove the standard or to set it to be current.

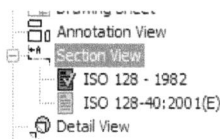

- Drawing Sheet
- Annotation View
- Section View
  - ISO 128 - 1982
  - ISO 128-40: 2001(E)
- Detail View

The settings that are established in the current standard for the Section View element control the appearance of the section line and annotation label when you draw a section line using the AMSECTIONLINE command.

You can set properties, such as the inclusion of a label and how it should display, the visibility and characteristics of the section line itself, and the appearance of its arrows and text.

The label pattern is a formula that automatically determines the section view label value that is in the drawing and increments the label to the next value. The initial text height and style are based on the text property settings for the overall standard. You can only change the text style or a custom height value if you are editing a custom standard.

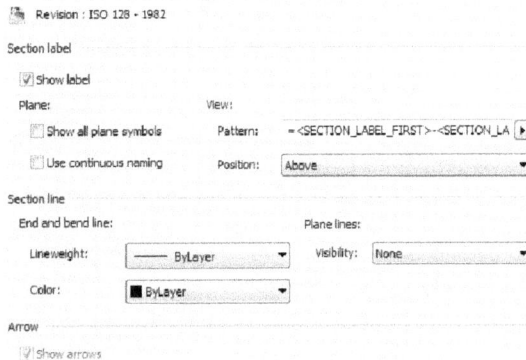

Detail Symbol Settings

In the Detail Symbol Settings dialog box, you can configure the text, label, and view border properties associated with the annotation of detail views. You can open this dialog box from the Options dialog box, in the AM:Standards tab, by double-clicking on the Detail View element.

The label pattern is a formula that automatically determines which detail view label value is in the drawing and increments the label to the next value. The initial text height and style are based on the text property settings for the overall standard. You can only change the text style or a custom height value if you are editing a custom standard.

By selecting or clearing the Show View Border and Show Connection Line checkboxes, you can preset the visibility of those items in the drawing.

Surface Texture Settings

Use the settings in the Surface Texture Settings dialog box to configure the default appearance of the surface texture symbol and the options from which the user can select when placing a surface texture symbol on a drawing. You can open this dialog box from the Options dialog box, in the *AM:Standards* tab, by double-clicking on the Surface Texture element.

Some industry standards might list multiple surface texture standards below the Surface Texture element. Right-click on the listed standard to insert or remove the standard or set it to current.

The options in the Surface Texture Settings dialog box enable you to do the following:

- Select what to include with the symbol.
- Create predefined lists of values and options for use when adding a surface texture symbol to a drawing.
- Select the appearance of the majority symbol.
- Configure the properties of the leader arrow and text.

To predefine a list of values and options, under Preset List, click Edit List that corresponds to the symbol notation that you want to define. After clicking one of the Edit List buttons, an edit dialog box opens with specific editing options for that symbol field. In the following illustration, the Edit List buttons for First Requirement A and Direction of Lay are identified with arrows.

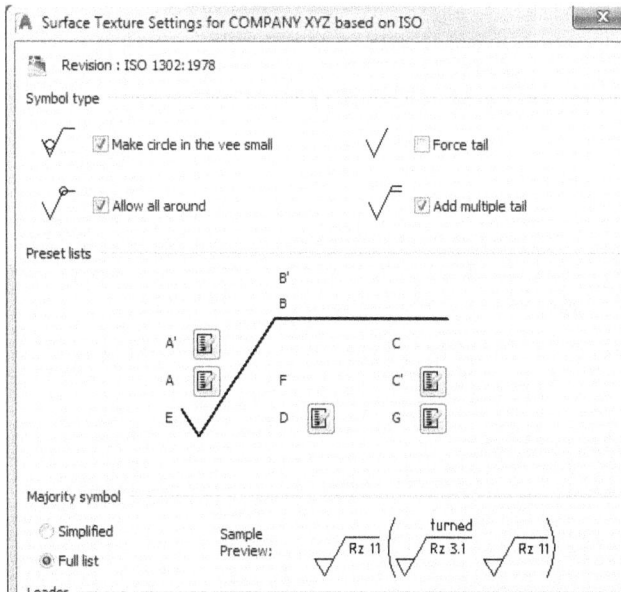

In the Edit list for First requirement A dialog box, you can add, edit, and remove values in the preset value list for the standard values of roughness, waviness, and cutoff. To change the preset values for a standard value, you first select it from the Standard Values list.

After the values display in the Preset Value list, you can change the order in which they are displayed so that they are listed in the order that is most efficient for you.

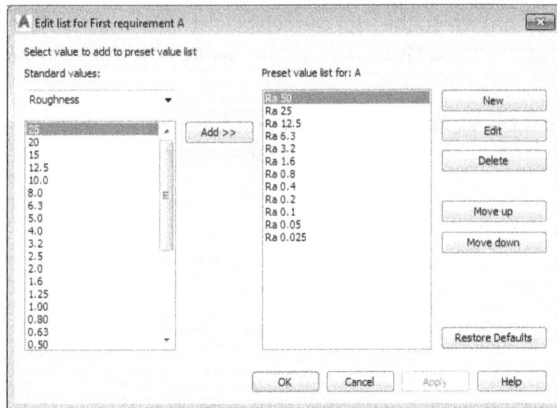

The Edit list for Direction of Lay D dialog box enables you to include or exclude values from the list and to change their listing order so that they are listed in the order that is most efficient for you.

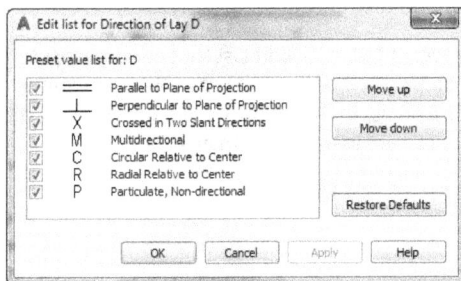

Welding Settings

Use the settings in the Welding Settings dialog box to configure the default options from which the user can select when placing a welding symbol on a drawing. You can also configure the properties of the leader arrow and text. You can open this dialog box from the Options dialog box, in the *AM:Standards* tab, by double-clicking on the Welding element.

The Identification Line area is only available as part of the standard when you are using any standard other than one based on ANSI or JIS. To change the linetype for the identification line, you must be editing a custom standard.

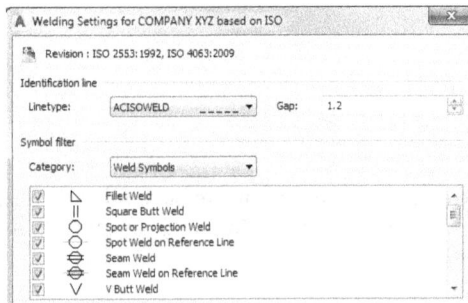

Feature Control Frame Settings

Use the settings in the Feature Control Frame Settings dialog box to configure the default appearance of the control frame and the options from which the user can select when they place a feature control frame on a drawing. You can also configure the properties of the leader arrow and text. You can open this dialog box from the Options dialog box, in the *AM:Standards* tab, by double-clicking on the Feature Control Frame element.

Edge Settings

You can open the Edge Settings dialog box from the Options dialog box, in the *AM:Standards* tab, by double-clicking on the Edges of Workpieces element. This element is only available for selection when you are configuring a standard based on the DIN, GB, ISO, or JIS drafting standard. Before double-clicking on the Edges of Workpieces element, ensure that the required version of the standard is set to be current.

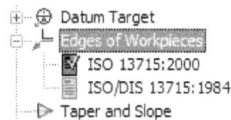

After opening the Edge Settings dialog box, click the representation, simplified, or full list that you want to configure as the default appearance for edge property symbols when the user selects the option to include the majority symbol next to the edge symbol on a drawing. You can also configure the required properties for the leader arrow and text.

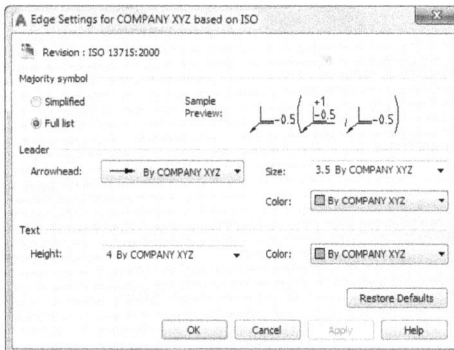

Datum Target Settings

Use the settings in the Datum Target Settings dialog box to configure the default appearance of the datum target symbols that the user places in a drawing. You can open this dialog box from the Options dialog box, in the *AM:Standards* tab, by double-clicking on the Datum Target element.

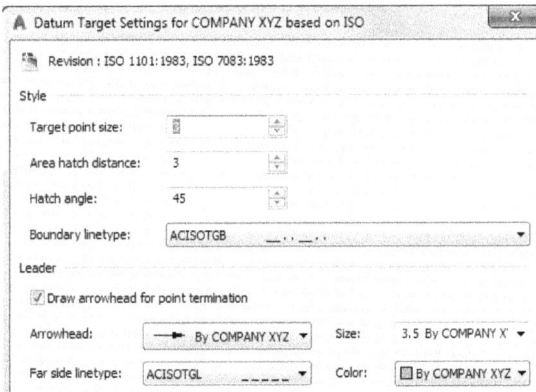

Taper and Slope Settings

In the Taper and Slope Settings dialog box, you can select the symbols that should be available to the user by default when they are annotating the drawing with a taper and slope symbol. You can also configure the properties of the leader arrow and text. You can open the dialog box from the Options dialog box, in the *AM:Standards* tab, by double-clicking on the Taper and Slope element.

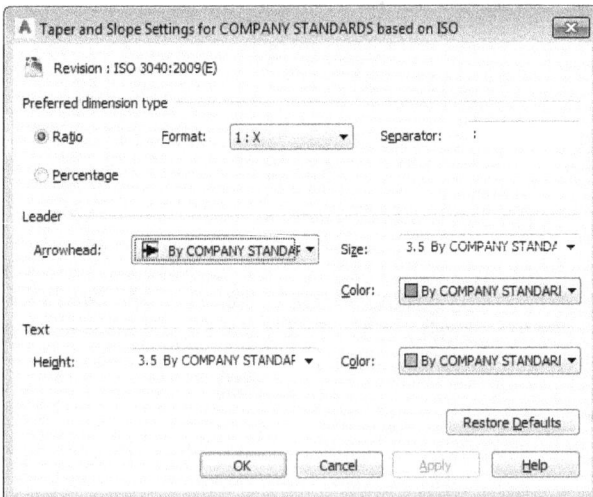

Exercise: Set Annotation Properties

In this exercise, you will make various changes to the configurations for dimensions, hole charts, title blocks, and notes as part of the process of preparing a drawing to become a template that contains your company standards.

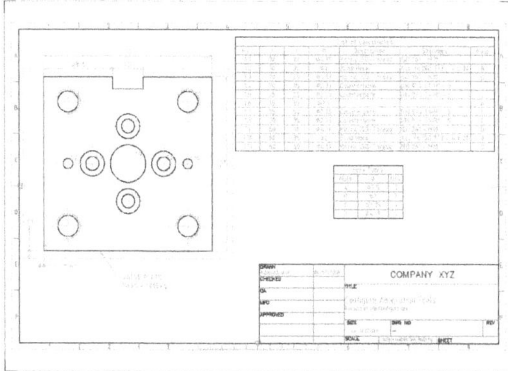

The completed exercise

1. Open *Configure Annotation Tools.dwg*.

2. To begin configuring the dimensions, do the following:

   - Click Application menu > Options.
   - On the *AM:Standards* tab, in the list of Standard elements, double-click on Dimension.

3. In the Dimension Settings dialog box, *Placement options* area, Display dimension text editor drop-down list, select Only on Demand.

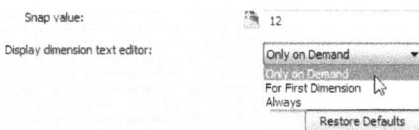

4. To begin modifying the dimension style, do the following:

   - Under Dimension style area, click Edit.
   - In the Edit Dimension Style dialog box, in the Dimension style list, select Company XYZ.
   - Click Modify.

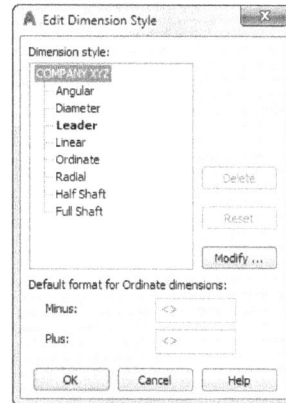

5. In the Modify dimension style dialog box, in the *Primary Units* tab, Linear dimensions area, in the Precision drop-down list, click 0.00. Click OK.

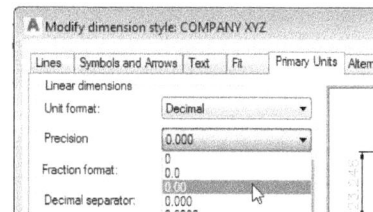

6. To change the unit precision for the substyle for linear dimensions, in the Edit Dimension Style dialog box, do the following:

   - In the Dimension style list, select Linear. Click Modify.
   - On the *Primary Units* tab, Linear dimensions area, in the Precision drop-down list, click 0.0.
   - Click OK.

7. To accept and apply these dimension changes to the standard, do the following:

   - In the Edit Dimension Style dialog box, click OK.
   - In the Dimensioning Settings dialog box, click OK.
   - In the Options dialog box, click Apply.

8. To begin configuring the hole charts, on the *AM:Standards* tab, in the list of Standard elements, double-click on Hole Chart.

9. To begin adding a column to the List of Ccoordinates hole table, in the Hole Chart Settings dialog box, click Hole table.

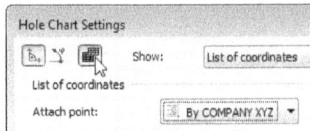

10. In the Hole Chart Settings dialog box, click Column Properties.

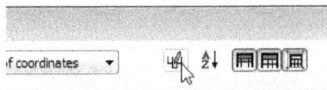

11. To add and configure a new column to the hole chart, in the Hole Chart Columns dialog box do the following:

- In the empty row at the bottom of the table, click the cell for the column titled Column.

- Enter **Hole Item** and press TAB.

- Enter **Hole** for the Caption column.

- Under Format columns, (1) Visible in hole chart, verify that Cartesian and Polar checkboxes are selected.

- Click OK.

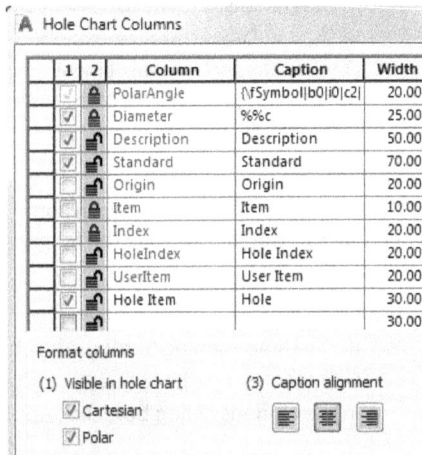

12. To change the insertion point of the chart List of coordinates, do the following:

- Under List of coordinates area, in the Attach point drop-down list, select Top Left.

- Click OK.

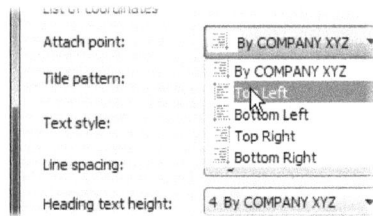

13. To add a custom title block to the drawing sheet configuration, do the following:

- On the *AM:Standards* tab, in the list of Standard elements, double-click on Drawing Sheet.

- In Drawing Sheet Settings dialog box, in the *Default title block* area, click Browse (...).

- Navigate to the folder location in which the Practice Files have been installed. Select *Co_XYZ-titleblock1.dwg* and click Open.

- Click OK.

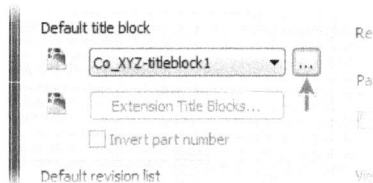

14. To begin configuring a new note as a library template, on the *AM:Standards* tab, in the list of Standard elements, double-click on Leader Note.

15. Begin to define the properties and format for the note. On the *Symbol* tab, Requirements area, in the Variables drop-down list, expand BOM ATTRIBUTES and select NAME.

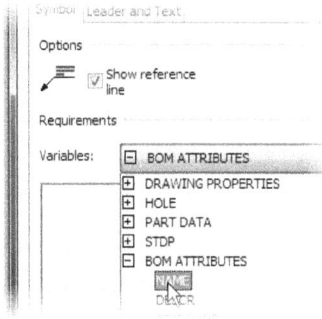

16. To specify the inclusion of the mass information, do the following:

- Press ENTER.
- In the second line of text, enter **MASS** =.
- On the Symbol tab, Requirements area, in the Variables drop-down list, expand BOM ATTRIBUTES and select MASS.

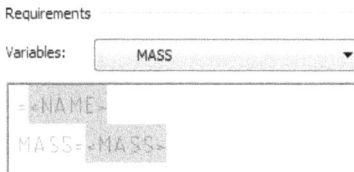

17. To add this configured note to the library, do the following:

- From the *Library* area, Category drop-down list, select OTHER TEMPLATES.
- Click Add.
- Enter **Part Name and Mass** and then press ENTER.

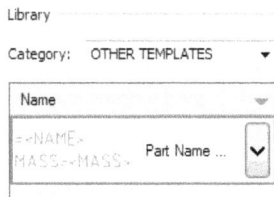

18. To format the leader line position to the note text, do the following:

- Click the *Leader and Text* tab.
- In the *Text* area, Leader justification drop-down list, select Middle of Top Line.
- Click OK.
- In the Options dialog box, click OK.

19. To review a drawing in which these settings were used during the annotation of the design, open *Configure Annotation Tools_Results.dwg*.

20. Save and close all of the files.

Lesson: Configure Component Properties, BOMs, Parts Lists, and Balloons

Overview

This lesson describes how to configure the component properties, BOM, parts list, and balloon elements of a standard within a drawing or template file.

By configuring and saving the standards for component properties, the BOM, parts list, and balloons in a template drawing and making that template available to other design team members, you ensure consistency for drawings and simplify the process of conforming to company and industry standards.

In the following illustration, the parts list and balloon configuration were changed to display the relevant data for the design of the bleacher substructure frame. The balloon is configured to display the cut length value for the piece and how many pieces need to be cut at that length.

9	1	Angle Steel	SS400	724.000	724.0
8	1	Angle Steel	SS400	791.300	791.3
7	1	Sloping Flange Channel Section	SS400	1130.000	1130.0
6	1	Angle Steel	SS400	318.000	318.0
5	1	Angle Steel	SS400	521.000	521.0
4	4	Angle Steel	SS400	600.000	2400.0
3	1	Angle Steel	SS400	927.000	927.0
2	5	Angle Steel	SS400	216.000	1080.0
1	1	Angle Steel	SS400	2577.500	2577.5
Item	Qty	Description	Material	Cut Length	Total Length

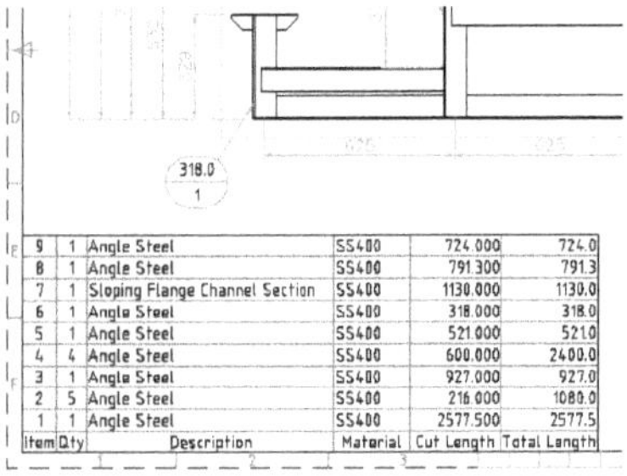

Objectives

After completing this lesson, you will be able to:

- Describe the importance and use of bill of materials data.
- Describe the process for configuring bill of materials settings for items related to bills of materials.
- State the purpose of the list of available component properties and identify what is configured for the different properties.
- Configure the component properties settings within the active standard.
- Configure the bill of materials settings within the active standard.
- Configure the parts list settings within the active standard.
- Configure the balloon settings within the active standard.

About BOM Data

A drawing file's bill of materials (BOM) plays a crucial role in annotating a drawing with balloons and a parts list. To better understand this relationship and importance, you need to learn about the BOM and its data.

In the following illustration, the BOM dialog box lists the contents of the bill of materials for the subassembly Bracket Bearing. This subassembly contains two distinct parts with two total parts used. Because Mechanical structure was used in this assembly design, this BOM data for the subassembly was automatically available for display.

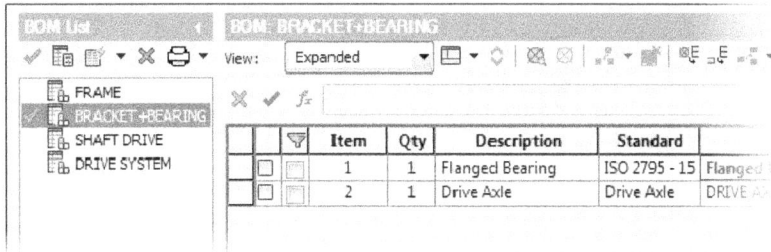

Definition of BOM Data

When you create an assembly, you typically want to list the parts and subassemblies, their quantities, and their specific properties in a table or chart format. The table that is placed on the drawing that lists this information is referred to as a parts list. To identify the different items in the drawing views, you can add balloons with item numbers that match the item numbers in the parts list. The information for the balloons and parts lists comes from a bill of materials (BOM) that is stored in the assembly file. The BOM often contains more information than you want to display on the drawing sheet. The BOM then becomes a central location for entering and editing data and can be exported for use in other software applications.

There are three methods of populating the data in the BOM. One method is to all of the data for the entire assembly manually. A second method is to the data associated with a part or subassembly into part references. The third method involves entering the values into the component properties for mechanically structured parts and subassemblies.

The second and third methods of populating BOM data are similar. In each of these methods, you can the properties for each unique part or subassembly and the BOM is then automatically populated with that information. By entering the data in the part reference or structured component properties, you can the data once and reuse it in multiple assemblies. For all of the assemblies in which the part or assembly is used, the BOM is automatically populated with that information. The quantity value in the BOM is then based on the number of instances of a part or subassembly in the overall assembly.

Example of BOM Data

Because the BOM is a central repository of information, you can use the data in many different ways. In the following illustration, the BOM dialog box is shown open below a parts list based on the BOM data. Note that there are more columns of data in the BOM dialog box than are being displayed in the parts list. The data in these other columns might exist so that it can be displayed in other parts lists or be included if you export the data to an external file for use in another software application.

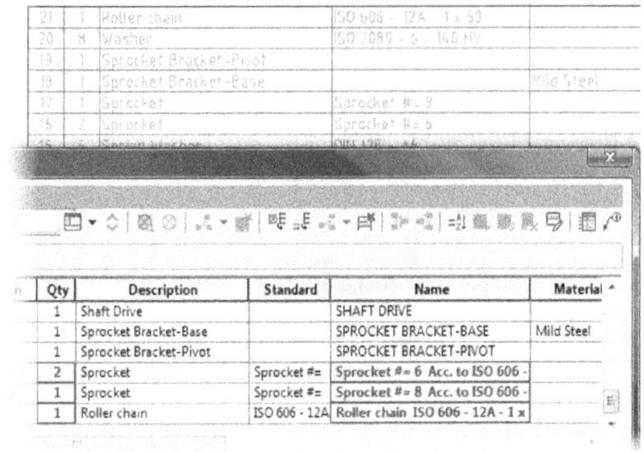

Configuring BOM Settings for BOM Related Items

You can configure the BOM settings for a standard to determine the information that should be stored in the drawing's BOM and component properties. You can also configure how that data should be formatted for display in the BOM dialog box and drawing parts list.

To make any required setting changes to the BOM and its related items, you need to learn the overall process of configuring the BOM settings for items related to the BOM.

In the following illustration, the dialog box for editing component properties, the listing of the parts in the BOM dialog box, and the parts list added to the drawing are shown. To list these properties in the correct order and with the correct settings in these areas, they first had to be configured to match the requirements.

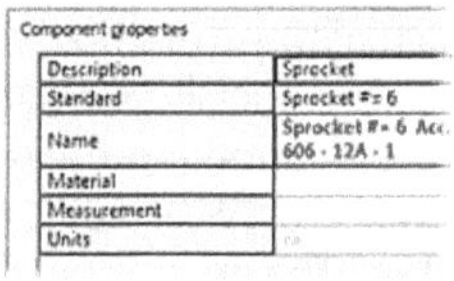

Component Properties 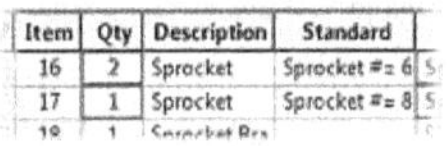   BOM 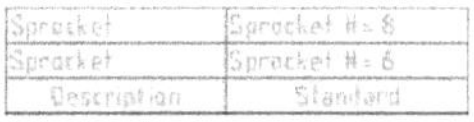   Parts List

Configuration Access

Because parts lists and balloons retrieve their data from the BOM, and the BOM can get its data from component properties, you can configure these items in the same dialog box. You can configure the BOM and its related items by changing the standard settings in the BOM Settings dialog box. You can open the dialog box from the Options dialog box, in the *AM:Standards* tab, by double-clicking on the Component Properties, BOM, Parts List, or Balloon element.

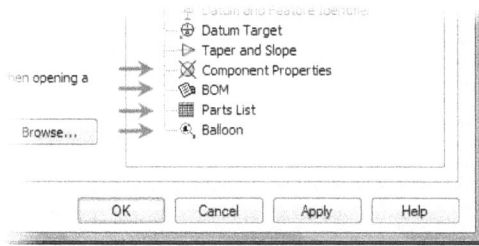

BOM Settings Dialog Box

When the BOM Settings dialog box opens, the tab that corresponds to the name of the standards element on which you double-clicked is initially active (2). For a component property to list on one of these tabs, the property must first exist in the list of available component properties (1).

Because the component property must first exist in the available component property field, you typically start configuring the BOM settings by creating and configuring the required component properties in the available component properties list (1). After the component property exists, you can add it to the list on the Component Properties, BOM, or Parts List tabs (2).

Adding an available property to the Component Properties or Parts List tabs automatically adds it to the BOM tab. Adding an available property to the BOM tab only adds it to the BOM tab. The list of component properties on the Balloon tab is based on the available properties on the BOM tab.

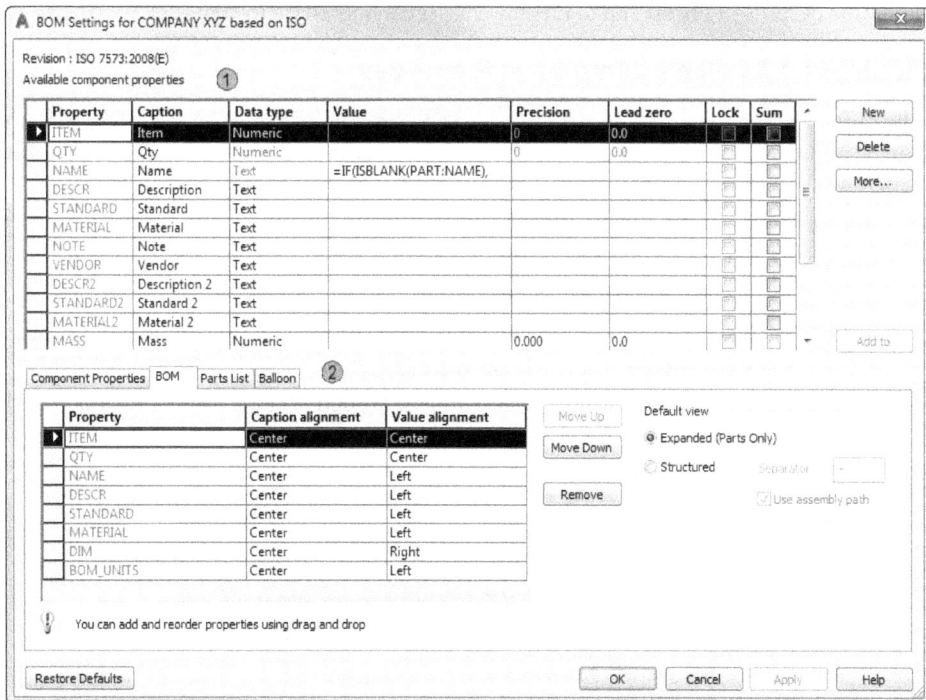

> To maintain consistency between the data captured for the different parts within a drawing and between drawings, configure and save the BOM settings to a template drawing before starting your drawings.

Process: Configuring BOM Settings for BOM-Related Items

An overview of configuring BOM settings for the BOM-related items of the component properties, BOMs, parts lists, and balloons is shown in the following steps:

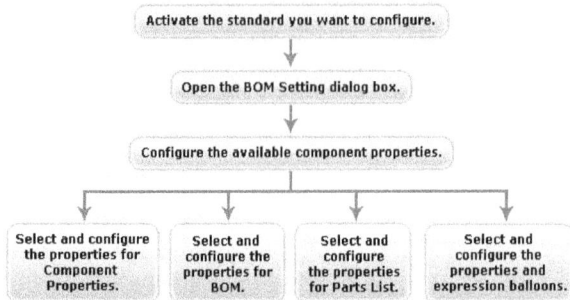

Activate the standard you want to configure.

↓

Open the BOM Setting dialog box.

↓

Configure the available component properties.

| Select and configure the properties for Component Properties. | Select and configure the properties for BOM. | Select and configure the properties for Parts List. | Select and configure the properties and expression balloons. |

Available Component Properties

Creating and configuring properties in the Available Component Properties list in the BOM Settings dialog box is an important part of configuring the component properties, BOM, parts list, and balloons. To add, delete, or modify properties in the Available Component Properties list, you need to know the purpose of the list and to identify what is configured for the different properties.

Settings for Available Component Properties

The Available Component Properties list in the BOM Settings dialog box indicates the properties that can be included in the component properties, BOM, or parts list. Within this list, you can control the following:

- The caption for the property value columns.
- The type of data stored in the property.
- Whether the value is based on an expression.
- The decimal precision and inclusion of leading zeros when set to the Numeric data type.
- Whether the value should be locked from manual editing.
- The summation of all of the values in the Numeric Property column when the option to show the results bar is toggled on.

BOM Settings for COMPANY XYZ based on ISO

Revision : ISO 7573:2008(E)

Available component properties

Property	Caption	Data type	Value	Precision	Lead zero	Lock	Sum	
ITEM	Item	Numeric		0	0.0			
QTY	Qty	Numeric		0	0.0			
NAME	Name	Text	=IF(ISBLANK(PART:NAME),					
DESCR	Description	Text						
STANDARD	Standard	Text						
MATERIAL	Material	Text						
NOTE	Note	Text						
VENDOR	Vendor	Text						
DESCR2	Description 2	Text						
STANDARD2	Standard 2	Text						
MATERIAL2	Material 2	Text						
MASS	Mass	Numeric		0.000	0.0			

New
Delete
More...
Add to

1. A unique name for storing the properties and values and for reference within formulas.

2. Use to the title of the column as indicated in the BOM dialog box and in the header in the parts list.

3. Select the type of data to be stored in the property as Text or Numeric.

4. Use to create and display a formula or expression for the calculation of the value for this column value. Your formula can contain attributes about the drawing, BOM, part, or features within the design. You can include numeric, logic, and string functions within the formula. You can also create a list of possible values from which you can select when specifying the property's value.

5. When the data type is numeric, select the decimal precision from a list. You can also select the number of leading zeros to include for the numeric value.

6. Select the checkbox for a property when you do not want the value to be directly editable by the user.

7. Select the checkbox for a property when you want the numeric value to be totaled for the column when the Show Results Bar option is selected in the BOM or parts list.

8. Click New to add a row to the list or select a row and click Delete to remove the row from the list.

9. Click to open the More Properties dialog box to select additional properties for inclusion in the list of available component properties.

Expression Builder

When you activate a cell in the Value column in the Available Component Properties list, you can manually an expression or you can click the button located on the right side of the active cell. When you click this button, the Expression Builder dialog box opens and you can create formulas or predefined lists of values.

Available component properties

Property	Caption	Data type	Value	Pre
ITEM	Item	Numeric		0
QTY	Qty	Numeric		0
NAME	Name	Text	=IF(ISBLANK(PART:NAME),	
DESCR	Description	Text		
STANDARD	Standard	Text		
MATERIAL	Material	Text		
NOTE	Note	Text		

Formulas

When the Expression Builder opens for a cell that is currently empty, by default you need to define a formula. You can add a property or function to the Expression box by selecting it in the Select list and clicking Add. The property or function is then added to the expression at the last cursor location. You can also directly the property or function in the Expression box.

Selecting numeric data type properties anding mathematical operators or functions causes the expression to calculate a new value based on that formula. Selecting properties with text, or noting an operator, causes the values of those properties to concatenate.

You can select properties or functions in the Component Properties, Drawing Properties, or Functions categories.

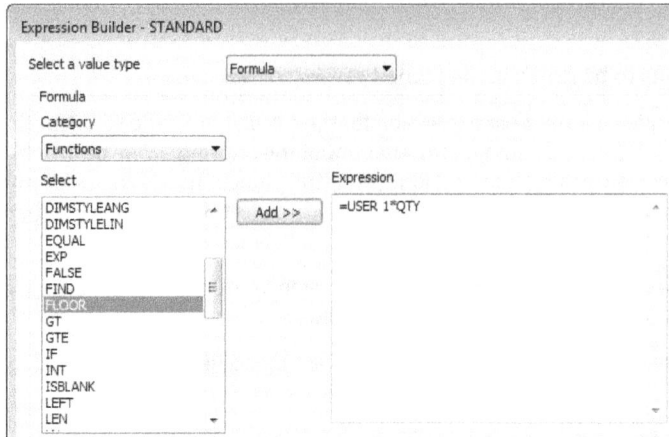

Predefined Lists

Properties can also include a predefined list of values from which the user can select when specifying values for properties of a part or assembly. To specify a list of values, in the Expression Builder, change the value type to Predefined List. Add rows to the list by clicking New or by clicking the last row in the list titled Click to Add.

You can select a row by clicking the gray button on the far left end of the row. After you select an existing row, you can click Delete to remove it from the list or change its position in the list by clicking Move Up or Move Down. You can also move a value up or down the list by clicking and dragging the gray button after selecting the row.

A checkmark icon in the column to the left of the Value column indicates that the value is assigned to the property by default. Select the row and click Set Default to assign the value as the default value. To set the default value to be an empty cell, do not set a value to be the default. To clear a default setting, select the row that is currently set to be the default and click Remove Default.

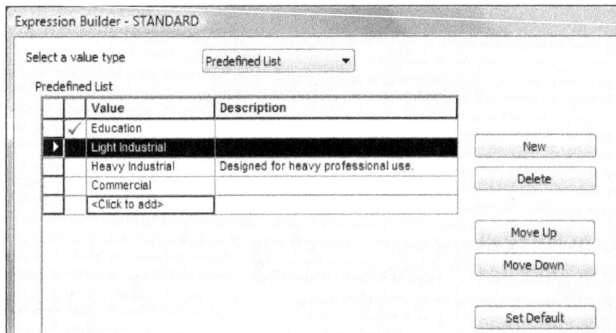

Configuring Component Properties

You can preconfigure the component properties in the standard and save the standard in the drawing template. When you edit the values of a mechanically structured component or a part reference in a drawing, the appropriate properties are listed for you and you can data.

In the following illustration, the Properties dialog box and the Part Reference dialog box show an example of the values of the configured component properties that are being edited.

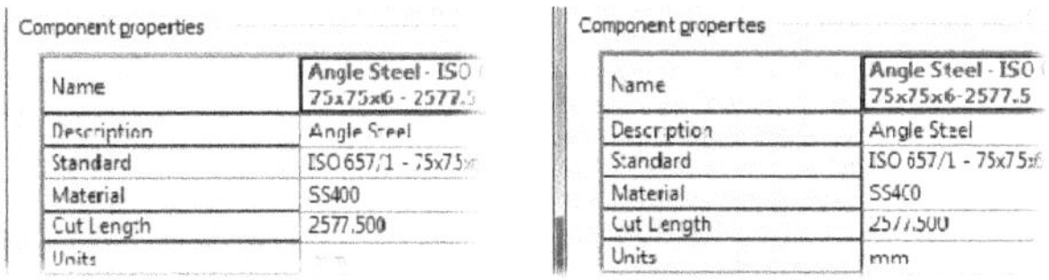

Component Properties

You can configure the component properties by changing the standard settings on the *Component Properties* tab in the BOM Settings dialog box.

The properties that are listed in the Component Properties list are those that are listed in the Properties or Part Reference dialog boxes. The values of the properties that are not set to be locked can be edited in these dialog boxes.

This list of properties does not have to contain all of the properties listed in the BOM. You can select the option to include only the properties that you want to edit in the Properties or Part Reference dialog boxes. To match the list of properties to the properties in the BOM, click Sync.

You can add individual properties to the list by first selecting them in the Available Component Properties list. After selecting the property that you want to add, you can drag it to the list in the Component Properties tab or click Add To. To select a row in the list, click the gray button located to the left of the row as shown by the arrows in the following illustration.

By selecting a row in the list on the Component Properties tab, you can change its order in the list by dragging it to a new location or by clicking Move Up or Move Down. When you click Remove, the property is removed from the Component Properties list but remains in the Available Component Properties list.

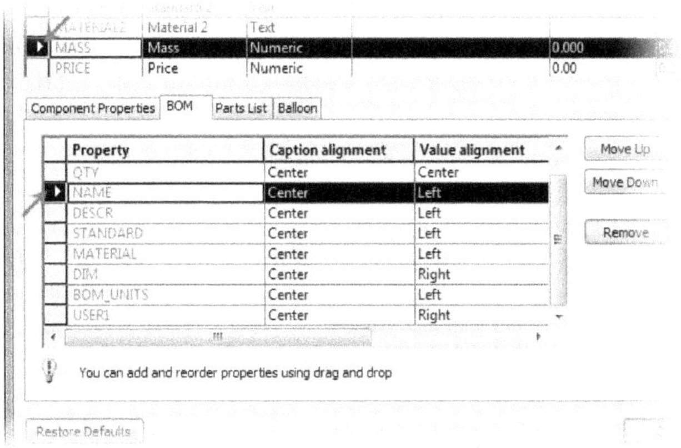

When you configure a property in the Available Component Property list, you can a caption for the property. The caption is used by the BOM and parts list as the header for that column of property data. This caption also becomes the default display prompt for the property in the Properties and Part Reference dialog boxes. Although the display prompt for a property defaults to its caption, you can a different display prompt for each property on the Component Properties tab in the Display Prompt field.

You can change the display prompt for a property to help the user determine the data that should be entered for that property and how it should be entered. For example, in the following illustration, the display prompt for the property MASS was changed to instruct the user to the value in kilograms.

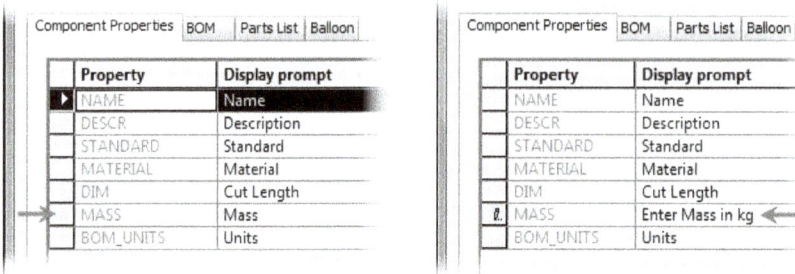

Procedure: Configuring Component Properties

An overview of configuring the component properties settings within the active standard is shown in the following steps:

1. Open the Options dialog box. Click the *AM:Standards* tab.

2. Double-click on the standard Component Properties element.

3. In the BOM Settings dialog box, in the *Component Properties* tab, you can add or remove properties, change the order in which the properties are listed, or a new prompt for the property.

Configuring the BOM

You can preconfigure the BOM in the standard and save it in the drawing template to determine the information that should be stored in the drawing's BOM. You can also establish how that data should be formatted for display in the BOM dialog box.

In the following illustration, the BOM tab in the BOM Settings dialog box is shown on top of the BOM dialog box listing the parts in a drawing file. This illustration shows the application of the BOM configuration. This configuration contains a column with a caption titled Total Length. The value in this column is stored in the property titled USER1. While the property configuration for USER1 is set under Available Component Options, the alignment for the caption and its values are configured on the BOM tab. The order of the columns in the BOM is also based on the order in which the properties are listed on the BOM tab.

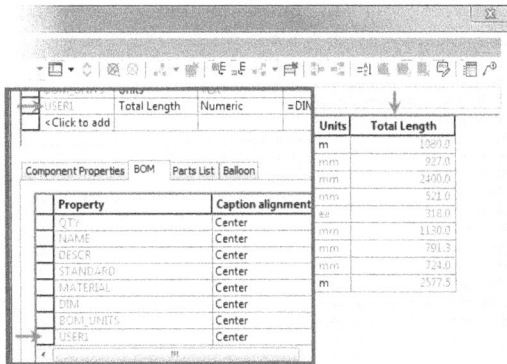

BOM

You can configure the BOM by changing the standard settings on the BOM tab in the BOM Settings dialog box.

On the BOM tab in the BOM Settings dialog box you can do the following:

- Add or remove component properties in the list.
- Change the order of the properties in the list.
- Change the alignment for the caption or value for each property.
- Set the BOM so that its display defaults to Expanded or Structured.

You can add individual properties to the list by first selecting them in the Available Component Properties list and then dragging it to the list on the BOM tab or clicking Add To. To select a row in the list, click the gray button located to the left of the row as shown by the arrows in the following illustration.

Properties are also added to the BOM automatically when you add a component property to the Available Component Properties list or you can add an available component property to the Parts List or Component Properties lists.

By selecting a row in the list on the BOM tab, you can change its order in the list by dragging it to a new location or by clicking Move Up or Move Down. When you click Remove, the property is removed from the BOM list but remains in the Available Component Properties list.

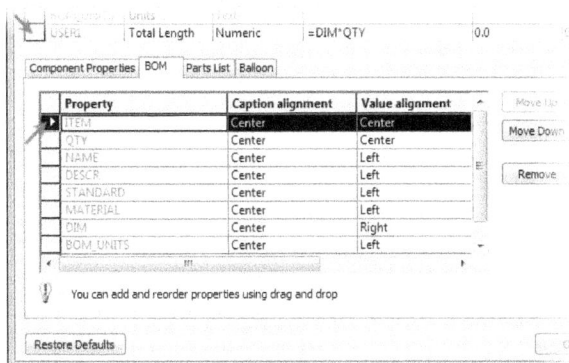

On the BOM tab, under Default View, you can set the default option for how you want to display the BOM subassembly information. When you click Expanded, you can display the subassemblies as a single line-item component. When you click Structured, the parts within the subassembly are elevated so that the subassembly entry is ignored. When you click Structured, you can preset the separator to use between the items numbers for the parts in the subassembly and the subassembly's item number.

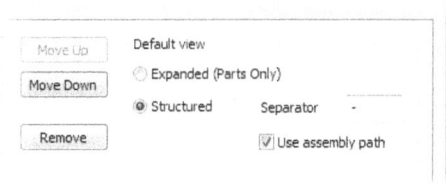

Procedure: Configuring the BOM

An overview of configuring the BOM in the active mechanical standard is shown in the following steps:

1. Display the Options dialog box. Click the *AM:Standards* tab.

2. Double-click on the standard BOM element.

3. In the BOM Settings dialog box, in the *BOM* tab, you can configure the property list to match your requirements by adding or removing properties, changing the order in which the properties are listed, or changing the alignment of the caption or value.

4. Set the default view for the BOM to Expanded or Structured. If you click Structured, set the separator value and the assembly use preference.

Configuring the Parts List

You can preconfigure the parts list in the standard and then save the standard in a drawing template. Drawings created based on the template then include the configured parts list within the saved standard. When a user adds a parts list to a drawing, the list displays the appropriate amount of information in the drawing based on that configuration.

In the following illustration, two parts list configurations display the same assembly BOM data, but the top parts list displays more BOM columns of information and with a different text height and color.

Parts List

You can configure the parts list by changing the standard settings on the *Parts List* tab in the BOM Settings dialog box.

On the Parts List tab in the BOM Settings dialog box you can do the following:

- Add or remove component properties from the list.
- Change the order in which the properties are displayed in the list.
- Change the alignment for the caption and value data.
- Set the width for each property so that the column in the parts list in the drawing has the required width for the value of that property.
- Select and set the properties of the parts list that is inserted into the drawing. Select between a parts list based on industry standards and a custom parts list block.

The properties are listed in the Parts List tab become columns of information in the Parts List dialog box and in the parts list that is added to the drawing.

This list of properties does not have to contain all of the properties listed in the BOM. You can add or remove individual properties so that the parts list that is added to the drawing only contains the required properties. To match the list of properties to the properties listed in the BOM, click Sync.

To add individual properties to the list, you first select the required property in the Available Component Properties list. Drag the property to the list on the Parts List tab, or click Add To. To select a row in the list, click the gray button located to the left of the row as shown by the arrows in the following illustration.

By selecting a row in the list on the *Parts List* tab, you can change the row's order in the list by dragging it to a new location or by clicking Move Up or Move Down. When you click Remove, the property is removed from the list on the Parts List tab but remains in the Available Component Properties list.

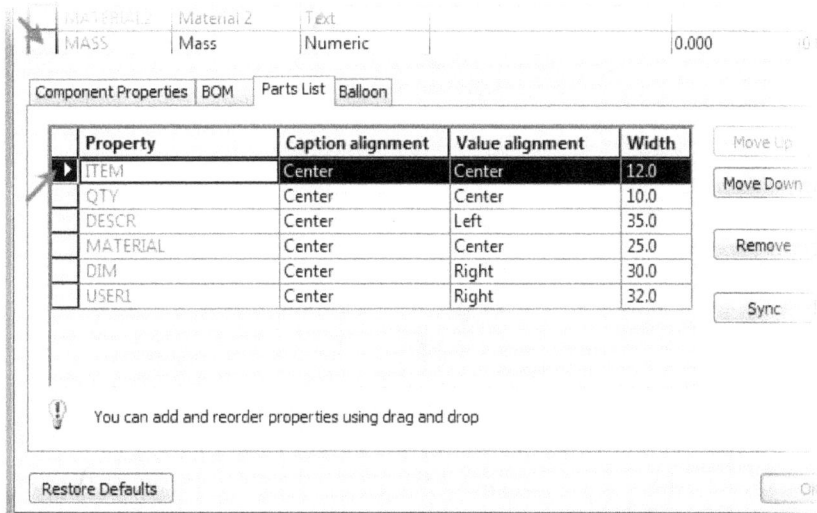

Parts List Style

In the *Parts List* tab, under Default Style, you can configure the parts list insertion appearance to follow a parts list based on industry standards or to use a custom parts list block. When you select the option to use a standards-based parts list, clicking Parts List Settings (shown by the arrow in the following illustration), opens the Parts List Settings dialog box.

In the Parts List Settings dialog box, you can set the parts list's insertion point, text properties (such as color and height), internal margins between the text and lines of the parts list, general layout, and column splitting. By enabling column splitting, you can set the parts list to repeat all of the property columns after so many rows or in so many sections. You can set it to wrap to the left or right of the insertion point.

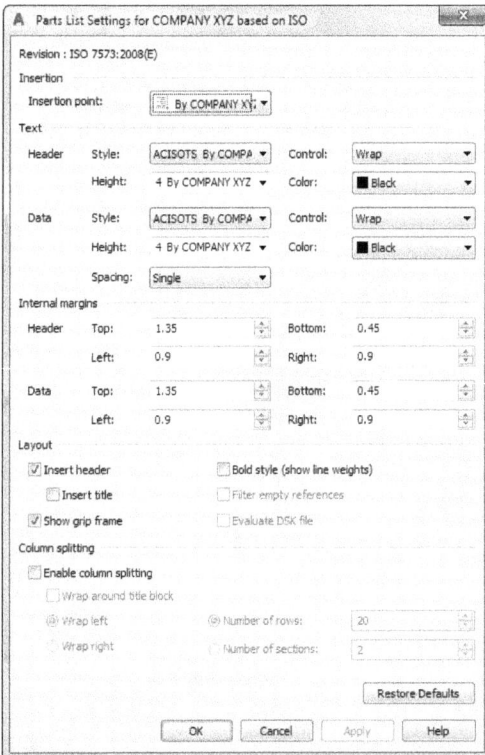

Procedure: Configuring the Parts List in the Active Standard

An overview of configuring the parts list in the active mechanical standard is shown in the following steps:

1. Open the Options dialog box. Click the *AM:Standards* tab.

2. Double-click on the standard Parts List element.

3. In the BOM Settings dialog box, on the Parts List tab, you can configure the property list as required by adding or removing properties, changing the order in which the properties are listed, changing the alignment of the caption or value, or entering a new column width.

4. In the *Parts List* tab, under Default style, set the parts list appearance to be based on an industry standard or a custom block.

5. If you set the parts list to use an industry-standard parts list, specify the properties and settings that match your requirements for parts list insertion, text, internal margins, layout, and column splitting.

Configuring the Balloons

As part of the process of creating a production-ready drawing, balloon callouts are added to identify the different parts and subassemblies that are represented in the drawing view. To have the balloons conform to your company drafting standards, configure them in the active standard and save the active standard in the template. In this way all new drawings created using the template are going to include balloons that meet the drafting standards requirements.

In the following illustration, the type of balloon was changed from the default circle to two other available standard balloon types. The balloons on the right show both the item number and quantity of the parts and subassemblies in the overall assembly.

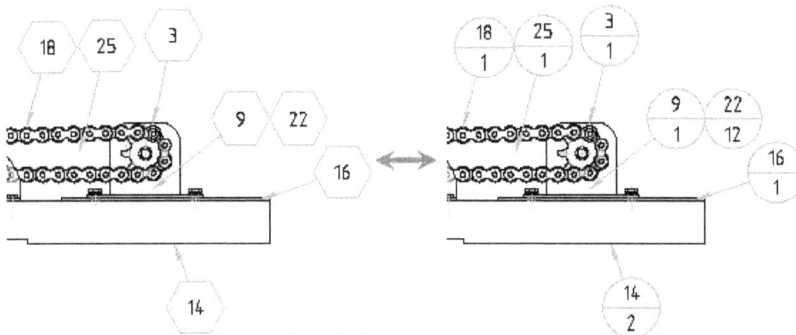

Balloon Properties

You can configure the balloon callouts by changing the standard settings in the *Balloon* tab in the BOM Settings dialog box.

In the Balloon tab in the BOM Settings dialog box, you can do the following:

- Specify whether the balloon is based on an industry standard or on a selected block.
- If the balloon is based on an industry standard, you can set the balloon type, size and spacing values, leader arrow type, and text properties.
- Define an expression for the balloon value.

Defining an expression for the balloon value is similar to specifying an expression for a property's Value field in the Available Component Property list. The list from which you can select properties for the Component Properties category is based on the properties listed in the BOM list. In the Category list you can also select Drawing Properties and Functions to have the Select list contain the properties or functions for that category. If you have selected the option to use the industry standard balloon type of Circular 2 Text, you can define two expressions: one for the value displayed on top and another for the value on the bottom.

Before defining an expression for the balloon, you should select the option to use a standards-based balloon or custom block. When you use an industry standard, you can an expression. When you use a custom block, you cannot define an expression for the block's value.

When you select the industry standard, you can click Balloon Settings to open the Balloon Settings dialog box and further define the appearance of the balloon.

Balloon Settings

In the Balloon Settings dialog box, for balloons based on industry standards, you can specify the balloon type, size factor, distance between automatically placed balloons, arrowhead type on its leader line, and text height and color.

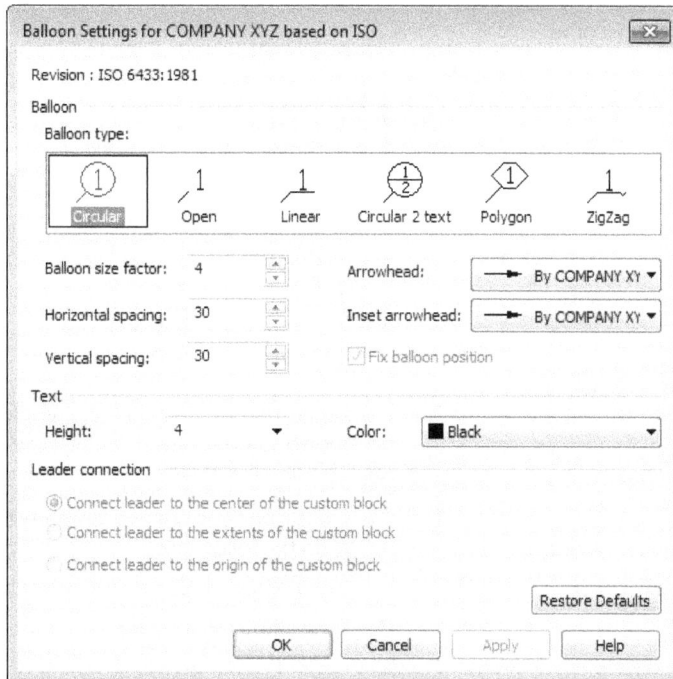

Procedure: Configuring the Balloons in the Active Standard

An overview of configuring the balloon settings in the active mechanical standard is shown in the following steps:

1. Open the Options dialog box. Click the *AM:Standards* tab.

2. Double-click on the standard Balloon element.

3. In the BOM Settings dialog box, in the *Balloon* tab, under Default style, select to have the balloon's appearance based on an industry standard or custom block.

4. If the balloons are based on an industry standard, in the Balloon Settings dialog box, select the balloon type and set the properties for the balloons, arrows, and text.

5. If your balloons are based on an industry standard, select or an expression of properties and functions to specify the value for the balloons.

Exercise: Configure Properties, BOM, Parts List, and Balloons

In this exercise, you will configure the available properties for component properties, BOM, parts lists, and balloons. You will then configure the BOM, component properties, parts list, and balloons. After configuring those items, you will open another drawing to review the same settings in a partially completed design.

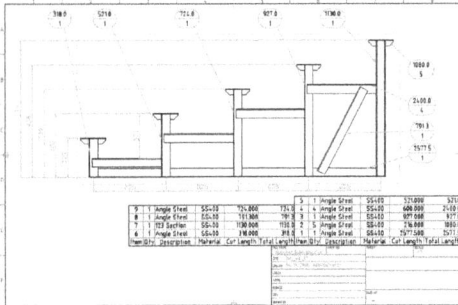

The completed exercise

1. Open *Configure BOM-PartsList-Balloons.dwg*.

2. To begin configuring the BOM, do the following:
    - Click Application menu > Options.
    - In the *AM:Standards* tab, in the list of Standard elements, double-click on BOM.

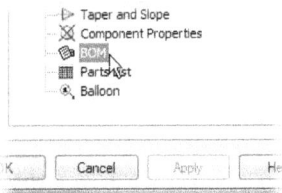

3. In the BOM Settings dialog box, in the Caption field for the property DIM, enter **Cut Length** to modify it.

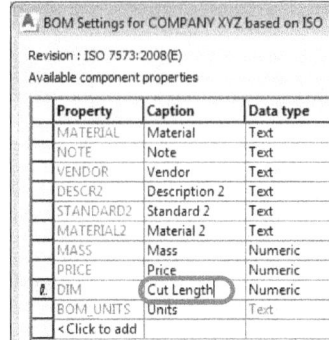

4. To display the list of additional predefined component properties, in the BOM Settings dialog box, click More.

5. To add the first custom user property to the BOM, do the following:
    - In the Move Properties list, select User 1.
    - Click OK.

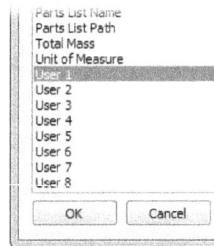

6. In the Caption field, for the property USER1, enter **Total Length**.

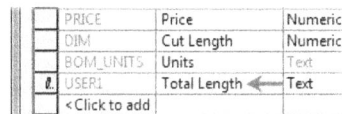

7. In the Data type cell for the USER1 property, select Numeric from the drop-down list.

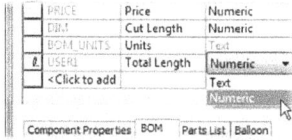

8. To begin entering a formula so that the USER1 value is a calculation of other property values, do the following:

- Click the Value cell for the USER1 property.
- Click the ellipsis (...) button as shown in the following illustration.

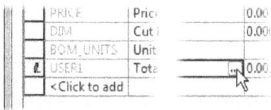

9. To specify the formula, in the Expression Builder dialog box, do the following:

- In the Select list, select DIM. Click Add>>.
- In the Expression box, after DIM, enter *.
- In the Select list, select QTY. Click Add>>.
- Note the expression and click OK.

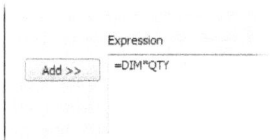

10. In the Precision cell for the USER1 property, select 0.0 from the drop-down list.

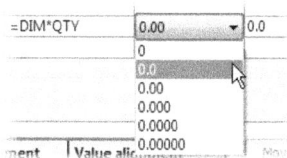

11. In the Lock cell for the USER1 property, select the checkbox to lock the value for this property.

12. On the *BOM* tab, note that the USER1 property was automatically added to the list of properties being tracked in the BOM.

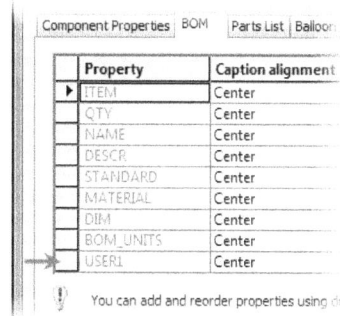

13. To add the available MASS property to the BOM, do the following:

- In the Available component properties list, click the gray square on the left of the MASS row to select the row.
- Click and drag the property to the *BOM* tab and drop it on the DIM row as shown in the following illustration.
- Note that the Mass row is added before the DIM row in the *BOM* tab list.

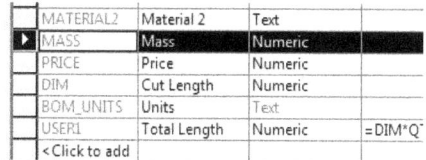

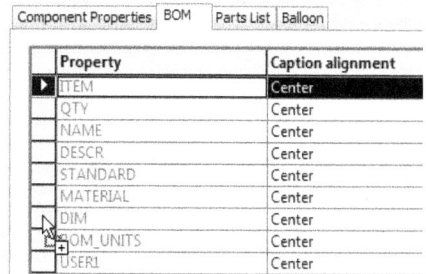

14. To add the MASS property to the listed fields when editing a component's properties, do the following:

- Click the *Component Properties* tab.
- Click and drag the MASS property from the Available component properties list and drop it on BOM_UNITS in the Component Properties list. This adds the MASS row in the Component Properties list.

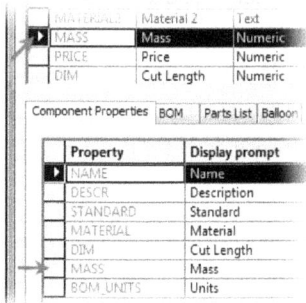

15. In the Display prompt field for the property MASS, enter **Enter Mass in kg**.

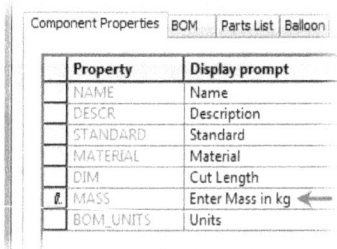

16. To begin configuring the parts list, click the *Parts List* tab.

17. Click the row for the STANDARD property. Click Remove.

18. To add columns to display in the parts list, do the following:

- In the Available component properties list, select the DIM property row. Click Add to.
- Select the USER1 property row. Click Add to. The parts list now displays as shown in the following illustration.

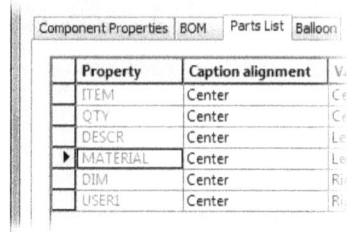

19. To set a different value alignment for the parts list for the material value, in the Value alignment field for the MATERIAL property, select Center from the drop-down list.

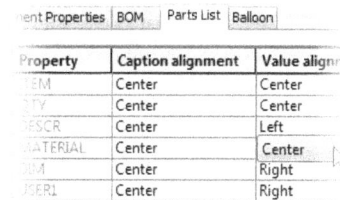

20. To change the column splitting settings for the parts list, in the Default style area, click the Parts List Settings ellipsis (...) button.

21. To set the parts list to wrap between two columns, do the following:

- In the Parts List Settings dialog box, in the Column splitting area, select the Enable column splitting checkbox.
- Click Number of sections.
- Click OK.

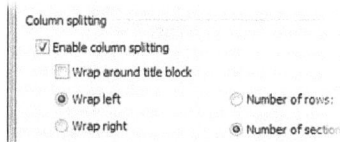

22. To begin configuring the balloon's appearance and values, click the *Balloon* tab.

23. To select a different balloon type, do the following:

- In the Default style area, click the Balloon Settings ellipsis (...) button.
- In the Balloon Settings dialog box, Balloon area, in the Balloon type list, click Circular 2 text.
- Click OK.

24. To change the value that is displayed at the top of the balloon, in the top Expression box, do the following:

- Delete the text <ITEM>.
- Select and add or enter =**<USER1>**.

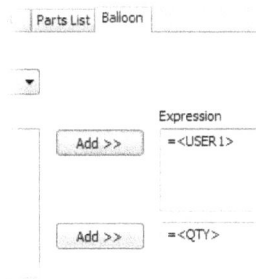

25. In the BOM Settings dialog box, click OK.

26. In the Options dialog box, click OK to save all of the changes to the active standard.

27. Open *Configure BOM-PartsList-Balloon_Results.dwg*.

28. Review the contents and the display of balloons and the parts list. They are displayed as they were configured in the other drawing.

29. Save and close all of the files.

Chapter Summary

In this chapter, you learned how to create a custom standard and how to configure layer, text, and symbol properties within a standard. You also learned how to configure the BOM, parts list, and balloon elements of a standard within a drawing or template file, and describe the configuration of the elements of a standard that pertain to various annotation tools.

Having completed this chapter, you can:

- Create and activate standards and set a default standards template.
- Configure layer, text, and object properties within a standard.
- Configure the elements of a standard within a drawing or template file that relate to annotation tools.
- Configure the component properties, BOM, parts list, and balloon standards within a drawing or template file.

www.ingramcontent.com/pod-product-compliance
Lightning Source LLC
Chambersburg PA
CBHW060938210326
41598CB00031B/4667